Studies in Celtic History XIII

SAINT PATRICK,

A.D. 493–1993

STUDIES IN CELTIC HISTORY

General editor David Dumville

Editorial manager Clare Orchard

ISSN 0261–9865

Already published

I · THE SAINTS OF GWYNEDD
Molly Miller

II · CELTIC BRITAIN IN THE EARLY MIDDLE AGES
Kathleen Hughes

III · THE INSULAR LATIN GRAMMARIANS
Vivien Law

IV · CHRONICLES AND ANNALS OF MEDIAEVAL IRELAND AND WALES
Kathryn Grabowski & David Dumville

V · GILDAS: NEW APPROACHES
M. Lapidge & D. Dumville (edd.)

VI · SAINT GERMANUS OF AUXERRE AND THE END OF ROMAN BRITAIN
E. A. Thompson

VII · FROM KINGS TO WARLORDS
Katharine Simms

VIII · THE CHURCH AND THE WELSH BORDER
IN THE CENTRAL MIDDLE AGES
C. N. L. Brooke

IX · THE LITURGY AND RITUAL OF THE CELTIC CHURCH
F. E. Warren (2nd edn, by Jane Stevenson)

X · THE MONKS OF REDON
Caroline Brett (ed. & transl.)

XI · EARLY MONASTERIES IN CORNWALL
Lynette Olson

XII · IRELAND, WALES, AND ENGLAND IN THE
ELEVENTH CENTURY
K. L. Maund

In press

XIV · MILITARY INSTITUTIONS ON THE WELSH MARCHES
Frederick C. Suppe

XV · UNDERSTANDING THE UNIVERSE IN SEVENTH-CENTURY IRELAND
Marina Smyth

XVI · EXTERNAL CONTACTS AND THE ECONOMY OF
LATE ROMAN AND POST-ROMAN BRITAIN
K. R. Dark (ed.)

XVII · COLUMBANUS: THE LATIN WRITINGS
M. Lapidge (ed.)

SAINT PATRICK,

A.D. 493 – 1993

DAVID N. DUMVILLE
with
LESLEY ABRAMS
T. M. CHARLES-EDWARDS
ALICIA CORRÊA
K. R. DARK
K. L. MAUND
and
A. P. McD. ORCHARD

THE BOYDELL PRESS

First published 1993 by The Boydell Press, Woodbridge

The Boydell Press is an imprint of Boydell & Brewer Ltd
PO Box 9, Woodbridge, Suffolk IP12 3DF, UK
and of Boydell & Brewer Inc.
PO Box 41026, Rochester, NY 14604, USA.

ISBN 0 85115 332 1

British Library Cataloguing-in-Publication Data
Dumville, David
Saint Patrick, A.D.493–1993. – (Studies in Celtic History, ISSN 0261–9865;Vol.13)
I. Title II. Series
270.092
ISBN 0–85115–332–1

Library of Congress Cataloging-in-Publication Data
Saint Patrick, A. D. 493–1993 / David N. Dumville, with Lesley Abrams . . . [et al.].
p. cm. – (Studies in Celtic history, ISSN 0261–9865 ; 13)
Includes bibliographical references and index.
ISBN 0–85115–332–1 (alk. paper)
1. Patrick, Saint, 373?–463? 2. Christian saints – Ireland – Biography. 3. Ireland – Church history – To 1172. 4. Ireland – History – To 1172. I. Dumville, David N. II. Series.
BR1720.P26S25 1993
270.2'092 – dc20
[B] 93–9235

The paper used in this publication meets the minimum requirements of American National Standard for Information Sciences – Permanence of Paper for Printed Library Materials, ANSI Z39.48–1984.

Printed in Great Britain by
St Edmundsbury Press Ltd, Bury St Edmunds, Suffolk

CONTENTS

GENERAL EDITOR'S FOREWORD

This collection of essays is to commemorate the 1500th anniversary of the death of St Patrick – 17 March, 1993. As befits a subject of such complexity and controversy, this will be the second commemoration: the last, in 1961, provoked an avalanche of academic and popular literature, comparable with that which occurred in England on the 900th anniversary of the Norman conquest. Yet there is every reason to think that the death-date in 461 is unsustainable. That 'first' death of St Patrick was, however, celebrated at its fifteenth centenary with an outpouring of controversy, bilious writing, and deplorable behaviour which led one observer to remark that in Patrician studies scholars have left no stone unthrown. As a result no writing on this subject can be uncontroversial. However, the combatants of 1961 are no longer active and there is no sign that the passions of that generation's debate are still alive. The purpose of the present volume is therefore in considerable measure to take stock now that the smoke of battle has drifted away. Various difficult issues, both large and small, are identifiable which require reassessment. In many instances what is needed is no more than a straightforward presentation of the evidence, accompanied by some discussion of the range of deductions possible from it. Most of the essays in this volume are short, aiming above all at clarity and simplicity of exposition of individual subjects. Together they cover a wide range of topics disputed in the 1950s and '60s, where the questions have been left in an unsatisfactory condition. It is hoped that this collection can stand as a fair summary of the evidence and its credible interpretations as well as serving as a reliable point of departure for the next generation's thinking.

Some texts are also presented in a fashion which is intended to be helpful for further study. The subject of the British apostle of Ireland has been one of perennial fascination to students of the history of Ireland, of the end of Roman Britain, and of the Church and its missions: it is hoped that this book will appeal to all of these groups.

David N. Dumville
Girton College,
Cambridge

This volume is inscribed
to the memory of
Ludwig Bieler.

PREFACE

This volume is a fifteenth-centenary tribute to St Patrick, a Briton whose contribution to Irish history has been much celebrated but also the subject of intense controversy. The book might have been called 'Studies in the Life and Legend of St Patrick': there has been no attempt here to discuss every possible aspect of the saint's career, much less of the legends about him. Indeed, the message of many of the chapters is that a conventional biography is almost impossible: we have Patrick's own impassioned *apologia pro uita sua*, but it is a text to whose detailed message access is not easy. The later Irish sources about St Patrick are also difficult: but they cannot be cast aside, as some historians have seen fit to do. It is doubtful whether they tell us much more about St Patrick, yet they may bring us material about Palladius, sent from Rome in A.D. 431 as first bishop for Irish christians but left ultimately without subsequent history or cult in his adopted country. The invention of two Patricks seems to belong, at the latest, to the eighth century and may be a reflex of the largely successful seventh-century conflation of the careers of Palladius and Patrick. The continuing mediaeval development of the legend and cult of St Patrick has its own interest as well as illuminating a wide variety of other historical and literary-historical issues, several of which are explored in this volume.

I cannot conclude this preface without offering my thanks to my collaborators in this project. They are at once fewer and more numerous than the group which first embarked on this voyage. They have met stringent deadlines, borne with many impositions, and produced fine chapters. I am very grateful to them. And, as so often, my thanks must be extended also to my friends at Boydell & Brewer for their imaginative and helpful response to this enterprise.

D.N.D.

PALLADIUS, PROSPER, AND LEO THE GREAT: MISSION AND PRIMATIAL AUTHORITY

T. M. Charles-Edwards

> Ad Scottos in Christo credentes ordinatus a papa Caelestino Palladius primus episcopus mittitur.
>
> 'Palladius, having been ordained by Pope Celestine, is sent, as their first bishop, to the Irish who believe in Christ.'
>
> (Prosper, Chronicle, *s.a.* 431)[1]

> Nec uero segniore cura ab hoc eodem morbo Britannias liberauit, quando, quosdam inimicos gratiae solum suae originis occupantes etiam ab illo secreto exclusit Oceani, et ordinato Scotis episcopo, dum romanam insulam studet seruare catholicam, fecit etiam barbaram christianam.
>
> 'He (Celestine) has been, however, no less energetic in freeing the British provinces from this same disease (the Pelagian heresy): he removed from that hiding-place certain enemies of grace who had occupied the land of their origin; also, having ordained a bishop for the Irish, while he labours to keep the Roman island catholic, he has also made the barbarian island christian.'
>
> (Prosper, *Contra Collatorem*, § 21)[2]

In a sermon preached to his Roman flock in 441, on the feast-day of the apostles Peter and Paul, the two columns of the Roman Church, Leo the Great proudly proclaimed that the authority of christian Rome had surpassed the farthest boundaries limiting the power of imperial Rome. Moreover, the comparison was not with the contemporary authority of the western Empire, but with imperial Rome at her apogee.[3]

These men [Peter and Paul, as opposed to the fratricide Romulus and his victim Remus] are the ones who promoted you [Rome] to such glory that, as a holy race, a chosen people, a priestly and a royal city, and having been made the head of the whole world through the holy see of the blessed Peter, you came to rule over a wider territory

1 *Chronica Minora*, ed. Mommsen, I.473.

2 *Patrologia latina*, ed. Migne, LI.271.

3 *Tractatus*, § 82.1 (ed. Chavasse, *Sancti Leonis Magni Romani Pontificis Tractatus*, p. 509). Cf. *Epistolae*, X.1 (ed. Migne, *Patrologia latina*, LIV.628–9). The Latin text of *Sermo LXXXII* is given below, p. 6, together with a parallel passage from Prosper, *De uocatione omnium gentium*. On Romulus as a fratricide, compare Augustine, *De ciuitate Dei*, XV.5.

through the worship of God than by earthly domination. For although you were exalted by many victories and thereby extended the authority of your empire by land and by sea, nevertheless what the toils of war subjected to you is less than that which a christian peace has made obedient.

The claim was appropriate to the feast-day, for Rome was the resting place of Paul, apostle to the Gentiles, as well as Peter, chief of the apostles and pre-eminent pastor of the sheep of Christ. Who then were these new subjects of christian Rome living beyond the bounds of the Empire? And was there any reason, apart from the honour due to the apostles Peter and Paul, and to their city, Rome, why Leo should have concerned himself with such distant missionary successes?[4]

Leo was unlikely to have been referring to Arian Goths (or Vandals). In the first place, they were Arians, and their Arianism may already, by the mid-fifth century, have become a badge of their distinctness from the Romans. Arian Goths, then, would hardly have been a feather in the cap of catholic Rome. Secondly, Ulfila was consecrated bishop by Eusebius of Nicomedia, who became bishop of Constantinople.[5] The context of the consecration was an embassy to the Emperor. This link between Imperial diplomacy, the leading court-bishop, and the consecration of a bishop for the barbarians finds an echo, of crucial importance for Leo the Great, in canon 28 of the Council of Chalcedon.[6] There the patriarchal status of the bishop of Constantinople is explicitly associated with a claim to consecrate bishops to work among barbarians in certain Imperial dioceses, notably Thrace.[7] New Rome, like Old Rome, was to have the authority to intervene beyond its own metropolitan province in order to promote the preaching of the Gospel among barbarian pagans. The phrasing of the relevant passage in the proceedings of the Council suggests that settlements south of the Danube in the heyday of Attila's empire may have been the principal subject of concern. In the early 450s any matter affecting relations with Attila was of critical importance for the Emperor Marcian; the opportunity of developing that close collaboration with the Patriarch Flavian, which had been a mark of the Council, must have been attractive. The bishop of Constantinople, therefore, had to have the authority to intervene far to the north; the source claimed for such an authority was his status as the bishop of New Rome, enjoying an authority derived from, and inferior only to, Old Rome. Yet Leo and his representatives at the Council would have none of such arguments. For the pope, Alexandria was the patriarchate second in rank to Rome, and its privileges were not to be abrogated. So began the long quarrel over the 'ecumenical' patriarchate which troubled several subsequent

4 McShane, *La Romanitas*, pp. 86–91, 97–107.

5 Philostorgius, *Historia ecclesiastica*, II.5, in *Die gotische Bibel*, ed. Streitberg, pp. xix–xx; Thompson, *The Visigoths*, pp. xiv–xvii. It is unclear whether Eusebius was already bishop of Constantinople when he consecrated Ulfila. (See Heather & Matthews, *The Goths*, pp. 133–43.) This would hardly matter by 441: for Leo, Eusebius would have been known as the leader of the Arian party and bishop of Constantinople.

6 *Sacrorum conciliorum nova et amplissima collectio*, ed. Mansi, VII.427 = *Acta Conciliorum Oecumenicorum*, First series, edd. Schwartz & Straub, II.448.

7 Cf. Herman, 'Chalkedon und die Ausgestaltung', p. 474.

popes, among them Gregory the Great in the very years when he despatched the mission to the English. In the 450s, therefore, missionary activity among the barbarians, and especially the right to consecrate a bishop to care for barbarian christians, was a matter of concern in the highest circles of christendom. Ulfila's mission, sponsored by a bishop of Constantinople, succeeded only in creating a nation of Arian heretics who subsequently sacked Rome.[8] If Leo thought of the Goths when he was preaching in honour of the apostles Peter and Paul, it was as an example to illustrate not his proud claim but rather its false shadow in Constantinople.

At the time when he was considering what arguments to address to the warring theological parties in the East, Prosper of Aquitaine was at least his friend and, very possibly, his adviser.[9] Prosper, however, was the author of three works which bear upon the theme of missionary work beyond the frontiers of the Empire: *De uocatione omnium gentium*, *Contra Collatorem*, and his continuation of the Chronicle of Eusebius.[10]

De uocatione omnium gentium was probably composed in Rome in the 440s, and thus within the circle of Leo and within a very few years of the Council of Chalcedon.[11] It was designed to counter arguments against Augustine's position on grace, but in a more eirenic manner than he had adopted in *Contra Collatorem* written *ca* 434. One of the issues addressed was a possible Pelagian argument from the goodness of non-christians.[12] If saving grace came to men through Christ, and if a primary and necessary consequence of grace was belief in Christ, good men before the Incarnation could not have been given saving grace. The same argument applied to those beyond the reach of the christian

8 Cf. Leo, *Tractatus* no. 84, on the anniversary of Alaric's sack, and withdrawal from, Rome.

9 Gennadius, *De uiris inlustribus*, § 85 (ed. Richardson, p. 90) (the term *consiliarius* is in only one manuscript, but McShane has argued that it seems to represent the situation in the period running up to the Council of Chalcedon: *La Romanitas*, pp. 370–1). This has been doubted by Markus, 'Chronicle and theology', pp. 34–6, but for reasons which, as will be clear from the discussion below, I cannot entirely share; Markus has, however, been content to see Prosper as Leo's friend. Cf. Valentin, *Saint Prosper*, pp. 135–9.

10 The authenticity of *De uocatione* was convincingly defended by Cappuyns, 'L'auteur'; his view was supported, with some further arguments, by Lorenz, 'Der Augustinismus Prospers', p. 233, n. 129; the doubts expressed by de Plinval, 'Prosper d'Aquitaine interprète', p. 351, were not supported by any argument. For earlier discussion, see Valentin, *Saint Prosper*, pp. 687–713.

11 Cappuyns, 'L'auteur', p. 226, dated the text *ca* 450. If this date is correct, the textual links with Leo's *Sermo LXXXII* would then suggest that Prosper (if he was not involved with the composition of the sermon) borrowed from Leo rather than the other way round. Apparently on the basis of Cappuyns's date, Markus, 'Chronicle and theology', pp. 36–9, assumed without any further argument that Prosper was indebted to Leo. But a date towards the beginning of Leo's pontificate and thus close to the date of *Sermo LXXXII* is entirely possible. A date *ca* 440 was adopted by Lorenz, 'Der Augustinismus Prospers', p. 233, n. 129; Lorenz's discussion of the doctrine of *De uocatione* is on pp. 247–51.

12 Cf. the argument put by Germanus in Cassian's *Conlatio XIII*, *De protectione Dei*, § 4 (*Iohannis Cassiani Conlationes*, ed. Petschenig, p. 365), with Prosper, *De uocatione omnium gentium*, II.17: 'Quod si forte, quemadmodum gentes non olim in consortium filiorum Dei nouimus adoptatas, ita etiam nunc in extremis mundi partibus sunt aliquae nationes quibus nondum gratia Saluatoris illuxit, non ambigimus, etiam circa illos occulto iudicio Dei tempus uocationis eius esse dispositum, quo Euangelium, quod non audierunt, audient atque suscipient'.

missionary. Men who had never heard even the name of Christ could not believe in him. If, then, faith in Christ was a necessary consequence of grace, such a person was denied salvation by an accident, the time or the place of his birth. So, it could be argued, an Augustinian position on grace must imply that most of the human race was beyond even the possibility of salvation. But it was the will of God that all men be saved (I Tim. 2:3–4, accepted wholeheartedly by Prosper in the *De uocatione*); hence the Augustinian view of grace and salvation must be false. In its place one could uphold a rival view, that just as Melchisedech and Job were not of the chosen people of Israel, and yet were pleasing to God,[13] so too in the New Covenant in Christ's blood there might be those beyond the bounds of the Church, ignorant of Christ, who were nevertheless worthy of Paradise.

For both parties the good pagan was a difficulty. Both had to uphold the doctrine that the passion and resurrexion of Christ were instrumental in the salvation of the human race. Yet how could that be if most of human history lay in the long centuries before the Incarnation, and even afterwards whole nations lay beyond the reach of the Church? Augustine appealed to prophecy: the Old-Testament prophet has faith in the Christ whom he foresees by the power of supernatural grace.[14] Grace, therefore, can confer faith, in Christ not just in God, before the Incarnation. Augustine was also prepared to argue, however, that prophecy, even among the Jews, could be unconscious and, before the beginnings of the Jewish people, could be 'by signs and symbols appropriate to the times'.[15] The role of prophecy is thus expanded to include the Mosaic law, the rites, the sacred calendar, the priestly organisation, and even the equipment of the Temple – 'all these were symbols and predictions which found their fulfilment in Christ'. This argument removed the distinction between prophecy and typology: everything which pointed to Christ, consciously or unconsciously, was prophecy. In the Old Testament, we may conclude, faith in Christ may be unconscious, not only in the prophet (or type) but in those who heard the prophet (or were aware of the type). Not only Job may be saved but even his companions. Pelagius's reaction was different. Prophecy is not necessary, and the type of Christ is not the same as the prophet. Job prefigured Christ through his virtuous life: he confessed a living God in the midst of his sufferings rather than prophesying a future Christ. Yet if the Pelagian upheld the claims of natural goodness, he loosened the link between Christ and human salvation. No longer would the Cross be the necessary condition of redemption from sin and eternal happiness. The controversy thus made the pagan nations beyond the Empire into a pressing problem, alongside unbaptised infants and the Gentiles of the Old Testament, such as Job.

13 Pelagius, *Ad Demetriadem*, V.2 (Melchisedech), VI.3 (Job, 'a man of the gospel before the gospel was known, a man of the apostles before their commands were uttered'), ed. Migne, *Patrologia latina*, XXX.20, 21 or XXXIII.1102, 1103; transl. Rees, *The Letters of Pelagius*, pp. 40, 43. So Prosper, *De uocatione*, II.5 (*Patrologia latina*, ed. Migne, LI.691) admitted that before Christ some non-Jews were saved just as, after Christ, some Jews are still saved (II.9, *Patrologia latina*, ed. Migne, LI.694).

14 Augustine, *De ciuitate Dei*, XVIII.47; *De peccatorum meritis et remissione*, II.11; *De perfectione iustitiae hominis*, XIX.

15 *De ciuitate Dei*, VII.32.

Prosper's *De uocatione omnium gentium* shows evidence of careful thought both theoretical and practical. As an example of the latter we may consider that central event in Patrick's career, the taking of Roman provincials into slavery beyond the frontier. Patrick was not just concerned with slave-raids in his own case where Irishmen were responsible; in the letter to Coroticus he showed a passionate concern for Irish men and women captured by raiders, as well as knowledge of Gallo-Roman efforts to ransom christian captives taken by the Franks.[16] Prosper, however, saw in these christian slaves the unconscious instruments of divine grace. The christian Roman taken by the pagan barbarian often converts his master to christianity.[17]

Quidam Ecclesiae filii ab hostibus capti, dominos suos Christi Euangelio mancipauerunt, et quibus conditione bellica seruiebant, eisdem fidei magisterio praefuerunt.

'Some sons of the Church who have been captured by enemies have handed their masters into the possession of Christ's gospel; and by virtue of teaching the faith they have had charge of those whom they were serving as slaves taken in war.'

Even barbarians raiding within Roman territory may learn of christianity 'in our lands' and so take the faith back with them to their homes beyond the frontier. This perception that the weakness of imperial Rome could help to spread christianity might have been a comment on the career of Patrick, if only one had any reason to believe that Prosper had heard of the *papa* of the Irish.[18]

In the long term the Irish Church was to follow its British counterpart in refusing, or not perceiving the need, to anathematise Pelagius, although in the short term there was an active anti-Pelagian party in Britain able to request Germanus to come to its aid.[19] This small network of anti-Pelagians linking Rome, Gaul, and Britain was instrumental in setting the mission to Ireland on a formal footing. Prosper, with his links to Celestine and especially Leo the Great, and probably also to Germanus of Auxerre, was a central figure in this network. He was also the person who, in two other works, his Chronicle and *Contra Collatorem*, provided us with the evidence for the mission of Palladius to the Irish. *De uocatione omnium gentium* is thus a key-text if one wishes to understand the reasons for Palladius's mission.[20]

We need to pause, however, before claiming that Leo the Great had the Irish in mind when he was preaching to the people of Rome on the feast of the apostles Peter and Paul in 441. The sermon exists in three forms of which the third differs little from the second, but the second represents a considerable expansion of the first.[21] Both the first and the second have links in content with *De uocatione omnium gentium*. To make the parallels clear I shall print the two texts side by side.

16 *Epistola ad Coroticum*, § 14.

17 *De uocatione omnium gentium*, II.33 (*Patrologia latina*, ed. Migne, LI.717–18).

18 'sanctus Patricius papa noster': Cummian, *De controuersia paschali*, edd. & transl. Walsh & Ó Cróinín, *Cummian's Letter*, p. 84, lines 208–9.

19 Dumville, 'Late-seventh- or eighth-century evidence' (with extensive bibliography on pp. 39–40).

20 This has been recognised by Thompson, *Who was Saint Patrick?*, pp. 58–65, 169–75, with whose discussion mine should be compared.

21 *Sancti Leonis Magni Romani Pontificis Tractatus*, ed. Chavasse, p. 506.

Leo, Sermon 82

[β: Isti sunt qui te ad hanc gloriam prouexerunt,] ut *gens sancta, populus electus*, ciuitas *sacerdotalis et regia*, per sacram beati Petri sedem caput totius (*om.* β) orbis effecta, latius praesideres religione diuina quam dominatione terrena. Quamuis enim multis aucta uictoriis ius imperii tui terra marique distenderes (protuleris β), minus tamen est quod tibi bellicus labor subdidit quam quod pax christiana subiecit. . . .
[β: Vt autem huius inenarrabilis gratiae per totam mundum diffunderetur effectus, romanum regnum diuina prouidentia praeparauit, cuius ad eos limites incrementa perducta sunt, quibus cunctarum undique gentium uicina et contigua esset uniuersitas. Disposito enim diuinitus operi maxime congruebat, ut multa regna uno confoederarentur imperio, et cito peruios haberet populos praedicatio generalis, quos unius teneret regimen ciuitatis.

Prosper, *De uocatione*, II.16–17

Parthi et Medi et Elamitae . . . et Arabes: audiuimus eos loquentes nostris linguis magnalia Dei? [Acts 2:9–12] Ad cuius rei effectum credimus prouidentia Dei romani regni latitudinem praeparatam, ut nationes uocandae ad unitatem corporis Christi, prius iure unius consociarentur imperii. Quamuis gratia christiana non contenta sit eosdem limites habere quos Roma, multosque iam populos sceptro crucis Christi illa subdiderit, quos armis ista non domuit. Quae tamen per apostolici sacerdotii principatum amplior facta est arce religionis quam solio potestatis.

The purpose of appealing to the spread of the Faith beyond the boundaries of the Empire is different for the two authors. For Leo it demonstrates the superiority of christian over pagan Rome; for Prosper it shows how divine grace is extended to the barbarians. For Leo (in the β-version) the Roman empire was designed by God so that its frontier should be contiguous with all the nations of the earth. He thus makes a more elaborate connexion than does Prosper between the size of the Roman empire, its role in bringing many nations under one rule so as to facilitate their conversion, and also its role in thereby transmitting christianity to nations contiguous with its boundaries. The latter point (the Empire is contiguous with the barbarians) is illustrated by Prosper elsewhere with his observations about, first, Roman slaves and barbarian masters, and, secondly, barbarian raiders taking christianity back to their native land. Leo's starting point is Rome's possession of both Peter and Paul; Prosper's is the apostles at Pentecost addressing 'Parthians and Medes and Elamites' and the rest, some from within, some from without the Empire. From the very beginning of the christian mission, therefore, the Gospel had been preached to those outside the Roman empire. That empire was indeed part of divine providence: Augustine himself had argued that the peace created by the city of this world could assist the city of God.[22] His disciple Orosius was prepared to go further than his master in recognising the providential role of the Roman empire.[23] For

22 *De ciuitate Dei*, XIX.17, 26.

23 Markus, 'Chronicle and theology', pp. 38–9, has suggested that Prosper was here indebted to Orosius. For Orosius's views see Markus, *Saeculum*, pp. 161–2.

Prosper, however, the Empire was one instrument of divine providence among others; the well-being of the Empire was not a necessary condition of the well-being of the Church.

In the 430s and 440s the mission of Palladius was the most immediate example of this mission to all peoples through which the divine 'calling of all nations' (*uocatio omnium gentium*) could be realised. It was also a dramatic instance, well known to Leo and Prosper, both of whom were in Rome *ca* 431, of the role of the see of Rome in preaching the gospel to the barbarians. The apostles preaching to Parthians and Medes at Pentecost would serve as the starting point of Prosper's argument in the *De uocatione*, quoted above, but he concludes by declaring that by the *principatus* of the apostolic see the authority of Rome has been extended farther than it had been by force of arms. For Leo's argument, Rome was the starting point and the conclusion, and therefore the mission to the Irish was crucial: Celestine had ordained and sent Palladius. Admittedly he did not cite it openly in his sermon: a Roman audience might be expected to take more interest in an eloquent statement of its enhanced authority under the christian dispensation than in any details about the Irish, that people sodden in porage.[24] The Irish mattered to Leo rather than to the Romans.

They also mattered, however, to his adviser, Prosper. He might start from a different point and seek to exalt divine grace more than the city of Rome, but the links between the *De uocatione* and Leo's sermon are sufficiently close to make it clear that they are different applications of a single idea, namely that the christian gospel has surpassed the Roman empire in territorial extent. This idea was under development by Leo and his advisers from early in his pontificate, as is shown by putting the three versions of the sermon and Prosper's work side by side. From this period of intense discussion in the 440s we may then turn to Prosper's earlier works, *Contra Collatorem* of *ca* 434 and the Chronicle, whose first version may be assigned to much the same period. At this point in *Contra Collatorem* (§ 21), Prosper is praising the initiatives taken by Celestine in defence of the doctrine of grace and against the Pelagian heresy. The conclusion of his argument is that the authority of Rome has spoken decisively against Pelagius and his disciples. Celestine's energy in defence of the Faith was demonstrated, for Prosper, by his having rescued Britain from heresy and Ireland from paganism. In his Chronicle he says that in 429 Celestine sent Germanus *uice sua*, as his representative, to rid Britain of Pelagianism, and in 431 he sent Palladius as bishop for the Irish who believed in Christ. At this period, *ca* 430, we are close to Prosper's first visit to Rome where the archdeacon Leo was already in a position of influence not confined to the city, as is shown by his friendship with Cassian.[25]

There is a link between Germanus's expedition to Britain and Palladius's to Ireland which goes beyond the probability that the latter was Germanus's deacon and was sent by him to Rome to gain papal authority for the visit to Britain. On 30 April, 418, the Emperor Honorius enacted a law by which anyone giving vent to Pelagian opinions was to be brought before the civil authorities and

24 Jerome, *In Ieremiam Prophetam*, III, *Praefatio*. Cf. Bury, 'The origin of Pelagius'.
25 O. Chadwick, *John Cassian*, pp. 141–2.

condemned to exile.[26] Yet this was ten years after Britain had rid itself of the authority of Ravenna.[27] The tactic employed by Augustine and his allies of appealing to secular authority against their theological opponents could have no effect in Britain. Yet what was beyond the reach of Imperial power was not beyond the authority of the pope. He could commission Germanus to rally the Britons to orthodoxy. Germanus himself, with his aristocratic birth and his background in government-service, was in a position to appreciate the limitations of secular authority and the necessity of appealing to something different.[28] The events of 409/10 had brought about the final detachment of Britain from the prefecture of Gaul.[29] A man of Germanus's standing in Gaul was best placed to perceive that papal authority given to a Gallic bishop might prevail when the Emperor could do nothing. Augustine and his allies had appealed both to the Emperor and to the bishop of Rome. His Gallic supporters, confronted with British independence from the Empire, had only one central authority to which they could turn.

The Pelagian party in Britain in the 420s may have been created by Imperial power and its limitations. Robert Markus has argued that the prevailing attitude in Britain is better described as 'pre-Pelagian'.[30] In other words, current assumptions about human morality, about free will, and about grace were not founded upon any conscious rejection of Augustinian opinions, but they were such as to impel most cultured christians to side more with Pelagius than with Augustine if the issue arose. Support for Pelagius was implicit and unformulated. The issue arose, however, in the 420s, probably because the law of 418 envisaged exile as the weapon to be used against the heretic. Prosper's *Contra Collatorem* implies that Germanus's opponents, 'the enemies of grace', had taken refuge in their native island: they were Britons but had, in the immediate past, been resident elsewhere, perhaps in Gaul or in Italy. The reason for their return to Britain may have been the law of 418, for, by crossing the Channel, they put themselves beyond the reach of Imperial laws. If the Emperor had decisively aided the Augustinian party in Gaul, he had perhaps created for the first time a consciously Pelagian party in Britain.

According to Constantius's Life of St Germanus, the weapon used by the bishop of Auxerre when he won over the Britons and thus cornered the Pelagian party was the same as that envisaged by the law of 418 – namely exile.[31] The danger was, however, also the same as with the law of 418, that the penalty would only displace the disease, not cure it. This may be a practical reason why Palladius was ordained by Celestine as bishop for the Irish who believed in Christ. His task was partly to safeguard the orthodoxy of existing Irish christians, partly, in the words of Prosper's *Contra Collatorem*, 'to make the barbarian island christian'.

26 *Patrologia latina*, ed. Migne, LVI.492.
27 Thompson, 'Zosimus 6.10.2'.
28 Stroheker, *Der senatorische Adel*, Prosopography, no. 178.
29 Thompson, *Saint Germanus*, pp. 32–8.
30 Markus, 'Pelagianism: Britain and the Continent', pp. 198–200, and 'The legacy'.
31 Constantius, *Vita S. Germani*, § 27, edd. [Krusch &] Levison, *Passiones*, VII.270; discussed by Thompson, *Saint Germanus*, pp. 28–30.

The words of Prosper – *dum romanam insulam studet seruare catholicam, fecit etiam barbaram christianam* – written only two or three years after Palladius was sent to Ireland, already oppose Roman empire and barbarian christianity in a manner which anticipates Leo's Sermon 82. Yet they represent aspiration rather than achievement, continued hopes for Palladius's mission entertained in Rome and in Gaul rather than congratulations addressed to a pope whose emissary has completed his task. Irish texts concerning St Patrick, from the late seventh century, were concerned to extract what they could from the notice of Palladius in Prosper's Chronicle, but to pass over in silence or to minimise the achievements of this bishop of the Irish christians. It is tempting to follow them in so far as Palladius may be supposed to have disappeared from the concerns of popes and Gallican bishops once he had crossed the Irish Sea. At the theoretical level, at least, the evidence of Prosper's *De uocatione omnium gentium* and of Leo's Sermon 82 shows that this is wholly untrue. For twenty years at least Palladius's mission remained a matter of deep concern for both Leo and Prosper. Moreover the consecration of a bishop by the pope for the Irish was directly relevant to canon 28 of the Council of Chalcedon and thus to papal relations both with the Eastern emperor and with the bishop of Constantinople. One of the main impulses behind the theoretical elaboration of the papal primacy – from Damasus to Gelasius – was fear of Imperial domination.[32] Imperial laws had indeed conferred major powers upon the bishop of Rome by which he might intervene in other provinces,[33] but that only made it the more important to base the papal primacy on something other than Imperial decrees. Otherwise the bishop of Rome would become merely an imperial official. The activities of Germanus and of Palladius, in Britain and in Ireland, demonstrated that a christian and papal Rome, the Rome of Peter and Paul, could intervene to safeguard and to spread the Faith in an island which had thrown off Imperial authority and also in another island which had never been subject to the sway of the Emperor. The christian faith and the authority of christian Rome extended not only to Roman citizens, not just to Parthians, Medes, and Elamites, but to rebellious Britons and even to the barbarian Irish.

There is no reason to believe that Leo the Great's interest in Britain and Ireland was merely theoretical. The second mission of Germanus to Britain, which E. A. Thompson would date to 437 (or possibly 436) but others to the 440s and therefore within Leo's pontificate, demonstrates that the concerns of 429–431 remained pressing, in spite of a slackening of the Pelagian controversy in Gaul.[34] As D. A. Binchy showed, there is no reason to argue from the silence of Patrick's *Confessio* and *Epistola ad Coroticum* about Palladius, that the latter's mission had been cut short.[35] It remains exceedingly likely that the lack of later evidence about Palladius, other than passages seeking to remove him

32 McShane, *La Romanitas*, p. 112.

33 Notably by Gratian, in A.D. 378/9: *Epistulae*, ed. Guenther, p. 58.

34 Thompson, *Saint Germanus*, pp. 55–70. Wood, 'The end of Roman Britain', p. 16, has suggested *ca* 435 although a date *ca* 440 is possible. In favour of a later date see Mathisen, 'The last year'.

35 Binchy, 'Patrick and his biographers', pp. 144–8.

from the scene before Patrick's arrival, is due simply to Patrician hagiographers' skill in transferring elements from the career of Palladius to that of Patrick.[36] Columbanus's reference, in his letter to Pope Boniface, to Irish preservation of the 'fides catholica sicut a uobis primum, sanctorum scilicet apostolorum successoribus, tradita est' is reasonably taken as a reference to the mission of Palladius.[37] When Columbanus left Ireland for Gaul *ca* 590 much more may have been remembered about the first bishop of the Irish than has come down to us.

In the last years of Leo's pontificate it was becoming increasingly difficult to maintain lines of communication between Rome, southern Gaul and the British Isles. The Gallic chronicler of A.D. 452 does not reveal triumphs of bishops against Pelagians or missions to the Irish, in part perhaps because his theological sympathies ran counter to those of Prosper. What he does record is the subjection of the Britons to Saxon power.[38] The appeal of the Britons to Aetius confirms the approximate accuracy of the Chronicle's entry in so far as it shows the Britons in grave difficulties, although Gildas himself sets the letter in the context of Irish and Pictish, not Saxon, attacks.[39] A Britain and Ireland under the benign authority of papal Rome, in which Leo had delighted in 441, was only a brief interval between the end of Imperial authority and the devastating expansion of Saxon power in the 440s. Prosper's hopes of barbarian inroads leading to barbarian conversion were borne out in the long run, but the next dramatic advance, the conversion of Clovis, saw a Frankish king concerned to advance his relations with the Emperor Anastasius more than with the pope. Clovis secured the blessing of Anastasius rather than of Symmachus for the new christian kingdom centred on Paris.[40] The pope for his part could hardly give a public blessing since he had to maintain good relations with Theodoric.

By the time of Gregory the Great, however, conditions were more propitious for a Roman mission. The papacy could be of more use to the Franks once it no longer lay within an Ostrogothic kingdom. Ecclesiastical relations with the East had been soured for a generation by the Trecapitoline Schism,[41] but the Austrasian court had attempted to coöperate, within limits, with Maurice's campaign

36 Todd, *St. Patrick*, pp. 265–345, 393–9; Binchy, 'Patrick and his biographers', pp. 27–31, 142–4. See below, pp. 65–84.

37 *Epistolae*, V.3: *Sancti Columbani Opera*, edd. & transl. Walker & Bieler, p. 38. Cf. Binchy, 'Patrick and his biographers', pp. 12, 169.

38 *Chronica Minora*, ed. Mommsen, I.660. See Ian Wood's very helpful discussion, 'The end of Roman Britain', pp. 17–20.

39 Gildas, *De excidio Britanniae*, I.20 (ed. & transl. Winterbottom, *Gildas*, p. 95). On the difficulties of reconciling the evidence of the 'Chronicle of 452' with Gildas's use of the letter, see Wood, 'The end of Roman Britain', p. 20, 'The fall', and, more recently, 'Continuity or calamity?'.

40 It is worth noting, however, the gift of 'a diadem with precious jewels' whish is said by *Liber Pontificalis* to have been sent by Clovis to Pope Hormisdas (*The Book of Pontiffs*, transl. Davis, p. 48). The chronology is impossible (Hormisdas became pope in 514, and therefore after Clovis's death), but the incident may have been displaced from the account of his predecessor, Symmachus. (I owe this suggestion to Ian Wood.)

41 Frankish concern is shown by canon 1 of the Council of Orléans, A.D. 549: *Concilia Galliae, A. 511–A. 695*, ed. De Clercq, pp. 148–9; cf. Wallace-Hadrill, *The Frankish Church*, p. 100.

of 590 against the Lombards.[42] What the Franks now had to offer the papacy was their influence in Kent and both logistic and moral support for a mission. Who first conceived the idea of a Roman mission to the English – whether pope or Franks – is unclear.[43] What is certain is that, in Gregory the Great's eyes, the mission entailed coöperation between three parties, as with Germanus and Palladius 150 years previously. There had to be an indication from Britain that a mission would be welcome, papal authority for the party sent to Britain, and support and practical assistance from Gaul. Syagrius of Autun was the most influential and enthusiastic supporter of the English mission among the Frankish bishops, a counterpart to Germanus of Auxerre.[44] Gregory the Great seems to have conceived the idea of a Roman mission to the English after being told that *sacerdotes e uicino*, namely Franks, were unwilling to undertake the task.[45] The strongest support for the mission seems to have come from Burgundy, which was not directly *e uicino* but was the kingdom in which Columbanus (who had clear missionary interests, as well as memories of Palladius) had already settled and was enjoying strong royal support from a régime headed by Brunhild.[46] In the first batch of letters to Francia concerning the mission of Augustine, and among two to Brunhild, was a letter accompanying a gift of relics of the apostles Peter and Paul.[47] Her favourite among the bishops seems to have been Syagrius.[48] Perhaps someone had been reading the Chronicle of Prosper and had seen the opportunity which lay close at hand. Perhaps the presence of Columbanus had drawn to the attention of Brunhild and Syagrius a lesson of history. It is impossible to do more than speculate, but if the stimulus came from Burgundy one cannot deny the possibility that the mission to the English was conceived after the model of Palladius's mission to the Irish.

That Gregory was aware of the links between his actions and the missionary endeavours of the fifth century is suggested by a passage in his *Moralia in Iob*.[49] The text upon which he is commenting is Job, 36:29–30: 'Si uoluerit extendere nubes quasi tentorium suum, et fulgurare lumine suo desuper, cardines quoque maris operiet'. Although he had begun the *Moralia* as long ago as 579, the date of this section cannot be before 596, since he goes on to say that the *lingua Britanniae*, which had known nothing other than barbarian gnashing of teeth,

42 *Epistolae Austrasicae*, nos 40–42 (*Epistolae*, edd. Dümmler *et al.*, I.145–9).

43 Hunter Blair, *The World of Bede*, pp. 41–8.

44 *S. Gregorii Magni Registrum*, IX.223 (ed. Norberg, II.794–7); Stroheker, *Der senatorische Adel*, pp. 221–2, Prosopography, no. 375.

45 *S. Gregorii Magni Registrum*, VI.51, 60 (ed. Norberg, I.423–4, 433).

46 The missionary interests of Columbanus have been denied by Schieffer, *Winfrid-Bonifatius*, p. 86, but are clear from *Epistolae*, IV.5: 'Mei uoti fuit gentes uisitare, et euangelium eis a nobis praedicari', *Sancti Columbani Opera*, edd. & transl. Walker & Bieler, p. 30, although at the stage when the letter was written, probably in 610, he had decided that circumstances were not propitious; with the evidence of *Epistolae*, IV.5, one may compare Ionas, *Vita S. Columbani*, the concluding sentence of I.4 (*Ionae uitae sanctorum*, ed. Krusch, p. 160).

47 *S. Gregorii Magni Registrum*, VI.58 (ed. Norberg, I.431).

48 Wallace-Hadrill, *The Frankish Church*, pp. 116–18.

49 Gregory the Great, *Moralia in Iob*, XXVII.xi, 20–1 (ed. Adriaen, III.1345–6).

had recently begun to sing the Hebrew Alleluia in praise of God.[50] One section of Gregory's commentary on these verses of Job is good evidence that he had read Leo's Sermon 82 and had appreciated its message:

Ecce quondam tumidus, iam substratus sanctorum pedibus seruit Oceanus; eiusque barbaros motus, quos terreni principes edomare ferro nequiuerant, hos pro diuina formidine sacerdotum ora simplicibus uerbis ligant; et qui cateruas pugnantium infidelis nequaquam metuerat, iam nunc fidelis humilium linguas timet.

'Behold how the Ocean, previously raging, has now paved the way for the feet of holy men; its barbarian heavings, which earthly rulers were unable to tame by the sword, the mouths of priests bind with simple words by virtue of the fear inspired by God; and the one who, when an unbeliever, never had the least fear of bands of warriors, now, as a believer, already fears the tongues of humble men.'

The ocean, in its barbarian wildness, is both the sea which Augustine and his companions must cross and also an image of the untamed heart of the pagan barbarian in the island beyond the sea. The *terreni principes*, by whom Gregory must mean the Roman emperors, were unable to tame the barbarian by the violence of the sword, whereas the envoys of papal Rome have prevailed over ocean and barbarian alike.

There is another aspect of Gregory's plans which looks to a British past. The mission was to the English but it was also to Britain. Augustine was to have authority over the whole of Britain, while the two metropolitical sees envisaged by Gregory, London and York, were to govern a christian Britain between them.[51] Gregory may have known very little about contemporary British christians, but he was clear that he wished to restore a christian Britain making full use of British bishops under the authority of his personal envoy, Augustine. The initial stimulus may therefore have been approaches by Æthelberht of Kent to his wife's people, the Franks, which came to nothing in the short term; but the task was taken up, perhaps through communications between Burgundy and Rome, and as his mind gave shape to his schemes of conversion Gregory turned more and more to the past, to Leo the Great, to a late Roman and christian Britain, and perhaps even to the Chronicle of Prosper, written largely in Rome, which would have told him of another papal initiative in converting the barbarian beyond the ocean.[52]

50 Fritze, 'Universalis gentium confessio', p. 109, following Caspar, *Geschichte des Papsttums*, II.505, n. 3, has argued that this text refers to the Celtic areas of Britain, on the grounds that the *Moralia* were written before the English mission set out. This is implausible (the British had long been christian) and unnecessary (the *Moralia* cannot be shown to have been completed before 600 or 602 at the latest: see Adriaen's introduction to his edition, I.v–vi).

51 Bede, *Historia ecclesiastica gentis Anglorum*, I.27, no. VII; I.29.

52 I am very grateful to Ian Wood for reading a draft and both saving me from error and suggesting improvements.

THE FLORUIT OF ST PATRICK – COMMON AND LESS COMMON GROUND

'The date of St Patrick' has been an issue which has proved obsessive for some scholars. It was given a new lease of life as a subject for controversy when T. F. O'Rahilly published his pamphlet, *The Two Patricks*, in 1942. In particular, the bitter controversies of the decade from 1955 failed to establish common ground on this matter,[1] although it is probably fair to say that most Irish scholars who wrote on that subject eventually came to favour a Patrician floruit in Ireland in the second half of the fifth century.[2] On the other hand, from 1965 onwards R. P. C. Hanson argued a case that the traditional date of St Patrick's arrival as bishop in Ireland, A.D. 432, was correct and that Patrick was therefore unlikely to have outlived the 450s or 460s.[3] Initially sober and impressive,[4] Hanson's case nevertheless depended both on rejection of all native Irish sources[5] and on a series of unsubstantiable assumptions about the nature of life in late Roman and sub-Roman Britain.[6] For twenty years Hanson maintained a determined output of publication about St Patrick, including new translations and edition of his works.[7] But, perhaps sensing a largely unspoken (or at any rate unpublished) unwillingness on the part of Irish scholars to accept his dating and perhaps also aware of some of the weaknesses which underlay his arguments, he became ever more shrill and thus incredible on the subject.[8]

The question has therefore been left in a rather unsatisfactory position. The most visible modern scholarship – Hanson's – was published around the world but contained ever more strident defence of a position which could not be seen to be under attack. The purpose of the present short essay is to establish where the common ground lies and to probe one or two of the most immediate

1 I count from the publication of Carney, *Studies*, pp. 324–73, 394–412.

2 Hanson, *The Life*, p. 20, had the impudence to say that 'Most scholars have accepted the later tradition that he landed in Ireland as a bishop in 432, and therefore his career must be placed wholly or largely in the first half of the fifth century. . . . More recently some have argued that his career covered largely the second half of the fifth century.'

3 Hanson, *St. Patrick, a British Missionary Bishop*, was the first of these publications.

4 His principal early work was *Saint Patrick, his Origins*.

5 *Ibid.*, especially chapter III. While the principle of depending only on contemporary sources was and is admirable, Hanson did not have the scholarly equipment to evaluate the native Irish witnesses which he therefore rejected after what appears to have been an over-hasty assessment of secondary literature on the subject.

6 *Ibid.*, especially chapters I–II and V–VI.

7 *Saint Patrick*, edd. & transl. Hanson & Blanc; *The Life*, transl. Hanson (his second published translation).

8 Hanson, 'The date' and *The Life*.

difficulties which underlie opinions about an 'early' or a 'late' Patrick. Problems arising from later Irish sources will be discussed in subsequent chapters.

It is undoubtedly the case that scholars have generally been content to situate St Patrick in the fifth century. Occasionally an effort has been made to give him an earlier career. An extreme example occurred in a book entitled *St Patrick A.D. 180*. The most promising of such attempts seemed at the time of its publication to be that which the distinguished Hiberno-Latinist, Mario Esposito,[9] published in 1956, arguing that Patrick's career occupied the years *ca* 350–*ca* 430. However, there do indeed seem to be two strands of evidence which together define an approximate period within which Patrick must have worked.

That he wrote in the fifth century is suggested by his observation in §14 of his tract about Coroticus.

Consuetudo Romanorum Gallorum christianorum: mittunt uiros sanctos idoneos ad Francos et ceteras gentes cum tot milia solidorum ad redimendos captiuos baptizatos.

Ludwig Bieler translated:[10]

This is the custom of the Roman christians of Gaul: they send holy and able men to the Franks and other heathen with so many thousand *solidi* to ransom baptised captives.

If the Franks were heathen in Patrick's time, that was unlikely to be in the sixth century, for Clovis (*ob.* 511/12) was the first Frankish king to be converted, a sensational event. The conventional date for his baptism has been 496: it is now clear that precisely when this occurred must be a matter of some doubt.[11] Equally, we cannot guess how quickly a bishop in Ireland might have heard such news. Nor should we be so naïve as to suppose that the taking and ransoming of captives would cease,[12] or all the Franks become suddenly christian, as a result of Clovis's baptism. Nevertheless, the usual deduction from this passage seems not unwarranted: Patrick is perhaps unlikely to have referred to the situation in Gaul in this way if he had been writing in the sixth century.

The evidence which effectively excludes the fourth century as at least a period of Patrick's adult life is of a very different sort. It turns on the nature of the biblical text known to him. Before we consider that, however, it is necessary first to review the internal chronology of Patrick's career before his apostolate began. He came of a family of high status in his locality – his father was both decurion and deacon, his grandfather a priest.[13] Yet the christianity of his parents' household may have been comfortable and conventional: commenting

9 'The Patrician problem'; cf. Binchy, 'Patrick and his biographers', pp. 30–3.

10 *The Works*, transl. Bieler, p. 45. Hanson (*The Life*, p. 68) translated rather differently because he resisted the equation of *gentes* and 'heathen'; consideration of Patrick's usage in general (cf. Devine, *A Computer-generated Concordance*, pp. 109–10) suggests that Hanson was mistaken.

11 Wood, 'Gregory of Tours and Clovis': a date as late as 508 is evidently possible.

12 Bieler (*The Works*, p. 92, n. 38) drew attention to the continuance of ransoming captives as a charitable act in Gaul, as displayed in *The Vitas*, ed. & transl. Garvin, pp. 420–1.

13 *Confessio*, §1; *Epistola ad Coroticum*, §10.

from the fervour of his later belief, he wrote that at the age of fourteen or fifteen or sixteen 'Deum enim uerum ignorabam' and 'Deum uiuum non credebam, neque ex infantia mea, sed in morte et in incredulitate mansi'.[14] He was taken captive by Irish raiders at the age of sixteen and escaped from Ireland after six years' captivity. Of the events immediately following his escape he tells us nothing, save to say that 'post paucos annos in Brittanniis eram cum parentibus meis, qui me ut filium susceperunt et ex fide rogauerunt me ut uel modo ego post tantas tribulationes quas ego pertuli nusquam ab illis discederem'.[15] It was at this time that a vision called him to his apostolate. The next years are even more obscure, but presumably they were dedicated to christian education and passing through the clerical grades, perhaps also to entry to monastic life. Before he was a deacon he confided a boyhood sin to a friend:[16] thirty years later this confidence was betrayed at a critical moment and he was denied promotion to the episcopate.[17] At an absolute minimum, then, Patrick was 15 + 30 = 45 years old at the time of that rejection: this makes no allowance for the *paucos annos* between his escape from captivity and his return to his parents nor for however long might have elapsed between his vision and his confiding his sin to his friend. When he eventually became a bishop we do not know, for he tells us nothing of the process. It is not surprising that some have concluded that he was a self-appointed bishop. That is no doubt to go too far. But Patrick was, one must presume, at the very least about fifty before he became a bishop.[18] For the moment, at any rate, the point is that his christian education and preparation for holy orders are unlikely to have begun before his mid-twenties. Unless we suppose that more of the Latin bible had rubbed off on him as a child than he later cared to admit, he would have begun to acquire his thorough knowledge of Holy Writ only in his middle years.

What was the Bible which he studied? In 1947 Ludwig Bieler published a substantial paper in which he analysed Patrick's biblical citations. This examination revealed that the Bible which Patrick knew was textually composite. The various biblical books were of three origins.[19]

(*a*) He knew a wholly Old Latin text of all the Old Testament (save for the Psalter), and, in the New Testament, of Revelation.
(*b*) He knew a Vulgate text of Acts.

14 *Confessio*, §§1, 27. For an extraordinarily misguided new argument developed from this sentence, see Powell, 'Christianity or solar monotheism'.
15 *Ibid.*, §23. See below, pp. 134–5, for discussion of this passage. If the 'few years' are really to be placed after his escape from Ireland, we can allow ourselves to imagine Patrick wandering across western Europe in search of home.
16 *Ibid.*, §27.
17 Cf. Bieler's assessment of the import of this episode: *The Works*, p. 86, n. 68. The crucial question is 'thirty years later than what?' – his sin in perhaps his fifteenth year, or his confiding the details to his friend. Cf. p. 137, below.
18 He could conceivably have been a priest in Ireland before that: cf. pp. 25–8, below.
19 Bieler, 'Der Bibeltext'; cf. the summary and discussion by Hanson, *Saint Patrick, his Origins*, pp. 179–84. It is extraordinary that Hanson could subsequently write (*The Life*, p. 45) that 'there is no clear indication that Patrick knew or used Jerome's Vulgate'! Reference to Mras, 'St. Patricius als Lateiner', p. 100, or to Mras's review (of Bieler's 'Libri') in *Anzeiger für die Altertumswissenschaft* 8 (1955) col. 73, is no basis for a challenge to Bieler's conclusions.

(*c*) His citations of the Psalter and of the New Testament (except Acts and Revelation) is contaminated – essentially pre-Vulgate but with some Vulgate readings.

Bieler summarised his findings in the statement that Patrick's quotations from the Bible were 'from a text at the point of transition from Old Latin to Vulgate'.[20] Numerous cautions attach themselves to this kind of evidence. We cannot be certain that his citations (or, rather, in many cases, reminiscences) are all of the Bible as he first learned it rather than as mutated by subsequent contact with varying texts. The citations could have been contaminated with Vulgate readings in the mediaeval transmission of Patrick's writings. However, the untidy distribution of Vulgate-readings in the Psalter, Gospels, and Epistles, the absolute dominance of the Vulgate Acts of the Apostles, and the clearly Old Latin nature of the remainder are, in their very inconsistency with one another, as good a guarantee of general authenticity as could be wished for.

St Jerome's Vulgate New Testament was completed in 383. His first Psalter-translations date from the 380s, and the remainder of the Old Testament was translated in the 390s and completed in 404. Jerome worked first in Rome and then in Palestine but where he remained in contact with the West. By A.D. 400 we have evidence for citation of the Vulgate in Latin North Africa. It would be astonishing, therefore, if Patrick's religious education, wherever we might reasonably deduce him to have gained it, occurred before the fifth century. How much later we should place the *terminus post quem* is a matter of guesswork. Early acquisition of a copy of Acts could be explained by all manner of hypotheses; but the infiltration of Vulgate readings into the Psalter, Gospels, and Epistles would, one imagines, have been a process of rather long duration.[21]

The other issue which certainly affects dating and is in some degree measurable is the progress of monasticism. St Patrick's writing contains what might be thought to be a surprising number of monastic references – at any rate, the point has certainly been downplayed by most commentators. Consider the following passages.

Confessio, §41. Vnde autem Hiberione qui numquam notitiam Dei habuerunt nisi idola et inmunda usque nunc semper coluerunt quo modo nuper perfecta est plebs Domini et filii Dei nuncupantur, filii Scottorum et filiae regulorum monachi et uirgines Christi esse uidentur?

§42. Et etiam una benedicta Scotta genetiua nobilis pulcherrima adulta erat, quam ego baptizaui; et post paucos dies una causa uenit ad nos, insinuauit nobis responsum accepisse a nuntio Dei et monuit eam ut esset uirgo Christi et ipso Deo proximaret. Deo gratias, sexta ab hac die optime et auidissime

20 Bieler, *The Life*, p. 38.

21 Bieler, *ibid.*, thought that the textual state of Patrick's Bible 'suggest[s] a date in the middle of the fifth century'. He perhaps did not see the chronological import of this assessment. Another textual issue which has been thought to have chronological implications is the nature of St Patrick's Creed (*Confessio*, §4; cf. §14). Extensive discussion has proved inconclusive, it seems to me. See Oulton, *The Credal Statements*; Bieler, 'The "creeds" '; Hanson, *Tradition*, 'Patrick and the *mensura fidei*', 'Dogma and formula', and 'The rule of faith'; Bradley, 'The doctrinal formula'; Hanson, 'Witness', *The Search*, and 'The *Profession*'.

arripuit illud quod etiam omnes uirgines Dei ita hoc faciunt, non sponte patrum earum, sed et persecutiones patiuntur et improperia falsa a parentibus suis et nihilominus plus augetur numerus – et de genere nostro qui ibi nati sunt nescimus numerus eorum – praeter uiduas et continentes.[22]

§49. Nam etsi imperitus sum in omnibus tamen conatus sum quippiam seruare me etiam et fratribus christianis et uirginibus Christi . . .

Epistola, §12. Lupi rapaces deglutierunt gregem Domini, qui utique Hiberione cum summa diligentia optime crescebat, et filii Scottorum et filiae regulorum monachi et uirgines Christi enumerare nequeo.

There can be no doubt, on this information, that Patrick was encouraging monasticism for men and women. We may therefore wish to consider whether Patrick himself had taken monastic vows.[23] One approach to this problem is to examine his use of the word *frater* to see whether it carries a monastic bias.[24] In general, in the *Confessio* and *Epistola*, it does not seem to do so, but one might note the juxtaposition *fratribus christianis et uirginibus Christi* in the passage just quoted from §49. Patrick's latinity requires new scrutiny from this point of view. The question must be put, however, whether a fifth-century bishop who was not himself a monk would so actively encourage monasticism. That same question might indeed be given a sharper chronological edge: by what date in the fifth century had the monastic movement grown sufficiently strong that the monastic developments revealed by Patrick's writings could have taken place?[25] The fourth century is out of the question; but how much of the fifth century is also ruled out?

I come last to an issue which has provoked some controversy. It has been said that one cannot prove that Patrick's episcopate succeded that of Palladius.[26] For all that, most students of the period have accepted Prosper Tiro's statement that Palladius was the first bishop for the Irish. What is certain is that Patrick was not the first missionary in some areas for – as he tells us in *Confessio*, §51 – 'ubique pergebam . . . in multis periculis etiam usque ad exteras partes, ubi nemo ultra erat et ubi numquam aliquis peruenerat qui baptizaret aut clericos ordinaret aut populum consummaret', (in Bieler's translation) 'I went . . . everywhere for your sake in many dangers, even to the farthest districts beyond which there lived nobody and where nobody had ever come to baptise, or to ordain clergy, or to confirm the people').[27] This provides the clearest indication

22 The reader should be warned that, even by the standards of Patrician criticism, there has been a remarkable variety of translations of this sentence.

23 Mohrmann, *The Latin of Saint Patrick*, p. 50, was adamant against this: 'The absence of monastic terminology in the works of Patrick is decisive'.

24 *Confessio*, §§6, 14, 32, 43, 47, 49; *Epistola ad Coroticum*, §§9, 16, 21.

25 Cf. the discussions by Grosjean ('S. Patrice à Auxerre sous S. Germain', p. 173) and Binchy ('Patrick and his biographers', p. 33). See also below, pp. 56–7, 139–40, and especially 180.

26 Binchy, *ibid.*

27 *The Works*, transl. Bieler, p. 37. Hanson (*Saint Patrick, his Origins*, pp. 184–5) offered the interesting observation that this notion of preaching to the end of the earth is to be connected with ideas of the approaching end of the world, themselves drawing strength from the fall and sack of Rome in A.D. 410.

that Patrick was not working virgin-territory. That he preached as far as the north or west or south coast of Ireland (or all of them) might be held to be indicated by his remark in §34, 'ecce testes sumus quia euangelium praedicatum est usque ubi nemo ultra est', 'indeed, we are witnesses that the Gospel has been preached into those parts beyond which there lives nobody',[28] although it is possible that this is simply a reference to Ireland as the last inhabited territory before the Western ocean.

There have been both minimal and maximalist reactions to the question of Patrick's relationship to his christian predecessors in Ireland. The mediaeval Irish response was minimalist. Palladius was a failure.[29] Patrick therefore came the following year, 432.[30] On the other hand, those who have thought of Patrick as working in the late fifth century have considered different possible scenarios in the transition from Palladius's papally directed enterprise to Patrick's British-supported mission. Suddenly, however, we have new and exciting material. As Thomas Charles-Edwards has shown, at the head of this volume, the papacy was still involved with its colleagues in Ireland at the outset of the pontificate of Leo I (440–461); and through the 450s 'missionary activity among the barbarians . . . was a matter of concern in the highest circles of christendom'. He has envisaged a situation in which the sudden expansion of Anglo-Saxon power at the expense of the Britons from the 440s onwards made communications between Rome, Gaul, and Ireland increasingly difficult.[31] It was presumably in these circumstances that the British Churches – which might in any case have provided from the first a significant part of the manpower for the new Irish Church – took over responsibility for the development of christianity in Ireland.[32] There are inevitable chronological conclusions to be drawn from this picture.

28 *The Works*, transl. Bieler, p. 31. That he perhaps reached or returned to (despite Bieler, *The Works*, p. 85, n. 61, and 'The problem') those 'qui erant iuxta siluam Uocluti quae est prope mare occidentale' and who had cried out to him in his vision (*Confessio*, §23) may be a further indication of the same point – unless *mare occidentale* is simply the Irish Sea, rather than the Atlantic.

29 See the material assembled by Bieler, 'The mission of Palladius'.

30 See my discussion of this date, pp. 39–43, below.

31 See above, pp. 1–12 (quotation from p. 3), especially 9–10 on Britain.

32 See further pp. 133–45, below.

ST PATRICK'S *UILLULA* AND THE FIFTH-CENTURY OCCUPATION OF ROMANO-BRITISH VILLAS

K. R. Dark

In his *Confessio* Patrick says that he was taken prisoner, aged sixteen, at a *uillula*.[1] This could mean a 'farm', an 'estate', or even a 'hill-fort', but interest has understandably concentrated on the possibility that this was a 'villa' in the modern archaeological sense of the term.[2] If Patrick was referring to a villa in this latter sense, he would either provide us with the latest evidence for the Romano-British villa or have lived in one in, at latest, the first quarter of the fifth century. In Britain, unlike Gaul, villas (in the modern archaeological sense) fell into disuse by the early fifth century, and probably closer to A.D. 400 than to 450.[3] A boy growing up in, say, the 430s or 440s is not likely to have lived in what archaeologists today would call 'a villa'.

Patrick's *uillula* is unlikely to have been a hill-fort. There is no certain evidence that '*uilla*' could be used in this way by (sub-)Roman Britons, and the suburban context of Patrick's *uillula*, near a *uicus*, militates against such a view.[4] As Sheppard Frere has famously remarked, Gildas does not call any site a 'villa', but he did have reason to describe hill-forts.[5] It is unlikely that Patrick was referring to such a site, and in any case we might expect that he would have used another term, for example, *burgus*.[6]

If we assume that we are seeking a farm, and not an area of land, then there are again only a few options in the known archaeology of sub-Roman Britain.[7] It must, of course, be noted that this is a period in which domestic sites, such as

1 *Confessio*, §1.

2 Frere, *Britannia*, p. 366; Hanson, *St Patrick, his Origins*, pp. 114–15. For a recent archaeological definition of 'the Romano-British villa' see Hingley, *Rural Settlement*, pp. 30–54 (especially 31). Hingley has noted six defining characteristics which need not all be present on every villa-site: partly built of stone, tile- or slate-roofed, mosaics and/or tessellated pavements, heated room(s), bath-house, painted plaster.

3 Percival, *The Roman Villa*, pp. 171–82; Frere, *Britannia*, pp. 366–7; Esmonde Cleary, *The Ending*, p. 134; Percival, 'The fifth-century villa'.

4 For the juxtaposition see Patrick, *Confessio*, §1. For Sidonius's use of *uilla* for a fifth-century hill-fort see Percival, *The Roman Villa*, pp. 174–6.

5 Frere, *Britannia*, p. 367. I take Gildas, *De excidio Britanniae*, I.25 and II.32 to be referring to hill-forts.

6 Percival, *The Roman Villa*, pp. 174–5, has noted that Sidonius used *burgus* for a hill-fort.

7 The most recent complete survey of the relevant archaeological evidence is that of Dark, 'High Status Sites', pp. 128–237.

farms, are notoriously difficult to identify and seem not to offer any diagnostic artefacts whatsoever. But, if we suppose that the sites at present identified as fifth- or sixth-century farms represent the range of such settlements originally in existence, then we can divide them all into two categories: 'enclosed' or 'unenclosed homesteads' similar to those found in Late Roman Britain and 'squatter-occupation' in disused Late Roman villas.

If Patrick was referring to a fifth-century British farm, then, as far as we can judge, he must have been referring to a site falling within these two groups. Two factors make it unlikely that the site concerned was a 'native' 'unenclosed' or 'enclosed homestead'. Patrick's *uillula* was owned by a decurion who was also a deacon and the son of a priest, who had a literate son with a Roman name.[8] This level of romanisation far exceeds what is conventionally seen as that of the equivalent sites in Late Roman Britain.[9] Secondly, it is doubtful whether these low- to middle-status homesteads housed the urban élite, even in the fourth century.[10] It might, therefore, be supposed that the *uillula* was something more romanised than a native homestead.

This brings us to the sites with 'squatter-occupation' in villas. What archaeologists call 'squatter-occupation' is small-scale domestic use usually involving the repair of a few rooms of a villa-building or their alteration in such a way as to presuppose a lack of romanised building techniques.[11] It is a characteristic of such occupation that, instead of new mosaics, hearths were built on, and post-holes cut through, mosaic floors. Baths and hypocaust-systems fell into disuse, and sometimes simple timber-buildings were erected in the courtyards of, or near, fourth-century villa-sites. Occasionally, as at Latimer,[12] more sophisticated timber-buildings replaced the mortared-stone structures of the villa. This pattern of re-use is extremely widespread throughout the area where Roman villas existed.

There are hints in Patrick's text that it is such a site which he meant by *uillula*. Patrick tells us that his father's *uillula* was near a *uicus*, and that his father was a decurion.[13] His information helps us to fit *uillula* into the known pattern of Romano-British settlement. A *uicus* is probably what some modern archaeologists would call a 'small town' and others would call a 'village'.[14] Such a place is extremely unlikely to have been governed by a romanised town-council, an *ordo*, necessary for the existence of the rank of decurion.[15] The only

8 *Confessio*, §1.

9 Collingwood *et al.*, *The Archaeology of Roman Britain*, p. 175. On romanisation in fourth-century Britain see Millett, *The Romanization of Britain*, pp. 186–211.

10 Even allowing that such sites might contain the rural élite: see Hingley, *Rural Settlement*, pp. 159–61, 123–7, 147.

11 Usefully summarised by Esmonde Cleary, *The Ending*, p. 134.

12 Branigan, *Latimer*.

13 *Confessio*, §1.

14 Todd, 'The vici of western England'. The authors of the latest comprehensive study (Burnham & Wacher, *The 'Small Towns' of Roman Britain*) have taken 'small town' to encompass a range of sites: for example, fortified examples range from under 100m. x 100m. to *circa* 600m. x 400m.. Others would call such sites 'villages', but I shall accept Burnham and Wacher's usage here.

15 Thomas, *Christianity*, p. 311; Hanson, *St Patrick, his Origins*, pp. 117–18.

towns likely to have been governed in this way were *ciuitas*-capitals. The zone referred to is, therefore, somewhere where *ciuitas*-capitas[16] and 'small towns' both occurred. Moreover, villas are more often found grouped around small towns than around *ciuitas*-capitals, and it would be conventional in the study of Roman Britain to assert that the urban élite owned villas surrounding 'small towns'. In other words, Patrick's *Confessio* contains a brief account of the settlement-pattern which we might otherwise find evidenced in the archaeology of Roman Britain.

If Patrick was a fourth-century Briton, we should have no hesitation in fitting him into the known settlement-pattern. In a sub-Roman situation, for Patrick to have dwelt in a secular settlement at a villa-site, he must have lived in what we would call a 'villa with squatter-occupation'. The evidence of Patrick's romanised upbringing might be felt to be in conflict with such a view, but this need not be the case.

In his study of 'squatter-occupation' in the Byzantine Mediterranean, Simon Ellis[17] has observed that modifications refurbishing romanised structures in an apparently piecemeal way would have resulted in the maintenance of a superficially romanised building. He has noted that even members of the Byzantine bureaucratic élite lived in some very modest buildings, as inscriptions incorporated into them show. It is possible, therefore, that we have too restricted a view of how the urban élite in fifth-century Britain lived, that its members might be resident in similarly humble surroundings, and that we can use Ellis's work to recognise that, far from a simple retreat into barbarism, 'squatter-occupation' represents a final phase of rebuilding at what originated as Romano-British sites.

The *romanitas* of villa-sites might bestow tenurial legitimacy on their sub-Roman occupants, whether or not they were the descendants of the landed élite of fourth-century Britain. Although we must recognise that the diminutive element in Patrick's word *uillula* might have lost its meaning in his Latin,[18] that diminutive would certainly convey an accurate description of the reduced occupation evidenced at such sites.

It cannot of course be claimed that this identification is certain, but it does fit all the evidence of Patrick's text. It may be that we can even go some way further towards identifying Patrick's home, by using two more pieces of information provided in his *Confessio*. Patrick says that he was taken prisoner during an Irish raid and that he returned to his family six or more years later.[19] Assuming that my argument thus far is correct, these pieces of information limit the area in which his family-home could have been located.

The combination of *ciuitas*-capital, 'small town', and villa necessitates a lowland, civilian-zone, location.[20] On this basis alone we can effectively rule

16 For small towns, including their relationship to villas, see Burnham & Wacher, *The 'Small Towns' of Roman Britain*; Hingley, *Rural Settlement*, pp. 116–18.

17 Ellis, 'An Archaeological Study'.

18 Hanson, *St Patrick, his Origins*, pp. 114–15.

19 Patrick, *Confessio*, §§1 and 23.

20 For the relevant distributions see Jones & Mattingly, *An Atlas*, p. 154, map 5:11; p. 156, map 5:12; p. 241, map 7:6. Although villas are found in the North (cf. Branigan, 'Villas in the North'), they are far rarer, and the relevant areas cannot satisfy the other criteria inferred here from Patrick's text.

out most of what is now Wales and northwestern England, as well as the southwestern peninsula to the west of the Exeter-district. But if we were to go further and say that Patrick returned to his home after the middle of the fifth century, it is also highly unlikely that this was in the areas settled by the Anglo-Saxons by that time.[21] What is now eastern England, from Humberside to Kent and as far west as Oxfordshire, is, therefore, unlikely to be the area referred to.

This leaves little of the civilian zone in which to locate Patrick. The mention of Irish raids might narrow the area still further. Although it is possible that such attacks would leave no archaeological trace, there is one, and only one, part of Roman Britain which has produced convincing archaeological evidence for Irish maritime raids in the later fourth or early fifth century – the West Country.[22] This is an area with villas, 'small towns', and *ciuitas*-capitals (Cirencester and Dorchester). It was among the most romanised parts of the Late Roman diocese and has convincing evidence for a strongly established rural Church from the fourth century onwards.[23] Villas in this area often show 'squatter-occupation', and there is evidence for the survival of 'small towns' into the fifth and sixth centuries.[24] The West Country might, then, satisfy all the requirements derived from Patrick's *Confessio*.

It seems to me that the argument put forward by Susan Pearce, that villas in this area were converted into religious sites in the fifth century, has greater strength than has often been appreciated.[25] Pearce's view is based upon the coincidence of Late Roman villas, sub-Roman cemeteries, and the sites of Anglo-Saxon minsters. Few of these sites have been the subject of excavations carried out to modern standards, but continuity from Late Roman villa to sub-Roman monastery might be expected on the analogy of Gallic sites producing similar sequences, where textual evidence assures us of this interpretation. Clearly, if villa-owners changed their villas into monasteries, villa-estates may

21 Hawkes, 'The South-east after the Romans'; Hines, 'Philology, archaeology'.

22 Branigan, *The Roman Villa in South-west England*, pp. 93–8, and 'Villa settlement in the West Country'. Although archaeological distribution-maps can be misleading in that they reflect mere survival of evidence, distributions of archaeological work, and/or distributions of distinctive artefacts, the sort of data upon which this particular distribution is based would be recognisable in even the most basic of excavations. As excavators have often expected villas to end in massacre or burning, material suggesting this has been widely sought. It is well known among British archaeologists that such material has not usually been forthcoming, and so it seems reasonable to place importance upon the only large regional group of sites showing evidence of destruction. That these are mostly situated along river-valleys accessible from the sea suggests that they represent maritime raiding, while numismatic evidence provides dates after which the relevant deposits must have occurred. For a discussion of the relevant textual information see Sims-Williams, 'Gildas and the Anglo-Saxons', pp. 9–15.

23 Thomas, *Christianity*, p. 138, fig. 15.

24 Branigan, *The Roman Villa in South-west England*, pp. 100–6; Dark, 'High Status Sites', pp. 193–9.

25 Pearce, 'The early church in the landscape', 'Estates and church sites', and 'Church and society in South Devon'; cf. Dark, 'High Status Sites', pp. 389 and 408. As Richard Morris has pointed out, these sites were not chosen for Anglo-Saxon minsters because they provided ready supplies of building stone, for such churches were almost certainly built of wood in the relevant period: Morris, *Churches in the Landscape*, p. 102.

have become monastic estates, whether or not these were later transferred to Anglo-Saxon minsters. If her interpretation is correct, then there is also evidence that sub-Roman tenurial continuity was to be found in the West Country.[26]

There is, then, a case for localising Patrick's British home in the West Country, perhaps specifically in an area close to a 'small town' near to a *ciuitas*-capital. The possible areas are further limited by the distribution of 'small towns'. Southern Dorset and the Cotswolds would seem to be the most likely areas. Of these, southern Dorset contains the only evidence for fourth-century chi-rho symbols in villa-mosaics, and the evidence from Poundbury suggests that church-members held high rank in the local community.[27] There is less evidence for either of these characteristics in the Cirencester-area but the town itself had perhaps been a bishopric from the fourth century.[28]

There are no other areas of Roman Britain which fit Patrick's description of his home so well. It must be remembered, however, that this interpretation rests ultimately on three assumptions: that Patrick refers to a site rather than an area when he uses the term *uillula*, that the range of sub-Roman British settlement-types, at present known, is, in general terms, representative of that which once existed, and that Patrick grew up in, was kidnapped from, and returned to his home-area in the fifth century.

I have employed these assumptions to consider the possible meaning of Patrick's *uillula* and its implications for localising his British home. In conclusion we might note some of the implications for Romano-British villa-studies if my interpretation of the evidence is found acceptable.

First, this interpretation would help to confirm that the social and tenurial relationships conventionally proposed for villas, 'small towns', and *ciuitas*-capitals, are correct. Secondly, it would suggest that what has often been dismissed as 'squatter-occupation' represents a final phase of 'high-status' secular occupation of villas.[29] Thirdly, it would imply that the final occupation of villas continued in sub-Roman Britain at least until the middle of the fifth century. Fourthly, we should have to suppose that much of the fabric of Romano-British life, including urban administration, was still in place in Patrick's home-region until that time. These conclusions are, it seems to me, in accordance with broader interpretations supportable on a wide range of other archaeological and historical sources.[30]

We should not, however, forget that Patrick's *uillula* could mean 'estate', and that any attempt to correlate his term with an archaeologically identifiable site can therefore only be tentative. If we were to adopt the interpretation proposed

26 Evidence from a villa at Halstock (Dorset) may show extensive rebuilding of the site in timber, during the fifth century or later. If so, then this too supports the view that, at least in some cases, continuity of tenure occurred at West-Country villas. I owe this information to C. Sparey Green, who was able to observe the site while it was under excavation by the late R. Lucas.

27 Thomas, *Christianity*, p. 104, cf. p. 137, fig. 15; Sparey Green, 'The cemetery of a Romano-British community at Poundbury'.

28 Thomas, *Christianity*, pp. 133–4.

29 Recently suggested on archaeological grounds by Higham, *Rome, Britain*, p. 116.

30 Dark, *Civitas to Kingdom*.

here, it would significantly alter our perception of the end of the Roman villa in Britain and of the 'squatter-occupation' found so frequently on villa-sites. Even if the interpretation proposed here is correct, it does not, however, necessitate tenurial continuity between the fourth and fifth centuries and does not show that Patrick was of, or descended from, the villa-owning classes of Late Roman Britain. For all we know, Patrick's father may have been the first of his family to hold secular office, and/or to acquire the *uillula* concerned. There seems to be a strong case, however, for considering the final, fifth-century, phase of occupation at villa-sites to be just that, and for abandoning the term 'squatter-occupation' once and for all.

ST PATRICK'S MISSING YEARS

One of the difficulties presented by St Patrick's only initially chronological review of his career, which constituted his *Confessio* or 'Declaration' *antequam moriar*,[1] is that most of his mature years are passed over: accounts of his origins, Irish captivity in his youth, and his 'laborious episcopate' in Ireland dominate his autobiographical account.[2] A great deal of speculation has attempted to fill this void. The question may reasonably be put, therefore, whether there is any realistic hope of recovering or deducing anything about these missing years.[3]

I have already discussed those aspects of the question which bear directly on the internal chronology of Patrick's life. Here I wish rather to consider some geographical issues. It has often been suggested that Patrick spent part of these missing years in Gaul. His Latin has been studied with a view to determining whether any elements are discoverable in it which can underpin such a theory. Christine Mohrmann, that most distinguished of Late Latinists, pronounced that 'There are in the language of Saint Patrick many elements of living Late Latin, which cannot possibly be traced back to British Latin. Therefore we must allow for a contact of Patrick with the Continent.'[4] Her conclusions are uniformly vitiated by her not having understood that Britain too had its own living Latin in that period, but that such of it as we can recover does not provide a basis for comparison with Patrick's latinity.[5] In the absence of a British equivalent of *Itinerarium Egeriae*, such study is hamstrung at the outset. Since Mohrmann could not define features of syntax or vocabulary separating the Latin of Gaul from that of Britain, there was from the outset no possibility of coming to an informed conclusion on the point at issue. The question must be resolved from what Patrick says (or does not say), not from how he constructed his language.

We have already encountered one of Patrick's two references to affairs in Gaul, his notice of how Gallo-Roman christians ransomed captives from the barbarians.[6] It is a nice question whether that need show any direct knowledge rather than having been gained from a Gallo-Roman informant or through common report in Insular christian circles. The other reference has occasioned a good deal more debate. In *Confessio*, §43, apparently explaining why he cannot

1 For the rendering of *Confessio* as *Declaration*, see *St. Patrick*, ed. & transl. Hood.

2 Bieler's quite reasonable translation (*The Works*, p. 29) of Patrick's *laboriosum episcopatum* is unfortunate because of another famous Briton who was to claim that as his lot – John Bale, in mid-sixteenth-century Ossory.

3 For their extent, perhaps from his mid-twenties to his mid-forties or fifties, see my discussion above, pp. 14–15. Cf. pp. 134–7, below.

4 *The Latin of Saint Patrick*, p. 50.

5 Cf. Hanson, *The Life*, p. 30.

6 *Epistola ad Coroticum*, §14. See above, p. 14.

leave Ireland (to answer his critics, perhaps at the instance of a formal summons from his superiors), Patrick asserts that 'libentissime paratus eram quasi ad patriam et parentes – non id solum sed etiam usque ad Gallias uisitare fratres et ut uiderem faciem sanctorum Domini mei'; 'how I should have loved to go to my country and my parents, and also to Gaul in order to visit the brethren and to see the face of the saints of my Lord!'[7] Gaul emerges from these two references as an object of admiration and desire – but it is hard to deduce with conviction from either that Patrick had prior, direct knowledge of that region. As E. A. Thompson has put it, Patrick's 'wish tells neither for nor against any such visit'.[8]

Another part of Patrick's *Confessio* has often been interpreted as referring to a stay of his in Gaul. Writing of the occasion when he was betrayed by his closest friend as he was being considered for promotion to the episcopate, he tells us:[9]

Et comperi ab aliquantis fratribus ante defensionem illam – quod ego non interfui nec in Brittanniis eram, nec a me oriebatur – ut et ille in mea absentia pulsaret pro me. Etiam mihi ipse ore suo dixerat, "Ecce dandus es tu ad gradum episcopatus", quod ego non eram dignus.

This difficult passage has given rise to radically different translations, all heavy in interpretation. Consider first that of Ludwig Bieler.[10]

And I was told by some of the brethren before that defence – at which I was not present, nor was I in Britain, nor was it suggested by me – that he would stand up for me in my absence. He had even said to me in person: "Look, you should be raised to the rank of bishop!" – of which I was not worthy.

Richard Hanson had a very different version.[11]

And I learned from some of the brothers that before that occasion for defending myself (at a time when I was not present nor was I even in Britain nor was the matter initiated by me) he, even he, was canvassing for me. He even had said to me with his own mouth, "Listen! You are to be promoted to the rank of bishop," though I was not worthy.

Patrick tells us quite explicitly that he was not in Britain at that time, but says no more. There are only two obvious possibilities – that he was in Gaul or in Ireland. Since Patrick never says anything about ever having been in Gaul, it might seem reasonable to start instead with the latter possibility. Hanson, with the dogmatism characteristic of his later writings, wrote that Patrick 'could not

7 *The Works*, transl. Bieler, p. 35 (with one minor alteration).

8 *Who was Saint Patrick?*, pp. 148–9. The episode of twenty-eight days' wandering in a desert (*Confessio*, §§19–20 and 22) has also often been taken as evidence for Patrick's having visited Gaul: we can be grateful to E. A. Thompson (*ibid.*, pp. 30–4) for his final demolition of literal (including Gallic) interpretations of Patrick's story.

9 *Confessio*, §32.

10 Bieler, *The Works*, p. 30.

11 *The Life*, p. 102 (with commentary on pp. 103, 105).

possibly have been in Ireland'.[12] The only grounds for such a view would be that Patrick 'could not possibly' have gone to Ireland before he became a bishop. But one has only to state this to see its weakness. Its logic is only that of those mediaeval *uitae* of Patrick which send the saint for eighty years' training in Gaul before allowing him to return to Ireland as a missionary.[13]

We must consider Patrick's account, in the *Confessio*, of his spiritual journey. After he had finally returned to his parents (six or more years after being snatched from them by Irish raiders), he had a vision in which he understood the Irish to be calling him back to them. This episode concludes with Patrick's reflexion, 'Deo gratias, quia post plurimos annos praestitit illis Dominus secundum clamorem illorum'.[14] The problem is a very familiar one: how many are *plurimos annos*?[15] Does this authorise us to suppose, with the authors of the mediaeval *uitae*, that when Patrick next set foot in Ireland he was a missionary bishop? One might think it strange that, if Patrick felt the call, he did not make great efforts to return as soon as he might have the necessary qualifications.

Many imponderables surround the question of how Patrick might equip himself to become a missionary. At the minimum he must assume holy orders and get himself posted to an office in the Irish Church. But here too we come up against a question of chronology. On some views of Patrick's life, there was no Irish Church, there were no Irish christians indeed, at the time when he returned from captivity. We do not know how or when christianity first reached Ireland. We do know, thanks to Prosper Tiro, that there were christians there in 431, and presumably therefore for some few years previously at least. However, if Patrick escaped from Ireland in 400x420, this might not have been so. In such a situation it could indeed have been a life's work to argue the case for a British mission to the Gaelic heathen. In recent years, however, we have been reminded forcefully by E. A. Thompson of those lost souls, the Britons who like Patrick were carried off to slavery in Ireland but who unlike him did not escape home.[16] It would perhaps have been a lesser difficulty to plead the cause of organising a mission (ostensibly) to bring pastoral care to them.

If, on the other hand, Patrick escaped after the events of 431, the possibility of joining the new Irish Church need not have seemed so remote. The number of ecclesiastics with experience of Irish conditions and the Irish language – and a willingness to work in Ireland! – must have been exiguous at best. Patrick, once trained, should have been a very welcome addition to the Church headed by Palladius or any successor. The closer in time that his training brought him to the point at which the Roman and Gallican Churches could no longer routinely sustain a team of clergy in Ireland,[17] the better would be Patrick's chances of

12 *Ibid.*, p. 105.

13 See below, pp. 65–84.

14 *Confessio*, §23.

15 His other uses of *plurimus* are not of much help: Devine, *A Computer-generated Concordance*, p. 209.

16 Thompson, 'St. Patrick and Coroticus'; and cf. *The Visigoths*. See also below, p. 108. The Britons taken in captivity were *tot milia hominum* (*Confessio*, §1); those whom Patrick subsequently baptised were counted thus too, perhaps significantly (*Confessio*, §§14, 50).

17 Cf. above, pp. 9–10, 18.

finding an outlet there for his personal mission. In a post-431 context, therefore, Patrick's *plurimos annos* could have been no more years than were necessary to acquire suitable ecclesiastical training.

This turns the spotlight on the circumstances in which Patrick finally was made bishop. He never tells us in so many words the nature of his episcopal responsibility. The nearest is the strange statement at the beginning of the tract about Coroticus: 'Patricius, peccator indoctus scilicet, Hiberione constitutus, episcopum me esse fateor', 'I, Patrick, an unlearned sinner resident in Ireland, declare that I am a bishop'.[18] He may have been a successor of Palladius. In theory he might have worked under or alongside Palladius. He might have been made 'bishop of Ireland' or merely bishop of some part of Ireland. None of these things do we know. But we might think it certain that if he had had experience as a priest in Ireland, he would both have started to realise his own personal mission and have acquired invaluable experience which could have persuaded his British superiors to consider his promotion when need struck.

The only certain point is that Patrick was not in Britain at his personal moment of crisis, described in §32 of the *Confessio*. We know that only because he tells us so. To deduce that he was in Gaul is unfounded guesswork. To deduce that he was in Ireland is also unfounded guesswork: but it has the merit of taking him where we know him to have been and where he would have been gaining further relevant experience, satisfying his own spiritual need at the same time.

Nevertheless, St Patrick's lost years remain mislaid. But some of the middle portion of his life may have been spent in the mission-field. Twice he tells us that he had baptised *tot milia hominum*:[19] not all of that work need have been part of his *laboriosum episcopatum*.[20]

18 *Epistola*, §1. The declaration becomes stranger still as it proceeds.
19 *Confessio*, §§14 and 50.
20 *Ibid.*, §26.

THE DEATH-DATE OF ST PATRICK

In this chapter, I do not seek to establish when St Patrick died. Rather, my concern is with the dates offered in mediaeval sources. The collection and digestion of this material is an essential preliminary to any deduction about the value of these overt statements on the subject.

I turn first to the annalistic evidence, which constitutes the least ambiguous corpus of such references. As is well known there are two principal groups of annal-entries. The one places the saint's death *ca* A.D. 460. Most members of this group refer to Patrick in his guise as *Senex Patricius*, Sen-Phátric.

AB[1] *s.a.* 458	Dormitatio sancti Senis Patricii.
AC[2] (A) *s.a.* 13 [= 457]	Sanctus Patricius ad Dominum migratur.
AFM[3] 457.3	Sean Patraicc do faoidhedh a spioraide.
ALL[4] §3	Secundinus et Senex Patricius quieuerunt.
ARC[5] §98	Dormitatio sancti Senis Patricii episcopi Golstomensis ecclesiae.
AU[6] 457.2	Quies Senis Patricii, ut alii libri dicunt.
AU[7] 461.2	Hic alii quietem Patrici dicunt.
CS[8] *s.a.* K.4	Dormitatio sancti Senis Patricii episcopi, id est Glosdoniensis ecclesiae.

The exceptions are therefore the entry in *Annales Cambriae* (which know nothing of distinctions among Patricks) and the second of the *alii* entries in the 'Annals of Ulster'. It is a question whether AU 461.2 represents an alternative to the obit at 457.2 or rather to a date in the 490s: but, to this, the chronicles seem unable to provide an answer. One point does, however, emerge with some clarity from the presentation of these entries, namely that the 'Chronicle of Ireland' is very unlikely to have contained such a notice of the death of *Senex Patricius*: that could be established *prima facie* only by the agreement of the

1 The 'Annals of Boyle': see 'The annals in Cotton MS. Titus A. XXV', ed. Freeman, p. 319.
2 *Annales Cambriae*: see 'The *Annales Cambriæ*', ed. Phillimore, p. 153. I have prepared a new edition and translation of the A-text.
3 The 'Annals of the Four Masters': see *Annala Rioghachta Eireann*, ed. & transl. O'Donovan, I.142/3.
4 The 'Annals from the Book of Leinster': see *The Book of Leinster*, edd. Best *et al.*, I.94 (lines 3000–1).
5 'The Annals of Roscrea', edd. Gleeson & Mac Airt, p. 151 (§98).
6 *The Annals of Ulster*, edd. & transl. Mac Airt & Mac Niocaill, I.44/5.
7 *Ibid.*, I.46/7.
8 *Chronicum Scotorum*, ed. & transl. Hennessy, pp. 24/5.

'Annals of Ulster' and the Clonmacnoise-group.[9] Such a requirement is not met by the distribution of the evidence, for the entries in the 'Annals of Ulster' must be placed among its early accretions to the underlying 'Chronicle of Ireland' in as much as the references to *alii* are a defining aspect of such augmentation. The entry at 457 is best explained as one of the borrowings from the Clonmacnoise-group tradition and therefore no earlier in date than the first half of the tenth century. On the other hand the entry at 461 remains unexplained within the narrow context of the Irish chronicling tradition. If we were to consider only the annalistic evidence, it would be possible to argue that *Senex Patricius* was a tenth-century Clonmacnoise invention.[10]

The obit of Patrick *ipse* at 493 is, however, comprehensively attested in the corpus of mediaeval Irish chronicles.

AB[11] *s.a.* 493	Ab initio mundi secundum Dionisium <anni> .v^{m}.dclx. usque ad transitum sancti Patricii episcopi, ab incarnatione uero Domini .ccccxlviii.; Patricius archiepiscopus et apostolus Hiberniensium anno etatis sue .c^{o}.ix^{o}., .xvi^{o}. die kal. Aprilis quieuit.
AClon[12] [487–496].8	Saint Patrick the Apostle and Archbushopp died in the hundred and twentieth yeare of his age, the sixteenth day of the Calends of Aprill.
AFM[13] 493.1	Patraicc, mac Calpuirn, mic Potaide, airdeaspuc, ceitt priomhaidh 7 ardapstol Ereann, do chuir an céd Celestinus Papa do phroicept soiscela . . . O ro comhfoicc-sigh aimsir eitsechta naomh Patriacc hi Sabhall, ro thochaith corp Chríost a lámhaibh an naoimh epscoip Tassach, isin 122 a aoisi, 7 no fhaidh a spirat do chum nimhe. . . . As do bhliadhnaibh bais naomh Patraicc atrubradh. O genair Criost, áiremh ait, .cccc. for caomh nochait, teora bliadhna fair iarsoin, go bás Patraicc priomhapstoil.
AI[14] [496].1	Quies Patricii hi .xvi. kl. April., anno .cccc.xxxii. a pasione Domini.
ALL[15] §14	Patricius Scottorum episcopus quieuit.

9 For discussion of the principles involved, see Grabowski & Dumville, *Chronicles and Annals*, chapters I–II.

10 For the date of the 'Clonmacnoise Chronicle' see *ibid.*, chapter IV. For some study of the earliest elements in the 'Chronicle of Ireland', see Smyth, 'The earliest Irish annals'. On the non-annalistic evidence for *Senex Patricius* see below, pp. 59–64.

11 'The annals in Cotton MS. Titus A. XXV', ed. Freeman, p. 319; cf. pp. 35–7, below.

12 *The Annals of Clonmacnoise*, ed. Murphy, p. 73; I have quoted directly from the copy in London, British Library, MS. Additional 4817, fo 38(34)r. The most significant difference is that the printed text gives his age as 'ye 123rd yeare'.

13 *Annala Rioghachta Eireann*, ed. & transl. O'Donovan, I.154–9, a vast entry from which I give only brief extracts.

14 *The Annals of Inisfallen*, ed. & transl. Mac Airt, pp. 64/5.

15 *The Book of Leinster*, edd. Best *et al.*, I.94 (line 3011).

AT[16] *s.a.* K.6.2 — PATRICIUS ARCIEPISCOPUS ET APOSTOLUS Hibernensium anno etatis sue centesimo uigessimo, .xvi. die kl. Aprilis, quieuit.

O genemain Crist ceim ait
cethri cét for caemnochaid,
teora bliadna sáer<a> iar soin
co bass Patraic primapstail.

AU[17] *s.a.* 491 [= 492].1 — Dicunt Scoiti hic Patricium archi<e>piscopum defunctum (fore).

AU^2 *s.a.* 491.1 — Tri .xx^{it}. bliadan, tearc dinn,
Ar nae diamhair a nErinn
[ ] go n-imad fert
Do bhi Padraig ag brogecht.

AU[18] *s.a.* 492 [= 493].2 — Patricius archi<a>postulus Scotorum quieuit .c^{mo}.xx. anno etatis sue, .lx^{o}. autem quo uenit ad Hiberniam ad babtisandos Scotos.

CS[19] *s.a.* K.3 — Patricius archiepiscopus et apostolus Hibernensium anno aetatis suae centessimo .xxii^{o}., .xvi. kl. Aprilis, quieuit, ut dicitur:

O genair Criost, airem ait
Cethre céd for caom nochait
Teora bliadhna beacht iar sin
Go bás Padraig, príomh aspail.

What seems clear is that underlying the 'Annals of Ulster' and the other (viz, the Clonmacnoise-group) texts is a core-entry for the year 493 in the 'Chronicle of Ireland' which read something like **Patricius archiepiscopus et apostolus Scotorum quieuit centesimo uicesimo anno etatis sue*. The chronicling traditions then diverged, that of Clonmacnoise acquiring the festival date and a computistical quatrain while that represented by the 'Annals of Ulster' received a statement (and, in due course, two) of the length of Patrick's mission. There is plenty of evidence in the several discrepancies between these ten witnesses that much chronological speculation, and a certain amount of scribal error, caused the annalistically supplied information to diversify: for example, Patrick died at various ages from 109 to 123, and after a mission of sixty or sixty-nine years. By the beginning of the tenth century at the very latest, St Patrick's mission in

16 'The Annals of Tigernach', ed. Stokes, p. 121.

17 *The Annals of Ulster*, edd. & transl. Mac Airt & Mac Niocaill, I.54/5. The last word is an addition in a more recent hand. AU^2 in the second item quoted here refers to the same phase of addition. There is every reason to think that the annotator took the dislocated dates in the principal manuscript (H) at face-value.

18 *Ibid.*, I.56/7. On this entry, cf. the misguided remarks of O'Rahilly, *Early Irish History and Mythology*, p. 246. The entry 553.3 refers to an event 'i cinn tri fichit bliadnae iar n-etsecht Patraic' (viz, in 493) but this is attributed to *Liber Cuanach*, a Clonmacnoise-group text. Other such references back are found at 571.1 (also in the 'Annals of Roscrea', §49, and the 'Annals of Tigernach'), *A morte Patricii .c. anni*, and 664.6 (also in the 'Annals of Tigernach' and *Chronicum Scotorum*), *A morte Patricii .cciii. anni*: on the latter, cf. O'Rahilly, *ibid.*, pp. 242 and 245(–6), n. 6.

19 *Chronicum Scotorum*, ed. & transl. Hennessy, pp. 32/3.

Ireland was deemed in the 'Chronicle of Ireland' to have extended from A.D. 432 to 493: this remained the native chroniclers' universal perception throughout the middle ages and beyond. In the first half of the tenth century, an awareness of a complication in Patrician hagiology and chronology was admitted by the reception into the chronicling tradition of the obit of *Senex Patricius* at A.D. 457; again, this remained integral thenceforth to native chronicles.

In so far as there was ever a single mediaeval Irish view of Patrician chronology, it seems to have been that of an approximately sixty-year mission, A.D. 432–493, St Patrick dying at the Mosaic age of 120;[20] but another and older St Patrick was admitted who died in 457. The only item from the chronicle-texts which is not obviously accounted for thus is the obit (of Patrick *ipse*) which *alii dicunt* should be placed in 461, according to the 'Annals of Ulster'.

Within the chronicle-literature are one or two further hints of knowledge of a death-date for St Patrick at A.D. 461. They are not such, however, as to encourage us to allow a great antiquity to that record. Thomas O'Rahilly drew attention to a notice of St Patrick's birth in the 'Annals of Tigernach' in the following sequence.[21]

K.vi. Constantinus a ducibus Constanti(nu)s fratris sui in bello occisus est. PAITRICIUS NUNC NATUS EST.
K.vii. Constans Arianus effeactus catholicos toto orbe persequitur.

The implication of this is that a Mosaic life-span has been combined with a death-date of 461 or thereabouts. That same date is implied by an *annus mundi* dating in the 'Annals of Boyle'.[22] Likewise an *annus Passionis* dating in the 'Annals of Inisfallen' implies an A.D. date of 459 or 464.[23] The text-historical evidence makes it very unlikely that there is any direct connexion between these few items: rather, they attest to continuing access to sources which asserted such a date for Patrick's death.

Dates in the 460s are calculable from the seventh-century hagiography of Patrick. A.D. 463 or 468 can be reckoned from an *annus Passionis* dating in the B-prologue to Muirchú's *uita.* Likewise, Tírechán's text offers an *annus Passionis* resolvable as A.D. 460 or 465, and cross-checking with other information suggests that 460 was the intended year. Equally, Muirchú at least of these hagiographers seems to have been aware of the death-date in the early 490s.[24]

If we may surmise that all the known or calculated death-dates in the range A.D. 457–463 (or 468) ultimately derive from the same information or calculation, we can turn – if briefly – to the unresolved question of the origin of this

20 On this matter see Dumville, 'Celtic-Latin texts', pp. 30–3, and Hennig, 'The literary tradition of Moses'. Cf. pp. 47–8, below, for various great ages attributed to Patrick. Hughes (*The Church in Early Irish Society*, p. 72) summarised a text printed in *Councils*, edd. Haddan & Stubbs, I.138–40 (cf. Kenney, *The Sources*, pp. 687–8), which had Patrick living to 143!

21 *The Two Patricks*, p. 71; cf. 'The Annals of Tigernach', ed. Stokes, p. 31. On the chronology, cf. Hanson, *Saint Patrick, his Origins*, p. 219.

22 See the discussion by K. L. Maund, below, pp. 35–7.

23 Cf. *ibid.*; on the alternative equations, see also below, pp. 36, 47.

24 For edition and translation of the works by Muirchú and Tírechán see *The Patrician Texts*, edd. & transl. Bieler & Kelly (on the B-prologue, see *ibid.*, p. 194); cf. also below, pp. 45–64, for further discussion.

date. It is unlikely, as we have seen, that it has great antiquity within the Irish chronicling tradition. It would therefore be simpler to suppose that its place lies ultimately in the hagiographical literature or the underlying hagiological lore (although it must be admitted that there is one item within the chronicling tradition which is otherwise unexplained and of which the hagiography is innocent – that of the *probatio Patricii in fide catholica*).[25] It is from the hagiography that an argument has been mounted that we have access through it to lost *acta* of Palladius: a death-date from him *ca* 460 would not necessarily be incredible and would cohere with the simplest explanation – Tírechán's and O'Rahilly's – of the identity of the mysterious *Senex Patricius*.[26]

Of the later dating for St Patrick's death one further point should be made here. The question of the earliest point in the 'Chronicle of Ireland' at which contemporary recording may be found is still in dispute. Dates *ca* 550,[27] *ca* 600,[28] and *ca* 680[29] have been advanced for this archival horizon. In debate about St Patrick's dates, much weight has been given to D. A. Binchy's view that the fifth-century annals contain nothing of independent value for that period. Indeed, R. P. C. Hanson used Binchy's authority as an excuse for his own comprehensive failure to engage with Irish source-material: such crude rejection of a whole class of evidence allowed Hanson to develop his own theories about dating untrammelled by the doubts which Irish sources would necessarily have inculcated.[30] A single observation should suffice here. If the earliest suggested date for the beginning of contemporaneity of record in the 'Chronicle of Ireland' should prove to be correct, one would have to admit that events in the 490s would have occurred within (if only just within) what was then living memory. That is not to say that the annalistic record of St Patrick's death in 493 was made *ca* 550, much less in the 490s, but it is to admit that a chronicler of Irish events writing in the mid-sixth century might think the death of Patrick in the 490s to provide an appropriate element of or even frame for his record. The possibility of early recording exists: it is up to scholars to provide reasons for and against the relationship of extant and reconstructable annalistic statements to sixth-century chronicling and fifth-century events.

25 Found in the annal for A.D. 441 in the 'Annals of Ulster' (edd. & transl. Mac Airt & Mac Niocaill, I.40/1) and the 'Annals of Inisfallen' (ed. & transl. Mac Airt, pp. 56/7). For discussion, cf. O'Rahilly, *Early Irish History and Mythology*, pp. 251–2, 509–10; Carney, *The Problem*, p. 34; Hanson, *Saint Patrick, his Origins*, pp. 100–3; and below, pp. 79–80, 85. For an important discussion see Morris, 'The dates of the Celtic saints', pp. 364–5.

26 See further below, pp. 59–64.

27 Byrne, 'Seventh-century documents'; Smyth, 'The earliest Irish annals'; Harrison, 'Epacts'; Dumville, 'Latin and Irish', p. 322 (cf. 'Sub-Roman Britain', p. 189).

28 Herbert, *Iona, Kells*, pp. 21–3.

29 Hughes, *Early Christian Ireland*, pp. 117–18.

30 Hanson, *Saint Patrick, his Origins*, pp. 96–105. Cf. Binchy, 'Patrick and his biographers', pp. 70–5.

THE SECOND OBIT OF ST PATRICK IN THE 'ANNALS OF BOYLE'

K. L. Maund

The 'Annals of Boyle',[1] preserved in a thirteenth-century manuscript – London, British Library, MS. Cotton Titus A.xxv –,[2] contain two notices of the death of St Patrick. The first, found *s.a.* 458, reads, 'Dormitatio sancti senis Patricii'.[3] In both its wording and its position within the text, this is a very close analogue to the equivalent entry in *Chronicum Scotorum*[4] to which the 'Annals of Boyle' are related in this section. It is of no special interest in the present context except in so far as it is testimony to the mediaeval development of the 'Two Patricks' theory.

The second obit, found *s.a.* 493, is our particular concern here. It reads as follows.[5]

Ab initio mundi secundum Dionisium <anni> .v^{m}.dclx. usque ad transitum sancti Patricii episcopi, ab incarnatione uero Domini .ccccxlviii.; Patricius archiepiscopus et apostolus Hiberniensium anno etatis sue .c^{o}.ix^{o}., .xvi^{o}. die kal. Aprilis quieuit.

The initial dating clause is unique to the 'Annals of Boyle'. The clause beginning 'Patricius archiepiscopus . . .' is identical in form and almost identical in detail to the corresponding entries in other Clonmacnoise-group chronicles.[6]

It is the dating clause which is of particular interest here, for it may be taken to suggest that this obit was once attached to a different year, whether in the exemplar of the extant 'Annals of Boyle' or in a precursor.[7] Within the internal chronological structure of the 'Annals of Boyle', this second obit now stands at

1 For text and partial translation, see 'The annals in Cotton MS. Titus A. XXV', ed. Freeman. I have prepared a new edition and translation under the auspices of the School of Celtic Studies, Dublin Institute for Advanced Studies.
2 For description of the manuscript, see O'Grady *et al.*, *Catalogue*, I.4–14, and the remarks by Robin Flower on (1927) pp. 339–44 of Freeman's edition.
3 'The annals in Cotton MS. Titus A. XXV', ed. Freeman, p. 319.
4 *Chronicum Scotorum*, ed. & transl. Hennessy, p. 24 (*s.a.* K.iiii); the equivalent entry in the 'Annals of Roscrea' (edd. Gleeson & Mac Airt, p. 151, §98) is equally close. The 'Annals of Tigernach' suffer from a physical lacuna at this point.
5 'The annals in Cotton MS. Titus A. XXV', ed. Freeman, p. 319 (the text printed above is the result of reëdition).
6 See above, pp. 30–1.
7 For previous discussion see O'Rahilly, *The Two Patricks*, p. 57.

A.D. 493. But the statements of date, *annus mundi* 4660 in the Dionysiac era and A.D. 448, clearly do not belong with that year. Nor do these two stated dates – A.M. 4660 and A.D. 448 – belong together. A.M. 4660 in the Dionysiac scheme requires an A.D. date of 461 (4199 being equivalent to the year of the Incarnation). A.D. 448, on the other hand, needs a Dionysiac A.M. date of 4647.

Given that the first obit of St Patrick – *Senex Patricius* – in the 'Annals of Boyle' occurs *s.a.* 458, it seems quite possible that the A.D. date 448 is a scribal error for 458 and pertains properly to the entry for that year (or with an entry which the obit of *Senex Patricius* might have supplanted). It could indeed be the case that this A.D. date and the clause beginning 'Patricius archiepiscopus . . .' had been moved wholesale in the Clonmacnoise-group ancestor from *ca* 458 to 493; but the general text-historical evidence is probably against this.[8] Equally, .ccccx*l*viii. could conceivably be an error for .ccccx*c*iii. rather than for .ccccl viii.. In either event we must admit that at least scribal error has rendered the extant entry in the 'Annals of Boyle' inaccurate and internally inconsistent.

What should one make, however, of the Dionysiac A.M. date, 4660 (= A.D. 461)? A.D. 461 is found as an alternative death-date for St Patrick in the 'Annals of Ulster', albeit with a different (subsequently added) A.M. date.[9] In that text A.M. dates are routinely given only for years from 432 to 493, St Patrick's career in Ireland! The 'Annals of Inisfallen' also have a (different) misplaced obit for Patrick in their entry [496] – an *annus Passionis* dating of 432;[10] this could refer either to A.D. 459 (by Victorian calculation) or to 464 (by Dionysiac reckoning). The possibility of a death-date *ca* A.D. 461 is undoubtedly present in the Irish chronicling tradition: therefore the date A.M. 4660 in the 'Annals of Boyle' should not be dismissed as a mere scribal error.[11]

The entry in the 'Annals of Boyle' neatly encapsulates the mediaeval debate about the date of St Patrick's death. (*Plus ça change . . .*) It is positioned to reflect the later death-date; the place of the earlier is occupied by a notice of *Senex Patricius*. It seems as if the scribe of the 'Annals of Boyle' was following his exemplar with insufficient intelligence. Either he copied (and made worse) an inconsistent pair of dates in an annal to which they did not belong or he failed to understand a complex exemplar which bore cross-references or marks of transposition. In either event, his annal for 493 bears all too evidently the remains of an obit pertaining to an earlier date. The appearance of these fossilised traces must raise a final question.

This second Patrician obit in the 'Annals of Boyle' is almost identical to those found in the 'Annals of Tigernach' and *Chronicum Scotorum* for the same year,

8 See above, pp. 29–33, for remarks on the place of the Patrician obits in the general textual history of the Irish chronicles.

9 *The Annals of Ulster*, edd. & transl. Mac Airt & Mac Niocaill, I.46: A.M. 4665 added in the hand of the principal annotator (called H^2 by the editors).

10 *The Annals of Inisfallen*, ed. & transl. Mac Airt, p. 64.

11 In the reckoning used in the additions to the 'Annals of Ulster' A.M. 4660 would correspond to A.D. 456. This form of *annus mundi* dating is in the eras of the Septuagint and of the Hebrews.

A.D. 493. But the version in the 'Annals of Boyle' is fuller in as much as it still carries a prose dating clause. Is it possible that that dating was original to the entry inherited by the Clonmacnoise chronicler whose handiwork we still recognise in the main clause of the entry?[12]

[12] For some of the methods employed in the Clonmacnoise revision of the 'Chronicle of Ireland' see Grabowski & Dumville, *Chronicles and Annals*, chapters I–II; much still remains to be done in reconstructing the textual development of the lost 'Clonmacnoise Chronicle' to the point at which it issued in the extant members of the so-called 'Clonmacnoise group' of chronicles.

THE DATE 432

In the historical and hagiological literature of mediaeval Ireland there was but one date for the arrival of Patrick as missionary bishop, the nation's apostolic saint. As a result it has attracted a remarkable degree of loyalty, even in unlikely quarters.[1] None of the types of doubt which have long affected the principal death-dates has undermined reception of the traditional year of arrival. When modern writers began to feel uncomfortable with the mediaeval attribution of a sixty-year apostolate to St Patrick, they first questioned the traditional death-date.[2]

As in so many other respects, Thomas O'Rahilly's epoch-making lecture and pamphlet, *The Two Patricks*, caused in 1942 the beginnings of doubt. O'Rahilly argued that the sixty-year apostolate should be divided between two missionaries. The derision which would naturally have attended his further assertion – that both men happened to bear the name Patrick[3] – was restrained not just by a nervous awareness of O'Rahilly's formidable personality and scholarship but by the fact that such a solution had ancient authority: Bishop Tírechán, in the late seventh century, had written that Palladius was also called Patrick and that his successor was *Patricius secundus*.[4]

Such a division, if accepted, immediately deprives the date 432 of any particular significance for either the biography of St Patrick or the history of Irish christianity. Unfortunately, O'Rahilly pursued his argument – which could have stood in perfect simplicty – into the entrails of the Irish chronicles.[5] Seizing on the entry for 432 in the 'Annals of Inisfallen',[6] he argued that that year had originally been famous for the initial impact of Palladius on the Irish people.

AI §390 Patricius episcopus Hiberniam tenet atque Scotos babtizare inchoat, nono anno regni Teothosi Minoris et primo anno episcopatus Xisti .xl. secundi episcopi romanae aeclesiae et in quarto anno regni Laegare meicc Neill. Finit.

Palladius autem hic uno anno mansit .xii^{o}. anno regni Teothosii

1 The most striking is that of R. P. C. Hanson in all his publications, from *St Patrick, a British Missionary Bishop* onwards, in spite of his repeated disavowal of all evidence drawn from Irish sources.

2 For discussion, see above, pp. 29–33.

3 *The Two Patricks*, pp. 9–10.

4 §56: see *The Patrician Texts*, edd. & transl. Bieler & Kelly, pp. 164–7.

5 *The Two Patricks*, pp. 11–13.

6 *The Annals of Inisfallen*, ed. Mac Airt, p. 45 (§390), an annal which seems to stand for A.D. 431, notwithstanding various indications to the contrary. It is worth consulting the facsimile-edition for this passage: *The Annals of Inisfallen*, edd. Best & MacNeill, fo 9va. For discussion, see Bieler, 'Was Palladius surnamed Patricius?', but cf. Binchy, 'Patrick and his biographers', p. 131.

> Minoris. Patricius uero .xiii., uel ut alii dicunt .xiiii°., anno eiusdem uenit ad Scottos. Patricius ergo Palladius ad Romam nec peruenit, sed in Brittania quieuit in Christo.

O'Rahilly quoted as far as the eighth word of this remarkable annal,[7] pronouncing it to have 'fortunately been preserved intact' here in the form which it had had in the lost 'Bangor Chronicle' of *ca* A.D. 740: for O'Rahilly had recognised this as a significant stage in the development of Irish chronicling.[8] Referring also back to the preceding annal in the 'Annals of Inisfallen', which is derivative of Prosper's annal for 431, he wrote, 'Nothing, it will be observed, is said in these entries under 431 and 432 concerning either the departure of Palladius or the arrival of Patricius'.[9] In fact this is only correct as long as one truncates the annal at the word *Finit.*

It is clear that the annals for the years 428–433 in the 'Annals of Inisfallen' are drawn from a variety of sources. Collectively they constitute a remarkable and unique – if ultimately very confusing – monument to an act of mediaeval scholarship.[10] The annal quoted above bears witness to a range of chronological and biographical speculation, including the ideas that Palladius spent one year in Ireland in 434/5 and that Patrick came to Ireland in 435/6 or 436/7, in effect causing 'Patricius Palladius' to leave the country.

Whatever the sources of the extraordinary annal quoted above, O'Rahilly's assertion that the 'Annals of Inisfallen' have uniquely preserved an item from the 'Chronicle of Ireland' is unacceptable. Our knowledge of the general textual history of the Irish chronicles renders almost impossible the notion of such a pattern of preservation.[11] Furthermore, the specific evidence of the other chronicles' annals for A.D. 432 shows what the entry in the 'Chronicle of Ireland' must have looked like.

AB[12] §144	Patricius archiepiscopus in Hiberniam uenit atque Scotos baptizare inchoauit.
ARC[13] §1	Patricius archiepiscopus in Hiberniam uenit atque Scottos baptizare inchoat nono anno Theodosi Minoris et 1° anno episcopatus Xisti .xlii. episcopi romanae ecclesiae, in 4 anno regni Loegaire.
AU[14] 432.1	Patricius peruenit ad Hiberniam nono anno regni Teodosii Minoris, primo anno episcopatus Xisti .xlii. episcopi romane ęclesie. Sic enumerant Beda et Marcillinus et Issiodorus in cronicis suis.
CS[15] K.iii.	Ab incarnatione Domini .cccc.xxxii°.
K.vi.	A morte Concculaind herois usque ad hunc annum .cccc.xxxi., a

7 *The Two Patricks*, p. 12.
8 *Early Irish History and Mythology*, pp. 235–59.
9 *The Two Patricks*, p. 12.
10 *The Annals of Inisfallen*, ed. Mac Airt, pp. 44–5 and 56 (§§387–391 and *an.* [433]).
11 On this point see Grabowski & Dumville, *Chronicles and Annals*, chapters I–II.
12 'Annals of Boyle': 'The annals from Cotton MS. Titus A. XXV', ed. Freeman, p. 318.
13 'The Annals of Roscrea', edd. Gleeson & Mac Airt, p. 145.
14 *The Annals of Ulster*, edd. & transl. Mac Airt & Mac Niocaill, I.38/9.
15 *Chronicum Scotorum*, ed. & transl. Hennessy, pp. 20–3: cf. AI §389 (as n. 6). For discussion see Dumville, 'Ulster heroes'.

morte Concupair mic Nessa .cccc.xii. anni sunt.
Patricius, id est archiepiscopus, in Hiberniam uenit atque Scotos baptizare inchoat, nono anno Teodisi Minoris, primo anno episcopatus Sixti .xlv. episcopi romanae ecclesiae, in .iiii°. anno regni Laeghaire mic Nell.

To these we may perhaps add the second relevant annal in the 'Annals of Inisfallen'.

AI[16] §391 Patricius ad Hiberniam mittitur, Teothosio Minore Arcadi filio regnante, in quo anno angelus cui nomen est Uictor a loco in quo Patricii crux posita Patricium uocauit. Item illo tempore Loegare mac Neill Hiberniam regnauit annis .xxxviii.; quarto autem anno regni eius Patricius peruenit ad Scottos.

It is fairly straightforward to reconstruct from this evidence the text of the 'Clonmacnoise Chronicle' for A.D. 432.[17]

K.vi. Ab incarnatione Domini .cccc.xxxii. A morte Con Chulainn herois usque ad hunc annum .ccccxxxi., a morte Conchobuir meic Nessa .ccccxii. anni sunt. Patricius archiepiscopus in Hiberniam uenit atque Scotos baptizare inchoat, nono anno Theodosi Minoris, primo anno episcopatus Xisti .xlii. episcopi romanae ecclesiae, in quarto anno regni Loegaire meic Néill.

The 'Chronicle of Ireland' seems to have contained, as so often, a less elaborate entry.

Patricius peruenit ad Hiberniam nono anno regni Teodosii Minoris, primo anno episcopatus Xisti .xlii. episcopi romanae ecclesiae.

Needless to say, there is no trace here of contemporary recording: this is a learned and chronographic reconstruction in the synchronising mode. It is also clear that the entry by which O'Rahilly set such store is a rewriting (whether in the tenth century or the eleventh) of that which originated in the 'Clonmacnoise Chronicle': *tenet* has been substituted for *uenit*,[18] whether by a simple scribal error or under the impact of the surrounding and complicating surfeit of information with which the chronicler was struggling. He perhaps realised what O'Rahilly did not, that an equation of Palladius and Patrick immediately deprives the year 432 of any particular significance in the history of the early development of Irish christianity.

It was left to James Carney to carry O'Rahilly's arguments to their logical conclusion.[19] If Palladius continued as bishop in Ireland, to be succeeded in due

[16] *The Annals of Inisfallen*, ed. Mac Airt, p. 45.
[17] For the principles on which the two following acts of reconstruction have been executed, see Grabowski & Dumville, *Chronicles and Annals*. For specific discussion of the chronological data in the Clonmacnoise annal reconstructed here, see Dumville, 'Ulster heroes'.
[18] Rather than the reverse, espoused by O'Rahilly, *The Two Patricks*, p. 13.
[19] Carney, *Studies*, pp. 324–73, 394–412.

course by the Briton Patrick who died in or by 493,[20] then Patrick could hardly have come to Ireland in 432. The date must be a phantom. How, therefore, did it come to have such significance?

Our first glimpses of the cult of St Patrick and of Irish knowledge of Palladius come in the seventh century. The impression which these have left on modern scholarship is that there was national recognition of the significance of Patrick as father of the Irish Church but that his cult-centre was at Downpatrick in Ulster; increasingly, however, it was the church of Armagh with which his name was associated.[21] At the end of the sixth century Columbanus of Bangor and Bobbio, writing to Pope Boniface, had allowed that Irish christianity had Roman origins:[22] but whether he would have attributed these to Palladius or Patrick or both we do not know. Palladius seems to have left no direct impression of himself on the memory, whether popular or institutional, of Irish christianity. No church is associated with his name. No feast-day is recorded for him. His name appears in late seventh-century writing, but only to be dismissed as an irrelevance.[23]

The sequence of events appears to have been as follows. Palladius left no cult: he may not have been regarded as a saint; he may have died outside Ireland; he may have ministered to Romano-British rather than native Irish christians; his principal church(es) may not have had a continuous history. Patrick, on the other hand, left tracts which survive and which convey an impression of an heroic ministry; a cult-site was associated with him which presumably had a continuous history from the fifth century and was able to promote his memory, in particular through his feast-day on 17 March. However, the only possible absolute date associated with him was an obit in 493; even this is controversial, and it seems to have been so already in the seventh century.[24]

When Prosper's Chronicle came to the attention of Irish scholars, whether in Columbanus's time or in the seventh century, there was no appeal against its record that Palladius was sent in 431 by Pope Celestine to be the first bishop for Irish christians.[25] In as much as nothing was known of Palladius in Ireland it was imperative both to explain why and to close or fill the gap between 431 and whatever date or dates might have been known for Patrick. The date 493 might have been available. Or it might already have been cult-knowledge that, in the year of Patrick's death, 17 March was a Wednesday:[26] if so, 493 could have been

20 It should perhaps be stressed that there is no warrant in St Patrick's writings (and therefore no evidence at all) for regarding Patrick as the immediate successor of Palladius: it is even possible that they had quite different jurisdictions. Cf. Thompson, *Who was Saint Patrick?*, pp. 66–78, 166–75. We simply have no evidence about fifth-century Irish episcopal succession. See also below, pp. 89–105, for the question of other foreign clerics associated with Palladius or Patrick.

21 For recent discussion see Sharpe, 'St Patrick and the see of Armagh'.

22 *Epistolae*, V.3: *Sancti Columbani Opera*, edd. & transl. Walker & Bieler, pp. 38/9.

23 For a valuable collection of materials about Palladius, see Bieler, 'The mission of Palladius'. For Palladius in an Irish guise as **Colldae*, see O'Rahilly, *The Two Patricks*, p. 9; Mulchrone, 'The Old-Irish form of *Palladius*', pp. 36 and 42 (*Collait* and *Collidan*); Binchy, 'Patrick and his biographers', p. 143 and n. 370. Cf. Sims-Williams, 'Dating the transition', pp. 229–30.

24 Cf. above, pp. 29–33. For cult, see Gougaud, 'Les plus anciennes attestations'.

25 *Chronica Minora*, ed. Mommsen, I.473 (§1307).

26 Carney, *The Problem*, pp. 27–8: it would be interesting and important to identify the first attestation of the Wednesday dating. Cf. Binchy, 'Patrick and his biographers', p. 113.

the result of calculation, but it would be a nice question why that, rather than an earlier date, was chosen. Perhaps the determining factor was provided by known death-dates of other ecclesiastics thought to have been associated with Patrick.[27] Nevertheless, in as much as Palladius's Irish career was unknown, it was easiest to suppose that he had had little impact and had died or retreated from Ireland at the earliest possible moment. His presumed successor's arrival should therefore be attributed to the following year (and the same agent, Pope Celestine I).

It remained to try to fill the intervening sixty years between arrival and death. The annalistic chronology at least seems to have grown backwards from a historical horizon at the end of the fifth century; one might now add that it had probably already extended thus from an archival horizon in the mid- or later sixth century. O'Rahilly provided the first hints as to the nature of the process as it affected the record of Ireland's secular history also: he discovered in Tírechán's account of St Patrick two statements which seemed to stand in direct contradiction of the remainder of his narrative. O'Rahilly argued that replacement of Loeguire, as the king of Tara whom Patrick met, with Ailill Molt, his alleged successor in that dignity, would restore the information provided by Tírechán's source.[28] As we shall see, James Carney took matters a step further and argued that an extensive reconstruction of the chronology of fifth-century secular Irish history was another response to the problems created by extending Patrick's history back to 432.[29]

Although the date 432 is universal in mediaeval Irish historical writing for the arrival of St Patrick as a missionary, it may be seen that it is a learned, if simple, response to discovery of the date 431 for Pope Celestine's despatch of Bishop Palladius to Ireland. A.D. 432 has no validity for the event which is attached to it and which occurred in an unknown year.[30] It had originated by the second half of the seventh century, as we can learn from the Patrician hagiographers:[31] but their work, and particularly that of Tírechán,[32] shows that the adoption of this date had already had chronological and historiographical consequences for Irish scholars.

27 See below, pp. 51–7.
28 *The Two Patricks*, pp. 36–7.
29 See below, pp. 45–50.
30 Carney's date for this event, A.D. 456, is based on an inadequate analysis of an unacceptable source: see below, pp. 279–88.
31 Notably from Muirchú, I.8–9: *The Patrician Texts*, edd. & transl. Bieler & Kelly, pp. 72–5.
32 §§9, 26: *ibid.*, pp. 132/3, 142/3. Cf. n. 28, above.

ST PATRICK AND FIFTH-CENTURY IRISH CHRONOLOGY: THE KINGS

In 1949 the study of Patrician chronology was put on a wholly new footing by James Carney, in a lecture published in expanded form in 1955 as 'Patrick and the kings'.[1] Reacting to T. F. O'Rahilly's epoch-making lecture of seven years earlier,[2] Carney showed how annalistic evidence could be used to display a view of fifth-century chronology gravely at variance with that required by the idea that Patrick's mission to Ireland extended from 432 to 457 or 461. A few years earlier, H. M. Chadwick had been moving in the same direction as Carney, but his work was published posthumously only in 1949.[3]

Before we proceed, it will be well to have before us the relevant entries from the 'Annals of Ulster', the Irish secular events from A.D. 431 to 535.[4]

435.1: Mors Bressail regis Laighen.
436.1: Uel hic mors Bresail.
440.2: Alii libri dicunt Maine filium Neill in isto anno perisse.
445.1: Nath I mac Fiachrach.
446.1: Bellum Femhin in quo cecidit filius Coerthin filii Coelboth.
Alii dicunt di Chruithnibh fuise.
452.2: Interfectio magna Lagenarum.
454.1: Cena Temhra apud Loeghaire filium Neill.
456.1: Mors Ennai maic Cathbotha et natiuitas sancte Brigide ut alii dicunt.
458.1: Cath Atho Dara for Laighaire re Laighnibh.
461.3: Loeghaire filius Neill post cenam Temhro annis .vii. et mensibus .vii. et dies .vii. uixit.
462.1: Mors Laeghaire filii Neill oc Greallaigh Daphil etir in da chnoc, .i. Eiriu ocus Albu a n-anmanda.
464.1: Primum bellum Ardda.
465.2: Eogan mac Neill mortuus est.
467.2: Cena Temhra la hAilill Molt. Sic in Libro Cuanach inueni.
468.2: Bellum Dumai Achir, .i. for Oilill Molt. Inueni in Libro Cuanach.
470.1: Feis Temra la hAilill Molt, ut alii dicunt.

1 *Studies*, pp. 324–73 (cf. 394–412).
2 *The Two Patricks*.
3 *Early Scotland*, pp. 133–6.
4 *The Annals of Ulster*, edd. & transl. Mac Airt & Mac Niocaill. The choice of concluding date relates to the content of 535.1 and its connexion with the arguments about Patrician chronology. See below, pp. 51–7.

475.1: Bellum Breg Heile re nAilill Molt for Laighniu. Sic in Libro Cuanach inueni.
477.1: Mors Tocco maic Aedha regis Cualann.
478.1: Bellum Bregh Heile.
480.1: Mors Conaill Cramthainne maic Neill.
482.1: Bellum Oche in quo cecidit Ailill Molt. A Conchobro filio Nesae usque ad Cormac filium Airt anni .ccc.viii.. A Cormac usque hoc bellum .cxvi., ut Cuana scripsit.
483.1: Ingulatio Chraumthain maic Ennai Ceinnselaig regis Lagen.
485.1: Bellum primum Granærad – Coirpri uictor erat – in quo cecidit Fincath; uel filius Erce uictor, ut alii dicunt.
490.2: Bellum Cinn Losnado ubi cecidit Oengus filius Nat Fraich, ut Cuana scriphsit.
493.1: Bellum Srotha.
493.3: Bellum secundum Granairet.
494.1: Cath Taillten for Laigniu ria Cairpri m. Neill.
495.1: Bellum secundum Granairet in quo cecidid Fraech mac Finchada, ri Laigen; Eochu filius Coirpri uictor fuit.
496.3: Expugnatio Duin Lethghlaissi.
498.1: Expugnatio Duin Lethglaisse.
498.2: Bellum Inni Moer i crich Oa nGabla for Laegniu; Muirchertach uictor erat.
499.2: Bellum in quo Mac Eirce uictor erat.
500.1: Bellum.
501.1: Muirchertach uictor fuit . . .
502.1: Bellum Segaisse in quo cecidit Daui Tinga Umhai; Muirchertach uictor fuit.
507.1: Bellum Arda Corann et mors Lugdach filii Loegaire; et, ut alii dicunt, Domhangart mac Nisse Reti secessit anno .xxxv^{o}..
508.1: Et mors Lughdach filii Læghaire 7 cath Arda Corrand.
510.1: Bellum Fremhonn for Fiachaigh mc. Neill; Failghi Berraide uictor fuit.
514.1: Cairpri Daim Argit, ri Airgiall.
516.1: Bellum Droma Derge for Failghi: Fiacha uictor erat; deinde Campus Midhe a Lagenis sublatus est.
520.2: Bellum Detnę i nDrumbaibh Bregh in quo cecidit Arddgal filius Conaill filii Neill; Colgu Moo Cluęthi, rex Orientalium, ocus Muirchertach Mac Erca uictores erant.
524.1: Bellum Cainrí filii Neill . . .
527.2: Mors Illaind maic Dunlainge.
528.2: Bellum Cinn Eich et bellum Atha Sighe for Laighniu; Muirchertach mac Ercę uictor fuit.
533.1: .iii. bellum in hoc anno gesta uno posito ergense ecc Leccan Lias.
533.3: Bellum Ebhlinne ria Muirchertach mc. Erce.
534.1: Demersio Muirchertaig filii Erce in dolio pleno uino in a<rc>e Cletig supra Boinn.
535.2: Bellum Lochara eiter da Inber ria Tuathal Maelgarb for Ciannacht.

These annal-entries represent a number of strands of the accumulating textual history of the 'Annals of Ulster'. In a full analysis these entries would have to be sorted by language, by named source, as variants, and in respect of their position in relation to entries drawn fron non-Irish chronicles (Prosper, Marcellinus, Bede). For the moment, it is necessary only to notice that the variants (436.1; 440.2; 446.1a; 456.1?; 470.1; 485.1a; 493.3 *or* 495.1; 496.3 *or* 498.1; 499.2 *or* 500.1; 501.1 *or* 502.1; 507.1a; 508.1) and the derivatives of the 'Book of Cuanu', a member of the Clonmacnoise group of chronicles (467.2; 468.2; 475.1; 482.1; 490.2), should be excluded to give a view of the chronology and structure of the earliest certainly recoverable stage of the text, that belonging to the (now lost) 'Chronicle of Ireland' as it stood in A.D. 911.[5]

The arguments advanced by Chadwick and Carney may be reduced to their bare essentials. The fifth-century chronology of the 'Chronicle of Ireland' embodied a contradiction. It brought first to Ireland Palladius in 431 (following Prosper's Chronicle) and then Patrick in 432; it placed Patrick's death in 492/3 in the sixtieth year of his mission and the 120th of his life. The entries relating to Patrick's career cluster in the 430s and 440s. He has no stated connexion with the secular rulers whose battles and deaths are noted in surrounding entries and annals.

The hagiography must, on the other hand, bring him into association with the lay world as he preaches to the heathen and receives land-grants for the foundation of churches. Already in the late seventh century Muirchú reported that 'the great difficulties which the telling of the story presents and the conflicting opinions and many doubts voiced by many a person have prevented them from ever arriving at one undisputed sequence of events'.[6] Patrick's first Easter in Ireland was also the time at which Loeguire mac Néill, king of Tara, was celebrating *Feis Temro* ('the Feast of Tara'). After a conflict between the two, Patrick prophesies that none of Loeguire's seed will ever succeed him as king of Tara.[7] The only other indication of absolute chronology occurs in the prologue found in MS. B: 'A passione autem domini nostri Iesu Christi colliguntur anni .cccc.xxx.vi. usque ad obitum Patricii';[8] this gives either A.P. (Victorius) 436 + 27 = A.D. 463 or, less likely, A.P. (Dionysius) 436 + 32 = A.D. 468.[9] These calculations are consistent enough with an early date for Patrick's death and therefore admission of an arrival-date of A.D. 432: Muirchú had reported the death of Palladius in Britain shortly before Patrick's consecration as bishop and departure for Ireland.[10] What is more, Muirchú gave him a life of 16 + 6 + 8 + 30/40 years (viz, 60 or 70 years) before he came to Ireland;[11] when he died he

5 For a start on some of these questions, see Smyth, 'The earliest Irish annals'; Dumville, 'Ulster heroes' and 'Latin and Irish'; Grabowski & Dumville, *Chronicles and Annals*.
6 Muirchú, *Vita S. Patricii*, preface: *The Patrician Texts*, edd. & transl. Bieler & Kelly, pp. 62–3.
7 Muirchú, I.13–21 (*ibid.*, pp. 82–99). Cf. Binchy, 'The Fair'.
8 *Ibid.*, p. 62.
9 For this type of calculation see Dumville, 'Some aspects of the chronology'.
10 Muirchú, I.8(7)–9(8).
11 I.1, 5, 7(6).

was 120.[12] Here at last is a clear contradiction: a death-date *ca* 492 is presupposed thus.

Tírechán, in his opening chapter, has a comparable calculation: 16 + 6 + 7 + 30.[13] He too has an A.P. calculation: 433 years (+ 27 = A.D. 460, or + 32 = A.D. 465). Loeguire is said to have reigned two or five years after Patrick's death:[14] those death-dates would therefore appear to have been 457 or 460, given the annalistic obit for Loeguire at 462; the figures seem consistent. Tírechán reckoned that Loeguire's reign lasted 36 years, therefore 426–62.[15] Some unspecified wondrous deeds were done by Patrick in the fifth year of Loeguire's reign, 431.[16] In §28 we are told that 'Interest autem inter mortem Patricii et Cerani natiuitatem, ut peritissimi numerorum aestimant, centum quadraginta anorum'.[17] This figure is not helpful, however, for Ciarán of Clonmacnoise is supposed to have died at the age of 33 in A.D. 549, being born therefore in 516.[18] In §40 the reign of Coirpre Nioth Fer is placed 100 years before Patrick's present.[19] §53 has another statement of his life-span: '6 (= 7th year) + 3 (= 10th year) + 7 + 30 + 72 = 120 (as Moses)'; this is not quite an accurate calculation.[20] His 72 years' teaching is a figure not otherwise met with.[21] Finally §56 tells us that Palladius (*qui Patricius alio nomine appellabatur*) was sent first as bishop but was martyred by the Irish, *ut tradunt sancti antiqui*; Patrick was then sent by Pope Celestine as the second bishop – in the thirteenth year of the Emperor Theodosius, an impossible synchronism.[22]

There is much evidence here for the difficulties, controversies, and doubts of which Muirchú spoke in his prologue. The early death-date for Patrick is apparent, as is the Mosaic life-span: but this does not indicate a life *ca* 340–*ca* 460, for sixty years (or more) are assigned to Patrick's missionary career. We may therefore be certain that by the late seventh century there was knowledge of: Prosper's date (431) for Palladius's mission; two different fates for Palladius; an equation of Palladius and Patrick; an arrival-date of 432 for Patrick; the conflict with Loeguire mac Néill in 432; death-dates of 457 x 460 (or x 465) and *ca* 492. As much as anything else, there is evidence here for experimentation with the available data but without the final achievement of a satisfactory result. For Patrick the eventual mediaeval solution was firmly established with his arrival in 432 and his death in the 490s. But this determination caused problems for secular chronology.

12 II.7(6).

13 §1 (*The Patrician Texts*, edd. & transl. Bieler & Kelly, pp. 124–5); in §49 (*ibid.*, pp. 162–3) he refers to seven years' captivity.

14 §2 (*ibid.*, pp. 126–7).

15 *Ibid.*

16 §1 (*ibid.*, pp. 126–7).

17 *Ibid.*, p. 146.

18 'Annals of Ulster' 549.1. Was the span from Patrick's *birth* at a date in the 370s, 120 years before his death in the 490s?

19 *The Patrician Texts*, edd. & transl. Bieler & Kelly, pp. 154–5.

20 *Ibid.*, pp. 164–5.

21 Cf. Dumville, 'Celtic-Latin texts', pp. 30–3; Hennig, 'The literary tradition of Moses'.

22 *The Patrician Texts*, edd. & transl. Bieler & Kelly, pp. 164–7. It was this equation of Palladius and Patrick which helped to launch the famous theory of O'Rahilly, *The Two Patricks*.

A full study is required of the rulers with whom each hagiographer brings Patrick into association. For the moment we may follow James Carney's consideration of the kings of Tara.[23] For him, Tírechán's chronology of the reign of Loeguire mac Néill is torpedoed by the chronicle-evidence, in particular that of the 'Annals of Ulster'. He saw two items as critical. AU 445.1 records the name of Nath Í mac Fiachrach, presumably indicating his death. Carney considered that this showed that Nath Í was king of Tara until that year.[24] Furthermore, the annalistic notices of Loeguire mac Néill place his celebration of *Feis Temro* in 454, which is likely to have been close to his date of accession and perhaps followed the *interfectio magna Lagenarum* recorded for 452.[25] In 458 Loeguire was defeated by the Leinstermen. We are told at 461 that he ruled seven years, months, and days after celebrating the Feast of Tara and at 462 that he died in that year. The death of his son Lugaid is placed in 507. His brothers' deaths are given at 465 (Eogan) and 480 (Conall), while two more brothers are active in 485 and 494 (Coirpre), and in 510 and 516 (Fiacha); other grandsons of Niall (apart from Lugaid) appear in 495 (Eochu mac Coirpri) and die from 520 (Arddgal mac Conaill) onwards. These dates are fairly consistent with one another.[26]

What Muirchú was undoubtedly recording in his account of Loeguire's Easter-activities at Tara was the celebration of *Feis Temro*.[27] In annalistic terms, then, this event should be placed in the 450s and, if Muirchú's internal chronology is to be retained, Patrick's arrival in Ireland should also be dated then.

In Tírechán's account, Patrick is brought into association serially with three sons of Niall Noígiallach: Loeguire at Tara (§§8, 12), Coirpre at Teltown (§9), and Conall at Domnach Pátraic Mór (§10).[28] We must imagine either that Tírechán, with all his concern for chronology, was extraordinarily muddle-headed or that the chronology which he was using (or creating?) placed the reigns of these figures a generation or more earlier than the chronology provided by the 'Annals of Ulster'.

In sum, it seems hard to gainsay the thrust of Carney's argument. If the annalistic dates for secular rulers of the period represent a consistent chronology, as they appear to do, then it must be accepted as having superior status to the chronologies provided by the hagiographical witnesses. As Carney has demonstrated, the testimony of the Clonmacnoise-group chronicles shows a tenth-century (or later) process of revision of the annalistic chronology.[29] Only if we could show that the fifth-century secular sequence displayed by the 'Chronicle of Ireland' is itself a revision of an earlier and more elongated

23 *Studies*, pp. 324–39, 364–71.

24 *Ibid.*, pp. 330–3. For an earlier study, reaching rather different conclusions, see O'Rahilly, *Early Irish History and Mythology*, pp. 209–15; cf. also *The Two Patricks*, pp. 36–7, on Ailill Molt.

25 Carney, *Studies*, pp. 333–9.

26 They are all drawn from the 'Annals of Ulster': cf. pp. 45–6, above. See the discussion by O'Rahilly, *The Two Patricks*, p. 40 and pp. 76–7 (n. 47).

27 For a different view, see Binchy, 'The Fair', pp. 128–32. Muirchú, I.15 (14): *The Patrician Texts*, edd. & transl. Bieler & Kelly, pp. 84–5.

28 *Ibid.*, pp. 130–3.

29 *Studies*, pp. 332–3.

scheme of events, should we be able to controvert these findings. The oldest core of annal-entries for the first century or so of (christian) Irish history could be as old as *ca* 550 or as young as *ca* 900, but in so far as it appears to defy various political doctrines which soon became current – for example, about the relations of Uí Néill with their neighbours –, we should do well to treat that core with respect.[30] None of this enables us to assign Patrick's Irish mission to the second half of the fifth century, but it adds to the weight of evidence and deduction which tells against an earlier date.

30 Cf. Smyth, 'The Húi Néill and the Leinstermen' and *Celtic Leinster*.

ST PATRICK AND FIFTH-CENTURY IRISH CHRONOLOGY: THE SAINTS

A measure of how Irish writers of the seventh and later centuries perceived St Patrick's chronological relationship with other founding figures of Gaelic christianity may be obtained from a number of sources and has seemed to scholars of the last generation to present some hope of anchoring St Patrick in time in a way which other approaches have failed to do uncontroversially or with sufficient precision. As in so many other respects, the method was exemplified by Thomas O'Rahilly. He provided a list of bishops whose lifetimes he thought to have overlapped St Patrick's own.[1]

> Thus the annals of the period 488–513 record the deaths of the following [twelve] bishops who are elsewhere associated with St. Patrick . . . . Of the deacon Justus the obit is not recorded in the annals, but, according to Tírechán, in his old age he baptised Ciarán mac an tSaír (born 512 or 517). Other contemporaries of Patrick were the presbyter Maucteus or Mochta (*ob.* 535 or 537) . . .; Ailbe, bishop of Emly, whose death is recorded in 527 or 534; his less well-known namesake, the presbyter Ailbe of Senchua (in Co. Sligo), who died in 542; and the Bishop Ném, who died about 544.

O'Rahilly's summary of his method and results was as follows: 'The fact that Patrick died towards the end of the fifth century is abundantly confirmed by the known obits of many of his disciples . . .'.[2] His information was reduced to tabular form by James Carney from whose list I draw.[3]

Name	*obit*	*source of association with St Patrick*
Secundinus	447	Tírechán, §§6, 34; *Liber Angeli*, §30; 'Chronicle of Ireland' [AU 439]
Auxilius	459	Muirchú, I.9; Tírechán, §§6, 51; *Liber Angeli*, §30
Benignus/Benineus	467	Muirchú, I.20 and 28 (II.3); Tírechán, §§5, 6, 8, 24, 30; *Liber Angeli*, §30
Iserninus/Eserninus	468	Muirchú, I.9; Tírechán, §51
Mel	487	Tírechán, §§6, 16
Cianán (Cennannus)	489	Tírechán, §6; 'Chronicle of Ireland'

1 *The Two Patricks*, p. 75, n. 46.
2 *Ibid.*, p. 40; cf. p. 6.
3 *The Problem*, pp. 14–15. The dates are drawn (except for 544) from the 'Annals of Ulster'. To the O'Rahilly-Carney list I have added Beo-aed and Brigit.

Mac Caille	490	?[4]
Mac Cuilinn of Lusk	496	?[5]
Cormac	497	'Chronicle of Ireland'; tract in *Leabhar Breac*[6]
Mo Choe of Nendrum	497	*Vita tripartita*[7]
Íbar	500/501	Tírechán, §6
Cerpán	504	Tírechán, §13
Mac Cáirthinn of Clogher	506	Tírechán, §16 (?);[8] *Additamenta*, §8
Mac Nisse of Connor	507	*Vita tripartita* (cf. *Notulae*, §58)[9]
Brón	512	Tírechán, §§6, 19, 25, 30, 43, 45
Erc of Slane	513	Muirchú, I.17; Tírechán, §13
Beo-aed	524	*Vita tripartita*[10]
Brigit	524/526	*Liber Angeli*, §32 (cf. Mac Caille & Mac Cáirthinn: Tírechán, §16)
Ailbe (of Emly)	527/534	*Vita tripartita* (Emly not specified, but in Munster)[11]
Mochta/Maucteus	535	Adomnán; 'Chronicle of Ireland'; *Vita tripartita*[12]
Ailbe (of Senchua)	542	*Vita tripartita* (cf. Tírechán, §19, and *Notulae*, §1)[13]
Ném	[544]	*Vita tripartita* (cf. *Notulae*, §11)[14]
Mac Táil of Kilcullen	549	Tírechán, §§6, 51

The sources of this list are very various. The number of ecclesiastics associated with Patrick in his hagiography is great and the list could be expanded considerably if less overtly dated characters were to be included.

The list above falls into two principal parts. The first four persons have latinate names, three of them (according to the hagiographers) were Continentals, and their obits are separated from the others' by a span of some twenty years.[15] Various deductions may be made from this division. Auxilius, Iserninus,

4 O'Rahilly (as n. 1) attributed this connexion with Patrick to Tírechán, but in §16 Mac Caille (bishop of Uisnech? – the syntax is not clear) is not directly presented thus. The episode does not recur in the *Vita tripartita*.

5 Again, O'Rahilly attributed the connexion to Tírechán. I have not been able to see why, or to find such a link in the later hagiography of Patrick.

6 Cormac was dropped by Carney from his list (*The Problem*, p. 15). The tract from *Leabhar Breac* is to be found in *The Tripartite Life*, ed. & transl. Stokes, II.550–5.

7 *Ibid.*, I.40/1.

8 Tírechán's wording is somewhat ambiguous; the connexion is absolutely plain in the 'Book of Armagh' *additamenta*: see *The Patrician Texts*, edd. & transl. Bieler & Kelly, pp. 136/7 and 172/3. On Mac Cáirthinn as Patrick's strong man, see Kenney, *The Sources*, pp. 351–2.

9 The *notulae* (*ibid.*, p. 182) provide an indication of a story, but it emerges fully into our knowledge only in the *Vita tripartita*: *The Tripartite Life*, ed. & transl. Stokes, I.162/3 and 166/7.

10 *Ibid.*, I.160/1.

11 *Ibid.*, I.198–201.

12 *Ibid.*, I.226–9, 264/5.

13 *Ibid.*, I.94/5.

14 *Ibid.*, I.162/3.

15 A.D. 469–486. Within this period the only other ecclesiastics memorialised are Docco 'of the

and Secundinus, in so far as they are presented as Continentals, are natural candidates for association with the efforts of Bishop Palladius and accordingly their received chronology would not be especially controversial.[16]

Benignus is the odd man out among this group (and his name-form is not stable): it is therefore of some interest that he is presented as Patrick's heir and successor. The annalistic notice of his death gives him no more precise title than 'bishop'. But the next two such in the chronicle-sources are Iarlaithe (*ob.* 481), described as 'third bishop of Armagh',[17] and Cormac (*ob.* 497), described as *heres Patrici.*[18] Presumably Iarlaithe's intended predecessors are Patrick and Benignus:[19] but, in as much as Iarlaithe is unknown before the Tripartite Life of St Patrick,[20] he is probably a late – viz, ninth-century – addition to Armagh story and therefore to the 'Chronicle of Ireland'. At what may have been an historical horizon, the 490s, Cormac is quite unkown to Patrician hagiography: this could be a point in favour of his historicity!

The ecclesiastics from Mel onwards, whom the seventh-century and later hagiography associates with Patrick,[21] have obits spreading over a period of some sixty years (487–549), down to the plague which marks the end of Irish christianity's apostolic era and of the protohistoric period of Gaelic history. If the historian is able to feel that he is in the context of evidence which genuinely pertains to this period, he may also acknowledge that all these persons could have been associated with Patrick if the apostle of Ireland had lived to 493 or thereabouts; that would be an effective impossibility for many on the list, however, if Patrick had died *ca* 460.[22] The only ways to admit the first premise (the effective historicity of these obits as a group) but deny the chronological deduction would be either to denounce the associations with St Patrick as hagiographical fancies or to insist that the chronology had been revised upwards to admit a new-fangled late date of his death. The former course is not incredible, but its weakest point is that it must deny a consistent body of association drawn from a number of not necessarily interdependent sources. The latter proposition, however, seems to run counter to the direction of chronographic manipulation. We might rather say that the chronicler has resisted the temptation to which historians of secular society partly succumbed and has failed to

Britons' (477) and Iarlaithe of Armagh (481: see n. 17, below). Before Patrick's death-notices (492/3) there is one other – Mac Caille (490).

16 See below, pp. 89–105.

17 In the 'Annals of Inisfallen' he appears (in Irish) as 'third abbot'. The entry's presence there, as well as in the 'Annals of Ulster', shows that it was in the 'Chronicle of Ireland' by A.D. 911.

18 That his obit appears in the 'Annals of Inisfallen' and *Chronicum Scotorum*, as well as in the 'Annals of Ulster', is a guarantee of its presence in the 'Chronicle of Ireland'.

19 Cf. the discussion below, pp. 273–8.

20 *The Tripartite Life*, ed. & transl. Stokes, I.218–21. The 'Book of Armagh' *notulae* (§26) have his father and brother (as they appear in the episode in the Tripartite Life): *The Patrician Texts*, edd. Bieler & Kelly, p. 181. So does *Vita IV S. Patricii*, §80 (xxxvii): *Four Latin Lives*, ed. Bieler, pp. 107–8.

21 Mel and Brón are consistently associated with St Patrick in the seventh-century hagiography of St Brigit: cf. Morris, 'The dates of the Celtic saints', p. 373, n. 2, and Sharpe, 'Saint Mauchteus', p. 86.

22 Morris, 'The dates of the Celtic saints', pp. 371–2; Sharpe, 'Saint Mauchteus', pp. 85–7.

draw these obits back in time by a generation or more to accommodate an elongated Patrician chronology.[23] If Irish sources never speak with a single voice, nevertheless their relative consistency in offering a view of Patrick's survival to a late fifth-century date is impressive, as many Irish scholars have allowed.[24]

Such students of the subject have used the 'Chronicle of Ireland' to provide obit-dates which may be independent of Patrician hagiography. It is worth considering what that text had to say directly on the matter at issue. We find two points at which explicit links are made between Patrick and another saint.

AU 489:[25] Quies sancti Ciannaini cui sanctus Patricius euangelium largitus est.

Although St Cianán of Duleek does not loom large in Patrician hagiography, he is nonetheless to be found there;[26] this particular story does not, however, occur in the *Vita tripartita* or its predecessors. On the other hand, a saint who has seemed to scholars to have an impressively documented connexion with St Patrick and whose annalistic death-date (535) is late in this sequence has been able to be presented as the flagship of this approach to identifying the dates of St Patrick's life and death.

St Mochta gains our attention by the unusual nature of his annalistic record.

AU 535.1:[27] Dormitatio Muchti discipuli Patricii, .xiii. kl. Septembris. Sic ipse scripsit in epistola sua: 'Mauchteus peccator, presbiter, sancti Patrici discipulus, in Domino salutem'.

Formally, it would be possible to assert that M(a)uchte was an indirect, or second-generation, pupil of St Patrick: but the reminiscences of Patrick's own epistolary style have encouraged assent to the idea of a direct relationship.[28] It is frustrating that the addressee of the letter is unspecified in the quotation or its annalistic introduction. Equally, its contents are unknown.[29]

23 Cf. above, pp. 45–50.

24 Cf. the comments of Sharpe, 'Saint Mauchteus', pp. 85–7, taking a rather different tack, and the references given there.

25 The entry is also found in representatives of the Clonmacnoise group of chronicles and therefore goes back to the 'Chronicle of Ireland'. Sharpe (*ibid.*, p. 86) overlooked this entry when he wrote that Irish chronicles 'do not directly associate anyone with St Patrick – except St Mauchteus' (Secundinus, Auxilius, and Iserninus must also be exempted from this statement).

26 *The Tripartite Life*, ed. & transl. Stokes, I.160/1. Unfortunately we have next to no hagiography of St Cianán: cf. Sharpe, *Medieval Irish Saints' Lives*, pp. 374–7, and Hughes, *Church and Society*, chapter V.

27 I quote from *The Annals of Ulster*, edd. & transl. Mac Airt & Mac Niocaill, I.70.

28 Morris, 'The dates of the Celtic saints', p. 374, n. 2; cf. Sharpe, 'Saint Mauchteus', pp. 88–90, for the literary question and its ramifications. For earlier study, see MacInerny, 'St. Mochta'.

29 For a comparably frustrating epistolary quotation, albeit in a rather different context, see Derolez, 'Dubthach's cryptogram'.

M(a)uchte has more surprises in store for us, however. In the 'Annals of Ulster' for 471 we read the following entry.[30]

Praeda secunda Saxonum de Hibernia, ut alii dicunt, in isto anno deducta est, ut Maucteus dicit. Sic in libro Cuanach inueni.

The 'Book of Cuanu' was a chronicle of the Clonmacnoise group which was collated against an ancestor of the 'Annals of Ulster' not earlier than about the middle of the tenth century.[31] The *alii dicunt* formula may (as is usual) refer to a variation in chronology among copies of the chronicle. What the *praeda secunda Saxonum* was, in fact or in legend, is quite unknown; this notice is tied to another – in Irish and presumptively later[32] – at A.D. 434 (for which *Liber Cuanach* is not blamed) recording the first such prey. Was this a subject of M(a)uchte's letter? This item, however, we cannot trace back before the first half of the tenth century.

Of much earlier origin is another reference to and quotation from M(a)uchte. In the 'second preface' of Adomnán's Life of St Columba, written shortly before 700, St Mochta is presented as prophesying Colum Cille's birth. Here the prophet is presented as not merely a disciple of Patrick but as *proselytus brito*, a British pilgrim.[33]

Hic igitur noster praesul non inmerito non solum a diebus infantiae hoc uocabulo Deo donante adornatus proprio ditatus est, sed etiam praemisis multorum cyclis annorum ante suae natiuitatis diem cuidam Christi militi spiritu reuelante sancto quasi filius repromisionis mirabili profetatione nominatus est. Nam quidam proselytus brito homo sanctus sancti Patricii episcopi discipulus Maucteus[34] nomine ita de nostro profetizauit patrono sicuti nobis ab antiquis traditum expertis conpertum habetur. 'In nouissimis' ait 'saeculi temporibus filius nasciturus est cuius nomen Columba per omnes insularum ociani prouincias deuulgabitur notum, nouissimaque orbis tempora clare inlustrabit. Mei et ipsius duorum monasteriolorum agelluli unius sepisculae interuallo disterminabuntur. Homo ualde Deo carus et grandis coram ipso meriti.'

Richard Sharpe has recently pointed to the importance of taking Adomnán and the annalistic evidence together.[35] It is not unlikely that the annal-entry originated at Iona before *ca* 700[36] and that a body of information about St Mochta was available there. If Mochta was important to the Iona community as a prophet of Columba, he may have been so too as a link to the apostle of Ireland. Sharpe's further comment that the hypothetical 'Iona annalist had no interest in St Patrick's dates and did not attempt to place Mauchteus's death at a plausible point in the Patrician chronology' is, however, unwise and the reasoning

30 *The Annals of Ulster*, edd. & transl. Mac Airt & Mac Niocaill, I.50. The entry (but without any reference to St Mochta) also occurs in the 'Annals of Inisfallen'.
31 For the date of the 'Clonmacnoise Chronicle', see Grabowski & Dumville, *Chronicles and Annals*.
32 Cf. Dumville, 'Latin and Irish'.
33 *Adomnán's Life of Columba*, edd. & transl. Anderson & Anderson, p. 4.
34 *Macteus*, β.
35 Sharpe, 'Saint Mauchteus'.
36 *Ibid.*, p. 88.

circular.[37] The original annalistic record of Patrick's death might derive from the lost 'Chronicle of Iona'.[38]

St Mochta was identified by Adomnán as a Briton connected – by prophecy – with Columba. The latter had also had a British teacher, Uinniau, who may have conveyed to Columba the enthusiastic fervour for the monastic life which had developed in Britain by the mid-sixth century.[39] In any event, St Mochta's prophecy also foresaw a close physical association between a monastery of his and one of Columba's – identification of the juxtaposed pair has nevertheless proved elusive. A local connexion, presumably known to Adomnán, remains to be discovered – perhaps, but not necessarily, in Co. Louth.

The place of St Mochta in Patrician hagiography has not, I think, been fully understood, The *Vita tripartita* contains the clue in an episode (treated as two by editors and commentators) which I now quote in full.[40]

Luid da*no* *for* cúlu co Firu Ross, co torinscan congbáil hi nDruim Mór hi crích Ross os Chlúain Caín. Is and do dechaid int aingel a dóchum 7 dixit: 'Ní sund rorath duit airisem.' 'Cest, cairm?' ol Pátraic. 'Saig in Machai fothúaid,' ol int aingel. 'Is caín ém in chlúain se tís,' ol Pátraic. 'Bid ed a ainm,' ol int aingel, 'Clúain Caín. Ticfea ailither di Bretn*aib* congéba and 7 bid lat-su íar tain.' 'Deo g*r*atias ago,' ol Patraic.

Is ed dochóid Pátraic íar sin do Ardd Pátraic fri Lúgmag anair, 7 folámadair congb*áil* and. Dodechoid Dál Rúntir inna diaid día astud, feib doucc cách díib di alailiu. Ros bendach Pátraic íar suidiu, 7 *for*áccaib ordnidi loech 7 cléirech díib 7 ardrach *for*ru fría tír anechtar, fódég dodechotar asa tír i ndegaid Pátraic.

Ticed Pátraic anair cech día ó Ard Pátraic, 7 Mochtae aníar ó Lúgmag, co comraictis immaccaldaim cach día oc Licc Mochtae. Láa n-ánd tucc int aingel epistil eturru. Arléga Pátraic in n-epistil, 7 is ed ro baí hi suidiu:

'Mochta craibdech credal
bííd i n-airm i rragab:
téit Pátraic la bréithir a Ríg
i mMachai mín anad.'

Ro aithni Pátraic na dá chlam déac do Mochtai *for*ácaib i nArdd Pátraic, 7 nu b*er*thi acnamad ó Mochtai doáib cech n-aidchi.

While this associates St Mochta with Louth,[41] the point of the story is to tie him and therefore St Patrick to Cluain Caín (Clonkeen, Co. Louth).[42] An angel prophesies to Patrick that *ailither di Bretnaib*, 'a British pilgrim' – *proselytus brito*,[43] will come to take charge of it in Patrick's interest. Towards the end of the episode an angel is again important, but this time in bringing a short letter

37 *Ibid.*, p. 91.
38 For the role of such a text, see Smyth, 'The earliest Irish annals', and above, p. 33.
39 Cf. Dumville, 'Gildas and Uinniau'; Sharpe, 'Saint Mauchteus', p. 89.
40 *Bethu Phátraic*, ed. Mulchrone, pp. 135–6 (lines 2672–96); cf. *The Tripartite Life*, ed. & transl. Stokes, I.226–9.
41 Cf. Sharpe, 'Saint Mauchteus', p. 87, for the point at issue.
42 Gwynn & Hadcock, *Medieval Religious Houses*, p. 377, following a different track (cf. pp. 185–6 on Louth).
43 See above, p. 55.

(in Irish verse) which is placed between the two saints. Prophecies and letters seem to be peculiarly associated with this particular British pilgrim.

As Richard Sharpe has remarked,[44] there is no reason to disbelieve St Mochta's existence, He was one of a possibly very numerous group of Britons who bridged the century after Patrick's death, perhaps until Irish christianity and monasticism were securely established.[45] Likewise there is little basis for a challenge to the received early mediaeval chronology of St Mochta. In so far as any of the evidence discussed here is admissible for the sixth or fifth century, it goes to confirm a strongly held view that Patrick's floruit (whenever it began) lasted through much of the second half of the fifth century.

44 'Saint Mauchteus', pp. 88–90, 92–3.
45 See below, pp. 133–45.

PATRICK SENIOR AND JUNIOR

In a Life of St Dunstan written *ca* A.D. 1000 we read the following about the cult of St Patrick at Glastonbury Abbey.[1]

Porro Hibernensium peregrini locum, quem dixi, Glestoniae, sicut ut ceterae fidelium turbae, magno colebant affectu, et maxime ob beati Patricii iunioris/senioris honorem, qui faustus ibidem in Domino quieuisse narratur.

Now Irish pilgrims, as well as other flocks of the faithful, sought this aforementioned place called Glastonbury with great veneration, especially because of the renown of the younger/older St Patrick, who is said to lie buried in that church.

The time in question is the first half of the tenth century. It is an interesting fact that the 'Clonmacnoise Chronicle', which records the death of *Senex Patricius* / Sen-Phátric in A.D. 457 and calls him bishop of the church of Glastonbury, was written in that very same period.[2] The presumption might seem to be that the original reading of the text of B's Life of St Dunstan was *Patricii senioris*. Each of the three surviving manuscripts of that work presents a rather different text:[3] the received textual history would suggest that the earliest surviving form of the text is that offered by the Arras manuscript, which alone reads *Patricii iunioris*.[4] That a change was effected *ca* A.D. 1000, and almost certainly at the Canterbury abbey of St Augustine, may reflect an increased English awareness of Irish debates about and solutions to the problems of Patrician chronology. It is noteworthy that the Canterbury (and presumptively the Glastonbury) kalendars of this period display the cult of *Bishop* Patrick at 17 March and Patrick *senior* at 24 August, of which the latter feast has the higher grading.[5]

The problem of the two Patricks had spilled over into England, therefore. As we have already seen, however, the difficulty was by the tenth century of long standing. In the early ninth century, Bishop Oengus mac Oíblén of Tallaght in

1 *Memorials of Saint Dunstan*, ed. Stubbs, pp. 10–11 (cf. p. 10, n. 8, and p. 461 for the variant reading). The translation is that of Lapidge, 'The cult of St Indract', p. 182 (cf., more generally, 179–84). For further discussion, see Lesley Abrams, below, pp. 233–42. (On St Dunstan's rather odd place in Irish literature, see Ó Cuív, 'St Gregory and St Dunstan'.)

2 See above, pp. 29–30. Cf. Grabowski & Dumville, *Chronicles and Annals*.

3 Arras, Bibliothèque municipale, MS. 1029 (812); London, British Library, MS. Cotton Cleopatra B.xiii, fos 59–90; Sankt Gallen, Stadtbibliothek, MS. 337. All were written soon after A.D. 1000 in Style-II Anglo-Caroline minuscule: for the implications see Dumville, *English Caroline Script*, pp. 84, 90, 147.

4 *Memorials of Saint Dunstan*, ed. Stubbs, pp. xxvi–xxx. It remains to be seen whether this view will be revised by the current work of reëdition by Michael Lapidge and Michael Winterbottom.

5 See Dumville, *Liturgy*, chapter II.

his metrical martyrology wrote of Sen-Phátric thus, in the second half of his stanza for 24 August:[6]

> Sen-Phátric, cing catha,
> coemaite ar srotha.
>
> Patrick Senior, a champion of battle,
> the dear fosterer of our sage.

The presumption must be that the *sruith*, 'sage', of the last line is the national apostle, the 'younger' Patrick, notwithstanding the semantic clash implied thereby. If that is so, a story is implied, according to which Sen-Phátric fostered Patrick the apostle. A similarly close relationship is implied by the originally Old Irish verse text 'Génair Pátraicc i nNemthuir' in which the penultimate stanza reads as follows.[7]

> In tan con-hualai Pátraic,
> ad-ella in Pátraicc n-aile;
> is malle connucabsat,
> dochum nÍsu maicc Maire.
>
> When Patrick flew upwards,
> he went to the other Patrick;
> together they rose
> to Jesus, Mary's son.

Who, then, was this 'other' Patrick? In the early ninth-century 'Martyrology of Tallaght', under 24 August, we find the following listed as the first two entries of Irish saints:[8]

> Patricii abbatis et episcopi Ruis Dela;
> Patricii hostiarii et abbatis Aird Macha.

Although the manuscript evidence for the 'Martyrology of Tallaght' does not antedate the second half of the twelfth century, scholars have seen fit to accept the transmitted text as essentially faithful to the original. What this offers us is not merely a second Patrick but a third:[9] I see no indication that the compiler intended these two entries to be alternatives to one another.[10] In 1950 Paul

6 For the text see *Félire Óengusso*, ed. & transl. Stokes, p. 178. For the authorship see *ibid*., pp. xxiv–xxviii, and Carney, 'The date and authorship of *Saltair na rann*'. For the date see Ó Riain, 'The Tallaght martyrologies, redated', where A.D. 828 x 833 is proposed.

7 Found in two eleventh-century manuscripts: see *Thesaurus Palaeohibernicus*, edd. & transl. Stokes & Strachan, II.xxxvii–xxxviii and 307–21; for this stanza see pp. 320–1. Binchy, 'Patrick and his biographers', pp. 124–6, assigned the text to the mid-eighth century on linguistic grounds; for his correction of the editors' translation of *con-hualai* see *ibid*., p. 125, n. 328.

8 *The Martyrology of Tallaght*, edd. Best & Lawlor; for a newly proposed date, A.D. 828 x 833, see Ó Riain, 'The Tallaght martyrologies, redated'. For the text given here, see *The Book of Leinster*, edd. Best *et al*., VI.1629 (lines 49940–1),

9 For three 'other' Patricks, see *Trias Thaumaturga*, ed. Colgan, p. 122 ('S. Patricii Septima Vita', § XXXIV).

10 As suggested by Binchy, 'Patrick and his biographers', pp. 127–8.

Grosjean showed that this entry took its origin in a misidentification of the apostle of Ireland with St Patrick of Nevers whose feast-day fell on 24 August.[11] An essential qualification of his case was entered in 1962 by D. A. Binchy who argued convincingly that 'the misunderstanding arose because Sen-Phátric was already a familiar figure':[12] the compiler of the 'Martyrology of Tallaght', seeing a Patrick at 24 August in his source-text (*Martyrologium hieronymianum*), thought that that saint must be the 'second/other Patrick' with whom he was familiar. Perhaps he covered himself by allowing a Patrick of Armagh also on this day. I must, however, register uncertainty as to whether this was the first attribution of the date 24 August to Sen-Phátric. No evidence has been brought forward which establishes beyond reasonable doubt that the moment of adoption of this date was the moment of compilation of the 'Martyrology of Tallaght'.[13]

Who was Sen-Phátric of Ros Dela? Not only is there little evidence of any sort but there is no agreement as to which of two places bearing this name should be accorded the honour of Patrician identification. One further work of Tallaght association requires passing mention here. The description of Patrick as '(abbot and) bishop of Ros Dela' in the 'Martyrology of Tallaght' finds partial confirmation in what Francis Shaw called, in an attempt to minimise its significance,[14] 'the long list of those remembered in the Mass' in the 'Stowe Missal', fos 32r–33v.[15] I quote from 32vb–c.[16]

Item episcoporum
Martini
Grigori
Maximi
Felicis
Patrici
Patrici
Secundini
Auxili
Isernini
Cerbani
Erci
Catheri
Ibori
Ailbi
Conlai
Maic Nissæ
Moinenn

11 Grosjean, 'S. Patrice d'Irlande'; cf. d'Arbois de Jubainville, 'Saint Patrice et Sen Patricc'.
12 Binchy, 'Patrick and his biographers', pp. 125–9 (quotation from p. 127).
13 I cannot share Binchy's generosity (*ibid.*, especially p. 126) to the argument to that effect by Shaw, 'The myth'.
14 *Ibid.*, p. 24.
15 On the 'Stowe Missal' – Dublin, Royal Irish Academy, MS. Stowe D.ii.3 (1238) – see Mac Niocaill, 'Fragments d'un coutumier', pp. 231–2; Breen, 'The text'; Ó Riain, 'The shrine'; Dumville, *Liturgy*, pp. 128–9. The manuscript is datable after A.D. 792, but how much later is very uncertain: a date in the first half of the ninth century is unlikely to be seriously misleading.
16 For facsimile and edition see *The Stowe Missal*, ed. Warner. The edited text of this passage (*ibid.*, II.15–16) is rather badly laid out.

With this name it is apparent that we have passed beyond a simple list of bishops. But to this point the 'Irish' saints read like a roll-call from Patrician hagiography.[17] One is bound to greet with derision Francis Shaw's statement about this list that 'It is not improbable that the second *Patrici* . . . is the Gallic Saint Patrick . . . honoured on 24 August'.[18] It is as clear as anything can be that in the culdee circle associated with Tallaght in the early ninth century there was a belief in two Bishops Patrick of Irish provenance.

Ros Dela has been identified with the modern Hiberno-English toponym Rostalla. Two such places are known. Amid the Middle and Early Modern Irish scholia on *Félire Oengusso* (of which no manuscript is earlier than the fourteenth century) are some observations on the point. To the name Sen-Phátric in the text we find the following notes.[19]

(*a*) .i. ic Ros Dela i Maig Lacha atá Sen-Pátraicc. (MS. L)
(*b*) .i. o Rus Dela i mMidi .i. i mMaig Locha araithi atá side. (MS. R^1)
(*c*) Sen-Phátraicc o Ross Dela i mMaig Locha . . . atá Sen-Phátraicc. (MS. R^2)
(*d*) Sen-Pátraic o Rus Dela a Muig Locha . . .
acht atáit athaisi i n-ulaid Sen-Pátraic i n-Ard Macha. (MS. LB)

I have omitted from all of these a variety of references to Glastonbury.[20] The essential point on which the witnesses agree, presumably therefore the original statement, is that Sen-Phátric was associated with Ros Dela in Mag Locha.[21]

This coincides with evidence from a much earlier pair of manuscript witnesses. The poem 'Génair Pátraicc i nNemthuir', whose origin has been placed in the eighth century, is transmitted in the two eleventh-century manuscripts of the Irish *Liber hymnorum*.[22] By that date it too had attracted a quantity of scholia – which must in part stand in a close relationship to the scholia on *Félire Oengusso*. To the text's *in Patraicc n-aile* we find the following commentary.[23]

.i. Sen-Phátraic
.i. iss ed ro-gell Pátraic mac Calpuirn do Shenphátraic commad immalle no-regtais dochum nime ocus iss ed inniset co rabai Pátraic otá .xvii. kl. Apr. co .ix. kl. Septimbir co dered in cetmís do fogomur arath immaig ocus aingil imme oc ernaide Shenphátraicc. Dicunt alii cumad i Ross Dela i mMag Locha no-betis taissi Senpátraic; sed uerius est i <n>Glastimber na nGoedel, .i. cathair i ndesciurt Saxan.

Once again we meet Ros Dela in Mag Locha, as well as Glastonbury. The doctrine that the younger Patrick predeceased Sen-Phátric in the same year is

17 Cf. above, pp. 51–2.
18 'The myth', p. 24.
19 I draw these from the two editions by Whitley Stokes: *On the Calendar of Oengus*, pp. cxxxii–cxxxiii (MS. LB); *Félire Óengusso*, pp. 188/9. The manuscripts are Dublin, Royal Irish Academy, MS. 23.P.16 (1230), known as *Leabhar Breac* (MS. LB); Oxford, Bodleian Library, MSS. Laud misc. 610 (*S.C.* 1132) (= MS. L), Rawlinson B.505 (*S.C.* 11852) (= MS. R^1), and Rawlinson B.512 (*S.C.* 11859) (= MS. R^2).
20 See further below, pp. 233–42; cf. above, pp. 29, 59.
21 A detailed study of these scholia is a considerable desideratum of Irish hagiological research.
22 See above, n. 7, and Bieler, 'The Irish Book of Hymns'.
23 *Thesaurus Palaeohibernicus*, edd. & transl. Stokes & Strachan, II.320–1.

one which would have excited the chronologists who established a gap of some thirty-five years between the death of Sen-Phátric and the subsequent demise of his younger namesake.[24] It is a story which derives from the liturgical perspective of the ecclesiastical kalendar.

'Ros Dela in Mag Locha' is Ros Deala / Rostalla in Ossory.[25] The scholiast on *Félire Oengusso* in Oxford, Bodleian Library, MS. Rawlinson B.505 (*S.C.* 11852) was therefore in error in assigning it to Mide.[26] That manuscript seems likely to have originated at Saints' Island in Lough Ree (Co. Longford)[27] and we need suppose no particular local knowledge of the patron-saint of Ros Deala / Rostalla in Co. Westmeath (next door to Durrow), merely an awareness of the place's existence. One must agree with Paul Walsh that the association of Sen-Phátric with Westmeath is mistaken[28] – although various scholars including D. A. Binchy have affirmed it[29] –, and that by the eleventh century at the latest (and possibly by the early ninth) the 'other, elder' Bishop Patrick had a cult localised at Rostalla in Ossory. Whether he had already acquired a feast-day on 24 August is a matter for dispute.

We are no nearer the identity of this other and elder Patrick. But that awareness of his existence goes back to the second half of the seventh century is a fair deduction from the treatment of two Patricks at the end of Tírechán's text (as transmitted uniquely in the 'Book of Armagh').[30] There has been much dispute as to whether the concluding sections of that work are genuine.[31] If they are additions they may be as late as the second half of the eighth century. However, no decisive or even reasonably convincing argument has ever been brought against their authenticity, and the bitty ending parallels the comparably scrappy beginning.[32] We may remind ourselves of what Tírechán had to say.[33]

Tertio decimo anno Teothosii imperatoris a Celestino episcopo papa Romae Patricius episcopus ad doctrinam Scottorum mittitur, qui Celestinus quadragesimus quintus episcopus a Petro apostolo in urbe Roma. Paladius episcopus primo mittitur, qui Patricius alio nomine appellabatur, qui martyrium passus est apud Scottos, ut tradunt sancti antiqui. Deinde Patricius secundus ab anguelo Dei Uictor nomine et a Celestino papa mittitur, cui Hibernia tota credidit, qui eam pene totam babtizauit.

In the thirteenth year of the Emperor Theodosius Bishop Patricius is sent by Bishop Celestinus, the pope of Rome, for the teaching of the Irish. This Celestinus (was) the forty-fifth bishop, (beginning) from Peter the apostle, in the city of Rome. Bishop Paladius is sent first, who was named Patricius with another name, who suffered

24 On the annalistic dimension, see above, pp. 29–37.
25 Walsh, *The Placenames of Westmeath*, pp. 270–1.
26 MS. R[1] above (cf. n. 19).
27 Sharpe, *Medieval Irish Saints' Lives*, pp. 247–65 (his MS. I).
28 Walsh, *The Placenames of Westmeath*, pp. 270–1.
29 Binchy, 'Patrick and his biographers', p. 128.
30 §§52–57: *The Patrician Texts*, edd. & transl. Bieler & Kelly, pp. 164–7.
31 Summarised by Binchy, 'Patrick and his biographers', pp. 129–33.
32 §§1–7: *The Patrician Texts*, edd. & transl. Bieler & Kelly, pp. 124–31.
33 §56: *ibid.*, pp. 164–7. I have made some minor alterations to the editing of the text and to the translation. With this passage, compare *The Annals of Inisfallen*, ed. & transl. Mac Airt, p. 45 (§§389–391): cf. above, pp. 39–43.

martyrdom at the hands of the Irish, as is the tradition of the holy men of old. Then Patricius is sent as second (bishop) by the angel Victor and by Pope Celestinus: he was believed by all Ireland, and he baptised almost all of it.

Whether chronological difficulties had first prompted the theory of two Patricks[34] – with subsequent localisation of the less famous one, by a mixture of cynicism and piety –, whether the knowledge of a Patrick of Ossory itself prompted such a solution, or whether Palladius was associated with Rostalla, is unknown.

There are two underlying possibilities. Either there is fact beneath the idea of two Patricks or there is not.[35] The 'other' Patrick could, it must be admitted, be simply the result of learned struggles in seventh-century Ireland with Prosper's annal about Bishop Palladius's appointment and despatch in A.D. 431. It has been doubted whether such an error could have been the origin of a long-lasting mediaeval conviction of the existence of another St Patrick. If there is another person whose true identity is waiting to be discovered beneath the misnomer of 'Sen-Phátric', scholars have another struggle on their hands.

In the opinion of D. A. Binchy, 'It is almost entirely due to [Thomas] O'Rahilly's brilliant advocacy that Palladius has now become the principal candidate' for identification as the other Patrick[36] – in other words, for an identification which would confirm what Tírechán had to say in his *Collectanea* thirteen hundred years ago.

34 See above, pp. 29–33.

35 The first appearance of the phrase *in dá Patraic*, 'the two Patricks', seems to be in a ninth-century preface to an ecclesiastical law-tract: *Cáin Adamnáin*, ed. & transl. Meyer, pp. 12/13 (§22); for the date see Ryan, 'The Cáin Adomnáin'. For a rather hysterical treatment of its evidence see Shaw, 'The myth', p. 24.

36 'Patrick and his biographers', p. 129. He referred to Malone, 'Sen (old) Patrick', as the modern author of the theory.

'ACTA PALLADII' PRESERVED IN PATRICIAN HAGIOGRAPHY?

In 1864 J. H. Todd explored the idea that acts of Bishop Palladius,[1] whom he thought to have been a Gallo-Roman (perhaps from the Auvergne) and an official of the church of Auxerre,[2] had been available to seventh-century and later Irish hagiographers. These writers had 'fathered on' St Patrick biographical details which properly belonged to Palladius. Following Tírechán, Todd admitted (as T. F. O'Rahilly was later to do) that Palladius bore also the name Patricius,[3] although in his reasoning he did not make as much use of this coincidence as he might therefore have been expected to do. Indeed, his discussion of the fusion of Palladian and Patrician biography was rather unsystematic. He saw it now as a deliberate, now as a chaotic, process; now recognition of it could be used as an analytic tool, now one had to admit that its effects overpowered attempts at critical investigation.

After a lengthy discussion, Todd came to the reasons why such confusion of two bishops' acts should have taken place.[4]

> We infer that the whole story of Patrick's connexion with St. Germain and mission from Celestine should be regarded as a fragment of the lost history of Palladius, transferred to the second and more celebrated Patrick, by those who undertook to interpolate the authentic records of his Life. The object of these interpolaters was evidently to exalt their hero. They could not rest satisfied with the simple and humble position in which his own writings, his Confession, and his Letter to Coroticus, had placed him. They could not concede to Palladius the honour of a great mission from Rome, without claiming for Patrick a similar honour; they should not be content that their own Patrick should be regarded as an unlearned, a rude, and uneducated man, even though he had so described himself. The biography of Palladius, 'alio nomine Patricius', supplied them with the means of effecting their object, and gave to the interpolated story the appearance of antient support.

In other words, the motivation for the fusion of biographies was deliberate, and comparable with that which has been claimed for the abridgment of St Patrick's *Confessio* and abandonment of his *Epistola* in the 'Book of Armagh' or its exemplar.[5]

1 Todd, *St. Patrick*, pp. 265–345.
2 *Ibid.*, pp. 276–8, 305–6.
3 *Ibid.*, pp. 305–8; cf. O'Rahilly, *The Two Patricks*.
4 *St. Patrick*, pp. 320–1. For the elements of the discussion see especially his pp. 293, 303, 308–9, 310, 312, 314; cf. pp. 322, 324, 332–3, 334–5, 335–6, 338, 338–9, 340, 342, 344, 344–5.
5 See below, pp. 191–202.

It was Todd's perception, moreover, that an awareness of the hagiographical fusion of Palladius and Patrick was maintained as late as the twelfth century.[6] Therefore the repeated acts of fusion of Palladian and Patrician biography which Todd saw as taking place each time a new Life of St Patrick came to be written were for the most part done as part of a continuing tradition and in full knowledge of the interpolatory character of the work. Only occasionally does a text manifest a form of this fusion which can be described as accidental or innocent. In as much as accounts of St Patrick written later than the seventh century drew in new ways upon the now lost 'acts of Palladius', those *acta* must have remained available for use (perhaps at Armagh) into the central middle ages – although Todd never made this point explicit.

Much of Todd's lengthy discussion of the place of Palladius in the growth of Irish christianity and in the Patrician legend was concerned with examination of the discrepancies between the various accounts and of internal inconsistencies in individual narratives.[7] This work needs to be done again – given the availability of new texts, better editions, and sharper critical techniques – in order to establish what traces of sources surivive in the various *uitae* and what the relationships of the several accounts of Palladius and of Patrick's Continental history are to one another.

We should be wary, however, of the supposition that any great riches are available thus. The part of the Patrician narrative in which any confusion with Palladius could have taken place is small indeed. I present here, therefore, from Ludwig Bieler's editions,[8] the relevant section of Muirchú's *Vita S. Patricii* and the parallel passages from *Vitae II/III/IV S. Patricii* and Probus's *Vita S. Patricii*. The comparable portion of the *Historia Brittonum* may be found elsewhere in this book.[9] I add also the few relevant passages from Tírechán's *Collectanea*,[10] an excerpt from the notes which follow Muirchú's text in the 'Book of Armagh',[11] and one bilingual passage from the so-called '*Additamenta*' (the 'alia pauca serotinis temporibus inuenta') in the same manuscript.[12]

Muirchú

I.6 (5) Transnauigato igitur mari dextro britannico ac cepto itinere per Gallias, Alpes ad extremum, ut corde proposuerat, transcensurus <Romamque petiturus> quendam sanctisimum episcopum Al<ti>siodori ciuitate principem Germanum summum donum inuenit, aput quem non paruo tempore demoratus, iuxta id quod Paulus ad pedes Gamaliel fuerat, in omni subiectione et patientia atque oboedientia scientiam sapientiam castitatemque et omnem utilitatem tam

6 *St. Patrick*, pp. 307–9.

7 *Ibid.*, pp. 287–345. Cf. Bieler, 'The mission of Palladius'. For a significantly developed role for Palladius in a Life of St Ailbe (whose author had read *Vita III S. Patricii*) see Sharpe, 'Quatuor', p. 391.

8 *Four Latin Lives*, ed. Bieler; *The Patrician Texts*, edd. & transl. Bieler & Kelly.

9 See below, pp. 221–32.

10 *The Patrician Texts*, edd. & transl. Bieler & Kelly, pp. 124–31, 164–7.

11 *Ibid.*, pp. 122/3.

12 *Ibid.*, pp. 174/5.

spiritus quam animae cum magno Dei timore et amore in bonitate et simplicitate cordis, corpore et spiritu uirgo, toto animi desiderio didicit dilexit custodiuit.

I.7 (6) Peractisque ibi multis temporibus quasi ut alii quadraginta alii triginta annis ille antiquus ualde fidelis Victoricus nomine, qui omnia sibi in hibernica seruitute possito antequam essent dixerat, eum crebris uissionibus uissitauit dicens ei adesse tempus ut ueniret et aeuanguelico rete nationes feras et barbaras ad quas docendas misserat illum Deus ut piscaret, ibique ei dictum est in uissione: 'Vocant te filii et filiae siluae Foclitae', et caetera.

I.8 (7) Oportuno ergo tempore imperante comitante diuino auxilio coeptum ingreditur iter ad opus in quod ollim praeparatus fuerat, utique aeuanguelii, et missit Germanus seniorem cum illo, hoc est Segitium praespiterum, ut testem comitem haberet, quia nec adhuc a sancto domino Germano in pontificali gradu ordinatus est. Certi enim erant quod Paladius archidiaconus pape Caelestini urbis Romae episcopi, qui tunc tenebat sedem apostolicam quadragensimus quintus a sancto Petro apostolo, ille (Palladius) ordinatus et missus fuerat ad hanc insolam sub brumali rigore possitam conuertendam. Sed prohibuit illum quia nemo potest accipere quicquam de terra nissi datum ei fuerit de caelo. Nam neque hii fieri et inmites homines facile reciperunt doctrinam eius neque et ipse longum uoluit transegere tempus in terra non sua, sed reuersus ad eum qui missit illum. Reuertente uero eo hinc et primo mari transito coeptoque terrarum itenere in Britonum finibus uita functus.

I.9 (8) Audita itaque morte sancti Paladii in Britannis, quia discipuli Paladii, id est Augustinus et Benedictus et caeteri, redeuntes retulerant in Ebmoria de morte eius, Patricius et qui cum eo erant declinauerunt iter ad quendam mirabilem hominem summum aepiscopum Amathorege nomine in propinquo loco habitantem, ibique sanctus Patricius sciens quae euentura essent <s>ibi episcopalem gradum ab Amathorege sancto episcopo accepit; etiam Auxilius Isarninusque et caeteri inferioris gradus eodem die quo sanctus Patricius ordinatus est. Tum acceptis benedictionibus perfectis omnibus secundum morem, cantato etiam Patricio quasi specialiter et conuenienter hoc psalmistae uorsu, 'Tu es sacerdos in aeternum secundum ordinem Melchisedech', uenerabilis uiator paratam nauim in nomine sanctae Trinitatis ascendit et peruenit Brittannias et omissis omnibus ambulandi anfractibus praeter commone uiae officium – nemo enim dissidia quaerit Dominum – cum omni uelocitate flatuque prospero mare nostrum contendit.

Vita Secunda

§22 Dehinc transnauigato mari dextro britannico, ut corde proposuerat, petiturus quendam sanctissimum et in fide probatissimum et principem paene Galliarum omnium Autisiodori ciuitatis episcopum Germanum nomine, apud quem non paruo tempore demoratus iuxta quod Paulus ad pedes Gamaliel in omni subiectione et oboedientia sapientiae studium et scripturarum notitiam sanctarum feruente animi desiderio didicit. Peractis itaque multis temporibus ibi, quasi annis ut alii triginta alii quadraginta, solebat eum uisitare Victoricus dicens ad eum crebro tempus adesse ut gentes inter quas antea seruierat a diaboli iugo liberaret et nomen Christi seminaret inter ipsos ibique euangelica fluenta diffunderet. Aralanensis nomen est insulae in qua Germanus docuit Patricium triginta annis. Triginta enim annorum aetas eius erat quando peruenit ad sanctum Germanum, triginta annis legit cum illo, sexaginta annis praedicauit in Hibernia.

§23 Oportuno ergo tempore imperante consilio Dei coeptum graditur iter ad opus in quod olim praeparatus fuerat, utique euangelii praedicationem. Et misit Germanus seniorem cum illo, hoc est Segitium presbiterum, ut testem et comitem haberet idoneum, qui nec adhuc a sancto Germano in pontificali gradu ordinatus est. Certi etenim erant quod Palladius archidiaconus papae Caelestini urbis Romae, qui tunc tenebat sedem apostolicam quadragesimus quintus ab apostolo Petro, a sancto papa ordinatus et missus fuerat ad hanc insulam sub brumali frigore positam conuertendam. Sed prohibuit illum Deus, quia nemo potest accipere quicquam de terra nisi datum fuerit ei de caelo. Nam neque immites homines receperunt doctrinam eius neque et ipse longum uoluit transigere tempus non sua in terra, sed reuersus est ad eum a quo missus fuerat. Ipso itaque reuertente et hinc primo mari transito coeptoque terrarum itinere in Pictorum finibus defunctus est.

§24 Nam beatissimus papa Caelestinus romanae ecclesiae archidiaconum nomine Palladium episcopum ordinauit et in Hiberniam insulam traditis sibi beati Petri et Pauli et aliorum sanctorum reliquiis, ueteris quoque et noui testamenti uoluminibus datis transmisit. Palladius ergo in terram Scotorum intrans Lagenensium ad fines peruenit, in quo Nathi filius Garrchon comes erat, qui sibi contrarius erat. Alii uero uiri diuina misericordia ad diuinum cultum a beato Palladio in nomine sanctae Trinitatis baptizati sunt, et tres ecclesias in eodem pago construxit: unam quae dicitur Cellfine, in qua usque hodie libri sui, quos a sancto Caelestino accepit, et capsa reliquiarum beati Petri et Pauli et aliorum sanctorum cum magna ueneratione habentur, et tabulae in quibus scribere solebat, quae ex ipsius Palladii nomine scotice Pallere, id est onus Palladii, uocantur; altera uero ecclesia ex discipulis Palladii, id est Thech na Róman; tertia uero ecclesia, id est Domnach Arte, in qua sunt sancti uiri de familia Palladii Siluester et Solonius, et postero tempore reliquiae eorum ad Inis Baitheni <portatae sunt> et ibi uenerantur cum reliquiis Baitheni. Post paruum denique interuallum defuncto Palladio in campo Girgin in loco qui dicitur Forddun – dicunt enim alii martyrio coronatum esse eum illic –,

§25 Patricius ab eodem papa Celestino in Hiberniam transmissus peruenit ad hostium eiusdem fluminis, id est Deae, et ibi erat iniquus comes Nathi, qui sancto Palladio ante restitit, et beato Patricio eiusque doctrinae contradicebat. Sinell uero filius Findchatho per praedicationem sancti Patricii omnipotenti Deo credidit et a sancto Patricio primus ex gente Scotorum baptizatus est. Propter hoc etiam et sibi et semini eius benedixit.

§26 Audita itaque morte Palladii sancti in Britannia, quia discipuli eius Augustinus et Benedictus et ceteri redeuntes retulerunt in Eboria de morte eius, Patricius et qui cum eo erant declinauerunt iter ad quendam mirabilem hominem summum episcopum Amathoregem nomine in propinquo habitantem loco, ibique sanctus Patricius sciens quae uentura essent illi episcopalem gradum ab Amathorege sancto episcopo accepit. Sed etiam Auxilius et Serenus et ceteri inferioris gradus ordinati sunt eodem die quo sanctus Patricius. Tunc accepta licentia et benedictione perfectisque omnibus, cantato etiam Patricio quasi specialiter et conuenienter hoc psalmistae uersu, 'Tu es sacerdos in aeternum', et reliqua, uenerabilis uiator paratam nauim in nomine sanctae Trinitatis conscendit et peruenit ad Britanniam, et postea peruenit ad Hiberniam cum omni uelocitate et flatu prospero.

Vita Quarta

§26 Dehinc, ut ab angelo admonitus fuerat, transnauigato mari britannico dextro, ut corde proposuerat, petiit quendam sanctissimum et in fide probatissimum episcopum et principem Galliarum pene omnium, spetialiter autem Alciadri principem nomine Germanum, a quo summa cum ueneratione susceptus est et apud eum non paruo tempore demoratus iuxta exemplum Pauli ad pedes Gamalihel in omni subiectione et obedientia permanens sapientiae studium et scripturarum notitiam sanctarum feruente animi desiderio didicit. Arelatensis autem nomen insulae fuit in qua sanctus Germanus docuit sanctum Patricium per .xxx^{ta}. annos. Triginta annorum aetas eius erat quando peruenit ad Germanum et .xxx^{ta}. annis apud eum mansit, sexaginta uero annos in Hibernia praedicauit. Ex hac igitur serie annorum apparet quod .c^{tum}. xx^{ti}. annis in hac uita mansit.

§27 Peractis igitur multis temporibus solebat angelus Domini uisitare eum dicens ei crebro tempus adesse ut gentes inter quas antea seruierat diaboli iugo liberaret et nomen Christi seminaret inter eos ibique euangelica fluenta diffunderet. Oportuno ergo tempore inspirante Deo ceptum iter ingreditur ad opus in quod olim paratus fuerat, id est euangelii praedicationem. Et misit sanctus Germanus seniorem cum eo Segetium presbyterum, ut testem et comitem haberet idoneum. Sed nec adhuc a sancto Germano in pontificali gradu ordinatus est. Sciebat enim quod Palladius archidiaconus papae Celestini urbis Romae episcopi qui tunc tenebat sedem apostolicam quadragesimus .v^{tus}. a Petro apostolo, ab eodem papa ordinatus in Hyberniam ad praedicandum missus esset.

§28 Cum ergo illuc perueniret, intra Laginensium fines uerbum Domini incaepit praedicare. Sed quia non per eum omnipotens Dominus hibernienses gentes de errore gentilitatis ad inuiolabilem sanctae atque indiuiduae Trinitatis fidem perducere predestinauit, paucis ibi diebus permansit. Pauci tamen crediderunt per eum, et in eodem pago tres aecclesias constituit: unam quae dicitur aecclesia Finte, in qua usque hodie libri eius, quos a sancto Celestino accepit, habentur et capsa cum reliquiis beati Petri apostoli et Pauli et aliorum sanctorum, et tabulae in quibus scribere solebat, quae ex ipsius Palladii nomine scotice Palladię, id est onus Palladii, nuncupantur, cum magna ueneratione habentur; alia aecclesia a discipulis Palladii constructa est, quae Domus Romanorum dicitur; tertia est aecclesia, quae Dominica Archa uocatur, in qua sancti uiri ex sociis Palladii sunt, id est Siluester et Solinus, quorum reliquiae post aliquantum tempus ad insulam Boetheni portatae sunt et ibi cum digno honore habentur. Videns autem sanctus Palladius quod non multum illic prodesse potuit, Romam reuerti uolens in regione Pictorum ad Dominum migrauit. Alii autem affirmant quod in Hybernia martirio coronatus est.

§29 Misit ergo, ut praefati sumus, sanctus Germanus beatum Patricium Romam, ut cum apostolicae sedis episcopi licentia ad praedicationem exiret; sic enim ordo exigebat. Igitur per mare Tyrrenum nauigando transiuit, et accepit baculum Iesu a quodam iuuene in quadam insula hospitium Christo tribuente. Et locutus est Dominus cum Patricio in monte et praecepit ei ut ad Hyberniam ueniret. Perueniente uero illo Romam a sancto papa Celestino honorifice est susceptus et traditis sibi sanctorum reliquiis ab eodem papa Celestino in Hyberniam missus est.

§30 Accepta ergo apostolica licentia beatus Patricius per Italiam Galliasque recto tramite perambulans peruenit ad mare inter Gallias et Brittannias positum. In cuius litore duos inuenit uiros inter se pugnantes; quos beatus Patricius admonens ut pacifice uiuerent responderunt dicentes quod nemo inter illos pacem facere ualeret nisi qui de minutis harenis illic adherentibus unum lapidem facere potuisset. Audiens haec beatus Patricius baculo Iesu, quem manu tenebat, harenas in modum circuli circumdans in unum transformauit lapidem. Videntes autem homines miraculum dantes gloriam Deo pacificati sunt. Lapis autem secutus est sanctum Patricium, qui auro et argento ornatus in quadam ciuitacula cum magno usque in hodiernum diem habetur honore.

§31 Audita itaque morte sancti Palladii in Brittannia, quam discipuli eius Augustinus et Benedictus et caeteri redeuntes retulerunt in Eboria, Patricius et qui cum eo erant declinauerunt ad quendam sanctum ac uenerabilem episcopum Amathoregem nomine in proximo habitantem loco, ibique sanctus Patricius sciens quae uentura essent ei episcopalem gradum a supradicto sancto episcopo ordinatus accepit. Sed etiam Auxilius atque Esserinus et caeteri inferioris gradus ordinati sunt. Et accepta licentia et benedictione perfectisque omnibus, cantato etiam Patricio quasi specialiter et conuenienter hoc psalmistae uersu, 'Tu es sacerdos in aeternum secundum ordinem Melchisedech', uenerabilis uiator paratam nauim in nomine sanctae Trinitatis cum suis comitibus ascendens prospero flatu ad Hiberniam nauigando peruenit.

Vita Tertia

§21 Tunc sanctus Patricius cogitauit per angelicam uisionem exire, ut sanctas scripturas disceret, ut posset eos docere. Perrexit ergo ad regiones Gallorum et uenit ad sanctum episcopum Germanum, uirum sapientissimum et honoratum ab omnibus Gallis, principem Altisiodori[13] ciuitatis, et mansit apud eum quadraginta annis legens et implens diuinas scripturas, et uirgo corpore et spiritu.

[13] *Autisiodori*, Π.

§22 Et postea uenit ad Martinum et mansit quadraginta dies secum. Et angelus ad Martinum dixit, ut iret Patricius ad Tamerensem insulam.[14] Transactis ibi quadraginta annis uoluit Patricius uisitare Romam, caput uidelicet omnium aecclesiarum, ad quam christiani ab omnibus mundi partibus conueniebant; et hoc placuit sancto Germano. Misitque Germanus seniorem cum illo, hoc est Segitium presbiterum, ut testem haberet idoneum.

§23 Tunc Patricius iter ingressus perrexit ad quendam heremitam in quodam loco habitantem, a quo Patricius portauit baculum qui fuit in manu Iesu Christi Domini nostri, ut per huius comitis auxilium prosperum haberet iter. Et baculus usque hodie manet in ciuitate Patricii, et uocatur baculus Iesu.

§24 Patricius quoque declinauit iter ad quendam mirabilem hominem, summum episcopum et sanctum, Amatorege[15] nomine, et ab illo sanctus Patricius gradum episcopalem accepit.

§25 Cum ergo Patricius Romam ingressus esset, inuenit gloriam et honorem apud Caelestinum, qui erat papa urbis Romae quadragesimus quintus a Petro apostolo. Cum autem esset sanctus Patricius Romae, audiuit uocem angeli de caelo dicentis: 'Vade ad Hiberniam insulam et adiuua eos qui te inuocant'. Et dixit Patricius: 'Non ibo donec Dominum salutem'. Et angelus duxit eum ad montem Arnon in Armairc Lete super petram[16] maris Tyrreni in ciuitate quae uocatur Capua, et salutauit Dominum ut Moyses.

§26 Tunc papa Caelestinus misit Patricium ad hanc insulam. Nam iste Celestinus alium predicatorem nomine Palladium miserat ante Patricium ad hanc insulam. Sed habitatores huius insulae non receperunt doctrinam eius, quia non illi Deus donauit istam insulam, sed sancto Patricio reseruauit eam. Palladius uero reuersus est ab hac insula, ut iret Romam; sed ille mortuus est in regione Brittonum.

§27 Tunc sanctus Patricius ex imperio papae Celestini reuersus est ad hanc insulam.

Vita auctore Probo

§12 Cumque adhuc esset in patria cum patre Calpurnio et matre Concessa, fratre etiam Ructhi ac sorore Mila nomine, in ciuitate eorum Arimuric, facta est seditio magna in partibus illis; nam filii Rethmiti regis de Britannia uastantes Arimuric et alia circum posita loca iugulauerunt Calpurnium et uxorem eius Concessam, filios autem eorum Patricium et fratrem eius Ructhi una cum sorore captiuos abducentes Hiberniam ingressi sunt, et uendiderunt Patricium Milchoni regi, Ructi uero fratrem eius ac sororem alteri principi; ubi et post multum temporis data est fratri suo Ructi in coniugium, at ille sciens esse sororem suam non tetigit eam, mansit tamen cum ea in continentia.

14 On this episode and the name of this island, see Dumville, 'St Patrick in Cornwall?'.
15 *Amoto*, Π.
16 *ripam*, Π.

§13 Post haec uenit angelus Domini ad beatum Patricium iuxta petram montis Egli et dixit illi: 'Vade ad hereditatem tuam de qua uenisti'. Qui statim fugiens de captiuitate perrexit iter unius diei, usque dum ueniret ad domum cuiusdam uiri in Arcennacte ciuitate; de cuius domo cum exiret, suscepit eum uir in nauim suam et uendidit eum in Galliam, et portauit pretium eius domum, solidos scilicet triginta. Suscipientes ergo Galli beatum Patricium duxerunt eum in naui in terram suam; qui cum nauigare coepissent, fuit illis uentus contrarius multis diebus. Rogauit autem sanctus Patricius Dominum et dedit illis uentum congruum.

§14 Deinde uenit cum Gallis post dies duodecim ad Brotgalum, inde Traiectum; ubi cum uenisset beatus Patricius, absolutus est a christianis de captiuitate. Et fugiens inde peruenit ad Martinum episcopum Turonis et quattuor annis mansit cum eo et tonso capite ordinatus est ab eo in clericum et tenuit lectionem et doctrinam ab eo.

§15 Peracto uero quadriennio apparuit ei angelus Domini et dixit illi: 'Vade ad plebem Dei, id est eremitas et solitarios nudis pedibus, et conuersare cum eis, ut proberis per aliquod tempus'. Et uenit in solitudinem et mansit cum eremitis per octo annos.

§16 Venitque iterum ad eum angelus Domini et dixit ei: 'Vade ad illos qui sunt in insula inter montes et mare'. Exiens igitur de solitudine uenit ad insulanos sicut praeceptum erat illi, et fuit uita cotidiana eius Domino disponente dimidius panis. Cumque mansisset inter insulanos illos et longo tempore laborem pro Christo sustinuisset, dixerunt insulani illi: 'Non potest homo habitare nobiscum, qui non possit portare aquam nobis de fonte'. Erat enim bestia magna iuxta fontem in circuitu per totum annum, nisi in uno mense, id est Maio. Tunc orauit ad Dominum sanctus Patricius et fugata est bestia a fonte sicque permansit cum insulanis illis nouem annis habitus ab eis in magna ueneratione.

§17 Rursus angelus Domini apparuit sancto Patricio dicens: 'Vade ad sanctum seniorem episcopum, qui est in monte Hermon', in dextro latere maris oceani, et uallata est ciuitas eius septem muris. Cumque uenisset illuc, mansit cum eo per aliquot dies. Deinde ordinauit eum episcopus ille in sacerdotem et lectitauit cum eo multis temporibus.

§18 Dum autem ibi moraretur, nocte quadam audiuit in uisione uoces puerorum de sinu et de uentre matrum, qui fuerunt in Hibernia, dicentium: 'Veni, sancte Patrici, saluos nos fac ab ira uentura'. Eadem quoque hora dixit angelus ad eum: 'Vade ad Hiberniam et eris apostolus insulae illius'. Patricius respondit: 'Non possum ire, quia mali sunt homines qui habitant in ea'. Angelus dixit: 'Vade'. Patricius econtra: 'Non possum', ait, 'nisi uidero Dominum'. Dicit ei angelus: 'Ascende cacumen montis Hermon et uidebis ibi Dominum'. Exiuit ergo Patricius cum nouem uiris et uidit Dominum. Dixitque Dominus ad eum: 'Veni ad dexteram meam'. Et iuit Patricius ad dexteram Domini. Tunc ait illi Dominus: 'Vade in Hiberniam et praedica in ea uerbum salutis aeternae'. Patricius respondit: 'Tres petitiones postulo a te, Domine: ut homines uidelicet Hiberniae diuites sint in auro et argento, et ego sim patronus eorum, et post hanc uitam sedeam ad dexteram tuam in caelo'. Ait illi Dominus: 'Habebis, Patrici, sicut rogasti, et insuper qui commemorauerit te in die uirtutis in nocte non peribit in aeternum'.

§19 Surgens igitur Patricius uenit in Hiberniam statimque uaticinati sunt prophetae Hiberniae quod uenisset Patricius illuc. Cum autem praedicantem illum diebus ac noctibus spernerent insulani, qui tamen resistere non poterant Dei ordinationi, sanctus Patricius fudit ad Dominum huiusmodi preces: 'Domine Iesu Christe, qui iter meum per Gallias atque per Italiam ad has insulas direxisti, perduc me, obsecro, ad sedem sanctae romanae ecclesiae, ut accepta inde auctoritate praedicandi cum fiducia uerbum tuum fiant christiani per me populi Hibernorum'.

§20 Nec multo post progressus ab Hibernia uir Domini Patricius uenit ad caput, ut postularat, omnium ecclesiarum Romam ibique benedictione apostolica petita et accepta reuersus est itinere quo uenerat illuc.

§21 Transnauigato uero mari britannico et arrepto uersus Gallias itinere uenit, ut corde proposuerat, ad hominem sanctissimum ac probatissimum in fide et doctrina omnium paene Galliarum primatem eximium, Germanum uidelicet Autisiodorensis ecclesiae episcopum; apud quem non paruo tempore demoratus est in omni subiectione, cum patientia, oboedientia, caritate, castimonia et omni tam spiritus quam animae munditia, uirgo manens in timore Domini, ambulans in bonitate et simplicitate cordis omnibus diebus uitae suae.

§22 Interim autem, dum ibi per multos dies demoraretur, angelus Domini, qui ei indesinenter apparuerat, etiam modo crebris uisionibus uisitauit eum dicens iam adesse tempus, ut ueniret in Hiberniam et euangelico ore nationes feras ac barbaras, ad quas docendas destinatus fuerat, conuerteret ad Christum. Nactus ergo tempus opportunum comitante consilio diuino aggreditur iter ad quod illum Dominus uocare dignatus est, misitque cum illo sanctus Germanus presbyterum nomine Regirum, ut testem et comitem eum haberet idoneum in omnibus uiis et operibus suis.

§23 Necdum tamen uir Domini Patricius ad pontificalem gradum fuerat promotus, quod ideo nimirum distulerat, quia sciebat quod Palladius archidiaconus Caelestini papae, qui quadragesimus quintus a sancto Petro apostolicae sedi praeerat, ordinatus ab eodem papa directus fuerat ad hanc insulam sub brumali rigore positam conuertendam; sed prohibuit illum Deus conuertere gentem illam, quia nemo potest accipere quidquam in terra nisi datum fuerit ei de caelo. Immites enim et feri homines recipere nolebant doctrinam eius, neque ipse longum uoluit transigere tempus in terra non sua, sed reuerti disposuit ad eum qui misit illum. Cumque aggressus Palladius mare transmeasset et ad fines Pictorum peruenisset, ibidem uita decessit.

§24 Audientes itaque de morte Palladii archidiaconi discipuli ipsius qui erant in Britannis, id est Augustinus, Benedictus et ceteri, uenerunt ad sanctum Patricium in Euboriam et mortem Palladii ei denuntiabant. Patricius autem et qui cum eo erant declinauerunt iter ad quendam mirae sanctitatis hominem summum episcopum Amatorem nomine in propinquo loco habitantem ibique sanctus Patricius, sciens quae superuentura essent illi, episcopali gradu ab eodem archipraesule Amatore sublimatus est; sed et alii nonnulli clerici ad officium inferioris gradus ordinati sunt. Eodem uero die quo sanctus Patricius sacris benedictionibus ordinatus est conuenienter hoc psalmistae canticum in choro psallentium clericorum decantatum est: 'Tu es sacerdos in aeternum secundum ordinem Melchisedech'.

§25 Tunc uenerabilis sacerdos Domini Patricius nauem celeriter ascendit et peruenit Britannias, omissisque omnibus ambulandi anfractibus cum omni uelocitate prospero fluctu mare nostrum in nomine sanctae Trinitatis adiuit.

Tírechán

Tirechan episcopus haec scripsit ex ore uel libro Ultani episcopi, cuius ipse alumpnus uel discipulus fuit.

§1 Inueni quattuor nomina in libro scripta Patricio apud Ultanum episcopum Conchuburnensium: sanctus Magonus, qui est clarus; Succetus, qui est <deus belli; Patricius, qui est> pater ciuium; Cothirthiacus, quia seruiuit quattuor domibus magorum; et empsit illum unus ex eis, cui nomen erat Miliuc maccu Boin magus, et seruiuit illi septem annis omni seruitute ac duplici labore, et porcarium possuit eum in montanis conuallibus. Deinde autem uissitauit illum anguelus Domini in somniis in cacuminibus montis Scirte iuxta montem Miss. Finita autem angueli sententia, 'Ecce nauis tua parata: surge et ambula', et secessit ab illo in caelum, surrexit et ambulauit, (et) ut dixit illi anguelus Domini Uictor nomine. In septimo decimo aetatis suae anno captus ductus, uenditus est in Hiberniam. In uicesimo secundo anno laboris magis relinquere potuit. Septem aliis annis ambulauit et naugiauit in fluctibus et in campistribus locis et in conuallibus montanis per Gallias atque Italiam totam atque in insolis quae sunt in mari Terreno, ut ipse dixit in commemoratione laborum. Erat autem in una ex insolis, quae dicitur Aralanensis, annis triginta mihi testante Ultano episcopo. Omnia autem quae euenierunt inuenietis in plana illius historia scripta. Haec sunt nouissima illius mirabilia in quinto regni anno Loiguiri maicc Neill finita atque feliciter facta.

§2 A passione autem Christi colleguntur anni quadringenti triginta tres usque ad mortem Patricii. Duobus autem uel quinque annis regnauit Loiguire post mortem Patricii. Omnis autem regni illius tempus triginta sex, ut putamus.

§3 Uenit uero Patricius cum Gallis ad insolas Maccu Chor et insola orientali, quae dicitur Insola Patricii, et secum fuit multitudo episcoporum sanctorum et praespiterorum et diaconorum ac exorcistarum, hostiariorum lectorumque nec non filiorum quos ordinauit.

* * * * *

§6 De episcoporum numero quos ordinauit in Hibernia quadringentos quinquaginta. De praespiteris non possimus ordinare, quia babtitzabat cotidie homines et illis litteras legebat ac abgatorias <scribebat>, et de aliis episcopos ac praespiteros faciebat, qui in aetate babtismum acciperunt sobria.

De episcopis
Benignus
Bronus
Sachellus
Cethiacus
Carthacus
Cartenus
Connanus
Firtranus
Siggeus
Aeternus
Sencaticus
Olcanus
Iborus
Ordius
Nazarius
Miserneus
Senachus
Secundinus
Gosach<t>us
Camulacus
Auxilius
Uictoricus
Bressialus
Feccus
Menathus
Cennannus
Nazarus
Melus
Maceleus
Mactaleus
Culeneus
Asacus
Bitheus
Falertus
Sesc<e>neus
Muireth<a>chus
Temoreris, qui fundauit aeclessiam sanctam Cairce, quam tenuit familia Clónó Auiss
Daigreus
Iustianus mac Híi
Daiméne
Olcanus
Domnallus et alii quamplurimi

De praespiteris
Anicius
Brocidius
Amirgenus
Lommanus
Catideus
Catus
Catanus
Broscus
Ailbeus
Trianus episcopus

§7 De nominibus Francorum Patricii episcopi tres:
Inaepius
Bernicius
Hernicius subdiaconus
Seman
Semen
Cancem
Bernicius diaconus
et Ernicius
Franci uiri quindecim cum sorore una aut sex uel tribus

Cassanus
Conlang
Erclang
Brocanus
Roddanus
Brigsón et alter Roddanus, qui fundauit aeclessiam Senem nepotum Ailello, quam tenuerunt monachi Patricii Genget et Sannuch.

De diaconis
Diaconus Iuostus qui babtitzauit Ceranum filium artificis ex libro Patricii.
Diaconus Coimmanus, carus Patricio, qui fuit in aeclessia magna Aird Licce.
Olcanus monachus, qui fuit in cellola magna Muaide praespiter; duo exorcistas scimus apud illum, exorcista Losca in Dorso Dairi in regionibus Tuirtri, exorcista alius in campo Liphi.

* * * * *

§56 Tertio decimo anno Teothosii imperatoris a Celestino episcopo papa Romae Patricius episcopus ad doctrinam Scottorum mittitur, qui Celestinus quadragesimus quintus episcopus a Petro apostolo in urbe Roma. Paladius episcopus primo mittitur, qui Patricius alio nomine appellabatur, qui martyrium passus est apud Scottos, ut tradunt sancti antiqui. Deinde Patricius secundus ab anguelo Dei Uictor nomine et a Celestino papa mittitur, cui Hibernia tota credidit, qui eam pene totam babtitzauit.

Notes following Muirchú's Life of St Patrick

§2 Patricius sexto anno babtitzatus est, uigesimo captus est, quindecim seruiuit, quadraginta legit, sexaginta unum docuit. Tota uero aetas centum undecim. Haec Constans in Gallis inuenit.

Additamenta

§12 Patricius et Isserninus \`id est episcopus Fith´ cum Germano fuerunt in Olsiodora ciuitate. Germanus uero Isernino dixit ut praedicare in Hiberniam ueniret atque prumptus fuit obedire etiam in quamcumque partem mitteretur n(iss)i in Hiberniam. Germanus dixit Patricio: 'Et tu anoboediens eris?' Patricius dixit: 'Fiat sicut uis'. Germanus dixit: 'Hoc inter uos erit, et non potuerit Iserninus in Hiberniam non transire'. Patricius uenit in Hiberniam, Isserninus uero missus est in aliam regionem; sed uentus contrarius detulit illum in dexteram partem Hiberniae.

Dutét iar sin dia chennadich, aicme becc i Clíu, Catrige a ainmm. Dulluid di suidiu concongab Toicuile. Facab noíb dia muintir and. Luid iarsuidiu concongab Ráith Foalascich. Facib noíb n-aile i suidiu. Dulluid di suidiu du Láthruch Da Arad i nDib Maigib. Dullotar cuci i suidiu secht maicc Cathboth; pridchis duaib et crediderunt et babtitzati sunt, ocus luid leo fades dia mmennut. Fusocart Éndæ Cennsalach fu bíthin creit<m>e ria cách. Luid epscop Fith leo for longis, cách a leth ódib. Ránic Patricc ier suidiu et crediderunt sibi septem filii Dúnlinge. Luid iar suidiu cu Crimthan macc nÉndi Ceinnselich, et ipse credidit ucc Raith Bilich. Áilsi Patricc iarna baitzed ara tailced maccu Cathbad ocus Isserninum leo, ocus adcotedae inn itge.

§12 Patrick and Isserninus, that is Bishop Fith, were with Germanus in the city of Auxerre. Germanus told Iserninus to go and preach in Ireland; and he was willing to obey, in whatever part (of the world) he might be sent, except to Ireland. Germanus said to Patrick: 'Will you also be disobedient?' Patrick said: 'Be it as you wish'. Germanus said: 'This will be (a difference) between you, and (yet) Iserninus will not be able not to go to Ireland'. Patrick went to Ireland, but Iserninus was sent to a different region; but the wind was against him and carried him to the southern part of Ireland.

Then he (Iserninus) comes to his district, a small sept in Clíu, named Catrige. He came thence and founded Toicuile. He left there a saint of his community. After this he went and founded Ráith Foalascich. There he left another saint. Thence he came to Láthrach Dá Arad in the Two Plains. There the seven sons of Cathboth went to him; he preached to them, and they believed and were baptized, and he went with them southwards to their abode. Énde Cennselach outlawed them because of their believing before everyone (else). Bishop Fith went with them into exile, each of them apart. Afterwards Patrick arrived, and the seven sons of Dúnlang believed him. Then he went to Crimthann son of Éndæ Cennselach, and he (Crimthann) believed at Ráith Bilech. After baptizing him, Patrick besought him to let back the sons of Cathboth, and Iserninus along with them, and he obtained the request.

The latest of these *uitae* may belong to the eleventh century.[17] A progressive elaboration of the story-line and deterioration in the quality of the information transmitted may be noted. Nevertheless, a full re-analysis of this material remains an indispensable need.

It would seem to be an essential deduction both from the remarks of Muirchú and Tírechán and from the necessity of textual history that in the later seventh century there already existed written accounts of St Patrick which no longer survive. What these contained about the Continental background to the Patrician mission is (as yet, at least) unknown. That some research on this question had been undertaken in Gaul is strongly suggested by the note quoted above from the 'Book of Armagh' in which one Constans is said to have found information there. By *ca* 700 a story of Patrick's formation in Gaul is thought to have been available to Abbot Cellán of Perrona Scottorum (Péronne in Picardy), as is briefly evidenced by some verses which were attributed to Cellán by Ludwig Traube:[18]

> 'Calpurnus genuit, istum alma Britannia misit;
> Gallia nutriuit, tenet ossaque Scottia felix'.

It is not clear, however, whether Cellán had access to the work of Muirchú or rather to some other source; nor is it known whether the antecedent hagiography circulated on the Continent.

The nature of the Continental episodes recounted in Patrician hagiography is such that we must suppose them either to derive from information about Palladius or to be the result of research into the context which would be presupposed by a Patrician mission beginning in A.D. 432. The confusions

17 The dates assigned to them by modern scholarship are neither precise nor very securely based. For discussion, see *Four Latin Lives*, ed. Bieler, pp. 1–42.

18 Traube, 'Perrona', pp. 488–9; Meyer, 'Verses from a chapel'; Kenney, *The Sources*, p. 507 (no. 306); Levison, 'Zu den Versen'; Grosjean, 'Les inscriptions métriques'; Lapidge, 'Some remnants', pp. 804–5 (no. 9). Péronne was drawn back into Irish discussion of the development of the cult of St Patrick by a remark of Best, 'Palaeographical notes, III, the Book of Armagh', p. 102, who argued that the exemplar of the 'Book of Armagh' had been written in a Continental scriptorium. Cf. Binchy, 'Patrick and his biographers', pp. 83–4.

which are found in these episodes suggest, at any rate, that they offer no straightforward reproduction of any fifth-century source.

In so far as J. H. Todd worked out his theory of an account of the 'acts of Palladius', its implication was that this was either a text composed in Ireland or one drawing rather precisely on Irish information. The reason for this deduction is that Todd thought it to have contained the episode of the bishop's rejection by King Nath Í mac Garrchon.[19] Many difficulties are offered by such a theory, however. Unless we are to suppose that Palladius's episcopate ended early in martyrdom or in abandonment of his position in Ireland, we should have to allow the writing of a source which knew of Palladius's arrival and perhaps early months in Ireland but of no subsequent event. If the hypothetical text had been written in Ireland, this would seem rather odd. Otherwise, we should have to suppose that it depended on a first despatch from Palladius in Ireland, recounting his first experiences; no subsequent reports would have been available to the author of the *acta*.

One has only to consider the logic thus to see difficulties multiply beyond endurance. Undoubtedly the simplest solution is to allow that no such Irish episode could have belonged to the *acta*, which would therefore have been solely concerned with the Continental background to the sending of Palladius to Ireland. In this way too, problematic questions about the form in which Irish names would have been recorded in the 430s and about how they would have been inherited and handled in the seventh century can be avoided.

If a locally specific Irish dimension to such information be excluded, the question about the place(s) of survival of the Palladian/Patrician Continental *acta* from the mid-fifth to the late seventh century is left completely open. There is perhaps one further argument which can be brought forward against Irish origin or transmission of such *acta* at that early date, although the point can be held to depend on prior acceptance of another – concerning the significance of the date 432 in Patrician history – which may be controversial. If this hypothetical text was preserved and known in Ireland in the sixth and earlier seventh centuries, then the discovery of Prosper's annal for A.D. 431 should not have caused the great shock to Irish historiography and chronography which evidently it did provoke. One might object that the text could have been preserved in Ireland but neglected, only to be rediscovered under the impetus of the questioning and research occasioned newly acquired knowledge of the true chronology of Palladius's appointment as bishop for Ireland. However, such complications move what is already exceedingly hypothetical beyond the bounds of plausibility, for they can be intended only to sustain a theory in imminent danger of self-destruction. We must conclude, therefore, that it is unlikely that Palladian *acta* were preserved in Ireland – say, at a church associated with Palladius or one of his co-workers – from the fifth century to the seventh; and if we choose to think of comparable Patrician, rather than Palladian, *acta* these too are disqualified but in this case for the reason that an early fifth-century Continental history for Patrick would have been a work of research (and perhaps even deliberate fraud) in the seventh century. The

[19] *St. Patrick*, pp. 338–45 (cf. 253–4).

connexion of Patrick with the same sources of authority – Auxerre and Rome – as Palladius was associated with cannot be separated from the claims put forward on behalf of the church of Armagh in *Liber angeli* in the mid-seventh century.[20]

By a process of exclusion of options, we are seemingly left with one rather broad conclusion, if the core-hypothesis of the former existence of *Acta* (*S.*) *Palladii episcopi* be admitted. We must suppose that an account written in Gaul or at Rome in the fifth century was found by Irish research-activity on the Continent in the seventh century under the stimulus of the discovery that Prosper's Chronicle provided a date, a papal commission, and an episcopal name for the beginning of organised christianity in Ireland.

The central difficulty which the hypothesis of fifth-century *acta Palladii* must face is that on the evidence of the Patrician hagiography which has provided the raw material for the theory, the subject treated was very limited – some aspects of the background to the despatch of Palladius to Ireland in 431. It is only when the range of source-material admitted as derivative of such *acta* is widened that a larger account of a connexion between Rome, Auxerre, and Ireland in the second quarter (and just possibly also the third) of the fifth century becomes imaginable. From the hagiographic extracts printed above it will have become apparent how restricted is the range of information deployed there about the Continental background to the Irish episcopates of Palladius and Patrick. Some well known names attached to this phase of Irish Church-history make scarcely an appearance, in particular those of Auxilius, Iserninus, and Secundinus.[21]

If we turn to Irish chronicle-evidence we can see the extent and different nature (and Patrician context) of the references to these men who are treated in passing, if at all, in the hagiography. I draw the following items from the 'Annals of Ulster'.[22]

439 Secundus, Auxilius, et Serninus mituntur, et episcopi ipsi, in Hiberniam in auxilium Patricii.
441 Probatus est in fide catolica Patricius episcopus.
443 Patricius episcopus ardore fidei et doctrina Christi florens in nostra prouincia.
444 Ard Macha fundata est: ab Urbe condita usque ad hanc ciuitatem fundatam .m.cxc.iiii..
447 Quies Secundini sancti .lxxv°. anno etatis sue.
454 Cena Temhra apud Loeghaire filium Néill.
457 Quies Senis Patricii, ut alii libri dicunt.
459 Auxilius episcopus quieuit.
461 Hic alii quietem Patricii dicunt.
467 Quies Benigni episcopi.
468 Isserninus episcopus moritur.

20 For the date of *Liber angeli*, see Sharpe, 'Armagh and Rome'.
21 On these figures, see below, pp. 89–105.
22 *The Annals of Ulster*, edd. & transl. Mac Airt & Mac Niocaill, I.40–9.

Here the fundamental underlying assumption is that a second mission, to assist Patrick, was sent some years after his arrival in Ireland:[23] this was led by three bishops (named but not particularly prominent in the hagiography, and certainly not in the parts dealing with the Continental background), two of whom (Auxilius and Iserninus) we meet elsewhere as associates of St Patrick – in the heading of the problematic conciliar text, *Synodus episcoporum*.[24] The obvious parallel to the situation envisaged by the chronicler (who may or may not have been responsible for the idea) is Pope Gregory's despatch of a supplementary mission to England in 601, following the initial successes of the team led by Augustine and sent five years earlier.[25] If we translate this into the context of Palladius's activities in Ireland, we might think that Palladius's initial successes (if Prosper's *Contra Collatorem* has been understood correctly)[26] had led to a need for more clergy (and perhaps bishops), and now indeed to an overtly missionary strategy perhaps not immediately envisaged by Pope Celestine in 431.

In 1962 D. A. Binchy wrote that 'It is high time for scholars to realise that the Patrician "entries" in the annals have simply been extracted from the Patrician documents and thus are in no sense independent evidence'.[27] In reply, one may say in Binchyesque language that 'Nothing could be further from the truth'. There is no simple relationship here at all. What is so striking is the different approach of the chronicler: however his methods may be characterised, it is as certain as anything can be that he did not simply extract his information from the hagiography.

In dealing with the range of problems thrown up by these sources we seem to be left with two mutually exclusive hypotheses. The first may be stated thus. Under the impact of the twin discovery of the fact of Palladius's appointment to Ireland in 431 and the absence of Irish knowledge of his history there, Irish hagiographers and historians felt the need to bring the missions of Palladius and Patricius into the closest association with one another. Research in Gaul (and perhaps at Rome, given that lines of communication were – briefly? – opened in

23 The annal for 439, as given here, is found in more elaborate (and rather defensive) form in texts of the 'Clonmacnoise group':

AI K.i: Secundinus et Auxiliarius et Esserinus mittuntur in auxilium Patricii, nec tamen tenuerunt apostolatum nisi Patricius solus (*The Annals of Inisfallen*, ed. & transl. Mac Airt, pp. 56/7, *s.a.* [439]).

ARC §6 (= ?437): Secundinus et Auxilius et Hesserninus mittuntur ad Hibernenses, ac[h]t ni ro gabsatt aireac[h]as na auctarás i rré Patraic nammá ('The Annals of Roscrea', edd. Gleeson & Mac Airt, p. 145).

CS K.vi.: Secundinus et Auxilius et Esserninus mittuntur ad Hibernenses, acht ní ro gabsad airechus na ughdarras i ré Padraic nama (*Chronicum Scotorum*, ed. & transl. Hennessy, pp. 22/3, *s.a.* [438]).

In general it is striking how much these Patrician entries have been developed in the 'Clonmacnoise Chronicle'.

24 See below, pp. 175–8.

25 Bede, *Historia ecclesiastica gentis Anglorum*, I.29–32. Cf. Wallace-Hadrill, *Bede's* Ecclesiastical History, pp. 42–7, and Deanesly, *Augustine of Canterbury*, pp. 44–59; see also Stancliffe, 'Kings and conversion'.

26 On this see above, pp. 1–12.

27 'Patrick and his biographers', p. 145, n. 374 (cf. pp. 73–4); see also pp. 150–1 on the annalistic notice of the foundation of Armagh.

the 630s)[28] provided some information about the background to Palladius's appointment;[29] but this was not wholly comprehended, given the distance in time and culture between the researchers and the events. It was decided to work what had been discovered into the biography of Patrick, exploiting both gaps and hints in his *Confessio* and admitting the fact (but no more) of Palladius's appointment and departure to Ireland as first bishop. The result was the type of Patrician hagiography which survives first from the later seventh century.

The alternative hypothesis would derive from a search for a historical context not for the manipulation of information but rather for the episcopate of Palladius in the light (if that is what it be) of what Irish sources have to tell us. The anti-Pelagian mission of Germanus, bishop of Auxerre, to Britain in A.D. 429 is now generally admitted to have had great importance in the history of Insular christianity.[30] What Germanus learned in Britain may have led directly to the establishment of an Irish diocese by Pope Celestine two years later. Certainly, two years later still, Prosper was able to link the two events as aspects of Celestine's wise policy. If Prosper is correctly understood as indicating that Bishop Palladius was perceived in Rome as having discharged his mission with success,[31] there is some scope for considering further developments in both islands as belonging to the context defined in 429–31. It now seems likely that Bishop Germanus returned to Britain in 436/7, shortly before his death, in a further effort to combat adherents of Pelagianism.[32] It would be no surprise, given the sequence of events in 429–31, if a result of his second mission to Britain were the strengthening of Palladius's team in Ireland. Thomas Charles-Edwards has suggested that the Germanic inroads in Britain in the 440s might have had the effect of weakening the links of Rome and Gaul with the Irish Church;[33] in these circumstances the British Church(es) might eventually have acquired a dominant influence in the ecclesiastical affairs of the neighbouring island.[34] But one should expect that foreign clergy sent to Ireland before 440 might survive in their adopted country for up to a generation. If the Roman mission in early seventh-century England be taken as a guide, such missionaries whose dates are approximately known because they occupied episcopal office died *ca* 604/5 (Augustine, the leader of the mission of A.D. 596/7), in 619 (Laurentius), 624 (Mellitus, already an abbot in 601), in 624/5 (Romanus), in 627x631 (Iustus), and 644 (Paulinus).[35] Mellitus had therefore lived twenty-

28 Cf. Sharpe, 'Armagh and Rome'; *Cummian's Paschal Letter*, edd. & transl. Walsh & Ó Cróinín, ' "New heresy for old" '.
29 One might compare the researches of Nothhelm, priest of London, in the papal archives on Bede's behalf and at the instance of Albinus, abbot of St Augustine's, Canterbury: Bede, *Historia ecclesiastica gentis Anglorum*, preface; cf. Wallace-Hadrill, *Bede's* Ecclesiastical History, pp. 37–8.
30 On Germanus and his context see Thompson, *Saint Germanus*, and *Who was Saint Patrick?*
31 Cf. above, pp. 1–12.
32 Wood, 'The end of Roman Britain', pp. 8–17; Thompson, *Saint Germanus*, pp. 55–70.
33 See above, pp. 9–10.
34 Cf. discussion below, pp. 133–45.
35 For these dates see Simon Keynes in *Handbook of British Chronology*, edd. Fryde *et al.*, p. 213: he has placed Augustine's death in 604x609. To these bishops should be added Abbot Peter (of St Augustine's, Canterbury) who died at an uncertain but early date (Bede, *Historia*

three, and Paulinus forty-three, years from the time of their departure from Rome in 601. Argument from such analogy would place the possible death-dates of the longest-surviving companions of Bishop Palladius in Ireland in the earlier 470s and of the members of any supplementary team up to ten years later still. (On this argument, whenever Patrick worked in Ireland there would probably have been companions of Bishop Palladius still active in the island.) What the Irish chronicles have to tell us is therefore by no means incredible in principle, if we supply Palladius's name for Patrick's in the quoted entries for A.D. 439, 441, 443 (not to mention 457 and 461, which are discussed elsewhere in this book):[36] but there is no reason why an early mediaeval writer, armed either with common sense and an intention to rewrite history or with a copy of Bede's History, could not have worked out such a scheme for himself.

In the last generation's scholarship there has been a tendency to talk rather glibly about a Continental mission to Ireland (as well as the British one associated with the name of Patrick) and about the presence of Continental bishops other than Palladius.[37] Recently it has been pointed out that, if we wish, we can organise – on the evidence of Prosper and Patrick alone – a single episcopal succession in fifth-century Ireland in which Patrick might be the third bishop.[38] What we deduce about the intervening period will probably colour our attitude to the testimony offered so determinedly by Irish sources.

Two arguments have been advanced which show the extent to which historians' thinking has strayed from hard evidence and first principles. Against T. F. O'Rahilly John Ryan urged that (in Binchy's exposition of Gerard Murphy's summary) 'the appointment of Patrick to succeed Palladius as head of the Irish mission in 461 would have amounted to a sharp disparagement of the other Continental bishops, at least three in number, who survived their leader and had already been labouring for several years in the vineyard. On the face of it, one of their number would seem to be a more suitable choice than this comparatively unknown and uncultured Briton.'[39] This was an objection taken seriously by both Bieler and Binchy.[40] But how do we know that there were other Continental bishops? For a follower of Muirchú there would be relatively little difficulty: he reported that Auxilius and Iserninus/Isarninus/Sa<r>ninus were ordained in Gaul by Bishop Amathorex when Patrick was consecrated bishop.[41] (If we do not allow that Patrick was a Gaul, we need not admit it for these two either: but, with the scholars just named, we may ignore this difficulty.) There is no indication that the chronicler who wrote the annal-entries quoted above thought them to be Continentals: they arrived to help Patrick; if Patrick was a

---

ecclesiastica gentis Anglorum, I.33 – and cf. I.27). Also to be considered is Honorius, archbishop of Canterbury from 627x631 until his death in 653: but it is not known when he first came to England (cf. Wallace-Hadrill, *Bede's* Ecclesiastical History, p. 116).

36 See above, pp. 29–37, 59–64.

37 Cf. Binchy, 'Patrick and his biographers', pp. 145–8 *et passim*, who did just this.

38 Thompson, *Who was Saint Patrick?*, pp. 66–102, 166–75.

39 Ryan, 'The two Patricks', p. 243; Murphy, 'The two Patricks', p. 304; Binchy, 'Patrick and his biographers', p. 145.

40 Binchy, *ibid.*; Bieler, 'The mission of Palladius', p. 14.

41 I.9 (8).

Briton, they too could as well be Britons. In sum, the only reasonably certain way to make these bishops with Latin names Continentals is, with O'Rahilly, to substitute Palladius for Patrick and to assume that all his helpers were also Continentals.[42] In other words, one must admit a first hypothesis in order to allow a second!

The other argument is that advanced by D. A. Binchy to deal with the objection to O'Rahilly raised by Ryan.[43] Patrick 'regarded himself as primarily responsible to the bishops in Britain who had organised and financed his own mission; but there is nothing to suggest that he claimed authority over the Gaulish bishops who were working in other parts of Ireland. Should we not think in terms of two missions, one conducted by Palladius and his compatriot bishops, the other by Patrick and his British helpers . . .?'[44] The situation envisaged might or might not have existed in fifth-century Ireland. But, once again, Palladius's 'compatriot bishops' have been conjured into existence without any stated justification. We stand at a considerable distance from the primary sources.

Given what we have seen of the literary materials with which the scholar must work and of the uncertain state of the principal hypothesis which has been advanced to explain what they have to say about St Patrick's Continental sojourn, we may reasonably think that there is no conclusion to be drawn about whether usable information concerning the papally established Irish Church has been transmitted through Irish sources. The discrepancies between the hagiographical and annalistic accounts make confusion worse confounded. There are two possible escape-routes from this dilemma.

The question of Sen-Phátric, *Senex Patricius*, has already been broached in this book.[45] If one were to agree with T. F. O'Rahilly that the 'older Patrick', whose obit was in the tenth century set at A.D. 457, should be identified with Palladius, this would go some way towards validating the idea of a deliberate conflation of the two bishops' *acta*.[46] However, there is a very real danger of circularity in any such train of thought. Nevertheless, it is worth hesitating for a moment to think of some implications. Sen-Phátric has a feast-day of 24 August

42 O'Rahilly, *The Two Patricks*.

43 Cf. nn. 39–40, above; Binchy, 'Patrick and his biographers', pp. 145–6.

44 Binchy's passing remarks on the 'Continental bishops' Sacellus and Caetiacus are not happy: *ibid.*, pp. 145 ('other missionary bishops from Gaul, such as Iserninus and Sacellus') and 148 (Patrick's 'principal "helpers", Auxilius, Secundinus, Iserninus and Cetiacus', according to the theory of the 'orthodox' Patriciologists). Although Sacellus is certainly a Latin name, the notes supplementary to Muirchú's *Vita S. Patricii* in the 'Book of Armagh' (§3: *The Patrician Texts*, edd. & transl. Bieler & Kelly, pp. 122/3) present him as an Irishman called Feradach who was a disciple of Patrick and who is particularly associated with the Roman martyr-relics preserved at Armagh (cf. Sheehy, 'The relics'; Sharpe, 'Armagh and Rome'). Likewise, Caetiacus/Cethiacus (for his name see p. 103, below) is presented by Tírechán (§27: *The Patrician Texts*, edd. & transl. Bieler & Kelly, pp. 144–7) as of Uí Ailello of Connaught (cf. §30: *ibid.*, pp. 148/9). These associations need to be explained before the Continental argument can be pressed further in the case of these two figures. Cf. pp. 102–3, below.

45 See above, pp. 59–64, for discussion. It is curious that Todd (*St. Patrick*, p. 307), having mentioned an 'embarrassment' of Patricks, referred to 'an older Patrick, called Sen-Patrick, or senior Patrick, of whom we shall say more presently', but seems never to have returned to the topic.

46 O'Rahilly, *The Two Patricks*.

which has almost certainly been acquired by a *furta sacra* from another saint called Patrick. In other words, Palladius may on this ground as on others be argued to have left no cult in Ireland.[47] Given the proliferation of saintly cults, and particularly cults of church-founders, among the mediaeval Irish, we might think it strange that this was so. However, we must remember Palladius's role. He was not sent as a missionary but as a first bishop – an administrator as well as a sacramental figure – for an existing christian community. His papal instructions seem to have been to secure Irish christianity against infection from British Pelagianism.[48] And nothing of the little which we know about him encourages us to think of him as a saintly or charismatic figure. Perhaps, in other words, there was no basis for a cult. Nevertheless, in historical terms, we have little option but to see Palladius as an apostolic figure in the founding era of Irish christianity. It is curious that all the Churches of modern Ireland have seen fit largely to ignore him: one might suggest that he deserves commemoration and that 24 August would be as well justified a day as any other. A full discussion of the problem of Sen-Phátric was offered in the previous chapter:[49] the reader may judge from it whether this problematic figure offers us any help in understanding the history of fifth-century Ireland or the sources which refer to it.

The second and perhaps more hopeful escape-route lies in study of the latinate personal names encountered in Patrician literature. There is a sufficient body of sufficiently unusual names for us to be able to ask what they might tell us of the sources from which they have been drawn. A first attempt at such an investigation will be made in a subsequent chapter:[50] but this is specialist work and needs detailed consideration by a variety of experts.

What, then, is the balance of this enquiry? If there were *acta Palladii*, they seem to have contained either precious little or just little of use to their excerptors. If such acts did not exist, we must at least posit Irish archival research among Continental churches' records in the seventh century and the somewhat mischievous use of what was discovered. The different information and different perspectives offered by the various genres of Irish sources may at first seem in some measure complementary but second thoughts suggest that they appear to indicate divergences of approach and opinion as well as perhaps to hint at access to sources lost to us. The possibility of some records (possibly letters, and obits in kalendars) having survived, whether in Ireland or on the Continent, cannot wholly be excluded, even though – on the basis of the evidence so far surveyed – it can nonetheless not be confirmed. What is certain is that there is not much scope here for confident statements about the *dramatis personae* of the 'Palladian' Church of mid-fifth-century Ireland.

47 For Sen-Phátric and Rostalla in Ossory, see above, pp. 59–64.
48 For the context, see above, pp. 1–12.
49 See pp. 59–64.
50 See below, pp. 89–105.

BISHOP PALLADIUS'S COMPUTUS?

Fusion, whether deliberate or accidental in origin, between records of Bishops Palladius and Patrick seems to have occurred in Ireland by the second half of the seventh century at the latest – and perhaps one can speculate that confusion could have been prevalent even as much as a century earlier. When Prosper's Chronicle, with its crucial annal for A.D. 431,[1] became known in Ireland – probably as part of a sequence of chronicles beginning with Eusebius-Jerome and ending with Isidore of Seville[2] –, a new clarity had perforce to be achieved. It has been argued that that revision was historically misleading in that it shortened and radically minimised Palladius's contribution to the development of Irish christianity.[3] So far, the recognised results of this process have been twofold.

In the annalistic literature, at a date which remains to be determined, Patrick's career was extended backwards in time until it abutted the one certain and datable notice of Palladius, that drawn from Prosper and referable to A.D. 431. The only elements of the annalistic treatment of St Patrick which might be argued to have been the result of borrowing from a Palladian record are the notice of the arrival of Bishops Secund(in)us, Auxilius, and (I)serninus (439) and the mention of the *probatio* of Patrick (441); possibly the death-notices of Secundinus (447), Auxilius (459), and Iserninus (468)[4] could be added but, as we have seen, chronological markers are very troublesome elements of this picture.[5]

Fusion may have occurred first in the more strictly hagiological context. However, since Muirchú and Tírechán in the late seventh century show awareness of Palladius and accept the necessity to despatch him rapidly from the Irish scene,[6] it seems clear that Patrician hagiography too was in this period driven by the results of the discovery of Prosper's annalistic record of Palladius's appointment to Ireland; the chronological confusion manifest in both authors' works bespeaks reactions (and perhaps recent reactions) to the receipt of new and different data.[7]

How far the identification of Patrick and Palladius had proceeded in other

1 *Chronica Minora*, ed. Mommsen, I.473 (§1307).
2 *Ibid.*, I.341–84, for discussion of the manuscript tradition.
3 See above, pp. 29–84.
4 *The Annals of Ulster*, edd. & transl. Mac Airt & Mac Niocaill, I.38–43, 46–9, for all these entries. The death of Benignus at 467 (*ibid.*, I.48/9) might be included here, but Benignus occupies a position in the record which is difficult to understand: cf. pp. 99–101, below.
5 Cf. pp. 51–7, above.
6 See above, pp. 65–84.
7 For their confusions, see above, pp. 29–33, 42–3, 49, 63–4, 65–84.

divisions of Irish ecclesiastical thought has not been clearly addressed. The 'invention' of Sen-Phátric (*Senex Patricius*) might be taken as a reflection of an ineradicable awareness of a pre-Patrician dimension to Irish christianity; but the development of a liturgical cult at a date (24 August) dependent on the name 'Patricius' indicates that that awareness had nonetheless lost a complete understanding of and continuous Irish connexion with the history of Bishop Palladius.[8]

The reference in Cummian's *Epistola de controuersia paschali*, written probably in A.D. 632, to Patrick as *papa noster* has been taken as evidence that in the earlier seventh century there was national recognition of the British apostle's role in the origins of Irish christianity.[9] Recently, however, Dáibhí Ó Cróinín has suggested that we find in this mention evidence for further confusion of Palladius and Patrick.[10] The context is Cummian's recital to his correspondent, Ségéne of Iona, of the various and differing paschal cycles which he has consulted.[11]

> Postremo ad cyclos computationum diuersarum quid unaquaeque lingua de cursu solis et lunae sentiret, conuersus totus, licet diuerse alium in die, alium in luna, alium in mense, alium in bissexto, alium in epacta, alium in aucmento lunari, quod uos saltum dicitis, inueni cyclos contra hunc, quem uos tenetis, esse contrarios.
>
> Primum illum quem sanctus Patricius papa noster tulit et fecit, in quo luna a .xiiii. usque in .xxi. regulariter, et equinoctium a .xii. kalendis Aprilis obseruatur.

The details provided by Cummian have indicated that this Patrician cycle was in line with the teachings of the school of Alexandria, which were gaining adherents in Latin Europe in the fourth and fifth centuries.[12] Easter was to be observed within the lunar limits 14–21 and after a Spring-equinox set at 21 March.

These data have seemed to present difficulties for scholars viewing Patrick within the twin context of the fifth-century British Church and the history of paschal observance in late sixth- and early seventh-century Ireland. That such a text was in circulation in seventh-century Ireland under the name of Patrick has been demonstrated by Dáibhí Ó Cróinín's important discovery of an excerpt from a prologue of Patrick to an Easter-cycle.[13]

8 On all this, see above, pp. 59–64.

9 *Cummian's Letter*, edd. & transl. Walsh & Ó Cróinín, pp. 84/5 (lines 208–10). For discussion, cf. Sharpe, 'St Patrick and the see of Armagh', pp. 36–9.

10 'New light'.

11 *Cummian's Letter*, edd. & transl. Walsh & Ó Cróinín, pp. 82–5 (lines 204–10); discussion on pp. 29–32. Some aspects of their translation at this point are slightly tendentious. In quoting the text here I have suppressed one editorial diacritic, expanded one abbreviation, and introduced paragraphing.

12 For further discussion see *Bedae opera de temporibus*, ed. Jones, pp. 17–68; cf. Strobel, *Ursprung*, and *Texte*; cf. Zelzer, 'Zum Osterfestbrief'. See also Harrison, 'Episodes', pp. 311–12.

13 The following text is derived from Oxford, Bodleian Library, MS. Bodley 309 (*S.C.* 8837), fol 106v, via *Cummian's Letter*, edd. Walsh & Ó Cróinín, p. 31, where a generally better text is given than by Ó Cróinín, 'New light', pp. 277–8. In republishing this excerpt here, I have repunctuated the text and made some minor changes in the treatment of abbreviations. On

Patricius in prologo suo, secundum rationem Anatolii, hoc ius ostendit. 'Notandum est quod in .xviiii. ciclo quattuor anni contrariae regulae inueniuntur, quorum ratio diligenter arguteque animaduertenda est. Hoc est annus .viii. lunaris secundum rationem Grecorum, et annus .xxvii.; item secundum rationem Latinorum .iiii. lunaris annus et .xxx.. Item tribus annis in .xviiii. ciclo eadem aetas super kalendas Aprilis et Maii inuenitur: hoc est in anno .xxvi. lunari super kalendas Ianuarii et in anno .xxviiii. et in anno .xxvii..'

If we ignore the possibility that the Patrick mentioned in these references was someone other than the apostle of Ireland, the difficulty has seemed to lie in understanding how St Patrick could have promoted the use of a decennovenal cycle of wholly Alexandrian sort when all British and Irish Churches have been reckoned as users, in the later sixth and earlier seventh centuries, of the old 84-year cycle known as *romana supputatio*, perhaps introduced to Britain under Roman influence in the early fourth century.[14]

In considering this problem, Ó Cróinín has thought to find in the different pre-Irish histories which can be created for Bishops Palladius and Patrick the explanation for the apparent incongruity of the attribution of this Patrician Easter-reckoning. Noting that Palladius's background lay at Auxerre and perhaps at Rome, Ó Cróinín has reckoned this to have been 'the perfect milieu for Cummian's "Patrician" table'. The conclusion which he offered drew on the conflation, otherwise attested, of Palladius and Patrick: 'Cummian's *papa noster* was Palladius, not Patrick'.[15] On the one hand, this deduction might be strengthened somewhat: Palladius's demonstrable connexions were with Rome rather than Auxerre,[16] and we must admit that it is difficult to know what paschal usage was followed at Auxerre in his time; the presumption, if one must be made, would however be in favour of *romana supputatio* rather than Alexandrian practice.

On the other hand, this method of approach contains the seeds of its own destruction. In so far as the anti-Pelagian mission of Germanus of Auxerre to Britain in A.D. 429 was encouraged by the papal curia,[17] we might allow that various aspects of papal influence would be felt in Britain – as they would be in Ireland following the appointment of Bishop Palladius in 431; there is reason to think of these two initiatives having a connexion with one another, as various scholars have observed.[18] We have no reason to think that, while there were diverse views and influences within the Italian and Gallican Churches, there

the 'Sirmond collection' of *computistica*, of which MS. Bodley 309 is the best representative, see Ó Cróinín, 'The Irish provenance' and cf. 'A seventh-century Irish computus'.

14 *Bedae opera de temporibus*, ed. Jones, pp. 16–17; cf. Ó Cróinín, 'New light', p. 278.

15 *Ibid.*, p. 282.

16 In other words, I reject the views of Hanson, *Saint Patrick, his Origins*, pp. 52–4 (cf. O'Rahilly, *The Two Patricks*, pp. 19, 52; Binchy, 'Patrick and his biographers', pp. 133–5 and 86–7), followed by Ó Cróinín, 'New light', p. 282, and (against the trend of his own argument) by Thompson, *Saint Germanus*, pp. 79–81. See Grosjean, 'Notes chronologiques sur le séjour de S. Patrice en Gaule', pp. 76–86 (especially 76–81), and Bieler, 'The mission of Palladius', p. 2.

17 Thompson, *Saint Germanus*, pp. 79–81.

18 Cf. Thompson, *Who was Saint Patrick?*, pp. 51–65.

were not comparable tensions and varying opinions among British churchmen, not least because of the long-running history of debate about paschal computation in the Church at large. If Patrick was in some sense, as many scholars have argued, a successor of Palladius[19] – and might even have worked in Ireland as a missionary priest before his elevation to the episcopate[20] –, there would have been pressures on him other than those of conservative clergymen at home in Britain; and we have in any case good reason to think that Patrick was out of step with such people in other respects.[21]

Ó Cróinín has pointed to the interest which the author of the Patrician prologue showed in comparing Greek and Latin reckoning: he has noted that this is a feature of fourth- and fifth-century Italian ecclesiastical culture.[22] Such comparison was formally empanelled in the cycle of Victorius of Aquitaine in 457. While this remained in use, comparative discussion would continue as an agendum of ecclesiastical business.[23] To the extent that the Victorian tables were officially adopted in Gaul eighty-four years later, in 541, one may suspect that discussion would have been lively there in the intervening period. The presumed impact of the Gaulish decision in Britain and Ireland meant that the issue was current in the Insular Churches down to Cummian's own time.[24] Columbanus is a witness to such a fact.[25] While Cummian plainly thought the Patrician cycle old, we cannot guarantee that its origin belonged to the fifth century. And that it emanated directly from Rome or Roman usage remains too narrow a conclusion. As so often in Patrician studies we are being asked to make judgments based on argument from our ignorance of fifth-century Britain. Whether the 'Easter-cycle of Patrick' was Palladius's or St Patrick's, or belonged to neither, remains an open question.

19 *Ibid.*, and pp. 169–75. However, we must remember the possibility that Palladius's work and Patrick's were differently localised and in that sense not in succession: cf. Ó Cróinín, 'New light', pp. 282–3.

20 For this conjecture, see above, pp. 25–8; cf. Thompson, *Who was Saint Patrick?*, p. 175.

21 See the recent conjecture on this point by Sharpe, 'Saint Mauchteus', pp. 92–3; but he has gone too far in his general assertion that it is 'apparent from his own *Confessio* that his ministry was conducted without the support of the British hierarchy' (p. 92).

22 'New light', pp. 278–80.

23 Cf. Harrison, 'Episodes', pp. 309–11.

24 *Ibid.*, pp. 318–19.

25 *Epistulae: Sancti Columbani Opera*, edd. & transl. Walker & Bieler, pp. 2–59 (*passim*).

AUXILIUS, ISERNINUS, SECUNDINUS, AND BENIGNUS*

Mediaeval Irish hagiography, secular and canon law, chronicling, and story all attribute to St Patrick a number of ecclesiastical colleagues with non-Irish names. Since the beginning of modern scholarly criticism of the Patrician legend, it has become almost customary to associate these figures with Palladius and a so-called 'Continental mission' to Ireland,[1] whether or not a theory of 'two Patricks' was also being admitted. However, that we possess any records of Palladius's government of the Irish Church more detailed than those which Prosper has left us is itself an issue for discussion and hypothesis.[2] It is perhaps surprising that there has not been more consideration of the possibility that some or all of these names were given to imaginary characters invented in the seventh century and later. The joke – rather in the manner of Vergilius Maro Grammaticus, one might think – that Auxilius was Patrick's helper, Secundinus his second in command, Iserninus the hard man of the mission, and Benignus its kindly face, points the way to such an assessment.

To advance a sceptical case of such a sort would of course require discussion of the sources from which Latin names for invented figures of hagiology could have been drawn in the early and central middle ages.[3] Classical and Late Latin texts (including *patristica*), inscriptions, list or catalogues of authors and recipients of literary works, documents, early mediaeval hagiography from the Continent – all these represent possible resources; and, if Irish scholars were indeed searching libraries and archives on the Continent in the seventh and later centuries for information about the origins of Irish christianity,[4] they would no doubt have had formidable onomastic resources at their disposal in the event that they might begin inventing assistants for St Patrick. That such creation of members of a Patrician penumbra was under way by and from the later seventh century can in fact be demonstrated by considering the literary history of Patrick's own family. In his *Confessio* Patrick identified himself by naming his father as Calpornius and his grandfather as Potitus. Both of these names are found attested here and there in Late Latin records.[5]

* I am greatly obliged to Ellis Evans for reading this chapter and giving me the benefit of his learning and judgment.

1 On 'missionary bishops from Gaul' see Binchy, 'Patrick and his biographers', p. 145.

2 Cf. pp. 59–88, above.

3 Michael Lapidge has drawn my attention to the detailed list of St Augustine's writings in Roma, Biblioteca Apostolica Vaticana, MS. Reg. lat. 596, fos 24–25 (a stray bifolium in Continental Caroline minuscule, perhaps of *saec.* x/xi), as a kind of convenient source of ancient names which might have potential for mediaeval writers.

4 Cf. discussion above, pp. 65–84.

5 For Calpurnius, see *Inscriptiones latinae christianae ueteres*, ed. Diehl, III.32–3; cf. Kajanto, *The Latin Cognomina*, pp. 32 and 143 (Calpurnianus), 36 and 161 (Calpurnia). For Potitus,

Two centuries later, however, Patrick himself has acquired a remarkable onomastic repertoire, as the opening of Tírechán's *Collectanea* indicates.[6]

Inueni quattuor nomina in libro scripta Patricio apud Ultanum episcopum Conchuburnensium: sanctus Magonus, qui est clarus; Succetus, qui est <deus belli; Patricius, qui est> pater ciuium; Cothirthiacus, quia seruiuit quattuor domibus magorum.

I have found four names for Patrick in a book written by Ultán, bishop of maccu Conchubair: the saint (was named) Magonus, that is, famous; Succetus, that is, <god of war; Patricius, that is,> father of the citizens; Cothirthiacus, because he served four houses of druids.

The opening words of Ludwig Bieler's *Libri epistolarum sancti Patricii episcopi*, published in 1951, reflect this information.[7] 'Magonus[8] Sucatus Patricius, generally known as Saint Patrick, the Apostle of Ireland, has so far been almost completely neglected by students of Latin language and literature'. One can imagine that students of Latin, seeing such a name, would feel strongly tempted to run in the opposite direction. It is characteristic of the dubious selectiveness too often practised in Patrician studies that Cothirthiacus has been quietly dropped from this tripartite latinate name.[9]

The opening chapter of Muirchú's *Vita S. Patricii* gives us a little more information.[10]

Patricius, qui et Sochet uocabatur, Brito natione in Britannis natus, <patre> Cualfarni<o> diacon<o> ortus filio – ut ipse ait – Potiti presbiteri, qui fuit uico Bannauem Thaburniae, chaut procul a mari nostro, quem uicum constanter indubitanterque conperimus esse Uentre, matre etiam conceptus Concessa nomine . . .

Patrick, also named Sochet, a Briton by race, was born in Britain. His father was Cualfarnius, a deacon, the son (as Patrick himself says) of a priest, Potitus, who hailed from Bannauem Thaburniae, a place not far from our sea. This place, as I am informed beyond hesitation or doubt, is Uentre. His mother's name was Concessa.

Concessa is a reasonably well attested Late Latin name.[11] However, unless we are to suppose an unbroken oral tradition proceeding ultimately from Patrick's lips to the late seventh century, we cannot allow this name, any more than the

see *ibid.*, pp. 95, 178, 354; *Inscriptiones latinae christianae ueteres*, ed. Diehl, III.129; for a British example (from Lundy), see Thomas, 'Beacon Hill revisited'. Bury, *The Life*, pp. 289–90, appears to have overstated the case when he remarked that Calpurnius 'does not seem to occur often' but 'Potitus was a common cognomen in the Roman empire'.

6 §1: *The Patrician Texts*, edd. & transl. Bieler & Kelly, pp. 124/5. Bieler reconstructed the corrupted text with the aid of derivative *uitae*. I have altered his translation at two points.

7 'Libri', ed. Bieler, I.5.

8 *Vitae* II and IV offer *Magonius*: *Four Latin Lives*, ed. Bieler, p. 63. The *Historia Brittonum* (see below, pp. 223, 227, 230) alone has Old Welsh *Maun* which would descend regularly from a British **Magunos*, 'servant-lad', but in defiance of the etymology provided by Tírechán. For discussion, see Bury, *The Life*, p. 292.

9 Cf. Harvey, 'The significance of *Cothraige*'.

10 I.1: *The Patrician Texts*, edd. & transl. Bieler & Kelly, pp. 66/7.

11 On *Concessus* and derivatives, see Kajanto, *The Latin Cognomina*, p. 350. The ninth-century 'Old English Martyrology' has a mysterious *Contablata* as the name of Patrick's mother: Kotzor, 'St. Patrick' (cf. Page, 'The lost leaf'); Cross, 'The influence', pp. 173–6.

others of person or place, to be more than an invention. However, it imposed itself so far on scholars that in 1952 Bieler could say that 'The *Q. Calpurnius Concessinus praefectus equitum* [named on a Romano-British inscription] is possibly a relative of Patrick':[12] this absurd deduction can be derivative only of acceptance that Concessa was indeed Patrick's mother's name. By the time of writing of *Vita IV S. Patricii*, the hagiographer was going so far as to quote the saint's *liber epistolarum* as a source for Patrick's mother's name.[13] In *Vita III S. Patricii* Conches (Concessa) has acquired a mother called Ochmis.[14]

By the time when the *alia pauca serotinis temporibus inuenta* were being written, perhaps in the early eighth century, Patrick's family had started to undergo significant and radical development. The following table will make this clear.[15]

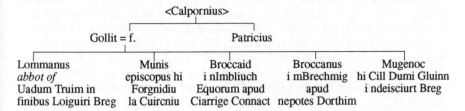

<Calpornius>

Gollit = f. — Patricius

Lommanus *abbot of* Uadum Truim in finibus Loiguiri Breg	Munis episcopus hi Forgnidiu la Cuircniu	Broccaid i nImbliuch Equorum apud Ciarrige Connact	Broccanus i mBrechmig apud nepotes Dorthim	Mugenoc hi Cill Dumi Gluinn i ndeisciurt Breg

The account ends with the statement, 'Haec autem progenies Patricii propria est consanguinitate et gratia, fide et babtismate et doctrina', 'These are Patrick's own relations by blood and by grace, by faith, baptism, and teaching'.[16]

The texts in the 'Book of Armagh' offer one further development. Alongside the text of §1 of the *Confessio* a marginale gives a further generation to the author's patriline: *filii Odissi* has been added in a hand of the same type as the main scribe's.[17] This difficult name recurs in the eleventh-century manuscripts of the Irish *Liber hymnorum* (albeit in a text, 'Génair Pátraic', assigned to the eighth century) and thereafter in a variety of later sources.[18]

I shall mention one further development in the Latin hagiography before turning away from Patrick's expanding, holy family. In the *Vita S. Patricii* of Probus we find that, in addition to Calpurnius and Concessa, Patrick has

12 'Libri', ed. Bieler, II.87. The notion seems to have originated with MacNeill, 'The native place', p. 138. For the inscription, at Hexham, see *Inscriptiones Britanniae Latinae*, ed. Hübner, p. 98 (no. 481): *Q. CALPVRN`I´VS CONCESSINIVS.*

13 §1: 'Ex illa ergo dispersione parentes eius in regionem Srato Cluade perrexerunt, in qua terra conceptus et natus est Patricius patre Kalfurno et matre Concessa, ut ipse dixit in libro epistolarum: "Ego sum Patricius filius Kalfurni, matrem habens Concessam" ' (*Four Latin Lives*, ed. Bieler, p. 51). Patrick's parents are that *uita* presented as Armorican exiles in Strathclyde.

14 *Ibid.*, p. 122 (§12).

15 For the text (§§2–3), see *The Patrician Texts*, edd. & transl. Bieler & Kelly, pp. 168–71.

16 In §10 of the *Additamenta* (*ibid.*, pp. 172/3), we meet 'Naó et Naí filii fratris Patricii'. But it is not clear who they were.

17 See below, p. 192 and n. 7.

18 *The Irish Liber Hymnorum*, edd. & transl. Bernard & Atkinson, I.97 and II.32 and 177. See also Anscombe, 'The pedigree of Patrick'. For some inconclusive discussion of the name, see 'Libri', ed. Bieler, II.88.

acquired a brother Ructhi and a sister Mila. These too were carried into Irish captivity, only to be married to one another in slavery.[19] On the other hand, in *Vitae* II, III, and IV, Patrick has a sister Lupita, with no brother mentioned. She too was carried off into captivity, in due course to be married to Patrick by his master.[20] Lupita's relics, we are told, are now in Armagh.[21]

While Patrick's ostensibly biological family was proliferating, his ecclesiastical family had shown a quite remarkable propensity to growth. On the one hand, the development which we first encounter in Tírechán's *Collectanea* – of bringing numerous local church-founders into association with Patrick – was carried further in that hagiographical tradition which ultimately issued in the Tripartite Life. On the other hand, Tírechán's work itself seems to represent a high point in respect of the list which it contains of ecclesiastics who accompanied St Patrick.[22] Tírechán there referred quite specifically to Continental clergy. About seventy persons are named. A good many are recognisably Irish, and of the remainder some are well known figures of Patrician legend. There is a substantial residuum, however, which cannot be placed in either category. A thorough commentary is required on this list, identifying names in their proper linguistic traditions; furthermore, it would be desirable to have accounts of the persons intended by the compiler of the list and notes on their roles in Patrican hagiology.

No such attempt will be made here, however. The purpose of the present chapter is rather to offer some remarks on the principal literary associates of Patrick who bear latinate names, in order to establish whether or not the name-forms are genuine, whether they could have been borne by fifth-century persons, and what the chances are of their having been available to a seventh-century creator of fictional associates of St Patrick.

Auxilius

As the compilers of the *Recueil des inscriptions chrétiennes de la Gaule antérieures à la renaissance carolingienne* have noted, Auxilius is a name-form not particularly frequently encountered.[23] It is a *cognomen* formed from the noun *auxilium* and belongs to a class of names of broad religious significance which in the late Empire were neither specifically pagan nor christian. Two christian examples are known from inscriptions in Gaul, from Besançon and Vienne, of the fourth or fifth century.[24] An Auxilius is found in a list of bishops of

19 §12: *Four Latin Lives*, ed. Bieler, p. 195.

20 *Ibid.*, pp. 61–7 (*Vita II*, §§11–16; *Vita IV*, §§15–20) and p. 121 (*Vita III*, preliminary section, §11, which has an abruptly incomplete account of this episode).

21 *Vita II*, §1 (*ibid.*, p. 51); *Vita III*, §1 (*ibid.*, p. 118).

22 *Collectanea*, §§6–7 (*The Patrician Texts*, edd. & transl. Bieler & Kelly, pp. 126–31). See above, p. 75.

23 *Recueil*, gen. ed. Marrou, XV.484–5: 'peu répandu'. Cf. Kajanto, *The Latin Cognomina*, pp. 117, 120–1, 363.

24 *Inscriptions chrétiennes de la Gaule*, ed. Le Blant, II.572 (no. 679, Besançon), and II.142 (no. 459, Vienne); for a more modern treatment of the latter, see *Recueil*, gen. ed. Marrou, XV.484–5 (no. 144). For two other epigraphic occurrences, see *Inscriptiones latinae christianae ueteres*, ed. Diehl, III.25.

Angers,[25] while two fifth-century Auxilii, both bishops, are known from christian Africa.[26]

The logic of this distribution is that, in as much as Auxilius was apparently not a widely used name, it would not have been very readily available to a seventh-century Irishman seeking to invent a helper for Patrick; on the other hand, if there were such an etymological motive, no knowledge of the antecedent use of such a name need be deemed necessary – this is an obvious and potentially polygenetic formation.

The name appears as a borrowing in mediaeval Irish in a number of variant forms: Ausaile, Ausaille, Usaile, Usaille;[27] the *-s-* reflects either sound-substitution or the possibility that the loan occurred from a Vulgar Latin form in which *-x-* had already become *-s-*.[28] The name is neither common nor widely distributed geographically, being found first and principally in the ecclesiastical settlement-name *Cell Ausaile* (Killashee),[29] near Naas (Co. Kildare) in Leinster. The mediaeval Irish perception was that this was the church of the Auxilius who was the colleague of St Patrick. Further evidence for the cult of St Auxilius/Usaille in Leinster is the development by (and perhaps in) the eleventh century of the personal name Gilla Usaille, 'servant of (St) Usaille', for Leinstermen.[30] It looks as though this was a localised cult in the central middle ages,[31] and perhaps one of very long standing. What significance we are to draw

25 Duchesne, *Fastes*, II.354.

26 Mandouze, *Prosopographie chrétienne du bas-empire*, I.132.

27 Ó Cuív, 'Aspects of Irish personal names', p. 163: *Usail(l)e* is reported as occurring with long or short *U-*.

28 Grandgent, *An Introduction*, p. 108 (§255); cf. Jackson, *Language and History*, pp. 37 and 522, n. 1.

29 Other modern Hiberno-English names for this place are Killishea (Bury, *The Life*, p. 163 and n. 3), Killassy and Killossy (Hogan, *Onomasticon*, p. 176).

30 Ó Cuív, 'Aspects of Irish personal names', p. 163.

31 Kenney, *The Sources*, pp. 169–70 (cf. p. 260, n. 314, on Auxilius's legendary family). Two feast-days are associated with him in Irish martyrologies and kalendars of the central middle ages: 19 March and 16 September. See *The Martyrology of Tallaght*, edd. Best & Lawlor, pp. 25, 71, 100–1; *Félire Húi Gormáin*, ed. & transl. Stokes, pp. 58–9, 178–9, 298 (*s.n.* Cell Ausailli), 333, 402. In the latter *félire*, a twelfth-century work, two more dates are found: 7 February (*ibid.*, pp. 32/3) and 27 August (*ibid.*, pp. 164/5, 400). The name-forms offered in *Félire Húi Gormáin* are *Auxil* (19 March), *Auxilius* (16 Sept.), *Uasaille* (27 Aug., where a gloss describes him as *mac húi Baird* [= maccu Baird]; cf. p. 347 on Cormac mac húi Baird and p. 400), and *Úsaille* (7 Feb.). In the 'Martyrology of Tallaght', at 19 March he has the form *Auxilinus* which is accompanied by a marginal note: 'Auxilinus episcopus et coepiscopus et frater sancti Patricii episcopi uel Auxilinus nomen eius' (presumably the second of the occurrences of the name should have read 'Auxilius'); a following note offers supplementary information that there were '.VII. filii Restiti de Longbardis .i. Sechnall, Nectain, Dabonna, Mogornan, Daríoc, Auxilinus, Lugnath' (edd. Best & Lawlor, pp. 100–1), which is presumably to be associated with the designation maccu Baird in the gloss to *Félire Húi Gormáin*, 27 August, noted above. It seems as though each variant name-form was associated with a feast-day: what this tells us about mediaeval practice at Cell Ausaile remains to be determined. For one further complication, see *Félire Húi Gormáin*, ed. & transl. Stokes, pp. 178/9, n. a: 'This bishop and confessor (a quo Cell Ausailli, now Killossy, near Naas) is commemorated in *Mart. Chr. Ch.* on Oct. 19'.

from its location in Leinster (and close to Naas, a notable power-centre in early mediaeval Leinster)[32] is altogether another question.[33]

Isarninus, Iserninus

This is only superficially a Latin name. The starting point is Celtic *isarn-*, 'iron', which is attested in Old Celtic, though not plentifully, as a name-forming element for both persons and places.[34] There is, however, substantial neo-Celtic evidence for the extensive use of derivative forms in personal names.[35] The simplex, Gallo-Latin *Isarnus*, Celtic *Isarnos*, is found in early mediaeval usage in southern France and northern Spain, for example an inscription from Minerve (Languedoc) and coin-legends from the Marseille mint.[36]

One of the features which came to distinguish Continental from Insular Celtic is that intervocalic *s* was weakened and then lost in British and Goidelic.[37] In British, as Kenneth Jackson has shown, *Isarn-* had become **Iarn-* or **Ịarn* by *ca* A.D. 100.[38] It is, however, far from clear to what extent the writing of the word in a latinate context would have been affected by this sound-change, if the *Isarn-* form had already established itself as conventional; and Continental usage might have continued to exert pressure on spelling conventions.[39]

Be that as it may, the only attestation of the name *Isarninus* from an ancient context is on a group of Late Roman pewter vessels unearthed in 1853 at Icklingham in Suffolk:[40] six pewter cups (of which only one can now be identified) bore the informal inscription *ISARNINUS*.[41] The goods are portable and the person may not have been a Briton: but the evidence of find-spot deserves to

32 For references see Hogan, *Onomasticon*, p. 554, *s.n.* Nás. Cf. Byrne, *Irish Kings*, pp. 138, 150, 152, 163; Smyth, *Celtic Leinster*, pp. 27–8, 34, 42–3, 49, 65–7; MacNeill, *Saint Patrick*, p. 83.

33 For a notably cautious statement about Killashee in this context, not even mentioning Auxilius except as part of the place-name, see Smyth, *Celtic Leinster*, p. 20.

34 Holder, *Alt-celtischer Sprachschatz*, II, cols 75–6; Rhys, *Lectures*, pp. 418–22.

35 Loth, *Chrestomathie bretonne*, pp. 139–41; cf. Jackson, *Language and History*, pp. 359–61, 522, and *A Historical Phonology*, pp. 230–1; Birkhan, *Germanen und Kelten*, p. 135.

36 Holder, *Alt-celtischer Sprachschatz*, II, col. 76; *Inscriptions chrétiennes de la Gaule*, ed. Le Blant, II.444 (no. 609.63), for the inscription from Minerve. See also Whatmough, *The Dialects*, p. 1084.

37 Rhys, *Lectures*, p. 418; Morris Jones, *A Welsh Grammar*, p. 134 (§94.ii). For Irish *IARNI*, see McManus, *A Guide to Ogam*, pp. 84, 107.

38 Jackson, *Language and History*, pp. 521–5 (§117), 694.

39 For considerations of this sort, cf. *ibid.*, pp. 523–4.

40 For their first publication see *Inscriptiones Britanniae Latinae*, ed. Hübner, p. 230 (no. 1270); for recent republication, see *The Roman Inscriptions of Britain*, edd. Collingwood & Wright, II, fasc. 2, pp. 72–83 (no. 2417.3, 12–20, 22). There have been three discoveries of hoards of pewter vessels at Icklingham – in 1839, 1853, and 1956. For the discovery there of christian lead-tanks, see *ibid.*, pp. 68–9 (no. 2416.9–10).

41 In 1873 Hübner (*Inscriptiones Britanniae Latinae*, p. 230, no. 1270) had reported the existence of vessels bearing the variant spellings ISXARNINVS and IXARNINVS. In so far as the vessels can be identified, the spellings appear to be IXARINVS, without the first *-N-*, thus raising other problems. For comment based on the older publication, see Morris Jones, *A Welsh Grammar*, p. 134 (§94.iii), and Jackson, *Language and History*, pp. 37 and 522, n. 1.

be stressed. Supporting evidence for the presumed former existence of the name in British is provided by Old Breton *Hoiernin*[42] and Old Welsh *Hiernin*.[43]

The only mediaeval attestation of the name is in connexion with the bishop presented in Irish sources as a colleague of St Patrick. The form *Isarninus* is attested once, in the oldest (late eighth-century) manuscript of Muirchú's *Vita S. Patricii*;[44] but otherwise *Is(s)erninus* (and *Es[s]erninus*) is the invariable usage in hagiographical and canon-law contexts.[45] The name does not appear to have been borrowed into Irish: in the hagiography, Iserninus is identified with a Bishop Fith of whom very little is otherwise known, and the equation seems inscrutable.[46] In the Patrician *Additamenta* in the 'Book of Armagh',[47] an Irish-language passage associates him with the Catrige of Clíu (barony of Idrone [< Uí Dróna], Co. Carlow). The following churches are attributed to him: Toicuile, Ráith Foalascich, Láthrach Da Arad i nDib Maigib, and Áth Fithot. There is an identification of modest certainty for only the last – Ahade (Co. Carlow)[48] – but it is agreed that all are places in Leinster, probably in Co. Carlow, although a Co. Wicklow location has been suggested for Láthrach Da Arad.[49]

How to explain the apparent *i*-affection of the form *Iserninus* (< *Isarninus*) is problematic. The phonetic development poses no difficulty in itself, but in which language-context did it occur? If the name had been reborrowed into British or Brittonic after the sixth century, we could imagine the change taking place there in the seventh or eighth century before our earliest mediaeval manuscript containing the name.[50] Alternatively, one could suppose that the change was purely graphic. After the Roman period the name, known only in written form, had no meaning and suffered from the common (if unexplained) scribal interchange of *a*/*e* found in Insular-script contexts. Hypercorrection of *ar* > *er* would be possible, in awareness of British-Latin mispronunciation of the

42 In a document of A.D. 860x866 copied in the eleventh-century cartulary of Redon Abbey (*Cartulaire de l'abbaye de Redon*, ed. De Courson, pp. 70–1, no. XCIII); cf. Loth, *Chrestomathie bretonne*, p. 140, who recognised beneath scribal corruption a variant form of the same name in a charter of A.D. 833 in the same source – *Huiernim* (for **Huiernin*).

43 Identified by Rhys, *Lectures*, p. 419; see *The Text*, edd. Evans & Rhys, p. 150 (two occurrences).

44 I.9 (8): this reading (MS. C) was adopted into the text published in *The Patrician Texts*, edd. & transl. Bieler & Kelly, p. 74, line 4. The reading of the eleventh-century MS. B is *Sanninus* (presumably an erroneous copying of an earlier **Sarninus*, itself an error but preserving the hypothetically original vocalism). MS. A (the 'Book of Armagh'), in common with all other Irish witnesses to the name, has a form with *-e-*.

45 For his appearance (as *Issernini*, *Isserninus*) in the heading to the unique copy of *Synodus episcoporum*, see below, pp. 175–8.

46 Cf. Smyth, *Celtic Leinster*, p. 127, n. 16, where the equation is simply accepted.

47 *The Patrican Texts*, edd. & transl. Bieler & Kelly, pp. 174–7 (§12). For discussion, see MacNeill, *Saint Patrick*, pp. 81–2, 83.

48 Hogan, *Onomasticon*, p. 61, *s.n.* Áth Fithot; cf. pp. 476 (on Láthrach Da Arad) and 641 (on Toicuile).

49 *The Patrician Texts*, edd. & transl. Bieler & Kelly, p. 260; cf. Smyth, *Celtic Leinster*, p. 127, n. 16.

50 On *i*-affection in Brittonic, see Jackson, *Language and History*, pp. 579–619 (§§155–176), 697.

sort *Garmani* for *Germani*.[51] The variations *-s-/-ss-* and *I-/E-* in the attested spellings of the name are indications of how the form might be affected by early mediaeval Celtic Latin graphic conventions. But neither of these contexts, of British sound-change or scribal error, provides a particularly satisfying solution to the shape of a name whose proper literary place was in Ireland.

In summary, we have a genuine and old Celtic-Latin name-form in Isarninus. In the seventh century, unless it was found in an inscription now unknown, we may be fairly certain that it would have been unlikely to have been invented in the British Isles. It could probably still have been created in Gaul or Spain at that date. The name had a continuous history from British into neo-Brittonic but might have been unrecognisable in the form *Isarn-* from not long after the first century A.D..[52] If it was borrowed from Gallo-Latin into British usage thereafter,[53] it might have been analysed as **Issarninus*; the *-ss-* would then have survived into neo-Brittonic and in due course *i*-affection would have produced **Issernin*; but this is to presuppose that the mediaeval spelling *Is(s)erninus* represents a genuine Brittonic vernacular form **Is(s)ernin*, which is very uncertain. The name seems to have no history in Irish.

How to take the name in its literary context is uncertain, therefore. If weight be given to attestations of the name or its derivatives, it will be declared British, even though the nearest possible British pronunciation would in the fifth century have been **Σi̯arninǝ̑s*.[54] On the other hand, if the *-s-* be deemed determinative, the name – as belonging to a fifth-century person – must be reckoned as Gallo-Latin.[55] The spelling with *-e-* would then have to be explained graphically.

There remains the question of survival. Unless the rather desperate hypothesis of a post-first-century Gaulish or Gallo-Latin loan into British be adopted, Muirchú could not have relied on British or Irish vernacular transmission of information: we must suppose that he had a written Latin source or a Continental informant. Either Bishop Isarninus was invented in Gaul in the seventh century or he is a documentary survivor from an earlier era. In either event, no continuous knowledge of a Bishop Isarninus in Britain or Ireland is presupposed, and the association with churches in Leinster is not certainly of any greater antiquity than *ca* A.D. 700:[56] evidence for cult of Iserninus is not available.

51 *Ibid.*, pp. 280–1. Cf. Bede, *Historia ecclesiastica gentis Anglorum*, V.9, on British pronunciation. Cf. Hamp, 'Latin *er* in British Celtic'.

52 Thereafter it would have been *Iarn-*, *Ii̯arn-*, or *Σiarn* (in the conventions of Jackson, *Language and History*, pp. 521–2).

53 We have to hypothesise such a form in Gallo-Latin, however, for the distribution of the form is purely Insular. For the likely result in British, cf. *ibid.*, p. 82.

54 *Ibid.*, p. 522: Jackson's alternative development of **isarno-* is preferable and is adopted here, for it offers a more natural explanation of the Brittonic forms in *h-*. For further discussion, see Hamp, '**isa* in British Celtic'.

55 Rhys, *Lectures*, p. 419, bluntly called it Gaulish.

56 For much more optimistic treatment of Iserninus in Leinster history, see Smyth, *Celtic Leinster*, pp. 9, 18, 20, 32.

Secundinus

Secundinus is a well known Late Latin name, a derivative of Secundus, itself long attested in the language; other variants are Secundio and Secundius.[57] Several known fifth-century bishops bore the name[58] and in Gaul it continued to be used into the seventh century when we find bishops of Lyon and Sisteron called Secundinus.[59] The name seems to have been used across the Latin world.[60]

In Irish sources the vernacular name-form Sechnall is found for Secundinus. The equation has been accepted by scholars but the detailed philological history of the loan has never been worked out. The *-ch-* implies borrowing as *-c-*,[61] subsequently lenited in Irish. On the other hand, the early development *-nd-* > *-n-* is not Irish and British influence has been invoked to explain it,[62] since that British sound-change took place from the late fifth century to the late sixth, according to Kenneth Jackson,[63] whereas it is a late eighth- or early ninth-century development in Irish.[64] Rudolf Thurneysen compared the development of *Columbán* > *Colmán* already by the seventh century, although *mb* > *m* is in Irish again a late eighth- or ninth-century development.[65] The explanation may rather be that, in a context of syncope, the creation of a complex consonant-group (ch + nd in the one case, l + mb in the other) led to an early assimilation of the original group. We must also allow the reduction of the *-ī-* of Secundinus to a short and oblique sound with the change of stress-pattern in the host-language. A sequence *Secundīnus* > **Sechundīnəs* > **Sechundīn* > **Sechndən* > **Sechnən* must be supposed; this was completed by dissimilation > **Sechnəl*, written *Sechnall*.[66] A later variant, Sechlann, was created by the operation of metathesis.

If this history is correctly deduced, we have to do with a borrowing from a Latin which failed to show British lenition of intervocalic *-c-*. Equally we have a

57 Kajanto, *The Latin Cognomina*, p. 292, and *Onomastic Studies*, pp. 30, 62, 64.
58 Cf. Mandouze, *Prosopographie chrétienne du bas-empire*, I.1049–52.
59 Duchesne, *Fastes*, II.169 (Lyon, A.D. 602–x614), and I.278 (Sisteron, *fl.* 614).
60 Cf. Jones *et al.*, *The Prosopography*, I.813–14 and II.985–6.
61 And therefore either from a British source before British lenition had taken place, or from a Latin speaker of other origin whose intervocal /k/ had not been voiced to /g/. For discussion of such matters, see Jackson, *Language and History*, pp. 76–148, and the publications cited on p. 105, n. 130, below.
62 Thurneysen, *A Grammar*, p. 93 (§151[c]).
63 *Language and History*, pp. 511–13 (§112 [2]) 695–6.
64 Thurneysen, *A Grammar*, p. 93: 'The spelling *-n(n)* first becomes common in' the Old Irish glosses on a psalter-commentary in Milano, Biblioteca Ambrosiana, MS. C.301 inf., of the mid- or later ninth century (cf. *ibid.*, p. 5). However, James Carney gave reasons for returning to a purely palaeographical dating of *saec.* viii/ix, noting also that the 'glosses seem to be copied from an earlier source': 'The Lambeth Commentary', edd. Bieler & Carney, pp. 5–7; but the matter is uncertain and, as in the case of the Old Irish glosses of an earlier period in Würzburg, Universitätsbibliothek, MS. M.p.th.f.12, new palaeographical study is needed (cf. Dumville, 'Language, literature, and law', p. 93 and n. 8) and will probably lead to reëvaluation of linguistic history.
65 Thurneysen, *A Grammar*, p. 94 (§152[c]).
66 For this explanation see *ibid.*, p. 93 (§151[c]).

name which, having been received into Irish, underwent there a complex development.[67]

St Sechnall is known as the patron of Dunshaughlin (Domnach Sechnaill, later Domnach Sechlainn) in Co. Meath, a short distance from Tara.[68] His cult seems to be attested from as early as appropriate sources are available: his feast-day is 27 November.[69] As in the case of Auxilius/Ausaile, compound personal names embodying the saint's name were created in the central middle ages. Mael Sechnaill (later Mael Sechlainn) is found from the ninth century, while in the eleventh and twelfth centuries Gilla Sechnaill enjoyed a certain vogue. Both gave rise to surnames from the eleventh century: Ua Maíl Shechnaill and Ua Maíl Shechlainn; Mac Gilla Shechnaill. All these names had particular currency in Mide and no doubt reflect devotion to St Sechnall in his adoptive home-territory.[70]

On this basis, while it would be possible to allow that Bishop Secundinus could have been a literary invention of the seventh century, the existence of the vernacular name (and everything which pertains to it) effectively disallows such speculation. It is simplest to suppose that Secundinus was a fifth-century cleric (though not necessarily a bishop) who worked in Ireland; it is at least possible that he was a Continental and *could* thus be assigned to a date as early as the mid-fifth century if we associate him with the Palladian Church. The possibility is not to be excluded, however, that he was a christian and perhaps a cleric of an earlier time: his date is defined solely by a *terminus ante quem* provided by the completion of lenition of intervocalic stops in Irish.[71]

67 For a much later borrowing, see *Secundin* for the martyrs called Secundinus and commemorated in *Félire Húi Gormáin* at 21 February and 29 April: ed. & transl. Stokes, p. 393, for details.

68 MacNeill, *Saint Patrick*, p. 81: 'about seven miles from Tara'. The commentaries on the metrical *féliri* place it *i ndeisciurt Breg*, 'in the south of Brega': *Félire Óengusso Céli Dé*, ed. & transl. Stokes, p. 248; *Félire Húi Gormáin*, ed. & transl. Stokes, pp. 226/7.

69 *Félire Óengusso Céli Dé*, ed. & transl. Stokes, p. 237 (referring already to Sechnall as author of a poem in praise of St Patrick); the portion of the 'Martyrology of Tallaght' for this date is lost. For the strange distribution of the earlier notices of Secundinus, see Bury, *The Life*, p. 292. As his (and the Patrician) legend expanded, he was identified (anachronistically: cf. Bury, *ibid.*) as a Lombard, whence presumably the affiliation *moccu Baird* (but therefore before *ca* 700? – Kenney, *The Sources*, p. 260, n. 214; cf. MacNeill, 'Mocu, maccu'). Cf. discussion in n. 31, above. He acquired a father Restitutus, which is a fairly common Late Latin name, especially popular among christians: cf. Jones *et al.*, *The Prosopography*, II.940–1 (two examples); Duchesne, *Fastes*, I.255(–7), a bishop of Trois-Châteaux; Mandouze, *Prosopographie chrétienne du bas-empire*, I.968–83 (thirty-five examples from christian Africa); *Inscriptiones latinae christianae ueteres*, ed. Diehl, III.136; see also Kajanto, *The Latin Cognomina*, p. 356, and *Onomastic Studies*, pp. 57, 62, 118. For the story of the quarrel and reconciliation between Sechnall and Patrick, Sechnall's despatch to Rome, and his return thence with relics, see the preface to the hymn of St Sechnall in *The Irish Liber Hymnorum*, edd. & transl. Bernard & Atkinson, I.3–6 and II.3–7; it is curiously parallel to the account of Sachellus in the 'Book of Armagh', for which see below, pp. 102–3. Cf. Doherty, 'The use', pp. 92–4.

70 Ó Cuív, 'Aspects of Irish personal names', pp. 163–4.

71 Dated by Jackson, *Language and History*, pp. 142–3, to the second half of the fifth century (and earlier rather than later in this period); but, as Harvey, 'The significance of *Cothraige*', has pointed out, Jackson's arguments (and therefore his conclusions) have been contaminated by non-linguistic considerations (which cannot now be admitted) and must accordingly be wholly reconsidered.

Benignus

We come now to a group of saints bearing Latin names but for whom Irish origins are claimed by the earliest sources to refer to them.[72] Benignus is the one most often mentioned, but Sacellus is another example of the same development. Both are figures of hagiography, although Benignus does make appearances in other contexts – in the chronicles, in *Liber Angeli*,[73] and in Patrick's company or as his representative in a variety of other situations, legal and pseudohistorical.[74] Benignus, who is found first in the work of Muirchú and Tírechán, is always presented as Patrick's heir or successor; in Tírechán's *Collectanea* he is described also as a bishop.[75] His associations, therefore, are with Armagh, but the *Additamenta* in the 'Book of Armagh' have him living seventeen years at a church *i nDruimm Daro .i. Druim Lias*, Drumlease in Co. Leitrim.[76] Irish origin is attributed to him[77] – he is made to come from the area of *hostium Ailbine*, 'the estuary of [the River] Ailbine', identified as the River Delvin (Co. Dublin/Meath)[78] – but without a great deal of accompanying detail.

In Irish Benignus normally appears as Benén. In Latin, the word was at once an adjective ('kindly', etc.) and a name which derived from it.[79] The name was well known, but perhaps less widely used in Late Antiquity and the early middle ages than one might have expected.[80] As to its persistence, a Benignus is recorded as being bishop of Angers in the first half of the eighth century.[81] In late Vulgar Latin vowels were lengthened before *-gn-*.[82] What is more, *e* and *i* had fallen together in many phonetic contexts in many dialects of Vulgar Latin.[83] We therefore find the inscriptional spelling BENEGNVS, for a possible *benēgnus*;[84] furthermore the *-g-* in such contexts was in due course vocalised,[85] so that **benīnus* and **benēnus* would have been possible Latin forms (cf. *rēnum* for *regnum*[86]). It is also possible that both forms were known in Ireland, giving (for the name) **Benín* and *Benén*.[87]

72 For a straightforward discussion, see MacNeill, *Saint Patrick*, p. 103.

73 §30, in a list of those who issued the *Liber* – Auxilius, Patricius, Secundinus, Benignus: *The Patrician Texts*, edd. & transl. Bieler & Kelly, pp. 190/1.

74 McCone, *Pagan Past*, pp. 97, 177, 200; *Lebor na Cert*, ed. & transl. Dillon, pp. ix, 2/3, *et passim.*

75 Muirchú, *Vita S. Patricii*, I.20 and 28; Tírechán, *Collectanea*, §§5, 6, 8 (= Muirchú, I.20), 24 (where he has a sister Mathona), 30. In Muirchú's account Benignus is still only *puer Patricii*, albeit his successor designate.

76 §8: *The Patrician Texts*, edd. & transl. Bieler & Kelly, pp. 172/3.

77 Tírechán, *Collectanea*, §5 (*ibid.*, pp. 126/7).

78 Hogan, *Onomasticon*, pp. 16, 456–7. Cf. MacNeill, 'Colonisation', p. 102.

79 Kajanto, *The Latin Cognomina*, p. 255.

80 For examples, see *Inscriptiones latinae christianae ueteres*, ed. Diehl, III.27.

81 Duchesne, *Fastes*, II.355.

82 Grandgent, *An Introduction*, pp. 74–5 (§172 [2]).

83 *Ibid.*, pp. 83–5 (§§196–201).

84 *Ibid.*, pp. 74–5; the inscription is at Vienne; the form quoted is adjectival, not a personal name.

85 *Ibid.*, pp. 110 (§259) and 114 (§269).

86 This example quoted by Grandgent, *ibid.*, p. 114.

87 For an Irish explanation of Benén, see below. Other possible Vulgar Latin forms would be **binīnus*, **binēnus*, of which the latter could explain Irish Binén (see below), otherwise problematic.

At least the falling together of Latin ē̆ and ī̆ is required by any theory as to how *Benignus* became Irish *Benén*. Given the developments in Vulgar Latin mentioned above, all that need be hypothesised in or subsequent to borrowing is loss of the final syllable. However, that may not be the whole story. The only parallel Latin > Irish borrowing known to me is *signum*, giving Irish *sén*.[88] Precisely the same development may be supposed as for *Benignus*. Nevertheless, the existence of Welsh *swyn*, earlier **sēn*, gives pause.[89] This could be explained in exactly the same way. A further comparandum, found in British only, is *lignum*, giving Vulgar Latin **lēnum*, Brittonic **lēn*, Welsh **lwyn* (Old Welsh *loin*) > *llwyn*.[90] These three examples are, I think, sufficient to establish that *Benignus* > *Benén* is part of a pattern. The Irish name could have been borrowed directly from Vulgar Latin, or it might have been mediated through British Latin or Brittonic. Since one cannot prove, I think, that the name reached Irish before the later seventh century, the precise source must remain open.

Some other Hiberno-Latin spellings of the name may tell a more complicated story. For *Benignus*, in I.20 the manuscripts of Muirchú's *Vita S. Patricii* have *Bineus* (MS. A, A.D. 807), *Binemus* (< *Binenius*) (MS. B, eleventh-century), *Bineneus* (MS. C, late eighth-century), and at the second occurrence *Benineus* (MS. A), while the other two repeat their previous forms.[91] It seems to me that this tells us something about developments in the vernacular. Latin terminations *-eus* and *-ius* were simple enough to add to vernacular name-forms. An implication of *Benin(eus)*, unless we wish to invoke Insular Latin spelling conventions (in which free variation of *e* and *i* was possible) is that Irish *Benén* had been analysed as containing the native hypocoristic suffix *-én*: **Benín* would then be an acceptable alternative, and that is (I suspect) reflected in this Latin form.[92] *Binen-* is not open to such an explanation, and might be better accounted for by Vulgar Latin developments.[93] That it does, however, reflect a genuine vernacular usage is suggested by the Tripartite Life of St Patrick which, alongside the regular Benén, does present also Binén.[94]

Ro-foided immurgu *Benén* isin leth crín ocus tunach in drúad im suide. Ro-híadad in tech iarom, ocus doratad crann archleith airi immach ar bélaib int slúaig, ocus adadar tene ind. Forcoemnacair firt mór and tre irraigthe Pátraic. Ro-loisced a lleth n-úr den taig ocus in druí i mmedón na caslae, ocus níro-mill a becc din chasail. Níro-loisced

88 Vendryes, *De hibernicis vocabulis*, pp. 176–7, and *Lexique étymologique*, S, pp. 84–5.

89 Cf. Jackson, *Language and History*, pp. 324–35, 697: Welsh ē was diphthongised in a period extending from the second half of the seventh century to the middle of the eighth.

90 For discussion of this see Jones, 'Etymological notes', pp. 43–6.

91 *The Patrician Texts*, edd. & transl. Bieler & Kelly, p. 96, lines 6 and 10.

92 For an alternative (Vulgar Latin) explanation, see above. For another Irish-language dimension to the complex development of this name, see Kenney, *The Sources*, p. 274 and n. 369.

93 See above, n. 87.

94 *Bethu Phátraic*, ed. Mulchrone, pp. 35–6, lines 603–10 (three occurrences of the name, as against Muirchú's two). The conclusion is not absolutely certain, however, since the author of this text could have been slavishly following his source (hypothetically reading *Binenius* or *Bineneus* at this point). Another Binén is, however, found in the 'Book of Armagh', in *Additamenta*, §7 (*The Patrician Texts*, edd. & transl. Bieler & Kelly, pp. 172/3): *Binean filius Lugu*. Cf. Grosjean, 'An early fragment', p. 43.

immurgu a lleth crín i rrabai *Benen*, ocus ro-anacht Día *Binén* i mmedón tonaigi in drúad ocus ro-loisced immurgu in tunach co ndérnai luaith di.

According to the last editor of the Tripartite Life, the witnesses are in precise agreement in the distribution of variant name-forms.[95]

If it were the case that the variant Irish forms – Benén, Binén, and *Benín (hypothesised from Hiberno-Latin Benineus) – all directly reflected variant uses in Vulgar Latin, we might do well to suppose that the borrowing was relatively early, when varied and widespread contact with Vulgar Latin was more likely (although the impact of seventh-century Continental vulgar usage on the Irish should perhaps not be overlooked). On the other hand, if the forms other than Benén were later and Irish developments, there is no necessity for such a conclusion. Likewise the possibilities concerning an actual fifth-century bishop called Benignus are not easily adjudicated.[96] Benignus may be a hagiographical fiction: if so, however, the Latin and Irish names have adhered firmly to him from the first. At the other extreme, he might have been a British or Continental cleric who did indeed bear that Latin name, a member of staff of one of the early bishops (even perhaps as a boy, as he is presented in the hagiography). If so, then he acquired (like some other foreign clerics) a native Irish identity by the late seventh century.[97] A third possibility is that the core of what the earliest hagiographers asserted about him is correct: that he was an Irish convert, perhaps as a boy, who was one of the early native bishops. Parallels are available from seventh-century England, although in that context the names chosen seem to have been more overtly christian (like Deusdedit) or else biblical.[98] That Benignus was bishop of Armagh, let alone Patrick's successor there, is an altogether more uncertain proposition for which no controlling testimony is readily available.[99]

95 *Bethu Phátraic*, ed. Mulchrone, p. 36, line 609, apparatus.

96 How early his cult began is uncertain. He was named already (with Patrick, Auxilius, and Secundinus) in the mid-seventh-century Armagh text, *Liber Angeli*, §30 (see n. 73, above): he was presumably therefore already a figure of note in Armagh's (pseudo-)history. He does not appear in the early ninth-century *Félire Oengusso*, and the section of the 'Martyrology of Tallaght' containing 9 November (his feast-day as later attested) is wanting. In the twelfth-century *Félire Húi Gormáin* (ed. & transl. Stokes, pp. 214/15, 335), at 9 November, he is Benignus, not Benén. He is the subject of an Irish Life, edited with Latin translation by Paul Grosjean in *Acta Sanctorum*, edd. Bolland *et al.*, November, IV.175–8 (for further discussion of part of the text, see Grosjean, 'An early fragment'). The monks of Glastonbury transported him thither to join St Patrick in their house-legends: Kenney, *The Sources*, pp. 307–8, 350–1, 606–8; Finberg, *West-Country Historical Studies*, pp. 82–3; Lesley Abrams, below, pp. 233–42 (cf. pp. 243–4).

97 For examples, see below, pp. 81–2. For this dimension of Benignus's 'history', see O'Rahilly, *The Two Patricks*, pp. 27–8, 59 (n. 28).

98 The earliest native bishops there were Deusdedit at Canterbury, Ithamar and Damianus at Rochester, Thomas at Dunwich. For further discussion, see above, pp. 82–3.

99 For Benignus in the Armagh coarbial lists, see below, pp. 273–8.

Sachellus and Caetiacus

D. A. Binchy drew attention to Sacellus as possibly the name of an early Continental bishop in Ireland.[100] As a Latin name it is not well attested. It is a diminutive of *sacer* and can be placed within a recognised group of Latin names of ultimately religious significance. The feminine *Sacella* is found.[101]

The Sachellus of Irish hagiography is not a substantial figure. He appears three times in Tírechán's *Collectanea*[102] and in the notes which follow Muirchú's *Vita S. Patricii* in the 'Book of Armagh' but which have been conjectured to be strays from Tírechán's work.[103] He is *Sachelus Basilice Móire hi Cíarraigiu* in the Tripartite Life of St Patrick.[104] Tírechán presents him, obliquely, as bishop of Baislec (Baslick, Co. Roscommon)[105] and also as exercising episcopal functions in Mag nAí.[106]

The latter episode has generated a considerable secondary literature, but pointlessly so. What has interested scholars is the implication of a once-surviving letter attributed to Patrick – what has been called his 'circular letter' to the bishops of Mag nAí:[107] the other bishop in question was one Caetiacus. In the *Additamenta* Sachellus appears as bishop of the Ciarraige of Connaught.[108]

Sachellus is presented as an Irishman called Feradach – who is located in terms of his father, *Hercaith nomine, de genere Nothi*, a man who is presented as having saved Patrick's life from a crowd of hostile pagans. We are told that[109]

> Credidit Deo Patricii, et babtitzauit illum Patricius et Feradachum filium eius; et immolauit filium Patricio. Et exiuit cum Patricio ad legendum triginta annis. Et ordinauit illum in urbe Roma et dedit nomen nouum Sachellum. Et scripsit illi librum psalmorum, quem uidi. Et portauit ab illo partem de reliquis Petri et Pauli, Laurentii et Stefani, quae sunt in Machi.

As in the last sentence, so in most references to Sachellus, he is tied closely to Armagh as well as Patrick. A notable historical romance was woven around Sachellus by T. F. O'Rahilly in a remarkable exercise of imagination: it has no substance.[110] The relics, on the other hand, were considered of great importance and it is notable that they are presented as having been acquired from Baslick,

100 'Patrick and his biographers', p. 145. Cf. O'Rahilly, *The Two Patricks*, p. 28: 'his Irish descent is an obvious fiction' (cf. *ibid.*, p. 59, n. 29). Cf. MacNeill, 'Beginnings', p. 42, for discussion of the reception of the name.

101 Kajanto, *The Latin Cognomina*, p. 211.

102 §§6, 30, 32.

103 §3 (*The Patrician Texts*, edd. & transl. Bieler & Kelly, pp. 122–5).

104 *Bethu Phátraic*, ed. Mulchrone, p. 67, lines 1212–13.

105 Cf. Doherty, 'The basilica'. Tírechán, §32 (*The Patrician Texts*, edd. & transl. Bieler & Kelly, pp. 148/9).

106 Cf. n. 103 for the text, which is uncertainly attributable to Tírechán; for discussion, see *ibid.*, pp. 213–14.

107 Cf. *ibid.*, p. 214, with further references, and Bieler, *The Life*, pp. 33, 75; O'Rahilly, *The Two Patricks*, pp. 28–9; Carney, *The Problem*, pp. 160–7.

108 §6: *The Patrician Texts*, edd. & transl. Bieler & Kelly, pp. 170–3. Cf. n. 104, above.

109 *Ibid.*, p. 122. I have repunctuated the text. It is not clear who is the subject of the penultimate sentence. Sachellus is presumably, but not certainly, the subject of the last.

110 *Early Irish History and Mythology*, pp. 250–1 (cf. *The Two Patricks*, pp. 28–9).

as was Sachellus's submission.[111] The stories of Sachellus do not seem entirely consistent with one another: they look like varying attempts to insist on the comprehensive submission and subordination of Baslick to Armagh; we may imagine that this testifies to controversy in the seventh century.

It is a nice question whether the name Sacellus might more naturally have been borne by a fifth- or sixth-century bishop (whether taken as a name in religion by an Irish convert or owned by a foreign cleric) or invented in the seventh century. We may simply note a parallel borrowing, of Latin *sagellum* as Irish *sachill*, 'cloth', 'shroud', 'napkin'.[112] But there is nothing other than the name to suggest that in the hagiographical notices of him we possess hidden traces of an early foreign missionary.[113]

His partner in crime in Mag nAí, Bishop Caetiacus (also Cethiacus/Cethiachus, the forms in the body of Tírechán's *Collectanea*),[114] is placed firmly in the area of the modern Co. Roscommon. Tírechán attributes to him paternal kindred of Uí Ailello and maternal descent from Corcu Sai of the Ciannacht of Co. Meath.[115] He has nevertheless been described as a Continental bishop[116] and a Continental Celtic etymology suggested for his name:[117] but in that case he would sound rather like a toponym. His name has not been satisfactorily explained and he is an even more intangible figure than Sac(h)ellus.[118]

In general, then, the Latin names attached to clerics of the Patrician legend do not lead in a single direction.[119] There seems certainly to be some material best

111 For discussion and references to the relics, see above, p. 83, n. 44, and p. 98, n. 69. A possibility pointed out by Whitley Stokes is striking in this regard: 'The name seems borrowed from or cognate with the Lat. *sacellum*, a shrine for receiving relics' (*Félire Húi Gormáin*, ed. & transl. Stokes, p. 392). Was Sacellus created from a story, like St Amphibalus of St Albans?

112 Vendryes, *De hibernicis vocabulis*, pp. 173 and 196, and *Lexique étymologique*, S, p. 5; *Dictionary of the Irish Language*, gen. edd. Quin *et al.*, S, col. 4.

113 He first appears in the native kalendars and martyrologies in the twelfth century: *Félire Húi Gormáin*, ed. & transl. Stokes, pp. 148/9 and 392, at 1 August, where he is *Sacell* (Sacéll, according to Stokes, *ibid.*, p. 392, with an Early Modern Irish form Soicheall). According to Stokes, *ibid.*, he is also found in the ninth-century 'Martyrology of Tallaght' but the reference is to a place-name, Cúil Sachaille, allegedly Taney (*olim* Saeoyle), near Dundrum (Co. Dublin); it must be admitted that the context is suggestive, given what we are told in the 'Book of Armagh' about his family (cf. O'Rahilly, *The Two Patricks*, p. 59, n. 29), for the entry memorialises one 'Nath Í Cule Sachaille' (*The Martyrology of Tallaght*, edd. Best & Lawlor, pp. 59, 221).

114 §§6, 14, 27, 29, 30, 32. We find *Caetiacus* in the passage of uncertain authorship referred to in n. 106, above.

115 §27.

116 Binchy, 'Patrick and his biographers', p. 148, no doubt following O'Rahilly.

117 O'Rahilly, *The Two Patricks*, pp. 28 and 59, n. 30.

118 He appears in the 'Martyrology of Tallaght' at 16 June: 'Cethig episcopi sancti Patricii' (edd. Best & Lawlor, p. 50); cf. *Félire Húi Gormáin*, ed. & transl. Stokes, pp. 116/17, 341, for the same information.

119 Continental scholars have devoted some attention to the ostensibly Continental place-names in Patrician hagiography: for the fullest and most recent treatment, see Grosjean, 'S. Patrice à Auxerre sous S. Germain'. The discussions seem to me to produce at best uncertain conclusions, at worst misleading ones: on two such points, see Dumville, 'St Patrick in Cornwall?'.

explicable in terms of an early origin. We have some evidence for localised cult in the cases of Auxilius and Secundinus. Isarninus seems difficult to explain in a seventh-century context. But there is much uncertainty and we should not underestimate the research-skills of seventh-century Irish hagiologists. We can certainly see Latin names being acquired for use in the growing family-tree of Patrick himself.[120] Secundinus also acquired an extended foreign pedigree, beginning with a father called Restitutus, a very well attested christian Late Latin name.[121] Patrick's mysterious postman, Uictoricus,[122] developed a remarkable life in both mediaeval hagiography and modern writing, accompanied by various name-changes. As I remarked at the outset, the names of Patrick's hagiographical associates require very thorough study. There is certainly much to discover.[123] What do we make of one of Patrick's aliases, Magon(i)us, which has been deemed to have a British or Continental Celtic etymology?[124] What is the significance of the treatment of the name of Amator, bishop of Auxerre, who – to the evident confusion of the Irish hagiographers – had become Amathorex (genitive, Amathoregis) in their ultimate source?[125] And the *senior* whom Bishop Germanus sent with Patrick, according to the hagiographers,[126] was one Segitius or Segetius:[127] again, a Celtic etymology has been seen for this rare name which has been found (as Segetius) in an inscription from second-century Spain and in a christian inscription from Firenze.[128] This *name* in particular seems a very unlikely invention of seventh-century date but that point by itself would not disallow the deduction that the *character* in Patrician hagiography

120 Cf. above, pp. 89–92.

121 Cf. above, p. 98 and n. 69.

122 *Confessio*, §23. There has been a repeated tendency to associate him with Uictricius, bishop of Rouen and monastic missionary of rural Gaul, who also visited Britain in mysterious circumstances at the beginning of the fifth century. See, for example, Grosjean, 'S. Patrice et S. Victrice'.

123 Patrick's *Franci* (Tírechán, *Collectanea*, §§7 and 29) require consideration: they lead us to Baslick again (cf. n. 111, above).

124 Cf. n. 8, above. To the references there add Holder, *Alt-celtischer Sprachschatz*, II, cols 385, 616.

125 Muirchú, *Vita S. Patricii*, I.9 (8) and *capitulum*, and derivatives. Cf. the comment of Grosjean, 'Notes chronologiques sur le séjour de S. Patrice en Gaule', p. 75, n. 6: 'L'ablatif *Amathorege* montre l'utilisation d'une source irlandaise, plus que probablement écrit, où l'évêque était appelé Amathorig'. This seems doubtful to me, but an explanation is certainly needed. Cf. O'Rahilly, *The Two Patricks*, p. 52, and Binchy, 'Patrick and his biographers', p. 86.

126 The choice of the word *senior* is interesting, given its role in Patrick's *Confessio*, especially §§26 and 27.

127 The tradition begins with Muirchú, *Vita S. Patricii*, I.8 (7). MSS. A and B testify to *Segitium*, while MS. C perhaps implies an original *Segetium*, as do *Historia Brittonum* (cf. below, pp. 223, 227, 230) and *Vita IV: The Patrician Texts*, edd. & transl. Bieler & Kelly, pp. 72(–3), line 9 and apparatus.

128 Holder, *Alt-celtischer Sprachschatz*, II, cols 1440–1. The Florentine inscription, whose context was not satisfactorily discussed on publication, reads 'Hic iacit Segetius d. scola gentilium' and thus raises many questions.

was a creation of such an era. We may see fit to be more immediately suspicious of the two disciples attributed by Muirchú to Bishop Palladius – Augustinus and Benedictus[129] – whose names would not have been difficult to find in the seventh century.[130]

129 Muirchú, *Vita S. Patricii*, I.9 (8): *The Patrician Texts*, edd. & transl. Bieler & Kelly, pp. 72–5.

130 One should not perhaps end this discussion without noting that the two most securely attested names in the whole story of the beginnings of christianity in Ireland, Palladius and Patricius, are extremely commonly attested in Roman history. See Jones *et al.*, *The Prosopography*, I.658–62, 673, and II.819–24, 837–43; Mandouze, *Prospographie chrétienne du bas-empire*, I.810–11, 833–5 (two Patricii were close relatives of Augustine of Hippo); Duchesne, *Fastes*, *passim* (nine Palladii in eight dioceses, four Patricii in four); *Inscriptions chrétiennes de la Gaule*, ed. Le Blant, II, nos 504, 570, and 649 (Palladius), and 641 (Patricius); *Inscriptiones latinae christianae ueteres*, ed. Diehl, III.120, 122; Kajanto, *The Latin Cognomina*, pp. 115 (Palladius) and 313 (Patricius). For an interesting early sixth-century inscription from Gaul (which reads '[In hunc] tumulum [req]uiescit bone [me]moriae Patri[ci]us, qui uixet an[no]s LXV; obiit in [pa]ce idus marti[as]'), see *Recueil*, gen. ed. Marrou, XV.560–2 (no. 190); the volume-editor's comment includes the odd idea that the name Patricius was 'rendu célèbre à partir du Ve s. par l'apôtre d'Irlande' – one of our problems is precisely that Patrick seems to have been unknown to general historical record until (at best) the seventh century!

COROTICUS

Coroticus was a ruler whose warriors had attacked a settlement where Patrick, in his episcopal capacity, had very recently conducted a ceremony of baptism.[1] They had killed some of his neophyte christians, carried others off into captivity, and taken a quantity of booty. It was, we might think, activity of a sort frequent enough in the fifth century (as in many others). Patrick was still close by, for on the next day he 'sent a letter with a holy priest whom I had taught from early childhood, and he was accompanied by some clerics; the letter requested that they grant us some of the booty and of the baptised prisoners whom they had seized'.[2] The captives asked for were women, it seems, although men had also been taken away. Not surprisingly, the soldiers of Coroticus 'roared with laughter at them'.[3] The letter in question does not survive.

What we do have is the source from which all the foregoing information has been taken. That is a text preserved in five manuscripts,[4] in none of which it bears a title. It is nowadays usually described as a letter and called 'Epistola ad Coroticum' or 'Epistola ad milites Corotici'. If it is a letter – and that seems very uncertain to me – then it is an open letter.[5] It is a tract stating what has happened, commenting on these events, offering (in the manner familiar from Patrick's *Confessio*) a defence of his own position, inviting publicity for his own account, and finally asking for its widespread circulation and even that it might be read out 'in the presence of Coroticus himself'.[6] Coroticus and his men are only once directly addressed.[7] This is largely a recital in the first and third persons. Patrick's text does imply and assume, however, that they are to hand, are known to the people, and can be addressed.[8] His extant *litterae* on the subject effectively state Coroticus's excommunication and that of his men – in so far as they were christians.[9]

A number of issues arises from this consideration of Patrick's text. The motives for the attack are at least partially discoverable in the result. Men, women, and other booty were carried off. The raiders would 'allot [these] poor

1 In this chapter, unadorned references to text are to the so-called *Epistola ad Coroticum*. For the information about Coroticus's raid, see §12. Coroticus was probably not present on that occasion, to judge by what Patrick has to say in this work.

2 §3.

3 §21.

4 For these sigla and a concordance with those used by other editors, see *Saint Patrick*, edd. & transl. Hanson & Blanc, pp. 56–8.

5 See the discussion below, pp. 117–27.

6 §§2, 21.

7 In §14. 'You' are otherwise his christian readers. Cf. Thompson, *Who was Saint Patrick*?, pp. 113–24, 134.

8 §21.

9 §7.

baptised women as prizes'.[10] The male captives were destined for slavery in foreign parts:[11] 'the Church mourns for its sons and daughters who have so far not been put to the sword but have been carried far off and transported to distant lands where sin is rife, openly, grievously, and shamelessly; and there freeborn men have been sold, christians reduced to slavery – and, what is more, as slaves of the utterly iniquitous, evil, and apostate Picts'.[12] But the tone of Patrick's tract leads one to wonder whether the very fact of the converts' baptism made them targets. The Devil 'shows his resentment through the unjust rule (*per tyrannidem*) of Coroticus who does not fear God or His priests'.[13]

Where was Coroticus ruler? Until recently, 'Britain' was the invariable answer to that question. In so far as Patrick's text (rather than later hagiography) provided grounds for that deduction, the evidence lies in the long-distance transportation of the captives, the references to the Picts,[14] and Patrick's refusal to call Coroticus and his men fellow-citizens: 'non dico ciuibus meis neque ciuibus sanctorum romanorum sed ciuibus daemoniorum'.[15] These are uncertain testimony, however. We have already seen how an apparent distinction between the fates of the various captives may suggest that Coroticus was involved in an organised slave-trade and was himself not necessarily a very distant ruler. Patrick is denying that the raiders and their ruler are christians – it is unwise to press the word *ciues* to a specific association with Roman citizenship; the clue is provided by the *sancti romani*, the Roman saints.

In 1980, however, Professor E. A. Thompson turned the subject on its head by insisting on a single point.[16] If Patrick was excommunicating Coroticus and his men, they must have been living in Ireland where he had episcopal jurisdiction. Otherwise, he would be invading a fellow-bishop's jurisdiction. Once the idea of Coroticus's residence in Britain has been shed, much in the text can be seen to fall into line with Thompson's interpretation. This has allowed him to construct a context for both Coroticus and Patrick for which he has offered an insistent parallel at the other end of the Roman world:[17] Patrick's mission in Ireland was not primarily to the native Irish but to the many British captives carried thither in the preceding decades, as Patrick himself had once been. Coroticus and his men represented a renegade, freedman element among that population. Interpreted thus, Patrick's words shed further light. That Coroticus was well known to Patrick's audience is explained. That Patrick could rapidly and successfully despatch clerical emissaries to his soldiers becomes easy to understand. And Patrick's apparently disparaging references to the Irish become more intelligible: these have offered a particular puzzle, although they have hardly been recognised as such. Writing of Coroticus, Patrick says, 'Far from

10 §19.
11 §15.
12 In §14 the Picts are 'a foreign people which does not know God'.
13 §6.
14 §§2, 12, 15.
15 §2.
16 'St. Patrick and Coroticus'.
17 Cf. Thompson, *The Visigoths*, on the means by which christianity was carried to the Goths. On that subject cf. also Green, *The Carolingian Lord*; Heather & Matthews, *The Goths*; Heather, *Goths and Romans*.

God's love is the man who delivers christians into the hands of Irish (*Scottorum*) and Picts'.[18] He continues: 'Ravening wolves have devoured the Lord's flock, which was in fact increasing excellently and most actively, and sons of the Irish (*filii Scottorum*) and daughters of petty kings (*regulorum*) were monks or virgins of Christ[19] – I cannot count their number'. He had already written, 'Like the Devil they live in death, allies of Irish (*Scottorum*) and of Picts and apostates'.[20]

On the other hand, Patrick – as in the *Confessio* – very clearly identifies himself with the native Irish. Again in reference to Coroticus and his men, he writes,[21] 'The wickedness of the wicked has prevailed over us. We have become like outsiders (*extranei*). Perhaps they do not believe that we have received one baptism or have one God as father. It is an affront to them that we are Irish (*Hiberionaci*). As it is written, "Have you not one God? Why have you one and all abandoned your neighbour?".'

There is an implied contrast here. It is as though *scottus* meant specifically 'pagan Irish',[22] whereas *hibernus* or *hiberionacus* had a more neutral connotation. But there is also a problem arising from uncertainty as to Patrick's self-identification. What did he mean in saying, with apparent reference to Coroticus and his men, 'And if my own people do not recognise me, well, a prophet does not have honour in his own country'?[23] This was said just after Patrick had described his 'Roman' background and called himself 'a slave in Christ to a foreign people (*genti exterae*)'.[24] The apparent presumption throughout the text is that, although Coroticus and his men are agents of the Devil, they are renegades, unfaithful to their christian origins, and a suitable target for excommunication, not pagans.

We are returned to the question of location. Coroticus and his men appear to be being described as Britons, or at any rate 'Romans'. Patrick has written his open letter in Latin. He supposes that his audience will know Coroticus, may know Patrick himself, and will understand the context. Although the assumption is not absolutely necessary, we may wish to deduce that his text was for circulation not merely among christians in Ireland but to a wider (and presumptively British) audience. Just as the Irish raided western Britain, a process to which Patrick himself was living testimony, so we cannot rule out the possibility that British raiders assaulted Ireland, whether inspired by Irish example or acting in revenge. Certainly we find such activity two centuries later, *ca* A.D. 700.[25]

If we admit this scenario, as scholars have generally done, then we see that a

18 §12.
19 Cf. *Confessio*, §41, for a similar remark about converts and monasticism.
20 §2.
21 §16.
22 Or perhaps a specific group – defined by tribal origin or by behaviour – among the Irish. Perhaps *Scotti* were those Irish given to piracy and raiding from the sea: were they the vikings of their day?
23 §11 (§§10–11 must be taken together: cf. pp. 121–2, below).
24 §10. In §14 the same phrase is used in reference to the Picts (and *Scotti*?) to whom captives are being sold.
25 See, for example, Mac Niocaill, *Ireland before the Vikings*, pp. 112–13; Cf. Byrne, *Irish Kings*, pp. 111–12, and Binchy, 'A pre-christian survival', pp. 176–7.

		HG 5	**HG 6**	**HG 7**
		Con(fer)		
		Fer		
		Cursalem		
		Cluim		
		Cinhil		
		Cynloyp		
522	452	Ceritic guletic		
547	482	Cinuit		
572	512	Dumngual hen		
597	542	Guipno	Clinoch	Cinbelim
622	572	Neithon	Tutagual	[C]linog Eitin
647	602	Beli	[R]iderch hen [*fl. ante* 597, *VC*] [*fl.* 585 x 592, *HB*]	
672	632	Eugein [*fl.* 642]		
697	662	Elfin		
722	692	Beli [† 722 *AC*]		
747	722	Teudebur [† 750 *AC*]		
772	752	Dumnagual [† 760 *AC*]		
797	782	Eugein		
822	812	Riderch		
847	842	Dumnagual		
872	872	Arthgal [† 872 *AU*]		
897	902	[R]un		

GENEALOGY OF RHUN AB ARTHAL, KING OF STRATHCLYDE

temptation arises. Can Coroticus be identified in other sources and thus be placed in more precise geographical and chronological contexts? Not until E. A. Thompson's work has any scholarly hesitation been shown on this point. The Romano-British form *Coroticus* represents a British name which was eventually to become Ceredig in Welsh. Already by the time of the mid-tenth-century 'Harleian Genealogies' of British kings, the forms *Ceretic* and *Ceritic* had arisen.[26] These royal genealogies present two figures called Ceredig: students of Patrician matters have long vied with one another in arguing for an identification of one or the other with Patrick's *Coroticus*. We may take each in turn.

The first to be found among the 'Harleian Genealogies' occurs in a pedigree of the late ninth-century king of Strathclyde, Rhun ab Arthal.[27]

26 HG §§5, 26, 32 (ed. Bartrum, *Early Welsh Genealogical Tracts*, pp. 10, 12, 13).
27 HG §§5–7 (*ibid.*, p. 10). See my tabular representation of the genealogy.

Calculation of the absolute death-date of 'Ceritic guletic' from this genealogy is a process fraught with every kind of possible difficulty. Counting from the most proximate recoverable date, that of the killing of Arthal in 872,[28] one finds that fourteen generations of Arthal's patriline must be reckoned with. Applying a generation-average of twenty-five years would give one a notional death-date for 'Ceritic guletic' in A.D. 522. In so far as the cumulative process of subtraction can be checked, this generation-average seems to justify itself back to Eugein (Owain) who was victor in the battle of Strathcarron in 642.[29] In a verse commemorating the event he is described as *ŵyr Nwython*, 'grandson of Nwython', where *Nwython* is probably a false modernisation of **Nēthon* which should have been updated as *Neithon*;[30] the pedigree appears to be vindicated at this point. To the early seventh century, therefore, the pedigree may be chronologically accurate. If the further four generations be allowed, the date suggested can be arrived at.

However, the collateral lines present a real difficulty. Rhydderch Hen – ostensibly of the same generation as Beli, father of Owain the victor at Strathcarron – was, according to two independent sources, active as king in the last third, perhaps even the last fifteen years, of the sixth century.[31] Although he is reported to have died peacefully and may therefore have lived long,[32] the genealogical position seems untenable. Rhydderch appears to be placed one or two generations too late.

Above Neithon and Tudwal (*Tutagual*) there are difficulties. The names *Guipno* and *Clinoch* both stand in need of uncertain emendation.[33] Dyfnwal hen, as an ancestor-figure (like his father Cynwyd too) in Brittonic genealogy, may have attracted false junctures with various lines or, more mechanically, may have stood (in an earlier copy) in a position, as immediate ancestor of a

28 Annals of Ulster 872.5 (edd. & transl. Mac Airt & Mac Niocaill, I.328/9).

29 Annals of Ulster 642.1 (*ibid.*, I.122/3), locating the battle in December but not stating (in the original text) who was the victor.

30 For the verse see *Canu Aneirin*, ed. Williams, p. 39 (line 969); transl. Jackson, *The Gododdin*, pp. 98–9, 147. In the B-version of this text we find the comparable (but opposite) error *eir Nwython* (for *ŵyr Neithon*), a doubly false updating of *ēr Nēthon*!

31 Adomnán's Life of St Columba, written in the late seventh century, has Rhydderch as being a (no doubt much younger) contemporary of the saint, therefore before 597: the relevant chapter is I.15 (edd. & transl. Anderson & Anderson, pp. 38–41) whose heading reads 'De rege Roderco filio Tothail qui in petra Cloithe regnauit'. The other source is the *Historia Brittonum* (written in Wales A.D. 829/30) whose author synchronised Rhydderch with Hussa, king of Bernicia 585–592.

32 For further discussion of Rhydderch and consideration of his place in the hagiography of Kentigern (who supposedly died in 612), see Jackson, 'The sources', pp. 318–20, 326–7, 341; cf. Macquarrie, 'The career'.

33 For *Guipno* see n. 35. *Clinoch* has been taken as an error for *Clitgno*, Clydno, who has then been identified as the father of a hero of the British poem *Y Gododdin*, one Cynon of Aeron. If all this is justified, then the position of Cli<tgno> Eitin as the father of a son active *ca* 550 (for the date cf. Dumville, 'Early Welsh poetry'), who would have been an uncle of Rhydderch, is quite satisfactory. However a '[C]linog Eitin', a better candidate for the identification, occurs in a collateral line (HG §7). If he is not a doublet of 'Clinoch' grandfather of Rhydderch, his position relative to the latter also suggests corruption or false construction in the genealogy.

number of lines, which invited confusion when read or transcribed.[34] The simplest act of restoration of the text would be to suppose that one or two names had been lost before, after, or in the middle of the problematic name *Guipno*.[35] However, the process might have been more complex. Nevertheless, if applied, this emendation would give 'Ceritic guletic' a notional death-date of 497 or 472.

The other candidate for indentification with Patrick's Coroticus has been the eponym of Ceredigion, 'Cardigan(shire)'. He too is found in the 'Harleian Genealogies'.[36]

In so far as students of St Patrick have tried to use this genealogy to date Ceredig of Ceredigion, they have shown a quite extraordinary degree of credulousness and incompetence. Most recently, R. P. C. Hanson, while denouncing Irish chronicles, hagiography, and vernacular literature as universally untrustworthy for this period, put absolute faith in this tenth-century Welsh collection of royal pedigrees and in his ability to make deductions from its contents;[37] such faith was doubly misplaced. The procedure which Hanson was the latest of many students to adopt was to date Ceredig by dating Cunedda. The only known date for Cunedda, as a quasi-eponym for Gwynedd by no means certainly a historical figure, has him flourishing in 388, for which there is a clear ideological motive.[38] Numerous arbitrary redatings have been offered, often to secure a preferred date for Ceredig and therefore for St Patrick. The only sound procedure is to calculate from the latest person named in, that is to say the owner of, the pedigree – in this case King Gwgon of Ceredigion (*ob.* 871, according to the A-text of *Annales Cambriae*).[39] Applying a generation-average of twenty-five years brings us to A.D. 596 for the death of Ceredig; with a thirty-year average, we reach A.D. 541; only an Irish-style 35 or 37.5-year generation-average[40] could push Ceredig back into the fifth century and that would conflict with the ninth-century evidence which is consistent with the shortest of these averages.[41]

34 Compare the position of the kings of Lindsey in the Anglian collection of genealogies (ed. Dumville, p. 31; cf. pp. 45–7). For further comment, see Dumville, 'Kingship, genealogies', p. 90.

35 It was proposed by Phillimore ('The *Annales Cambriæ*', p. 172, n. 5) that *Guipno* arose from miscopying of **Guiþno*, where the Old English runic character had been used, and that this was in reality the name found as Gwyddno in Welsh. But this requires an alarming series of unlikelinesses. The extant form needs discussion before any such course of speculation is embarked upon.

36 HG §26. See my tabular representation of the genealogy (p. 113).

37 Hanson, *Saint Patrick, his Origins*, pp. 22–7; cf. *The Life*, transl. Hanson, pp. 11, 24–5.

38 Dumville, 'Sub-Roman Britain', pp. 181–3.

39 For the text, see 'The *Annales Cambriæ*', ed. Phillimore, p. 166.

40 For such calculation, see Miller, 'Date-guessing and pedigrees', pp. 99–100.

41 The only externally datable section of the pedigree of the kings of Ceredigion is that from Gwgon (*ob.* 871) back to his great-grandfather Arthen (*ob.* 807), a three-generation span of sixty-four years, a generation-average of 21.3 years.

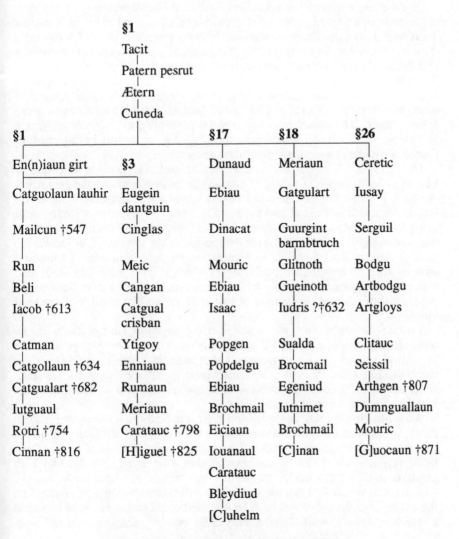

§1
Tacit
Patern pesrut
Ætern
Cuneda

§1	§3	§17	§18	§26
En(n)iaun girt		Dunaud	Meriaun	Ceretic
Catguolaun lauhir	Eugein dantguin	Ebiau	Gatgulart	Iusay
Mailcun †547	Cinglas	Dinacat	Guurgint barmbtruch	Serguil
Run	Meic	Mouric	Glitnoth	Bodgu
Beli	Cangan	Ebiau	Gueinoth	Artbodgu
Iacob †613	Catgual crisban	Isaac	Iudris ?†632	Artgloys
Catman	Ytigoy	Popgen	Sualda	Clitauc
Catgollaun †634	Enniaun	Popdelgu	Brocmail	Seissil
Catgualart †682	Rumaun	Ebiau	Egeniud	Arthgen †807
Iutguaul	Meriaun	Brochmail	Iutnimet	Dumnguallaun
Rotri †754	Caratauc †798	Eiciaun	Brochmail	Mouric
Cinnan †816	[H]iguel †825	Iouanaul	[C]inan	[G]uocaun †871
		Caratauc		
		Bleydiud		
		[C]uhelm		

GENEALOGY OF THE FAMILY OF CUNEDDA
FROM THE HARLEIAN COLLECTION

On this, the only evidence available, Ceredig of Ceredigion may with modest confidence be assigned to the sixth century and eliminated from the Patrician question.[42] It is clear from comparison of the pedigree of King Gwgon with those for the other kingdoms of Greater Gwynedd that it has a different origin and history, more comparable with that for Dunoding than with the others. Though of the same length as the other three pedigrees,[43] its terminal figure is two or three *generations* later in date than theirs. In this latter respect, it corresponds to the pedigree of Cuhelyn of Dunoding (which is, however, three *names* longer). The conclusion to be drawn is probably that an existing pedigree ascending to the eponymous ancestor, Ceredig, was simply attached to Cunedda's name at a moment of political necessity.[44]

The elimination of Ceredigion does not of itself validate identification of Patrick's Coroticus with Ceredig of Strathclyde. In favour of it is the geographical position of Strathclyde, between Patrick's presumed northeasterly or northern mission-area in Ireland and the Picts to whom the captive christians were being traded, and outside the former Imperial diocese of Britain. But there are many reasons for hesitation. The most important is the simplest. Our knowledge of fifth-century British politics is minimal: to suppose that, even if Coroticus were a king in Britain, we could identify him from a surviving mediaeval collection of genealogies simply by his name, would be folly. Hundreds (if not thousands) of relevant names must be lost to us, as must knowledge of scores of kingdoms.

Turning to Strathclyde, we must recall the apparent fault or faults in the transmitted genealogy. Much has been made of Ceredig's epithet, *gwledig*, but in reality we can see its etymology rather than its current significance:[45] a derivative of *gwlad*, 'country', 'area of sovereignty', it need mean no more than 'ruler' although it could of course seek to convey the idea of 'founder of the kingdom'; but of what date is its evidence?

What has directed scholars' attention most insistently to Strathclyde has been the description of Coroticus in the *capitula* to Muirchú's *Vita Sancti Patricii* in the 'Book of Armagh' as *rex Aloo*: 'De conflictu sancti Patricii aduersum Coirthech regem Aloo'.[46] On the assumption that *Aloo* stands for the Old Irish genitive, *alo*, of *ail*, 'rock',[47] the further assumption has been made that *Ail Cluaide*, Old Welsh *Alt Clut*, Modern Welsh Allt Glud, was intended. Even if so, the evidence dates only from *ca* A.D. 800, and could be the result of historical research.[48] Muirchú himself speaks only of the evil of 'cuiusdam regis britannici

42 Cf. Dumville, 'Some aspects of the chronology', p. 445, n. 2, for a comparable calculation from a Welsh pedigree.

43 HG §§1, 3, 18 (ed. Bartrum, *Early Welsh Genealogical Tracts*, pp. 9, 10, 11): see my table.

44 For discusion see Miller, 'Date-guessing and Dyfed', pp. 55–60; and Dumville, 'Gildas and Maelgwn'.

45 Cf. *Geiriadur Prifysgol Cymru*, edd. Thomas *et al.*, II.1682, *s.v. gwledig*.

46 *The Patrician Texts*, edd. & transl. Bieler & Kelly, p. 66. (Cf. p. 207, below.)

47 Cf. Fergus Kelly, *ibid.*, p. 242. Note also the marginale in *Liber Ardmachanus*, fo 16ra: *ymnus Colmán Alo* (*ibid.*, p. 166).

48 Cf. Thompson, 'St. Patrick and Coroticus', p. 13; and his *Who was Saint Patrick?*, pp. 126–9. The text in the 'Book of Armagh' is almost certainly a copy and this identification can therefore be pressed back into the eighth century (though perhaps only just so).

nomine Corictic[49] infausti crudelisque tyrranni'.[50] Another explanation of the deduction now presents itself, however. In seeking to explain the origin of the name Co(i)thr(a)ige which attaches to St Patrick in some of the hagiography, Anthony Harvey has drawn attention to two different places called *Ail Coithrigi*;[51] it could have been such an equation which was in the mind of the capitularist whose work is represented in the 'Book of Armagh'.

A final pair of considerations may be offered. The form *Coirthech* found in the *capitulum* in the 'Book of Armagh' is what would be expected in Old Irish if the name had developed naturally in Irish from the fifth century.[52] It is seen elsewhere in the hagiography only at one point, towards the end of the Tripartite Life.[53] In the Latin hagiography the form *Coritic* usually found is best taken as Brittonic, showing *i*-affection in the second syllable and loss of British final syllable, if it has any linguistic reality.[54] If Coirthech in the 'Book of Armagh' is a genuine Irish name-form, it is a reminder of another point which has not received its due of attention in the scholarly literature. In the fifth century *Coroticus* would have been a natural latinisation of a form common to British and Irish which would become Old Welsh (and presumably Cumbric) *Ceritic/Ceretic* but Old Irish *Coirthech.* On his name alone, St Patrick's adversary cannot be shown to be British rather than Irish.[55]

49 Various forms appear in later Patrician hagiography: *Chairtic* in the Life by Probus (*Four Latin Lives*, ed. Bieler, p. 215); *Coritic* in *Vita III* (Γ) and *Ceritic* in *Vita III* (Π), §72 (*ibid.*, p. 169). On *Vita III*, see also Dumville, 'St Patrick in Cornwall?'.

50 Muirchú, *Vita S. Patricii*, I.29 (edd. & transl. Bieler & Kelly, *The Patrician Texts*, p. 100).

51 Harvey, 'The significance of *Cothraige*', pp. 7–8.

52 I am indebted to the late Kenneth Jackson for confirming this for me.

53 *Coirt(h)ech, rí Bretan: The Tripartite Life*, ed. & transl. Stokes, I.248.

54 But the *i*-affection has not spread here to the first syllable: on 'double *i*-affection', see Jackson, *Language and History*, pp. 591–2 (§164).

55 Once again I must record my obligation to the late Kenneth Jackson for lengthy discussion of the relation of the linguistic evidence to the historical problems.

VERBA MILITIBUS MITTENDA COROTICI
An Analysis of St Patrick's Tract on the Crimes of Coroticus

It is striking that in spite of a detailed commentary by Ludwig Bieler, of numerous annotated translations, and of a vast outpouring of books and articles, there has been no straightforward attempt to understand the structure of Patrick's tract on Coroticus and to follow the progress of his argument. If such an analysis had been undertaken, it seems unlikely that the text would be known simply as the 'Letter to Coroticus'.[1]

Where the notion of a letter derives from is a nice question. In the 'Book of Armagh', in a celebrated colophon to the Patrician dossier, we read, 'Hucusque uolumen quod Patricius manu conscripsit sua: septima decima martii die translatus est Patricius ad cælos'.[2] In 'quod Patricius manu conscripsit sua' it is hard not to see a reminiscence of 'Coroticus' §2, 'Manu mea scripsi atque condidi uerba ista', even though that work is not contained in *Liber Ardmachanus*.[3] If we turn to the head of the *Confessio* in that manuscript, we find an introductory rubric: 'Incipiunt libri sancti Patricii episcopi'.[4] The matter will require further discussion,[5] but it seems that the exemplar contained both works: it was a *uolumen* containing two *libri*; the first *liber* was the *Confessio*, the second the tract on Coroticus. This is made quite explicit in three manuscripts, Hanson's CFG, which have a formally rubricated division into two *libri*.[6]

Patrick's work on the crimes of Coroticus opens in a way which is clearly comparable with the beginning of the *Confessio*. He states who he is and what is most important about his situation. The themes so apparent in the other work recur powerfully, even bluntly, here.

1 Patricius, peccator indoctus scilicet Hiberione constitutus, episcopum me esse fateor. Certissime reor a Deo accepi id quod sum. Inter barbaras itaque gentes habito, proselitus et profuga ob amorem Dei; testis est ille si ita est. Non quod optabam tam dure et tam aspere aliquid ex ore meo effundere; sed cogor zelo Dei, et ueritas Christi excitauit, pro dilectione proximorum atque filiorum, pro quibus tradidi patriam et parentes et animam meam usque ad mortem. Si dignus sum, uiuo Deo meo docere gentes, etsi contempnor aliquibus.

1 For further discussion, cf. above, pp. 107–9.
2 *Liber Ardmachanus*, fo 24va, *ad fin.*: cf. below, pp. 191 (discussion) and 202 (text).
3 Cf. below, p. 191.
4 For the text, see below, pp. 192–202.
5 See below, p. 205.
6 For the sigla, see *Saint Patrick*, edd. & transl. Hanson & Blanc, pp. 56–8. The text and translation which follow have been adapted from those by Hood, *St. Patrick*.

1 I, Patrick, a sinner, yes, and unlearned, established in Ireland, put on record that I am bishop. I am strongly convinced that what I am I have received from God. And so I live among barbarian peoples, a stranger and an exile for the love of God; He is my witness if it is so. Not that I wanted to utter anything from my lips so harshly and bluntly, but I am compelled by my zeal for God, and Christ's truth has roused me to do so, for the love of my neighbour and my children, for whose sakes I gave up homeland and family and my life even to the point of death. If I so deserve, I live for my God, to teach the heathen, even if I am despised by some.

He then turns to explain the sequence of events which have brought him to write. His words are to find their way to the soldiers of Coroticus – but not directly, for one attempt has already proved futile. By implication he seeks to bring the force of public opinion to bear on these sinners. This, then, is at best an 'open letter'. Even so, it is not one written in a direct form of address to these men.

2 Manu mea scripsi atque condidi uerba ista danda et tradenda, militibus mittenda Corotici – non dico ciuibus meis neque ciuibus sanctorum Romanorum sed ciuibus daemoniorum, ob mala opera ipsorum. Ritu hostili in morte uiuunt, socii Scottorum atque Pictorum apostatarumque. Sanguilentos sanguinare de sanguine innocentium christianorum, quos ego innumerum <numerum> Deo genui atque in Christo confirmaui!

3 Postera die qua crismati neophyti in ueste candidi – flagrabat in fronte ipsorum dum crudeliter trucidati atque mactati gladio supradictis –, misi epistolam cum sancto presbytero quem ego ex infantia docui, cum clericis, ut nobis aliquid indulgerent de praeda uel de captiuis baptizatis quos ceperunt; cachinnos fecerunt de illis.

2 With my own hand I have written and composed these words to be given, delivered, and sent to the soldiers of Coroticus – I do not say to my fellow-citizens nor to fellow-citizens of the holy Romans, but to fellow-citizens of the demons, because of their evil actions. Like the enemy they live in death, as allies of Irish and of Picts and apostates. These bloodthirsty men are bloody with the blood of innocent christians, whom I have begotten for God in countless numbers and have confirmed in Christ!

3 On the day after the neophytes, clothed in white, had received the chrism (its fragrance was on their brows as they were butchered and put to the sword by those whom I have mentioned), I sent a letter with a holy priest whom I had taught from early childhood, and he was accompanied by some clerics; the letter requested that they should grant us some of the booty and baptised prisoners that they had captured; they roared with laughter at them.

He reflects on his own feelings for those attacked by Coroticus's forces, but also on the fate of the criminals – hell is theirs.

4 Idcirco nescio quid magis lugeam; an qui interfecti uel quos ceperunt uel quos grauiter zabulus inlaqueauit. Perenni poena gehennae pariter cum ipso mancipabunt<ur>, quia utique qui facit peccatum seruus est et filius zabuli nuncupatur.

4 And so I do not know what to lament more, those who were killed or those whom they took prisoner or those whom Satan has sorely ensnared. They shall be delivered up to hell along with him in eternal punishment because undoubtedly he who commits a sin is a slave and is called the son of Satan.

Patrick excommunicates Coroticus and his men. He does not use that word but he leaves no doubt – they are estranged from Patrick and from God; no one should take food and drink with them; alms should not be accepted from them. Patrick also justifies his action and his right to take it: *non usurpo*.[7]

5 Quapropter resciat omnis homo timens Deum quod a me alieni sunt et a Christo Deo meo, pro quo legationem fungor; patricida, fratricida, lupi rapaces deuorantes plebem Domini ut cibum panis, sicut ait: 'Iniqui dissipauerunt legem tuam, Domine,' quam in supremis temporibus Hiberione optime benigne plantauerat, atque instructa erat fauente Deo.

6 Non usurpo; partem habeo cum his quos aduocauit et praedestinauit euangelium praedicare in persecutionibus non paruis usque ad extremum terrae, etsi inuidet inimicus per tyrannidem Corotici, qui Deum non ueretur nec sacerdotes ipsius, quos elegit et indulsit illis summam diuinam sublimam potestatem, quos ligarent super terram ligatos esse et in caelis.

7 Unde ergo quaeso plurimum, sancti et humiles corde; adulari talibus non licet nec cibum nec potum sumere cum ipsis, nec elemosinas ipsorum recipi debeat, donec crudeliter <per> paenitentiam effusis lacrimis satis Deo faciant et liberent seruos Dei et ancillas Christi baptizatas, pro quibus mortuus est et crucifixus.

5 Therefore let every man who fears God acknowledge that they are estranged from me and from Christ my God, for whom I am an ambassador; the man is a patricide, a fratricide, they are ravening wolves, devouring God's people like so much bread, as is said: 'The wicked have destroyed Your Law, O Lord' (Psalms 118.126) – which in these last times He had most graciously planted in Ireland and which had become established with God's favour.

6 I am not claiming more than my due; I have a share with those whom He called and predestined to preach the gospel right to the ends of the earth in the midst of no small persecution, even if the enemy shows his resentment through the unjust rule of Coroticus, who does not fear God or His priests

7 On usurpation of episcopal jurisdiction, see Thompson, 'St. Patrick and Coroticus', and *Who was Saint Patrick?*, pp. 132–3.

whom He has chosen and endowed with the supreme, divine, and exalted power that those whom they bound on earth should be bound in heaven also.

7 And therefore I make this earnest appeal to all you men of piety and humble heart; it is not right to curry favour with such as these nor to take food or drink with them, nor ought one to accept their alms, until they make amends to God by gruelling penance, with shedding of tears, and free God's servants and the baptised handmaids of Christ, for whom He died and was crucified.

At last we have had a direct indication of an apparent intended audience for this tract – *sancti et humiles corde*: this vocative is, however, the only such indication in this otherwise first- and third-person statement.

Patrick now turns to summon some biblical support for his views and actions.

8 'Dona iniquorum reprobat Altissimus. Qui offert sacrificium ex substantia pauperum quasi qui uictimat filium in conspectu patris sui.' 'Diuitias,' inquit, 'quas congregauit iniuste euomentur de uentre eius, trahit illum angelus mortis, ira draconum mulcabitur, interficiet illum lingua colubris, comedit autem eum ignis inextinguibilis.' Ideoque, 'Uae qui replent se quae non sunt sua;' uel, 'Quid prodest homini ut totum mundum lucretur et animae suae detrimentum patiatur?'

9 Longum est per singula discutere uel insinuare, per totam legem carpere testimonia de tali cupiditate. Auaritia mortale crimen. 'Non concupisces rem proximi tui. Non occides.' Homicida non potest esse cum Christo. 'Qui odit fratrem suum homicida adscribitur;' uel, 'Qui non diligit fratrem suum in morte manet.' Quanto magis reus est qui manus suas coinquinauit in sanguine filiorum Dei, quos nuper adquisiuit in ultimis terrae per exhortationem paruitatis nostrae!

8 'The Most High rejects the gifts of the wicked. He who offers sacrifice from the goods of the poor is like the man who sacrifices the son before his father's eyes' (Ecclesiasticus 34.23–24). 'The wealth,' it is written, 'which he has amassed unjustly will be vomited from out of his belly; the angel of death drags him away; he will be tormented by the wrath of dragons; the serpent's tongue will kill him, and unquenchable fire devours him' (Job 20.15ff.). And so, 'Woe to those who fill themselves with what is not theirs' (Habakkuk 2.6); or, 'What does it profit a man to gain the whole world and suffer the loss of his own soul?' (Matthew 16.26).

9 It would be tedious to deal with each individual point, to make declarations and to collect texts on such greed from the whole Law. Avarice is a mortal sin. 'Thou shalt not covet thy neighbour's property. Thou shalt not kill' (Exodus 20.17, 13). A murderer cannot be with Christ. 'He who hates his brother is reckoned a murderer' (1 John 3.15); or, 'He who does not love his brother dwells in death' (1 John 3.14). How much more guilty is he who

has sullied his hands with the blood of the sons of God, whom He recently won in the ends of the earth thanks to the exhortation of one as insignificant as I am!

He seeks brevity of biblical exposition but leaves no doubt as to his message. The last sentence effectively sums up the point, but Patrick cannot resist (as so often) the temptation to state (with however militant a modesty) his own role as a fisher of souls in Ireland.

This need to refer to his own contribution leads him to return to a restatement of his own history and motives, picking up on what he said in §1. The implication seems to be that the recipients of his work would know his story – but it could be deduced in part from these remarks.

10 Numquid sine Deo uel secundum carnem Hiberione ueni? Quis me compulit? Alligatus sum Spiritu ut non uideam aliquem de cognatione mea. Numquid a me, piam misericordiam quod ago erga gentem illam qui me aliquando ceperunt et deuastauerunt seruos et ancillas domus patris mei? Ingenuus fui secundum carnem; decorione patre nascor. Uendidi enim nobilitatem meam – non erubesco neque me paenitet – pro utilitate aliorum. Denique seruus sum in Christo genti exterae ob gloriam ineffabilem perennis uitae quae est in Christo Iesu Domino nostro.

10 Did I come to Ireland without God's favour or according to the flesh? Who forced me? I am obliged by the Spirit not to see any of my kinsfolk. Does it come from me that I show devout mercy towards the very people which once took me captive and harried the slaves of my father's house, male and female? I was free-born according to the flesh; my father was a decurion. I sold my good birth (not that I am ashamed or regret it) in the interest of others. In short, I am a slave in Christ to a foreign people for the ineffable glory of the everlasting life which is in Christ Jesus our Lord.

Patrick assumes that his christian audience ('in Christo Iesu Domino *nostro*') will know what a decurion is or was; the recipients were certainly not all expected to be Irish, therefore.[8]

He now continues the theme of the poor opinion which some have of him. The implication is that in the eyes of Britons he is not well regarded.

11 Et si mei me non cognoscunt, propheta in patria sua honorem non habet. Forte non sumus ex uno ouili neque unum Deum patrem habemus, sicut ait: 'Qui non est mecum contra me est, et qui non congregat mecum spargit'. Non conuenit; unus destruit, alter aedificat. Non quaero quae mea sunt. Non mea gratia sed Deus qui dedit hanc sollicitudinem in corde meo, ut unus essem de uenatoribus siue piscatoribus quos olim Deus in nouissimis diebus ante praenuntiauit.

11 And if my own people do not recognise me, well, a prophet does not have honour in his own country. Perhaps we are not of one fold and do not have

[8] For discussion of the *decurio*, see Hanson, *Saint Patrick, his Origins*, pp. 112–18, 176–9.

one God as father, as Christ says: 'He who is not with Me is against Me, and he who does not gather with Me scatters' (Matthew 12.30). We are at cross purposes; one destroys, another builds. I am not seeking what is my own. It is not my grace but God who laid this responsibility in my heart, to be one of His hunters or fishers whom God once foretold would appear in the last days.

Therefore he must seek God's aid directly. He turns to address the Almighty.

12 Inuidetur mihi. Quid faciam, Domine? Ualde despicior. Ecce oues tuae circa me laniantur atque depraedantur, et supradictis latrunculis, iubente Corotico hostili mente.

12 I am resented. What should I do, Lord? I am very much despised. See, Your sheep are torn to pieces around me and are carried off, and by the raiders whom I have mentioned, on the aggressive orders of Coroticus.

Patrick's direct appeal to God is brief. He resumes his commentary.

Longe est a caritate Dei traditor christianorum in manus Scottorum atque Pictorum. Lupi rapaces deglutierunt gregem Domini, qui utique Hiberione cum summa diligentia optime crescebat, et filii Scottorum et filiae regulorum monachi et uirgines Christi – enumerare nequeo.

Far from God's love is the man who delivers christians into the hands of *Scotti* and Picts. Ravening wolves have devoured the Lord's flock, which everywhere in Ireland was in fact increasing excellently and most actively, and sons of the *Scotti* and daughters of underkings were monks and virgins of Christ – I cannot count their number.

Suddenly we meet a direct address.

Quam ob rem iniuria iustorum non te placeat; etiam usque ad inferos non placebit.

Therefore be not pleased at the wrong done to the righteous; even as far as hell it shall not be pleasing.

What is more, the addressee is singular. It is hard to see that such a remark could be addressed even to the most unfriendly British ecclesiastic. It seems rather as though Patrick has without warning turned to speak to Coroticus, warning him of the extent of revulsion against his action: only in hell, perhaps not even there, will the criminal's actions be approved.

Patrick now returns, it seems, to those whom he addressed previously – the *sancti et humiles corde*, true christians. He chooses to assume rhetorically that all such people will themselves recoil from contact with the criminals, that they will in effect not need to follow Patrick's formal excommunication of the malefactors but on receiving his account of events react thus spontaneously.

13 Quis sanctorum non horreat iocundare uel conuiuium fruere cum talibus?

13 Which of the saints would not shudder at the thought of making merry or feasting with such men?

The subject changes again. Patrick picks up once more the narrative description of the raiders' evil and his commentary upon it.

De spoliis defunctorum christianorum repleuerunt domus suas, de rapinis uiuunt. Nesciunt miseri, uenenum letale cibum porrigunt ad amicos et filios suos, sicut Eua non intellexit quod utique mortem tradidit uiro suo. Sic sunt omnes qui male agunt; mortem perennem poenam operantur.

They have filled their homes with spoils taken from dead christians, they live by plunder. The wretches do not realise it, they are offering deadly poison as food to their friends and children, just as Eve did not realise that she in fact handed death to her husband. All who do evil are so; they bring death on themselves as their eternal punishment.

Patrick now turns to seek a more satisfactory, christian example of transfer of wealth by 'Romans' to the barbarians. He finds it in the practice of paying to redeem baptized captives from the Franks and other pagan peoples. But this leads him into a direct comparison in which he addresses Coroticus in the second person.

14 Consuetudo Romanorum Gallorum christianorum: mittunt uiros sanctos idoneos ad Francos et ceteras gentes cum tot milia solidorum ad redimendos captiuos baptizatos. Tu potius interficis et uendis illos genti exterae ignoranti Deum; quasi in lupanar tradis membra Christi. Qualem spem habes in Deum, uel qui te consentit aut qui te communicat uerbis adulationis? Deus iudicabit. Scriptum est enim: 'Non solum facientes mala sed etiam consentientes damnandi sunt'.

14 Here is the custom of the Roman christians in Gaul; they send suitable holy men to the Franks and other peoples with so many thousand *solidi* to ransom baptised captives; whereas you kill them or sell them to a foreign people which does not know God; you commit the members of Christ as though to a brothel. What hope do you have in God, or indeed anyone who agrees with you or converses with you in words of flattery? God will judge; for it is written, 'Not only those who do evil but also those who agree with them are to be damned' (Romans 1.32).

Patrick next picks up a theme begun in §4. He grieves for those who have been killed, but he can do no more. But he and the Church mourn still for those carried off – not yet killed, but sold in slavery to the vile Picts.

15 Nescio quid dicam uel quid loquar amplius de defunctis filiorum Dei, quos gladius supra modum dure tetigit. Scriptum est enim, 'Flete cum flentibus;' et iterum, 'Si dolet unum membrum, condoleant omnia membra'. Quapropter ecclesia plorat et plangit filios et filias suas quas adhuc gladius nondum interfecit, sed prolongati et exportati in longa terrarum, ubi peccatum manifeste grauiter impudenter abundat; ibi uenundati ingenui homines, christiani in seruitute redacti sunt, praesertim indignissimorum pessimorum apostatarumque Pictorum.

15 I do not know what more to say or speak concerning those of the sons of God who have departed, whom the sword struck all too hard. For it is written, 'Weep with those that weep' (Romans 12.15); and again, 'If one member grieves, let all the members share that grief' (1 Corinthians 12.26). Therefore the Church mourns and weeps for its sons and daughters who so far have not been put to the sword but have been carried far off and transported to distant lands, where sin is rife, openly, grievously, and shamelessly; and there freeborn men have been sold, christians reduced to slavery – and what is more, as slaves of the utterly iniquitous, evil, and apostate Picts.

With another shift in attention he directs his succeeding remarks to those captives. He follows them, verbally, with grief and encouragement. He identifies himself with them: the wicked have prevailed 'over us'; 'it is an affront to them that *we are* Irish'. They will find eternal salvation; their captors will get everlasting fire.

16 Idcirco cum tristitia et maerore uociferabo, o speciosissimi atque amantissimi fratres et filii quos in Christo genui – enumerare nequeo –, quid faciam uobis? Non sum dignus Deo neque hominibus subuenire. Praeualuit iniquitas iniquorum super nos. Quasi extranei facti sumus. Forte non credunt unum baptismum precepimus uel unum Deum patrem habemus. Indignum est illis Hiberi<o>na<c>i sumus. Sicut ait: 'Nonne unum Deum habetis? Quid dereliquistis unusquisque proximum suum?'

17 Idcirco doleo pro uobis, doleo, carissimi mihi. Sed iterum gaudeo intra meipsum: non gratis laboraui uel peregrinatio mea in uacuum non fuit. Et contigit scelus tam horrendum ineffabile; Deo gratias, creduli baptizati de saeculo recessistis ad paradisum. Cerno uos; migrare coepistis ubi nox non erit neque luctus neque mors amplius, sed exultabitis sicut uituli ex uinculis resoluti et conculcabitis iniquos et erunt cinis sub pedibus uestris.

18 Uos ergo regnabitis cum apostolis et prophetis atque martyribus. Aeterna regna capietis, sicut ipse testatur. Inquit: 'Uenient ab oriente et occidente et recumbent cum Abraham et Isaac et Iacob in regno caelorum'.

16 Therefore I shall lift up my voice in grief and sorrow. You most radiant and beloved brothers and children whom I have begotten in Christ (I cannot count your number), what can I do for you? I am not worthy to help God or man. The wickedness of the wicked has prevailed over us. We have become like outsiders. Perhaps they do not believe that we have received one baptism or have one God as Father. It is an affront to them that we are

Irish. As is written: 'Have you not one God? Why have you one and all abandoned your neighbour?' (Malachia 2.10).

17 Therefore I grieve for you, I grieve, my dearly beloved friends, Yet there again, I rejoice within myself; I have not laboured for nothing and my travels have not been in vain. And yet such an unspeakably horrible crime took place; but thank God, it was as baptised believers that you departed from this world to go to Paradise. I can see you; you have begun your journey to where there will be no night or mourning or death any more, but you will leap for joy like calves freed of their bonds and will trample on the wicked, and they will be ashes under your feet.

18 And so you will reign with the apostles and prophets and martyrs. You will gain the eternal realms, just as He bears witness, saying, 'They shall come from the East and from the West and shall lie down with Abraham and Isaac and Jacob in the kingdom of heaven' (Matthew 8.11).

The sequence of thought has followed exactly what was foreshadowed in §4 (that too, like §§16 and 17, begins with *Idcirco*): first the dead christians, then the captives, finally the captors weigh on Patrick's mind.

'Foris canes et uenefici et homicidae;' et, 'Mendacibus periuris pars eorum in stagnum ignis aeterni.' Non immerito ait apostolus: 'Ubi iustus uix saluus erit, peccator et impius transgressor legis ubi se recognoscet?'

19 Unde enim Coroticus cum suis sceleratissimis, rebellatores Christi, ubi se uidebunt, qui mulierculas baptizatas praemia distribuunt, ob miserum regnum temporale quod utique in momento transeat? Sicut nubes uel fumus qui utique uento dispergitur, ita peccatores fraudulenti a facie Domini peribunt; iusti autem epulentur in magna constantia cum Christo, iudicabunt nationes et regibus iniquis dominabuntur in saecula saeculorum. Amen.

18 (ctd) 'Outside are dogs and sorcerers and murderers' (Revelation 22.15); and, 'As for lying oath-breakers, their lot will be in the lake of everlasting fire' (Revelation 21.8). Not without cause does the apostle say: 'When the just shall scarcely be saved, where will the sinner and ungodly transgressor of the Law find himself?' (1 Peter 4.18).

19 So then, what of Coroticus and his villains, these rebels against Christ, where will they see themselves, they who allot poor baptised women as prizes, for the sake of a miserable temporal kingdom which will in any case pass away in a moment? Like clouds or smoke which is soon scattered by the wind, so deceitful sinners shall perish from before the Lord's face; but the righteous shall feast in full assurance with Christ; they shall judge the nations and hold sway over wicked kings for ever and ever, Amen.

Coroticus and his men are damned. So too are all unbelievers. Patrick states his faith in this fundamental truth.

20 Testificor coram Deo et angelis suis quod ita erit sicut intimauit imperitiae meae. Non mea uerba sed Dei et apostolorum atque prophetarum, quod ego Latinum exposui, qui nunquam enim mentiti sunt. 'Qui crediderit saluus erit, qui uero non crediderit condempnabitur;' Deus locutus est.

20 I testify before God and His angels that it will be just as He has indicated to me in my ignorance. These are not my words but those of God and His apostles and prophets, which I have set out in Latin – and they have never lied. 'He who believes will be saved, but he who does not believe will be damned' (Mark 16.16); God has spoken.

Concluding his tract, Patrick resumes the appeal which he launched in §7 – *quaeso plurimum* – addressed to the *sancti et humiles corde*. Here we find the same rhetorical target – *quicumque famulus Dei*. While there the plea was to shun the wicked, the excommunicate, here it is to spread Patrick's message and even to bring it to Coroticus himself. He concludes on an optimistic or merciful note. May Coroticus and his men repent, 'however late', and be made whole!

21 Quaeso plurimum ut quicumque famulus Dei promptus fuerit ut sit gerulus litterarum harum, ut nequaquam subtrahatur uel abscondatur a nemine, sed magis potius legatur coram cunctis plebibus et praesente ipso Corotico. Quod si Deus inspirat illos ut quandoque Deo resipiscant, ita ut uel sero paeniteant quod tam impie gesserunt – homicida erga fratres Domini! – et liberent captiuas baptizatas quas ante ceperunt, ita ut mereantur Deo uiuere et sani efficiantur hic et in aeternum! Pax Patri et Filio et Spiritui Sancto!

21 I earnestly beg that whichever servant of God is ready and willing should be the bearer of this letter, so that it may not be suppressed or hidden on any account by anyone, but rather be read out in front of all peoples and in the presence of Coroticus himself. But if only God may inspire them to come to their senses eventually and return to God, so that, however late, they repent of acting so sacreligiously (murderer that he is of the Lord's brethren!) and free the baptised women whom they previously took captive, so that they may be found worthy to live for God and may be made whole here and for ever! Peace to Father, Son, and Holy Ghost. Amen.

Patrick seems to allow himself the suspicion that there may be those who will seek to subvert his intentions, suppressing his words. The next British writer known to us, Gildas, had the same suspicion because he too denounced politically motivated evil.[9] Patrick nevertheless hopes that his message will get through, that repentance will prevail.

Patrick's highly rhetorical 'open letter' has stated a fair amount about himself, shown his pride in his missionary labours and their results, told about the

9 For editions and translations of his *De excidio Britanniae*, see Williams, *Gildas*, and Winterbottom, *Gildas*. For further discussion see *Gildas: New Approaches*, edd. Lapidge & Dumville, and references cited there. See also Brooks, 'Gildas' *De excidio*'.

specific evils perpetrated by Coroticus and his men, Patrick's failed attempt to retrieve the position. He announces their excommunication. He addresses his fellow christians, urges their support, and marshals biblical authority behind his case. He puts rhetorical questions, testing his own motives. He addresses God, seeking guidance. He reflects repeatedly on the sins of these transgressors. In two separated passages he appears to address Coroticus.[10] He addresses the captives – rhetorically, for they can hardly expect to hear his words in their Pictish exile. Finally, he reiterates his appeal for circulation and reading of his tract. May it bring these wicked men to their senses!

This is a powerful, ornate, rhetorical piece of writing. Its structure is at once complex and direct. It seems to have been written while the events were still fairly recent, perhaps when Patrick had learnt the Pictish fate of some of the captives. He involves all interested parties – christians, raiders, God, captives – and seeks to bind them with his concerns. His tract on the evils of Coroticus was not a historical statement, not an autobiographical account: rather it was an urgent plea for action and justice. It was not the letter to Coroticus:[11] that is lost. Rather it addressed a latinate and christian community. Whether it achieved any results we shall probably never know.

10 §§12 (see above, p. 122) and 14 (see above, p. 123). Cf. Thompson, *Who was Saint Patrick?*, pp. 117, 134 (and, more generally, 113–24).
11 §3 makes this clear.

PICTI APOSTATAE(QUE)

In his tract against Coroticus, Patrick thrice mentions the Picts,[1] twice in association with the idea of apostasy.

§2: Manu mea scripsi atque condidi uerba ista danda et tradenda militibus mittenda Corotici – non dico ciuibus meis neque ciuibus sanctorum romanorum sed ciuibus daemoniorum, ob mala opera ipsorum. Ritu hostili in morte uiuunt, socii Scottorum atque Pictorum apostatarumque. Sanguilentos sanguinare de sanguine innocentium christianorum quos ego in numero Deo genui atque in Christo confirmaui!

§15: Quapropter ecclesia plorat et plangit filios et filias suas quas adhuc gladius nondum interfecit, sed, prolongati et exportati in longa terrarum ubi peccatum manifeste grauiter impudenter habundat, ibi uenundati ingenui homines, christiani in seruitute redacti sunt, praesertim indignissimorum pessimorum apostatarumque Pictorum.

These passages have been used in attempts to date both the floruit of St Patrick and the mission of St Ninian to the southern Picts.[2] The result has been circularity of argument, but the interdependence of the two attempts has by no means generally been apparent to individual practitioners.

Bede tells us, in an aside to his account of St Columba of Iona, that (*ut perhibent*) christianity was first brought to the southern Picts by a British bishop, Nynia by name, whose own see was at Whithorn in Galloway (far, as it would appear, from Pictish territory). Bede says nothing about when this occurred – merely that in respect of St Columba's day it was *multo ante tempore*.[3] Nor does he give any impression that these Picts had subsequently apostasised. The picture is fleshed out somewhat by hagiography of St Ninian beginning *ca* 800 with an Anglo-Latin verse text which appears to have drawn on antecedent British information (probably also written in Latin);[4] however, the additional details do not seem to help the present enquiry.

Three immediate issues arise. Is Patrick's text sound and authorial in both places? Did he in §2 use the pleonastic idiom *atque X X′que* for simple *atque X X′*? What did he mean by *apostatae*? Only then can we consider what his words may mean for British and Irish history.

In both places there is no significant variation among the manuscript witnesses. (The apparatus of the most recent edition is filled at these points with

1 §§2, 12, 15. The standard discussion is that of Grosjean, 'Les Pictes apostats'.

2 For the latter, see Bede, *Historia ecclesiastica gentis Anglorum*, III.4.

3 The context in which Bede mentioned Nynia is crucial, as is his use of his characteristic qualifier (*ut perhibent*). For discussion, see MacQueen, *St. Nynia*.

4 For discussion see Levison, 'An eighth-century poem'. For a useful translation of the Anglo-Latin text, see W. W. MacQueen, 'Miracula Nynie episcopi'.

modern scholars' conjectures.[5]) This means that we must in the first instance seek to understand the text as transmitted, before resorting to conjectural emendation. The archetypal text is not in doubt at these points but that might have been transmitted in a manuscript only as old as the ninth or tenth century, albeit in Insular script.[6]

We may therefore approach a translation of the relevant sentences.

§2: 'They live, like the Devil, in death, allies of the *Scotti* and *Picti* and apostates'.

§15: 'carried far off and transported into distant lands . . . there, freeborn men have been sold, christians reduced to slavery – what is more, (as slaves) of utterly iniquitous and evil men *apostatarumque Pictorum*.

The first-declension Latin noun *apostata* derives from Greek ἀποστάτης and was used to mean 'a rebel against God' or 'a fallen christian' – what is conveyed in Modern English by 'apostate'. A third-declension Latin feminine *apostatrix* was a secondary development. A first-conjugation verb, *apostato*, an adjective *apostaticus*, and (by *ca* 400) a third-declension abstract noun *apostatio* were all created. The semantic range of *apostata* came to be extended, however, in development of the sense of 'rebel'. It could now be applied to a heretic. Eventually it became a term of abuse and could be employed of anyone regarded as a serious transgressor.[7] We are faced with the problem of locating Patrick's usage within that semantic range.

Ludwig Bieler proposed that §15 should be emended to read 'indignissimorum pessimorum <atque> apostatarumque Pictorum':[8] 'seeing how constantly Patrick repeats himself, one might expect the same pleonasm here as in' §2. There are difficulties with this approach. It is by no means clear (as Bieler chose to think) that in §2 'Scottorum atque Pictorum apostatarumque' means 'of *Scotti* and apostate Picts' with the pleonastic Late or Vulgar Latin usage mentioned by Bieler:[9] that is certainly not the most natural translation. It would require *apostatarum* to be adjectival, retaining first-declension flexion when describing a second-declension masculine noun. We may wonder whether such a nicety should be expected here. If one had to emend to achieve consistency between these passages, it would be better to read in §15 'indignissimorum pessimorum apostatarumque <atque> Pictorum'.

We should remember that Patrick in this text was describing Coroticus as a rebel against God.[10] This point comes through repeatedly, but is made quite explicit in §19: 'Coroticus cum suis sceleratissimis, rebellatores Christi'. They were apostates, therefore, in a currently accepted sense of that word. What is more, those with whom they lived and dealt were morally reprehensible in similar measure. In §15 Patrick wrote that 'They have filled their homes with

5 *Saint Patrick*, edd. & transl. Hanson & Blanc, p. 136.
6 *Ibid*., pp. 58–62, for discussion.
7 Souter, *A Glossary of Later Latin*, p. 20.
8 'Libri', II.194, n. 165.
9 *Ibid*., pp. 193–4.
10 See the discussion above, pp. 125–7 (cf. 107–9).

spoils taken from dead christians. They live by plunder. The wretches do not realise it, they are offering deadly poison as food to their friends and children . . .'. That Coroticus and his men are '*socii* of *Scotti* and Picts **and apostates** (*apostatarumque*)' is in these terms quite an accurate rendering of Patrick's views.

A further difficulty with Bieler's approach lies in the idea of repetition. While seeking to accommodate *Picti* and *apostatae* to one another, he overlooked the presence of *Scotti* in §2 and their absence from §15. On the other hand, in §12, *Scotti* and *Picti* are mentioned together without notice of *apostatae*: 'Longe est a caritate Dei traditor christianorum in manus Scottorum atque Pictorum'.

What all this teaches us, it seems to me, is that there are overlapping categories here and that the principal requirement being served is the development of Patrick's rhetorical need. Coroticus and his men are *apostatae*, but in as much as others share in their crimes they too come into that category. Furthermore, unless *Scotti* carried a narrower sense than 'Irish',[11] not all Irish belonged to the category of persons denounced – for Patrick could say *Hiberionaci sumus*, thinking of his relationship with his flock.[12] In short, whether *apostatae* is to be taken as noun or adjective in either passage, the result is essentially the same. If Picts are *apostatae* they are not necessarily so because their nation has abandoned christianity but because the Picts denounced by Patrick have a share in the crimes of the *rebellatores Christi*.[13] We may therefore translate the crucial passage in §15: 'what is more, (as slaves) of utterly iniquitous men, of evil men, and of apostates – the Picts'. For us to invoke apposition here is probably the simplest solution to the apparent textual difficulty.

I conclude, therefore, that Patrick's words convey no historical information about whether the Picts had accepted christianity or gone on to renounce it. Their history cannot be used to date St Patrick's endeavours, nor St Patrick's *floruit* to date St Ninian's.[14] The gain from a closer look at these passages has been a clearer understanding of Patrick's sense of the meaning of *apostata* and of his perception of the relationship of Coroticus with other groups.

11 Cf. pp. 108–9, above.
12 §16.
13 In §14 the Picts are a people ignorant of God.
14 For discussions of St Ninian/Nynia (supplementary to those in nn. 3–4, above), see Fahy, 'The historical reality', and Macquarrie, 'The date'.

BRITISH MISSIONARY ACTIVITY IN IRELAND

We have seen there to be an argument that the religious situation in Britain, as observed by Germanus of Auxerre and Lupus of Troyes in 429, may be held to explain the papal decision to organise the Church in the neighbouring island in 431.[1] It is doubtful that British ecclesiastics were thereafter without interest or influence in the developing Irish Church(es). Not the least reason for their concern, as E. A. Thompson has pointed out in recent years,[2] was the position of numerous British christians carried into slavery in the Gaelic world as a result of the raids which had been taking place along the western British seaboard, perhaps already for a considerable period of time before *ca* 430.[3] It is of course well known that St Patrick himself had been one such captive, a principal motivation for his subsequent desire to bring the Irish to christianity. Thompson has speculated that what was most controversial about St Patrick's activities in Ireland was his very determination to carry the gospel to the heathen.[4] One may doubt whether he was the first ecclesiastic in Ireland to be involved in missionary work: Thomas Charles-Edwards has shown how in the years around 440 the question of the relationship of the Church to heathen, barbarian peoples beyond the Empire's frontiers had become a subject of concern at the papal curia.[5] While Palladius's appointment in 431 may not have had a predominantly missionary motivation, the development of papal thinking and the exigencies of the local situation would probably have conspired to push the newly organised Irish Church into a partially evangelistic stance.

On the other hand the geopolitical context must increasingly have inhibited Roman (and more generally Continental) efforts to assist the nascent Irish Church or to exert influence in the Gaelic world. Charles-Edwards has suspected that, because of successful and extensive Germanic military penetration of Britain in the course of the 440s,[6] the principal external role in evangelising the Irish passed out of Continental hands and – paradoxically – to the Britons in their own time of travail. Scholars have indeed generally agreed (since the effective abandonment of the mediaeval notion of Patrick's Roman or Gaulish, commission) that a British hierarchy was responsible for directing and supporting Bishop Patrick's activities in Ireland.

Such an idea has been easier to state than to define, however. E. A. Thompson

1 See above, p. 81.
2 'St. Patrick and Coroticus'.
3 On this movement in general see Thomas, 'The Irish settlements'; on Dál Riata in particular, see below, pp. 183–9 and references given there.
4 *Who was Saint Patrick?*, pp. 79–102.
5 See above, pp. 1–12.
6 See above, pp. 8–9.

has directed some searching questions at the theory of British ecclesiastical financing of Patrick's missionary work.[7] The practicalities are indeed difficult to envisage. So too are the issues of order and responsibility – of the constitutional position of the Irish Church or Churches in relation to external authority. Nor should we imagine that we are so well informed about fifth-century Britain that a statement of the organisation of the British Church(es) can easily be offered.

Much turns, in the first place, on two considerations. Was Patrick's episcopate a pan-Irish commission or were his efforts and responsibility concentrated in one area – for example, Ulster –, perhaps in partial or effective independence of christian clergy working elsewhere in the island? Respectable arguments can in fact be made for both of these mutually exclusive propositions.[8] Secondly, is it the case that Patrick's own writings show him to have been responsible to and indeed dependent upon a British Church (among whose members there were people critical of his character and conduct)? In a brilliant analysis of the *Confessio*, E. A. Thompson has shown how the principal audience of the work may be taken to be a foreign – and presumptively British – community resident in Ireland.[9] This interpretation solves some problems but intensifies or creates others. In particular, it warns us that Patrick's role as bishop of a mission emanating from Britain is an assumption rather than a demonstrated fact.

Indeed, one is led to wonder whether it is even demonstrable. If one reads *Confessio* and *Epistola* without this preconception, the evidence which emerges to support it is not extensive. It is slightly alarming to realise that the details of his origins offered in *Confessio* §1 do not tell us that Patrick was a Briton – given that his father Calpornius and grandfather Potitus are not otherwise known,[10] and that the *uicus* of *Bannauenta Berniae* has never been identified.[11] At this stage a British location is indicated only by the statement that the adolescent Patrick – among so many others – had been carried off from his home into captivity in Ireland.[12] (Western Britain in its whole length is known to have been subject to Irish raiding and settlement in the fifth century, but no reliable information has been brought forward to suggest that such activities ever extended to Continental Europe.) It is only when we read on to §§23 and 43 that Patrick's British origins are made certain. After relating his escape from Ireland (§§17–22) he tells us – in a famous sentence which has fuelled much debate – of his reunion with his family (§23): 'Et iterum post paucos annos in Britaniis

7 *Who was Saint Patrick?*, pp. 95–102.

8 The most recent case is Thompson's (*ibid.*, especially pp. 66–102, 144–57, 166–75) for a single bishopric of Ireland to which Patrick was the third appointee.

9 *Ibid.*, pp. 103–24, extending insights first displayed in 'St. Patrick and Coroticus'.

10 An apparently sixth-century inscription from Lundy Island in the Bristol Channel bears the inscription *Potiti* (cf. Thomas, 'Beacon Hill revisited', and Thomas *et al.*, 'Lundy, 1969'), but there is of course no basis for associating him with Patrick's grandfather.

11 For the suggestion of a double error in the manuscripts' reading *Bannauem Taberniae*, which would give not just *Bannauenta Berniae* but *Bannauenta Taberniae*, cf. 'Libri', ed. Bieler, I.56. MS. P of the *Confessio* (Paris, Bibliothèque nationale, MS. latin 17626: cf. White, 'The Paris manuscript') has *Taburniae*, as has the sole direct witness (Bruxelles, Bibliothèque royale, MS. 64 [3129]) to Muirchú, *Vita S. Patricii*, I.1 (cf. *The Patrician Texts*, edd. & transl. Bieler & Kelly, pp. 66/7). Scholars have generally preferred the reading with *-u-*.

12 *Confessio*, §1.

eram cum parentibus meis, . . .'.[13] Much later, in explaining why he cannot and will not interrupt his 'laborious episcopate', he states that 'Unde autem etsi uoluero amittere illas [*sc.* ancillas Domini] et ut pergens in Brittannias – et libentissime paratus eram quasi ad patriam et parentes . . . . – . . . timeo perdere laborem quem inchoaui'.[14]

Patrick's *patria* lay in Britain, therefore.[15] This does not of itself authorise us to deduce straightforwardly that his episcopal commission was derived thence. There are, however, some pointers in that direction. First, we may note that two of the direct references to Britain seem to bear on the matter. In the passage just quoted from §43 the implication is that, if Patrick returned to base, it would be to Britain: it is a nice question whether there is a further implication that Patrick is resisting a call to account for himself there – certainly nothing is said directly to that effect. In §32 Patrick is concluding a discussion (§§26–32) of the circumstances in which because of the treachery of one of his supporters he failed to be elected bishop – when, presumably, someone else was appointed instead.[16] 'Et comperi ab aliquantis fratribus ante defensionem illam – quod ego non interfui nec in Britanniis eram nec a me orie<ba>tur – ut et ille in mea absentia pulsaret pro me. Etiam mihi ipse ore suo dixerat, "Ecce dandus es tu ad gradum episcopatus".' 'And I learned from a number of the brethren before that defence [of my case] – at which I was not present, nor was I in Britain, nor did I initiate it – that he would take up the cudgels for me. He had even told me himself from his own mouth, "See, you should be raised to the rank of bishop".' The *defensio* to which Patrick is here referring is presumably the occasion mentioned in §26, at the start of the discussion of this episode. 'Et quando temptatus sum ab aliquantis senioribus meis, qui uenerunt et peccata mea contra laboriosum episcopatum meum <obiecerunt>,[17] utique illo die fortiter impulsus sum ut caderem

[13] The apparently straightforward translation, 'And again after a few years I was in Britain with my parents', has provoked a huge and long-running debate about where Patrick was in the 'few years' which separated his escape from Ireland and his reunion with his parents. Cf. above, pp. 14–15, 25–8. A different translation may suggest that such a controversy has been unnecessary: 'And [so] after [these] few years [in captivity] I was again with my parents in Britain'. It is difficult to know whether Patrick's *paucos* would cover his six years in Irish slavery: he uses the word on only one other occasion – which offers no help (Devine, *A Computer-generated Concordance*, p. 201). For me, what makes it certain that Patrick's escape brought him straight back to Britain is the wording of his visionary message in §17: 'cito iturus ad patriam tuam', 'soon you will be going to your *patria*'. In the spirit of the discussion below (and cf. n. 15), I take *patria* to be his home-region in Britain, where his parents were.

[14] §43. His word *illas* refers back to those women mentioned in §42 who need his support. On *amittere*, cf. §§36 (below, n. 19) and 58: his usage looks significant; it seems to imply the loss of people (and place) to whom he is deeply attached and has especial responsibilities.

[15] On *patria* see the important discussion by Thompson, *Who was Saint Patrick?*, pp. 109–13. For another Insular problem of identifying a *patria* – Gildas's – see Dumville, 'The chronology', pp. 62, 71, 73–4, 77; Wright, 'Gildas's geographical perspective', pp. 102–4.

[16] On this point, see the discussion by Thompson, *Who was Saint Patrick?*, pp. 66–78, 166–75.

[17] This emendation has been admitted in *St. Patrick*, ed. & transl. Hood, p. 28, following Bury's observation that a verb is missing hence (*The Life*, p. 318). I should prefer to suggest that, rather than suppose such a radical loss, we pinpoint the fault at †*uenerunt* (*et*)† for which *obiecerunt* would be an adequate replacement. Not only does the sense 'came' appear to be redundant, but it might indeed be held to introduce undesirable complications into Patrick's account.

hic et in aeternum; sed Dominus pepercit proselito et peregrino propter nomen suum benigne. . . .' 'And when I was attacked by a number of my elders, who came and brought up my sins against my arduous episcopate, certainly that day I was struck a heavy blow so that I might fall here and for ever; but the Lord spared me, a stranger in a foreign land for His name's sake. . . .' The situation which we have to imagine, it seems, is that at a meeting in Britain Patrick and at least one other were being discussed as candidates for episcopacy in Ireland. Patrick was already a missionary (and presumably a priest) in Ireland where he was at the time when the meeting in question took place.[18] His promising case was sabotaged by his friend's treachery.

Patrick's suitability for this position was opposed, it seems, by *aliquantis senioribus meis*. Pursuit of his *seniores* may help our comprehension of Patrick's case. In §§33–46 Patrick gives an emotional account of how he came to realise the nature of his vocation. In §36 he asks 'Unde mihi postmodum donum tam magnum, tam salubre, Deum agnoscere uel diligere, sed ut patriam et parentes amitterem?',[19] 'From where did that gift so great and so salutary afterwards come, the gift of knowing and loving God – but at the cost of losing family and homeland?' Referring first to his *parentes*,[20] he answers himself. 'Et munera multa mihi offerebantur cum fletu et lacrimis, et offendi illos; necnon contra uotum aliquantis de senioribus meis, sed gubernante Deo nullo modo consensi neque adquieui illis – non mea gratia sed Deus qui uincit in me et resistit illis omnibus, ut ego ueneram ad Hibernas gentes euangelium praedicare . . .', 'And I was offered many gifts, with weeping and tears, and I offended them [*parentes*]; and I also acted against the wishes of a number of my elders [*seniores*], but under God's guidance I refused to agree or defer to them – not that it was my grace, it is God who is victorious in me and withstands them all, when I came to the [heathen] peoples of Ireland to preach the gospel . . .'. The situation which we must envisage, I think, is that Patrick (presumably after training for holy orders in his home-region) has decided to go to work in the Irish Church, with the intent to evangelise the heathen. His parents beseech him not to go; and indeed some more senior clergy advise against it. But Patrick, having found his vocation, is not to be dissuaded. The cost of his following his calling was to lose indefinitely *patriam et parentes*.

That this was not a sudden decision on Patrick's part is made clear by §46 which states the point at some length. For our immediate purpose, however, the core of his account is this: 'multi hanc legationem prohibebant, etiam inter se ipsos post tergum meum narrabant – et dicebant, "Iste quare se mittit in periculo inter hostes qui Deum non nouerunt?" –, non ut causa malitiae, sed non sapiebat illis . . .'; 'many tried to prevent this mission and talked among themselves behind my back – and said, "Why is this fellow walking into danger among enemies who do not know God?" –, not that they were being malicious, but they did not like the idea . . .'.

18 Cf. discussion above, pp. 25–8.

19 On the force of *amitterem*, cf. the parallel instances cited in n. 14, above.

20 This seems to be the natural interpretation, but it has not usually been taken so.

It is clear, then, that there was opposition in his homeland to Patrick's idea of carrying the gospel to the heathen Irish. Later, when at about the age of forty-five he was being considered for the episcopacy,[21] this same opposition formed (we may conjecture) the basis of the case against him. If so, we may suppose not merely that British *seniores*, presumably bishops, were appointing to a diocese in Ireland but that this was not perceived as a missionary bishopric. What made Patrick's position disturbingly revolutionary was that (as E. A. Thompson has deduced) he proposed to lead his Church into evangelistic endeavour among the Gaelic heathen.[22]

When Pope Celestine appointed Palladius as bishop of the Irish christians in A.D. 431, he must have given some thought to the question of the constitutional position of the new diocese. In as much as the impetus to the appointment seems to have come from the state of affairs in Britain two years earlier,[23] we may suspect that a natural option for him would have been to attach it to one of the British provinces. Already by the year 314 we see evidence for a structured Church in the Roman part of the island of Britain, in as much as in the proceedings of the Council of Arles we find subscriptions of a bishop of York (*Eborius episcopus de ciuitate Eboracensi*) and one of London (*Restitutus episcopus de ciuitate Londinensi*),[24] as well as a bishop (Adelfius) of an unknown *colonia*, perhaps Lincoln. All of these are described as coming from *prouincia Britania*, which is clearly an ecclesiastical province.[25] From then until the 430s we have no reason to think of the British Church(es) as other than regularly organised and in full communion and contact with the rest of christendom[26] – save in so far as political difficulties and outbreaks of heresy might introduce complications. However, we know nothing of its internal hierarchical structures – whether, for example, there were archbishops or metropolitans.[27] After the

21 The details of his age are simply calculated from *Confessio*, §27. He was, he thought, not (quite?) yet fifteen when he committed a sin which, (at least) thirty years later, was held against him. Cf. p. 15, above.

22 Thompson, *Who was Saint Patrick?*, pp. 79–102.

23 Cf. discussion above, pp. 1–12, 81.

24 This is the name which, in the later literature of Irish (and especially Patrician) hagiology, is used for that of St Secundinus's father: cf. pp. 98, n. 69, and 104, above.

25 For the *acta* see *Conciles gaulois du IVe siècle*, ed. & transl. Gaudemet, pp. 35–67. These subscriptions are printed on p. 60.

26 *Councils*, edd. Haddan & Stubbs, I.1–40, remains the fundamental (if yet incomplete) collection of materials bearing on this point, even though it is padded somewhat with mediaeval *testimonia* of no value.

27 Haddan & Stubbs, *Councils*, I.10, n. a, raised by implication the position of Britain within a larger ecclesiastical sphere. Referring to Sulpicius Seuerus's account of the Council of Rimini (A.D. 359) at which British bishops were present, they wrote that ' "Galliæ" here, as in Lactantius above quoted (p. 6), includes Britain'. Whether that be the case or not, the bishops at the Council of Arles in 314 were referred to as belonging to a *prouincia Britania* (n. 25, above) and their subscriptions were placed between those of bishops from the provinces of Gaul and Spain (the observation of Haddan & Stubbs, *Councils*, I.7, that their signatures are 'included among those of the Bishops of Gaul' is mistaken). If Britain had, in the last century of Roman rule, been administratively part of the Church of Gaul, that would have interesting implications for the activities of Germanus and Palladius in 429–37; but I can find no convincing evidence to support the basic premise.

430s and the second visit of Germanus of Auxerre,[28] nothing is clear for a century. When Gildas, writing his *De excidio Britanniae* perhaps *ca* 540,[29] offers us information, the situation seems to have changed significantly. Patrick's mature years stand at an uncertain point in that century of transition. If we suppose that Pope Celestine assigned the diocese of Ireland to the British ecclesiastical province, we can indeed imagine that British bishops would have had significant influence in the choice of Palladius's eventual successor. But who, in the British circumstances of the half-century from *ca* 440, would have constituted the bishops of the British province? Indeed, by this stage, might there have been more than one ecclesiastical province? – and, if so, which would have inherited responsibility for the Irish bishopric? Furthermore, at what point would the question have arisen of constituting more than one Irish see? None of these questions can be answered but they all point legitimately to potential complications – in the historical development of the Churches of the British Isles – with which we must reckon in any attempt to comprehend Patrick's circumstances.

In so far as we see the British Church involved in the government (and, from Patrick's time, in the missionary transformation) of the Irish Church, we must suppose that significant numbers of British clergy were committed to pastoral work in Ireland. Furthermore, we have seen reason to think that there was a British community in Ireland which arose partly from slave-raiding but perhaps also from commercial and other natural relationships between neighbouring islands.[30] And Gildas's words about the early effects of Anglo-Saxon invasion could be understood to refer to British migration not merely to the Continent but also to Ireland.[31] All in all, whatever the Continental contribution to the growth of Irish christianity may have been, we have every reason to think that from the outset Britons would have played a large part in the building of the Irish Church.

Before we leave Patrick, one further question demands to be put. There have been many attempts to identify his birthplace, his *patria*, and thus to define the geographical source of the British mission to Ireland. It is not quite clear that this procedure is logical, for it supposes a very localised origin for Patrick's Church and the British contribution to Ireland. Nevertheless, two areas have been pushed forward in the modern literature of the subject (to say nothing of

28 On the date of Germanus's second visit to Britain, see Wood, 'The end of Roman Britain: Continental evidence', pp. 8–17, and Thompson, *Saint Germanus*, pp. 55–70.

29 On the date of the *De excidio* see Dumville, 'The chronology', for a review. I have seen nothing convincing in the attempts to move Gildas's life and work to a significantly earlier date. Those which rely – however reasonably – on comparison and contrast with Continental Latin authors of the fifth and sixth centuries automatically make unverifiable assumptions thereby about the development of British social and ecclesiastical institutions and literary culture in a context for which we have no direct evidence. Such arguments from silence are in effect of the same sort as those made by R. P. C. Hanson to justify a dubiously early date for St Patrick's floruit.

30 See above, pp. 27–8 and 107–27.

31 On this possibility see Dumville, 'The chronology', pp. 73–5, commenting on Thompson, 'Gildas' (and *ibid.*, p. 209, for British colonists in Ireland). Kenney, *The Sources*, pp. 170 and 171, long ago considered the possibility of British exiles in Ireland. Nor should we forget in this context the brilliant, if now discarded, hypothesis of fifth-century Continental scholars' migration to Ireland put forward by Meyer, *Learning*.

what mediaeval hagiographers attempted to do). The lands on either side of the Bristol Channel have proved a favourite in this regard and indeed a case is made for the southern shore in the present volume.[32] On the other hand, a northerly location has been advanced, and in particular the Carlisle region.[33] The only credible specific argument in favour of this source of British missionary efforts in Ireland derives from consideration of the area of Patrick's work there. If it be conceded that Patrick's mission was directed specifically and exclusively to the north of Ireland (leaving the remainder as the preserve of one or more other bishops), then a case may exist for allowing a north British source for that endeavour. How one would set out to prove such a situation is not clear. It may not be especially controversial to say that Patrick laboured – and died – in Ulster, being buried perhaps at Downpatrick (Dún Lethglaisse) itself.[34] But to present that as an exclusive proposition is altogether another matter. Ulster may have been the missionary front-line in Patrick's last years. He may have been active in several parts of the island. If he was sole bishop for Ireland, he could have travelled and preached very widely across the country. To argue back to Britain for deductions about developments in fifth-century Ireland is to try to explain *ignotum per ignotius*.

Nothing is known of Patrick's British contemporaries in Ireland. Although he must have had a staff of priests and lesser clergy, some (at least) of whom are likely to have been Britons, he never names one. Those persons of latinate name with whom he is associated in later sources are at least as likely to have been Continentals as Britons.[35] Auxilius, Iserninus, and Secundinus might have been British,[36] but nothing is otherwise known about them save that in Patrician hagiography they are represented as having been ordained in Gaul:[37] we have no means of dating them within reasonable limits or of understanding their role in Irish Church-history.[38] Among members of the Irish Church who were subsequently reputed to be associated with Patrick is perhaps one hope: Maucteus, St Mochta, who has been discussed above in connexion with problems of Patrician chronology, seems to have been a Briton whose name was already linked to Patrick's before the late seventh century[39] – but the gap remains long.

St Maucteus, if he was a pupil of St Patrick and lived on into the 530s, bridges another gap – that between the Patrician era itself and the period from which we next have contemporary evidence about Hiberno-British contacts, the middle of the sixth century. Much modern (and indeed mediaeval) writing on the subject has long been coloured by the schematic presentation of historical periodisation offered by a text known as *Catalogus sanctorum Hiberniae per*

32 See the remarks of K. R. Dark, above, pp. 19–24.

33 Thomas, 'Saint Patrick and fifth-century Britain', and *Christianity*, pp. 310–14. (For the method, cf. n. 63, below.) For Thompson's comments on this see *Who was Saint Patrick?*, p. 10(–11), n. 8.

34 On this, cf. below, pp. 147–52, 183–9.

35 See above, pp. 89–105.

36 But there are linguistic difficulties in respect of both Iserninus and Secundinus.

37 Muirchú, *Vita S. Patricii*, I.9 (8), and its derivatives.

38 On the question of their possible association with Bishop Palladius, see above, pp. 65–84.

39 See above, pp. 54–7.

diuersa tempora which may have been written *ca* A.D. 900.[40] This text describes three *ordines* of *sancti* in Ireland, with changes occurring *ca* 550 and *ca* 600:[41] the first two *ordines* are presented as under British influence, the former led by St Patrick and the latter receiving a mass from SS. David, Gildas, and Doccus.[42] The implication of this text is that the monastic movement took root in Ireland from Britain: on the evidence of contemporary sources beginning with Patrick himself, there is little reason to quarrel with this.[43] Amid the British ecclesiastical practices introduced into Ireland was a naming-method, involving the use of hypocoristic prefixes and suffixes, which may have been a peculiarly monastic fashion.[44]

Uinniau, shown by his name to be a Briton, was resident in Ireland in the middle of the sixth century.[45] We have a penitential attributed to him and fragments of a letter which Gildas wrote in reply to a request from Uinniau for advice on certain problems of monastic discipline. What happened to memory of him in Ireland is a warning of what may lurk beneath the surface of other Gaelic hagiological evidence. Before *ca* 700 he had been naturalised in two widely separated Irish locations:[46] at Clonard in Meath he became a saint of a local tribe, moccu Telduib; at Moville (Mag Bile) in Co. Down he was adopted by moccu Fiatach, Dál Fiatach, one of the principal peoples of the Ulaid. Uinniau thus became an Irishman, or rather two Irishmen, with two localisations, two pedigrees and therefore separate identities, and two different sixth-century chronologies.[47] Something similar may have happened to St Cairnech whose history is not well attested but who is also found localised in Meath and Ulster and with two different chronologies.[48]

On both sides of the Irish Sea (as also in Brittany) the subsequent historiographical idealogy of the 'Age of the Saints' gave rise to doctrines or assump-

40 'Édition', ed. Grosjean.

41 For discussion see Hughes, *The Church in Early Irish Society*, pp. 69–70, 72, 79.

42 The identification of Doccus has always been a problem: Kenney, *The Sources*, p. 172; Morris, 'The dates of the Celtic saints', pp. 372–3; Brooke, *The Church and the Welsh Border*, pp. 80–1 (cf. p. 85, n. 157). Although Hughes (*The Church in Early Irish Society*, p. 70) observed that 'The author of the Catalogue used sources like those available to the men who compiled the annals' found in the 'Chronicle of Ireland' at about the same time, the two texts' treatments of St Doccus are incompatible. For the death of Doccus in 473 see *The Annals of Ulster*, edd. & transl. Mac Airt & Mac Niocaill, I.50/1: 'Quies Docci episcopi sancti Britonum abbatis'.

43 Hughes, *The Church in Early Irish Society*, pp. 71–4, was remarkably unwilling to admit this conclusion, and for no readily apparent reasons.

44 Cf. Dumville, 'Some British aspects', pp. 19–20, and the references given there.

45 On all this, cf. Dumville, 'Gildas and Uinniau'.

46 The dating depends on the use of the obsolescent *moccu* formula for localisation: MacNeill, 'Mocu, maccu'.

47 See Ó Riain, 'St Finnbarr: a study in a cult', for yet other manifestations of Uinniau in Irish hagiology.

48 St Cairnech ('the Cornishman', according to Kenney, *The Sources*, pp. 180, 352), otherwise St Cernach (according to Carney, *Studies*, pp. 407–12), identified not later than the twelfth century with St Carannog (Old Welsh *Carantoc*): for further discussion, see Kenney, *The Sources*, pp. 172, 180, 350–2. Whether there is an historical figure to be found beneath all this must be open to some doubt. The better documented case of Uinniau allows that point to be argued in either direction.

tions about the free movement and settlement of saints between and in the various Celtic lands.[49] This, combined with what appears to have been an almost complete collapse of knowledge about the period before the mid-sixth-century plagues,[50] makes it difficult to draw conclusions about the travels of individual ecclesiastics. For example, the hagiography of St Gildas,[51] as also a late text of *Annales Cambriae*,[52] takes him to Ireland. The hagiography contributes the interesting idea that there was a serious pagan reaction and widespread apostasy in Ireland after Patrick's time – by no means an incredible notion but one for which an eleventh-century *uita* is hardly acceptable evidence – which Gildas helped to overcome.[53] That Gildas might have gone to Ireland is by no means incredible. His death is recorded at 570 in the earliest recoverable stratum of the 'Chronicle of Ireland'.[54] In Ireland he was taken to be an authority in matters of ecclesiastical discipline from his own time to at least the eighth century.[55] Nevertheless, none of this requires the conclusion that he ever set foot on Irish soil.

By the time of the earliest Irish hagiography, in the second half of the seventh century, a number of companions or associates of the saints thus memorialised – the *trias thaumaturga* of Patrick, Brigit, and Columba – was already shown as associated in one way or another with British ecclesiastics.[56] We have already mentioned the case of St Mochta in Adomnán's Life of St Columba, where Uinniau is also presented as teacher of Columba.[57] In the Lives of St Brigit, Mel, bishop of Ardagh, is a prominent figure who is described as a Briton.[58] Whether by imitation and extension of such examples or simply by use of knowledge of the British origins of certain early ecclesiastics, the appearance of British *sancti*

49 Expounded most enthusiastically in modern times by Chadwick, *The Age of the Saints*, and Bowen, *The Settlements*. My O'Donnell Lecture in the University of Wales (publication forthcoming) was devoted to a reconsideration of this question.

50 Cf. Hughes, *The Church in Early Irish Society*, pp. 64–6.

51 *Gildas*, ed. & transl. Williams, II.315–413, for the two *uitae* in question.

52 *Annales Cambriæ*, ed. Williams (Ab Ithel), p. 5, for the entry from the B-text (*ca* A.D. 1300), apparently relating to the year 565: 'Nauigacio Gilde in Hibernia'. For more detail on the B-text, and on its connexions with hagiography, see below, pp. 279–88.

53 For this episode, see *Vita I S. Gildae*, §§10–13 (*Gildas*, ed. & transl. Williams, II.338–43), where the king of Ireland is represented as one Ainmericus – presumably derived from the genitive of mediaeval Irish Ainmire; a king by this name died in the 560s or 570s and was father of a well known Uí Néill king of Tara, Aed (cf. Mac Niocaill, *Ireland before the Vikings*, pp. 70–2). For Gildas in Ireland in *Vita II* (by Caradog of Llancarfan), see §§4–5 (*Gildas*, ed. & transl. Williams, II.400–3): it does not contain the more colourful story offered in *Vita I*; for its story of the reason for Gildas's departure for Ireland, the impending birth of St David, which in the hagiography of St David was told of Patrick's departure, see below, pp. 279–88.

54 *The Annals of Ulster*, edd. & transl. Mac Airt & Mac Niocaill, I.84/5 (570.3: 'Gillas obiit'); 'The Annals of Roscrea', edd. Gleeson & Mac Airt, p. 147 (§48: 'Gillas'); *The Annals of Inisfallen*, ed. & transl. Mac Airt, pp. 74/5 (*s.a.* [567]: 'Quies Gilldais epscoip').

55 Cf. Sharpe, 'Gildas as a Father'.

56 *Vita I S. Samsonis*, whose date is highly controversial, has also sometimes been assigned to the second half of the seventh century (a rival attribution to the first half of that century is on any reckoning incredible). For its testimony to links between Britain and Ireland – and in particular the creation of a 'federation' of churches across the sea, cf. Hughes, *The Church in Early Irish Society*, pp. 72–3, 76–7.

57 See above, pp. 54–7, 139–40.

58 *Trias Thaumaturga*, ed. Colgan, pp. 527, 546, 567–8, for example.

became more widespread in subsequent Irish hagiography and notably in that of St Patrick. In the 'Book of Armagh', for example, we meet St Lommanus, founder of Trim (Áth Truim) in Meath, who is presented quite graphically as a Briton.[59] Later, in the Tripartite Life of St Patrick, one of the Britons encountered is Malach Brit of Cell Malaich in the territory of the Déisi deiscirt.[60] Such examples could be multiplied from the hagiography of Patrick and other Irish saints.

From the seventh century onwards we can see that a number of Irish ecclesiastical bodies commemorated a British founder, called their churches 'of the Britons',[61] or enjoyed links with particular British communities. The ties which we find expressed in the hagiography therefore had some contemporary resonance, whether general or specific, in early and central mediaeval Ireland. We find such transmarine links reciprocated in Brittonic hagiography, although most of the relevant texts date from no earlier than the late eleventh and twelfth centuries.[62] In addition to the general historiographic ideology which dictated the portrayal of Hiberno-British saintly connexions,[63] we have reason to think

59 *Additamenta*, §§1–4: *The Patrician Texts*, edd. & transl. Bieler & Kelly, pp. 166–71. Cf. O'Rahilly, *The Two Patricks*, p. 76; Byrne, 'A note'.

60 *The Tripartite Life*, ed. & transl. Stokes, I.198/9.

61 See for example, the cases of Dairmag (Durrow) in Southern Brega and Gailinne (Gallen, Co. Offaly): *The Annals of Ulster*, edd. & transl. Mac Airt & Mac Niocaill, I.294/5 (*s.a.* 836.7, 'Prima praeda gentilium o deisciurt Bregh, .i. o Telcaibh Droman ocus o Dermaigh Britonum, et captiuos plures portauerunt et mortificauerunt multos et captiuos plurimos apstulerunt', where Durrow is called 'of the Britons' presumably to distinguish it from other Durrows farther south) and I.280/1 (*s.a.* 823.9, 'Galinne na mBretan exha<u>stum est o Feidlimtidh cum tota habitatione sua et cum oratorio'). Elsewhere in that text we find comparable epithets being applied to persons with (in at least one instance) no implication of British nationality: *ibid.*, I.206/7, *s.a.* 751.6, 'Mors Colman na mBretan maic Faelain abbatis Slaine' (it was presumably Colmán rather than Faelán who was abbot of Slane [Co. Meath]; for a Colmán na mBretan, see *Additamenta*, §11 [4], edd. & transl. Bieler & Kelly, *The Patrician Texts*, pp. 174/5); *ibid.*, I.320/1, *s.a.* 864.5, 'Aedgen Britt, episcopus Cille Daro et scriba et anchorita et senex fere .cxvi. annorum, pausauit' (but cf. 865.2, 'Cellach mac Ailella, abbas Cille Daro et abbas Ia, dormiuit in regione Pictorum', which might hint why an official of Kildare could at that time be called British). On British clerics and their foundations, cf. Smyth, *Celtic Leinster*, p. 9.

62 St Gildas (nn. 51–55, above) and St Samson (n. 56, above), have already been mentioned. The Welsh *uitae sanctorum* (most may be found in *Vitae*, edd. & transl. Wade-Evans) in which the British saint is given an Irish connexion are those of Cadog, Carannog (see above, n. 48), Cybi, and Padarn (Paternus, whose father, Petranus, had already gone to Ireland as a religious exile).

63 We should note also the ties which are said to have bound Whithorn (Old English *Hwitærn*, Latin *Candida Casa*) in Galloway to Irish churches: for a straightforward assertion of this, see Mac Niocaill, *Ireland before the Vikings*, p. 24. However, the Hiberno-Latin *uitae* in which the connexion is found – those of Abbess Darerca-Moninna of Killeevy (Co. Armagh), Énda of Aran (Co. Galway), Eogan of Ardstraw (Co. Tyrone), and Tigernach of Clones (Co. Monaghan), for which see *Vitae*, ed. Plummer, II.62–3 (Énda, §§6–7), 68–9 (Énda, §20), 263 (Tigernach, §4), and *Vitae*, ed. Heist, pp. 91 (Darerca, §25), 108 (Tigernach, §4, as above), 400–1 (Eogan, §§1–2) – do not refer clearly to Whithorn, but rather to a place called Rosnat, Rostat, and Rostnat, a *monasterium* (also called *Alba* according to the Life of St Tigernach) whose holy man was one Monend/Monenn, or – in the Life of St Eogan of Ardstraw – 'uir sanctus ac sapiens Nennyo, qui Maucennus dicitur'. The identification with Whithorn has proceeded from the identification of this 'Nennyo' (Middle Welsh Nynniaw) with St Ninian

that specific ties bound Llancarfan and Mynyw (St Davids) to Irish churches.[64] Unfortunately, evidence does not survive to allow us to say whether such connexions were very old or continuous to the tenth-century point of record. And there may have been many such specific links between communities, of which no traces have been identified.

The hagiography on the whole reflects a general ecclesiastical culture which allowed – and even in some measure celebrated – the significant British element in the origins and formation of Irish christianity. It admitted too the continuing interaction with churchmen from neighbouring Brittonic regions.[65] Such continuing relationships do not rely for their documentation on hagiography, however. Chronicle-evidence, for example, points to the continuing presence of British ecclesiastics in Ireland,[66] something which remained the case throughout the period before the twelfth century brought so many changes on both sides of the Irish Sea.[67] But a wider range of evidence testifies to the changes in relationships and attitudes which inevitably developed with time.

That missionary conditions created some uncontrolled enthusiasm among British ecclesiastics for work in Ireland may be suggested by a clause in that problematic and undated text, *Synodus episcoporum*: 'A cleric who comes from the Britons without letters, even though he be resident in the *plebs*, is not allowed to minister'. Whether the canon dates from the fifth century or the

---

(Nynia) of Whithorn, and no doubt from the observation that the relevant *uitae* are all of saints of the north of Ireland. The identification was demolished by Wilson, 'St. Ninian and Candida Casa' and 'St. Ninian: Irish evidence'. Attempting to pick up the pieces, Thomas, '*Rosnat*', proposed that that *monasterium* should instead be identified with a site at Tintagel (Cornwall) – contrary to the geographical procedure which he adopted in seeking the origins of St Patrick's mission (see n. 33, above); however, the collapse of the ecclesiastical interpretation of Dark-Age Tintagel (cf. Burrow, 'Tintagel', Thomas, 'East and West', and Dark, 'The plan and interpretation of Tintagel', for discussion) effectively removes that rather hopeful identification and makes the *uallis rosina* of Mynyw (St Davids) in Dyfed once again the favourite candidate (cf. Thomas, '*Rosnat*', p. 104). However, a completely different location may await identification: nothing is certain, save that Whithorn is not a credible option; however, see Thomas, *ibid.*, p. 100, and Kenney, *The Sources*, p. 263 (no. 90), for a certain appearance of Whithorn in Irish hagiological legend.

64 For Llancarfan and Clonard, see Hughes, *Church and Society in Ireland*, chapters II–VI, and Brooke, *The Church and the Welsh Border*, pp. 74–81. On Mynyw and Ireland, see for repetition of the claims of mediaeval hagiography Mac Niocaill, *Ireland before the Vikings*, p. 24; for specific contact between St Davids and Clonmacnoise, see Grabowski & Dumville, *Chronicles and Annals*, chapter IV.

65 A relationship between St Patrick and St Mac Cuill moccu Greccae (an Ulsterman), bishop of the Isle of Mann (and specifically bishop of *Arddæ Huimnonn*), was advanced already by Muirchú, *Vita S. Patricii*, I.23 (22), who also noted the claims of Bishops Conindrus and Rumilus as apostles of the island (*The Patrician Texts*, edd. & transl. Bieler & Kelly, pp. 102–7). On Mac Cuill, cf. O'Rahilly, *Early Irish History and Mythology*, pp. 470–1.

66 For an example from A.D. 913, see *The Annals of Ulster*, edd. & transl. Mac Airt & Mac Niocaill, I.360/1: 'Mael Brigte mac Tornáin du techt i mMumain do fhuaslucud ailithir do Bretnaibh', 'Mael Brigte mac Tornáin went to Munster to ransom a Welsh pilgrim'.

67 For the connexions of the family of Sulien of Llanbadarn and Mynyw with Ireland in the late eleventh century, see Lapidge, 'The Welsh-Latin poetry'; cf. Huws, 'A Welsh manuscript of Bede's *De natura rerum*'.

seventh, it is evidence for regulation by bishops of the clergy who minister in their areas of jurisdiction.[68] That British ecclesiastics were available thus should occasion no surprise at either date. As the seventh century wore on, Irish churchmen began to take decisions which put them on collision-course with British colleagues. Two significant bones of contention must have been reactions to Roman and Gaulish pressure on the paschal question and the involvement of Irish missionaries in evangelising the English, the Britons' hated enemies. By the early eighth century the strains are clearly apparent[69] while a century later still one Irish cleric is found writing to another with undisguised contempt for the intellectual capacity of British ecclesiastics.[70]

We may suspect, then, that by or soon after the middle of the seventh century the continuous and full-hearted British contribution to the evangelisation of Ireland and development of Irish christianity had come to an end. As we have seen, there were later and indeed close relationships, but the era in which British ecclesiastical influence was a seminal force in Gaelic christendom was over. That that influence had indeed in its time been fundamental is demonstrable from linguistic evidence above all. In addition to the question of clerical name-formation, mentioned above,[71] and specific evidence of lexical borrowing from Brittonic,[72] there is overwhelming testimony to the impact of British churchmen in two other respects. First, of the very substantial body of Latin loanwords in mediaeval Irish,[73] the greater part has been borrowed in a phonetic shape which shows provenance to have been the lips of Britons.[74] Secondly, the relationship of alphabet to sound-system in Old Irish has indicated that the principal tradition of vernacular literacy in early mediaeval Ireland derives from the adaptation to

68 §33. On this clause, see Hughes, *The Church in Early Irish Society*, p. 49; for more general discussion of the text, see below, pp. 175–8.

69 See *Collectio canonum hibernensis*, XX.6 (*Die irische Kanonensammlung*, ed. Wasserschleben, pp. 61–2): '*De prouinciis et personis deuitandis ad iudicandum.* Institutio Romana: Cauendum, ne ad alias prouincias aut ecclesias referantur causae, quae alio more et alia regione utuntur; siue ad Iudeos qui umbrae magis quam ueritati deseruiunt, aut ad Britones qui omnibus contrarii sunt et a romano more et ab unitate ecclesiae se abscidunt, aut hereticos quamuis in ecclesiasticis causis docti et studiosi fuerint.' The placing of the Britons between Jews and heretics is as eloquent as what is actually said of them. Cf. Hughes, *The Church in Early Irish Society*, p. 49.

70 Derolez, 'Dubthach's cryptogram'.

71 See p. 140.

72 Thurneysen, *A Grammar of Old Irish*, pp. 565–76, for discussion. Cf. Pedersen, *Vergleichende Grammatik*, I.23–4.

73 Güterbock, *Bemerkungen*, and Vendryes, *De hibernicis vocabulis*, remain the principal studies. See also n. 75, below.

74 The major treatment remains that of Jackson, *Language and History*, pp. 122–48. For subsequent discussion see the review by Binchy, *Celtica* 4 (1958) 288–92; cf. Jackson, 'Final syllables'. See also De Búrca, 'The Patricks', and Greene, 'The making of Insular Celtic' and 'Some linguistic evidence'. For refinement before the event see Mulchrone, 'The Old-Irish form of *Palladius*'. More recent controversy was unleashed by Gratwick, 'Latinitas britannica'; cf. Russell, 'Recent work', and McManus, '*Linguarum diversitas*'.

the Irish language of the Latin alphabet as realised phonetically by Britons. There could be no clearer demonstration than these testimonies provide to the formative (but not exclusive) role played by British ecclesiastics in the creation and development of Irish christianity.[75]

[75] Kenneth Jackson used the interaction between British/Brittonic, Latin, and Irish as a means of dating linguistic developments in the Insular Celtic languages. For demolition of a central support of his conclusions, see Harvey, 'The significance of *Cothraige*'. The help which it has been thought that linguistic chronology might give to the solution of historical problems now seems largely illusory. The specificity formerly achieved in linguistic chronology rested on false interpretation of essentially historical evidence. Interpretation of the historical development of both British and Irish in the approximate period A.D. 300–600 is now in flux. For British there are important discussions by Sims-Williams, 'Dating the transition', and in numerous papers by Koch, especially 'The loss of final syllables', 'When was Welsh literature first written down?', and 'The cynfeirdd poetry'; Koch's direct contribution to the Patrician question, '**Cothairche*, Esposito's theory', whatever its linguistic merits, is however a great step backwards in terms of historical method. Cf. Schmidt, 'Late British'. For Irish, see McManus, 'A chronology of the Latin loan-words', 'On final syllables', 'The so-called *Cothrige* and *Pátraic* strata', 'Ogam', and *A Guide to Ogam*; Harvey, 'The ogam inscriptions', 'Early literacy in Ireland', 'Some significant points', and 'Latin, literacy and the Celtic vernaculars'; Stevenson, 'The beginnings'. However, to speak of the arrival (at least on the Irish side) of an 'emerging orthodoxy' (as Harvey has done, 'Early literacy in Ireland', p. 15, n. 53) is to mistake the enthusiasm of the moment for a promised land which still seems far off.

EMAIN MACHA, ARD MACHA

Armagh presents a number of difficulties to the student of fifth-century Ireland. When was that church founded which would in time become the head of christianity in the island? Why was Armagh chosen as the site for a church-foundation? What is the nature of the connexion between Armagh and St Patrick?

To the first question mediaeval sources offer us conflicting testimony, but none of it inspires confidence. The probably early eighth-century *additamenta* to Tírechán's *Collectanea* in the 'Book of Armagh' record in §1 the foundation of Áth Truimm (Trim, Co. Meath), apparently in the first year of Patrick's mission and therefore (by the traditional chronology) in A.D. 432;[1] this is described as having occurred 'uigesimo quinto anno antequam fundata esset aeclessia Alti Machae', 'in the twenty-fifth year before the church of Armagh was founded'.[2] This date was taken over into the 'Annals of the Four Masters'.[3] On the other hand, the 'Annals of Ulster' refer this event to the year 444:[4] 'Ard Macha fundata est: ab Urbe condita usque ad hanc ciuitatem fundatam .m.cxc.iiii.'. The Clonmacnoise-group texts have nothing to say on the matter, and this has led to the not unreasonable deduction that the entry in the 'Annals of Ulster' was written after A.D. 911:[5] indeed, on this basis one might go so far as to say that it was written at Armagh between 911 and 1166.[6] Here, therefore, is no information which could with any plausibility be used for writing fifth-century history.

The dating of the establishment of the church of Armagh, as perhaps also the answer to the next question, is a matter for archaeology. One cannot therefore expect that a very precise chronological conclusion is likely to be achieved,

1 §§1–4 of the *Additamenta* deal with Trim: see *The Patrician Texts*, edd. & transl. Bieler & Kelly, pp. 166–71. The dating has been established by study of the Irish linguistic forms: *ibid.*, pp. 246–8.

2 *Ibid.*, pp. 168/9; comment on p. 236.

3 *Annale Rioghachta Eireann*, ed. O'Donovan, I.142/3 (*s.a.* 457).

4 *The Annals of Ulster*, edd. & transl. Mac Airt & Mac Niocaill, I.42/3. The 'Annals from the Book of Leinster' offer the same opening four words (*The Book of Leinster*, edd. Best *et al.*, I.94) but are (given their lack of an explicit chronology and thin scatter of entries) ambiguous as to the date intended: either 444 or 457 is possible. *Annales Cambriae* (A) were once thought to begin with 444, therefore the year of the foundation of Armagh, and some significance was attached to this (notwithstanding the absence of the entry itself): more recently it has become apparent that the opening year is 445 (cf. Miller, 'The final stages'), and the association with that foundation has been quietly dropped.

5 Binchy, 'Patrick and his biographers', pp. 150–1, reporting the views of John V. Kelleher. For the principles by which the contents of the 'Chronicle of Ireland' may be established, see Grabowski & Dumville, *Chronicles and Annals*, chapters I–II, and chapter I for the date 911.

6 I use 1166 here as the date of the 'Book of Leinster'.

unless some extraordinarily good luck should be experienced.[7] As matters stand, we see pre-christian Armagh as a pagan religious site which had at some date before the seventh century been transformed into an ecclesiastical establishment aligned with the cult of St Patrick.[8] There is no historical evidence which can credibly associate Bishop Patrick himself with Armagh, nor any which tells us that there was a church there (whether devoted to St Patrick or not) in the sixth. Eventually archaeology should be able to fill the sixth-century lacuna, but – save for the possibility of discovery of an exceptionally informative inscription of fifth-century date – it is unlikely ever to be able to provide us with more than a balance of probabilities concerning Patrick's alleged connexion with Armagh. What we are already offered by physical survival, however, is a view of a pagan sanctuary of some importance.[9] The same message about the site's pre-christian function seems to come from literary sources – ranging from the testimony of Muirchú's *Vita S. Patricii* to that of vernacular saga and toponymic aetiology in the late Old Irish period.[10] It must remain unclear, of course, to what extent such sources can have been well informed about pre-christian Armagh and whether we can speak with conviction about a goddess Machae who was culted at Ard Macha and Emain Macha.

The toponymic association of Armagh (Ard Macha) and Navan (Emain Macha) naturally leads to a search for a connexion of function. As yet, this remains to be demonstrated. Both sites have been provisionally interpreted as pre-christian ritual sites, but without its being clear that they were in use contemporaneously. As a result, the theory has been put forward that Ard Macha succeeded Emain Macha in this role.[11] This is likely to remain a matter for speculation, however well meaning or well informed, for some considerable time to come. Emain Macha is a complex and substantial site of which only two relatively small portions have been excavated: the results, of which details are beginning to emerge into print, are of the greatest interest but seem to leave considerable scope for interpretation.[12] For the present purpose the historian needs to know what the site was used for, if it was used at all, in the fourth, fifth, and sixth centuries A.D.. The historian's secondary requirement is some sense of whether any earlier function would have left traces which might have given rise to local legends about the site. At some point not later than the beginning of the Old Irish linguistic period Emain Macha had become the focus of a cycle of heroic stories about a prehistoric kingdom of the Ulaid which occupied much of northernmost Ireland and whose capital it is presented as having been.[13] It remains to be seen whether this association of Ulidian capital and Emain Macha is more than literary. That the site shares physical features, possible pagan ritual

7 The best hope is no doubt that some timber may be recovered which will allow dendrochronological dating: for an example of the remarkable achievements for Ireland of the Belfast Palaeoecology Centre, see Baillie, 'The central post from Navan Fort'.

8 For a statement of this position, see Sharpe, 'St Patrick and the see of Armagh', pp. 44–59.

9 *Ibid.*, pp. 53–4; cf. Rynne, 'Celtic stone idols in Ireland'.

10 Lambkin, 'Patrick, Armagh, and Emain Macha'; but cf. Lynn & McDowell, 'Muirchú's Armagh'.

11 Cf. Sharpe, 'St Patrick and the see of Armagh', p. 54.

12 Lynn, 'Navan Fort. A draft summary'.

13 For an introduction to the literature of the 'Ulster Cycle' see Knott & Murphy, *Early Irish Literature*, pp. 114–31.

use in prehistory, and legendary associations as a royal centre, with a number of other famous complex monuments elsewhere in Ireland – notably Tara (Temair) in Meath, Rathcroghan (Cruachain) in Connaught, and Knockaulin (Dún Ailinne) in Leinster – is a circumstance which has greatly complicated interpretation of the history of each.[14]

In the case of Emain Macha, historical thinking has suffered from diversions created by literary sources created to serve mediaeval political objectives. The most potent of all has been the ninth-century origin-legend of the Airgialla, containing the story of the Three Collas.[15] The Three Collas, ancestors of Airgiallan royalty, destroyed the Ulaid in a military campaign and forced them to retreat eastwards. (The work of reduction of the ancient province of Ulaid was then finished by Niall Noígiallach and his sons to whom the Airgialla were subject allies.) It is clear that this text reflects the circumstances which obtained after the battle of Leth Cam in 827, at which the Northern Uí Néill finally triumphed over the Airgialla[16] and thus completed their dominance of what was perceived as the ancient fifth, or province, of the Ulaid (save for the relatively narrow strip of east-coast territory occupied by Dál Fiatach, Dál nAraide, and Dál Riata, now collectively described as Ulaid). There is no message to be extrapolated from this about fifth-century (or earlier) affairs.

The anterior political situation envisaged by the Airgiallan origin-legend was one in which the Ulaid dominated Ireland north of a band of territory stretching from Connaught to Leinster and which was ruled from Tara. This was the political geography of the Old-Irish 'Ulster Cycle' of tales.[17] It is, however, a view which gives no comprehensive definition of the province's internal structure. In other words, we are not able to tell whether it was envisaged as a complex polity of the sort seen generally in early mediaeval Ireland, in which each province would have contained many *tuatha*, petty kingdoms, and a small number of *mórthuatha*, mesne kingdoms comprising an aggregation of *tuatha*. This is a crucial difficulty for our understanding of both the context in which the political geography of northern Ireland was given literary definition in the 'Ulster Cycle' and the early mediaeval history of that region.

The researches of the last generation have suggested that a critical turning point in the history of the Ulaid in the early middle ages was the battle of Mag Rath (Moira, Co. Down) in 637.[18] It was from this moment that the Ulaid were

14 Wailes, 'The Irish "royal sites" '.

15 'The oldest account', ed. & transl. O'Brien (cf. *Irish Origin Legends*, ed. O'Brien, pp. 9–16, and *Corpus*, ed. O'Brien, I.147–51). For a dating of the text to *ca* 900, see O'Brien, 'Irish origin-legends', p. 50; this has been modified slightly by Sharpe, 'St Patrick and the see of Armagh', p. 51, n. 74. Later versions of the origin-legend explicitly mention the destruction of Emain Macha: O'Rahilly, *Early Irish History and Mythology*, pp. 226–7; Byrne, *Irish Kings*, p. 74.

16 Sharpe, 'St Patrick and the see of Armagh', pp. 51–2. For Leth Cam, see *The Annals of Ulster*, edd. & transl. Mac Airt & Mac Niocaill, I.284/5 (*s.a.* 827.4): it should be noted that Ulaid and Airgialla were united against Uí Néill in this battle. For discussion of the context, see Ó Corráin, *Ireland before the Normans*, pp. 16–17.

17 Cf. *The Táin*, transl. Kinsella, pp. xiii–xiv, xvii–xxiii, for helpful mapping.

18 It must be said, however, that these new perceptions are not solidly based on first-class evidence: consultation of the 'Annals of Ulster' for A.D. 637 will show how little our earliest chronicle-source tells us about the battle. For discussion see Byrne, *Irish Kings*, pp. 112–14 (cf. 257);

effectively excluded from contention for the kingship of Tara,[19] presumably to be taken as the overkingship of the provinces of the 'Northern Half' of Ireland.[20] Henceforth, we may suppose, the relationships of the Ulaid (in the sense of Dál Fiatach, Dál nAraide, and Dál Fiatach) and the Airgialla would become particularly delicate.

It might be argued that it was in this political context that the principal political story-line of the 'Ulster-Cycle' tales was created. If the province of the Ulaid did once extend across the whole of northernmost Ireland, from Down to Donegal (to say nothing of more southerly districts) – and this has been assumed rather than argued or demonstrated – then that province seems to have been under sustained military assault and colonisation – at least in the west – through the sixth century.[21] The Northern Uí Néill had begun a process of conquest which was to culminate in 827 at the battle of Leth Cam. The Southern Uí Néill, by virtue of the damage which they had inflicted on the Laigin,[22] had become the principal contenders for the kingship of Tara and therefore major enemies of the Ulaid: to that extent we must see them as an important military and political threat to the Ulaid from the south. After 637 the Ulaid would have felt particularly beleaguered. In such circumstances the creation (albeit in part from traditional materials) of a legend of an Ulidian heroic age,[23] in which the province stood successfully (and notwithstanding the defection of some of its leading men to the enemy) against the might of the rest of Ireland, might seem an understandaable reaction. The church of Bangor (Co. Down), founded (according to the 'Annals of Ulster') in 555 or 559, has of course been seen as having a major role in the development and literary dissemination of this legend.[24]

For the present purpose, what is of interest is the role assigned in the 'Ulster Cycle' of tales to Emain Macha itself. That it could be presented as the capital of a great province when it was in the seventh and later centuries not part of the territory of Dál Fiatach (or the other two peoples of the Ulaid as now narrowly defined) must be a significant fact. Either Emain Macha had long been perceived as having occupied this role and present political realities could be ignored, or the promotion of this literary polity constituted an appeal by the

---

Mac Niocaill, *Ireland before the Vikings*, pp. 95–7; Sharpe, 'St Patrick and the see of Armagh', p. 58; Dumville, 'Cath Fedo Euin'.

19 Byrne, *Irish Kings*, pp. 112–17; cf. *Bechbretha*, edd. & transl. Charles-Edwards & Kelly, pp. 123–31, for a discussion of very great importance.

20 For discussion of the nature of the kingship of Tara, a controversial subject, see Byrne, *The Rise of the Uí Néill*, and *Irish Kings*, pp. 48–69.

21 See Byrne, *ibid.*, pp. 83–4, for a rather unsatisfactory account. Historians have usually not discussed this process in anything but the most general terms. But cf. MacNeill, 'Colonisation'.

22 Cf. Smyth, 'The Húi Néill and the Leinsterman', 'Húi Failgi relations', and *Celtic Leinster*.

23 For recent discussion, see Dumville, ' "Beowulf" and the Celtic world', pp. 132–55; Aitchison, 'The Ulster Cycle: heroic image'; Carney, 'Three Old Irish accentual poems', pp. 73–80, and 'Early Irish literature'; Olmsted, 'The earliest narrative version of the *Táin*'.

24 For the foundation, see *The Annals of Ulster*, edd. & transl. Mac Airt & Mac Niocaill, I.78–81; for the death of the founder, St Comgall, in 602, see *ibid.*, I.100/1. On the role of Bangor see the speculations of Flower, *The Irish Tradition*, pp. 1–23; Mac Cana, 'Mongán mac Fiachna and *Immram Brain*'.

Ulaid to the Airgialla (and the Conaille Muirthemne, who have a crucial role in the 'Ulster Cycle') to maintain or return to ancient political alliances, or the political realities of seventh- and eighth-century Ulster have been misunderstood.

It has been the custom of historians studying early mediaeval Ireland to work on the assumption that the Ulaid and the Airgialla had been separated politically not later than the fifth century. Indeed the relationship implied by juxtaposition of the names Ulaid and Airgialla has been projected back into prehistory. It is by no means clear, however, when or in what circumstances the name Airgialla was given to the peoples of mid-Ulster; it is dangerous to assume its extreme antiquity, for what is then effectively an attribution of origin is bound to colour views of subsequent history. That Airgialla are found associated with Dál Riata in the Gaelic colonies in North Britain may be an indication of weakness in the received history of the Airgialla.[25] Between 637 and 827 the political situation of the Airgiallan peoples was no doubt exceptionally sensitive. Before the end of the seventh century we can see one of them, the Airthir, explicitly associated with Uí Néill:[26] Armagh and Navan lay in the territory of the Airthir, and it is significant that we can see the church of Armagh adjusting its stance towards the Uí Néill kings of Tara in the second half of the century.[27] However, before 637 the situation may have been very different. Without good evidence it would be most unwise for us to feel certain that the Airgialla were not part of the province of Ulster and were not themselves considered to be Ulaid. In circumstances in which the two constituted one polity, or were known recently to have been parts of a single whole, the literary placing of an ancient Ulidian capital at Emain Macha need not have appeared at all strange. If Emain Macha had never been in that province and the Airthir never recognised as Ulaid, its situation there in the 'Ulster Cycle' of tales would have been and seemed work of pure fantasy. Muirchú's comment on the relationship of Airthir and Ulaid is an indication of how local political history was perceived towards the end of the seventh century: 'aliquando propinquales et propinquos, nunc . . . dirissimos hostes'; they were peoples 'at one time neighbourly and friendly, now bitter enemies'.[28]

The legend of the Three Collas, assuming as it does a political background of the sort offered by the 'Ulster Cycle' of tales, has had a wholly dominating effect on modern perceptions of the early mediaeval history of Ulster. It is essential that we divorce ourselves from its spell. If political schism between Airthir and Ulaid had occurred within living memory of Muirchú's generation, then 637 is the point at which it probably happened. The further implication offered by the literary role of Emain Macha may be that the Airthir were not previously just friendly neighbours but in fact members of the Ulidian polity.

25 See Bannerman, *Studies*, pp. 113, 115–18, 147.

26 Muirchú, *Vita S. Patricii*, II.13 (11): *The Patrician Texts*, edd. & transl. Bieler & Kelly, pp. 120/1 ('bellum . . . inter nepotes Néill et Orientales ex una parte <et inter Ultanos ex altera parte>').

27 The matter turns on whether Loeguire mac Néill, king of Tara, accepted christianity after his conflict with St Patrick: according to Tírechán, Loeguire remained a pagan, whereas Muirchú has Loeguire converting. See Sharpe, 'St Patrick and the see of Armagh', pp. 44–9, 57–9.

28 II.13 (11): *The Patrician Texts*, edd. & transl. Bieler & Kelly, pp. 120/1.

For Patrick and the fifth century the implications are less clear. We have no evidence that this was a period of particular upheaval in mid-Ulster. The possibility of Patrick's having founded a church at Armagh is not excluded if he was indeed an apostle to the people of Ulster, but neither is it validated. Whether the foundation of christian Armagh has anything to do with the proximity of Emain Macha could be answered only with the aid of an understanding of fifth-century perceptions of the functions and history of that site. Psycho-archaeology may be the only discipline which will offer a solution.

'AUDITE OMNES AMANTES': A HYMN IN PATRICK'S PRAISE

Andy Orchard

The abecedarian hymn in praise of St Patrick, 'Audite omnes amantes', has been frequently edited, and still more frequently discussed.[1] A brisk and unusually good-tempered scholarly debate has focussed almost exclusively on the related questions of the age of the hymn, and of the authenticity (or otherwise) of its attribution – first witnessed in the 'Martyrology of Oengus' under 27 November – to St Secundinus (Sechnall).[2] Arguments concerning this traditional attribution have been rehearsed by such scholars as Ludwig Bieler, J.B. Bury, and Eoin MacNeill (for), and (against) D. A. Binchy, James Carney, Michael Curran, and Mario Esposito.[3] Few have troubled to consider the literary value of the text; fewer still have found much to praise. Bury is typical in his assessment of the hymn that 'Literary merit it has none, and the historian deplores that, instead of singing the general praises of Patrick's virtues and weaving round him a mesh of religious phrases describing his work as pastor, messenger, and preacher, the author had thought well to mention some of his particular actions'.[4] F. Chatillon was equally dismissive in noting that 'le style est rocailleux; mais là n'est point la question'.[5] Here, by contrast, I propose to consider just these literary aspects of the hymn, to demonstrate the subtlety with which the author has addressed his theme, and finally to speculate on the literary context within which the author worked and on the relationship of this hymn with other, similar, rhythmical compositions.

'Audite omnes amantes' has been edited best by Bieler;[6] here in an appendix I print simply for convenience of reference the version of the hymn found in the earliest manuscript, the so-called 'Antiphonary of Bangor', usually thought to have been written A.D. 680 x 691, which appears to have preserved the best

1 The most important editions are *The Antiphonary of Bangor*, ed. Warren, II.14–16; *The Irish Liber Hymnorum*, edd. Bernard & Atkinson, I.7–13; *Analecta Hymnica*, edd. Dreves *et al.*, LI.340–6; 'The Hymn of St. Secundinus', ed. Bieler.

2 *Félire Óengusso*, ed. & transl. Stokes, p. 237; Doherty, 'The cult', pp. 88–9.

3 Bieler, *The Life*, pp. 78–9, 109–11, 130, and 136; 'The Hymn of St. Secundinus', p. 117; *The Works*, pp. 57–60. See also Binchy, 'Patrick and his biographers', pp. 52–5; Bury, *The Life*, pp. 117 and 246–7; Carney, *Studies*, pp. 399–401, and *The Problem*, pp. 40–6; Curran, *The Antiphonary of Bangor*, pp. 35–44; Esposito, 'Notes on Latin learning', pt I, pp. 229–30; MacNeill, 'The Hymn'.

4 Bury, *The Life*, p. 118.

5 Chatillon, 'Sur le thème *alpha-oméga*', p. 337.

6 'The Hymn of St. Secundinus', ed. Bieler.

readings.[7] The hymn is composed in alternate half-lines of eight and seven syllables, forming stanzas of four long lines of fifteen syllables each, without regular rhyme, but with a strict caesura. No account is taken of the principles of quantitative prosody, but there is a marked tendency towards fixed stress-patterning at the caesura (where the penultimate syllable is stressed), and the end of the line (where the antepenultimate syllable is stressed); according to the system devised by Dag Norberg, the verses can be classified as 8p + 7pp.[8] This rhythm, which may have begun as an imitation of the metrical trochaic septenarius, is not found in a pure form in 'Audite omnes amantes', the author of which apparently permitted certain licences. Therefore we find dissyllabic endings in a number of verses, technically producing a derivative rhythm 8p + 7p. It is striking, however, that the author of 'Audite omnes amantes' all but restricts these exceptions to a handful of repeated words, such as *Dei* (lines 23, 28, and 85), *Deum* (line 72), *bonis* (lines 22 and 46), and *bono* (line 24); other rhythmical infelicities are comparatively rare.[9] As with most rhythmical compositions, hiatus is permitted frequently, but there apears to be in 'Audite omnes amantes' a solitary case of elision.[10] The best specific metrical model for the form of rhythm adopted in 'Audite omnes amantes', the trochaic septenarius, is that used in an influential hymn often attributed to St Hilary, 'Hymnum dicat turba fratrum', which is the first hymn transcribed in the 'Antiphonary of Bangor', and which proved extremely popular in mediaeval Ireland.[11] In this hymn we find plentiful examples of both dissyllabic endings, all (as in 'Audite omnes amantes') with a short initial syllable, and therefore permissible in metrical verse, and elision. The hymn is indeed attributed to Hilary in the 'Antiphonary of Bangor', but Curran has given a detailed account of doubts concerning this traditional ascription and put forward an interesting – but to me finally unconvincing – case that 'Hymnum dicat turba fratrum' is of Hiberno-Latin origin.[12] If, however, the rhythmical model for 'Audite omnes amantes' is plausibly to be sought in hymns such as 'Hymnum dicat turba fratrum', other sources are required for its other formal features.

A number of christian authors wrote hymns and prayers in an abecedarian form; the most celebrated and influential of these were probably the hymn 'A

7 On this dating, see now Lapidge, 'Columbanus and the "Antiphonary of Bangor" ', p. 104, n. 22. The manuscript-evidence provides the same approximate *terminus ante* for the hymn as does its use by Muirchú (p. 160, below). For the origin of the manuscript, cf. Best, 'Palaeographical notes, III, the Book of Armagh', pp. 104–5.

8 Norberg, *Introduction*, pp. 90–1 and 112–14.

9 So in line 32, *in cruce* is probably to be thought of as a single trisyllabic rhythmical unit, scanned on the antepenultimate syllable. The only genuine rhythmical error is in line 66, where *indutus* should properly be stressed on the long penultimate syllable.

10 Elision occurs in *sibi elegit* (line 81), and, although several manuscripts have *sibi legit*, this appears to be the stronger reading – as Bieler argued ('The Hymn of St. Secundinus', p. 127), citing the parallel uses of *elegit* in lines 13 and 58. Bieler's reasoning seems sound enough but does nothing to explain why in both of these parallel cases, *illum elegit* (line 13) and *Dei elegit* (line 58), elision fails to take place.

11 'Hymnum dicat turba fratrum' was edited by Clemens Blume, in *Analecta Hymnica*, edd. Dreves *et al.*, LI.269–71. On the popularity of this hymn in Ireland, see *The Irish Liber Hymnorum*, edd. Bernard & Atkinson, II.127–8.

12 Curran, *The Antiphonary of Bangor*, pp. 22–34.

solis ortus cardine' of Caelius Sedulius, and Augustine's *Psalmus contra partem Donati*, but similar compositions were created by (for example) Venantius Fortunatus and Hilary of Poitiers.[13] Scholars have often searched for the inspiration for 'Audite omnes amantes' in one or more of these undoubtedly popular texts. But, as indeed Augustine's title suggests, there were also biblical models available, such as Psalms XXXVI, CI–CII, and CXVIII, or Lamentations I–IV, and it seems more probable in the context of the following study that these proved influential on the author of 'Audite omnes amantes'. Moreover, the abecedarian form seems to have been particularly attractive to Hiberno-Latin authors; many such poems are recorded both in the 'Antiphonary of Bangor' and in the Irish *Liber Hymnorum*.[14] Many of these Hiberno-Latin abecedarian compositions begin, moreover, with the invocation *Audite*, and several of these seem to have had some literary relationship.[15] It has been suggested that there are both biblical and Patristic models for commencing verses with such an invocation; the final section of Augustine's *Psalmus contra partem Donati* begins *Audite fratres quod dico*,[16] whilst the Canticle of Moses (Deut. XXXII), well known from liturgical practice, and which appears to have provided Augustine with his theme, begins *Audite caeli quod loquor*.[17] Once again the biblical source seems more likely in the particular case of 'Audite omnes amantes', and it is interesting that the Canticle of Moses is the first item in the 'Antiphonary of Bangor', followed after a brief gap by the only other items with a similar incipit, all abecedarian compositions which appear as an apparently related cluster (items 13–15): 'Audite omnes amantes' (the hymn for St Patrick), 'Audite pantes ta erga' (a hymn for St Comgall), and 'Audite bonum exemplum' (a hymn for St Camelacus).[18] The textual relations between these three hymns will be considered in detail below. Yet a further (and still closer) biblical model for the form of 'Audite omnes amantes' is suggested in the brief introduction to the version of the hymn in *Leabhar Breac*, a late fourteenth-century manuscript, where it is asserted that 'Audite omnes amantes' was written *similitudine Moysi dicentis Audite caeli quae loquor* (Deut. XXXII.1) *et David dicentis Audite haec omnes gentes* (Psalms XLVIII.2).[19] The latter quotation from the Psalms offers a particularly attractive model, since it begins with an invocation to the *gentes* ('peoples' or 'Gentiles') to forsake worldly things and turn towards under-

13 Norberg, *Introduction*, p. 56.

14 Stevenson, '*Altus Prosator*: a Seventh-century Hiberno-Latin Poem', p. 162.

15 See further below, pp. 160–4.

16 One might compare two compositions having apparently derivative titles, which can be described as Hiberno-Latin with some confidence: 'Audite fratres, facta', a hymn to St Monenna (*Analecta Hymnica*, edd. Dreves *et al.*, LI.337–40), and 'Audite fratres, famina', a hymn to St Peter (*ibid.*, LI.347–49).

17 On the use of the Canticle of Moses in the liturgy, see Curran, *The Antiphonary of Bangor*, pp. 186–8.

18 'Audite pantes ta erga' and 'Audite bonum exemplum' were both edited by Clemens Blume, in *Analecta Hymnica*, edd. Dreves *et al.*, LI.321–4. See further Coccia, 'La cultura', pp. 290–1; Curran, *The Antiphonary of Bangor*, pp. 44–6 and 81–2.

19 'In imitation of Moses saying: "Give ear, O ye heavens, and I will speak" and David, saying: "hear this, all ye people".' The *Leabhar Breac* ('Speckled Book'), Dublin, Royal Irish Academy, MS 23.P.16 (1230), was reproduced in facsimile by Ferguson, *Leabhar Breac*; the introduction to 'Audite omnes amantes' is found on p. 238a.

standing of God, a message which chimes well with that of the author of 'Audite omnes amantes', who (like Patrick) seems to have understood the term *gentes* to apply best to the unconverted Irish.[20] Moreover, similar allusion to and manipulation of biblical (and Patrician) diction is the hallmark of this author's style, as we shall see.

As is to be expected from a composition derived more closely from biblical and Patrician models than from Patristic sources, the style and rhetorical structure of 'Audite omnes amantes' are distinctly unostentatious, but there are still signs of careful syntactical patterning, and not merely for rhythmical reasons. The lack of a regular rhyme-scheme may indicate a date earlier than the ornate and multisyllabic rhymes found increasingly in Hiberno-Latin hymns during the course of the seventh century,[21] but there is close attention to other forms of sound-patterning. Alliteration is fairly frequent, but not at all intrusive, as in the following examples.

in cuius multiplicantur ut manna in manibus (36)
kastam qui custodit carnem ob amorem Domini (37)
suamque pascere plebem diuinis dogmatibus (59)
propinansque Dei plebem spiritale poculum (68)

In some verses, the use of alliteration points up a conscious chiastic patterning of syntax, as in

qui caeleste haurit uinum in uassis caelestibus (67)

where the adjective-and-noun pairs *caeleste . . . uinum* and *uassis caelestibus* are linked through sound and sense. Elsewhere, homoeoteleuton (rhyme) performs the same function, as in

qui quod uerbis docet sacris factis adimplet bonis (46)

where the carefully repeated patterning of noun-verb-adjective is underlined by the rhymes on *uerbis*: *factis*, *docet*: *adimplet*, and *sacris*: *bonis*. It is clear, then, that the apparent artlessness of the diction conceals a certain skill.

In the same way, Bieler's confident assertion that: 'vocabulary and phraseology have narrow limitations; repetition of words after short interval is common – a sort of mental perseveration' may be somewhat insensitive.[22] In part, this repetition can be seen in the same kind of striving after syntactical patterning which we have already seen, and such close repetition of identical and parallel diction is, after all, a mark of the 'biblical style' to which the author of 'Audite omnes amantes' so clearly aspires.[23] It even seems possible that some of the most blatant (and clearly deliberate) repetition may have served a structural function. It is certainly striking that key-phrases at the end of the first quarter of

20 Patrick used the term *gentes* no fewer than sixteen times in his two extant writings, often in biblical quotation, and always in this specialised sense. See further Devine, *A Computer-generated Concordance*, pp. 109–10; 'Libri', ed. & transl. White, p. 287.

21 Cf. Meyer, *Gesammelte Abhandlungen*, III.323–8.

22 Bieler, 'The Hymn of St. Secundinus', p. 124.

23 Cf. Howlett, 'Biblical style in early Insular Latin'.

the hymn (lines 21–3) are echoed closely at the half-way point (lines 46–7), and that the final couplet of the fifth stanza (lines 19–20) anticipates the diction of the final couplet of the whole hymn (lines 91–2). We might therefore compare the following examples.

(a) apostolicum exemplum formamque praebet bonis
qui tam uerbis quam et factis plebi praedicat Dei
ut quem dictis non conuertit actu prouocet bono. (22–4)

qui quod uerbis docet sacris factis adimplet bonis
bono praecedit exemplo formamque fidelium. (46–7)

(b) nauigi huius laboris tum opere praetium
cum Christo regni caelestis possessurus gaudium. (19–20)

cuius ingentis laboris percepturus praemium
cum apostolis regnabit sanctus super Israel. (91–2)

The first pair of passages (a) is linked not simply by diction (such as *exemplum formamque*, uniquely here), but by rhythm, in the repeated dissyllabic endings,[24] heightened in the first passage by the syntactic (and alliterative) patterning of *praebet . . . praedicat . . . prouocet*. The second pair of passages is linked by the curious (and again alliterative) jingle *praetium . . . praemium* (the spelling *praetium* is found in all manuscripts) and by the unique use here of the future participles *possessurus* and *percepturus*. The significance of such repetition, which in these cases underlines two important themes in the author's picture of Patrick, is a subject for further speculation, but the very fact that the author clearly intended his chosen diction to resonate at key-points of his hymn lends credence to the notion that any allusions to his sources need equally careful consideration.

The biblical flavour of the language of the hymn has been long recognised; Bieler signalled what at first glance seems to be an extraordinary number of verbal borrowings, and indeed his list of parallels can even be extended somewhat.[25] The verbal debt is overwhelming; several passages from 'Audite omnes amantes' are little more than reworkings of borrowed biblical diction, as the many examples which I have cited in the Appendix clearly show. Phrases such as *in Dei timore . . . inmobilis* (line 9), *in carne Christi portat stigmata* (line 31), *gloriatur in cruce* (line 32), and *ne . . . in uia deficiant* (line 34) have specific and easily identifiable biblical sources,[26] and so faithful is the borrowing in some cases that it has been argued that the author was using a form of the Bible similar to that used by Patrick, Pelagius, and Gildas, the so-called 'missing British form of the Old-Latin'.[27] So, for example, the source of the phrase *et in*

24 See above, p. 154.

25 So, for example, Warren's list of biblical parallels, produced in the course of his detailed commentary, *The Antiphonary of Bangor*, II.51–5, is of some use in indicating more general biblical themes than Bieler indicated. Other parallels in the appendix below I have traced for myself.

26 So we might indicate Tobias II.14 (*inmobilis in Dei timore*), Gal. VI.17 (*stigmata Iesu in corpore meo porto*), Gal. VI.14 (*gloriari in cruce*), and Matthew XV.32 (*ne deficiant in uia*).

27 *Pelagius's Expositions*, ed. Souter, I.146; see also Burkitt, 'On two early Irish hymns'.

caelis Patrem magnificant Dominum (line 8) is seen in the Old Latin reading of Matthew V.16: *et magnificent* (Vulgate *glorificent*) *Patrem vestrum qui est in caelis*, and a similar preference for the Old Latin is seen in, for example, *in cuius porte aduersum inferni non praeualent* (line 12), taken from Matthew XVI.18, *et portae inferni* (Vulgate *inferi*) *non praeualebunt aduersum eam, hostiam placentem uiuam offert Domino* (line 40), imitating Rom. XII.1, *hostiam uiuam . . .* (Vulgate *uiuentem*) *Deo placentem*, and *maximus . . . in regno caelorum uocabitur* (line 45), which borrows from Matthew V.19, *maximus* (Vulgate *magnus*) *uocabitur in regno caelorum*. The examples of borrowing quoted here are typical in their distribution; the author of 'Audite omnes amantes' seems to have relied almost exclusively for his diction on the New Testament, and there predominantly on the Gospel of Matthew.[28]

It is, moreover, clear that, as with Patrick's own writings, 'Audite omnes amantes' contains not merely biblical language, but implicit allusions beyond the explicit text.[29] Patrick is equated in turn with angels, and apostles, and especially with the figures of SS. Peter and Paul. Particular biblical themes and parables are repeatedly alluded to, giving the hymn a notable coherence of structure often lacking in other, later, abecedarian compositions. So, for example, one stanza clearly alludes to the parable from the Sermon on the Mount found in the Gospels of Matthew and Luke, about hiding one's light under a bushel. One might compare the following stanza

Lumenque mundi accensum ingens euangelicum
in candellabro leuatum toto fulgens saeculo
ciuitas regis munita supra montem possita
copia in qua est multa quam Domnius possedet (41–4)

with Luke VIII.16: *nemo autem lucernam accendens operit eam uaso . . . sed supra candelabrum ponit ut intrantes uideant lumen*, and Matthew V.14–15, and 35: *uos estis lux mundi non potest ciuitas abscondi supra montem posita . . . super candelabrum . . . ciuitas est magni Regis*. It is clear that the author of 'Audite omnes amantes' has here managed to combine the thought and wording of the two Gospel-accounts, and has ranged widely within the particular biblical chapter Matthew V. The same chapter is the source for the immediately following line, *Maximus namque in regno caelorum uocabitur* (line 45), which derives, as we have seen, from Matthew V.19: *hic maximus uocabitur in regno caelorum*. The next line of the hymn, *qui quod uerbis docet sacris factis adimplet bonis*

28 Bieler's notes to his edition of Patrick's own writings indicate a marginal preference (on Patrick's part) for Matthew among the evangelists: 'Libri', ed. Bieler, I.114–15; one might also note in passing that there exists a remarkable abecedarian rhythmical poem on the passion and resurrexion of Christ, beginning 'Audite omnes gentes', which consists almost entirely of biblical diction drawn from the Gospel of Matthew. The poem is preserved in only a single tenth-century manuscript, Bruxelles, Bibliothèque royale, MS. 8860–8867 (1351), perhaps from Sankt Gallen, and was edited by Karl Strecker, in *Poetae*, edd. von Winterfeld & Strecker, IV.501–3. Some relationship between this poem and 'Audite omnes amantes' seems possible, but cannot as yet be satisfactorily demonstrated.

29 The classic, if rather cautious, study of Patrick's use of biblical language remains that of Mohrmann, *The Latin of Saint Patrick*, pp. 32–44, but see now further the stimulating and provocative work by Howlett, 'Ex saliva scripturae meae'.

(line 46), is more loosely taken from the same biblical verse, Matthew V.19: *qui autem fecerit et docuerit.* Closely following these passages we find in 'Audite omnes amantes' the simple phrase *mundoque in corde* (line 48), used as a description of Patrick, and note that it recalls one of the Beatitudes, again from the same biblical chapter, Matthew V.8: *beati mundo corde quoniam ipsi Deo uidebunt* ('blessed are the pure in heart, for they shall see God'). In this case, however, the audience is presumably expected to extrapolate from the plain phrase *mundoque in corde*, found only here in the whole New Testament, to the entire biblical verse, which clearly alludes to a passage later in the hymn, *Israel uocatur huius anima uidens deum* (line 72), which itself implies that Patrick, who is, as we are told, *mundo . . . corde*, does indeed see God.[30] Similar extra-textual allusions are found in many passages of 'Audite omnes amantes', linking together many of the repeated themes which Bieler found so tiresome. A further example can be given where a simple phrase such as *cum usuris exigit* (line 18) – which again derives from a verbal borrowing from Luke XIX.23, *cum usuris exegissem*, with a further parallel in Matthew XXV.27, *cum usuris* (Vulgate *cum usura*) – introduces a wealth of allusions, again to a parable from a single chapter of the Gospel of Matthew. In this case, the parable of the talents, the biblical source is explicitly alluded to by verbal borrowing in the stanza in question (as the noted parallels which I have given in the Appendix make clear) and thematically linked to the rest of the hymn by later references to the sowing of seed (lines 77–80) and the finding of treasure (lines 69–72). It is perhaps also implicitly connected with Patrick's own personal history, since the parable opens by comparing the kingdom of heaven with *homo proficiscens peregre* ('a man travelling into a far country'). It seems clear that the extensive use of biblical language in 'Audite omnes amantes' is far from random and has a literary purpose far more subtle than previous scholars have supposed. Indeed, one might describe the activity of the author of 'Audite omnes amantes' in terms similar to those in which Christine Mohrmann chose to describe the part played by the Bible in Patrick's own works:[31] 'there is a sort of omnipresence of Holy Scripture. In every sentence, in every thought which he formulates, there are traces of biblical language. And not only his language but also his way of thinking is determined by the Bible.'

Moreover, the author of 'Audite omnes amantes' echoes in Patrick's praise not merely his manner of composition, but much of his phrasing. Alongside the many biblical borrowings there are some close parallels between the diction of 'Audite omnes amantes' and that of Patrick's own works, which again seem to have been selected in a calculating manner. Such parallels, from both Patrick's *Confessio* (henceforth *Conf.*) and his *Epistola ad Coroticum* (henceforth *Ep.*), have been noted for many years, after the extensive work of G. F. Hamilton, and it is the chief flaw of Bieler's otherwise exemplary edition of 'Audite omnes amantes' that he pays them so little account.[32] In some cases the author of

30 The interpretation of the word *Israel* as *uidens Deum* is a Patristic commonplace; see further Bieler, *The Works*, p. 103, n. 19.

31 Mohrmann, *The Latin of Saint Patrick*, p. 43.

32 Hamilton, *In Patrick's Praise*. Somewhat curiously, however, Bieler did note many of these parallels in his edition of Patrick's own works; see his 'Libri', I.117.

'Audite omnes amantes' has simply borrowed Patrick's phraseology in places where there is no biblical (or other) source, as in the phrase *in Trinitate sacri . . . nominis* (line 87), which must echo Patrick's *adoramus unum Deum in trinitate sacri nominis* (*Conf.* 4); or in the description of how Patrick *cum apostolis regnabit* (line 92), which repeats Patrick's own promise to the faithful, *regnabitis cum apostolis* (*Ep.* 18). The opening of Patrick's *Epistola ad Coroticum* includes a number of phrases which chime with those of 'Audite omnes amantes': Patrick says of himself that *inter barbaras gentes habito . . . profuga ob amorem Dei*, that for his flock *tradidi . . . animam meam usque ad mortem*, and that his purpose was *docere gentes* (*Ep.* 1); one might compare several lines in 'Audite omnes amantes'.

Dominus illum elegit ut doceret barbaras (13)
kastam qui custodit carnem ob amorem Domini (37)
pro qua a Christi exemplo suam tradidit animam (60)

Patrick's conviction that he was chosen by God to perform his task (the key word is *elegit*, as in *Conf.* 56 and *Ep.* 6) is echoed constantly in 'Audite omnes amantes' using the same verb (lines 13, 17, 58, and 81), while in the last example quoted (line 60) we can see Patrick and the author of his hymn drawing on the same biblical verse (Phil. II.30). In other ways, the author of 'Audite omnes amantes' shares with Patrick a fondness for the same biblical verses and the same borrowed phrases. So Patrick gives thanks to God *ut . . . offeram illi sacrificium ut hostiam uiuentem animam meam Christo domino meo* (*Conf.* 34), while the author of 'Audite omnes amantes' echoes more closely their shared biblical source (Rom. XII.1) when he describes how Patrick *hostiam placentem uiuam offert Domino* (line 40).[33] More often, however, in employing a common biblical source the author of 'Audite omnes amantes' prefers Patrick's reading of the text. When Patrick quotes a number of biblical authorities (Matthew IV.19 or Mark I.17, and Jer. XVI.16) and concludes that *oportet quidem bene et diligenter pascere . . . ualde oportebat retia nostra tendere* (*Conf.* 40), it is clear that the author of 'Audite omnes amantes' is echoing Patrick, rather than his biblical source, in describing how Patrick had been chosen *ut . . . piscaret per doctrinae retia* (line 14), just as Muirchú was later to echo 'Audite omnes amantes' in his own Life of Patrick.[34] Only Patrick and the author of 'Audite omnes amantes' (followed by Muirchú) employ *pisco* as an active verb; in the biblical passages which were the inspiration the deponent form *piscor* is exclusively used, as Bieler indicated.[35]

The further literary relationship of 'Audite omnes amantes' to other abecedarian hymns with a similar incipit has been the subject of only limited scholarly scrutiny. Chatillon provided a brief survey, but offered no conclusive analysis, while Carney, and later Curran, made particular comparisons with the hymn in

33 Note that in this case Patrick gives the Vulgate reading *uiuentem*, in place of the Old Latin *uiuam* of the author of 'Audite omnes amantes'. See further above, pp. 157–8.

34 See further Carney, *Studies*, pp. 400–1.

35 'Libri', II.169.

honour of St Camelacus, 'Audite bonum exemplum'.[36] Carney's remarks preface a discussion in which he suggested that a marginal note to Tírechán's *Collectanea* in the 'Book of Armagh' which describes 'Audite omnes amantes' as *Hymnus Colmán Alo* ('The hymn of Colmán of Lynally') is a correct attribution of authorship, and elaborated the point by ascribing 'Audite bonum exemplum' to the same hand.[37] The structural parallels between 'Audite omnes amantes' and 'Audite bonum exemplum' are indeed at first glance compelling: both are abecedarian hymns (employing identical words at certain points in the alphabetical sequence such as *Audite*, *Fidelis*, *Kastam*, *Quem*, *Regis*, and *Xristus*), both have but a single example of elision in the opening line of their *Xristus*-stanzas, and both employ the same unrhymed rhythmical structure (8p + 7pp). Moreover, some parallels of diction between the hymn for St Patrick and that for St Camelacus present themselves; we might compare *exemplum mirificum* ('Audite omnes amantes', line 7) with *bonum exemplum* ('Audite bonum exemplum', line 1); *exemplum . . . praebet* ('Audite omnes amantes', line 22) with *exemplum praebet* ('Audite bonum exemplum', line 5); *in aduersis laetatur* ('Audite omnes amantes', line 56) with *laetatur in paupertate* ('Audite bonum exemplum', line 11); *diebus ac noctibus . . . Deum orat Dominum* ('Audite omnes amantes', line 89–90) with *noctibus atque diebus orat Dominum suum* ('Audite bonum exemplum', line 13–14); *cum apostolis regnabit sanctus super Israel* ('Audite omnes amantes', line 92) with *yn paradiso regnabit cum sancto Elizaro* ('Audite bonum exemplum', line 24). The fact (which apparently escaped Carney and Curran) that these parallel passages occur in exactly the same sequence in each hymn may suggest literary borrowing rather than shared authorship, and indeed the differences in style and tone between the two hymns seem great. The hymn to Camelacus is rhythmically and syntactically inferior: as it stands, line 7 has a syllable too few, while the use of dissyllabic endings (lines 5, 7, 10, 14, and 18) is both more frequent and more varied than in the hymn for Patrick, and the sudden and untidy change of subject at lines 18–19 unparalleled. The hymn to Camelacus has demonstrative pronouns and pronominal adjectives as semantically redundant 'filler'-words (*hic*, line 10; *huic*, line 19; *suum*, lines 14 and 18) in a way quite without parallel in the hymn for Patrick, whose author (on the other hand) greatly favoured relative clauses (there is but one in the hymn to Camelacus) and avoided altogether the conjunction *atque* (cf. line 13), using *et* and (particularly) *-que* with an unmatched frequency. Even with such brief hymns, the possibility of shared authorship seems remote, and all indications are that in this case of literary borrowing it is the author of the hymn to Camelacus who is the borrower, indicating that the hymn to Patrick enjoyed a certain vogue.

But while Carney's assertions of joint authorship of 'Audite omnes amantes'

[36] Chatillon, 'Sur le thème *alpha-oméga*'; Carney, *The Problem*, pp. 42–3; Binchy, 'Patrick and his biographers', p. 55; Curran, *The Antiphonary of Bangor*, pp. 38 and 44–6. 'Audite bonum exemplum' is found only in the 'Antiphonary of Bangor', and was edited by Clemens Blume, in *Analecta Hymnica*, edd. Dreves *et al.*, LI.321; see further Coccia, 'La cultura', p. 290.

[37] Carney, *The Problem*, pp. 44–6. See too Binchy, 'Patrick and his biographers', p. 55; Curran, *The Antiphonary of Bangor*, p. 38. For the marginal note (and the text to which it refers) see *The Patrician Texts*, edd. & transl. Bieler & Kelly, p. 166 (§57).

and 'Audite bonum exemplum' are easily dismissed, his claims for Colmán Elo as the author of the hymn for Patrick are less simply refuted. There is no other material extant which can with confidence be ascribed to the hand of Colmán Elo with which to make any kind of objective stylistic comparison. A single brief extract of a Latin hymn is attributed to Colmán Elo in the 'Martyrology of Oengus', and reads as follows:

> Exurgam dilucolo, confitebor Domino
> quia non est inane sperare in Domino.

As Carney noted, the couplet is in part a rendering of a biblical passage, Psalm CVII.3–4: *exsurgam diluculo confitebor tibi in populis, Domine.*[38] One might add that the phrase *sperare in Domino* is common throughout the Psalms, and that a further possible parallel is found in I Cor. XV.58: *labor uester non est inanis in Domino*. While the technique of reworking biblical diction in rhythmical ways is notably close to what occurs in 'Audite omnes amantes', Colmán Elo (if indeed it is he) here employed a different rhythm (7p + 8pp, if we assume an error in *dilucolo*, or 7pp + 8pp, if we assume an error in *inane*)[39] and shows greater interest in rhyme (*dilucolo . . . Domino, inane sperare*, and *Domino . . . Domino*). It is also clear that the author of the hymn to Patrick, for all his repetition of diction, never repeats the same ending in consecutive lines, as here. The case for Colmán Elo's authorship of 'Audite omnes amantes' is on such slender evidence neither proved nor disproved, and must remain speculation.

The author of the hymn for St Camelacus does not seem to have been the only Hiberno-Latin poet who consciously imitated the diction and style of 'Audite omnes amantes'. Several others of the Hiberno-Latin abecedarian hymns beginning *Audite* seem equally indebted. In the case of the hymn to St Brigit, attributed to St Ultán, only the final three abecedarian stanzas survive – beginning, incidentally, as in 'Audite omnes amantes', with the words *Xristus . . . Ymnus . . . Zona* – and are followed in three manuscripts by a further stanza, presented as the opening of the entire hymn, as follows:[40]

> Audite uirginis laudes, sancta quoque merita:
> perfectionem quam promisit, uiriliter impleuit;
> Christi matrem se spopondit dictis et fecit factis.

The opening line is in the same rhythm as the hymn for St Patrick (8p + 7pp), the next two in the derivative rhythm (8p + 7p) found in those lines in 'Audite omnes amantes' which end in a dissyllable.[41] Apart from similarity of rhythm, however, this stanza demonstrates the same concern for alliteration (*perfectionem . . . promisit . . .impleuit; fecit factis*), and the same disregard for rhyme,

38 Carney, *The Problem*, p. 46.

39 Either rhythmical structure would be rare; in his list of fifteen-syllable forms Norberg, *Introduction*, p. 215, has given no parallel examples whatsoever.

40 The hymn to St Brigit was edited by Clemens Blume, in *Analecta Hymnica*, edd. Dreves *et al.*, LI.317–19; the stanza in question (which is found in both manuscripts of the Irish *Liber Hymnorum*), is printed on p. 318. See further Coccia, 'La cultura', pp. 307–8.

41 See above, p. 154.

as is found in the hymn for St Patrick.[42] Further parallels of diction strengthen the notion of literary borrowing; one might compare from 'Audite omnes amantes' such lines as the following.

Audite omnes amantes Deum sancta mereta (1)
qui tam uerbis quam et factis plebi praedicat Dei (23)
ut quem dictis non conuertit actu prouocet bono (24)
qui quod uerbis docet sacris factis adimplet bonis (46)

Given that the opening line of 'Audite omnes amantes' may have drawn its inspiration in part from Psalm XLVIII.2 (*Audite omnes gentes*), it is clear that the opening of this hymn for St Brigit has departed from the original source, and therefore this stanza is, as the debased rhythm and verbal parallels seem to show,[43] the borrower. Once again the literary influence of 'Audite omnes amantes' may be detected.

It is, however, quite clear that this stanza from a hymn for Brigit has no necessary connection with the preceding three stanzas with which it has been preserved; these last are in a different rhythm (8pp + 8pp),[44] with consistent monosyllabic rhyme, but with the same concern for alliteration. The preservation of only the last three verses – of an apparently now lost abecedarian hymn for St Brigit, followed by the opening stanza of what is presumably a quite separate hymn – recalls neatly the eleventh-century survival of the last three stanzas of 'Audite omnes amantes', followed by the first, as a quite separate item in Cambridge, Corpus Christi College, MS. 41, and the Irish tradition of the peculiar efficacy of the final three stanzas of 'Audite omnes amantes' in the salvation of souls.[45] That the surviving stanzas of the hymn for St Brigit begin with the same words as the equivalent lines of the hymn to St Patrick strengthens the case for literary borrowing, and there are further possible indications of borrowed diction. The opening four lines of the final stanza of the hymn for St Brigit read

Zona sanctae militiae
sanctos lumbos praecingere
haec consueuit diurno
nocturno quoque studio

42 It should be noted that the latest (twelfth-century) manuscript has the variant *factis fecit* in line 3, thereby providing monosyllabic (and monotonous!) caesural rhyme, but only in lines 2–3 (*promisit . . . impleuit* and *spopondit . . . fecit*). The preferred reading *fecit factis* offers exactly the same kind of parallel syntax in line 3 (*spopondit dictis et fecit factis*) as is so common in 'Audite omnes amantes', as we have seen.

43 One might also note the single example of synezesis in *perfectionem* (line 2) here; there are no examples in 'Audite omnes amantes', but the licence was to prove popular in later Hiberno-Latin verse.

44 The few exceptions to this rhythm, such as *felicem* (stanza 1, line 5), *diurno* (stanza 3, line 3), and *splendore* (stanza 3, line 7) are acceptable departures in the context of Hiberno-Latin octosyllables: similar 'errors' are found in (for example) 'Altus prosator'. See further Herren, 'The stress systems', pp. 70–3.

45 Cf. Bieler, *The Life*, pp. 109–10; *The Works*, p. 59. See further Ker, *Catalogue*, pp. 43–5 (no. 32).

and may consciously echo such phrasing from 'Audite omnes amantes' as

ut in caelesti moneret clericos militiae (62)
zona Domini praecinctus diebus ac noctibus (89).

Like its alleged 'opening stanza', the end of this hymn for St Brigit may owe something to 'Audite omnes amantes'.

A rather similar case for influence can be made with respect to a further abecedarian hymn for St Brigit, beginning 'Alta audite ta erga'.[46] This hymn, in monosyllablic *a*-rhyme throughout, has a regular rhythm (8pp + 8pp) and ornate and insistent alliteration. There are two alliterating allusions to St Patrick,[47] and the same use of identical alphabetical opening words both throughout the hymn (*Electa* and *Kasta*) and particularly with respect to the three closing stanzas (*Xristum*, *Ymnizans*, and *Zona*). Other parallels of diction present themselves, most interestingly and convincingly an alliterative allusion at the exact centre of the hymn, *mira ciuitas, consita / supra montis cacumina* (stanza 6, lines 3–4), to the same biblical image expressed as follows in 'Audite omnes amantes':

ciuitas regis munita supra montem possita (43).

The notion that this hymn for St Brigit has borrowed from 'Audite omnes amantes' is of considerable interest, since there seems also to be a literary link between this hymn and the celebrated hymn for St Comgall which immediately follows 'Audite omnes amantes' in the 'Antiphonary of Bangor'.[48] In particular the opening line of the hymn for St Brigit, 'Alta audite ta erga', sees in its use of Greek a conscious echo of the opening of the hymn for St Comgall, 'Audite pantes ta erga', which itself may simply derive from the pure Latin (borrowed from Psalm CVII) of 'Audite omnes amantes'. James F. Kenney put forward a case for deriving 'Audite pantes ta erga' from 'Audite omnes amantes' based on just such slim parallels; since there is little overlap of diction, however, and still less of style, it is unclear how a stronger case could be constructed.[49] As with a number of other hymns of a similar stamp, the influence of 'Audite omnes amantes' on the hymn for St Comgall remains unproven, a tantalising possibility not at all at odds with the other available evidence.

It is quite clear, however, from the brief survey already given, that 'Audite omnes amantes' exerted a fascination for a number of early Hiberno-Latin authors, who each attempted to imitate its individual form or diction. Some of these derivative pieces are themselves thought to be early in date, such as 'Audite bonum exemplum', which (like the hymn for St Patrick), Dag Norberg considered, 'appartient aux plus anciens chants latins composés en

46 Edited by Clemens Blume, in *Analecta Hymnica*, edd. Dreves *et al.*, LI.319–20. See further Coccia, 'La cultura', pp. 309–10.

47 *Patricii cum prudentia* (stanza 3, line 2) and *Patricii patrocinia* (stanza 9, line 4); both require synezesis, as elsewhere in the hymn.

48 'Audite pantes ta erga' was edited by Clemens Blume, in *Analecta Hymnica*, edd. Dreves *et al.*, LI.321–4, and has been discussed often; see Coccia, 'La cultura', p. 289, and Curran, *The Antiphonary of Bangor*, pp. 81–2.

49 Kenney, *The Sources*, p. 266; cf. too Binchy, 'Patrick and his biographers', pp. 54–5.

Irlande'.[50] There is, however, still little to dissent from in Esposito's judicious statement that the hymn 'may, in fact, have been composed at any time between the middle of the fifth and the middle of the seventh centuries, but the Latinity might perhaps point to an earlier date than those of other Hiberno-Latin hymns'.[51] Many of those who accepted the traditional attribution of the hymn to St Secundinus were impressed by the lack of legendary elements and allusions to the later burgeoning cult of St Patrick; many, like Bieler, thought that the hymn was composed in Patrick's own lifetime, 'in defence of Patrick against those critics whose hostility had been aroused by his demand to excommunicate Coroticus – a prelude, as it were, to Patrick's own apologia'.[52] One recalls that in that apologia Patrick addressed his critics with the famous words *uos domini cati rethorici audite et scrutamini* (*Conf.* 13), and it may be that it was in a further echo of Patrick that our author commenced his hymn with the reconciling words 'Audite omnes amantes'.

What I have tried to demonstrate here is that in his subtle use of predominantly biblical diction and biblical models the author of 'Audite omnes amantes' came close to the practice of St Patrick himself. Mediaeval audiences were clearly more appreciative of this occasionally tortuous technique than modern scholarship has been; the extent to which the hymn was itself taken as a model is sufficient indication. Still more telling, perhaps, is the brief prayer appended to 'Audite omnes amantes' in the Irish *Liber Hymnorum* and in the *Leabhar Breac: In memoria aeterna erit iustus / ab auditione mala non timebit.*[53] F. E. Warren noted that this was a biblical phrase, taken verbatim from Psalm CXI.7.[54] But there is perhaps a greater significance, for like the hymn itself the phrase is in a perfect rhythm (8p + 4p), recorded in hymns elsewhere.[55] The psalm in question, like 'Audite omnes amantes', is an abecedarian piece, and the phrase in question is, somewhat intriguingly, taken from the heart of the piece, exactly half-way through the psalm. And the subject of the psalm, most fittingly of all for a prayer appended to this hymn for St Patrick, is revealed in its opening line: *Beatus uir qui timet Dominum.* In short, the very techniques of biblical quotation and extra-textual allusion employed in 'Audite omnes amantes' are here used to conclude the hymn.

'Audite omnes amantes' is a well-wrought and highly influential hymn the literary merits of which have been overlooked too long; other early Hiberno-Latin hymns might indeed repay similar attention. The modern scholar cannot afford simply to identify sources and move on; more sensitivity to the way in which each source is used in context is clearly required. Close study of 'Audite omnes amantes' can teach much about how one early mediaeval text was understood and read, and similar study of related texts may yet reap similar rewards; in biblical terms (Mark IV.9), *qui habet aures audiendi audiat* ('he that hath ears to hear, let him hear').

50 Norberg, *Introduction*, p. 113, n. 3.
51 Esposito, 'Notes on Latin learning', pt I, p. 230.
52 Bieler, *The Works*, pp. 57–8.
53 Bieler, 'The Hymn of St. Secundinus', p. 122.
54 *The Antiphonary of Bangor*, ed. Warren, II.54–5.
55 Norberg, *Introduction*, p. 154.

APPENDIX

Text, translation, sources, and parallels[56]

YMNUM SANCTI PATRICI MAGISTER SCOTORUM

Audite omnes amantes deum sancta mereta
uiri in christo beati Patrici episcupi
quomodo bonum ob actum similatur angelis
perfectamque propter uitam aequatur apostolis.

Beata christi custodit mandata in omnibus
cuius opera refulgent clara inter homines
sanctumque cuius sequuntur exemplum mirificum
unde et in caelis Patrem magnificant Dominum.

Constans in dei timore et fide inmobilis
super quem aedificatur ut Petrus aecclesia
cuiusque apostolatum a deo sortitus est
in cuius porte aduersum inferni non praeualent.

Dominus illum elegit ut doceret barbaras
nationes et piscaret per doctrinae retia
et de saeculo credentes traheret ad gratiam
Dominum qui sequerentur sedem ad etheream.

1 cf. Deut. XXXII.1: *audite caeli quod loquor*
cf. Psalms XLVIII.2: *audite haec omnes gentes*
cf. Patrick, *Conf.* 13: *et uos dominicati rethorici audite et scrutamini*
4 cf. Patrick, *Conf.* 44: *uitam perfectam ego non egi*
5 *custodit mandata*, a biblical commonplace
8 Matthew V.16: *et magnificent* (Vulgate *glorificent*) *Patrem uestrum qui in caelis est*
9 Tobias II.14: *sed inmobilis in Dei timore permansit agens gratias Deo omnibus diebus uitae suae*
cf. *timor(em) Dei*, Patrick, *Conf.* 16, 18, and 44
10 Matthew XVI.18: *super hanc petram aedificabo ecclesiam meam*
11 Acts I.15–17: *Petrus . . . sortitus est sortem ministerii huius*
cf. Heb. VIII.6: *melius sortitus est ministerium*

[56] The text printed here is basically that found in the 'Antiphonary of Bangor', retaining original spellings, and with minimal alterations in only the following two cases: *lauacri* for *lauacris* (line 50) and *caelesti salleantur* for *caelestis alleantur* (line 76). Detailed notes on the language and diction of the hymn were given by Bieler, 'The Hymn of St. Secundinus', pp. 117–19 and 124–7.

THE HYMN OF SAINT PATRICK, TEACHER OF THE IRISH

Listen, all who love God, to the holy qualities
of Bishop Patrick, a sainted man in Christ,
how through good action he is likened to angels
and by his perfect life he is matched with apostles.

He keeps Christ's blessed commands in all things,
and his deeds shine bright among men;
whose marvellous and holy example they follow
by which they magnify the Lord their Father even in heaven.

He is constant in the fear of God and firm in faith
on whom, like Peter, the Church is built,
and whose apostolate he has from God,
and against whom the gates of Hell do not prevail.

The Lord chose him to teach the heathen nations,
that he might fish with doctrine's nets,
that he might bring believers from worldly things to grace
and they might follow the Lord to the seat of heaven.

12 Matthew XVI.18: *et portae inferi non praeualebunt aduersum eam*
13 cf. Luke VI.13: *uocauit discipulos et elegit duodecim ex ipsis*
cf. Matthew XXVIII.19: *euntes ergo docete omnes gentes*
cf. Patrick, *Ep.* 1: *inter barbaras itaque gentes habito*
cf. use of *elegit* in Patrick, *Conf.* 56; Patrick, *Ep.* 6
14 cf. Jer. XVI.16: *ecce ego mittam piscatores multos dicit Dominus et piscabuntur eos*
cf. John XXI.3: *Dicit eis Simon Petrus uado piscari*
cf. Patrick, *Conf.* 40: *oportet quidem bene et diligenter piscare . . . ualde oportebat retia nostra tendere*
cf. Patrick, *Ep.* 17: *creduli baptizati, de saeculo recessistis ad paradisum*
16 cf. Patrick, *Conf.* 16: *cotidie itaque pecora pascebam et frequens in die orabam*

Electa Christi talenta uendit euangelica
quae Hibernas inter gentes cum usuris exigit.
nauigi huius laboris tum opere praetium
cum Christo regni caelestis possessurus gaudium.

Fidelis dei minister insignisque nuntius
apostolicum exemplum formamque praebet bonis
qui tam uerbis quam et factis plebi praedicat Dei
ut quem dictis non conuertit actu prouocet bono.

Gloriam habet cum Christo honorem in saeculo
qui ab omnibus ut Dei ueneratur angelus
quem Deus misit ut Paulum ad gentes apostolum
ut hominibus ducatum praeberet regno Dei.

Humilis Dei ob metum spiritu et corpore
super quem bonum ob actum requiescit Dominus
cuiusque iusta in carne Christi portat stigmata
in cuius sola sustentans gloriatur in cruce.

Impiger credentes pascit dapibus caelestibus
ne qui uidentur cum Christo in uia deficiant
quibus erogat ut panes uerba euangelica
in cuius multiplicantur ut manna in manibus.

Kastam qui custodit carnem ob amorem Domini
quam carnem templum parauit sanctoque Spiritui
a quo constanter cum mundis possedetur actibus
quam et hostiam placentem uiuam offert Domino.

18 Matthew XXV.27: *et ueniens ego recepissem utique quod meum est cum usura*
Luke XIX.23: *et ego ueniens cum usuris utique exegissem illud*
cf. Patrick, *Conf.* 37: *ut ego ueneram ad Hibernas gentes euangelium praedicare*
19 Apoc. XVIII.19
19–20 cf. Matthew XXV.21, 23, 34: *euge bone serue et fidelis . . . euge serue bone et fidelis . . . possidete paratum uobis regnum a constitutione mundi*
21 cf. Ephes. VI.21: *fidelis minister in Domino* (cf. Col. I.7; IV.7)
cf. Patrick, *Conf.* 56: *ut unus essem de suis minimis minister*
22 Tit. II.7: *in omnibus te ipsum praebe exemplum bonorum operum*
23 cf. Acts XV.36: *praedicauimus uerbum Domini*
cf. Acts XVII.13: *praedicatum est a Paulo uerbum Dei*
24 cf. Heb. X.24: *et consideremus inuicem in prouocationem caritatis et bonorum operum*
25 *habet gloriam et honorem*, a biblical commonplace
26 cf. Gal. IV.14: *sed sicut angelum Dei excepistis me sicut Christum Iesum*
cf. Matthew XXII.30: *sed sicut angeli Dei in caelo*
27 cf. Acts XXVI.17: *eripiens te de populo et gentibus in quas nunc ego mitto te*
cf. Rom. XI.13: *ego sum gentium apostolus*
cf. use of *gentes*, Patrick, *Conf.* 18, 37, 38, 40, 48; Patrick, *Ep.* 1 (x2), 14

He sells the choice talents of Christ's gospel
and claims payment with interest from the heathen Irish;
as his price for the toil of the labour of this voyage
he will gain the joy of the heavenly kingdom with Christ.

He is a faithful servant of God, a splendid messenger
who provides an apostolic example and model for the good,
who preaches to God's people as much in words as deeds,
that him whom he does not convert with words he incites by good action.

He has glory with Christ and honour in the world,
and is adored by all as an angel of God,
whom God sent, like Paul, as an apostle to the Gentiles
to offer men guidance to the kingdom of God.

He is humble in mind and body through fear of God,
on whom because of his good deeds the Lord rests,
and he carries the stigmata of Christ on his just flesh,
he glories in the Cross, which alone sustains him.

Briskly he feeds the faithful with heaven's feast,
lest those who are seen with Christ should falter on the way;
he offers the words of the gospel like loaves of bread,
which are multiplied like manna in his hands.

He keeps his body chaste for love of the Lord,
the flesh which he has prepared as a temple for the Holy Spirit,
by which it is always possessed in pure actions,
the flesh which he offers as a living sacrifice, pleasing to the Lord.

28 cf. Matthew XV.14: *caecus autem si caeco ducatum praestet ambo in foueam cadunt*
29 cf. Ps. XXXIII.19: *et humiles spiritu saluabit*
cf. Prov. XXIX.23: *superbum sequitur humilitas et humilem spiritu suscipiet gloria*
31 Gal. VI.17: *ego enim stigmata Iesu in corpore meo porto*
32 cf. Gal. VI.14: *mihi autem absit gloriari nisi in cruce Domini nostri Iesu Christi*
34 Matthew XV.32: *et dimittere eos ieiunos nolo ne deficiant in uia*
cf. Mark VIII.3: *et si dimisero eos ieiunos in domum suam deficient in uia*
37 cf. I Tim. V.22: *te ipsum castum custodi*
cf. Patrick, *Ep.* 1: *profuga ob amorem Domini*
38 I Cor. VI.19: *an nescitis quoniam membra uestra templum est Spiritus Sancti qui in uobis est*
40 Rom. XII.1: *ut exhibeatis corpora uestra hostiam uiuentem sanctam Deo placentem*
cf. Phil. IV.18: *hostiam acceptam placentem Deo*
Patrick, *Conf.* 34: *offeram illi sacrificium ut hostiam uiuentem animam meam Christo Domino meo*

Lumenque mundi accensum ingens euangelicum
in candellabro leuatum toto fulgens saeculo
ciuitas regis munita supra montem possita
copia in qua est multa quam Domnius possedet.

Maximus namque in regno caelorum uocabitur
qui quod uerbis docet sacris factis adimplet bonis
bono praecedit exemplo formamque fidelium
mundoque in corde habet ad deum fiduciam.

Nomen Domini audenter adnuntiat gentibus
quibus lauacri salutis aeternam dat gratiam
pro quorum orat delictis ad Deum cotidie
pro quibus ut Deo dignas immolatque hostias.

Omnem pro diuina lege mundi spernit gloriam
qui cuncta ad cuius mensam aestimat quiscilia
nec ingruenti mouetur mundi huius fulmine
sed in aduersis laetatur cum pro Christo patitur.

Pastor bonus et fidelis gregis euangelici
quem Deus Dei elegit custodire populum
suamque pascere plebem diuinis dogmatibus
pro qua a Christi exemplo suam tradit animam.

Quem pro meretis saluator prouexit pontificem
ut in caelesti moneret clericos militiae
caelestem quibus annonam erogat cum uestibus
quod in diuinis inpletur sacrisque affatibus.

Regis nuntius inuitans credentes ad nuptias
qui ornatur uestimento nuptiali indutus
qui caeleste haurit uinum in uassis caelestibus
propinansque Dei plebem spiritale poculum.

41 cf. Patrick, *Conf.* 38: *posui te lumen in gentibus*
41–3 Matthew V.14–15, 35: *non potest ciuitas abscondi supra montem posita . . . super candelabrum . . . ciuitas est magni Regis*
Luke VIII.16: *nemo autem lucernam accendens operit eam uaso . . . sed supra candelabrum ponit ut intrantes uideant lumen*
45 Matthew V.19: *hic magnus uocabitur in regno caelorum*
cf. Patrick, *Ep.* 18: *et recumbent cum Abraham et Isaac et Iacob in regno caelorum*
47 cf. Tit. II.7: *in omnibus te ipsum praebe exemplum bonorum operum*
48 Matthew V.8: *beati mundo corde quoniam ipsi Deum uidebunt*
I John III.21: *carissimi si cor non reprehenderit nos fiduciam habemus ad Deum*
cf. II Cor. III.4: *fiduciam talem habemus per Christum ad Deum*
49 cf. Acts XXVI.20: *et in omnem regionem Iudaeae et gentibus adnuntiabam*
cf. Acts XXVI.23: *lumen adnuntiaturus est populo et gentibus*
52 *immolat hostiam*, common in Psalms
55 cf. Patrick, *Conf.* 13: *huius mundi*

Like a great evangelical light burning on the earth,
raised high on a candelabrum, shining for the whole world,
the fortified citadel of the King placed on a mountain-top,
in which there is the great abundance which the Lord possesses.

For he will be called the greatest in the kingdom of heaven,
who fulfils in good deeds what he teaches in sacred words,
who provides a model in good example for the faithful
and has confidence towards God in his pure heart.

Boldly he announces the Lord's name to the heathens,
to whom he grants eternal grace of the bath of salvation,
for whose sins he prays daily to God,
for whom he offers sacrifices worthy of God.

For God's law he despises all the glory of the world,
at whose table he reckons all else worthless,
nor is he moved by the violent lightning of the world,
but rejoices in adversity, since he suffers for Christ.

He is a good shepherd, faithful to the gospel flock,
whom God has chosen to guard God's people,
and to feed His people with sacred teaching,
for whom, after Christ's example, he lays down his life.

For his qualities the Saviour has made him a bishop,
to advise the clerics in their heavenly service,
to whom he dispenses food and clothing,
which he supplements with holy and sacred sayings.

He is the King's messenger inviting the faithful to the wedding-feast,
who is adorned and clothed in wedding garb,
who drinks heavenly wine in heavenly vessels
and gives God's people a drink from the spiritual cup.

57 John X.11: *ego sum pastor bonus; pastor bonus animam suam dat pro ouibus*
58 cf. use of *elegit*, Patrick, *Conf.* 56; Patrick, *Ep.* 6
cf. Patrick, *Conf.* 58: *plebem suam*
60 cf. Phil. II.30: *quoniam propter opus Christi usque ad mortem accessit tradens animam suam*
cf. Acts XV.26: *hominibus qui tradiderunt animas suas pro nomine Domini nostri Iesu Christi*
cf. Patrick, *Ep.* 1: *tradidi . . . animam meam usque ad mortem*
cf. Patrick, *Conf.* 24: *Qui dedit animam suam pro te*
65 cf. Matthew XXII.3: *et misit seruos uocare inuitatos ad nuptias*
66 Matthew XXII.11–12: *et uidit ibi hominem non uestitum ueste nuptiali, et ait illi amice quo modo huc intrasti non habens uestem nuptialem*
68 cf. I Cor. X.4: *et omnes eundem potum spiritalem biberunt*

Sacrum inuenit thesaurum sacro in uolumine
saluatoris in carne deitatem peruidet
quem thesaurum emit sanctis perfectisque meritis
Israel uocatur huius anima uidens Deum.

Testis Domini fidelis in lege catholica
cuius uerba sunt diuinis condida oraculis
ne humane putent carnes aessæque a uermibus
sed caelesti salleantur sapore ad uictimam.

Verus cultor et insignis agri euangelici
cuius semina uidentur Christi euangelia
quae diuino serit ore in aures prudentium
quorumque corda ac mentes sancto arat Spiritu.

Xpistus illum sibi elegit in teris uicarium
qui de gemino captiuos liberat seruitio
plerosque de seruitute quos redemit hominum
innumeros de zaboli absoluit dominio.

Ymnos cum apocalipsi salmosque cantat Dei
quosque ad aedificandum Dei tractat populum
quam legem in Trinitate sacri credit nominis
tribusque personis unam docetque substantiam.

Zona Domini praecinctus diebus ac noctibus
sine intermisione Deum orat Dominum
cuius ingentis laboris percepturus praemium
cum apostolis regnabit sanctus super Israel.

69 cf. Matthew XIII.44: *simile est regnum caelorum thesauro abscondito in agro*
73 Apoc. I.5; III.14; II.13: *testis fidelis*
Patrick, *Conf.* 58: *ut reddam illi testem fidelem*
75 cf. Mark IX.43, 45, 47: *ubi uermis eorum non moritur*
76 cf. Mark IX.48: *omnis enim igne sallietur et omnis uictima sallietur*
81 cf. use of *elegit*, Patrick, *Conf.* 56; Patrick, *Ep.* 6
83 cf. Patrick, *Conf.* 35: *Deus de seruitute saepe liberauit*
87 Patrick, *Conf.* 4: *adoramus unum Deum in trinitate sacri nominis*

He finds a sacred treasure-store in the sacred volume,
he sees the divinity of the Saviour in the flesh,
a treasure-store he purchases with holy and perfect qualities;
his soul is called Israel – 'seeing God'.

He is a faithful witness of the Lord in the catholic law,
whose words are seasoned with the prophecies of heaven,
that human flesh may not rot, eaten by worms,
but be salted for sacrifice with the savour of heaven.

He is a true and splendid tiller of the gospel-field,
whose seeds seem to be Christ's gospels,
which he sows with heavenly mouth in the ears of the wise,
and he ploughs their hearts and minds with the Holy Spirit.

Christ chose him to be His vicar on earth,
who frees captives from a twin servitude:
many he frees from bondage to men,
and countless sets free from the Devil's domain.

He sings hymns and the psalms of God, together with the Apocalypse,
which he recites to edify the people of God.
He believes as a law in the Trinity of sacred name
and teaches one substance in three persons.

Girt with the girdle of the Lord, night and day,
he prays to the Lord God without ceasing;
he will receive his reward for that huge labour:
holy, he will reign with the apostles over Israel.

89 cf. Apoc. I.13: *praecinctum ad mamillas zonam auream*
cf. Apoc. XV.6: *praecincti circa pectora zonis aureis*
90 II Tim. I.3: *quam sine intermissione habeam tui memoriam in orationibus meis nocte ac die*
92 cf. Matthew XIX.28: *sedebitis et uos super sedes duodecim iudicantes duodecim tribus Israhel*
cf. Luke XXII.30: *et sedeatis super thronos iudicantes duodecim tribus Israhel*
Patrick, *Ep.* 18: *uos ergo regnabitis cum apostolis et prophetis atque martyribus*

ST PATRICK AT HIS 'FIRST SYNOD'?

A conciliar text known to scholarship as 'the First Synod of St Patrick' (Pa. 1) or (by an abbreviation of the manuscript-title) *Sinodus episcoporum* survives in a unique copy, written at Tours in the second half of the ninth century.[1] This short series of canons has been an object of controversy both because of its alleged connexion with St Patrick and on account of its remarkable testimony to an early stage of Irish christianity. The sole copy of the text occurs in the company of other Hiberno-Latin matter in Cambridge, Corpus Christi College, MS. 279.[2] It is introduced very elaborately with a rubric written in display-scripts and occupying a whole page: 'Incipit sinodus episcoporum id est Patrici Auxilii Issernini'. More than a third of the next page is occupied by another statement, a salutation, in lesser display-scripts: 'Gratias agimus Deo patri et filio et Spiritui Sancto. Presbiteris et diaconibus et omni clero Patricius Auxilius Isserninus episcopi salutem.'[3] The text presents itself to us, therefore, as a statement of the *acta* of a synod led by three bishops famous in Patrician legend.

Interpretations of this document have varied greatly. A good many scholars of the first half of this century, following J.B. Bury,[4] were prepared to accept it as the record of a synod of Patrick's own time, often attributing a remarkably precise date to the event. Ludwig Bieler probably stood last in that tradition.[5] On the other hand, there has been a willingness to see in some of its provisions references either to circumstances unlikely to have obtained in Patrick's lifetime or to issues proper to a very much later date. As a result, a date as late as the seventh century has had to be seriously considered.[6] On the other hand, those who have accepted a date earlier than that have had to allow – if admitting that some elements point to a subsequent era – for interpolation of the text; however, this process was carried so far that it discredited itself.[7] The function of the text

1 For text and translation see *The Irish Penitentials*, edd. & transl. Bieler & Binchy, pp. 1–2, 15 (MS. W), 54–9, 240; *The Bishops' Synod*, ed. Faris. For a reproduction of pp. 1–11 of the manuscript, see *ibid.*, pp. 65–75 (but p. 2 of the manuscript has there been placed before p. 1).

2 For a recent description, with references to older scholarship, see De Brún & Herbert, *Catalogue*, p. 109 (no. 52).

3 In its display-scripts the manuscript corresponds to the classic practices of the Tours scriptorium: Rand, *Studies in the Script of Tours*, I.

4 *The Life*, pp. 233–45.

5 *The Irish Penitentials*, edd. & transl. Bieler & Binchy, p. 2, for Bieler's view.

6 Binchy, 'Patrick and his biographers', pp. 45–9 (and see also p. 168, n. 422), and 'St Patrick's "First Synod" '.

7 Bury and those who followed him allowed that §§25, 30, 33, 34 (and part of §6) were probably interpolations. To this list Bieler added §§8, 11, 14, 15, 24: 'Patrick's Synod' and 'Interpretationes patricianae'. Cf. Binchy, 'St Patrick's "First Synod" ', p. 54. Hughes, *The Church in Early Irish Society*, pp. 49–50, added §§2–3 to the tally of interpolated clauses.

is also greatly affected by these disputes: if taken at face-value this document is a record of conciliar proceedings in the fifth-century Irish Church; if it is a post-Patrician work, various interpretations are possible. It might have been an old and anonymous conciliar text which a subsequent copyist considered to derive from the apostolic era. It might have been an old document which an interpolator used as a vehicle for his own concerns and for which Patrician authority could be claimed. Finally, if it was a new creation of the seventh century, here was a deliberate attempt – in what was presumably therefore a text of private origin – to assert Patrician authority for currently controversial opinions on issues of the day. No doubt other interpretations of the claimed authorship are discoverable. In all this, the only points which are certain are the following. The document had been created by the end of the seventh century, for in the early eighth-century *Collectio canonum hibernensis* it is extensively quoted.[8] That source also shows that by that time our text was already travelling under the name of St Patrick.

It is not my purpose here to discuss, and reach a conclusion about, the date of *Sinodus episcoporum*. That problem will require separate treatment on another occasion. Instead I wish, first, to consider the factors which may be taken as difficulties in accepting its origin in a synod led by SS. Patrick, Auxilius, and Iserninus; having done that, I shall seek a context for its origin, which may ultimately help to explain some of the apparent contradictions which the document embodies.

We must begin by attempting to imagine the situation which would have obtained at the time at which Patrick, Auxilius, and Iserninus could have jointly presided at a synod. Leaving aside the dates in the range 447x459 which have been proposed on the basis of late evidence, we may say that any such gathering would have been held no more than sixty years after Palladius was sent to Ireland as first bishop, and, on one chronology of Patrick's life, no more than thirty. Nowadays no credence is, or can be, given to the hagiographical view that Patrick made Ireland wholly christian in the course of his lifetime: it is not possible to imagine that a missionary endeavour lasting one generation or two – however devoted it may have been – could have produced such a result. Patrick's *Confessio*, apparently written after a lengthy episcopate, leaves the impression that the struggle to establish the new religion had a long way still to run. While christianity might have been reasonably securely entrenched in some few petty kingdoms[9] (*reguli* were the class of rulers with whom St Patrick seems to have had to deal),[10] in general many local christian communities had no doubt been created but remained in a minority position. The latter might indeed seem to be the situation reflected in *Sinodus episcoporum*.

The more moderate case against a fifth-century origin for *Sinodus episcoporum* was put by Kathleen Hughes.[11]

[8] This relationship is most clearly laid out in the commentary in *The Bishops' Synod*, ed. Faris.
[9] That is to say, in those where christianity had first been introduced or in those where the new dispensation had particularly powerful supporters.
[10] Cf. Devine, *A Computer-generated Concordance*, p. 239 (*regulorum*); cf. p. 238 (*regibus*).
[11] *The Church in Early Irish Society*, pp. 44–5; cf. her *Early Christian Ireland*, p. 69.

It is very difficult to believe that the church depicted in these canons is the first-generation missionary church. Its organization is well developed, with *paruchiae* each under the control of their own bishops and having well-defined boundaries, for no one must invade the *paruchia* of another. All seven clerical grades are established, and lectors sing the office in each church. Clerics must come, when summoned, to sing the offices of matins and vespers (much as they were ordered to come by the Justinian Code) on pain of exclusion from the clergy. The last canon in the collection implies a form of monasticism no longer at its most primitive, for the monks live a community life under the rule of an abbot, and may not take journeys without his permission. It seems that the church would need some little time to reach this level of organizational development.

She also added the observation that §33, in rejecting the ministry of British clergy coming without proper letters of introduction, 'does not suggest the shortage of clergy you would expect in a first-generation church'.[12]

These points do not have equal weight. It is certainly the case that *Sinodus episcoporum* shows us a Church with a plurality of bishops. The jurisdiction (*parrochia*) of the bishop seems to be coterminous with the *plebs*, almost certainly the *tuath* ('tribe'; 'petty kingdom').[13] Within that jurisdiction the bishop should be supreme: but the necessity for legislation implies that that jurisdiction was being infringed by fellow-christians. In effect, this episcopal element in the text is the crucial point. Before all fifth-century dates for *Sinodus episcoporum* can be ruled out, scholars must satisfy themselves that a number of bishoprics coextensive with *plebes* could not have been created before the 490s; this requirement remains operative whether one considers that the three bishops named had any connexion with the promulgation of our document or not.[14] What is more, the rhetorical strategy of Patrick's *Confessio* prevents us from knowing whether or not he was at all times the sole bishop in Ireland.[15]

The questions about numbers of bishops and their interrelationships brings us to what seems to me to be the central issue for those who would seek to understand *Sinodus episcoporum* and to use its evidence in building a picture of the development of Irish christianity. The universal principle of interpretation of this text has been to consider it within a national framework.[16] In other words, the document has been taken as presenting the *acta* of a national synod. This has permitted the conditions displayed to be viewed as generally representative of the religious situation across the country. As a result, Kathleen Hughes was able to measure the state of development of christianity and the Church shown in this text against a linear, chronological scale which ran from universal paganism at

12 *The Church in Early Irish Society*, p. 49 and n. 1; she advanced further ideas in *Early Christian Ireland*, pp. 67–72.

13 Hughes, *The Church in Early Irish Society*, p. 50. For an objection to this point of view, see Sharpe, 'Some problems', p. 243, n. 2; and cf. Adams, 'Some linguistic problems'.

14 It is noteworthy – though of uncertain import – that the salutation opening *Sinodus episcoporum* implies that the three bishops named were the whole of the episcopate.

15 Patrick's opening statement in *Epistola ad Coroticum*, §1, could be taken to mean that he was one of a number of bishops in Ireland.

16 The only apparent exceptions to this have been Corish, *The Christian Mission*, p. 2 (a fifth-century Leinster synod's *acta*, albeit with interpolations), and R.H.M. Dolley in *The Bishops' Synod*, ed. Faris, p. 28 ('a document emanating from the Southern Irish church and taken over later for purposes of the Northern').

the beginning of the fifth century to predominant christianity in the seventh.[17] The result which she achieved was to place *Sinodus episcoporum* in the mid-sixth century.[18]

Yet to take the text as applying to a Church of the whole Irish nation is to sing the tune of the hagiographers who saw the work of conversion as a driving force across the country in Patrick's lifetime. One might indeed say also that to proceed thus is to take too seriously the rubric and salutation of *Sinodus episcoporum*. If one rejects the idea of a fully national synod, two possibilities of interpretation present themselves. One such would admit that these canons are the *acta* of a synod of the whole Irish Church but acknowledge also that that Church would have represented only a fraction of the national territory, significant parts of the island still having no christian population or organisation. That would in essence be an attempt to preserve the long-standing mode of interpretation while admitting what would nowadays be seen as the realities of the process of conversion. The other possibility would be to cut free completely from the notion that the synod represented the whole Irish Church.

The possibility that *Sinodus episcoporum* offers the *acta* of a gathering of a provincial Church opens up a broad range of potential datings – indeed, acknowledgment of that option demands that for the moment the widest available dating range be admitted for this text. It might indeed be argued that to recognise these *acta* as potentially those of a provincial synod would be to adapt better to the likely realities of political geography: it would probably have been politically difficult to organise a supraprovincial synod. In so far as the text shows a form of ecclesiastical organisation in which a bishop represents a *tuath*, a province would itself therefore contain a substantial number of bishops if each of the *tuatha* possessed organised christian communities.

The principal point to be recognised is that christianity is unlikely to have been carried into every *tuath*, or even every province, of the Gaelic world at the same time or in the same fashion. We surmise that christianity was introduced into Leinster and Ulster[19] (probably at that time a continuous band of east-coast territory)[20] in the fifth century. But when did it reach Munster or Connaught? If *Sinodus episcoporum* presents the *acta* of a synod of the province of Leinster, we shall be hard pressed (given that chronological basis) to deny that this could be a fifth-century text. On the other hand, if it represents a synod of a region more remote from the presumptively eastern-Irish sources of the island's christianity, one would have to hesitate before denying that both synod and text could belong to the seventh century.

17 Hughes, *The Church in Early Irish Society*, p. 45.

18 Hughes, *Early Christian Ireland*, p. 68. Given her procedure, it was illogical for her to say (*ibid.*, p. 71) that the evidence of *Sinodus episcoporum* 'invalidate[s] the old view of a conversion completed by 500'.

19 It has to be said, of course, that this geographical assessment rests heavily on the location of the cults of the alleged members of fifth-century missions. There is no contemporary evidence for the region(s) in which foreign clergy worked in the first generations of Irish christianity.

20 On the seizure of the plains of Mide, Brega, and Muirthemne by Uí Néill see Smyth, *Celtic Leinster*, as well as his more detailed study, 'The Húi Néill and the Leinstermen'.

CHURCH-GOVERNMENT AND THE SPREAD OF CHRISTIANITY IN IRELAND

One of the questions which have oppressed students of early mediaeval Irish history is how the government of the Church developed, indeed underwent revolutionary changes,[1] between the apostolic era and the seventh or eighth century. In the scholarship of the 1960s and 1970s the perception hardened that in the fifth and earlier sixth centuries foreign clerics had introduced into Ireland a system of Church-government like that known in the provinces of the late Roman empire.[2] The provisions of *Sinodus episcoporum* were used to give colour to what was in fact an *a priori* assumption. And, following the model of national applicability which I have described above,[3] that system was seen as extending to the entire country.

More recently, and particularly under the tutelage of Richard Sharpe,[4] scholars have learned to be more sceptical of these assumptions. It is far from clear that a universal, romanising governmental structure was introduced. Kathleen Hughes put it thus: 'Patrick's mission was distinctly unconventional . . . .[5] An ill-educated itinerant bishop, travelling with a paid retinue of young nobles, distributing largesse to petty kings, . . . Patrick's mission demonstrates that from the beginning the peculiar conditions of an extra-imperial, heroic society compelled unconventional measures of evangelization. . . . Yet the church . . . was the church already established elsewhere. It was not until later that its peculiarities hardened into a markedly different organization.'[6] Nevertheless, by the seventh century, in her view, a monastic form of government was becoming prominent in the Irish Church.[7] Sharpe has also taught us to be dubious about the universal applicability of the monastic model. He has wisely insisted upon what Hughes herself had stressed, the diversity apparent in so many aspects of Irish ecclesiastical culture in the early middle ages.[8]

It cannot be denied, however, that differences of organisational character are clearly evident between the Church portrayed in *Sinodus episcoporum* and that most commonly visible in eighth-century sources. Questions of the motivation, chronology, and mechanisms of change cannot therefore be avoided. However,

1 Hughes, *Early Christian Ireland*, p. 69.
2 This is particularly apparent in the discussions by Hughes, *The Church in Early Irish Society*, pp. 32–5, 50–2, 79–81, *et passim.*
3 See pp. 177–8.
4 See his fundamental essay, 'Some problems'.
5 *The Church in Early Irish Society*, p. 34.
6 *Ibid.*, p. 35.
7 *Ibid.*, p. 81, *et passim.*
8 Sharpe, 'Some problems', pp. 233–51; on diversity, cf. Hughes, *The Church in Early Irish Society*, pp. ix–x in particular.

one must avoid two traditional and associated ingredients of this discussion, the fallacy of universal applicability (which has always been assisted by the knowledge that such a view had already been taken in the middle ages by the author of *Catalogus sanctorum Hiberniae secundum diuersa tempora*)[9] and the desire to make change progress in a single linear chronological movement. What, then, were the major changes which affected the structure of the Irish Church as it grew during the early middle ages?

Inevitably the principal development must be admitted to be the rise of monasticism, but one would be unwise to be very confident about the chronology of this movement. It is clear that, already in the fifth century, Patrick was encouraging the monastic ideal – to the extent that one has felt obliged to ask whether he himself might have taken monastic vows.[10] In Britain, it is certain that there was a monastic element in the Church before the middle of the sixth century.[11] There seems to have been an explosion of enthusiasm and support for the monastic life in both Britain and Ireland in the central years of the sixth century,[12] leading to the earliest in a lengthy series of monastic foundations. Among these were monasteries of long-term significance in the history of the Gaelic Church – Bangor, Clonmacnoise, Iona, for example.

By the time when this process of monastic foundation was under way, the Irish Church cannot be pretended to have spread itself throughout the whole island, much less to have established organisational forms in every *tuath*. We simply do not know how rapidly or how slowly the process of evangelisation was advancing. From such a standpoint it is not surprising to be told that the last pagan king of the Southern Uí Néill was Diarmait mac Cerbaill (*ob.* 565), although whether this information has any historical validity is a nice question.[13] While major political dynasties remained pagan, the spread of the new religion might have remained restricted and the security of the Church precarious even in the east of Ireland.

A solution to the difficulty which has long troubled historians may therefore be in view. A traditional form of ecclesiastical government was established on Irish soil as christianity came to be made secure in its second generation. The primary unit of social and political organisation was the *tuath*, to which the diocese was therefore adapted. The number of bishops started to increase accordingly. Among the difficulties which Irish – like other west-European – bishops faced at this period was invasion of episcopal rights by founders of

9 Grosjean, 'Édition', and Sharpe, 'The origin'; cf. Sharpe, 'Some problems', p. 247 – 'This worthless text'.

10 Cf. above, pp. 16–17. For further discussion of interconnexions of episcopacy, missions, and monasticism, see Sheehy, 'Concerning the origin'; Hanson, 'The Church in fifth-century Gaul'; Herren, 'Mission'.

11 This is apparent from Gildas, *De excidio Britanniae*, I.27.

12 Gildas, *Fragmenta* (cf. Sharpe, 'Gildas as a Father') and *Praefatio de poenitentia* (*The Irish Penitentials*, edd. & transl. Bieler & Binchy, pp. 60–5, 240–2); Uinniau, *Penitentialis* (cf. Dumville, 'Gildas and Uinniau'); Columbanus, *Epistola I* (*Sancti Columbani opera*, edd. & transl. Walker & Bieler, pp. 2–13).

13 Binchy, 'The Fair' and 'A pre-christian survival'.

estate-churches and of monasteries.[14] As monastic enthusiasm increased, so would the problems of this sort multiply. Meanwhile, both the disorderly spread of christianity and the deliberate work of evangelisation would have continued. In this increasingly confused situation from the mid-sixth century it would not be surprising to find that the first evangelists to establish a christian community in a *tuath* were monks or that the first christians in a given area were a family of enthusiasts for the monastic life who gave their land to endow a monastic church. One might therefore argue that, whatever structural changes – revolutionary or otherwise – occurred within the earliest-organised dioceses, areas receiving christianity from the mid-sixth century onwards need never have been given such a form of ecclesiastical government, monastic churches being in such cases the primary factor. We should not deceive ourselves into thinking that a single, alternative form of administration is thus implied. There may have been executive monastic bishops in some *tuatha*, but managerial abbots with purely sacramental bishops in others. No doubt from the beginnings of substantial enthusiasm for the monastic life, bishops in the early-established dioceses felt acute pressures for change. Similarly one can imagine that, from not later than the seventh century, different systems may have begun to compete with one another. But there is little reason to allow that before the twelfth century there was any uniform pattern of Gaelic ecclesiastical government. Change there was in the early middle ages, but it was not such as to require us to see an all-encompassing transition from one system to another, occurring at much the same time across the country. Varying processes of conversion to christianity over a lengthy period seem likely to have been the determinants of continuing development and diversity in early mediaeval Irish Church-government.[15]

14 The evidence is provided by *Sinodus episcoporum*: cf. pp. 175–8, above. On the seventh and eighth centuries, see the discussions by Hughes, *The Church in Early Irish Society*, pp. 79–80, and Sharpe, 'Some problems'.

15 Hughes herself (*The Church in Early Irish Society*, p. 78) had observed that 'Ireland was hardly Christianized in a century, and early monastic churches may have been founded in places where the bishops had little influence'. For the survival of active paganism in seventh-century (and perhaps later) Ireland, see Binchy, 'St Patrick's "First Synod" ', p. 56; Sharpe, 'Hiberno-Latin *laicus*'; McCone, 'Werevolves'.

ST PATRICK AND THE CHRISTIANISATION OF DÁL RIATA

The geographical extent of Patrick's missionary labours in Ireland remains very uncertain. During the middle ages, following the lead given by Tírechán[1] Patrick's travels were extended to cover the entire island; this picture was systematised by modern historians whose efforts culminated in J. B. Bury's famous book, published in 1905.[2] Since then, a reaction has set in. It is fair to say that Patrick himself in his two surviving works gives no overt indication of his area of operations: he speaks of himself as a bishop in Ireland, perhaps even as a bishop for Ireland,[3] and tells his audience that he had carried the Gospel to districts – as far as the Ocean – beyond the point where other missionaries had reached.[4] We must accommodate within this a region which Coroticus and his men could assault; but, in view of the difficulties in identifying Coroticus and understanding his status and context, that does not help very much.[5]

The late seventh-century hagiographers of Patrick had their own agenda. Drawing in part on common sources or on one another, Muirchú and Tírechán certainly showed the saint in motion. Muirchú seems especially concerned to demonstrate Patrick's supremacy over the kings of Tara and in consequence took him to Meath.[6] But Muirchú also told of a particular determination of the saint, to visit the man who had owned Patrick during those years of his youth as a slave in Ireland.[7] Patrick himself, in the *Confessio*, offers little help to any reader who would identify the location of his captivity.[8] All he tells us is that he had to travel perhaps two hundred miles from his place of slavery to an unknown location in which he would find a ship. Some years later, when he was in Britain with his family, he dreamed that he saw a man called Uictoricus coming from Ireland bearing letters, of which one was for Patrick.[9] As he read its opening words, 'Vox Hiberionacum . . .', he imagined that he heard the voice of those who were 'beside the forest of Foclut (*iuxta siluam Focluti*)[10] which is near the western sea (*prope mare occidentale*)'. On these words have been

1 *The Patrician Texts*, edd. & transl. Bieler & Kelly, pp. 124–67.
2 Bury, *The Life*.
3 *Epistola*, §1: 'Patricius peccator indoctus, scilicet *Hiberione constitutus episcopum*, me esse fateor'. Cf. *Confessio*, §62: 'scripturam quam Patricius peccator indoctus scilicet Hiberione conscripsit'.
4 *Confessio*, §51.
5 See above, pp. 107–15.
6 I.14–22 (*The Patrician Texts*, edd. & transl. Bieler & Kelly, pp. 84–99).
7 Muirchú, I.11–12 (*ibid.*, pp. 76–81).
8 §§16–17 provide the evidence, such as it is.
9 *Confessio*, §23.
10 For the variant readings in the manuscripts, and for scholars' conjectural emendations, see *Saint Patrick*, edd. & transl. Hanson & Blanc, p. 96.

based identifications of Patrick's place of captivity. It has to be said that the linkage of the two is at best inspired interpretation: there is no necessary warrant for it in what Patrick wrote. Identifications of the place-name have been various and I have no desire to accept or reject any of them here. There is an outside possibility that the 'western ocean' is the Irish Sea – western to Britain, that is –, but the more natural interpretation would make it the Atlantic and *silua Focluti* a place on the oceanic coast of Ireland: from Donegal to Kerry there is, however, a wide choice of possible sites, although modern scholars have tended to prefer a location in Connaught – near Killala, Co. Mayo.[11]

The hagiographers did not hesitate, however: Patrick's slave-master was one Miliucc who was *moccu Bóin*[12] – of the Bónrige or Dál mBóin.[13] This anchored Patrick's Irish experiences firmly in Ulster. Consideration of their treatment of this story allows us to see what was the information available to these writers and what were some of their political concerns. St Patrick's first desire after he returned to Ireland as bishop was to go to convert Miliucc. He therefore set out for Ulster. His first convert was the result of a chance-encounter with one Díchu, 'habitans ibi ubi nunc est orreum Patricii nomine cognominatum', 'living in the place where there is now the barn named after Patrick': this is Saball Pátraic (Saul, Co. Down) in the territory of Dál Fiatach Ulad. Patrick then travelled by land 'in regiones Cruidnenorum donec peruenit ad montem Miss', 'to the territory of the Cruithni until he came to Slíab Miss', Slemish (Co. Antrim),[14] or (as Tírechán called it) *mons Miss Boonrigi*, 'Slemish of the Bónrige'.[15] Eoin MacNeill showed that this place was 'on or near the border between Dal Araidhe and Dal Riada'.[16] Rather than face his former slave, King Miliucc gathered all his wealth into his residence and burned it and himself. Patrick, aghast at the sight and the deed, prophesied that 'none of his sons shall sit on his throne as king of his kingdom in generations to come; what is more, his line shall be subordinate for ever'.[17] He then returned from the territory of the Cruithni (Dál nAraide) to Díchu in the territory of the Ulaid (Dál Fiatach). Díchu's territory was in Mag nInis, which has been identified as the barony of Lecale in Co. Down.[18] He 'stayed there for many days and travelled around the whole plain. He favoured and loved it, and the faith began to spread there.'

There is little doubt that a message is being conveyed here. Patrick's first conversions were in Ulster, but among Dál Fiatach not Dál nAraide; on the contrary, his contacts (both as a slave and as a missionary) with the Cruithni were unpleasant, and the Bónrige at least were politically damned as a result. What is more, within Dál Fiatach the place most favoured by Patrick was Saul

11 For a full discussion of the matter, see Bieler, 'The problem'.
12 Muirchú, I.11–12; Tírechán, §§1, 16, 49.
13 For the identification see MacNeill, 'Early Irish population-groups', pp. 70 and 75, and *Saint Patrick*, p. 51. Cf. Ó Briain, 'Studien', p. 224.
14 Muirchú, I.11.
15 §49 (*The Patrican Texts*, edd. & transl. Bieler & Kelly, pp. 162–3).
16 *Saint Patrick*, p. 155.
17 Muirchú, I.12.
18 *The Patrician Texts*, edd. & transl. Bieler & Kelly, p. 260, s.v. *Inis(s)*.

and its region.[19] When the time came for Patrick's death, an angel ordered him to go not to Armagh but to Saul; in the event he was buried at nearby Dún Lethglaisse (Downpatrick).[20]

These legends making Saul the place of Patrick's first successful missionary endeavour,[21] Mag nInis his most favoured region, and Downpatrick the place of his burial are known to us first from the late seventh century, two hundred years after the event. Nevertheless, they demand some respect from the historian partly because, with the date of a saint's death, the place of his burial and therefore cult is likely to be the oldest piece of information about him.[22] Perhaps an equally compelling reason for taking this information seriously is that Muirchú shows no sign of hostility towards Downpatrick or its association with St Patrick: it looks as though at that time the clergy of Armagh might have felt obliged to admit these old claims by the churches of Saul and Downpatrick.

The best which can be said is that the situation of Patrick's principal missionary endeavours among Dál Fiatach Ulad could be advanced with credibility in the late seventh century. We must be aware that the works of Muirchú and Tírechán, from which we draw this information, also show the saint active at Tara, Armagh, and in many other parts of Ireland: it is important that our perspective does not become distorted. What is clear, however, is that of the three principal peoples of early mediaeval Ulster only Dál Fiatach finds favour in these hagiographical accounts. Patrick's contacts with Dál nAraide are unhappy and those with Dál Riata non-existent. Only in the work of subsequent hagiographers were these peoples brought successfully within the ambit of Patrick's activities.

Patrick's literary excursion to the territory of the Bónrige brought him to the borderland of Dál nAraide and Dál Riata. Eoin MacNeill's remarks on this region are worth quoting. Having observed that King Miliucc and his people belonged to the Cruithni, MacNeill continued:[23]

> His sept is named Dal Buain and he himself is named with a corresponding surname, Miliucc Moccu Buain. His territory continued to bear the name Dal Buain until modern times. It appears to have extended from the eastern side of Lough Neagh northwards as far as Sliabh Mis (Slemish) within the present county of Antrim.

MacNeill noted that Slemish stood on the border of Dál nAraide and Dál Fiatach,[24] and discussed that borderland in some detail.[25]

19 Mag nInis and the Ulaid reappear twice in Muirchú's narrative (I.23, 26). In the first episode, which alone has useful detail, he encounters the brigand Macc Cuill moccu Greccae; the story leads on to an account of early christianity in the Isle of Mann (with which Ulster seems to have had or claimed some connexion).

20 Muirchú, II.4–14 (especially II.5 and 11).

21 Saul may also have been intended by Muirchú as the place of Patrick's death, but his narrative is not explicit on the point.

22 Cf. the discussion by Sharpe, 'St Patrick and the see of Armagh', pp. 39–44.

23 *Saint Patrick*, p. 51.

24 *Ibid.*, p. 155.

25 *Ibid.*, p. 208. In the quotation I have italicised the references to Hogan, *Onomasticon*, and expanded MacNeill's 'V T' to *Vita tripartita*.

Modern books show much confusion as regards the ancient extent and limits of the kingdom of Dál Riata in Ireland, and this confusion has unfortunately been continued by *Onomasticon Goedelicum*, which cites Usher and Colgan as authorities for identifying Dál Riata with the district named 'an Rúta', 'the Route'. In the Annals of Ulster, the latter name is found for the first time under date of 1357 in the form 'Rút Mic Uidhilin', under later dates in the form 'an Rúta'. I take this name to have been introduced by the feudal colonists and to represent the French *route* applied to the most northern section of the ancient main road, Slige Midluachra, which ended at Dún Sobairche, Dunseverick. Neither etymologically nor topographically is there any identity between Dál Riata and Rúta. The Route is a district in the north-west of Co. Antrim, and is still so named, its market centre being Ballymoney. Dál Riata is the north-eastern district of the same county, but extended as far west as the river Buas, Bush. The river Fregabal, now called in English the 'Ravel Water', appears to have formed part of the southern boundary; it now forms part of the boundary between the barony of Kilconway and the baronies of Lower Antrim and Lower Toome. Further east, Dál Riata, in the topography of *Vita tripartita*, did not extend to the river of Glenarm, for *Vita tripartita* places in Dál Araidi the church of Gluare, founded by Patrick. The site in 'the Glore', on the west side of the Glenarm river, is occupied by an ancient cemetery called 'the Old Church'. *Vita tripartita* locates Gluare in a district named Latharne, later Latharna, a name now represented by that of the town of Larne and Larne Glen, about nine miles distant from the Glore: one of many instances that show the risk of facile assumption in seeking to fix topographical bounds for any period by the topography of another period. The kingdom of Dál Riata in the seventh century should thus have extended no farther than from the Giant's Causeway to Glenarm Bay. *Onomasticon Goedelicum* makes it extend about twelve miles father southward, to Glenn Indechta or Gleann Finneachta, identifying this with the valley of Glynn, about two miles south of Larne. *Vita tripartita*, however, places Glenn Indechta in Dál Araidi, naming it immediately after Gluare and Latharne aforesaid. It would thus appear that, at a time later than the topography of *Vita tripartita*, Dál Riata gained territory southward along the coast.

In spite of the exclusion of Dál nAraide from Patrick's favourable attention in the works of Muirchú and Tírechán, it is clear that by the time of the creation of the *notulae* found in the 'Book of Armagh'[26] Dál Riata and Dál nAraide had been brought into the view of Patrician hagiotopography.[27] An intermediate point may be indicated by the situation envisaged in *Liber Angeli*, in which Armagh has a particular jurisdiction over a *terminus* (*termonn*) *uastissimus* comprehending the Airgialla, Dál Fiatach, and Dál nAraide, but excluding Dál Riata.[28]

If Patrick had indeed brought christianity to Dál Fiatach in the fifth century, it is a nice question how this would have affected Dál nAraide and Dál Riata. If they were under the overkingship of Dál Fiatach they might have been introduced or even subjected to christianity; equally we might suppose that the other peoples would have recoiled from a new religion associated with their rivals.

26 *The Patrician Texts*, edd. & transl. Bieler & Kelly, pp. 180–3, 238; cf. *The Tripartite Life*, ed. & transl. Stokes, II.348–51.

27 MacNeill, *Saint Patrick*, pp. 147, 150–1, 156.

28 *Ibid.*, pp. 155–6: for §7 of *Liber angeli*, see *The Patrician Texts*, edd. & transl. Bieler & Kelly, pp. 184–5.

Unfortunately the matter has a number of consequences for the history of northern Britain in the second half of the sixth century.

Speaking of the early mediaeval province of the Ulaid, Eoin MacNeill remarked[29] that it

> was divided into a number of minor kingdoms and none of these held a permanent headship over the others. The kingdom of Dal Riada in the northeastern corner facing Cantire [Kintyre], though it was small in extent and poor in fertility, had the advantage of lying nearest to the Irish settlements beyond the channel in the islands and forelands of southwestern Scotland. The kings of Dal Riada do not appear to have taken up their own abode in those parts until a time some years later than St. Patrick's death. Many years were yet to pass before Scotland was united under their sovereignty.

MacNeill envisaged a two-stage process by which Dál Riata was established in northern Britain. First, and presumably contemporaneously with the Gaelic assaults on and migrations to other parts of western Britain,[30] settlements took place on some of the Western Isles and on parts of the Argyll mainland. Subsequently, as the settlements became economically and politically more significant than the modest homeland, the rulers of Dál Riata removed themselves to Britain.[31] While this history is not unlikely in principle, no literary evidence exists to validate it. We await the development of archaeological investigation to the point where the establishment of Gaelic-speaking population and consequent Dalriadan authority in Britain can be dated.[32] Until that desideratum has been achieved, there is no compulsion to allow or reject either the earliest possible (fourth-century?) or the latest (early sixth-century?) date for that process – which could in any case have occupied a substantial period. We have no reason to accept the apparent origin-legend, attested first in the earlier tenth century, which brought an ancestor-figure to Britain *ca* A.D. 500:[33] 'Feargus Mor mac Earca cum gente Dalraida partem Britaniæ tenuit, et ibi mort<u>us est'. Even less will Bede's version do, although it is two centuries earlier, in which an eponymous ancestor (Reuda) of all Dál Riata was credited

29 *Saint Patrick*, p. 73.

30 For the geographical extent of such settlements, from Argyll to Cornwall, see Thomas, 'The Irish settlements'.

31 For discussion of this point see Bannerman, *Studies*, pp. 1, 124. Modern historians have added a phase of political separation of the two in the seventh century: Bannerman, *ibid.*, pp. 1–8; *Adomnán's Life of Columba*, edd. & transl. Anderson & Anderson, p. xxv. Cf. Dumville, 'Cath Fedo Euin'.

32 That this point has not yet been reached is clear from the paper by Nieke & Duncan, 'Dalriada'.

33 This is drawn from the 'Annals of Tigernach': it is not found in the 'Annals of Ulster', conforming instead to a type of entry proper to the 'Chronicle of Clonmacnoise' created in the first half of the tenth century; cf. Grabowski & Dumville, *Chronicles and Annals*, chapter II. Fergus Mór was the ancestor-figure for Cenél nGabráin and Cenél Comgaill but not the other two principal royal dynasties of (British) Dál Riata, Cenél nOengusso and Cenél Loairn. Bannerman (*Studies*, p. 1; cf. pp. 73–5, 86, 118–32) has accepted the historicity of the information offered by the 'Annals of Tigernach', unwisely in my view; indeed, he has gone so far as to assert (*ibid.*, p. 105; cf. p. 73) that 'In all probablity the Dál Riata in Ireland had been governed from Scotland since the time of Fergus mac Eirc'.

with leading Irish settlers into Pictland, gaining territory now by alliance and now by force.[34]

No early source tells us anything of the introduction of christianity to Dál Riata. Indeed, we have information about the British Dál Riata before we learn anything of the ecclesiastical history of their counterparts in Ulster. In 562 the future St Columba (Colum Cille) found himself excommunicated and thus apparently exiled from Ireland by a synod,[35] seemingly for his role in the battle of Cúil Dreimne, fought the previous year.[36] Obeying the letter rather than the spirit of the sentence passed upon him,[37] Columba took himself to a Hebridean island on what must then have been a border-zone between Dál Riata and Pictland.[38] While this may seem to have been in the best traditions of Gaelic asceticism, combining a sea-pilgrimage to find a desert in the ocean with eremitic settlement on a remote island,[39] it seems unlikely that Columba's exile was excessively humbling. We find him continuing to play a significant role in Gaelic secular and ecclesiastical politics. The element of that life which immediately concerns us is his place in the ecclesiastical history of Dál Riata.

Most of our information about Columba's activities in Dál Riata is drawn from the *Vita S. Columbae* written by the ninth abbot of Iona, Adomnán, a century after Columba's death.[40] The hagiographer's sources were no doubt largely associated with the house-traditions of Iona Abbey about its founder; the annalistic evidence from Iona, such as it is, is unlikely to be independent.[41] As Marjorie Anderson has noted, the Dál Riata of Columba's day 'seem to have been Christians' and there is no hint of his undertaking vigorous missionary work among them.[42] It was their eastern and northern neighbours, the Picts, who were heathen.[43] If the Dál Riata were christian, then we must suppose that by the mid-sixth century an ecclesiastical infrastructure had already been created, to which Iona was in the first instance but a monastic appendage.[44]

What is striking is the extent of the authority in northern Britain which Iona had apparently long since acquired by the time when Bede had occasion to refer to this matter. He repeatedly stressed that that church had become the head of an international organisation:[45] 'the monastery was for a very long time chief

34 *Historia ecclesiastica gentis Anglorum*, I.1 (ed. Plummer, I.12; cf. II.9–10).

35 Adomnán, *Vita S. Columbae*, III.3 (cf. I.7), on the Synod of Tailtiu (Teltown, Co. Meath).

36 'Annals of Ulster' 561.1: the entry concludes, 'Per orationes Coluim Cille uicerunt'.

37 Adomnán, *Vita S. Columbae*, III.4, for his voyage with twelve disciples. The founding of Iona was dated 565 by Bede (*Historia ecclesiastica gentis Anglorum*, III.4) but 563 by Gaelic sources probably all ultimately dependent on Adomnán, *Vita S. Columbae*, Secunda praef., I.7, III.22–23. That Columba made return-visits to Ireland is clear: see *Adomnán's Life of Columba*, edd. & transl. Anderson & Anderson, p. xxxv.

38 According to the 'Annals of Ulster' 574.2, it had been granted to him by King Conall mac Comgaill.

39 Cf. *Vita S. Columbae*, I.6 and II.42, on Cormac of Uí Léthain; cf. Dumville, '*Echtrae* and *immram*'.

40 *Adomnán's Life of Columba*, edd. & transl. Anderson & Anderson, p. xlii.

41 On these points see Herbert, *Iona, Kells*.

42 *Adomnán's Life of Columba*, edd. & transl. Anderson & Anderson, pp. xxxi, xxxii.

43 *Ibid.*, pp. xxxii–xxxv (especially xxxiv).

44 On the other hand the stories about Columba in the *uita* were drawn from all parts of his thirty-five-year career in Britain; it is not impossible that the earlier years of this period did see much missionary or Church-building effort.

45 *Historia ecclesiastica gentis Anglorum*, III.3, 4, 21; V.9.

among almost all the monasteries of the northern Irish and all those of the Picts, exercising supervision (*regendisque*) over their peoples'.[46] It may be that in Dál Riata this status was achieved because of the arrival there, in the second half of the sixth century and the first half of the seventh, of the new enthusiasm for the monastic life to which Columba was himself a witness. In Ireland that same process also created in the same period monasteries of dispersed jurisdictions and great status.[47] A further and perhaps equally important aspect of the rise of Iona may have been Columba's status, both as an ascetic and as a politically significant member of a major royal dynasty: he is said to have received the grant of Iona from Conall mac Comgaill, king of Cenél Comgaill and apparently overking of all Dál Riata, and Adomnán shows us Columba in the king's presence.[48] Columba is also associated by Adomnán with Conall's successor Aedán mac Gabráin, king of Cenél nGabráin, and with the subsequent fortunes of his dynasty.[49]

If we suppose that christianity had come to British Dál Riata before Columba's day (and therefore not later than the very middle of the sixth century), we are obliged to suppose that it had already spread in Irish Dál Riata not later than the first half of the century. This chain of reasoning must lead us to deduce that christianity was advancing in northern Ulster within a generation or two of Patrick's death.[50] Whether that permits the further deduction that St Patrick was himself active in Ulster is another question.

46 *Ibid.*, III.3.
47 Cf. Hughes, *The Church in Early Irish Society*, pp. 39–78.
48 'Annals of Ulster' 574.3; Adomnán, *Vita S. Columbae*, I.7. These do not make it certain that King Conall was a christian, but it is more likely than not, especially if his successor in 574 was.
49 *Vita S. Columbae*, I.9; III.15.
50 Cf. Sharpe, 'St Patrick and the see of Armagh', pp. 43, 55.

THE FORM OF ST PATRICK'S *CONFESSIO* IN THE 'BOOK OF ARMAGH'

Liber Ardmachanus, written at Armagh *ca* A.D. 800 (and partly at least in 807 at the instance of Torbach, coarb of St Patrick), contains on fos 22ra10–24va a copy of St Patrick's *Confessio* which the scribe Ferdomnach's colophon describes as 'uolumen quod Patricius manu conscripsit sua'. The introductory rubric, however, states that here begin '*libri* sancti Patricii episcopi'.[1] It has often been supposed that the exemplar contained also St Patrick's Letter about Coroticus and that that was omitted, for whatever reason, by Ferdomnach (or even that it had been omitted at an earlier stage of the textual history).[2] This view has seemed to agree well with the condition of the text of Patrick's *Confessio* in the 'Book of Armagh'. It is a version of the text which is significantly shorter than that found in other manuscripts. Thirty years of gentle controversy have explored the proposition that the short text in the 'Book of Armagh' was original, or an early draft:[3] in my view, the discussion has shown this view to be unsustainable. That conclusion does not, however, rob the shorter version of its interest. If, as D. A. Binchy suggested, large sections of the text were excised because they displayed Patrick's humility and sensitivity, as well as the frequent weakness of his position, in a way which would have seemed incomprehensible once Patrick was being presented by hagiographical propagandists as an all-conquering wonder-worker,[4] comparison of the two versions becomes important as a study in the ecclesiastical outlooks of two different ages. (One must, however, note that as the work progresses there are unmistakable signs of abbreviation for its own sake.) I therefore give here a full text of Patrick's *Confessio*, but with those chapters omitted from the copy in the 'Book of Armagh' reproduced in *italics*. I trust that this will give easy access to both versions and encourage fruitful study of their differences.

1 For a facsimile, see *Book of Armagh*, ed. E. Gwynn; for a diplomatic text, see *Liber Ardmachanus*, ed. J. Gwynn; for critical editions of the *Confessio* see 'Libri', ed. Bieler, and *Saint Patrick*, edd. & transl. Hanson & Blanc (there is an older edition, *Libri*, ed. White); for a plain (but edited) text, see *St. Patrick*, ed. & transl. Hood. For the palaeography of Dublin, Trinity College, MS. 52, the 'Book of Armagh', see Lowe, *Codices*, II, no. 270, and Sharpe, 'Palaeographical considerations'.

2 Cf. Binchy, 'Patrick and his biographers', pp. 65–6, and Sharpe, 'Palaeographical considerations', pp. 14–15.

3 Esposito, 'The Patrician problem'; Bieler, 'The Lives of St. Patrick'; Grosjean, 'The Confession'; Carney, *The Problem*, p. 93; Binchy, 'Patrick and his biographers', pp. 40–2; Powell, 'The textual integrity'; Hanson, 'The omissions'; Powell, 'St Patrick's Confession'; Hanson, 'The D-text'. For older treatments see Healy, *The Life*, p. 631; *Liber Ardmachanus*, ed. J. Gwynn, p. lxxx.

4 Binchy, 'Patrick and his biographers', pp. 41–2.

Incipiunt libri sancti Patricii episcopi.
<CONFESSIO>

1 Ego Patricius, peccator rusticissimus et minimus omnium fidelium et contemptibiliss<imus>[5] apud plurimos, [6]patrem habui Calpornium diaconum filium quondam Potiti `filii Odissi´[7] presbyteri qui fuit uico Bannauem Taberniæ; uillulam enim prope habuit ubi ego capturam dedi. Annorum eram tunc fere .xvi.. Deum uerum ignorabam et Hiberione in captiuitate adductus sum cum tot milia hominum secundum merita nostra quia a Deo recessimus et praecepta eius non custodiuimus et sacerdotibus nostris non oboedientes fuimus qui nostram salutem admonebant; et Dominus induxit super nos iram animationis suę et dispersit nos in gentibus multis etiam usque ad ultimum terrae ubi nunc paruitas mea esse uidetur inter alenigenas.

2 Et ibi Dominus aperuit sensum **<22rb>** incredulitatis meæ ut sero rememorarem dilicta mea ut confirmarem toto corde ad Dominum Deum meum qui respexit humilitatem meam et missertus est adoliscentiæ ignorantiæ meæ et custodiuit me antequam scirem eum et antequam saperem uel distinguerem inter bonum et malum et muniuit me et consulatus est me(i) ut pater filium.

3 Unde autem tacere non possum – neque expedit quidem – tanta beneficia et tantam gratiam quam mihi dignatus in terra captiuitatis meæ; quia haec est retributio (mea)[8] nostra ut post correptionem uel agnitionem Dei exaltare et confiteri mirabilia eius coram omni natione quae est sub omni caelo.

4 Quia non est alius Deus nec umquam fuit nec ante nec erit post haec praeter Deum Patrem ingenitum sine principio a quo est omne principium omnia tenentem ut dicimus; et eius filium Iesum Christum qui cum Patre scilicet semper fuisse testamur ante originem saeculi spiritaliter apud Patrem inerrabiliter genitum ante omne principium; et per ipsum facta sunt uissibilia; hominem factum morte deuicta in cælis; et dedit illi omnem potestatem super omne nomen caelestium et terrestrium et infernorum et omnis lingua confiteatur ei quia Dominus et Deus est Iesus Christus quem credimus et ex(ce)pectamus aduentum mox futurum iudex uiuorum atque mortuorum qui reddet unicuique secundum facta sua; et effudit in uobis habunde Spiritum Sanctum donum et pignus inmortalitatis qui facit credentes et oboedientes ut sint filii Dei et coheredes Christi; quem confitemur et adoramus unum Deum in Trinitate sacri nominis.

5 *contemptibilissem*, MS.
6 In the manuscript, the first twelve words of the text have been separated from the rest and written in a more elevated script.
7 A marginal addition in the manuscript.
8 In the manuscript, this word stands beneath a triangle of dots.

5 Ipse enim dixit per profetam: 'Inuoca me in die tribulationis tuæ et liberabo te et magnificabis me'. **<22va>** Et iterum inquit: 'Opera `autem´ Dei reuelare et confiteri honorificum est'.

6 Tamen etsi in multis inperfectus sum, opto fratribus et cogn(ot)atis meis scire qualitatem meam ut possint perficere uotum animæ meæ.

7 Non ignoro testimonium Domini mei qui in psalmo[9] testatur: 'Perdes eos qui loquntur mendacium'. Et iterum inquit: 'Os quod mentitur occidit animam'. Et idem Dominus: 'Uerbum otiossum quod locuti fuerint homines reddent rationem de eo in die iudicii'.

8 Unde autem uehimenter cum timore et tremore metuere hanc sententiam in die illa ubi nemo se poterit subtrahere uel abscondere sed omnes omnino reddituri sumus rationem etiam minimorum peccatorum ante tribunal Domini Christi.

9 Quapropter ollim cogitaui scribere sed et usque nunc hessitaui; timui enim ne incederem in linguam hominum quia non dedici sicut et caeteri qui optime itaque iure et sacras literas utroque pari modo combiberunt et sermones illorum ex infantia numquam motarunt sed magis ad perfectum semper addiderunt. Nam sermo et loquela nostra translata est in linguam alienam sicut facile potest probari ex aliue scripturæ meæ qualiter sum ego in sermonibus instructus atque eruditus quia inquit, 'sapiens per linguam dinoscetur et sensus et scientia et doctrina ueritatis'.

10 Sed quid prodest excussatio iuxta ueritatem praesertim cum praesumptione quatinus modo ipse adpeto in senectute mea quod in iuuentute non conparaui quod obstiterunt ut confirmarem quod ante perlegeram? Sed si quis me cre(di)dit etsi dixero quod ante praefatus sum? Adoliscens **<22vb>** immo pene puer inuerbis capturam dedi antequam scirem quid peterem uel quid adpeterem uel quid uitare debueram. Unde ergo hodie erubesco et uehimenter protimeo denudare imperitiam meam quia non (possum de)[10] deeritis breuitate sermone explicare nequeo sicut enim spiritus gestit et animas et sensus monstrat adfectus.

11 Sed si itaque datum mihi fuisset sicut et cæteris uerumtamen non silerem propter retributionem et si forte uidetur apud aliquantos me in hoc praeponere cum mea inscientia et tardiori lingua sed scriptum est: 'Linguæ balbutientes uelociter discent loqui pacem'. Quanto magis nos adpetere debemus qui sumus nos, 'aepistola Christi in salutem usque ad ultimum terrę', et si non deserta sed ratum fortissimum 'scriptum in cordibus uestris non atramento sed spiritu Dei uiui'. Et iterum Spiritus testatur et rusticationem ab Altissimo creata est.

[9] The scribe has used Greek ψ for *ps-*.
[10] In the manuscript, these words are surmounted by triangles of dots.

12 Unde ego primus rusticus profuga inductus scilicet qui nescio in posterum prouidere sed illud scio certissime quia utique priusquam humiliarer ego eram uelut lapis qui iacet in luto profundo; et uenit[11] qui potens est et in sua missericordia sustulit me et quidem scilicet sursum adleuauit et collocauit me in sua pariete; et inde fortiter debueram exclamare ad retribuendum quoque aliquid Domino pro tantis beneficiis eius hic et in aeternum quae mens hominum æstimare non potest.

13 Unde autem ammiramini **<23ra>** magni et pusilli et uos dominicati qui timetis Deum rethorici audite et scrutamini. Quis me stultum excitauit de medio eorum qui uidentur esse sapientes et legis periti et potentes in sermone et in omni re et me quidem detestabilis huius mundi `prae´ (de)[12] cæteris inspirauit si talis essem dummodo autem ut cum metu et reuerentia et sine querella fideliter genti ad quam caritas Christi transtulit et donauit me in uita mea si `dignus´ (uiuus)[12] fuero; denique ut cum humilitate et ueraciter deseruirem illis.

14 In mensura itaque fidei Trinitatis oportet distinguere sine reprehensione periculi notum facere donum Dei et consolationem æternam sine timore fiducialiter Dei nomen ubique expandere ut etiam post obitum meum exagallias[13] relinquere fratribus et filiis meis quos in Domino ego babtizaui tot milia hominum.

15 Et non eram dignus neque talis ut hoc Dominus seruulo suo concederet post erumpnas et tantas moles post captiuitatem post annos <m>ultos[14] in gentem illam tantam gratiam mihi donerat – quod ego aliquando in iuuentute mea numquam speraui neque cogitaui.

16 Sed postquam Hiberione deueneram cotidie itaque pecora pascebam et frequens in die orabam; magis ac magis accedebat amor Dei et timor ipsius et fides augebatur et spiritus agebatur ut in die una usque ad centum orationes et in nocte prope similiter ut etiam in siluis et monte manebam ante lucem excitabar ad orationem **<23rb>** per niuem per gelu per pluiam et nihil mali sentiebam neque ulla pigritia erat in me – sicut modo uideo quia tunc Spiritus in me feruebat.

17 Et ibi scilicet quadam nocte in somno audiui uocem dicentem (sibi)[15] mihi: 'Bene ieiunas cito (ieiunanus)[15] iturus ad patriam tuam'. Et iterum post paululum tempus audiui responsum dicentem mihi: 'Ecce nauis tua parata est'. Et non erat prope sed forte habebat .cc. milia passus et ibi numquam fueram nec ibi notum quemquam de hominibus habebam. Et deinde postmodum conuersus sum in fugam et intermissi hominem cum fueram .vi.

11 Altered from *ueniens* by adding subscript *-t* and placing a triangle of dots above *-ens*.
12 Transposition-marks stand above this word in the text and the preceding word in the margin.
13 In the margin stands a note tied to this place: 'Inc(erc)/ertus/ liber'.
14 *inultos*, MS.
15 Overpointed for deletion, MS.

annis et ueni in uirtute Dei qui uiam meam ad bonum dirigebat et nihil metuebam donec perueni ad nauem illam.

18 Et illa die qua perueni profecta est nauis de loco suo et locutus sum ut abirem unde nauigarem cum illis; et gubernatori displicuit illi et acriter cum interrogatione[16] respondit: 'Nequaquam tu nobiscum adpetes ire'. Et cum haec audiissem separaui me ab illis ut uenirem ad tegoriolum ubi hospitabam et in itenere cæpi orare et antequam orationem consummarem audiui unum ex illis et fortiter exclamabat post me: 'Ueni cito, quia uocant te homines isti'. Et statim ad illos reuersus sum et coeperunt mihi dicere: 'Ueni quia ex fide recipimus te; fac nobiscum amicitiam quomodo uolueris'; et in illa die itaque reppuli sugere mammellas eorum propter timorem Dei sed uerumtamen ab illis speraui uenire in fidem Iesu Christi quia gentes erant et ob hoc obtinui cum illis.

19 Et post triduum terram cæpimus **<23va>** et .xxviii. dies per disertum iter fecimus et cibus defuit illis et fames inualuit super eos et alio die coepit gubernator mihi dicere: 'Quid, christiane? Tu dicis deus tuus magnus et omnipotens est; quare ergo pro nobis orare non potes? Quia nos a fame periclitamur; difficile enim umquam ut aliquem hominem uideamus.' Ego enim euidenter dixi illis: 'Conuertemini ex fide ad Dominum Deum meum cui nihil est inpossibile ut cibum mittat uobis in uiam uestram usque dum satiamini; quia ubique habundat illi'. Et adiuante Deo ita factum est; ecce grex porcorum in uia ante oculos nostros apparuit et multos ex illis interficerunt et ibi .ii. noctes manserunt et bene refecti et canes eorum repleti sunt quia multi ex illis secus uiam semiuiui relicti sunt; et post haec summas gratias egerunt Deo et ego honorificatus sum sub oculis eorum. Etiam mel siluistre inuenierunt et mihi partem obtulerunt et unus ex illis dixit: 'Immolaticium est'. Deo gratias, exinde nihil gustaui.

20 Eadem uero eram dormiens et fortiter temptauit me Satanas quod memor ero quandiu fuero in hoc corpore; et cicidit super me ueluti saxum ingens et nihil membrorum praeualens. Sed unde mihi uenit in spiritum ut Heliam uocarem? Et in hoc uidi in caelum solem oriri et dum clamarem Heliam uiribus meis ecce splendor solis illius decidit super me et statim discussit a me grauitudinem; et credo quod a Christo domino meo clamabat pro me et spero quod sic erit in die praesuræ meæ sicut in æuangelio inquit: Dominus 'non uos estis'.

21 Multos adhuc capturam dedi. Ea nocte prima itaque mansi **<23vb>** cum illis. Responsum autem diuinum audiui: 'Duobus autem mensibus eris cum illis'. Quod ita factum est; nocte illa sexagensima liberauit me Dominus de manibus eorum.

[16] *indign-* written in the margin and attached with transposition-marks.

22 Etiam in itenere praeuidit nobis cibum et ignem et siccitatem cotidie donec (.x.)[17] decimo die peruenimus omnes. Sicut superius insinuaui .xx. et .viii. disertum iter f`e´cimus[18] et ea nocte qua peruenimus omnes de cibo uero nihil habuimus.

23 Et iterum post paucos annos in Britannis eram cum parentibus meis qui me ut filium susciperunt et ex fide rogauerunt me ut uel modo ego post tantas tribulationes quas ego pertuli nusquam ab illis discederem. Et ibi scilicet in sinu noctis uirum uenientem quasi de Hiberione cui nomen Uictoricus cum æpistolis innumerabilibus uidi et dedit mihi unam ex his et legi principium æpistolę continentem 'Uox Hyberionacum', et dum recitabam principium aepistolæ putabam enim ipse in mente audire uocem ipsorum qui erant iuxta siluam Focluti quae est prope mare occidentale et sic exclamauerunt: 'Rogamus te sancte puer ut uenias et adhuc ambulas inter nos'; et ualde conpunctus sum corde et[19] amplius non potui legere et sic expertus sum. Deo gratias quia post plurimos annos praestitit illis Dominus secundum clamorem illorum.

24 Et alia nocte nescio Deus scit utrum in me an iuxta me uerbis peritissime quos ego audiui et non potui intellegere nisi ad posterum orationis sic efficiatus est: 'Qui dedit animam suam pro te ipse est qui loquitur in te'; et sic expertus sum gaudibundus.

25 Et iterum uidi in me ipsum orantem et eram quasi intra corpus meum et audiui hoc est **<24ra>** super interiorem hominem et `i´bi fortiter orabat gemitibus et inter haec stupebam et ammirabam et cogitabam quis esset qui in me orabat sed ad postremum orationis sic efficiatus est ut sit episcopus et sic expertus sum et recordatus sum apostolo dicente: 'Spiritus adiuuat infirmitates orationis nostræ; nam quod oremus sicut oportet nescimus; sed ipse Spiritus postulat pro nobis gemitibus inerrabilibus quae uerbis expremi non possunt'; et iterum, 'Dominus aduocatus noster postulat pro nobis'.

26 Et quando temptatus sum ab aliquantis senioribus meis qui uenerunt et peccata mea contra laboriosum episcopatum meum obiecerunt utique illo die fortiter impulsus sum ut caderem hic et in aeternum; sed Dominus pepercit proselito et peregrino propter nomen suum benigne et ulade mihi subuenit in hac conculcatione. Quod in labe et in obprobrium non male deueni Deum oro ut non illis in peccatum reputetur.

27 Occasionem post annos triginta inuenerunt me aduersus uerbum quod confessus fueram antequam essem diaconus. Propter anxietatem maesto animo insinuaui amicissimo meo quae in pueritia mea una die gesseram

17 Overpointed for deletion, MS.

18 The scribe originally wrote *facimus*; *-e-* was interlined in correction.

19 After this the scribe began to write *ualde*, but after *-d-* stopped and overpointed what he had written.

immo in una hora quia necdum praeualebam. Nescio Deus scit si habebam tunc annos quindecim et Deum uiuum non credebam neque ex infantia mea; sed in morte et in incredulitate mansi donec ualde castigatus sum et in ueritate humiliatus sum a fame et nuditate et cotidie.

28 Contra Hiberione non sponte pergebam donec prope deficiebam; sed hoc potius bene mihi fuit qui ex hoc emendatus sum a Domino et aptauit me ut hodie essem quod aliquando longe a me erat ut ego curam haberem aut satagerem pro salute aliorum quando autem tunc etiam de me ipso non cogitabam.

29 Uidi in uissu noctis scriptum erat contra faciem meam sine honore et inter haec audiui responsum dicentem mihi: 'Male audiuimus faciem designati nudato nomine'. Nec sic praedixit: 'Male uidisti' sed 'male uidimus', quasi sibi se iunxisset, sicut dixit, 'Qui uos tanguit quasi qui tanguit pupillam oculi mei'.

30 Idcirco gratias ago ei qui me in omnibus confortauit ut non me inpediret a profectione qua statueram et de mea quoque opera quod a Christo Domino meo dedideram sed magis ex eo sensi uirtutem non paruam et fides mea probata est coram Deo et hominibus.

31 Unde autem audenter dico non me repraehendit conscientia mea hic et in futurum. Teste Deo abeo quia non sum mentitus in sermonibus quos ego retuli uobis.

32 Sed magis doleo pro amicissimo meo cur hoc meruimus audire tale responsum. Cui ego credidi etiam animam! Et comperi ab aliquantis fratribus ante defensionem illam quod ego non interfui nec in Britanniis eram nec a me oriebatur ut et ille in mea absentia pulsaret pro me; etiam mihi ipse ore suo dixerat: 'Ecce dandus es tu ad gradum episcopatus' – quod non eram dignus. Sed unde uenit illi postmodum ut coram cunctis bonis et malis et me publice dehonestaret quod ante sponte et laetus indulserat et Dominus qui maior omnibus est?

33 Satis dico. Sed tamen non debeo abscondere domum Dei quod largitus est nobis in terra captiuitatis meae, quia tunc fortiter inquisiui eum et ibi inueni illum et seruauit me ab omnibus iniquitatibus sic credo propter inhabitantem Spiritum eius qui operatus est usque in hanc diem in me. Audenter rursus; sed scit Deus si mihi homo hoc effatus fuisset forsitan tacuissem propter caritatem Christi.

34 Unde ergo indefessam gratiam ago Deo meo qui me fidelem seruauit in die temptationis meae ita ut hodie confidenter offeram illi sacrificium ut hostiam uiuentem animam meam Christo Domino meo qui me seruauit ab omnibus angustiis meis ut et dicam: quis ego sum Domine uel quae est uocatio mea qui mihi tanta diuinitate comparuisti ita ut hodie in gentibus constanter exaltarem et magnificarem nomen tuum ubicumque loco fuero nec non in secundis sed etiam in pressuris ut quicquid mihi euenerit siue bonum siue malum aequaliter debeo suscipere et Deo gratias semper agere qui mihi ostendit ut indubitalem eum sine fine crederem et qui me adiuuerit ut ego inscius et in nouissimis diebus hoc opus tam pium et tam mirificum auderem adgredere ita ut imitarem quippiam illos quos ante Dominus iam olim praedixerat praenuntiaturos euangelium suum in testimonium omnibus gentibus ante finem mundi – quod ita ergo uidimus itaque suppletum est; ecce testes sumus quia euangelium praedicatum est usque ubi nemo ultra est.

35 Longum est autem totum per singula enarrare laborem meum uel per partes. Breuiter dicam qualiter pissimus Deus de seruitute sepe liberauit et de periculis .xii. qua periclitata est anima mea praeter insidias multas et quae uerbis expraemere non ualeo. Nec iniuriam legentibus faciam; sed Deum auctorem qui nouit omnia etiam antequam fiant.

36 Unde mihi haec sapientia quae in me non erat qui nec numerum dierum noueram neque Deum sapiebam? Unde mihi postmodum donum tam magnum tam salubre Deum agnoscere uel diligere sed ut patriam et parentes amitterem?

37 Et munera multa mihi offerebantur cum fletu et lacrimis et offendi illos nec non contra uotum aliquantis de senioribus meis sed gubernante Deo nullo modo consensi neque adquieui illis – non mea gratia sed Deus qui uincit in me et resistit illis omnibus ut ego ueneram ad Hibernas gentes euangelium praedicare et ab incredulis contumelias perferre ut audirem obprobrium peregrinationis meae et persecutiones multas usque ad uincula et ut darem ingenuitatem meam pro utilitate aliorum et si dignus fuero promptus sum ut etiam animam meam incunctanter et libentissime pro nomine eius; et ibi opto impendere eam usque ad mortem si Dominus mihi indulgeret

38 Quia ualde debitor sum Deo qui mihi tantam gratiam donauit ut populi multi per me in Deum renascerentur et ut clerici ubique illis ordinarentur **<24rb>** ad plebem nuper uenientem ad credulitatem quam sumsit Dominus ab extremis terræ sicut olim promisserat per profetas suos: ‘Sicut falsa conparauerunt patres nostri idola et non est in eis utilitas’; et iterum, ‘Posui te lumen in gentibus ut sis in salutem usque ad extremum terrę’.

39 Et ibi uolo expectare promissum ipsius qui utique numquam fallit sicut in æuanguelio pollicetur: ‘Uenient ab oriente et occidente et ab austro et ab aquilone et recumbent cum Abraam et Issac et Iacob’; sicut credimus ab omni mundo uenturi sunt credentes.

40 Idcirco itaque oportet bene et diligenter piscare sicut Dominus praemonet et docet dicens, ‘Uenite post me et faciam uos fieri piscatores hominum’; et iterum, ‘Ecce mitto piscatores et uenatores multos dicit Deus’; et cætera. Unde autem ualde oportebat retia nostra tendere ita ut multitudo copiossa et turba Deo caperetur et ubique essent clerici qui babtizarent et exhortar-

ent populum indegentem et dissiderantem sicut Dominus in æuanguelio ammonet et docet dicens, 'Euntes ergo nunc docete omnes gentes babtizantes eas in nomine Patris et Filii et Spiritus Sancti', rl' usque dicit 'saeculi'; et iterum, 'Euntes ergo in mundum uniuersum praedicate æuanguelium omni creaturæ; qui crediderit et babtizatus fuerit saluus erit; qui uero non crediderit condempnabitur'. Reliqua sunt exempla.[20]

41 Unde autem Hiberione qui numquam notitiam Dei habuerunt **<24va>** nissi idula et inmunda usque semper coluerunt quomodo nuper facta est plebs Domini et filii Dei nuncupantur filii sanctorum et filiæ regulorum monachi et uirgines Christi esse uidentur?

42 Et etiam una benedicta Scotta genetiua nobilis pulcherrima adulta erat quam ego baptizaui; et post paucos dies una causa uenit ad nos insinuauit nobis responsum accepisse a nuntio Dei et monuit eam ut esset uirgo Christi et ipsa et Deo proximaret. Deo Gratias sexta ab hac die optime et auidissime arripuit illud quod etiam omnes uirgines Dei ita hoc faciunt – non sponte patrum earum sed et persecutiones patiuntur et improperia falsa a parentibus suis et nihilominus plus augetur numerus et de genere nostro qui ibi nati sunt nescimus numerum eorum praeter uiduas et continentes. Sed et illae maxime laborant quae seruitio detinentur; usque ad terrores et minas assidue perferunt; sed Dominus gratiam dedit multis ex ancillis suis nam etsi uetantur tamen fortiter imitantur.

43 Unde autem etsi uoluero amittere illas et ut pergens in Brittanniis – et libentissime paratus eram quasi ad patriam et parentes; non id solum sed etiam usque ad Gallias uisitare fratres et ut uiderem faciem sanctorum Domini mei; scit Deus quod ego ualde optabam sed alligatus Spiritu qui mihi protestatur si hoc fecero ut futurum reum me esse designat et timeo perdere laborem quem inchoaui – et non ego sed Christus Dominus qui me imperauit ut uenirem esse cum illis residuum aetatis meae si Dominus uoluerit et custodierit me ab omni uia mala ut non peccem coram illo.

44 Spero autem hoc debueram sed memetipsum non credo quamdiu fuero in hoc corpore mortis quia fortis est qui cotidie nititur subuertere me a fide et praeposita castitate religionis non fictae usque in finem uitae meae Christo Domino meo; sed caro inimica semper trahit ad mortem id est ad inlecebras inlicitate perficiendas; et scio ex parte quare uitam perfectam ego non egi sicut et ceteri credentes sed confiteor Domino meo et non erubesco in conspectu ipsius quia non mentior ex quo congoui eum a iuuentute mea creuit in me amor Dei et timor ipsius et usque nunc fauente Domino fidem seruaui.

45 Rideat autem et insultet qui uoluerit ego non silebo neque abscondo signa et mirabilia quae mihi a Domino monstrata sunt ante multos annos quam fierent quasi qui nouit omnia etiam ante tempora saecularia.

20 The whole of the rest of §40 has been dismissed with these few words.

46 *Unde autem debueram sine cessatione Deo gratias agere qui saepe indulsit insipientiae meae neglegentiae meae et de loco non in uno quoque ut non mihi uehementer irasceretur qui adiutor datus sum et non cito adquieui secundum quod mihi ostensum fuerat et sicut Spiritus suggerebat et misertus est mihi Dominus in milia milium quia uidit in me quod paratus eram sed quod mihi pro his nesciebam de statu meo quid facerem quia multi hanc legationem prohibebant etiam inter se ipsos pos tergum meum narrabant et dicebant: 'Iste quare se mittit in periculo inter hostes qui Deum non nouerunt?' Non ut causa malitiae sed non sapiebat illis sicut et ego ipse testor – intellige propter rusticitatem meam; et non cito agnoui gratiam quae tunc erat in me; nunc mihi sapit quod ante debueram.*

47 *Nunc ergo simpliciter insinuaui fratribus et conseruis meis qui mihi crediderunt propter quod praedixi et praedico ad roborandam et confirmandam fidem uestram. Utinam ut et uos imitemini maiora et potiora faciatis! Hoc erit gloria mea quia filius sapiens gloria patris est.*

48 *Uos scitis et Deus qualiter inter uos conuersatus sum a iuuentute mea in fide ueritatis et in sinceritate cordis. Etiam ad gentes illas inter quas habito ego fidem illis praestaui et praestabo. Deus scit neminem illorum circumueni nec cogito propter Deum et ecclesiam ipsius ne excitem illis et nobis omnibus persecutionem et ne per me blasphemaretur nomen Domini; quia scriptum est: 'Uae homini per quem nomen Domini blasphematur.'*

49 *Nam etsi imperitus sum in omnibus tamen conatus sum quippiam seruare me etiam et fratribus Christianis et uirginibus Christi et mulieribus religiosis quae mihi ultronea munuscula donabant et super altare iactabant ex ornamentis suis et iterum reddebam illis et aduersus me scandalizabantur cur hoc faciebam; sed ego propter spem perennitatis ut me in omnibus caute propterea conseruarem ita ut non me in aliquo titulo infideli caperent uel ministerium seruitutis meae nec etiam in minimo incredulis locum darem infamare siue detractare.*

50 *Forte autem quando baptizaui tot milia hominum sperauerim ab aliquo illorum uel dimidio scriptulae? Dicite mihi et reddam uobis. Aut quando ordinauit ubique Dominus clericos per modicitatem meam et ministerium gratis distribui illis si poposci ab aliquo illorum uel pretirum uel calciamenti mei dicite aduersus me et reddam uobis.*

51 *Magis ego impendi pro uobis ut me caperent et inter uos et ubique pergebam causa uestra in multis periculis etiam usque ad exteras partes ubi nemo ultra erat et ubi numquam aliquis peruenerat qui baptizaret aut clericos ordinaret aut populum consummaret; donante Domino diligenter et libentissime pro salute uestra omnia generaui.*

52 *Interim praemia dabam regibus praeter quod dabam mercedem fillis ipsorum qui mecum ambulant et nihilominus comprehenderunt me cum comitibus meis et illa die auidessime cupiebant interficere me sed tempus*

nondum uenerat; et omnia quaecumque nobiscum inuenerunt rapuerunt illud et me ipsum ferro uinxerunt et quartodecimo die absoluit me Dominus de potestate eorum et quicquid nostrum fuit redditum est nobis propter Deum et necessarios amicos quos ante praeuidimus.

53 Uos autem experti estis quantum ego erogaui illis qui iudicabant per omnes regiones quos ego frequentius uisitabam. Censeo enim non minimum quam pretium quindecim hominum distribui illis ita ut me fruamini et ego uobis semper fruar in Deum. Non me paenitet nec satis est mihi; adhuc impendo et superimpendam. Potens est Dominus ut det mihi postmodum ut meipsum impendar pro animabus uestris.

54 Ecce testem Deum inuoco in animam meam quia non mentior; neque ut sit occassio uobis neque ut honorem spero ab aliquo uestro; sufficit enim honor qui non mentitur.

55 Sed uideo iam in praesenti sæculo me supra modum exaltatus sum a Domino et non eram dignus neque talis ut hoc mihi praestaret dum scio melius conuenit paupertas et calamitas quam diuitiæ et diliciæ sed et Christus Dominus pauper fuit pro nobis ego uero miser et infelix etsi opes uoluero iam non habeo neque meipsum iudico quia quotidie spero aut internicionem aut circumueniri aut redigi in seruitutem siue occassio cuiuslibet.

56 Ecce nunc commendo animam meam fidelissimo Deo meo pro quo legationem fungor in ignobilitate mea sed quia personam non accipit et elegit me ad hoc officium ut unus essem de suis minimis minister.

57 Unde autem retribuam illi pro omnibus quae retribuit mihi. Sed quid dicam uel quid promittam Domino meo quia nihil ualeo nisi ipse mihi dederit? Sed scrutator corda et renes quia satis et nimis cupio et paratus eram ut donaret mihi bibere calicem eius sicut indulsit et ceteris amantibus se.

58 Quapropter non contingat mihi a Deo meo ut numquam amittam plebem suam quam adquisiuit in ultimis terrae. Oro Deum ut det mihi perseuerantiam et dignetur ut reddam illi testem fidelem usque ad transitum meum propter Deum meum.

59 Et si aliquid boni umquam imitatus sum propter Deum meum quem diligo peto illi det mihi ut cum illis proselitis et captiuis pro nomine suo effundam sanguinem meum etsi ipsam etiam caream sepulturam aut miserissime cadauer per singula membra diuidatur canibus aut bestiis asperis aut uolucres caeli comederent illud. Certissime reor si mihi hoc incurrisset lucratus sum animam cum corpore meo quia sine ulla dubitatione in die illa resurgemus in claritate solis hoc est in gloria Christi Iesu redemptoris nostri quasi filii Dei uiui et coheredes Christi et conformes futuri imaginis ipsius; quoniam ex ipso et per ipsum et in ipso regnaturi sumus.

60 *Nam sol ist quem uidemus ipso iubente propter nos cotidie oritur sed numquam regnabit neque permanebit splendor eius sed et omnes qui adorant eum in poenam miseri male deuenient; nos autem qui credimus et adoramus solem uerum Christum qui numquam interibit – neque qui fecerit uoluntatem ipsius sed manebit in aeternum quomodo et Christus manet in aeternum qui regnat cum Deo Patre omnipotente et cum Spiritu Sancto ante saecula et nunc et per omnia saecula saeculorum Amen.*

61 *Ecce iterum iterumque breuiter exponam uerba confessionis meae. Testificor in ueritate et in exultatione cordis coram Deo et sanctis angelis eius quia numquam habui aliquam occasionem praeter euangelium et promissa illius ut umquam redirem ad gentem illam unde prius uix euaseram.*

62 Sed praecor credentibus et timentibus Deum quicumque dignatus fuerit inspicere uel recipere hanc scripturam quam Patricius peccator indoctus scilicet Hiberione conscripsit ut nemo umquam dicat quod mea ignorantia si aliquid pussillum egi uel demonstrauerim secundum sed arbitramini et uerissime credatur quod donum Dei fuisset. Et hæc est confessio mea antequam moriar.

Hucusque uolumen quod Patricius manu conscripsit sua.
Septima decima Martii die translatus est Patricius ad cælos.

MUIRCHÚ'S LIFE OF ST PATRICK FROM THE 'BOOK OF ARMAGH'

The only straightforward publication of the 'Book of Armagh' text of Muirchú's Life of St Patrick was that in John Gwynn's magnificent diplomatic edition of the entire *Liber Ardmachanus*, issued in 1913. However, that volume is not readily accessible nor is its diplomatic text easy to use. Accordingly, there follows here an edited reproduction of the text in the 'Book of Armagh', intended to allow the reader both to see, in a straightforward fashion, what that important manuscript contains and to read the text with no more difficulty than Muirchú's Latin presents. This is necessary because the two most readily available editions of the Life have, for various reasons, departed radically from the text as presented by its Armagh scribe.[1] Allan Hood in 1978 gave a text of Book I only, omitting the fourteen chapters which constitute Book II on fos 7v–8v of the 'Book of Armagh'.[2] Ludwig Bieler in 1979 gave a drastically reorganised text with the most elaborate chapter-numeration: the reader must undertake significant research in order to attempt to reconstruct the order of the Armagh text.[3]

The manuscript does, however, offer some real difficulties too. The first folio, which would originally have contained I.1–6 and the beginning of I.7 (as well, perhaps, as an introductory rubric and elaborate initial),[4] has been lost 'as a result of the use of the open volume for oaths and for the production of miraculous water'.[5] The text as thus hypothetically completed would have been different in a number of respects from that presented by other manuscripts: three chapters (I.27–29) are missing from the end of Book I; Book II begins at a different point from other witnesses; only this manuscript has *capitula* to Book II; after these *capitula*, the concluding part of II.8 precedes II.1. At the end of the text, after the closing 'finit amen', two short paragraphs follow which contain notes on Patrick's career (five blank lines complete the leaf).[6]

This is not all, however. The collection of texts about St Patrick – which may

1 *St. Patrick*, ed. & transl. Hood; *The Patrician Texts*, edd. & transl. Bieler & Kelly.

2 This followed the objections against Muirchú's authorship of Book II (or, at any rate, against the textual integrity of the whole *uita*) expressed by Morris, 'The dates of the Celtic saints', pp. 365–6, and Hughes, *The Church in Early Irish Society*, p. 89, n. 4, and p. 275. For an older expression of doubt, see Zimmer, *The Celtic Church*, p. 13.

3 For the best discussion of Bieler's practice and its shortcomings, see Sharpe, 'The Patrician documents'.

4 This addition is necessary, for otherwise calculation shows that there is marginally too little text missing for a whole folio.

5 *St. Patrick*, ed. & transl. Hood, p. 20.

6 These paragraphs are reproduced below, p. 219. They require discussion as to their origins and any possible original relationship to Muirchú's text.

have consisted of two admitted elements, the *breuiarium* (fos [1]–16ra),[7] and the *alia pauca* (fos 16rb–18vb)[8] which seem to have been organised in three single-folio units – occupied two quires, was written by a single scribe, and ended with four hexameters:

Scripsi hunc ut potui librum; pulsare conetur
Omnis quicumque legerit ut euadere poena
Ad caelum ualeam et ad summi praemia regni,
Patricio Dominum pulsante, habitare per æuum.

We must suppose that the remainder of the column and two succeeding folios all remained blank. The lower half of 18vb and most of 19r were subsequently filled (perhaps by another scribe) with what have long been known as the *notulae* about St Patrick (and St Gregory the Great), all written in a noticeably smaller script.[9] At a later date, the last folio of quire II was excised.[10] Folio 19v has remained blank.

What has not been appreciated until recently is the significance of the following quire. As Richard Sharpe has shown, quire III (fos 20–24 and a following cancelled leaf, presumed blank) was written by the master-scribe Ferdomnach who also wrote fos 25–105 (Gospels) and fos 214–222 (the last quire of Sulpicius Seuerus's works on St Martin of Tours). Quires I–II, on the other hand, were the work of an anonymous scribe 'A', who otherwise contributed fos 106–126 (the first three quires of Pauline Epistles) and fos 192–213 (the first two quires of Martiniana). A third scribe, 'B', wrote seven quires (fos 127–191), completing the Pauline Epistles and continuing through the remainder of the New Testament (in the order, Catholic Epistles, Revelation, Acts).[11]

Ferdomnach's 'supplement' (as it now appears and has often been called) begins with a bold, decorated **Q***uonia***m**. Folio 20r–va5 is occupied by the preface of Muirchú's Life of St Patrick, thirty *capitula* to Book I of that text, and a four-line authorship-statement: 'Haec pauca de sancti Patricii peritia et uirtutibus Muirchú maccu Machtheni, dictante Aiduo Slebtiensis ciuitatis episcopo, conscripsit'. We now see the point of reference in the phrase *alia pauca* which introduces the section following the *breuiarium* on fo 16r.

7 That is to say, the texts of Muirchú (minus the preface and the *capitula* to Book I) and Tírechán, with any intervening matter (such as that printed under Tírechán's name in *The Patrician Texts*, edd. & transl. Bieler & Kelly, pp. 122.10–124.12). For discussion, see Sharpe, 'Palaeographical considerations'.

8 *The Patrician Texts*, edd. & transl. Bieler & Kelly, pp. 166–79, under the title '*Additamenta*'.

9 The palaeography of this section (ed. *ibid.*, pp. 180–3) requires a great deal more study. There is a potential inconsistency in Sharpe's handling of it ('Palaeographical considerations', pp. 14–19), for if the '*Notulae*' were not by Scribe A (an option considered but discounted by Sharpe), then the 'Book of Armagh' assumes a quite different place in the textual history.

10 I disagree with Sharpe ('Palaeographical considerations', pp. 14–15) in his opinion that Scribe A cancelled this last folio. His view depends on two assumptions, that Scribe A wrote the '*Notulae*' (which seems doubtful to me), and that if the last (now cancelled) folio had been left, Ferdomnach would have written on it. This second point seems to me to be at variance with his main thesis about the status of fos 20–24.

11 For Sharpe's superb analysis, see 'Palaeographical considerations', building on the brief remarks of Lindsay, *Notae Latinae*, p. 455, and Lowe, *Codices*, II, no. 270.

At fo 20va6 a new, five-line paragraph begins with a large initial and diminuendo continuation. This paragraph is a statement introducing the Armagh document known as *Liber angeli*.[12] Fo 20va11 is a rubric to the text, which then occupies the following pages until it concludes abruptly on 22ra7. After two blank lines we read another rubric, elaborately written (22ra10): *Incipiunt libri sancti Patricii, episcopi*. There follows an abbreviated text of St Patrick's *Confessio*[13] which concludes at the bottom of 24va with the well known colophon: 'Hucusque uolumen quod Patricius manu conscripsit sua. Septima decima Martii die translatus est Patricius ad cælos.' Much modern scholarly ink has been spilt in controversy about this colophon. However, there seems to be no reason to take it as an attempt at forgery by Ferdomnach: the *uolumen* is not the extant manuscript (nor even a predecessor claiming false authority) – although this is undoubtedly how it was read, later in the middle ages, as a Patrician autograph – but rather the *Confessio* itself. What is less clear is the identity of the *libri* named in the opening rubric: was the *Confessio* perceived as a work in two or more books, or did other work (most obviously, the Letter about Coroticus) follow in the exemplar but which has not been carried over into this copy?[14] Fo 24vb remained blank and the following leaf was cancelled.

Various possibilities arise from this distribution of evidence. (*a*) Quire III might originally have preceded quires I–II, *Liber angeli* and *Libri sancti Patricii episcopi* being interpolated before the body of Muirchú's text. (*b*) Ferdomnach might have rescued the beginning of Muirchú's work from his collaborating scribe's incompetent inattention – perhaps, to be charitable, we can suppose that the first leaf of the exemplar had become dislocated. (*c*) Muirchú's preface (and *capitula*) had been rejected by Scribe A as inappropriate to the plan of creating a *breuiarium* comprising the works of Muirchú and Tírechán with assorted minor additions.[15] (*d*) Scribe A's exemplar never contained the beginning of Muirchú's text, which Ferdomnach obtained from another source.[16] It is not necessary here to adjudicate between the competing claims of these variously incompatible deductions. Some observations about the *capitula* would seem to be in order, however.

In as much as *capitula* in Book II remain in Scribe A's text (fo 7va1–18), it is a reasonable deduction that the exemplar once contained *capitula* for Book I also. Ferdomnach's copy of the *capitula* to Book I contains entries pertaining to I.27–29, but these chapters are wanting from Scribe A's copy of the work itself. Infamously, the *capitulum* for I.29, the last of the book, reads 'De conflictu sancti Patricii aduersum Coirthech *regem Aloo*': the chapter in question, as retrieved from MS. B of Muirchú's work, describes *Corictic* as a British king, but does not call him *rex Alo*, thus giving him no geographical location; likewise, later *uitae* of Patrick, ultimately derivative of Muirchú, while calling the king variously *Coritic*, *Ceritic*, *Chairtic*, offer no attendant place-name. The

12 *The Patrician Texts*, edd. & transl. Bieler & Kelly, pp. 184–91. A new translation is badly needed.

13 See above, pp. 191–202.

14 For discussion of this point, see above, p. 191, and the references given there.

15 This is the explanation preferred by Sharpe, 'Palaeographical considerations', p. 15.

16 This possibility has been suggested by Hood, *St. Patrick*, p. 20.

information must have arisen from eighth-century research to find the identity of Patrick's persecutor.[17]

Reconstruction of the text of this Life of St Patrick to a state closer to that in which it left Muirchú's hands is a daunting task. No attempt is made here to improve upon Ludwig Bieler's work, although a new critical edition and translation are greatly to be desired. What follows is offered in the belief that the evidence of the 'Book of Armagh' needs to be more readily available for study.

<20ra> Quoniam quidem mi domine Aido multi conati sunt ordinare narrationem utique istam secundum quod patres eorum et qui ministri ab initio fuerunt sermonis tradiderunt illis sed propter difficillimum narrationis opus diuersasque opiniones et plurimorum plurimas suspiciones numquam ad unum certumque historiæ tramitem peruenierunt; ideo ni fallor iuxta hoc nostrorum prouerbium ut deducuntur pueri in ambiteathrum in hoc periculossum et profundum narrationis sanctæ pylagus turgentibus proterue gurgitum aggeribus inter acutissimos carubdes per ignota aequora insitos a nullis adhuc lintribus excepto tantum uno patris mei Cog<u>itosi[18] expertum atque occupatum ingenioli mei puerilem remi cymbam deduxi. Sed ne magnum de paruo uidear finguere pauca haec de multis sancti Patricii gestis parua peritia incertis auctoribus memoria labili attrito sensu uili sermone sed affectu pissimo caritatis (et)[19] sanctitatis tuæ et auctoritatis imperio oboedens carptim grauatimque explicare aggrediar.

[1] De ortu Patricii et eius prima captiuitate.

[2] De nauigio eius cum gentibus et uexatione diserti cibo sibi gentilibus diuinitus delato.

[3] De secunda captura quam senis decies diebus ab inimicis pertulerat.

[4] De susceptione sua a parentibus ubi agnouerunt eum.

[5] De ætate eius quando iens uidere sedem apostolicam uoluit discere sapientiam.

[6] De inuentione sancti Germani in Galliis et ideo non exiuit ultra. **<20rb>**

[7] De aetate eius quando uissitauit eum anguelus ut ueniret adhuc.

[8] De reuersione eius de Gallis et ordinatione Palladii et mox morte eius.

[9] De ordinatione eius ab Amatho rege episcopo defuncto Palladio.

[10] De rege gentili habeto in Temoria[20] quando uenerat sanctus Patricius babtismum portans.

[11] De primo eius itenere in hac insola ut seipsum redemeret o Miliucc priusquam alios a demonio traheret.

[12] De morte Milcon et uerbo Patricii de semine eius.

[13] De consilio sancti Patricii ubi hessitum est de celebratione primi pascæ.[21]

[14] De oblatione primo pasca in hac insola facta.

[15] De festiuitate gentili in Temoria eadem nocte qua sanctus Patricius pasca adorauit.

[17] For a robust treatment of this problem, see Thompson, 'St. Patrick and Coroticus'. For further discussion, suggesting that an Irish place-name was intended, see my remarks above, pp. 114–15.

[18] MS. *cognito si*

[19] MS. ⁊

[20] MS. altered from *Temeria*.

[21] Appears as two *capitula* in manuscript: *De* . . . *De* . . .

[16] De gressu regis Loiguri de Temoria ad Patricium in nocte pascæ.
[17] De uocatione Patricii ad regem et fide Eirc filii Dego morte magi in illa nocte.
[18] De ira regis et suorum ad Patricium et plaga Dei super eos et transfinctione Patricii coram gentilibus.
[19] De aduentu Patricii in die pascæ ad Temoriam et fide Dubthaich maccu Lugir.
[20] De conflictu Patricii aduersus magum in illa et mirabilibus uirtutibus.
[21] De conuersione Loiguiri regis (et conuersio)[22] et de uerbo Patricii de regno eius post se.
[22] De doctrina et babtismate signisque sancti Patricii secundum exemplum Christi.
[23] De Macc Cuill et conuersione eius ad uerbum Patricii.
[*] [23]De morte Moneisen.[23]
[25][24] De fabula Dairi et equo et oblatione Airddmachæ ad Patricium.
[24][24] De gentibus laborantibus die Dominica trans praeceptum Patricii.
[26] De fructifera terra in salsuginem uersa ad uerbum Patricii.
[27][25] De morte Moneisen Saxonissæ.
[28][25] De eo quod sanctus Patricius uidit caelum apertum et Filium Dei et anguelos eius. **<20va>**
[29][25] De conflictu sancti Patricii aduersum Coirthech regem Aloo.
Haec pauca de sancti Patricii peritia et uirtutibus Muirchu maccu Machtheni dictante Aiduo Slebtiensis ciuitatis episcopo conscripsit.

<Ferdomnach's portion of the text ends here.>

<The acephalous text of Scribe A begins here.>

[7] **<2ra>** sibi in hibernica seruitute possito antequam essent dixerat eum crebris uissionibus uissitauit dicens ei adesse tempus ut ueniret et aeuanguelico rete nationes feras et barbaras ad quas docendas misserat illum Deus ut piscaret; ibique ei dictum est in uissione: 'Uocant te filii et filiæ siluæ Foclitæ', et cętera.
[8] Oportuno ergo tempore imperante comitante diuino auxilio coeptum ingreditur iter ad opus in quod ollim praeparatus fuerat utique æuanguelii et missit Germanus seniorem cum illo – hoc est Segitium prespiterum – ut testem comitem haberet quia nec adhuc a sancto domino Germano in pontificali gradu ordinatus est. Certe enim erat quod Paladius – archidiaconus pape Caelestini urbis Romæ episcopi qui tunc tenebat sedem apostolicam quadragensimus quintus a sancto Petro apostolo –, ille Palladius ordinatus et missus fuerat ad hanc insolam sub brumali rigore possitam conuertendam. Sed prohibuit illum quia nemo potest accipere quicquam de terra nisi datum ei fuerit de cælo. Nam neque hii feri[26] et inmites homines facile reciperunt doctrinam eius neque et ipse

22 MS.: these words are overpointed for deletion.
23...23 MS.: surrounded by *z . . . z*.
24 MS.: §§24 and 25 are presented in opposed order in *capitula* and text.
25 Nos 27–29 not represented in this manuscript.
26 MS. *?fieri*.

uoluit transegere tempus in terra non sua; sed reuersus ad eum qui missit illum. Reuerte<nt>e[27] uero eo hinc et primo mari transito coeptoque terrarum itenere in Britonum finibus uita factus. **<2rb>**

[9] Audita itaque morte sancti Paladii in Britannis – quia discipuli Paladii id est Augustinus et Benedictus et cæteri redeuntes retulerant in Ebmoria de morte eius – Patricius et qui cum eo erant declinauerunt iter ad quendam mirabilem hominem summum æpiscopum Amatho rege nomine in propinquo loco habitantem; ibique sanctus Patricius sciens quae euentura essent ibi episcopalem gradum ab Matho rege sancto episcopo accepit. Etiam Auxilius Iserninusque et cæteri inferioris gradus eodem die quo sanctus Patricius ordinatus est.[28] Tum acceptis benedictionibus perfectis omnibus secundum morem cantato etiam Patricio quasi specialiter et conuenienter hoc psalmistæ uorsu, 'Tu es sacerdos in aeternum secundum ordinem Melchisedec', uenerabilis uiator paratam nauim in nomine sanctæ Trinitatis ascendit et peruenit Brittannias; et omissis omnibus ambulandi anfractibus praeter commone uiæ officium nemo enim dissidia quaerit Dominum cum omni uelocitate flatuque prospero mare nostrum contendit.

[10] In illis autem diebus quibus haec gesta sunt in praedictis regionibus fuit rex quidam magnus ferox gentilisque imperator barbarorum regnans in Temoria quae erat caput Scotorum Loiguire nomine filius Neill orig<inis>[29] stirpis regię huius pene insolae. Hic autem sciuos et magos et aurispices et incantatores et omnes malæ artis inuentores habuerat qui poterant **<2va>** omnia scire et prouidere ex more gentilitatis et idolatrię antequam essent; e quibus hii .ii. prae cæteris praeferebantur quorum nomina hæc sunt, Lothroch qui et Lochru et Lucetmael qui et Ronal. Et hii .ii. ex sua arte magica crebrius profetabant morem quendam exterum futurum in modum regni cum ignota quadam doctrina molesta lon<g>uinquo[30] trans maria aduectum a paucis dictatum a multis susceptum ab omnibusque honoratum regna subuersurum resistentes turbas seducturum omnes eorum deos distructurum et iectis omnibus illorum artis opibus in sęcula regnaturum. Portantem quoque suadentemque hunc morem signauerunt et profetauerunt hiis uerbis quasi in modum crebro ab hiisdem dictis maxime in antecedentibus aduentum Patriciique .ii. aut .iii. annis. Haec autem sunt uersiculi uerba pro linguę idiomo non tam manisfesta: 'Adueniet Asciciput cum suo ligno curui capite ex sua domu capite perforato. Incantabit nefas a sua mensa ex anteriore parte domus suæ; respondebit ei sua familia tota: "fiat fiat".' Quod nostris uerbis potest manifestius expraemi. 'Quando ergo[31] haec omnia fiant regnum nostrum quod est gentile non stabit.' Quod sic potest ea euenerat. Euersis enim in aduentu Patricii idulorum culturis fides Christi catholica nostra repleuit omnia. **<2vb>** De his ista sufficiant; redeamus ad propossitum.

[11] Consummato igitur nauigio sancto perfectoque honorata nauis sancti cum transmarinis mirabilibus spiritalibusque tessauris quasi in oportunum portum in regiones Coolennorum in portum apud nos clarum qui uocatur hostium Dee

27 MS. *reuertere*
28 MS. *-ti sunt* added in margin, as an alternative reading.
29 MS. *origo*
30 MS. *lonquinquo*
31 MS.: added in margin.

dilata est. Ubi uissum est ei nihil perfectius esse quam ut semetipsum primitus redemeret et inde appetens sinistrales fines ad illum hominem gentilem Milcoin apud quem quondam in captiuitate fuerat portansque geminum seruitutis praetium terrenum utique et cæleste ut de captiuitate liberaret illum cui ante captiuus seruierat ad anteriorem insolam quae eius nomine usque hodie nominatur prurim nauis conuertit. Tum deinde Brega Conalneosque fines necnon et fines Ulathorum in leuo dimittens ad extremum fretum quod est Brene se inmissit. Et discenderunt in terram ad hostium Slain ille et qui cum eo erant in naui et absconderunt nauiculam et uenierunt aliquantulum in regionem ut requiescerent ibi. Et inuenit eos porcinarius cuiusdam uiri natura boni licet gentilis cui nomen erat Dichu habitans ibi ubi nunc est Orreum Patricii nomine cognominatum. Porcinarius autem putans eos fures ac latrones exiuit et indicauit domino suo, du Dichoin, et induxit **<3ra>** illum super eos ignorantibus illis. Qui corde proposuerat occidere eos; sed uidens faciem sancti Patricii conuertit Dominus ad bonum cogitationes eius. Et praedicauit Patricius fidem illi et ibi credidit Patricio et requiescit ibi sanctus apud illum non multis diebus. Sed uolens cito ire ut uissitaret praedictum hominem Milcoin et portaret ei praetium suum et uel sic conuerteret ad Christi fidem relicta ibi nauis apud Dichoin coepit per terras diregere uiam in regiones Cruidnenorum donec peruenit ad montem Miss. De quo monte multo ante tempore quo ibi captiuus erat seruierat praesso uestigio in petra alterius montis expedito gradu uidit anguelum Uictoricum in conspectu eius ascendisse in caelum.

[12] Audiens autem Miliucc seruum suum iterum ad uissitandum eum ut morem quem nolebat in fine uitæ faceret quasi per uim ne seruo subiectus fieret et ille sibi dominaret instinctu diabuli sponte se igni tradidit et in domu in qua prius habitauerat rex congregato ad se omni instrumento substantię suæ incensus est. Stans autem sanctus Patricius in praedicto loco a latere dextero montis Miss ubi primum illam regionem in qua seruiuit cum tali gratia adueniens uidit ubi nunc usque crux habetur in signum ad uissum primum illius regionis ilico sub oculis rogum **<3rb>** regis incensum intuitus. Stupefactus igitur ad hoc opus duabus aut tribus fere horis nullum uerbum proferens suspirans et gemens lacrimansque atque haec uerba promens ait: 'Nescio, Deus scit, hic homo rex qui se ipsum igni tradidit ne crederet in fine uitæ suæ et ne seruiret Deo aeterno, nescio, Deus scit, nemo de filiis eius sedebit rex super sedem regni eius a generatione in generationem; insuper et semen eius seruiet in sempiternum. Et his dictis orans et armans se signo crucis conuertit cito iter suum ad regionem Ulothorum per eadem uestigia quibus uenerat; et rursum peruenit in campum Inis ad Dichoin; ibique mansit diebus multis et circumiit totum campum et elegit et amauit, et coepit fides crescere ibi.

[13] Adpropinquauit autem pasca in diebus illis quod pasca primum Deo in nostra Aegipto huius insolæ uelut quondam in Genesseon celebratum est. Et inuenierunt consilium ubi hoc primum pasca in gentibus ad quas missit illum Deus celebrarent; multisque super hac re consiliis iectis postremo inspirato diuinitus sancto Patricio uissum est hanc magnam Domini (re)[32] sollempnitatem quasi caput omnium sollempnitatum in campo maximo ubi erat regnum maximum nationum harum quod erat omnis gentilitatis et idolatriæ ne possit ulterius

[32] MS.: *re* overpointed.

liberari uti hic inuictus cuneus in caput totius idolatriæ ne possit ulterius aduersus Christi fidem insurgere sub malleo fortis operis cum fide **<3va>** iuncti sancti Patricii et suorum manibus spiritalibus primus inlideretur; et sic factum est.

[14] Eleuata igitur nauis ad mare et dimisso in fide plena et pace bono illo uiro Dichu migrantes de campo Iniss dexteraque manu demittentes omnia ad plentitudinem ministerii quae erant ante non incongrue leua in portum hostii Colpdi bene et prospere delati sunt. Relictaque ibi naui pedistri itenere uenierunt in praedictum maximum campum donec postremo ad uesperum peruenierunt ad Ferti uirorum Feec quam ut fabulæ ferunt fodorunt uiri id est serui Feccol Ferchertni qui fuerat unus e nouim magis profetis Bregg. Fixoque ibi tentorio debeta pascæ uota sacrificiumque laudis cum omni deuotione s<anctu>s[33] Patricius cum suis Deo altissimo secundum profetæ uocem reddidit.

[15] Contigit uero in illo anno idolatrię sollempnitatem quam gentiles incantationibus multis et magicis inuentionibus nonnullis aliis idolatrię[34] superstitionibus congregatis etiam regibus satrapis ducibus principibus et optimatibus populi insuper et magis incantatoribus auruspicibus et omnis artis omnisque doni inuentoribus doctoribusue uocatis ad Loigaireum uelut quondam ad Nabcodonossor regem in Temoria istorum Babylone exercere consuerant eadem nocte qua sanctus Patri**<3vb>**cius pasca illi illam adorarent exercerentque festiuitatem gentilem. Erat quoque quidam mos apud illos per edictum omnibus intimatus ut quicumque in cunctis regionibus siue procul siue iuxta in illa nocte incendisset ignem antequam in domu regia – id est in palatio Temoriæ – succenderetur periret anima eius de populo suo. Sanctus ergo Patricius sanctum pasca celebrans incendit diuinum ignem ualde lucidum et benedictum qui in nocte reffulgens a cunctis pene per plani campi habitantibus uissus est. Accidit ergo ut a Temoria uideretur uissoque eo conspexerunt omnes et mirati sunt. Conuocatisque senioribus[35] et[36] maioribus natu regi nesciisse illum qui hoc fecerit magi responderunt: 'Rex in æternum uiue. Hic ignis quem uidemus quique in hac nocte accensus est antequam succenderetur in domu tua[37] – id est in palatio Temorię – nissi extinctus fuerit in nocte hac qua accensus est numquam extinguetur in æternum; insuper et omnes ignes nostrę consuitudinis supergradietur; et ille qui incendit et regnum superueniens a quo incensus nocte in hac superabit nos omnes et te et omnes homines regni tui seducet et cadent ei omnia regna et ipsum inplebit omnia et regnabit in sæcula saeculorum.' **<4ra>**

[16] His ergo auditis turbatus est rex Loiguire ualde – ut ollim Erodis – et omnis ciuitas Temoria cum eo. Et respondens dixit: 'Non sic erit; sed nunc nos ibimus ut uideamus exitum rei et retinebimus et occidemus facientes tantum nefas in nostrum regnum'. Iunctis .viiii. curribus secundum deorum traditionem et assumptis his .ii. magis ad conflictionem prae omnibus optimis – id est Lucetmael et Lochru – in fine noctis illius perrexit Loiguire de Temoria ad Ferti uirorum Feec, hominum et equorum facies secundum congruum illis sensum ad leuam

33 MS.: *spiritus*.
34 MS.: added in the margin.
35 MS.: added in margin.
36 MS.: interlined.
37 MS.: *t-* altered from ?

uertentes. Euntibus autem illis dixerunt magi regi: 'Rex, nec tu ibis ad locum in quo ignis est, ne forte tu postea adoraueris illum qui incendit; sed eris foris iuxta et uocabitur ad te ille ut te adorauerit et tu ipse dominatus fueris, et sermocinabimur ad inuicem nos et ille in conspectu tuo, rex, et probabis nos sic'. Et respondens rex ait: 'Bonum consilium inuenistis; sic faciam ut locuti fuistis'. Et peruenierunt ad praefinitum locum; discendentibusque illis de[38] curribus suis et equis non intrauerunt in circuitum loci incensi sed sederunt iuxta.

[17] Et uocatus est sanctus Patricius ad regem (iuxta)[39] **<4rb>** extra locum incensi. Dixeruntque magi ad suos: 'Nec surgemus nos in aduentu istius: nam quicumque surrexerit a<d>[40] aduentum istius credet ei postea et adorabit eum'. Surgens denique sanctus Patricius et uidens multos currus et equos eorum huncque psalmistæ uersiculum non incongrue in labiis et in corde decantans, 'Hii in curribus et hii in equis, nos autem in nomine Dei nostri ambulabimus', uenit ad illos. Illi non surrexerunt in aduentu eius; sed unus tantum a Domino adiutus qui noluit oboedire dictis magorum – hoc est Ercc filius Dego cuius nunc reliquię adorantur in illa ciuitate quæ uocatur Slane – surrexit: et benedixit eum Patricius, et credidit Deo aeterno. Incipientibusque illis sermocinari ad inuicem alter magus nomine Lochru procax erit in conspectu sancti audens detrachere fidei catholicę tumulentis uerbis. Hunc autem intuens turuo oculo talia promentem sanctus Patricius ut quondam Petrus de Simone cum quadam potentia et magno clamore confidenter ad Dominum dixit: 'Domine qui omnia potes et in tua potestate consistunt quique me missisti huc hic impius qui blasfemat nomen tuum eleuetur nunc foras et cito moriatur'. Et his dictis eliuatus est in æthera magus et iterum dimissus foras desuper uerso ad lapidem cerebro comminutus et mortuus fuerat coram eis; et timuerunt gentiles. **<4va>**

[18] Iratusque cum suis rex Patricio super hoc uoluit eum occidere et dixit: 'Iniecite manus in istum perdentem nos'. Tunc uidens gentiles impios inruituros in eum sanctus Patricius surrexit claraque uoce dixit: 'Exsurgat Deus et dissipentur inimici eius et fugiant qui oderunt eum a facie eius'. Et statim inruerunt tenebrę et commotio quaedam horribilis et expugnauerunt impii semetipsos alter aduersus alterum insurgens; et terrę motus magnus factus est et collocauit axes curruum eorum et agebat eos cum ui; et praecipitauerunt se currus et equi per planitiem campi donec ad extremum pauci ex eis semiuiui euasserunt ad montem Monduirn; et prostrati sunt ab hac plaga coram rege ex suis sermonibus ad maledictum Patricii septem septies uiri donec ipse remanserat tantum hominibus, ipse et uxor eius et alii ex Scotis .ii., et timuerunt ualde. Ueniensque regina ad Patricium dixit ei: 'Homo iuste et potens, ne perdas regem: ueniens enim rex genua flectet et adorabit Dominum tuum'. Et uenit rex timore coactus et flexit genua coram sancto et finxit se adorare quem nolebat. Et postquam separauerunt ad inuicem paululum gradiens uocauit rex sanctum Patricium simulato uerbo uolens interficere eum quomodo. Sciens autem Patricius cogitationes regis pessimi **<4vb>** benedictis in nomine Iesu Christi sociis suis octo uiris cum puero uenit ad regem. Enumerat eos rex uenientes statimque nusquam conparuerunt ab oculis regis; sed uiderunt gentiles .viii. tantum ceruos cum

[38] MS.: *d-* altered from ?
[39] MS.: overpointed for deletion.
[40] MS.: *a*

hynulo euntes quasi ad dissertum. Et rex Loiguire mestus timidus et ignominiossus cum paucis euadentibus ad Temoriam uersus est deluculo.

[19] Sequenti uero die – hoc est in die pascæ – recumbentibus regibus et principibus et magis apud Loiguire festus enim dies maximus apud eos erat manducantibus illis et bibentibus uinum in palatio Temorię sermocinantibusque et aliis et aliis cogitantibus de his quae facta fuerant sanctus Patricius .v. tantum uiris ut contenderet et uerbum faceret de fide sancta in Temoria coram omnibus nationibus hostiis claussis secundum id quod de Christo legitur uenit. Adueniente ergo eo in caenacolum Temorię nemo de omnibus ad aduentum eius surrexit praeter unum tantum, id est Dubthoch Maccu Lugil, poetam optimum apud quem tunc temporis ibi erat quidam adoliscens poeta nomine Feec qui postea mirabilis episcopus fuit cuius reliquiæ adorantur hi Sleibti. Hic ut dixi **<5ra>** Dubthach solus ex gentibus in honorem sancti Patricii surrexit; et benedixit ei sanctus; crediditque primus in illa die Deo et repputatum est ei ad iustitiam. Uisso itaque Patricio uocatus est a gentibus ad uescendum ut probarent eum in uenturis rebus. Ille autem sciens quæ uentura essent non reffellit uesci.

[20] Cænantibus autem omnibus ille magus Lucetmail qui fuerat in nocturna conflictione etiam in illa die solicitus est extincto consocio suo confligere aduersus sanctum Patricium; et ut initium causæ haberet intuentibus aliis inmissit aliquid ex uasse suo in poculum Patricii ut probaret quid faceret. Uidensque sanctus Patricius hoc probationis genus uidentibus cunctis benedixit poculum suum; et uersus est liquor in modum gelu et conuerso uasse cicidit[41] gutta illa tantum quam inmisserat magus. Et iterum benedixit poculum: conuersus est liquor in naturam et mirati sunt omnes. Et post paululum ait magus: ‘Faciamus signa super hunc campum maximum in hoc campo maximo’. **<5rb>** Respondensque Patricius ait: ‘Quæ?’ Et dixit magus: ‘Inducamus niuem super terram’. Et ait pater: ‘Nolo contraria uoluntati Dei inducere’. Et dixit magus: ‘Ego inducam uidentibus cunctis’. Tunc incantationes magicas exorsus induxit niuem super totum campum pertinguentem ferenn; et uiderunt omnes et mirati sunt. Et ait sanctus: ‘Ecce uidemus hoc: depone nunc’. Et dixit: ‘Ante istam horam cras non possum deponere’. Et ait sanctus: ‘Potes malum et non bonum facere. Non sic ego’. Tunc benedicens per totum circuitum campum dicto citius absque ulla pluia aut nebulis aut uento euanuit nix. Et clamauerunt turbæ et mirati sunt corde. Et paulo post inuocatis demonibus induxit magus densissimas tenebras super terram in signum; et mormurauerunt omnes. Et ait sanctus: ‘Expelle tenebras’. At ille similiter non poterat. Sanctus autem orans benedixit et reppente expulsae sunt tenebrae et refulsit sol. Et exclamauerunt omnes et gratias egerunt. His autem omnibus in conspectu regis inter magum Patriciumque, ait rex ad illos: ‘Libros uestros in aquam mittite et illum cuius libri inlessi euasserunt adorabimus’. Respondit Patricius: ‘Faciam ego’. Et dixit magus: ‘Nolo ego ad iudicium aquæ uenire cum isto: aquam enim deum habet’. Certe audiuit babtisma per aquam a Patricio datum. Et respondens rex ait: ‘Permitte per ignem’. **<5va>** Et ait Patricius: ‘Prumptus sum’. At magus nolens dixit: ‘Hic homo uersa uice in alternos annos nunc aquam nunc ignem deum ueneratur’. Et ait sanctus: ‘Non sic. Sed tu ipse ibis et unus ex meis pueris ibi tecum in

41 MS.: *e* interlined above first *i*.

separatam et conclaussam domum et meum erga te et tuum erga me erit uestimentum et sic simul incendemini.' Et hoc consilium insedit et aedificata est eis domus cuius dimedium ex materia uiridi et alterum dimedium ex arida facta est. Et missus est magus in illam domum in partem eius uiridem et unus ex pueris sancti Patricii Bineus nomine cum ueste magica in partem domus. Conclussa itaque extrinsecus domus coram omni turba incensa est. Et factum est in illa hora orante Patricio ut consumeret flamma ignis magum cum demedia domu uiridi permanente cassula sancti Patricii tantum intacta quia ignis non tetigit. Felix autem Benineus e contrario cum demedia domu arida secundum quod de tribus pueris dictum est non tetigit eum ignis neque contristatus est nec quicquam molesti intulit; cassula tantum magi quae erga eum fuerat non sine Dei nutu exusta. Et iratus est ualde rex aduersus Patricium de morte magi sui et inruit poene in eum uolens occidere; sed prohibuit illum Deus. Ad praecem enim Patricii et ad uocem eius discendit ira Dei in uerticem suum. Et timuit rex uehimenter et commotum est cor eius et omnis **<5vb>** ciuitas cum eo.

[21] Congregatis igitur senioribus et omni senatu suo dixit eis rex Loiguire: 'Melius est credere me quam mori'. Initoque consilio ex suorum praecepto credidit in illa die et conuertit ad Dominum Deum Hisrael aeternum; et ibi crediderunt multi alii. Et ait sanctus Patricius ad regem: 'Quia resististi doctrinę meæ et fuisti scandalum mihi licet prolonguentur dies regni tui nullus tamen erit ex semine tuo rex in aeternum'.

[22] Sanctus autem Patricius secundum praeceptum Domini Iesu gentes babtitzansque eas in nomine Patris et Filii et Spiritus sancti profectus a Temoria praedicauit Domino cooperante Domino et sermonem confirmante sequentibus signis.

[23] Erat quidam homo in regionibus Ulothorum Patricii tempore Macuil Maccu Greccae et erat hic homo ualde impius sæuus tyrannus ut Cyclops nominaretur cogitationibus[43] prauus (prauus uerbis),[42] uerbis intemperatus, factis malignus, spiritu amarus, anima iracondus, corpore scelestus, mente crudelis, uita gentilis, conscientia inanis, in tantum uergens impietatis in profundum ita ut die quadam in montosso aspero altoque sedens loco hi nDruim Moccu Echach ubi ille tyrannidem cotidie **<6ra>** exercebat signa `diberca´ sumens nequissima crudelitatis et transeuntes hospites crudeli scelere interficiens sanctum quoque Patricium claro fidei lumine radiantem et miro quondam cælestis (patriæ) glorię deademate fulgentem uidens eum inconcussa doctrinæ fiducia per congruum uiæ iter ambulantem interficere cogitaret dicens satilitibus suis: 'Ecce seductor ille et peruersor hominum uenit cui mos facere praest(r)igias ut decipiat homines multosque seducat. Eamus ergo et temptemus eum et sciemus si habet potentiam aliquam ille Deus in quo se glorietur.' Temptaueruntque uirum sanctum in hoc mundo: temptauerunt et posuerunt unum ex semetipsis sanum in medio eorum sub sago iacentem infirmitatemque mortis simulantem ut probarent sanctum in huiusquemodi fallaci re sanctum seductorem uirtutis praest(r)igias et orationes ueneficia uel incantationes nominantes. Adueniente sancto Patricio cum discipulis suis, gentiles dixerunt ei: 'Ecce unus ex nobis nunc infirmatus est.

42 MS.: overpointed as for deletion.
43 MS. *cogitantibus*, subsequently altered with puncta delentia and `*oni*´ interlined.

Accede itaque et canta super eum aliquas incantationes sectæ tuę si forte sanari possit.' Sanctus Patricius sciens omnes dolos et fallacias eorum constanter et intripide ait: 'Nec mirum si infirmus fuisset'. Et reuelantes socii eius faciem insimulantis infirmitatem uiderunt eum iam **<6rb>** mortuum. At illi obstupescentes ammirantesque tale miraculum dixerunt intra se gentes: 'Uere hic homo Dei est; male fecimus temptantes eum'. Sanctus uero Patricius conuersus ad Maccuil ait: 'Quare temptare me uoluisti?' Respondensque ille tyrannus crudelis ait: 'Poeniteat me facti huius et quodcumque praeciperis mihi faciam et trado me nunc in potentiam Dei tui excelsi quem praedicas'. Et ait sanctus: 'Crede ergo in Deo meo Domino Iesu et confitere peccata tua et babtitzare in nomine Patris et Filii et Spiritus sancti'. Et conuersus in illa hora credidit Deo æterno. Babtitzatusque est insuper; et non addidit Maccuill dicens: 'Confiteor tibi, sancte domine mi Patrici, quia proposui te interficere. Iudica ergo quantum debuerit pro tanto ac tali cremine.' Et ait Patricius: 'Non possum iudicare sed Deus iudicabit. Tu tamen egredire nunc inermis ad mare et transi uelociter de regione hac hibernensi nihil tollens tecum de tua substantia praeter uile et paruum indumentum quo possit corpus tantum contegi nihil gustans nihilque bibens de fructu insolæ huius, habens insigne peccati tui in capite tuo; et postquam perueniás ad mare conliga pedes tuos conpede ferreo et proiece clauim eius in mari et mitte te in nauim unius pellis absque gubernaculo et absque remo et quocumque te duxerit uentus et mare esto paratus et terram in quamcumque defferat te diuina prouidentia inhabita et exerce tibi diuina mandata.' **<6va>** Dixitque Maccuill: 'Sic faciam ut dixisti. De uiro autem mortuo quid faciemus?' Et ait Patricius: 'Uiuet et exsurget sine dolore'. Et suscitauit eum Patricius in illa hora et reuixit sanus. Et migrauit inde Maccuil tam cito ad mare dexterum campi Inis habeta fiducia inconcussa fidei collegauitque se in litore ieciens clauim in mare secundum quod praeceptum est ei et ascendit mare in nauicula. Et inspirauit illi uentus aquilo et sustulit eum ad meridiem iecitque eum in insolam Euoniam nomine. Inuenitque ibi .ii. uiros ualde mirabiles in fide et doctrina fulgentes qui primi docuerunt uerbum Dei et babtismum in Euonia – et conuersi sunt homines insolę in doctrina eorum ad fidem catholicam – quorum nomina sunt Conindri et Rumili. Hii uero uidentes uirum unius habitus mirati sunt et miserti sunt illius eliuaueruntque de mari suscipientes cum gaudio. Ille igitur ubi inuenti sunt spiritales patres in regione a Deo sibi credita ad regulam eorum corpus et animam exercuit et totum uitæ tempus exegit apud istos. .ii. sanctos episcopus usque dum successor eorum in episcopatu effectus est. Hic est Maccuil di Mane, episcopus et antestes Arddæ Huimnonn.

[24] Alia uero uice sanctus requiescens Patricius in die dominica supra mare iuxta salsuginem quae est ad aquilonalem plagam a collo bouis distans non magno uice spatio audiuit sonum intemperatum gentilium in die Dominica laborantium facientium rathi uocatisque illis prohibuit eos Patricius ne laborarent in Dominico die. At illi non consentiebant uerbis sancti: quin immo inridentes deludebant eum. Et ait sanctus Patricius: 'Mudebroth, quamuis laboraueritis nec tamen proficiat'. Quod tamen completum est. In sequenti enim nocte uentus magnus adueniens turbauit mare et omne opus gentilium distruxit tempestas iuxta uerbum sancti. **<6vb>**

[25] Fuit quidam homo diues et honorabilis in regionibus Orientalium cui nomen erat Daire. Hunc autem rogauit Patricius ut aliquem locum ad exercen-

dam re`le´gionem daret ei. Dixitque diues ad sanctum: 'Quem locum petis?' – 'Peto', inquit sanctus, 'ut illam altitudinem terrę quae nominatur Dorsum Salicis dones mihi et construam ibi locum.' At ille noluit sancto terram illam dare altam; sed dedit illi locum alium in inferiori terra ubi nunc est Fertæ Martyrum iuxta Ardd Machę et habitauit ibi sanctus Patricius cum suis. Post uero aliquod tempus uenit eques (Doiri) Dairi ducens equum suum miraculum ut pasceretur in herbosso loco christianorum. Et offendit Patricium talis dilatio equi in locum suum et ait: 'Stulte fecit Daire bruta mittens animalia turbare locum [44]sanctum paruum [44]quem dedit Deo'. At uero eques tanquam sordus non audiebat et sicut mutus non aperiens os suum nihil loquebatur sed dimisso ibi equo nocte illa exiuit. Crastino autem die mane ueniens eques uissitare equum suum inuenit eum iam mortuum. Domique reuersus tristis ait ad dominum suum: 'Ecce christianus ille occidit equum tuum. Offendit enim illum turbatio loci sui.' Et dixit Daire: 'Occidatur et ille: nunc ite et interficite eum'. Euntibus autem illis foras dictu citius inruit mors super Daire. Et ait uxor eius: 'Caussa christiani est haec. Eat quis cito et portentur nobis beneficia eius et saluus eris; et prohibentur et reuocentur qui exierunt occidere eum.' Exieruntque .ii. uiri (occidere eum)[45] ad christianum qui dixerunt ei celantes quod factum est: 'Et ecce infirmatus est Daire: portetur illi aliquid a te si forte sanari possit'. **<7ra>** Sanctus autem Patricius sciens quae facta sunt dixit: 'Nimirum. Benedixitque aquam et dedit eis dicens: 'Ite, aspergite equum uestrum ex aqua ista, et portate illam uobiscum. Et fecerunt sic et reuixit equus; et portauerunt secum sanatusque est Daire asparsione aquæ sanctę (apersione[46] aquae sanctae). Et uenit Daire post haec ut honoraret sanctum Patricium portans secum eneum mirabilem transmarinum metritas ternas capientem. Dixitque Daire ad sanctum: 'Ecce hic æneus sit tecum'. Et ait sanctus Patricius: 'Grazacham'. Reuersusque Daire ad domum suam dixit: 'Stultus homo est qui nihil boni dixit praeter "Grazacham" pro æneo mirabili metritarum trium'. Additque Daire dicens seruis suis: 'Ite reportate nobis æneum nostrum'. Exierunt et dixerunt Patricio: 'Portabimus æneum'. Nihilominus et illa uice sanctus Patricius dixit: 'Gratzacham, portate'; et portauerunt. Interrogauitque Daire socios suos dicens: 'Quid dixit christianus quando reportasti æneum?' At illi responderunt: ' "Grazacham" dixit et ille'. Daire respondens dixit: ' "Gratzacham" in dato, "Grazacham" in ablato; eius dictum tam bonum est; cum "Grazacham" illis portabitur illi rursum æneus suus'. Et uenit Daire i<p>semet[47] illa uice et portauit æneum ad Patricium dicens ei: 'Fiat tecum æneus tuus. Constans enim et incommotabilis homo es. Insuper et partem illam agri quam ollim petisti do tibi nunc quantum habeo; et inhabita ibi.' Et illa est ciuitas quae nunc Ardd Machae **<7rb>** nominatur. Et exierunt ambo sanctus Patricius et Daire ut considerarent mirabile oblationis et beneplacitum munus et ascenderunt illam altitudinem terræ inuenieruntque ceruam cum uitulo suo paruo iaciente in loco in quo nunc altare est sinistralis aeclessiae in Ardd Machæ. Et uoluerunt comites Patricii tenere uitulum et occidere; sed noluit sanctus neque permissit; quin potius ipsemet sanctus tenuit

44...44 MS.: *sanctum* in the text is associated by a signe de renvoi with *paruum* in the margin.
45 MS.: these words marked by suprascript triangles of dots.
46 MS.: altered to *aparsione* or *apassione* by underpointing and interlining.
47 MS.: *insemet.*

uitulum portans eum in humeris suis. Et secuta illum cerua uelut amantissimaque ouis usquedum dimisserat uitulum in altero saltu situm ad aquilonalem plagam Airdd Mache: ubi usque hodie signa quædam uirtutis esse manentia periti dicunt.

[26] Uirum aliquem ualde durum et tam auarum in campo Inis habitantem in tantum stultitię auaritiæque incurrisse cremen periti ferunt ut .ii. boues carrarum Patricii uechentes alio die post sanctum laborem in pastu agili sui requiescentibus pascentibusque se bobus uiolenter inconstanter praesente sancto Patricio uanus ille homo per uim cocgit. Cui irascens sanctus Patricius cum maladictione dixit: 'Mudebrod, male fecisti. Nusquam proficiat tibi ager hic tuus neque semini tuo in aeternum; iam inutilis erit. Et factum est sic. Inundatio etenim maris tam habunda eodem ueniens die circumluit et operuit totum agrum et possitus est iuxta profetæ uerbum terra fructifera in salsuginem a malitia inhabitantis in ea. Arenossa ergo et infructuossa haec a die qua maledixit eam sanctus Patricius usque in hodiernum diem.

Finit primus incipit secundus liber. **<7va>**

[1] De Patricii deligentia orationis.
[2] De mortuo ad se loquente.
[3] De inluminata Dominica nocte ut equi inuenti sunt.
[4] De eo quod angelus eum prohibuit ne [48]i <Ma>chi[48] moriretur <et> de rubo ardente in qua erat angelus.[49]
[5] De .iiii. Patricii petitionibus.
[6] De die mortis eius et de tempore uitae .xxx. annorum.
[7][49] De termino contra noctem possita[50] <et> de caligine .xii. noctium abstersa.
[8] De uigilis primæ noctis iuxta corpus Patricii quas angeli fecerunt.
[9] De consilio sepulturae eius ab angelo.
[10] De (sæpulcro)[51] igne de sepulcro eius erumpente.
[11] De freto susrum surgente[52] ut non bellum de corpore fieret.
[12] De felici seductione populorum.

[53]Si quis autem terminum contra noctem et noctem non uissam esse in tota prouincia breui tempore in quo luctus Patricii peractus est abnegare infidiliter uoluit audiat et diligenter attendat qualiter Ezechiae languente in horalogiae Acaz demonstrato sanitatis indicio, rl'.[53]

[1] De dilegentia orationis. Omnes psalmos et ymnos et Apocalipsin Iohannis et omnia kantica spiritalia scripturarum cotidie decantans siue manens aut in itenere pergens tropeo etiam crucis in omni hora diei noctisque centies se signans et ad omnes cruces quascumque uidisset orationis gratią de curru discendens declinabat.

48...48 MS.: *innichi.*
49 This *capitulum* is written as two in the manuscript.
50 MS.: *uel -o* (interlined).
51 MS.: *sæpulcro*: stands beneath a series of dotted triangles.
52 MS.: altered from *rurgente*.
53...53 This appears to belong in II.7 at the point marked *.vi.* and with two marginal occurrences of *z*.

[2] Inde **<7vb>** etiam in die quadam ingrediens crucem quae erat iuxta uiam sitam non uidens praetergressus est. Hanc tamen auriga uidit; et ille dixit cum ad hospitium quoddam quo tenderat peruenissent et orare ante prandium coepissent dixit inquam auriga: 'Uidi crucem iuxta uiam per quam uenimus positam'. At ille Patricius dimisso hospitio per uiam quam uenerat(ur) ad crucem pergens orauit; et sepulcrum ibi uiderat et mortuum in illo busto sepultum. Interrogauit qua morte abierat et sub fide uixerat. Respondit mortuus: 'Gentilis uixi et hic sepultus fui. Quædam etiam mulier in alia prouincia degens mortuum filium qui se longue separatus erat habuit et illa absente sepultus est. At post aliquot dies lugens mater omissum filium planxit et indecreto errore sepulchrum gentilis hominis sui filii bustum esse putans crucem non iuxta gentilem possuit.' Et ob hanc caussam ut Patricius dixit crucem non uiderat quia sepulturæ gentilis locus fuit; et uirtus maior inde surrexerat ut mortuus loqueretur et qui sub fide defunctus erat Christi scieretur et iuxta illum almę crucis fieret meritum signo in uero terminio possito.

[3] Consuetudo autem illi erat ut a uespera Dominicę noctis usque ad mane secundæ ferię Patricius non ambularet. Inde in quadam Dominica die honore sacri temporis in campo pernoctans grauis pluia cum tempestate accederat. Sed cum grauis pluia in tota patria populata est **<8ra>** in loco ubi sanctus episcopus pernoctabat siccitas erat sicut in conca et in uellere Gedeon. Accederat auriga memorat equos amissos quasi amicos caros planguit quia illos quaerere tenebris arcentibus uissum non poterat. Inde pietas Patricii patris pii mota est et flebili aurigæ dixit: 'Deus in angustis in oportunitatibus adiutor prumptus adiutorium praestabit et equos quos ploras inuenies'. Exhinc manum spolians manica extensam (iugulauit)[54] eleuauit et. .v. digiti sicut luminaria ita proxima quaeque inluxerat et per lucem extensæ manus equos quos commisserat auriga solito gemitu inuenit. Sed hoc miraculum auriga comes usque ad Patricii obitum absconderat.

[4] Post uero miracula tanta quae alibi scripta sunt et quae ore fideli mundus celebrat adpropinquante die mortis eius uenit ad eum anguelus et dixit illi de morte sua. Ideo ad Ardd Machae missit quam prae omnibus terris dilexit. Ideo mandauit ut uenirent ad eum uiri multi ad eundem deducendum quo uoluit. Inde cum comittibus suis iter carpere coepit ad Machi uoluntarię tellurem cupitam satis. Sed iuxta uiam rubus quedam arserat et non comburetur sicut antea Moyses prouenerat in rubo. Uictor erat anguelus qui Patricium sepe uissitare solebat et Uictor alterum anguelum ad Patricium prohibendum ne pergat quo pergere cupit missit et dixit illi: 'Quare proficisceris sine Uictoris consilio? Quamobrem Uictor te uocat et ad eum declina.' Et ut ei iussum est declinauit et quid facere deberet interrogauit. Et respondens anguelus dixerat: 'Reuertere ad locum unde uenis – hoc est Sabul – et datæ sunt .iiii. petitiones tibi quas petisti.

[5] 'Prima petitio ut in Ardd Machæ fiat ordinatio tua. Secunda petitio ut quicumque ymnum qui de te compossitus est in die exitus de corpore contauerit **<8rb>** tu iudicabis poenitentiam eius de suis peccatis. .iii. petitio ut nepotes Dichon qui te benigne susciperunt missericordiam mereantur et non pereant. .iiii. petitio ut Hibernenses omnes in die iudicii a te iudicentur sicut dicitur ad

54 MS.: marked with suprascript triangles of dots.

apostolos, 'Et uos sedentes iudicabiti .xii. tribubus Israel', ut eos quibus apostolis fuerunt iudices fuistis.
[6] 'Reuertere igitur sicut tibi dico et moriens ingrediereis uiam patrum tuorum.' Quod in die .xvi. kl. Aprilis peractus totius eius uitæ annis .cxx. et prouenerat sicut omnbus totius Hyberniæ annis celebratur.
[7] 'Et contra noctem terminum pones.' Quia in illa die mortis eius nox non erat et per duodecimas dies in illa prouincia in qua mortis eius exequiæ peractæ sunt nox non inruit et fuscis tellurem non amplexerat alis et pallor non tantus erat noctis et astriferas non induxerat bosferus umbras. Et plebs Ulod dixit quod usque in finem anni totius in quo abierat numquam noctium tales tenebrę erant quales antea fuerunt. Quod ad tanti uiri meritum declarandum esse dubium est. *.vi.*[55] Adpropinquante autem hora obitus sui sacrificium ab episcopo Tassach sicut illi Uictor anguelus dixit ad uiaticum beatæ uitæ acciperat.
[8] In prima nocte exequiarum eius angueli uigilias psalmi corporis fecerunt in uigiliarum et psalmorum moribus omnibus quicumque ad uigilias in illa prima nocte ueniebant dormientibus. Homines orantes et psalmos cantantes corpus custodierunt. Postquam autem in caelum profecti sunt angueli odorem suauissimum quasi mellis et flagrantiam dulcidinis quasi uini dimisserunt; ut impleretur quod in benedictione[56] patriarchę Iacob dictum est: 'Ecce odor filii mei tamquam odor agri pleni quem benedixit Dominus'.
[9] *.viii.* Quando autem anguelus ad eum uenit consilium sepulturæ dedit illi: 'Elegantur .ii. boues indomiti et pergant quocumque uoluerint et ubicumque requiescunt æclessia in honorem corpusculi tui ædificetur'. Et sicut anguelus dixit instabiles electi sunt iuuenci et stabili plaustrum gestamine humeris inpossitum cum sancto corpore uechunt. **<8va>** Et a loco qui Clocher uocatur ab oriente Findubrec de pecoribus Conail electio clarificauit boues. Et exierunt Dei nutu regente ad Dun Lethglaisse ubi sepultus est Patricius.
[10] Et dixit ei: 'Ne reliquię a terra reducuntur corporis tui et cubitus de terra super corpus fiat'. Quod iussu Dei factum in nouissimis demonstratum est temporibus, quia quando aeclessia super corpus facta est fodientes humum antropi ignem a sepulchro inrumpere uiderunt et recedentes flammigerum timuerunt flammæ ignem.
[11] De reliquiis sancti Patricii in tempore obitus sui dira contensio ad bellum usque perueniens inter nepotes Neill et Orientales ex una parte inter aliquando propinquales et propinquos nunc inter dirissimos hostes irarum intrat certamen. Sed fretum quoddam quod Collum Bouis uocatur merito Patricii sanguis effunderetur et misericordia Dei altis crispantibusque intumescebant fluctibus et undarum uertices concaua rumpebant æra et dorsa in fluctibus tremula aliquando crispanti rissu et aliquando flauis uallibus in certamine rueba`n´t; quasi ad cohibendam animossitatem gentium dirarum tales enim populi sunt surrexit freti feritas et plebem pugnare prohibuit.
[12] Postea autem sepulto Patricio et freti tumore sepulto Orientales et contra Ultu nepotes Neill acriter ad certamen ruunt et certatim praeparati et armati ad bellum ad locum beati corporis prorumperat. Sed felici seducti sunt fallacia

55 This mysterious number is accompanied by *z* written twice in the margin. See n. 51 above.
56 Altered to *benediction`ibus´*, with the *i* subscript and the *-bus* suprascript, original final *-e* being ignored.

putantes se duos boues et plaustrum inuenire et corpus sanctum rapere æstimabant et cum corpore et tali praeparatu et armatura usque ad fluium Cabcenne peruenierunt et corpus tunc illis non conparuit. Inpossibile enim ut de tanto ac de beato corpore pax fieret nisi Dei nutu taliter uideretur uissio ad tempus ostensa: ne quod animarum salus innumerabilium in exitum et mortem uerteretur felici fallacia ostensum est. Sicut Siri antea excæcati, **<8vb>** ne sanctum profetam Helesseum occiderent, ad Helesseum diuina prouissione ad Samariam usque ducti sunt, haec etiam seductio ad concordiam populorum facta est.
[*][57] Iterum recurrat oratio. Anguelus in omni septima die septimanę semper uenire consuerat; et sicut homo cum homine loquitur ita conloquio angueli fruebatur Patricius. Etiam in .xvi. anno ætatis captus et .vi. annis seruiuit et per .xxx. uices conductionum anguelus ad eum uenerat et consiliis atque conloquiis fruebatur anguelicis. Antequam de Scotia ad Latinos pergeret centies in die et centies in nocte orabat. Aliquando sues custodiens perdidit eas et anguelus ueniens ad eum sues indicauit illi. Aliquando etiam anguelus illi loquens multa illi dixit; et postquam illi locutus est pedem super petram ponens in Scirit in montem Mis coram se ascendit. Uestigia pedis angueli in petra hucusque manentia cernuntur. Et in illo loco .xxx. uicibus ad eum locutus est et ille locus et ibi fidelium preces fructum felicissimum obtinent.

Finit. Amen.

[58]Portauit Patricius per Sininn secum L. clocos L. patinos L. calices altaria libros legis æuanguelii libros et reliquit illos in locis nouis.

Patricius .vi. anno babtitzatus est, .xx. captus est, .xv. seruiuit, .xl. legit, .lxi. docuit. Tota uero aetas eius .cxi.. Hæc Constans in Gallis inuenit.[58]

[57] This chapter is not mentioned in the list of *capitula*. In the other copies of Muirchú's work it occupies a place in the middle of Book I: see *The Patrician Texts*, edd. & transl. Bieler & Kelly, p. 15, for discussion; cf. pp. 80–3 (text), 201–2 (commentary).

[58...58] These two paragraphs follow Muirchú's work; after them, there are five blank lines before the end of the folio and the quire.

ST PATRICK IN THE *HISTORIA BRITTONUM*: THREE TEXTS

The *Historia Brittonum* was written in Wales in the year 829/30, as internal chronological indicators show. The author, an anonymous Welsh ecclesiastic, had access to a variety of Irish sources as his references to Irish informants and his use of texts of Irish origin demonstrate. Whether he himself was able to speak or read Irish has been a matter of some uncertainty.[1]

Among the Irish elements from which his synthetic history was woven is a short composite Life of St Patrick. This stands, slightly uneasily, between an even more obviously composite account of the visit to Britain of St Germanus of Auxerre (and in particular his destruction of the British ruler Gwrtheyrn) and the famous passage dealing with the martial exploits of Arthur, the undefeated *dux bellorum*, against the English invaders. Students of the *Historia Brittonum* have given a modest amount of attention to the Patrician section of the text,[2] concluding generally that the works of both Muirchú and Tírechán were probably obtained in one and the same manuscript and that both were laid under contribution by the Welsh writer. In 1942 Ludwig Bieler summed up the position by saying that this composite Life was 'probably compiled from various sources by' the author of the *Historia Brittonum*.[3]

This conclusion no longer seems convincing. The principal difficulty is that, as yet, students of neither the *Historia Brittonum* (in its various manifestations) nor the tradition of Patrician hagiography have integrated the last generation's work on either corpus of texts with the other. In particular, the considerable advances in the textual history of the *uitae Patricianae*[4] have occurred without much reference to the *Historia Brittonum*.[5] In as much as it seems clear that, from the time of the 'Book of Armagh' at least (and probably in fact from a date in the eighth century), there existed a composite mixed-language Life of St Patrick,[6] it would seem sensible to suppose that the Patrician section of the

1 For discussion of all these aspects of the *Historia Brittonum*, see Dumville, *Histories and Pseudo-histories*.

2 *The Tripartite Life*, ed. & transl. Stokes, I.cxvii–cxviii; Zimmer, *Nennius Vindicatus*, pp. 116, 121, 208–10; Bury, *The Life*, pp. 248, 257; *Nennius*, ed. Lot, I.46.

3 Bieler, *Codices Patriciani*, p. 21 (no. 21). Cf. *The Patrician Texts*, edd. & transl. Bieler & Kelly, p. 28: 'a conglomeration of Patrician lore from many sources, insufficiently analysed'.

4 Conveniently summarised in stemmata by Sharpe, 'Palaeographical considerations', p. 18 (subject to the possible caveat noted above on p. 204, n. 9). Cf. *The Patrician Texts*, edd. & transl. Bieler & Kelly, p. 30.

5 For one point where contact has been made, see *Four Latin Lives*, ed. Bieler, pp. 228–32.

6 For the starting point, see *The Tripartite Life*, ed. & transl. Stokes, I.xcv–xcix; for the advance, cf. Bieler, 'Bethu Phátraic'. In general see the collection of papers by Bieler, *Studies on the Life*.

Historia Brittonum is in principle likely to be derived from such a hybrid text. Meanwhile, our growing knowledge of the methods and outlook of the author of the *Historia Brittonum* enables us to see that, while he was capable of bringing different sources together, his methods of dealing with texts as he laid them under contribution were not such as to produce seamless transitions.

In order to bring the *Historia Brittonum* into the mainstream of Patrician criticism, I print here three texts which derive from my long-running studies of the textual tradition of the *Historia*.

I

The 'Harleian' recension

It is generally agreed that this anonymous text represents, in essentials, the original version of the work as it was first composed in A.D. 829/30.[1] The text (Harl. §§43–50) given below is drawn from a draft of my critical edition of this recension:[2] it depends on the following witnesses.

C London, British Library, MS. Cotton Vespasian B.xxv (*saec.* xii^{1}; Canterbury, Christ Church)

H London, British Library, MS. Harley 3859 (*saec.* xi/xii; origin unknown, probably Continental)

I Quotations in the *Cronica Imperfecta* of Christ Church, Canterbury (*saec.* xii^{1})[3]

L Quotations in the *Liber Floridus* of Lambert of Saint-Omer (*an.* 1120; Saint-Omer)[4]

R London, British Library, MS. Cotton Vespasian D.xxi, fos 1–17 (*saec.* xii^{1}; Rochester)[5]

V London, British Library, MS. Cotton Vitellius A.xiii, fos 91–100 (*saec.* xiii^{1}; Rochester)[6]

Their interrelationships may be summed up in a *stemma codicum*.

1 Cf. Dumville, *Histories and Pseudo-histories*, for discussion.

2 *The Historia Brittonum*, ed. Dumville.

3 Unpublished: to be edited in *The Anglo-Saxon Chronicle*, gen. edd. Dumville & Keynes. The manuscript is Oxford, Bodleian Library, MS. Lat. misc. d.13 (*S.C.* 30572).

4 For text and discussion, see Dumville, *Histories and Pseudo-histories*, chapter XII. The manuscript is Ghent, University Library, MS. 92.

5 A detached portion of London, British Library, MS. Royal 15.A.xxii.

6 A detached portion of London, British Library, MS. Royal 15.B.xi.

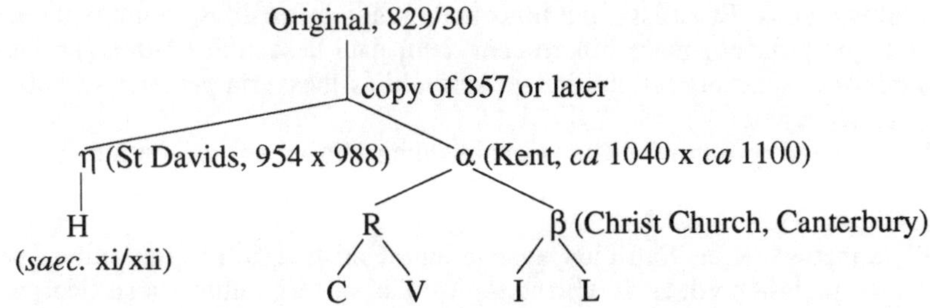

§43. Sanctus Germanus reuersus est post mortem illius ad patriam suam. Et sanctus Patricius erat in [1]illo tempore[1] captiuus apud Scottos, et dominus illius nominabatur Milchu, et porcarius cum illo erat. Et in septimo decimo anno[2] etatis sue reuersus est de captiuitate. Et nutu Dei eruditus est postea in sacris litteris. Et ad Romam usque peruenit, et per longum spatium mansit ibidem ad legendum et ad scrutanda misteria[3] Dei, et sanctarum scripturarum libros percurrit.[4] Nam cum ibi esset per annos septem, missus est Palladius[5] episcopus primitus a Scelestino[6] episcopo et papa Rome ad Scottos in Christum conuertendos; sed prohibuit illum Deus per quasdam tempestates, quia nemo potest accipere quicquam de terra nisi de celo datum fuerit[7] illi desuper. Et profectus est ille Palladius[8] de Hibernia[9] et peruenit ad Brittanniam; et ibi defunctus est in terra Pictorum.

§44. Audita morte Palladii episcopi alius legatus Patricius, Theodosio et Ualentiano regnantibus, a Scelestiano[1] papa romano et angelo Dei cui nomen erat Uictor, monente et[2] suadente[3] [4]sancto Germano[4] episcopo,[5] ad Scottos in fidem[6] Christi[7] conuertendos mittitur. Misit Germanus seniorem cum illo[8] Segerum ad quendam hominem mirabilem, summum episcopum Amatheam regem, in propinquo habitantem. Ibi, sanctus sciens omnia que uentura essent illi, episcopalem gradum [9]a Matheo rege[9] episcopus[10] sanctus accepit et nomen quod est Patricius sumpsit quia prius Maun uocabatur. Auxilius et Iserinus et ceteri inferiori gradu[11] simul ordinati sunt[12] cum eo.

§45. Tunc, acceptis benedictionibus perfectisque omnibus in nomine Sancte Trinitatis, paratam ascendit nauim et peruenit ad Brittanniam et predicauit ibi

§43
1...1 CHR; *tempore illo* V.
2 HL; om. CRV.
3 H; *mysteria* CLRV.
4 CH^{1}RV; *percucurrit* H^2.
5 CHLR; *Paladius* V.
6 CHR; *Cęlestino* L; *Celestino* V.
7 CRV; *datum fuerit* (*et* [H^2]) *datum fuerit* H.
8 CHR; *Paladius* V.
9 CHR; *Hybernia* V.

§44
1 C*HRV; *Celestiano* C^2; *Celestino* I; *Cęlestino* L.
2 H; om. CRV.
3 CRV; *suadente a* H.
4...4 CHR; *Germano sancto* V.
5 H; *episcopos* CRV.
6 CHR; om. V.
7 CHR; *Christum* V.
8 CHR; *eo* V.
9...9 Another corruption of the original *Amat(h)orex*; cf. MS. A of Muirchú (above, pp. 104, 206, 208).
10 CHR; om. V.
11 CHR; *gradus* V.
12 HI; om. CRV.

non multis diebus. Et amissis omnibus ambulandi anfractibus,[1] summa uelocitate flatuque prospero mare hibernicum[2] cum naui descendit.[3] Honerata[4] uero nauis cum transmarinis mirabilibus et spiritalibus thesauris perrexit ad Hiberniam;[5] et baptizauit eos.

§46. A mundi principio usque ad baptismum Hiberniensium[1] quinque milia trecenti triginta anni sunt. In quinto anno Loygare regis exorsus est predicare fidem Christi.

§47. Sanctus itaque Patricius euangelium Christi externis nationibus per annos quadraginta predicabat. Uirtutes apostolicas:[1] cecos illuminabat; leprosos mundabat; surdos audire faciebat; demones obsessis[2] corporibus fugabat;[3] mortuos numero[4] usque[5] ad nouem suscitauit.[6] Captiuos multos utriusque sexus suis propriis donis redemit. Scriptsit abegetoria trecenta sexaginta quinque aut eo amplius; ecclesias quoque eodem numero fundauit, trecentas sexaginta quinque; ordinauit episcopos trecentos sexaginta quinque, aut eo[7] amplius, in quibus spiritus Dei erat. Presbiteros autem usque ad tria milia ordinauit; et duodecim milia hominum in una regione Conachta[8] ad fidem Christi conuertit et baptizauit. [9]<Et septem reges qui erant filii Amolgith in uno die baptizauit.>[9] Quadraginta diebus et quadraginta noctibus in cacumine collis Eile ieiunauit, id est Cruachan Eile.

§48. In quo colle mare[1] inminente,[2] tres petitiones pro his qui fidem ex Hiberniensibus[3] receperunt clementer postulauit. Prima petitio eius est, ut dicunt Scotti, id est ut susciperet unusquisque penitentiam licet in extremo uite sue statu; secunda, ut ne a barbaris consumentur in eternum; tercia, ut non superuixerit aliquis Hiberniensium[4] in aduentu iudicii, quia delebuntur pro honore Patricii septem annis ante iudicium.

§49. In illo autem tumulo benedixit populis Hibernie,[1] et ideo ascendit ut oraret pro eis et uideret fructum laboris sui. Et uenerunt ad eum aues multi coloris innumerabiles ut benediceret illis, quod significat omnes sanctos utriusque sexus[2] Hiberniensium[3] peruenire ad eum in die iudicii, ad patrem et ad

§45

1 CHR; *amfractibus* V.

2 HV; *hybernicum* CR.

3 H; *conscendit* CR; *ascendit* V. No reading is satisfactory; a verb meaning 'to set sail' is needed here. The manuscripts of Muirchú's *Vita S. Patricii* read *contendit* (A) and *peruenit* (B).

4 CHR; *Onerata* V.

5 CHR; *Hyberniam* V.

§46

1 H; *Hibernensium* CLR; *Hyberniensium* V.

§47

1 A verb has presumably been omitted hence; alternatively, one might read '<Per> uirtutes apostolicas cecos illuminabat . . .'.

2 CHRV; *ab obsessis* H^{2}.

3 LV; *fugiebat* CHR.

4 C*HRV; *uero* C^{2}.

5 C^{2}H; *us* C^{1}R; om. V.

6 CHRV^{2}; *suscitabat* V^{1}; L has this clause twice, reading first *suscitabat* and then *suscitauit*.

7 H; om. CRV.

8 The Old Irish nominative. Either this is an error for the genitive (*Connacht*) or else an adjective, limiting *regione*, has been created.

9...9 My insertion, after comparison with the 'Vatican' and 'Gildasian' recensions.

§48

1 H; *in aere* CRV.

2 H; *imminente* CR; *īminente* V.

3 CHR; *Hyberniensibus* V.

4 H^{2}; *Hibernientium* H^{1}; *Hibernensium* CR; *Hybernensium* V.

§49

1 CHR; *Hybernie* V.

2 CRV; *sexus autem* H.

3 R; *Hibernensium* CH; *Hybernensium* V.

magistrum suum, ut sequantur illum ad iudicium. Postea in senectute bona migrauit ubi nunc letatur in secula seculorum, amen.

§50. Quattuor modis equantur Moyses et Patricius:[1] [2]id est,[2] angelo colloquente in rubo igneo; secundo modo, in monte quadraginta diebus et quadraginta noctibus ieiunauit;[3] tercio modo, similes fuerunt etate centum uiginti annis; quarto modo, sepulchrum illius[4] nemo scit, sed in occulto[5] humatus est nemine sciente.

Quindecim annis in captiuitate; in uicisimo[6] quinto anno ab Amatheo sancto episcopo subrogatur; octoginta[7] et quinque annorum in Hibernia[8] predicauit. Res autem exigebat amplius loqui de sancto Patricio, sed tamen pro compendio sermonis uolui breuiare.

II

The 'Vatican' recension

In A.D. 943/4, the *Historia Brittonum* – in a now lost recension which can be shown to have been created in Wales *ca* 875 x *ca* 925 – was rewritten in England.[1] The stylistic changes were exceptionally thorough; some parts of the text were omitted; and a reorganisation significant for the present purpose is apparent in the revised version. The principal manuscript-witness to this recension is an eleventh-century French copy, but one which clearly derives from an exemplar (now lost) in English Square-minuscule script. In this version the account of St Patrick stands as the last element of the text (§28), indeed in a form which makes it manifestly separable from the body of the work.[2] The result was that it seems generally to have been lost from the 'Vatican' tradition of the *Historia*: no otherwise complete copy contains the account of St Patrick. (However, we do have indirect evidence for the survival of the full text in England: a copy of the 'Vatican' recension was collated against a text of another recension at Bury St Edmunds, Suffolk, *ca* 1300; the result is eighteen excerpts from a witness to the 'Vatican' recension, one of which is drawn from the account of Patrick.) The

§50

1 HRV; *Patrius* C.

2...2 It is possible (though by no means necessary) that an earlier *.i.* = *primo* has been read as *id est*.

3 HRV; *iunauit* C.

4 H; om. CRV.

5 HRV; *oculto* C.

6 H[1]; *uicesimo* H[2]; *.xx^mo^*. CRV.

7 CLRV; *octingentorum* H[1]; *octinginta* H[2].

8 CHR; *Hybernia* V.

1 *The Historia Brittonum*, ed. Dumville, III.

2 The end of §27 of the text reads like the conclusion of the *Historia*. The only failure of separation is that the Patrician *uita* (§28) still begins (now very misleadingly) 'In illo tempore'. §28 also ends in MS. R with two statements of closure.

very fact of this section's separability produced the possibility of its travelling independently: a short *Vita S. Patricii* in a manuscript perhaps written at Metz in the second half of the twelfth century has proved to be a separate copy of §28 of the 'Vatican' recension.[3]

One matter remains to be discussed. It has not proved possible to identify the English church at which the 'Vatican' recension was created in the fifth year of King Edmund I. A speculation may perhaps be allowed. The special treatment accorded to the text's account of St Patrick inevitably raises the possibility that the church in question was one which had more than a passing interest in him. We know from B's Life of St Dunstan (written in 995x1004) that that was unusually true of Glastonbury in the first half of the tenth century, and we can see from the evidence rehearsed by Lesley Abrams that there is likely to have been a formal cult of St Patrick in tenth-century Glastonbury.[4]

I reproduce this text from my published edition of the 'Vatican' recension, where in this chapter the text is based wholly on R, but with some augmentation of the apparatus. The text depends on four witnesses.

B The Bury St Edmunds annotations
  a London, College of Arms, MS. Arundel 30 (*saec.* xiii/xiv)
  b Cambridge, University Library, MS. Ff.1.27 (1160), pp. 41–64 (*saec.* xiv^{1})
R Roma, Biblioteca Apostolica Vaticana, MS. Reginensis lat. 1964, fos 47r–58r (Soissons, *saec.* xi^{2})
W Paris, Bibliothèque nationale, MS. latin 8501A, fo 1r/v (?Metz, *saec.* xii^{2})

Their relationships may be summarised in a *stemma codicum*.

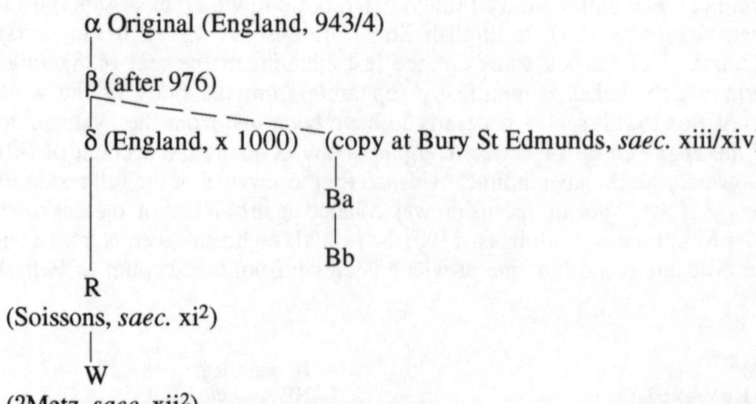

3 Noticed but not investigated by Bieler, *Codices Patriciani*, p. 45 (no. 56). For a full description, see Crick, *The Historia Regum Britannie*, III.284–6 (no. 183). This copy seems likely to be a derivative of the Soissons manuscript since it is followed by a Frankish genealogy (noted by Faral, *La Légende arthurienne*, I.288 and n. 2) which also occurs in that position in MS. R.

4 See below, pp. 233–42 (cf. 243–4); cf. Dumville, *Liturgy*, chapter II.

§28.[1] <I>n[2] illo tempore sanctus Patritius[3] erat apud Scottos;[4] et dominus illius nominabatur Milchu, et porcarius[5] cum illo fuit septem annis. In decimo septimo autem anno [6]etatis suae[6] reuersus est de captiuitate, Deo liberante. Et nutu Dei eruditus est in sacris scripturis. Et postea Romam petiit,[7] et longo tempore illic mansit legendo; et sacra misteria[8] sanctamque scripturam legit, Spiritu Sancto replente. Nam, cum esset ibi in studio lectionis,[9] missus est Palladius episcopus primus a Celestino, papa romano, ad Scottos Christo conuertendos. Sed per quasdam tempestates et signa illum Deus prohibuit – quia nemo potest [10]quicquam accipere[10] in terra, nisi fuerit[11] datum desuper –; [12]et ille[12] Palladius[13] rediens de Hibernia ad Bryttanniam[14] ibi defunctus est in terra Pictorum.

Conscia autem morte Palladii episcopi romanis patriciis Theodotio[15] et Ualentino[16] regnantibus, a Celestino papa romano – et angelo Dei comitante monente atque[17] adiuuante Uictore – et a Germano[18] episcopo a<d>[19] Scottos ad fidem Sanctae[20] Trinitatis conuertendos Patritius[21] missus est. Misit ergo Germanus seniorem cum illo Segerum ad quen<dam>[22] grandeuum laudandumque senem[23] episcopum et ad regem, Matheum nomine, in propinquo commorantem; ibique sanctus Patricius – quae[24] uentura illi erant praescius[25] – episcopalem gradum a Matheo rege pontificeque sancto accepit. Et illud nomen – Patricius – in ordinatu[26] sumpsit, quia[27] antea Mauun uocabatur. Auxilius uero[28] et Iserninus aliique fratres gradibus inferioribus simul ordinati sunt cum eo.

Tunc, acceptis benedictionibus perfectisque omnibus in nomine Sanctae[29] Trinitatis, peruenit ad mare quod est inter Gallos et Bryttones.[30] Inde prompto[31] nauigio descendit in Bryttanniam.[32] Et in ea praedicauit aliquo tempore. Praeparatis[33] autem sibi necessariis, angelo commonente, Ibernicum[34] mare petiit.[35] Impleta uero naue transmarinis muneribus et spiritalibus thesauris, Dei largitu peruenit ad Hiberniam. Et eis praedicauit, illosque[36] baptizauit.

A mundi siquid<em>[37] principio[38] usque ad baptismum Hibernensium[39] quinque milia trecenti triginta anni fuerunt. In quinto anno imperii Logiore regis

§28

1 No heading in R; *Incipit de ordinatione et uita sancti Patricii episcopi et apostoli Scotorum*, W.
2 [ ]*n* R; *In* W.
3 R; *Patricius* W.
4 R; *Scotos* W.
5 R; *portarius* W.
6...6 R; *etatis sue* W.
7 R; *peciit* W.
8 R; *misteria celebrando* W.
9 R; *leccionis* W.
10...10 R; *accipere quicquam* W.
11 R; *fuerit ei* W.
12...12 R; om. W.
13 R; *Palladius itaque* W.
14 R; *Brittanniam* W.
15 R; *Theodosio* W.
16 R; *Ualentiniano* W.
17 R; *et* W.
18 R; *Germano autisiod[ ]orensi* W (with deleted -*i*-).
19 *at* R; *ad* W.
20 R; *Sancte* W.
21 R; *Patricius* W.
22 *quen* R; *quendam* W.
23 R; *uirum senem* W.
24 R; *que* W.
25 R; *prescius* W.
26 R; *ordinatione* BbW.
27 R; *qui* W.
28 BbR; *autem* W.
29 R; *Sancte* W.
30 R; *Brittones* W.
31 *prom`p´to* R.
32 R; *Brittanniam* W.
33 R; *Preparatis* W.
34 R; *Hibernicum* W.
35 R; *peciit* W.
36 R; *eosque* W.
37 *siquid* R; *siquidem* W.
38 R; *initio* W.
39 R; *Hiberniensium* W.

Hibernię primum praedicatio uere fidei Trinitatis Almae[40] unitatisque indiuiduae[41] Hiberniensibus aduenit.

Sanctus itaque Patricius extraneis nationibus euangelium[42] Christi per annos quadraginta praedicauit. Uirtutes apostolicas fecit: cecos illuminauit; leprosos mundauit; surdos audire fecit; demones ab obsessis corporibus eiecit;[43] nouem mortuos suscitauit. Capituos multos utriusque sexus suis propriis muneribus redemit, et in nomine Sanctae[44] Trinitatis liberauit. Canonicos aliis[45] ad fidem catholicam pertinentibus libros scripsit trecentos sexaginta quinque; ęcclesias quoque eodem numero trecentas sexaginta quinque fundauit; [46]seruos Dei[46] docuit et ad episcopalem gradum, Spiritu Sancto affirmante, tali numero consecrauit – [47]id est[47] trecentos sexaginta quinque. Praesbiteros autem admodum tria milia ordinauit; et duodecim milia hominum in una regione Cunnehcta ad fidem christianam conuertit et baptizauit. Et septem reges, qui fuerunt septem[48] filii Amolgith, in una die baptizauit. Quadraginta diebus et quadraginta noctibus in cacumine montis Eli ieiunauit, id est Cruachan Ęli.[49]

In quo monte tres petitiones,[50] pro his Hiberniensibus qui fidem receperunt, clementer a Deo postulauit. Prima petitio[51] eius fuit, ut Scotti[52] affirmant, ut unusquisque plebis credibilis ad Dominum per illum penitentiam peccatorum recipiat, licet in extremo [53]uitae suae[53] statu; secunda autem ut numquam consumeretur a barbaris; tertia[54] uero [55]ut superrogetur[56] aquis septem annis ante aduentum Domini quo[57] uenturus est iudicare uiuos ac[58] mortuos, ut [59]pro oratione[59] sancti Patricii crimina populi abluuntur[60] et animae[61] ante iuditium[62] purgentur.[55]

De illo supercilio montis popul<i>s[63] Hibernię[64] dixit;[65] et ideo ascendit ut oraret pro eis et ut licentia Dei uideret fructus laboris sui. Et uenerunt ad illum aues coloris multi ualde innumerabiles ut benediceret eis; quae[66] significabant omnes sanctos utriusque sexus peruenire ad eum in die iuditii[67] de genere Hibernensium,[68] quasi ad patrem et apostolum suum, ut illum ad iuditium[69] ante tribunal Christi sequantur. Ipse autem sanctus Patricius post magnum laborem postque multas uirtutes et innumerabilia bona migrauit ad Dominum de hoc

40 R; *Alme* W.
41 R; *indiuidue* W.
42 *eauangelium* R.
43 Altered from *egecit* (an Anglo-Latin spelling), R.
44 R; *Sancte* W.
45 *aliis* glossed (interlineally) *scilicet libris*, R; *cum aliis libris*, W.
46...46 R; *Dei seruos* W.
47...47 R; om. W.
48 R; om. W.
49 R; *Eli* W.
50 R; *peticiones* W.
51 R; *peticio* W.
52 R; *Scoti* W.
53...53 R; *uitę sue* W.
54 R; *tercia* W.
55...55 This part also in B.
56 R; *superroretur* altered to *superrigetur* W; *superrigetur* Bb.
57 RW; *qui* Bb.
58 R; *et* BbW.
59...59 RW; *per orationem* Bb.
60 R (where the second *-u-* shows signs of alteration, perhaps to *-a-*); *abluantur* BbW.
61 R; *anime* BbW.
62 R; *iudicium* BbW.
63 My emendation; *populos* RW.
64 R; *Hibernie* W.
65 R; *benedixit* W.
66 R; *que* W.
67 R; *iudicii* W.
68 R; *Hiberniensium* W.
69 R; *iudicium* W.

mundo, uitam in[70] melius conuertens in senectute bona et perfecta, ubi semper cum sanctis et electis Dei gaudet in sęcula sęculorum, amen.[71]

Quattuor modis coęquantur[72] Moyses et Patricius: uno[73] modo angelo illi colloquente in rubo[74] igneo; alio modo in monte quadraginta diebus et quadraginta noctibus ieiunando; tertio[75] modo quod[76] similes fuerunt ętate centum uiginti annorum; quarto modo quod sepulchrum[77] illius[78] nemo scit, sed in occulto humatus est nemine sciente. Sedecim annis in captiuitate fuit; in uicesimo quinto anno a Matheo rege episcopus subrogatur; octoginta quinque annis in Hibernia[79] praedicauit. Profitiebat[80] amplius de Patritio[81] narrare, sed cumpendio[82] laboris breuiter nunc liceat terminare:[83] [84]explicit de sancto Patritio[85] episcopo.[84]

III

Cambridge, Corpus Christi College, MS. 139

This manuscript was written at the Cistercian abbey of Sawley (Yorkshire, West Riding) in 1164x1166.[1] Its copy of the *Historia Brittonum* belonged to a well defined subgroup of that recension of the *Historia Brittonum* which carries an attribution of the work to Gildas. However, soon after it was written, this copy was subjected to a detailed collation with another Cambro-Latin redaction of the *Historia* – that attributed to Ninnius and conventionally called the 'Nennian' recension. An unhappy fate has befallen the 'Nennian' version: the full Latin redaction is lost and the work is known as a continuous text only from a Middle Irish translation, *Lebor Bretnach*, 'the British Book', probably to be attributed to the eleventh century.[2] As a result, the collations in CCCC 139 have unusual authority as the sole direct witness to the Latin text. The interest of that manuscript does not end there. The collation just mentioned inaugurated a period of approximately a half-century in which CCCC 139 was repeatedly and variously

70 `*in*´ R.
71 In W, a concluding rubric: *Explicit uita sancti Patricii episcopi.*
72 R; *coequantur* W.
73 In R, altered from *una.*
74 R; *rubeo* W.
75 R; *tercio* W.
76 *quo`d*´ R.
77 *sepulc`h*´*rum* R.
78 R; *eius* W.
79 R; *Hibernia fuit et* W.
80 R; *Proficiebat* W.
81 R; *Patricio* W.
82 R; *compendio* W.
83 *termina[ ]re* R, with *-ra-* deleted.
84...84 In R only.
85 *Patrit`i*´*o* R.

1 Cf. Dumville, *Histories and Pseudo-histories*, for discussion.
2 For discussion see Dumville, 'The textual history of "Lebor Bretnach" '; for a further discovery (which may apply to the circulation of the Latin or the Irish text of the 'Nennian' recension in Ireland – this is not yet clear) see Ó Riain, 'The Psalter of Cashel'.

annotated. (The whole formed the basis for a new recension of the *Historia.*)[3] Among the additions applied to it is one in a hand of *ca* A.D. 1200 containing a quite remarkable discussion of the comparison of St Patrick with Moses,[4] which had long since become traditional in Patrician hagiography.

I give here a diplomatic transcript of CCCC MS. 139, fos 175(176)rb5–176(177)ra3, with alterations, interlineations, and marginalia presented in an apparatus, save that the discussion of Patrick and Moses is held over for separate printing (in edited form) after the base-text.

Beatus[1] uero germanus reuersus est post mortem guorthigirn[2] ad patriam suam. et sanctus patricius erat in illo tempore captiuuus apud scottos. et dominus illius dicebatur melchu et porcarius[3] cum illo erat. et in .xvii. anno ętatis suę de captiuitate reuersus est. et nutu dei eruditus est in sacris litteris. ac post romam usque perrexit. et per longum spacium ibidem mansit. ad legendum scrutandaque misteria dei. sanctasque percurrit scripturas. Nam cum ibi esset. per annos plurimos. missus est palladius episcopus primitus. á celestino papa. romano. ad scotos in christum conuertendos. qui prohibitus á deo per quasdas tempestates. quia nemo potest quicquam accipere in terra. nisi de celo datum illi fuerit. Et profectus est ille palladius de ibernia. peruenitque ad brittanniam. et ibi defunctus est in terra pictorum. Audita[4] morte palladii episcopi patricius theodosio et ualentino regnantibus á celestino papa romano. et angelo dei cui nomen erat uictor monente et germano sancto episcopo. ad scottos conuertendos in christum mittitur.

MISIT[5] ergo germanus cum illo seniorem segérum[6] ad [7]quendam hominem mirabilem summum episcopis á matheo rege[7] in propinquo habitantem. |

Ibi sanctus[8] sciens omnia quę uentura essent illic[9] gradum episcopalem á matheo rege et á sancto episcopo accepit. nomenque quod est patricius sumpsit.[10] quia maún[11] prius uocabatur. Auxilius[12] yserninus.[13] et ceteri inferiori gradu simul cum eo ordinati sunt.

TVNC[14] acceptis benedictionibus perfectisque omnibus[15] sancte trinitatis.

3 The early thirteenth-century 'Sawley' recension: *The Historia Brittonum*, ed. Dumville, VII.

4 For discussion, see Dumville, 'Celtic-Latin texts', pp. 30–3 (reprinted in *Histories and Pseudo-histories*, chapter XI).

1 Before this word a chapter-number has been added: *.LIII.*

2 *-i* has been added to the end of this word.

3 *-ca-* stands on erasure.

4 Before this word a chapter-number has been added: *.LIIII.*

5 Before this word a chapter-number has been added: *.LV.*

6 After this word *episcopum* has been added interlineally, C^2.

7...7 These eight words have been crossed out. They have been replaced – interlineally – by *amatheum regem*, C^2.

8 After this word *erat* has been added interlineally, C^6.

9 Altered to *illi. et illic*, C^7, by marginal intrusion.

10 *ibi* added interlineally here, C^2.

11 Perhaps altered from *mauun*, C^7.

12 *presbiter et* added interlineally here, C^6.

13 *diaconus* added interlineally here, C^6.

14 Before this word a chapter-number has been added: *.LVI.*

15 *in nomine* added interlineally here, C^2.

paratam ascendit nauim. et peruenit ad brittanniam insulam. et predicauit ibi non multis diebus. et amissis omnibus ambulandi anfractibus summa uelocitate flatuque prospero mare ibernicum[16] honerata uero naui cum transmarinis[17] mirabilibus. et spiritualibus thesauris perrexit ad hiberniam et baptizauit eos.

A[18] mundi principio usque ad baptismum hiberniensium .v^{m}.ccc.xxx. anni sunt in quinto loigere regis anno exorsus est[19] predicare fidem dei. Sanctus itaque patricius euangelium christi exteris nationibus per annos .xl. predicabat. uirtutes apostolicas.[20] cecos illuminabat. [21]surdos audire faciebat. demones ex obsessis corporibus fugábat. mortuos .íx. suscictabat.[22] capituos multos utriusque sexus suis propriis sumptibus redemit.

Scripsit[23] abietoria .ccc.lxv. et eo amplius numero. ęcclesias quoque eodem numero fundauit .ccc.lxv. Ordinauit episcopos eodem numero .ccc.lxv. et eo amplius in quibus spiritus dei erat. presbiteros autem usque tria .m.[24] ordinauit et .xii^{m}. hominum in una regione[25] connachta ad fidem[26] christi [27]conuertit. et baptizauit. et .vii. reges qui erant filii amolgith in uno |

die baptizauit .xl. diebus, totidemque noctibus in cacumine collis eli [28]ieiunauit. id est cruachaneli. In quo colle in aere tres peticiones pro his hibernensibus qui fidem christi receperint[29] clementer postulauit.

PRIMA[30] eius petitio fuit ut fertur[31] quod unusquisque susciperet penitentiam credentium licet in extremo uitę suę statu. Secunda ne á barbaris consummerentur[32] in ęternum. Tercia ut non superuiuat aliquis hiberniensium in aduentu iudicii. quia delebitur[33] pro honore[34] patricii .vii. annis ante diem iudicii. In illo autem tumulo[35] benedixit populo hiberniensium. et ideo ascendit ut oraret pro eis. et uideret fructum laboris sui. ueneruntque ad eum aues multicoloris[36] innumerabiles ut benediceret eis. quod significat omnes sanctos utriusque sexus hiberniensium peruenire ad eum in die iudicii.[37] patrem[38] magistrum suum ut sequantur illum ad iudicium. Postea in senectute bona migrauit ad dominum ubi nunc letatur in secula seculorum AMEN.

16 *transfretauit* added interlineally here in an uncertainly identified hand (but not C^1, C^2, or C^3).
17 *-marinis* has been crossed out and replaced (interlineally) by *-fretaret hoc mare magnum*, C^2.
18 Before this word a chapter-number has been added: *.LVII.*
19 *patricius* added interlineally here, C^2.
20 *faciebat* added interlineally here, C^2.
21 *leprosos mundabat* added interlineally here, C^2.
22 *-bat* underlined for deletion and replaced by *-uit*, apparently by the original scribe.
23 Before this word a chapter-number has been added: *.LVIII.*
24 In hand C^1 over an erasure.
25 *que uocatur* added interlineally here, C^2.
26 As it stands this word is an addition in hand C^2, although *fi-* may be by the original scribe.
27 *in una uici* added interlineally here, C^8.
28 A now erased interlinear gloss was once marked for insertion at this point.
29 Altered to *receperunt*, C^2.
30 Before this word a chapter-number has been added: *LIX.*
31 *á scottis* added here, C^2, as a marginale.
32 A gloss has been interlined here: *uel dominarentur*, C^8.
33 *aqua* added interlineally here, C^1.
34 *sancti* added interlineally here, C^1.
35 Altered to *cumulo* (hand unidentified).
36 The first *-i-* appears to be an addition.
37 *ad* inserted interlineally here, C^2.
38 *et ad* inserted interlineally here, C^2.

QVATVOR[39] modis equantur moyses. et patricius.[40] colloquente in rubo igneo. Secundo[41] in monte .xl. diebus[42] noctibus ieiunauit. Tercio similes fuerunt etate .cxx. annis. Quarto sepulcrum illius non inuenitur. sed in occulto humatus est. nemine sciente. Quindecim annis in captiuitate. in uigesimo .v. anno. ab amatheo sancto |

episcopo subrogatur. Octoginta .v. annorum in hibernia predicauit.[43] Res autem exigebat [44]amplius loqui de sancto[44] patricio sed tamen pro compendio sermonis uolui breuiare.

<MARGINALE ON FO 176(177)r, LOWER MARGIN>

Hic, ut mihi uidetur, †contradicet†[1] sibimet ipsi. Sed aliter audiuimus et scripta reperimus, ita: quadragenarius erat quando de captiuitate exiuit; et per .xl. annos didicit et Deo seruiuit; et .xl. predicauit. In his tribus quadragenariis uero maxime Patricius equatur Moysi. Nam sicut Moyses in .xl. annis in domo Pharahonis uelut in captiuitate et .xl. in exilio in terra Madian et .xl. in predicatione et in ducatu populi, [ita][2] Patricius .xl. in exilio inter Gallos et .xl. predicando et miracula faciendo atque resistendo Loygere [regi][2] et magis eius – sicut Moyses Pharaoni et eius magis – uiriliter et indefesse Deo seruiuit.

Nam bene potest fieri illum fuisse in captiuitate per .xv. annos et quadragenarius egressus fuisse. Sed hoc attende: Moyses quadragenarius fuit quando de Egypto exiuit †et in fugam†[3] ad Egyptum propter populos Dei missus rediit post quadraginta annos; et ipse Patri[ci]us[2] quadragenarius erat quando de †Roma†[4] in fugam exiuit, et post .xl. annos – missus ad populum Dei ex<c>ipiendum de manu diaboli – ad Hiberniam rediit. Et uterque per .xl. annos in studio predicationis manserunt, et simili fine et ieiunio non dissimili.

39 Before this word a chapter-number has been added: *.LX.*

40 After *patricius.* the text now continues in hand C^7 over an erasure: *Primo .i. angelo sibi.* I have not been able to read the original text here, which has been thoroughly eradicated.

41 *-o* appears to stand on an erasure.

42 *et* added interlineally here, C^7; *.xl.* then follows (also in hand C^7) on an erasure of original text.

43 The lengthy marginal gloss *Hic ut mihi uidetur* . . . (printed separately below), in hand C^5, is marked for insertion at this point.

44...44 Above these words stands an erased interlineation which I have been unable to recover.

1 Leg. *contradicit*?

2 Letters in square brackets are insertions in hand C^7.

3 Leg. *in fugam, et.*

4 Leg. *Hibernia.*

ST PATRICK AND GLASTONBURY ABBEY: *NIHIL EX NIHILO FIT*?

Lesley Abrams

Patrick appears to be one of those saints who died repeatedly, in different places, and at different times. The ecclesiastical community at Glastonbury in Somerset favoured a middling date for his death (A.D. 472) and a local venue. The subject of this paper is the monks' claim that the apostle of Ireland was buried at Glastonbury Abbey after serving as its abbot.

The in-house evidence for an association between St Patrick and the community at Glastonbury is provided by two sorts of source: charters and chronicles. The charter-evidence is slim and of doubtful integrity. In naming Glastonbury as the recipient of royal grants, three charters add St Patrick to the dedication of Glastonbury's church (otherwise cited as dedicated simply to Mary),[1] apparently indicating that at times during the period before the Norman conquest the minster-church had a double dedication. The surviving record of all three charters, however, is not original: it stands at at least one remove from the first version of the text, so that none of the three references to St Patrick is necessarily contemporary with the grant which the charter professes to record. The first, dated 681, is a charter in the name of King Baldred; it survives in a single-sheet copy probably of tenth-century date.[2] The next, a privilege in the name of King Ine (A.D. 688–726) and dated 704, exists only in texts of even later date; it first appears in the history of the abbey begun by William of Malmesbury, *De antiquitate Glastonie ecclesie*, and is thus datable – at the earliest – to 1129x1135 (or the mid-thirteenth century, the date of the earliest manuscript).[3] The last is a grant for which no text survives but about whose contents there is nevertheless some information: in the *De antiquitate*, in an apparent quotation from the charter, a certain Ealdred is said to have given land

1 Sawyer, *Anglo-Saxon Charters*, nos 236, 246, and – less straightforwardly – 1766.

2 *Ibid.*, no. 236. Edwards, *The Charters*, pp. 11–15. The script of the single sheet can be interpreted as an imitative Insular Hybrid minuscule or a protoform of Square minuscule; in neither case is it likely to antedate the tenth century. I am grateful to David Dumville for his expert advice on the script.

3 Sawyer, *Anglo-Saxon Charters*, no. 246. Later authors made interpolations to William's text of the *De antiquitate*. See Crick, 'The marshalling of antiquity', for a full description of the thirteenth-century manuscript – Cambridge, Trinity College, MS. R.5.33 (724) – in which the *De antiquitate* is found. The text has been edited and translated by John Scott: *The Early History*.

to the church of Mary and St Patrick during the reign of King Edgar (959–975).[4] This lost document may, therefore, also owe its reference to Patrick to a revision at the time when the *De antiquitate* was first composed or subsequently copied.

Of the three charter-references to dedications to Patrick, therefore, none was necessarily part of the original charter-text. It may seem mean-spirited to doubt that these purportedly seventh-, eighth-, and tenth-century charters with references to Patrick qualify as acceptable evidence of seventh-, eighth-, and tenth-century dedications, but the otherwise overwhelming evidence of a single dedication to Mary is hard to ignore. It may be that Patrick was inserted in retrospect when the charters were recast, as a kind of extra seasoning which added a dash of ancient authority. If so, it appears that the Irish saint was so used by the tenth century, if his appearance in the diploma of King Baldred was intended to represent a dedication of earlier times; if it was added to the charter in order to represent a contemporary tenth-century, rather than a late seventh-century, situation, however, the single sheet could be interpreted as evidence of a cult of Patrick at Glastonbury in the tenth century. Whichever interpretation is favoured, the tenth century seems to be the first firm context for the appearance of Patrick in Glastonbury's documentary record, whether as the object of contemporary cult or as adopted ancestor or as both.

Glastonbury's narrative sources offer much more about Patrick. The *De antiquitate* (followed closely by the later, expanded, chronicle of the abbey by John of Glastonbury, *Cronica siue antiquitates Glastoniensis ecclesie*),[5] opens with an attempt to consolidate the house-traditions concerning the various eminent founders of the abbey: Jesus himself, the disciples of St Philip (including Joseph of Arimathea), SS. Phagan and Deruvian, Glasteing and his eight-footed pig,[6] and St Patrick. Patrick, it is claimed, returned in his old age from Ireland to his native land, went to Glastonbury, found twelve brothers living there as hermits, organised them into a community, became their abbot, climbed Glastonbury Tor, and wrote the effusive document known as the *carta sancti Patricii episcopi*.[7] This work of fiction exhibits no signs of pre-Conquest or even twelfth-century composition and may in fact belong to the thirteenth century.[8] However, a chapter of biographical detail, including reference to Patrick's having spent thirty-nine years at Glastonbury and to his death and burial there in A.D. 472 (at the age of 111), was apparently part of the original *De antiquitate*.[9] So too was an interesting miracle-story: a certain brother who had expressed doubt about whether the apostle of Ireland had indeed been monk

4 Sawyer, *Anglo-Saxon Charters*, no. 1766; *De antiquitate*, §62 (ed. & transl. Scott, p. 130).

5 *The Chronicle* , edd. & transl. Carley & Townsend.

6 On Glasteing and his pig, see Thornton, 'Glastonbury and the Glastening'.

7 *De antiquitate*, §§8–9 (ed. & transl. Scott, pp. 54–8).

8 It is referred to among the *antiqua priuilegia* listed elsewhere in the manuscript (written in 1247 and corrected in the following year) which contains the *De antiquitate*. It is not found in the sections relating to Glastonbury in William of Malmesbury's *Gesta regum Anglorum*, although the succeeding chapter of the *De antiquitate*, on St Patrick's death, does occur in one of the later recensions of that work (1135x1140). See below, n. 9.

9 It was quoted by William of Malmesbury in the second edition (A.D. 1135) of his *Gesta regum Anglorum*, I.22 (ed. Stubbs, I.26–7). For Stubbs's discussion of the relationship between the *De antiquitate* and the recensions of *Gesta regum Anglorum*, see *Willelmi Malmesbiriensis monachi De gestis regum*, ed. Stubbs, I.xxxi, xxliii, lviii–lxii, and 23 (n. 8).

and abbot at Glastonbury (it seems that the question frequently arose and often troubled the brother, whose memory was not what it had once been) had a vision in which he was reassured that Patrick was indeed a monk and abbot after he had received the metropolitan's pallium. We are clearly in the realms of fantasy here, and the vision's omission of the name of Patrick's monastery should not worry us any more than its inclusion of an anachronistic pallium. The story is interesting, however, as an indication that Patrick's connexion with Glastonbury may have been considered debatable, even at that house itself, in the twelfth century.[10]

The in-house evidence offered by the charters and narrative sources reveals St Patrick's prominent place in Glastonbury's early house-traditions. This raises the larger question of the date and nature of Glastonbury's Irish connexion.[11] Very different views on this subject continue to be held. Glastonbury's geographical location and the immensely successful mediaeval advertising campaigns featuring its Celtic roots have made it a favoured candidate for 'Celtic continuity' – that is, the idea that a pre-English religious community crossed the divide of the *aduentus Saxonum* and survived to tell the tale, or, rather, the tales (of 'Celtic' saints).[12] If this is indeed what happened, it did so without leaving any reasonable evidence; the existence of a British church at Glastonbury has not been proved. In A.D. 995x1004, however, credible testimony of Irish links and of an active cult of St Patrick was offered by B, St Dunstan's earliest biographer, who stated in his Life of that saint (who was educated at Glastonbury and subsequently became abbot there) that during Dunstan's youth Irish *peregrini* flocked to Glastonbury, drawn especially by the cult of Patrick. B appears to have based his Life on personal knowledge, at least of this early stage of Dunstan's career.[13] This evidence would take the Irish associations of Glastonbury back to *ca* 910 x *ca* 940. B had only remarked on the presence of Irish *peregrini*, with the additional detail that they had books with them, which Dunstan studied.[14] Dunstan's later *uitae* by Osbern of Canterbury and William of Malmesbury describe a school at Glastonbury where the sons of the local nobility were taught by learned Irishmen; but, like B, Osbern and William did not discuss the first appearance of these Irish or the origins of the school.[15]

10 Might William of Malmesbury's inclusion of the tale in the *De antiquitate* and repetition of it in his *Gesta regum Anglorum* suggest that he had his own doubts about the connexion?

11 See H.P.R. Finberg's refreshingly sceptical treatment in his *West-Country Historical Studies*, pp. 70–88, and also Hughes, 'Evidence for contacts', pp. 57–8. Michael Lapidge has extended the discussion in 'The cult of St Indract'. See also the earlier studies by Slover, 'William of Malmesbury and the Irish', and 'Glastonbury Abbey and the fusing'.

12 Those who have declared Glastonbury to have been a 'Celtic' establishment taken over by the Anglo-Saxons in the seventh century are too numerous to mention here, but one member of this group who has been particularly influential is C. A. R. Radford; he has asserted that the Irish cults must have predated the English arrival ('Glastonbury Abbey', p. 104).

13 For the text of B's *Vita S. Dunstani*, see *Memorials of Saint Dunstan*, ed. Stubbs, pp. 3–52. For a brief discussion, see Lapidge, 'The cult of St Indract', p. 182 (and notes).

14 B, *Vita S. Dunstani*, §5 (*Memorials of Saint Dunstan*, ed. Stubbs, pp. 10–11).

15 Osbern, *Vita S. Dunstani*, §6 (*ibid.*, pp. 74–5); William of Malmesbury, *Vita S. Dunstani*, §4 (*ibid.*, pp. 256–7). William wrote that the Irish were brought to Glastonbury by their love of St Patrick who was buried there. Dunstan acquired sacred and secular learning from them, including instruction in poetry, mathematics, geometry, astronomy, and music.

H. P. R. Finberg argued that it had been established during the reign of Alfred, king of Wessex A.D. 871–899, in the context of that king's well known efforts to improve the state of education in his kingdom.[16]

The Irish scholars of Dunstan's day were not the first of their countrymen who were said to have been in the neighbourhood of Glastonbury after the English conquest of the region in the later sixth or the seventh century.[17] The development at the abbey of a cult of St Indract, an Irish abbot travelling home from Rome who may have been martyred near Glastonbury with his companions in A.D. 854, may suggest that the abbey acted as a stopping-off point for Irish ecclesiastics *en route* to and from the Continent in the ninth century.[18] Other suggestions of contact between Glastonbury and Ireland from the seventh century to the ninth have been cited,[19] but these are misconceived or inconclusive and take us away from the central question concerning St Patrick.

While the stories in the *De antiquitate* cannot be admitted as historical evidence of a Patrician foundation, other sources – originating both within the abbey and abroad – can provide some confirmation of a perceived connexion with the apostle of Ireland in the tenth century. An addition to the statement in *Vita III S. Patricii* that Patrick died *in regionibus Uloth iuxta Dun Lethglaisse* ('in the territory of the Ulaid near Downpatrick') reads 'quod nos dicimus in nostra lingua Glastingaberi'.[20]

16 Finberg, *West-Country Historical Studies*, pp. 76–8. We do know that Irishmen visited Alfred's court: Finberg supported his argument with a reference to the entry for A.D. 891 in the Anglo-Saxon Chronicle, which relates that 'three *Scottas* came to King Alfred in a boat without any oars from Ireland. . . . Their names were as follows: Dubslane, Maccbethu, and Maelinmun.' Cf. Dumville, '*Echtrae* and *immram*'.

17 The progress and chronology of the conquest of this part of Wessex are obscure.

18 See Lapidge, 'The cult of St Indract'.

19 A missionary called Wihtberht, on his arrival as a new recruit in Germany (A.D. 732x754), wrote a letter to the abbot and monks of Glastonbury, whom he evidently knew well (*Die Briefe*, ed. Tangl, pp. 224–5, no. 101; *English Historical Documents*, transl. Whitelock, pp. 760–1, no. 182); he has sometimes been identified with the missionary of the same name mentioned by Bede who had spent many years in Ireland and was renowned for his learning (Bede, *Historia ecclesiastica gentis Anglorum*, V.9; edd. & transl. Colgrave & Mynors, pp. 478–80). On a Wihtberht in Ireland, see Ó Cróinín, 'Rath Melsigi', pp. 24–6. But Bede's Wihtberht stayed in Frisia for only two years, during the reign of King Radbod (*ob*. 719); so the Irish-trained priest cannot have been the man – seemingly a West Saxon – who sent his greetings from the Continent to Glastonbury and another house in the same area after 732. For the seventh century, J. A. Robinson argued (*Somerset*, pp. 51–2) that the wording of a charter in the name of Cenwealh, king of Wessex A.D. 642–672 (Sawyer, *Anglo-Saxon Charters*, no. 227), suggested the presence at Glastonbury of a pre-Vulgate Old Latin version of the Pauline Epistles with a 'Celtic' or a 'mixed' text. For the ninth century, Finberg (*West-Country Historical Studies*, pp. 77–8) postulated the existence of Irish abbots at Glastonbury, but Lapidge has convincingly disposed of them ('The cult of St Indract', p. 181); on these see also Foot, 'Glastonbury's early abbots', pp. 174–5. For another approach, see Carley & Dooley, 'An early Irish fragment'.

20 *Vita tertia*, §88 (*Four Latin Lives*, ed. Bieler, p. 183). MSS. C (which reads *glestingabyri*) and D of recension Π alone share this addition. There must be some connexion between this text and the small Hiberno-Latin Life of St Patrick which Bieler identified as circulating in Herefordshire in the early thirteenth century, which ends abruptly with Patrick's body lying at *Dun Lethgles* ('Eine Patricksvita in Gloucester', ed. Bieler, pp. 346 and 359). Someone presumably saw this *uita* and, knowing of Glastonbury's house-tradition concerning Patrick's

St Indract's cult produced an early twelfth-century *passio* (with a putative Old English source of the second half of the tenth, now lost); it claims that Patrick was buried in a stone shrine to the south of the high altar.[21] The Old English list of saints' resting places, surviving in eleventh-century manuscripts but containing two groups of names, arguably of ninth- and tenth-century origin respectively, records Patrick at Glastonbury in the second, later, group, which concentrates on sites in Wessex or with a Wessex connexion.[22] A lost tenth- century kalendar of Glastonbury use may be represented by two late tenth-century English kalendars: they list Patrick *senior* under 24 August.[23] The kalendar of the 'Leofric Missal', datable 979x987, reads 'Sancti Patricii senioris', while that of the 'Bosworth Psalter', datable 988x1006, has 'Sancti Patricii senioris in Glæstonia'.[24]

It is under 24 August that a Patrick with Glastonbury connexions is found in Irish sources: manuscripts of the 'Martyrology of Oengus' (*ca* 800) and the twelfth-century 'Martyrology of Gorman' in surrounding commentary both record Patrick *senior* as buried at Glastonbury and amplify this with the information that it was a place sought out by *Scotti*.[25] The problem with the evidence of these martyrologies, however, is that it cannot be definitely dated: Glastonbury appears not in the original texts but in the glosses and commentaries added to

---

burial place, identified *Dún Lethglaisse* with the English abbey. William of Malmesbury also knew of a story whereby Patrick was buried at *Dún Lethglaisse* (as we can see from John Leland's excerpts from his lost Life of Patrick: see below, pp. 265–71).

21 Lapidge, 'The cult of St Indract', pp. 179 and 202. He has argued (pp. 184–6) that the lost Old English Life was not likely to have been written before the reforming abbacy of Dunstan. The reference to Patrick's shrine, if it was to be found in this lost source, could therefore have been made in the mid-tenth century. It could equally, however, have been added in the twelfth-century Latin version. B did not mention a shrine of St Patrick, nor did Osbern in his Life of St Dunstan; however, early twelfth-century references to the shrine occur in William of Malmesbury's *Gesta regum Anglorum* (I.22: ed. Stubbs, I.27) and *Vita S. Dunstani* (§4: *Memorials of Saint Dunstan*, ed. Stubbs, pp. 256–7); one is also found in the *De antiquitate* (§10: ed. & transl. Scott, p. 60). Lapidge has also drawn attention to a litany probably copied at an English nunnery in the second quarter of the eleventh century which has St Indract followed by St Patrick: Lapidge, 'The cult of St Indract', pp. 184–6; *Anglo-Saxon Litanies*, ed. Lapidge, p. 167 (cf. pp. 69–70).

22 *Die Heiligen Englands*, ed. Liebermann, pp. 9–23, especially p. 17; see also Rollason, 'Lists', especially pp. 62–8 and 92. The Old English text reached its present form by A.D. 1031, when it was entered in London, British Library, MS. Stowe 944 (*ibid.*, p. 68).

23 See the discussion by Dumville, *Liturgy*, chapter II. For newly discovered martyrological evidence, see below, pp. 243–4.

24 Oxford, Bodleian Library, MS. Bodley 579 (*S.C.* 2675): *The Leofric Missal*, ed. Warren, especially pp. lii–liv, 25, and 30. On the origin and provenance of this kalendar, see the analyses by Dumville, *Liturgy*, chapters II and III. Patrick *episcopus* appears under 17 March (ed. Warren, p. 25; *English Kalendars before A.D. 1100*, ed. Wormald, p. 51). For the entry in the 'Bosworth Psalter' (London, British Library, MS. Additional 37517), see *ibid.*, p. 65. August 24 is the feast-day of St Patrice of Nevers, whose feast became associated with the Irish Patrick due to the identity of their names; see Grosjean, 'S. Patrice d'Irlande', p. 156. For the significance of the epithet *senior*, see above, pp. 59–64.

25 *Félire Óengusso Céli Dé*, ed. & transl. Stokes, pp. 178 and 188; *Félire Húi Gormáin*, ed. & transl. Stokes, p. 162. A 'kalendar of Cashel' appears to have shared the same information (*Trias Thaumaturga*, ed. Colgan, p. 10). According to excerpts from this lost text, Glastonbury was described as a city in southern England where Irishmen lived and where there was a shrine with the relics of St Patrick *senior* of Armagh [*sic*].

them between the time of their composition and the writing of the surviving manuscripts. Thus the date of the associated material in the 'Martyrology of Oengus', for example, can be identified no more specifically than *ca* 800 (the date of the text) × *ca* 1350 (the earliest possible date for the earliest manuscript).[26]

The same difficulty applies with other Irish sources. Patrick and Glastonbury are also linked in a comment on 'Fiacc's Hymn'.[27] D. A. Binchy argued on linguistic grounds that this poem was composed in the mid-eighth century. Its earliest witness is apparently in the Irish *Liber Hymnorum*, the manuscripts being of the eleventh century.[28] The date of the additional matter is difficult to pin down; the reference to 'Glastonbury of the Irish' as the elder Patrick's burial place clearly transmits the same information as that in the martyrologies of Oengus and 'Gorman'.

Irish chronicles constitute a further type of evidence. *Chronicum Scotorum* and the Annals of Roscrea both identify Glastonbury as the burial place of Patrick *senis* (if indeed 'Glosdoniensis ecclesia' and 'Golstoniensis ecclesia' can be identified with the English house).[29] These are both witnesses to the lost 'Chronicle of Clonmacnoise' (datable 911x954):[30] if the equation goes back to that text, it is a piece of evidence even earlier than that of B's Life of St Dunstan (which nevertheless referred back to the first half of the tenth century).

These references all pertain to Patrick *senior* or *senex*, or *Sen-Phátric* as he is in Irish vernacular sources.[31] They therefore date from a period after the saint had been divided in two. Unfortunately, opinions vary as to the date of this division: a comment in the 'Book of Armagh', where Palladius is said to have also been called Patrick,[32] seems to be the first extant example of two Patricks.

26 *Félire Óengusso Céli Dé*, ed. & transl. Stokes, pp. vii–xxiv. The absence of the information from the main text of the 'Martyrology of Gorman', however, would suggest that the material had not yet accrued to Oengus's text when 'Gorman' was written (since 'Gorman' depended on the 'Martyrology of Oengus' or its source).

27 'In tan conhualai Pátraic, adella in Pátraic n-aile / is malle connucabsat dochum n-Ísu meicc Maire' ('When Patrick departed, he visited the other Patrick: together they ascended to Jesus, Mary's son'): 'Fiacc's Hymn', lines 65–6 (*The Irish Liber Hymnorum*, edd. Bernard & Atkinson, I.103 and II.35). (Cf. p. 60, n. 7, above.) To this is added the comment (in the eleventh-century manuscript, Killiney, Franciscan House of Studies, MS. A.2) that Sen-Phátric is in 'Glastimber na nGoedel' ('Glastonbury of the Irish'), a monastery in the south of England (*ibid.*, I.103).

28 Grosjean suggested the beginning of the eighth century as the date of composition of the poem, with early ninth-century interpolations ('S. Patrice d'Irlande', p. 156); Binchy placed it in the mid-eighth century and criticised O'Rahilly's date of *ca* 800 as too late ('Patrick and his biographers', pp. 124–5).

29 'Kl. .iiii. dormitatio sancti Patricii episcopi in Glosdoniensis ecclesiae': *Chronicum Scotorum*, ed. & transl. Hennessy, p. 24. 'Dormitatio sancti Patricii episcopi Golstomensis <*leg.* Golstoniensis?> ecclesiae': 'The Annals of Roscrea', edd. Gleeson & Mac Airt, p. 151 (§98).

30 Grabowski & Dumville, *Chronicles and Annals*, especially chapters II and IV.

31 See the discussion above, pp. 59–64.

32 'Paladius episcopus primo mittitur, qui Patricius alio nomine appellabatur, qui martyrium passus est apud Scottos, ut tradunt sancti antiqui': Tírechán, *Collectanea*, §56 (*The Patrician Texts*, edd. & transl. Bieler & Kelly, pp. 164–7).

Paul Grosjean dated this paragraph to the second half of the eighth century, D. A. Binchy to the mid-eighth;[33] T. F. O'Rahilly considered it to be part of the original late seventh-century work.[34] 'Fiacc's Hymn' also features two Patricks, the older waiting for his younger namesake before proceeding to heaven; opinions on the date of this text also vary, as we have seen.[35]

The question of whether the Patrician material should be applied to a single missionary or to two (or even three) men who have been conflated into a composite Patrick, is, fortunately, not one which greatly affects the issue of Glastonbury's involvement. According to Binchy, the association of the second Patrick with the saint of Nevers (commemorated on 24 August) followed closely on the first appearance of more than one Patrick.[36]

The Irish liturgical evidence for two Patricks should be noted here: a litany in the original hand in the 'Stowe Missal' has two consecutive *Patricii*.[37] Two Patricks appear in the martyrologies of Oengus and 'Gorman', as we have seen; the 'Martyrology of Tallaght' can be added to this testimony.[38] The existence of two Patricks therefore seems to be firmly established by the beginning of the ninth century.[39] Another source, the Law of Adomnán, included *in dá Pátraic*, 'the two Patricks', in a list of sureties.[40]

In all cases but one, it is the older of the two Patricks who is associated with Glastonbury. What has been taken to be the earliest version of B's Life of Dunstan mentions, however, not Patrick *senior* (as in the other two manuscripts which attest slightly variant texts), but Patrick *iunior*.[41] C. H. Slover interpreted this as an early incident in the war of attributions, 'a denial of a previous [Irish] statement that it was some other Patrick that was buried there'.[42] Patrick *senior*, argued Slover, might have owed his existence to the contradictory stories regarding the burial place of the apostle of Ireland: Irish ecclesiastics might have invented another Patrick in order to account for Glastonbury's claims and to keep the important one to themselves. If this were the case, the earliest instance of two Patricks anywhere would by itself take the Glastonbury claim back well before the time of B and the charter of Baldred – the first surviving, datable, sources explicitly to associate Patrick (any Patrick) with the house. But Slover's

33 Grosjean, 'S. Patrice d'Irlande', p. 170; Binchy, 'Patrick and his biographers', especially pp. 129–31.
34 O'Rahilly, *The Two Patricks*, pp. 10–11.
35 See above, n. 28.
36 Binchy, 'Patrick and his biographers', pp. 125–7.
37 Dublin, Royal Irish Academy, MS. Stowe D.ii.3, fo 32v; *The Stowe Missal*, ed. Warner, II.15.
38 *The Martyrology of Tallaght*, edd. Best & Lawlor, pp. 65–6. It omits the reference to Glastonbury from its commentary but cites two Patricks in its main text.
39 On the date of the 'Martyrology of Tallaght' and 'Martyrology of Oengus', see Ó Riain, 'The Tallaght martyrologies, redated'; Ó Riain has proposed a revised date of A.D. 828x833 (replacing 797x808). His date for the Stowe Missal (*ibid.*, p. 38: *ca* 830) is also slightly later than Warner's (*The Stowe Missal*, ed. Warner, II.xxxii–xxxvii).
40 *Cáin Adamnáin*, §22 (ed. & transl. Meyer, p. 12). Meyer dated it to 'probably . . . the ninth century' (*ibid.*, p. viii), Ryan to *ca* 900 ('The Cáin Adomnáin', p. 269).
41 *Vita S. Dunstani*, §5 (*Memorials of Saint Dunstan*, ed. Stubbs, p. 10).
42 Slover, 'William of Malmesbury and the Irish', pp. 272–3.

argument rests on the idea that Glastonbury's claims predated the creation of this second Patrick, rather than that the abbey appropriated this character for its own purposes.

This brings us back to where we started; apart from the uncertain significance for Glastonbury of the apparent early doubling of Patricks, the actual datable material for a Patrick at Glastonbury does seem to cluster in the tenth century, and its heritage is uncertain. Finberg, who had his suspicions about the abbey's Patrician claims, considered that they might have originated with Irish *peregrini* there during Dunstan's youth. He suggested that the fictions about St Patrick (and Glastonbury's other Irish saints – Indract, Benignus, and Brigit) were 'little more than extracts from the school prospectus'.[43] The apparent concentration of dates in the tenth century seems to support this; it may appear to be a less conclusive argument for the tenth-century origins of the abbey's cult of Patrick, however, if we consider the minimal survival of sources of any sort for the preceding centuries. So much has been lost that the absence of earlier corroboration for the origins and development of this (or any) cult must not be used to draw conclusions from silence. We can say only that the earliest credible evidence locates a cult of Patrick at Glastonbury in the early tenth century.[44]

The *Patricius senior* commemorated on 24 August in the kalendar of the 'Leofric Missal' had a graded feast (of the second rank), as opposed to the Patrick whose feast on 17 March was ungraded. Perhaps it was this distinction which lay behind C. E. Hohler's remark that *Patricius senior* was 'the man who,

43 Finberg, *West-Country Historical Studies*, p. 86.

44 Even so, in B's Life and the Latin Life of St Indract Glastonbury's church is dedicated simply to Mary: B, *Vita S. Dunstani*, §5 (*Memorials of Saint Dunstan*, ed. Stubbs, p. 10); Lapidge, 'The cult of St Indract', pp. 202–3. Patrick is not associated with any particular estate belonging to Glastonbury, except in the very late context of his so-called charter, which sets his display of asceticism on Glastonbury Tor. SS. Benignus and Brigit have more specific associations with places. The former is said (in the *De antiquitate*) to have come to Glastonbury in A.D. 460 on a visit to St Patrick and to have established himself at Meare; Benignus is reputed to have created the natural resources of the place and, 'after endless struggles', died and been buried there (*De antiquitate*, §13; ed. & transl. Scott, p. 62). (This means that two fifth-century 'archbishops of Armagh' are supposed to have abandoned their post in favour of monastic life in Somerset! – cf. Dumville, 'A seventeenth-century Hiberno-Breton hagiological exchange', p. 251.) St Brigit is said to have been living on the island of Beckery in A.D. 488, and, although she departed to return to Ireland, she left behind some personal memorabilia, including a bell and the place-name, Beckery, interpreted as meaning *Becc-Ériu*, 'Little Ireland' (*De antiquitate*, §§12 and 60; ed. & transl. Scott, pp. 60 and 124). (See also William of Malmesbury's *Gesta regum Anglorum*, where the possibility of Brigit having died at Glastonbury is raised: *Gesta regum Anglorum*, I.23; ed. Stubbs, I.27.) The Irish pedigree which these stories give to Glastonbury's relationship with Meare and Beckery may be spurious, but it is nonetheless the case that both these estates formed part of the very early endowment of the abbey. I do not mean to suggest that they were indeed linked to a 'Celtic' Glastonbury in the fifth century; but whoever did link these places with Irish visitors to Glastonbury knew enough to identify the saints with early (that is, possibly late seventh-century) possessions. Charters for these places were to hand in the archive for any approved story-writer to consult. No charter for Beckery now survives, but the author of the *De antiquitate* appears to have seen one (§§ 36 and 69; ed. & transl. Scott, pp. 90 and 140); texts of charters for Meare (Sawyer, *Anglo-Saxon Charters*, nos 227 and 1249) are in the abbey's cartularies.

I feel sure, was the actual founder of Glastonbury'.[45] Hohler's certainty is breathtaking, but unfortunately he did not share the genesis of his conviction with his readers.[46] An intriguing bit of arithmetic can perhaps further identify this Patrick *senior*. According to Glastonbury's house-tradition, as it had developed no later than the mid-thirteenth century, Patrick died in A.D. 472, after thirty-nine years as abbot; this would suppose that he had given up his apostolate in A.D. 433, a date suspiciously close to the one advanced in Irish sources for the end of Palladius's career.[47] Is Glastonbury's Patrick-tradition therefore perhaps one which, in as much as Patrick *senior* was equated with Palladius, referred to the bishop sent from Rome? Rumour had it that Palladius had died in Britain, and Irish ecclesiastics might have been delighted to be able to identify the precise locality.[48] The imponderable in all this is the role played by Glastonbury Abbey itself (in the early tenth century or earlier) in perhaps encouraging Irishmen to identify Glastonbury as Palladius-Patrick's burial place.[49]

This Palladian connexion should perhaps have been grist to T. F. O'Rahilly's mill in his study of the two Patricks. Instead, he attempted to associate Glastonbury with the younger Patrick, the apostle of Ireland. He identified the part of Britain where this Patrick had been raised as 'the eastern end of the Bristol Channel', this being the one area of Roman Britain which could support two of the very few known details of Patrick's life in England, the status of his father (which implied a nearby Roman town) and Patrick's capture by Irish raiders (implying a nearby stretch of the Irish Sea). It was, he thought, 'a very remarkable coincidence' that Glastonbury, with its claim of a special connexion with Patrick, lay in this area. Perhaps even more remarkable is what O'Rahilly proceeded to do with this claim: since more glory would accrue to the abbey if the great man was thought to have been buried there (as opposed to merely having been born in the region), O'Rahilly suggested that, although the Glastonbury area was Patrick's birthplace, the monks claimed a burial instead. O'Rahilly's evidence for this argument rested on his conversion of the name of the *uicus* mentioned by Patrick in the *Confessio*, *Bannauem taburniae*,[50] to *Bannauenta Burniae*, which he conjectured was a corruption of *Bannauenta Bruuiae*, Glastonbury's (unknown) Roman name (*Bannauenta* on the River Brue, the Brue being the river now running to the south of the town; that its

45 Hohler, 'Some service-books', p. 69.

46 He made the interesting observation, however, that the attachment of 24 August to the commemoration of the man buried to the right of the altar (according to the twelfth-century description) indicated that the monks did not know the proper anniversary of their founder, a situation which could not have pertained if the community had had an unbroken existence (*ibid.*, p. 222, n. 32).

47 Cf. Bieler, 'The mission of Palladius'.

48 For the legends of Palladius's death in Britain, see above, pp. 39–43, 65–84.

49 We may wonder how the subsequent story of Abingdon's spurious Irish founder, the eponymous Abbenus (St Abbán), relates to these developments at Glastonbury. Cf. Stenton, *The Early History*; Sharpe, *Medieval Irish Saints' Lives*, pp. 349–53; Heist, 'Over the writer's shoulder', p. 83.

50 *Confessio*, §1. *Bannauem* from MS. D and *taburniae* from MS. P are both unique readings. Otherwise the manuscripts read *banauem* (MSS. CFGPRV), *taberniae* (MSS. CDGRV), and *tabinę* (MS. F). See *Saint Patrick*, edd. & transl. Hanson & Blanc, p. 70.

name was Celtic apparently supported this argument.)[51] O'Rahilly was, by his own confession, led to this conclusion on the principle *nihil ex nihilo fit*.[52]

If the case of St Patrick is to be considered an apt illustration of this principle, it is clearly complicated by an embarrassment of Patricks, since there are at least two to choose from as candidates for Hohler's 'actual founder' of the abbey. Can the historical Palladius or the British apostle of Ireland really be associated with Glastonbury? What is the weight of the evidence? Is there really no smoke without fire, or is this an example of what Binchy described as 'that apparently insatiable urge to fill a vacuum'?[53] James Carney and R.P.C. Hanson considered it possible that Patrick might have had a monastic training in sub-Roman Britain, might have undertaken the evangelisation of Ireland from his monastery, and might have returned to his house in old age.[54] This monastery, they said, could have been Glastonbury.[55] Believers in 'Celtic' continuity will see in the evidence discussed above a hardy kernel of tradition surviving in elaborated form.[56] Sceptics will point out that the identification has as much to do with our ignorance of fifth-century sites as it has with the credibility of Glastonbury's association with Patrick; they will argue that Glastonbury's foundation might have postdated Palladius and Patrick by several hundred years, and that it is the tenth century which provides a suitable context for the genesis of the cult there. Confirmed sceptics will point out that early evidence for cults is so fragmentary that the clustering of sources in the tenth century is inevitable and therefore inconclusive. And hardened sceptics will not have expected to give a straight answer to a straight question, especially one concerning St Patrick.

51 O'Rahilly, *The Two Patricks*, pp. 32–4 and n. 32 (p. 59). The removal by cloud of St Cadog in the sixth century from Llancarfan to *Beneuentana ciuitas*, where there was a monastery, could, according to O'Rahilly (*ibid.*, pp. 59–60, n. 33), support this association: see the Life of St Cadog, §37 (*Vitae*, ed. & transl. Wade-Evans, pp. 102–6); for comment on this passage see Brooke, *The Church and the Welsh Border*, pp. 87–9; Dumville, 'St Teilo, St Cadog and St Buite in Italy?'; Goetinck, 'Lifris and the Italian connection'. For the name of the River Brue, see Ekwall, *English River-names*, pp. 55–6.

52 *The Two Patricks*, p. 34.

53 Binchy, 'Patrick and his biographers', p. 9.

54 An idea raised, but not necessarily supported, by Porter, *The Celtic Church in Somerset*, p. 73.

55 Carney, *The Problem*, p. 121; Hanson, *Saint Patrick, his Origins*, p. 157(–8), n. 1.

56 A maxim enunciated by Bieler might be supported by such believers: 'A tradition may be accepted as true if there is no reason to the contrary' (*The Life*, p. 26).

ST PATRICK IN AN ANGLO-SAXON MARTYROLOGY

Cambridge, Corpus Christi College, MS. 57 is a large-format book written in Phase-VII Anglo-Saxon Square-minuscule script *ca* A.D. 1000:[1] the dating is a rather precise one, for this flat-topped variety of Square minuscule seems to have been written for only a very few years, in the 990s and possibly in the succeeding decade.[2] The manuscript now comprises 162 folios but is incomplete at the end. It had suffered serious damage already before the middle of the eleventh century, for three whole leaves and part of another are supply written in imitative script attributable to that date.[3]

By the mid-eleventh century – in particular the period of Æthelstan's abbacy (1044–1047) – this book seems to have been the chapter-office book of Abingdon Abbey in the Thames Valley.[4] A considerable number of very detailed local additions was made to the martyrology which the manuscript contains: it was M. R. James who recognised the place of origin of these supplementary items and hence the provenance of the book as a whole.[5] Its contents are entirely Benedictine and in substantial measure Carolingian. The first four quires are devoted to a copy of the Rule of St Benedict (fos 2v–32v).[6] In the next (fos 33–40) are found three Carolingian texts pertaining to the Rule – *Memoriale qualiter*, *Epitoma* (or *Collectio capitularis*), and *Abbreuiatio*.[7] The next four quires (fos 41–96) are largely given over to an interpolated copy of Usuuard's

1 Catalogued in some detail by James, *A Descriptive Catalogue*, I.114–18; noticed, for a few Old English glosses to its copy of *Regula Sancti Benedicti*, by Ker, *Catalogue*, pp. 46–7 (no. 34); for Phase-VII Square minuscule, see Dumville, 'English Square minuscule script', p. 147, and 'Beowulf come lately', pp. 59–62; for its decoration, see Wormald, 'Decorated initials', p. 134, and Temple, *Anglo-Saxon Manuscripts*, pp. 55–8 (no. 30 [x]).

2 For the four specimens of this type, written at Canterbury (1) and perhaps Rochester (1), at Dorchester-on-Thames (1), and with later Abingdon provenances (2), see Dumville, 'Beowulf come lately', pp. 59–60, 61–2.

3 Cf. Ker, *Catalogue*, p. 46; Dumville, *English Caroline Script*, pp. 153–4 and plate XV. The supply-leaves are fos 8, 19, 22; fo 85 was repaired at the same time. The eleventh-century scribe was a practitioner of Style-IV Anglo-Caroline but sought to imitate the work of his Square-minuscule predecessor.

4 Cf. Gneuss, 'Liturgical books', pp. 128–31.

5 *A Descriptive Catalogue*, I.114; cf. Ker, *Catalogue*, p. 47.

6 Printed in *The Rule*, ed. Chamberlin; discussed *ibid.*, pp. 9–11, also by Meyvaert, 'Towards a history', pp. 100, 110, and by Gretsch, *Die Regula*, chapters II–III, and 'Æthelwold's translation', pp. 126–37. It has significant text-historical links with the eighth-century copy in Oxford, Bodleian Library, MS. Hatton 48 (*S.C.* 4118) – facsimile in *The Rule*, ed. Farmer – which may have been written at Worcester and was certainly there by the second half of the eleventh century.

7 Cf. *Wulfstan of Winchester*, edd. & transl. Lapidge & Winterbottom, pp. lv–lviii; *The Rule*, ed. Chamberlin, p. 9.

Martyrology.[8] On fos 95–96 are found the preliminaries to the *Diadema monachorum* of Smaragdus of Saint-Mihiel, while the body of the text, to the point at which it breaks off incomplete in §84, occupies the remaining eight quires (fos 97–162).[9]

The mid-eleventh-century additions to the manuscript adhere to the Martyrology. Many marginal and interlinear obituary additions were published by M. R. James and have recently been the subject of new attention by Jan Gerchow who has dated them to 1046/7.[10] These by no means exhaust the store of alterations which the Martyrology suffered in this period: palaeographical and liturgical analyses of the layers of change remain desiderata. Following this major text two small additions have been made rather elaborately on the originally blank fo 94v: these comprise two formula-letters for death-announcements; one is addressed to Abbot Æthelstan.[11]

The body of the Martyrology is the text of Usuuard's work but interpolated here and there with new material of great interest. At 17 March we find Usuuard's own entry about St Patrick. But the name recurs at 24 August (*.ix. kal. Sept.*) where Usuuard's brief entry about St Patrice of Nevers has been abandoned in favour of an altogether more expansive and remarkable account. After notices of the three hundred martyrs of Carthage and of St Audoenus of Rouen, the day's entry concludes with the following (fos 74v24–75r2).

In `H îbernia[12] sancti Patricii abbatis et Gildardi confessoris. Qui Patricius primus Iberniensium fertur fuisse magister; sed, quia nec eos correxisse potuit, in peregrinationem perrexit. Ad monasterium Glæstingense peruenit ibique uitam, uirtutibus clarescens, finiuit. Quod[13] et usque hodie mortua ossa ipsius contestari uidentur.

In Ireland the holy abbot Patricius and Gildardus the confessor. Patrick is said to have been the first teacher of the Irish; but, because he could not discipline them, he departed on pilgrimage. He came to Glastonbury Abbey and, growing famous for his miraculous powers, ended his life there. Even to the present his corporeal relics are seen to attest that.

The identity of this Gildardus is, in detail, a mystery, but here he is derived with Patricius from Nevers via the martyrological tradition.[14] Yet 'Abbot Patrick' can in the present text be none other than Senex Patricius or Palladius.[15] Here at last we have clear evidence from the English side that the source of the tenth-century Patrician cult at Glastonbury was Irish.[16] Furthermore we have a direct statement of what must have been the abbey's official view of the saint's history: but it is not clear to me whether the author of this martyrological notice was, in his use of *fertur*, distancing himself from that view. A full study of this fascinating Anglo-Saxon adaptation of Usuuard's work must be undertaken before the date, location, and outlook of the redactor can be established.

8 *Le Martyrologe d'Usuard*, ed. Dubois, for the original work.
9 Cf. Dumville, *English Caroline Script*, p. 8, n. 4.
10 James, *A Descriptive Catalogue*, I.115–18; Gerchow, *Die Gedenküberlieferung*, pp. 245–52, 335–8.
11 James, *A Descriptive Catalogue*, I.118. On Æthelstan, see Knowles *et al.*, *The Heads*, p. 24.
12 In the manuscript *H-* is represented by a rough-breathing mark above the vowel.
13 In the manuscript only *Q-* seems original.
14 Cf. Grosjean, 'S. Patrice d'Irlande', pp. 153–6, 160–1.
15 See above, pp. 59–64.
16 Cf. Lesley Abrams's discussion above, pp. 233–42.

A MASS FOR ST PATRICK IN AN ANGLO-SAXON SACRAMENTARY

Alicia Corrêa

No greater honour was given a saintly figure than to commemorate that individual's entry (the *natalis*) into the heavenly kingdom with an annual liturgical devotion. The most common expression of this devotion was to dedicate the mass on the day of the saint's death to that saint. In Anglo-Saxon England, the evidence from liturgical books suggests that St Patrick, apostle of Ireland, was seldom honoured in this way. Only one pre-Conquest service-book contains a mass for St Patrick, 'bishop', here on 17 March. This manuscript is London, British Library, MS. Cotton Vitellius A.xviii, a sacramentary (and benedictional) datable to the third quarter of the eleventh century. On account of the appearance of St Congar (27 November) in the kalendar, a confessor venerated in the diocese of Wells,[1] this manuscript has been assigned to Wells and, more particularly, to Bishop Giso (1061–1088).[2] However, St Congar is not awarded a high grading with a cross by his name in the kalendar. The following is a list of those saints in the Vitellius kalendar who *are* given a high grading. The three Insular saints in this category have associations with Christ Church, Canterbury; furthermore, according to post-Conquest accounts, the relics of St Ouen (Audoenus) were deposited there in the time of Archbishop Oda (941–958), and those of St Bartholomew during the reign of King Cnut (1016–1035). These 'Christ Church, Canterbury' saints are indicated by my italics.

1 Robinson, 'A fragment', where he edited *Vita S. Cungari*, and 'St Cungar'; Grosjean, 'Cyngar Sant'; Doble, 'St Congar'; and see also Fros, *Bibliotheca*, pp. 232–3 (no. 2013). For a brief discussion of St Congar, Wells, and the 'Vitellius Sacramentary', see Hohler, 'Some service-books', pp. 70–1 and 222.

2 Gasquet & Bishop, *The Bosworth Psalter*, pp. 162–4, and especially 61, n. 1, where the kalendar of the 'Vitellius Sacramentary' is categorised as the 'new' type on account of the presence there of Continental names which Bishop thought attributable probably to the influence of the 'Lorrainer' Giso, bishop of Wells. On Giso, see further Robinson, *The Saxon Bishops of Wells*, p. 52. This codex has been listed by Gneuss, 'Liturgical books', pp. 101 (no. A.5) and 133 (no. S.6). Its kalendar was edited by Wormald, *English Kalendars before A.D. 1100*, pp. 99–111; see especially p. 110. For the litanic evidence, see *Anglo-Saxon Litanies*, ed. Lapidge, pp. 305–6. The manuscript also contains sections from an *ordo confessionis* (fos 223v–226r), an *ordo de consecratione crismalis olei* (fos 227r–231v), and an *ordo in dedicatione ecclesie* (fos 232r–238v).

Gregory (12.3), the pope who first sent missionaries to England
Ælfheah (19.4)
Philip & James (1.5)
Invention of the Holy Cross (3.5)
Dunstan (& Potentiana) *(19.5)*
Augustine of Canterbury (26.5)
John the Baptist (24.6)
Passion of Peter (& Paul) (29.6)
St Paul (30.6)
James/Christopher (25.7)
Laurence (10.8)
Assumption of the Virgin Mary (15.8)
Bartholomew & Audoenus (24.8)
Nativity of the Virgin Mary/Hadrian, martyr (8.9)
Matthew (21.9)
Dedication of St Michael, archangel (29.9)
All Saints/Cesarius (1.11)
Martin/Mennes (11.11)
Clement/Felicity (23.11)
Andrew (30.11)
Thomas (21.12)
Nativity of Christ (25.12)
Stephen, protomartyr (26.12)
John the apostle (27.12)
Holy Innocents (28.12)

The Vitellius kalendar also commemorates the following saints whose cults are associated with English churches.

Winchester
Iudoc (9.1 = translation)
Eadburh (16.6) <should be 15 June>
Swithhun (2.7)
Grimbald (8.7)
Swithhun, translation (15.7)
Iustus of Beauvais (18.10)
Machutus (15.11)
Birinus (3.12)
Iudoc (13.12)

Elsewhere
Brigit (1.2) – Glastonbury?
Ceadda (2.3) – Lichfield
Patrick (17.3) – Glastonbury
Edward (18.3) – Shaftesbury
Cuthbert (20.3)
Aldhelm (25.5) – Sherborne
Boniface (5.6)
Alban (22.6) – St Albans
Ætheldryth (23.6) – Ely
Oswald, king and martyr (5.8)
Aidán (31.8) – Glastonbury
Cuthbert, translation (4.9)
Ceol(d)frith (25.9) – Glastonbury
The two Hewalds (3.10)
'Columbanus, bishop & martyr' (24.10) – identification uncertain
Edmund (20.11) – Bury St Edmunds
Congar (27.11) – Congresbury

In the list of Winchester saints, nine out of Edmund Bishop's defining list of sixteen Winchester feasts are present in the Vitellius kalendar.[3] The evidence points to a Winchester source-kalendar of 971x984, one compiled, that is, after the translation of Swithhun but before the death of Æthelwold.

In the list of saints from other localities, the Glastonbury trio of Patrick, Aidán, and Ceolfrith is mentioned, but not Benedict Biscop – hence Glastonbury is a source indicated, but no more than that. The conclusion which may be drawn from this analysis, then, is that the kalendar was produced at Christ Church, Canterbury (on account of the high grading given to the Canterbury saints); further, that the kalendar or *cultus* or both relied on connexions with Winchester and Glastonbury. For the moment, then, an attribution of this manuscript to Wells must be thought questionable until the evidence from the kalendar can be compared with other liturgical evidence, for instance, with the results of a full collation of this sacramentary with other Anglo-Saxon sacramentaries.

The compiler of the 'Vitellius Sacramentary', whoever he or she was, chose to include the unique mass for St Patrick published here, in addition to masses for two Irish saints, St Brigit (1 February) and St Aidán of Lindisfarne (31 August).[4] The rarity of an Anglo-Saxon mass for St Patrick warrants an edition, in conjunction with those for the two Gaelic saints mentioned.[5]

Any Anglo-Saxon liturgist who would have undertaken the composition of a mass in honour of a particular saint would have concerned himself with one of a number of 'proper' elements which together make up the mass-set. These elements vary according to the feast of that day, and consist of musical and spoken texts. A sacramentary would have contained only the spoken texts of the mass. A mass requiring a very high level of devotion would include: a collect, which introduces the subject for the day's mass; the secret, which is read immediately after the bread and wine have been offered and again refers to the saint's commemoration; the preface, a longer prayer which is read as an introduction to the Canon of the Mass, and which traditionally held great attraction

3 Gasquet & Bishop, *The Bosworth Psalter*, p. 60: the number may be increased to seventeen saints; see *ibid.*, p. 41.

4 For a discussion of the sanctoral, see Hohler, 'Some service-books', pp. 76–7 and 226–7. Another saint of some interest in the 'Vitellius Sacramentary' is Cuthbert, who is awarded two feasts: his deposition (fo 85r) and his translation (fo 117v). For one of the more useful discussions of the masses of St Cuthbert in Anglo-Saxon service-books, see *Two Anglo-Saxon Pontificals*, ed. Banting, pp. xliv–xlviii, and especially p. xlv where Banting noted that the Missal of the New Minster, Winchester (ed. Turner, pp. 154–5), and the 'Vitellius Sacramentary' are the only Anglo-Saxon service-books to provide a mass for his translation on 4 September. Banting (*Two Anglo-Saxon Pontificals*, pp. xlvi–xlvii) also pointed out that the postcommunion for St Aidán in the 'Vitellius Sacramentary' occurs in the deposition-mass for St Cuthbert in the 'Ratoldus Sacramentary' (Paris, Bibliothèque nationale, MS. latin 12052). On the mass(es) for St Cuthbert, see further Rollason, 'St Cuth[b]ert', pp. 416 and especially 419; Hohler & Hughes, 'The Durham services', pp. 157–8; Hohler, 'Some service-books', pp. 66–7 and 221–2, and 'Les Saints insulaires'.

5 First published in *The Leofric Collectar*, edd. Dewick & Frere, II.303, 306, but Brigit's mass was not included.

for writers of liturgical prayers;[6] and the postcommunion, a shorter prayer, similar to the collect, which concludes the Communion-proceedings. The masses for SS. Patrick, Brigit, and Aidán in the 'Vitellius Sacramentary' are limited to the three shorter prayers; the preface is not included in either of the three masses. Liturgically, this indicates that their commemorations in the daily liturgy were not of the highest order.[7] We should have to assume that the prefaces for their masses were taken from the Sunday mass.

The greater proportion of proper prayers in a sacramentary was inherited from older sources, although this inherited material was by no means static and new texts could be, and were, added to it. Any introduction of new prayers into that corpus meant that the writer had made a special effort to compose a prayer on behalf of particular saints, in this case, Insular ones. The significance, from a literary and cultural point of view, of these newly composed prayers for St Patrick, and those for SS. Brigit and Aidán should not be minimised.

As a general rule, liturgical books from later Anglo-Saxon England depended very heavily on Continental traditions of the sacramentary, most notably the supplemented Hadrianic Gregorians of the ninth century[8] and the mixed Gregorian-Gelasians of the tenth century.[9] Yet only a few of the prayers from the masses for these Insular saints in the 'Vitellius Sacramentary' can be identified with such Continental material. Of the three proper prayers for St Patrick, neither the collect nor a verbal echo of it can be found in the sacramentary

6 The *Uere dignum* coda, which introduces the (spoken) preface, is sung to music and was one of the first liturgical pieces to have been notated. For general remarks, see Treitler, 'Reading and singing', p. 161, and especially Stäblein, 'Präfation'. I am grateful to Dr Susan Rankin for these references.

7 In the 'Vitellius Sacramentary', prefaces are provided only for feasts of the highest grade. Of the list of high-grade sanctoral feasts given above, prefaces occur in the following masses: all masses associated with the Nativity of Christ, fos 16v–18v; the second (day) mass for John the Baptist, fo 103v; the (day) mass for Peter and Paul, fo 105v; Paul, fo 106r; the second (day) mass for Laurence, fo 125v; the (day) mass for the Assumption of the Virgin Mary, fo 127v; the Nativity of the Virgin Mary, fo 119r (this mass occurs within a misplaced quire: fos 112–119 should occur after fo 127); the Dedication of Michael the Archangel, fo 133r; the (day) mass for All Saints, fo 138r; Martin, fo 140r; Clement, fo 143v; the (day) mass for Andrew, fo 145v (the celebrant is instructed to take the preface from the Common of one apostle); and, lastly, the mass for Thomas, fo 148v (again, the celebrant is referred to the preface in the Common of one apostle).

8 The supplemented *Hadrianum* represented a sacramentary which had integrated the mass-book sent by Pope Hadrian to Charlemagne with a variety of other material required to make the *Hadrianum* more usable. Some of the more important extant representatives of this tradition have been edited by Deshusses, *Le Sacramentaire grégorien*, II–III. For general literature with further bibliography, see Gamber, *Sakramentartypen*, pp. 135–44; Deshusses, 'Les sacramentaires', pp. 40–4; and Vogel, *Medieval Liturgy*, pp. 85–92 and 125–7.

9 The mixed Gregorian-Gelasians represented a sacramentary which had combined the supplemented Gregorian of the ninth century with the Frankish Gelasians of the eighth. The eighth-century Gelasians have all been edited individually; see, for example, *Liber sacramentorum Gellonensis*, edd. Dumas & Deshusses. For a list of manuscripts with further bibliography, see Gamber, *Sakramentartypen*, pp. 99–119, and Vogel, *Medieval Liturgy*, pp. 70–8 and 117–21. On the fusion of the eighth-century Gelasians with the supplemented *Hadrianum*, see Andrieu, 'Quelques remarques', but his terminology can be misleading; Bishop & Wilmart, 'La réforme liturgique', pp. 205–7; and Vogel, *Medieval Liturgy*, pp. 102–5 and 132–3.

sources mentioned above. The same can be said for the secret. The postcommunion, however, derives from the Old Gelasian sacramentary,[10] where it appears as the postcommunion in the mass for St Priscus (1 September). Only the description of the saint has been altered, from *quoque martiris Prisci* to *pontificis Patricii*.

The three proper prayers in the mass for St Aidán cannot be found in the sacramentary sources. The postcommunion occurs in the mass for St Cuthbert in the 'Ratoldus Sacramentary', a book with Anglo-Saxon characteristics which was copied in the second half of the tenth century on the Continent; that prayer in the 'Ratoldus Sacramentary' is still used as a postcommunion, but it is rubricated with the older description, *ad complendum*.[11] The prayers for St Brigit are less localised. The collect, like that for St Patrick and St Aidán, does not appear in the sacramentary sources. The first part of the secret derives from a prayer in the 'Leonine',[12] and is found thereafter in the Old Gelasian for the feast of St Paul (30 June)[13] and in the *Hadrianum* for the same feast.[14] But, from the natural break at the *ut*-clause until the end, this prayer departs from its apparent source and offers a slightly more elaborate devotional concept – 'so that we, who humbly beseech your majesty on behalf of her merits, may experience your mercy by the aid of her prayers' – instead of the older, Continental one, 'so that what we celebrate, on behalf of her glory, may benefit us for [your] forgiveness'.[15] The postcommunion for St Brigit is a standard one for

10 The 'Old Gelasian' refers to one specific manuscript (Roma, B.A.V., MS. Reg. lat. 316), written perhaps at Chelles in the mid-eighth century. Although it is the oldest surviving example of the Roman sacramentary, it does not represent a purely Roman liturgy and preserves certain Gallican prayers. It has been edited, with the prayer for St Priscus, by Mohlberg *et al.*, *Liber sacramentorum romanae aeclesiae*, no. 1015. For further literature and bibliography, see Gamber, *Sakramentartypen*, p. 56; Chavasse, *Le Sacramentaire gélasien*; and Vogel, *Medieval Liturgy*, pp. 64–70 and 113–17. The usage of this prayer for St Priscus was thereafter canonised in the eighth-century Gelasians (*Liber sacramentorum Gellonensis*, edd. Dumas & Deshusses, no. 1422) and in the mixed Gregorian-Gelasians (*Le Sacramentaire grégorien*, ed. Deshusses, no. 3142).

11 Noted by Banting, *Two Anglo-Saxon Pontificals*, p. xlv (and see n. 4, above). For literature on the 'Ratoldus Sacramentary', a full edition of which does not yet exist, see Martimort, 'La documentation liturgique', p. 97 (no. 106). For a discussion of the English elements in that sacramentary, see Hohler, 'Some service-books', pp. 64–7. The 'Ratoldus sacramentary' is most commonly referred to for its version of the 'Edgar' coronation *ordo*: 'An early version', ed. Ward, pp. 350–61; discussed fully by Bouman, *Sacring and Crowning*, pp. 20–1, 117–21, and Nelson, *Politics and Ritual*, pp. 361–8.

12 The name 'Leonine Sacramentary' refers to the earliest collection of *libelli missarum*: this has survived uniquely in Verona, Biblioteca capitolare, MS. LXXXV (80), copied in the first quarter of the seventh century and probably at Verona, although this last is much disputed. Unlike the practice of the later sacramentaries noted above, the feasts in the 'Leonine' are arranged according to the Roman calendar, not the liturgical one. Hence the prayer in question occurs in the month of June: *Sacramentarium Veronense*, edd. Mohlberg *et al.*, no. 318. For literature and further bibliography, see Bourque, *Étude sur les sacramentaires*, I.65–77; Gamber, *Sakramentartypen*, pp. 48–50; Vogel, *Medieval Liturgy*, pp. 38–46 and 55–9; and Hope, *The Leonine Sacramentary*, with review by Martimort, *Bulletin de littérature ecclésiastique* 73 (1972) 267–8.

13 *Liber sacramentorum romanae aeclesiae*, edd. Mohlberg *et al.*, no. 919.

14 *Le Sacramentaire grégorien*, ed. Deshusses, no. 605.

15 'ut quod pro illius gloria caelebramus, nobis prosit ad ueniam', edited in one of the three sacramentary traditions mentioned in nn. 12–14, above.

virgins; it occurs in the Old Gelasian for St Sotheris (10 February)[16] and in the *Hadrianum* for St Agatha (5 February).[17] With these sources as guide, we can safely reconstruct the end of this prayer, the last word of which is missing on account of the loss of one leaf after fo 79.

Within the corpus of Anglo-Saxon service-books, where we might have expected a proliferation of masses held in honour of saints who had, in one way or another, affected Anglo-Saxon England, the evidence for St Patrick and St Aidán is surprisingly sparse. There is no evidence that these saints were commemorated with a proper mass outside the area where the 'Vitellius Sacramentary' was written and used. But we must always be aware that from the pre-Conquest period only a handful of sacramentaries has survived – of the hundreds of such books which must have been copied. By contrast, in Irish liturgy, where admittedly the evidence comes entirely from later sources, the survival of a mass for St Patrick is not uncommon; but the extant Irish mass is derivative of a tradition quite different from that of the 'Vitellius Sacramentary'.[18]

St Brigit enjoyed a much wider recognition in Anglo-Saxon liturgy.[19] A vestige of a mass for her appears in the 'Missal of Robert of Jumièges', where the 'Vitellius' collect, 'Caelorum atque terrarum conditor', with minor textual variants, occurs. The remainder of this mass was (for reasons no longer apparent) not copied: in mid-page (fo 112v), after a complete copy of the collect for St Brigit had been transcribed, a series of blessings for the feast of the Purification of the Virgin Mary was entered.[20] We cannot assume, however, that the secret and postcommunion would have corresponded with those in the 'Vitellius Sacramentary'. In the Missal of the New Minster, Winchester, St Brigit was honoured with a proper mass which included a proper preface unique to that

16 *Liber sacramentorum romanae aeclesiae*, edd. Mohlberg *et al.*, no. 714.

17 *Le Sacramentaire grégorien*, ed. Deshusses, no. 133.

18 On the mass of St Patrick in Irish service-books, see Hohler, 'Some service-books', p. 76 and p. 226, n. 75, where he has referred to a mass for St Patrick which has survived in the 'Corpus Missal' (Oxford, Corpus Christi College, MS. 282) and in Rouen, Bibliothèque municipale, MS. A.279 (313); and see Warren, *The Liturgy*, pp. 270–1, where the collect, secret, and postcommunion of the mass-set from the 'Corpus Missal' and from the 'Rosslyn Missal' (Edinburgh, National Library of Scotland, MS. Adv. 18.8.17) are printed, with a note on the Irish composition of these prayers. An Irish liturgical background must account for the mention of St Patrick in two mid-eleventh-century Anglo-Saxon service-books. The names of SS. Patrick and Brigit, and five other saints, are invoked in a charm/prayer (against the theft of cattle) which incorporates four stanzas from the hymn 'Audite omnes amantes' (see above, p. 163): see *Cambridge, Corpus Christi College 41: the Loricas*, ed. Grant, pp. 5–13. In London, British Library, MS. Cotton Galba A.xiv, a collect for St Patrick can be found on fo 152v (*A Pre-Conquest English Prayer-book*, ed. Muir, p. 191, no. 104), parallels for which occur in Irish missals.

19 In addition to the liturgical evidence from the mass-books discussed below, the invocation of her name occurs in most litanies, and her feast is noted in most kalendars. This is in stark contrast to the positions of St Patrick and St Aidán who are represented only sporadically in the litanies and kalendars (for discussion, cf. Dumville, *Liturgy*, chapter II). See *Anglo-Saxon Litanies*, ed. Lapidge, and *English Kalendars before A.D. 1100*, ed. Wormald.

20 *The Missal of Robert of Jumièges*, ed. Wilson, pp. 157–8. The sequence of feasts – Brigit, followed by the Purification – is correct. St Brigit's feast, on 1 February, would normally coincide with the vigil-feast for the Purification (2 February). See the arrangement in *The Missal of the New Minster*, ed. Turner, pp. 68–9.

particular book.[21] The collect is 'Caelorum atque terrarum conditor' and resembles the 'Vitellius' reading, not that of the 'Missal of Robert of Jumièges'. But the secret and postcommunion are quite different from those in the 'Vitellius Sacramentary'. It seems, then, that at least two (and possibly more) mass-sets for St Brigit were circulating in Anglo-Saxon England and that the collect 'Caelorum atque terrarum conditor' was the most commonly used of these mass-prayers, although variants did occur in the text.[22] When we compare Brigit's relatively frequent appearance in Anglo-Saxon service-books with the lack of information about her in Continental books, we are bound to conclude that her popularity was a peculiarity of later Anglo-Saxon England.

The transmission of these three particular mass-sets – for St Patrick, St Brigit, and St Aidán – does not appear to have survived the Conquest. The Sarum rite commemorates the feasts of St Patrick and St Brigit, but not that of St Aidán; and the masses are entirely different.[23] Only St Patrick is still remembered in the Roman Missal, where the sole proper prayer provided is the collect, different alike from the Anglo-Saxon and the Sarum liturgical traditions.[24] The texts of these prayers as purveyed by the 'Vitellius Sacramentary' are therefore peculiar to the liturgy of late Anglo-Saxon England. The words and concepts employed are accordingly of value to scholars of this period. Special emphasis should be placed on those prayers which cannot be traced among the earlier Continental material. These are six in number: the collect and secret from the mass for St Patrick; all three propers in the mass for St Aidán; and the collect for St Brigit.

21 *Ibid.*, p. 68.

22 The same collect, but with no other prayers from the mass-set, occurs in fragmentary form in London, British Library, MS. Cotton Galba A.xiv, fo 72v (*A Pre-Conquest English Prayer-book*, ed. Muir, p. 90, no. 35), from the Winchester Nunnaminster. In the Irish books, the mass for St Brigit retained the collect and secret as preserved in the 'Vitellius Sacramentary', but had a different postcommunion ('Adiuuent nos, quesumus, Domine, hec misteria sancta . . . ueneranda'): ed. Warren, *The Liturgy*, p. 270.

23 *Missale*, ed. Dickinson, pp. 695–6 (St Brigit) and 720–2 (St Patrick). The use of Sarum represented a modification of the Roman rite in use at the cathedral church of Salisbury, the first written records of which date from the thirteenth century. In the later middle ages, versions of the Sarum rite were followed in many other dioceses in England. For further literature, see Frere, *The Use of Sarum*, I, especially pp. xiii–xlii; and Pfaff, *New Liturgical Feasts*, pp. 8–9, 35–8.

24 For the other propers of this mass in the Roman Missal, the celebrant is referred to the Common of the Saints, where he is to select the propers either from the mass for missionaries or from that for bishops.

TEXTS

XVI Kl. Apr. Natale Sancti Patricii episcopi (fos 83v–84r)

Domine, Deus omnipotens, qui nobis sanctorum intercessione succurris, da, quesumus, ut sancti Patricii confessoris tui atque pontificis et exultemus meritis, et patrocinio gaudeamus. Per Dominum nostrum Iesum Christum filium tuum.

Secreta

Quesumus, benedictionis auctor et sanctificationis dator, quesumus, ut hoc sacrificium benedicere et sanctificare digneris, et interpellante beato pontifice Patricio, nobis famulis tuis remissionem tribue peccatorum. Per.

Postcommunio

Presta, quesumus, Domine, ut sacramenti tui participatione uegetati sancti pontificis Patricii precibus adiuuemur. Per.

* * *

Natale Sanctę Brigidę uirginis (fos 79v–80r)

Caelorum atque terrarum conditor et gubernator, omnipotens Deus, precanti populo continua pietate succurre, et presta ut qui in honore sanctę Brigidę presentis diei gerimus solemnitatem pro ipsius suffragia perenni misericordia tua potiamur. Per.

Secreta

Ecclesię tuę, quesumus, Domine, preces et hostias beatę Brigidę commendet oratio, ut qui pro illius meritis maiestatem tuam humiliter imploramus, eius precibus adiuti misericordiam tuam sentiamus. Per.

Postcommunio

Beatę Brigidę uirginis tuę, Domine, precibus confidentes, quesumus, clementiam tuam, ut per ea quę sumpsimus ęterna reme[dia capiamus. Per.]

* * *

II. Kl. Sept. Depositio Sancti Aidani episcopi (fos 116v–117r)

Deus, qui sanctorum tuorum meritis ecclesiam tuam toto orbe diffusam decorasti, presta, quesumus, ut intercessione beatissimi pontificis tui Aidani, in sorte iustorum tua optanda pietate censeamur. Per Dominum.

Secreta

Oblata, Domine, quę tibi offerimus, pię deuotionis intentu, in honore sanctissmi Aidani episcopi, tua preclara clementia sanctificet, et purificatos nos ea percipere tua faciat gratia in omnibus ubique laudanda. Per.

Postcommunio

Satiatis, Domine, munerum tuorum donis auxilium gratię tuę rogatus impende, et auribus tuę pietatis nostras miserando preces benignus exaudi, ut meritis sancti presulis Aidani et intercessione adiuti, in electorum tuorum numero ęterna in secula censeamur. Per.

THE AFTERLIFE OF *LIBER ANGELI*

Recent study of the Patrician dossier in the 'Book of Armagh' has stressed the physical division to be noted between quires I–II (now fos 2–19), containing what Richard Sharpe has described as the 'Composite Life' of St Patrick, and quire III (now fos 20–24) containing a supplement written by the master-scribe Ferdomnach.[1] The supplement contains the otherwise missing preface (and *capitula* for Book I) of Muirchú's *Vita S. Patricii*, the seventh-century Armagh documentary text known as *Liber angeli*, and an abridged version of Patrick's *Confessio*.[2]

Liber angeli was drawn upon by Tírechán in the making of his *Collectanea* of St Patrick: he shifted the emphasis of its claims and as a result that document's importance as an active quasi-legal record of the church of Armagh began at once to decline. The evidence of its position in the 'Book of Armagh' strongly supports Sharpe's contention that it did not form part of the Patrician dossier then current at Armagh. Just as the *Confessio* had been gutted by Muirchú, so Tírechán had absorbed the elements of *Liber angeli* which remained useful. The transcription of these texts in ninth-century Armagh was 'an act of antiquarianism'.[3]

Sharpe has hinted that by the beginning of the eleventh century the stock of *Liber angeli* might have been rising again.[4] From the eighth century, however, *Liber angeli* had 'passed into the background' with the *Confessio*.[5] In this context, and with an eye both to the question of the correctness of this judgment and to the dating of the Tripartite Life, I recall that Kathleen Mulchrone and Ludwig Bieler both noted the use of *Liber angeli* in the Tripartite Life.[6] §§1–9 of the former correspond to lines 2760–2773 of Mulchrone's edition. Here, then, whatever its date may eventually prove to be, is evidence that at a certain point after the eighth century and before the late middle ages *Liber angeli* was not wholly forgotten. Discovery of the date of this section of the Tripartite Life will determine just how significant was the use of *Liber angeli*.

1 Sharpe, 'Palaeographical considerations'.
2 See above, pp. 203–19 (Muirchú) and 191–202 (*Confessio*).
3 Sharpe, 'Palaeographical considerations', p. 26.
4 *Ibid.*, p. 28.
5 *Ibid.*, p. 26.
6 *Bethu Phátraic*, ed. Mulchrone, pp. 139–40 (cf. *The Tripartite Life*, ed. & transl. Stokes, I.232–5, where the parallel was not noted); *The Patrician Texts*, edd. & transl. Bieler & Kelly, pp. 184–5.

TRIPARTITE LIFE OF ST PATRICK, BOOK III (2760–73)
(ed. Mulchrone)

Fecht n-aili ro boí Pátraic inna chumsanud i ndered aidchi oc Tiprait Cernai hi Tír Tiprat. Dolluid int aingel a dóchum ⁊ doníusaig. Dixit ei Pátricius: 'Hin fil ní hi crádind do Día, nó in fail a baraind frim?' ol Pátraic. 'Nocon fail,' ol int aingel, '*Ocus* timarnad duit ó Día,' ol int aingel, 'masu ed as maith latt, cona bía cuit do nach ailiu i nHére acht duit t'oenur. *Ocus* is hé commus t*er*muind do chathrach ó Día co Droma Breg ⁊ co Slíab Miss ⁊ co Bri nAirigi.' Respondit Patricius: 'Mo débróth ém,' ol Pátraic, 'ticfat m*aic*c bethad imm diaid-se, ⁊ is maith lim-sa honóir dóib ó Día dimm ése-si isin tír.' Respondit angelus: 'Is dercaige són da*no* ⁊ dorat Día Héirind huili duit-siu,' ol int aingel, '⁊ nach sóer bías i nHére bid lat-su.' 'Deo gratias,' ol Pátraic.

LIBER ANGELI
(ed. Bieler), §§1–9

(1) Quo<n>dam itaque sanctus Patricius de Alti Mache urbe ad multitudines utriusque sexus humani generis babtizandas, docendas atque sanandas iuxta fontem in orientali praedictae urbis parte prope herentem pie perrexit. (2) Et ibi ante lucem multas undique ad notitiam fidei confluentes expectauit; subito ergo eum sopor prostrauit eo quod prius pro Christo uigiliis nocturnis fessus fuisset. (3) Et ecce tam cito uenit anguelus ad eum de caelo et excitauit eum leniter de sompno; et dixit sanctus Patricius, 'Ego adsum. Numquid inique gessi nuper in conspectu Altissimi? Si accidit, ueniam peto a Deo.' (4) Respondit anguelus: 'Non, sed missit me summus omnipotens ad te, id est ad animi tui consulationem, post conuersionem Hibernensium per te ad se in fidem, quos ei adquaessisti per durissimum laborem et per tuam ualde praedicationem, gratia Spiritus Sancti lucidissimam uniuersis gentibus fructuossam, (5) cum esses semper laboriossus multis temporibus in multis periculis a gentilibus per frigus et aestatem essuriens et sitiens deambulans impiger quotidie de gente in gentem ad utilitatem multarum gentium. (6) Scit ergo Dominus Deus tuum praesentem locum quem praesto uidemus in alto positum cum parua celula angustum, ab aliquibus quoque regionis habitatoribus coartatum, et suburbana eius non sufficiunt cunctis ad refugium. (7) Idcirco constituitur terminus a Domino uastissimus urbi Alti Mache, quam dilexisti prae omnibus Hibernensium telluribus, id est a pinna montis Berbicis usque ad montem Mis; a monte Miss usque ad Bri Erigi; a Bri Erigi usque ad Dorsos Breg – certe, si uolueris, erit huius magnitudinis. (8) Ac deinde donauit tibi Dominus Deus uniuersas Scotorum gentes in modum paruchiae et huic urbi tuae, quae cognominatur Scotorum lingua Ardd Machæ.' (9) Dixit sanctus Patricius prostrata facie deorsum in conspectu angueli: 'Gratias ago Deo meo Domino sempiterno, qui dignatus est tantam gloriam donare clementer famulo suo.'

THE DATING OF THE TRIPARTITE LIFE OF ST PATRICK

The Tripartite Life of St Patrick, a massive three-book account (mostly in Irish, but containing much scattered Latin) of the saint's life and travels throughout Ireland, has survived only in a small number of manuscripts, all belonging to a restricted period from the late fourteenth to the early sixteenth century. The first modern edition was that of Whitley Stokes, published in 1887.[1] From then until the work published by Kathleen Mulchrone from 1926 to 1943,[2] the general inclination of scholars seems to have been to place the composition of the text in the second half of the tenth century or even in the eleventh.[3] Mulchrone, however, took the view that the work had its origin in the period 895x901 and that a Cashel scribe made a copy in the years 927x936 from which one of the extant copies (London, British Library, MS. Egerton 93) was ultimately derived.[4] On the other hand, an interpolated version of the text has come down to us in Oxford, Bodleian Library, MS. Rawlinson B.512:[5] the date of the interpolations remains unclear. Although there seems to have been some initial resistance to Mulchrone's conclusions,[6] in the last generation her dating has held the field.

That very period has, however, seen the major work of Ludwig Bieler on the textual history of the Latin hagiography of St Patrick.[7] Doing his best to take on board the evidence provided by the Tripartite Life, Bieler accepted Mulchrone's

1 *The Tripartite Life*, ed. & transl. Stokes.

2 *Bethu Phátraic*, ed. Mulchrone. Cf. also 'Die Abfassungszeit'; 'The Tripartite Life of Patrick. Lost fragment discovered'; 'The Tripartite Life of Patrick. Fragments of Stowe copy found'.

3 *The Tripartite Life*, ed. & transl. Stokes, I.lxiii, lxxxix; Strachan, 'Contributions to the history of the deponent verb', p. 550.

4 *Bethu Phátraic*, ed. Mulchrone, p. v. The dates '927x936' derive from a reference in MS. E to one Iosep, who has been identified (tentatively by Stokes, with conviction by Mulchrone) as a tenth-century coarb of Patrick.

5 *Ibid.*, pp. vi–vii, Mulchrone described these sections of text peculiar to MS. R as 'valuable early language material', a doubly depressing statement. Given her assumptions about MS. E, it might in fact turn out that what she described as 'interpolations' in R have been omitted from the text represented by E. What is more, if her (admittedly vague) description of these passages' linguistic character is accurate, a later dating for *r* (the archetype) would place increasing strain on this aspect of her reconstructed textual history.

6 See MacNeill, *Saint Patrick*, pp. 159–220; O'Rahilly, *Early Irish History and Mythology*, pp. 409–10. (Cf. Binchy, 'Patrick and his biographers', pp. 68–9, 73–4.) A similar conclusion to O'Rahilly's was reached by Carney, 'The date and authorship of *Saltair na Rann*', who described the Tripartite Life as a compilation which he dated *ca* 870. Recently, Pádraig Ó Riain ('The shrine', p. 292) has written of 'the mid-ninth century, when materials were being collected in Munster for a new Life of St Patrick, the so-called "Tripartite Life" '.

7 His principal relevant works are: papers reprinted in his *Studies on the Life*, especially 'Bethu Phátraic'; *Four Latin Lives*, ed. Bieler; *The Patrician Texts*, edd. & transl. Bieler & Kelly.

date of origin *ca* 900.[8] This seemed to provide a fixed point in the welter of broad and uncertain datings for the various anonymous Latin *uitae*. In as much as the Tripartite Life represented the fullest written elaboration of Patrician hagiography, the development of that process could – in so far as it represented stages between what Muirchú and Tírechán had achieved shortly before A.D. 700 and the Tripartite Life itself – be constrained chronologically within the eighth and ninth centuries. This perception loomed large in Bieler's reconstructions of the textual tradition of the corpus of Patrician Lives.[9]

Suddenly, all is in flux again. In a paper published in 1982 Gearóid Mac Eoin systematically demolished the basis for Mulchrone's date, 895x901. He proposed instead that the references to Munster history contained in the Tripartite Life would allow only a *terminus post quem* of *ca* A.D. 940.[10] Meanwhile Frederic Mac Donncha had argued that Mulchrone's recognition of a copy by a Cashel scribe of the period 927x936 is a distraction, and that the Tripartite Life had taken its origin in its present shape *ca* A.D. 1100, being adapted into homiletic structure from an antecedent hagiographic form.[11] Gearóid Mac Eoin has seen much of the difficulty in dating the Tripartite Life as being a problem arising from the linguistically stratified character of the text. The Tripartite Life, he has argued, is 'usually regarded as the earliest considerable text of the Middle Irish period. Here, in the midst of language generally consistent with a date about 900, one finds a number of forms which one would not have expected before 1000. The opinions of scholars as to the date of the text have varied according as they saw the earlier or later stratum as the more significant.'[12] He himself has broadly accepted Mac Donncha's conclusion (as well as, in the preceding quotation, a view of the language as 'generally consistent with a date about 900') and has reconciled these by noting both the existence of 'some structural features which show that it was still in a state of development in the tenth century' and the general character of the Tripartite Life as 'a text in a state of growth'.[13] Ludwig Bieler had seen *r*, the ultimate common source of the extant copies of the Tripartite Life, as 'a free Irish-Latin version' of a text ancestral also to the common source of *Vita II* and *Vita IV*; that ancestor had likewise been bilingual, but predominantly Latin as against the Tripartite Life's predominantly vernacular character.[14] These views can be reconciled with one another, as Mac Eoin has pointed out.[15] The text may be seen in a continual condition of alteration in language, detailed content, and perhaps structure from at least the ninth century until whatever date can be attributed to *r*. What is more, the 'interpolations' peculiar to MS. R of the Tripartite Life may suggest that the process of accretion continued even beyond the time of *r*.

8 However, seeing in a longer Patrician perspective the specific evidence on which Mulchrone's dating was based, he regarded it as an accretion to the principal line of textual descent: 'Bethu Phátraic', pp. 260–1.

9 Cf. *The Patrician Texts*, edd. & transl. Bieler & Kelly, p. 30.

10 Mac Eoin, 'The dating', pp. 115, 127–34.

11 'Dáta Vita Tripartita'; cf. his earlier paper, 'Medieval Irish homilies'.

12 'The dating', p. 115.

13 *Ibid.*, p. 128.

14 *The Patrician Texts*, edd. & transl. Bieler & Kelly, p. 26.

15 'The dating', p. 128.

Most recently, in 1986 Kenneth Jackson, in one of his last publications, attacked the problem of dating the Tripartite Life.[16] Leaving aside the Latin evidence, and concentrating on Irish linguistic history, he concluded that the work was substantially created (using, *inter alia*, Old Irish sources) in the second half of the tenth century.[17] However, in broad agreement with Frederic Mac Donncha (though not with the latter's eventual dating),[18] he admitted 'a rather superficial re-edition . . . with the addition of the Prefaces and Perorations' in the eleventh century, and perhaps early in that century.[19] Finally, he tentatively accepted from Gearóid Mac Eoin a suggestion that *r*, the archetype of the surviving copies, should be dated to the twelfth century.[20] On the face of it, then, the dating *ca* 900 has been tested from all angles and found wanting.

Matters are unfortunately not so straightforward. In as much as, from an early stage of study, a premium has been placed on finding the date of origin of this text, the later stages of its transmission have received relatively little study. This lack was intensified by the use of criteria which were neither linguistic nor text-historical to achieve the date 895x901. The normal procedure in creating a textual history must be to reconstruct and date the proximate stage(s) of transmission. In Jackson's work we find the first attempt to set out systematically the linguistic features likely to have been peculiar to the archetype, *r*; however, he hesitated about assigning an absolute date to this stage.[21] More work on defining the latest linguistic stratum in *r* is clearly necessary.

Other approaches might also be attempted. Elsewhere I have discussed the significance of one of Patrick's petitions – that foreigners should not dominate Ireland – and noted the difficulty of deducing with certainty that the *barbari* in question were Scandinavians. I remarked that at the corresponding point the Tripartite Life spoke of *Saxain*, 'English', rather than foreigners.[22] If, for the sake of argument, I may reverse the direction of my earlier exposition, it would be a possible deduction that such a reference in *r* (if it had not been carried forward from an early mediaeval form of the petition which was more specific in its reference to foreigners than those texts which survive) would date that archetype no earlier than the last third of the twelfth century.

There is, in any case, a substantial difficulty in achieving an absolute linguistic dating for an Irish-language text of the period *ca* 900 – *ca* 1200. The elements of the problem were clearly laid out by Gearóid Mac Eoin in 1982.[23]

16 'The date of the Tripartite Life'. Jackson made no reference to Mac Eoin's paper, even though he recorded discussion with the latter.

17 *Ibid.*, p. 16. There is an apparent contradiction between this conclusion and his observation on p. 15 that, apart from Old Irish features borrowed from sources, 'Other linguistic points . . . suggest a stage of the language later than standard Old Irish but possibly earlier than [*Saltair na Rann*]. That is to say, they would belong to the first half or three quarters of the tenth century. . . . Still others . . . seem at any rate to be no later than the language of' that text. Presumably Jackson decided, in constructing his linguistic history of the Tripartite Life, to assimilate these two elements to one another. Cf. Jackson's detailed discussion, pp. 23–38.

18 For this disagreement, see Jackson, *ibid.*, pp. 9–10.

19 *Ibid.*, pp. 15–16.

20 *Ibid.*, p. 16.

21 *Ibid.*, pp. 15–16, 41–4.

22 Dumville, 'St Patrick in Cornwall?'.

23 'The dating', pp. 113–15.

Lack of satisfactory identification and detailed study of chronologically fixed points within the Middle Irish period remains the central issue. Most studies which have sought to give an absolute dating to Middle Irish texts have had to accept a framework constructed from dates given at an earlier stage of scholarship to other texts which themselves carry no overt indication of date. The element of circularity is very considerable.[24] The only effective controls have been the dates assigned to linguistic developments within Old Irish (themselves not always securely based, given inadequate attention to palaeographical and historical study of the principal manuscripts)[25] and, at the other end, the latest possible dates assignable to Irish manuscripts of the later eleventh century and the twelfth.[26] The ages assigned to the collection of homiletic texts from *Leabhar Breac*, for example, rest on logically very uncertain foundations.[27] As is clear from Kenneth Jackson's analysis of the language of the Tripartite Life, the central text for comparison has been the lengthy biblical poem, *Saltair na Rann*, to which the date 988 is attached.[28] Yet the historian looking at that text and the arguments brought forward from it must have grave doubts about the reasoning involved. Nor has the date escaped challenge from students of Irish language and literature.[29] And, finally, even if the date 988 could be established, questions would still need to be asked about the extent to which the linguistic register of a solemn verse text could be expected to be broadly comparable with that of narrative prose works.

Large questions await definition and resolution. Until much further progress has been made, Jackson's dating of the Tripartite Life must remain very uncertain. The gains of recent study are, however, that the dating to 895x901 has been demolished, that the Cashel copy of 927x936 has been brushed aside, that there is a greater willingness to accept later elements in the text, and that dating *r* to a period at least as late as the twelfth century has been contemplated. These conclusions may create havoc in the detailed study of the development of Patrician hagiography by elongating considerably its timescale: the subversion of Kathleen Mulchrone's confident attribution of *r* itself to 895x901 will have repercussions on the dating of Latin *uitae*.

24 Cf. Dumville, 'Language, literature, and law', pp. 92–3.

25 For one example, see *ibid.*, p. 93 and n. 8.

26 Principally the two manuscripts of the Irish *Liber Hymnorum* (edd. Bernard & Atkinson), *Lebor na hUidre* (edd. Best & Bergin), the 'Book of Glendalough' (*Rawlinson B.502*, facs. ed. Meyer), and the 'Book of Leinster' (edd. Best *et al.*).

27 *The Passions*, ed. & transl. Atkinson; Jackson, 'The date of the Tripartite Life', pp. 9–10, offered a date *ca* 1050, as against the dates *ca* 1100 or *ca* 1150 usually suggested in previous work.

28 For a statement of the case for that date, see Mac Eoin, 'The date and authorship' and 'Observations on Saltair na Rann'.

29 Carney, 'The dating of early Irish verse texts', pp. 184–7, 207–16, and 'The date and authorship of *Saltair na Rann*'.

ST PATRICK AND THE SCANDINAVIANS OF DUBLIN

An account of the role of St Patrick in Irish literature remains to be written. While the hagiography has received considerable – though still insufficient and patchy – attention, Patrick's much larger place and very varied functions in the literary tradition remain to be explored. In legal, onomastic, literary-historical, and poetic texts, in *fíannaigecht* and Ulster-Cycle tales, the apostle of Ireland has a part to play in the literature of the Old and Middle Irish periods.[1] There are obvious links, and yet surprising discrepancies, between Patrician hagiography and the tradition of historical record represented by the annalistic literature.[2] The development of formal hagiography of St Patrick seems to have ceased with the twelfth century but its subject-matter had long since become severely circumscribed: the elaborate account of the codifying of Irish law into the *Senchus Már* may, in the role which it assigned to Dubthach moccu Lugair,[3] stand in a relationship to Patrician hagiography,[4] but the full account was never incorporated into Lives of the apostle. Nevertheless, by *ca* 900 the annalistic literature came to record, *sub anno* 438, 'Senchus Mór do scribunn', albeit without any amplifying detail.[5] In the legal, as in the hagiographic, tradition St Benén (Benignus) plays a supporting role to Patrick – and indeed the same may be seen in the late Old Irish text *Siaburcharpat Con Chulainn*.[6]

A quasi-legal text in which Benén was given prominence is the late Middle Irish composite work, *Lebor na cert*, 'The Book of Rights'.[7] Now usually attributed to a Munster origin in the eleventh or twelfth century (the latter being more probable),[8] this work displays St Benén as reporter of the rights and obligations of the various peoples and political groupings of Ireland. As might be expected, however, not far behind the suppositious author stands St Patrick. In the poem (attributed to Benén) which follows, six of the eighteen stanzas are

1 Some of these have recently been explored by McCone, *Pagan Past*.
2 See above, pp. 79–84, for example.
3 McCone, 'Dubthach'; cf. Carey, 'The two laws'.
4 Cf. McCone, *Pagan Past*, pp. 90–101.
5 I quote from *The Annals of Ulster*, edd. & transl. Mac Airt & Mac Niocaill, I.40/1. That there is an entry of identical content but slightly variant wording found in two members of the Clonmacnoise group of chronicles ('The Annals of Roscrea', edd. Gleeson & Mac Airt, p. 145, §7; *Chronicum Scotorum*, ed. & transl. Hennessy, pp. 22/3, *s.a.* K.vi, item 2) suggests that by A.D. 911 the 'Chronicle of Ireland' contained such a notice. Given that the entry is wholly in Irish, it may not greatly antedate *ca* 900: for the evidence, cf. Dumville, 'Latin and Irish'.
6 For discussion, see McCone, *Pagan Past*, p. 200 (cf. 199–200).
7 *Lebor na cert*, ed. & transl. Dillon.
8 *Ibid.*, pp. ix–xiv; cf. Dillon, 'On the date'. For more recent comment, see Hughes, *Early Christian Ireland*, pp. 285–7, 289; Ó Corráin, *Ireland before the Normans*, p. 27; Byrne, *Irish Kings*, pp. 107, 126, 192.

put directly into the mouth of St Patrick. This text is an excellent example of how St Patrick, as a figure at once literary and authoritative, came to transcend the barriers of mere time: he is found coming to convert the vikings of Dublin, having left the unbelieving Loeguire at Tara with a curse.[9]

Benén ro chachain inso do shenchus Gall Átha Claith.	Benén sang this about the tradition of the Foreigners of Dublin.
Atá sund seanchas suairc seang is maith le fearaib Érind, sochar Átha Cliath, ní chél, amal forfhácaib Benén.	Here is a gay and graceful story, pleasing to the men of Ireland; the revenue of Dublin – I shall not conceal it – as Benén appointed it.
Dia táinic thuaid a Temraig Hua deochain in deigtheaglaig, d'apsdal Breatan ⁊ Breag nír chreit Laegairi lánmear.	When the Deacon's Grandson [viz, St Patrick] of the goodly household came to Tara in the north, vigorous Laegaire did not believe that apostle of the Britons and of Brega.
Luid deisil Banba buidi Hua deochain, in deagduine, co toracht dún na nGall ngeal do chobair Chland Mac Mílead.	That good man, the Deacon's Grandson, went sunwise around radiant Ireland until he reached the fortress of the fair Foreigners, helping the children of the sons of Míl.
Is hé ba rí a nÁth Chliath chruaid dia táinic Pádraic atuaid Ailpín mac Aeoil Ádaig do chloind Domnaill Dubdámaig.	The king of stalwart Dublin, when Patrick came south, was Ailpín son of Aeol Ádach of the descendants of Domnall Dubdámach.
In lá táinic co hÁth Cliath Pádraic Macha na mórfhiach is and ros fuc bás bágach aenmac Ailpín imnárach.	On the day when Pátraic of Macha of the great tributes came to Dublin, victorious death carried off the bashful son of Ailpín.
Adagar co Ua ndeochain aenmac ríg Gall gairg-Eochaid, dia chrád ⁊ dia chelgad; don apsdal rob imdeargad.	The son of the king of the Foreigners, uncouth Eochaid, is brought to the Deacon's Grandson to trouble and ensnare him: it was an insult to the apostle.
Dia tuca anmain andsin, a chléirig cháid chumachtaig, sléchtfad duit 'con choill cheanaind, sléchtfaid Gaill in glaisfheraind.'	'If you give him life, cleric revered and powerful, I shall bow before you at Coill Chenann, and the Foreigners of the green land will bow.'

[9] *Lebor na cert*, ed. & transl. Dillon, pp. 114–19 (§ VIII). In quoting this poem I have made some minor editorial changes and removed some infelicities from the translation. For earlier notices of its Patrician connexion, see Kenney, *The Sources*, p. 326, and Esposito, 'Notes on a Latin Life', p. 67 and n. 30 (on Probus's *Vita S. Patricii* where he detected a whiff of Glastonbury).

Luid ina deisiul fo thrí
int apsdal is int airdrí
cora érig 'na beathaid
féinnid álaind aird-Eachaid.

The apostle and the king made three circuits sunwise, and the fair warrior, Eochaid, arose alive.

Ar sin adnagat dó in slóg,
screpall cach fhir, unga d'ór,
unga cacha sróna ar sin,
is screball óir cach énfhir.

Then the host bring to him a *screpall* for each man, an ounce of gold, an ounce for each nose thus, a *screpall* of gold for each man.

Trí huingi forácbad thall
don cháin a ngarrdaib na nGall;
aircther fo thrí ind Áth Cliath
ó Gaeidelaib na nglainsciath.

Three ounces of the tax were left in the gardens of the Foreigners; Dublin is thrice plundered on account of it by the Gaedil of the bright shields.

'Dianam tora in cach bliadain
in cháin sea lib ó Liamain
nochon fhétfad fir thalman
bar ndún-si do díthfhaglad.

'If this tax is paid to me every year by you from Liamain, the men of the whole world will not be able to despoil your fortress.

In dún i táid co dreaman
nos scér-sa fri duibdeman;
bid hé in treas teine nach tim
bias fa deiread i nÉrind.

The fortress which you occupy in force I shall deliver from the black demon: it will be one of the three last surviving hearths in Ireland.

Fácbaim forsan Áth uili
buaid mban ar a mbanchuri,
buaid ara nGallaib geala,
buaid n-áilli ara n-ingena.

I bestow upon all Dublin supremacy in womanhood for their women, supremacy for their fair Foreigners, supremacy in beauty for their daughters.

Buaid snáma ar macaib a mban,
buaid cocaid is buaid comrom,
buaid dia ndaltaib co nóna,
im luad chorn is chom-óla.

Supremacy in swimming for their sons, supremacy in war and in strife, supremacy for their fosterlings till evening in sending round the drinking horns.

Buaid ríg chaidchi i nÁth Cliath chruaid
buaid n-amais, buaid n-óclaig uaig,
buaid cádusa 'na chellaib,
buaid n-árais is naímchendaig.

Supremacy for the king for ever in stalwart Dublin, supremacy for the hireling, supremacy for the perfect warrior, of reverence in its churches, supremacy for dwellings and sacred heights.

In dún asa tánac tuaid,
ná roib ara ríg robuaid;
is mór gallacht a gaili,
mo mallacht ar Laegairi.'

The fortress in the north [viz, Tara] from which I have come, may its king be without success; great is his fierceness in a fight, my curse on Laegaire.'

Is de nach bia síth na nGall
re ríg Midi na mórland
itir Theamair is Liamain
cen debaid cach énbliadain.

Therefore the Foreigners will give no peace to the king of Meath of the long blades, but there will be strife every year between Tara and Liamain.

Hé sin senchas Átha Cliath
indisim daíb tar ceand fhiach;
biaid i llebraib co bráth mbras
mar atá sund sa seanchas.

That is the tradition of Dublin, I tell it to you in return for (payment of your) debts (?); it will be in books for ever as it is here in the tradition.

The fundamental anachronism embedded in this text posed no problem for the poet or (we may be sure) his audience. For what was being offered here was a justification for a current political situation, whether achieved or merely desired. To find the clue we have only to look to the ecclesiastical history of twelfth-century Dublin.

In his edition of *Lebor na cert* Myles Dillon argued that this poem was in part dependent upon the Life of St Patrick by Jocelin of Furness, datable *ca* 1186.[10] The story (lines 1709–24) of the conversion of the fictitious Ailpín, king of Dublin, is first known in Patrician hagiography in that text.[11] However, we are by no means obliged to suppose that Jocelin was the creator of that legend – indeed his British origin renders that very unlikely – and it is worth noting that there is no other surviving Patrician *uita* certainly later than the ninth century in which such a story might be expected to be found.[12] Dillon's dating is too narrowly based and conflicts with his other arguments: it cannot stand. When the royal dynasty of Scandinavian Dublin was converted to christianity remains a deeply controversial question.[13] That event would provide an absolute *terminus post quem* for this poem.

The author of the poem is stating that St Patrick evangelised the presumed ancestors of the royal dynasty of Dublin. Patrick is therefore able to insist that he (and, by implication, his heirs) stand in a special relationship to that dynasty. We might think that that relationship was a certain fact. However, when Patrick speaks, his words are conditional: 'If this tax is paid to me every year by you . . .'. It is not difficult to envisage the situation in which this was written.

The first known bishop of Dublin belongs to the second half of the eleventh century.[14] The early bishops all eschewed a formal relationship with the churches of their Irish neighbours, looking instead to Anglo-Scandinavian (and subsequently Anglo-Norman) Canterbury as a source of consecration and therefore at least implied authority. As reform of the administrative structure of the Irish Church began – at the First Synod of Cashel (1101) and the Synods of Raith Bresail and Uisneach (1111) – Dublin initially stood aloof, secure both in

10 *Ibid.*, p. 117, n. 2.

11 *Trias Thaumaturga*, ed. Colgan, pp. 90–1 (§§69–71).

12 For Patrician hagiography after the 'Book of Armagh' see above, pp. 253–8; *Four Latin Lives*, ed. Bieler; and Bieler, *Studies on the Life*, chapters XIV–XIX; cf. Sharpe, *Medieval Irish Saints' Lives*, pp. 33–4 *et passim*.

13 For discussion see Gwynn, 'The origins of the see of Dublin'; Hughes, *The Church in Early Irish Society*, pp. 215 (delphic, but perhaps favouring the later tenth century), 255–7, and *Early Christian Ireland*, p. 261; Ó Corráin, *Ireland before the Normans*, p. 96 (ninth-century).

14 Gwynn, 'The origins of the see of Dublin'; Hughes, *The Church in Early Irish Society*, pp. 256–9.

its external relationship with Canterbury and in the access to reform-ideas which that must have brought.[15] Nevertheless, the creation of a diocesan and provincial system for the Irish Church caused the archbishop of Armagh to look askance at any imagined infringement of his jurisdiction. The anomalous constitutional position of the church of the kingdom of Dublin became a focus of attention for the clergy of Armagh. On the death of Samuel, bishop of Dublin, in 1121 an event occurred which is recorded thus in the 'Annals of Ulster'.[16]

Samuel H. Angli espoc Átha Cliath in pace quieuit. Ceallach comarba Pátraic do ghabáil epscopoiti Átha Cliath a togha Gall ocus Gaeidhel.

Samuel ua hAngli, bishop of Dublin, rested in peace. Cellach, coarb of Patrick, took the bishopric by the choice of foreigners and Irish.

The closing phrase suggests special pleading. We know from a letter of the clergy and people of Dublin to Ralph, archbishop of Canterbury (1114–22), that they felt threatened by the church of Armagh:[17] 'the bishops of Ireland have great jealousy towards us, and especially that bishop who dwells at Armagh, because we do not wish to be obedient to their ordination, but wish to be always under your rule'. How long the relationship described in the annal for 1121 lasted is not known.[18] By the time of the synod, that of Kells-Mellifont, which in 1152 decided the administrative structure of the Irish Church, the problem had been resolved by allowing Dublin its own archbishop but under the primacy of the archbishop of Armagh.

The outer limits of date for the poem are the christianisation of the royal dynasty of Dublin (or at any rate the establishment of a bishopric in that city) and the final resolution of Dublin's position vis-à-vis Armagh and therefore St Patrick in 1152. In practice, it must have been Church-reform which determined the origin of the dispute between them:[19] the date-range should accordingly be

[15] *Ibid.*, pp. 257–62; Gibson, *Lanfranc of Bec*, pp. 121–6; for Lanfranc's correspondence concerning Ireland, see *The Letters*, edd. & transl. Clover & Gibson, pp. 49–57 (no. 4), 64–7 (no. 8), 66–9 (no. 9), 70–3 (no. 10), 154–62 (no. 49); cf. pp. 184 and 186–7 for an *epistola uagans* and episcopal professions (texts ed. Richter, *Canterbury Professions*, nos 36 and 42).

[16] *The Annals of Ulster*, edd. & transl. Mac Airt & Mac Niocaill, I.566/7 (quoted with minor editorial changes and deliberate alteration of the translation of *do ghabáil*. For commentary on the course of events, see Gwynn, *The Twelfth-century Reform*, pp. 35, 40; Hughes, *The Church in Early Irish Society*, pp. 268–9.

[17] For the text see Ussher, *The Whole Works*, IV.532–3; cf. Hughes, *The Church in Early Irish Society*, pp. 268–9. It survives in London, British Library, MS. Cotton Claudius E.v, fo 255v.

[18] Gwynn, *The Twelfth-century Reform*, p. 54 (and cf. p. 35), suggested that by 1129 Gregory, bishop of Dublin, had accepted the authority of Armagh. But that seems to me to be wishful thinking based on naïve acceptance of the wording of the 'Annals of Ulster', whose entries were still being written at the church of Armagh. For discussion of the events of 1152, see *ibid.*, pp. 53–63.

[19] Many jurisdictional and other disputes were touched off by the process of establishment of territorially defined sees with fixed diocesan seats: for discussion, see Sheehy, *When the Normans came*, pp. 65–8; cf. Sharpe, 'Some problems', pp. 265–70.

narrowed to 1101x1152. And one might suggest that until the reforming Bishop Cellach had taken office at Armagh, the affairs of Dublin would not have been of particular interest: on such an argument the termini for our poem's composition might be narrowed slightly to 1105x1152.[20]

[20] It is a curious fact that Cellach's predecessor was taken critically ill at Dublin: *The Annals of Ulster*, edd. & transl. Mac Airt & Mac Niocaill, I.544/5 (*s.a.* 1105.3). For another poem thought to have emerged from the context of Anglo-Irish reforming contacts, see Ó Cuív, 'St Gregory and St Dunstan'.

WILLIAM OF MALMESBURY'S *VITA S. PATRICII* AND HIS SOURCE: TWO LOST LIVES OF ST PATRICK?

In his *Collectanea* John Leland devoted two pages to extracts from (and comments on) a Life of St Patrick in two books, yet still not complete, which was written by William of Malmesbury for the monks of Glastonbury.[1] William was one of the most learned and prolific English authors (and scribes) of the first half of the twelfth century.[2] The copy from which Leland made his extracts he had found at the house of Augustinian canons at Christchurch, Twinham (Hampshire);[3] but he had seen two others at Glastonbury Abbey.[4] All of them shared the peculiarity of ending with a statement that 'Nunc ad eius in patriam gratiosum reditum et ad celum gloriosum transitum dirigam mentem et stilum'. No manuscript of this Life is known to survive: we are left to wonder, with Leland, whether the author left the work unfinished or whether the copies which he had met all descended from a mutilated ancestor.

In the thirteenth century a text *De antiquitate Glastonie ecclesie* passed under the name of William of Malmesbury.[5] The surviving work is not, as it stands, what William wrote. An aim of the last century's scholarship has been to define what remnant of William's writing remains amid the interpolations and recension, but it cannot be said that progress has been considerable.[6] Opening the work, however, is a preface directed to Henry of Blois, bishop of Winchester (1129–1171) and abbot of Glastonbury (from 1126).[7] Although some doubts have been expressed about the fidelity of the extant preface to what William wrote, there has been among scholars a generally favourable impression of its authenticity.[8] In it the author tells us that he had already written a Life of St Patrick. William's *De antiquitate* had been composed by 1135, for at that time

1 Oxford, Bodleian Library, MS. Top. gen. c.2 (*S.C.* 3118), pp. 236–7. *Joannis Lelandi antiquarii De rebus britannicis collectanea*, ed. Hearne, III.273–6.

2 For an introduction to William as reader and writer, see Thomson, *William of Malmesbury*; cf. also Gransden, *Historical Writing*, I.166–85.

3 This item needs to be added to the entry for Christchurch (Twinham) given by Ker, *Medieval Libraries*, p. 51.

4 *Collectanea*, ed. Hearne, III.275–6.

5 *The Early History*, ed. & transl. Scott. The oldest manuscript (from whose text the other survivors seem to descend) is Cambridge, Trinity College, MS. R.5.33 (724), written at Glastonbury in 1247. Cf. Crick, 'The marshalling of antiquity'.

6 Newell, 'William of Malmesbury on the antiquity'; Robinson, *Somerset*, pp. 1–25 (cf. 26–53); Slover, 'William of Malmesbury and the Irish'; Faral, *La Légende arthurienne*, II.402–60; Gransden, 'The growth'; *The Early History*, ed. & transl. Scott, especially pp. 27–33, 180–2.

7 *Ibid.*, pp. 40–3.

8 Newell, 'William of Malmesbury on the antiquity', pp. 460, 466, for objections; cf. Robinson, *Somerset*, p. 4; *The Early History*, ed. & transl. Scott, pp. 185–6.

he incorporated excerpts of it in the second edition of his massive *Gesta regum Anglorum*.[9] We do not know, however, whether William ever revised the *De antiquitate*.[10] Before (1129x)1135, therefore, William may have composed his Life of St Patrick. What was it like?

I reproduce here the extracts which John Leland made from the Twinham copy, accompanied by the annotations which he attached to these excerpts. We are fortunate in having Leland's autograph, now Oxford, Bodleian Library, MS. Top. gen. c.2 (*S.C.* 3118), pp. 236–237. The text was first published in the eighteenth century by Thomas Hearne and was reproduced from his edition by Clark Slover in a discussion of William's Life of St Patrick.[11]

Ludwig Bieler agreed with Slover that William's *Vita S. Patricii* was based on the *Vita tertia*, and (further) that it was based on a Π-text, comparable with that now known from the thirteenth-century Ramsey manuscript (MS. O), a member of the sub-group containing an interpolation equating Dún Lethglaisse (Downpatrick) with Glastonbury.[12] However, these scholars displayed further information which greatly complicates the picture. William knew the contents of *Vita tertia*, §§1–11, which are found only in the Γ-text where they have been borrowed from a manuscript of *Vita secunda* or *Vita quarta*. Bieler concluded that 'A Life of Patrick of the *W*-type could easily have been at William's disposal in Glastonbury'.[13] This is easier to say than to demonstrate. Although these two *uitae* circulated in northern France and Belgium in areas with good contacts with England, knowledge of the text in England has not been shown.[14]

A further complication noted by Bieler is that William had access to details about Patrick's early life; he tracked these to Muirchú, I.1.[15] However, as Rodney Thomson has noted,[16] Patrick's *Confessio* supplies the necessary information – and Leland observed that William made great use of that text.[17] He could have seen it at either Salisbury or Worcester in manuscripts of the 'Cotton-Corpus Legendary'.[18]

9 The first edition was published in 1125: for the recensions see *Willelmi Malmesbiriensis monachi De gestis regum*, ed. Stubbs, I, introduction.

10 If he did, the surviving preface may have descended from a second edition (for which William's own death, *ca* 1143, would be the only *terminus ante quem*) rather than from the original.

11 Slover, 'William of Malmesbury's *Life of St. Patrick*', pp. 10–19, where Leland's excerpts may be found in parallel with the corresponding passages from the g-text of *Vita tertia*.

12 *Four Latin Lives*, ed. Bieler, pp. 22–5. (Cf. above, pp. 236–7.)

13 *Ibid.*, p. 24. *W* is the siglum given by Bury (followed by Bieler) to the conjectured common source of *Vita secunda* and *Vita quarta*.

14 *Ibid.*, pp. 1–13, on the circulation of these *uitae*.

15 *Ibid.*, p. 24. He seemed there to forget what he had known in 1949 (*The Life*, pp. 121–2), that William also had access to Patrick's *Confessio*.

16 *William of Malmesbury*, p. 70.

17 *Collectanea*, ed. Hearne, III.273, 274.

18 On the legendary, see Zettel, 'Saints' Lives in Old English'; cf. Dumville, *Liturgy*, pp. 139–41. The principal Salisbury copy is now Salisbury, Cathedral Library, MSS. 221 + 222 (*saec.* xi^{2}). There is also one in Salisbury, Cathedral Library, MS. 223 which is later than MSS. 221 + 222 but perhaps early enough for William to have been able to see. (Until 1985 the Salisbury manuscripts were in the Fell collection in the Bodleian Library, Oxford.) For the Worcester manuscript see Cambridge, Corpus Christi College, MS. 9 + London, British Library, MS. Cotton Nero E.i.

Whether it is economical to suppose that William used at least two different *uitae* (including one not known to have circulated in England) is a nice question. We may prefer to think that a text not yet discovered, representing another descent from the stem of Patrician hagiographical transmission, would be a more credible source. For the time being the question must remain open.

In the following edition, Leland's comments are at the head and foot of the text, and in the left-hand column, as in the manuscript.

<p. 236>

Hunc librum inueni apud canonicos Christicolas de Twinham, siue Medimnenses, in prouincia Auoniæ littoralis.

Ex `primo´ libro Gulielmi Meldunensis, quem de uita S. Patr[itii] ad monachos Glessoburgenses scripsit.

alias Lupida.

Patricius cog: Succet.

<§1> Auus eius Potitus presbyter, pater Calpurnius diaconus Romanorum morem, qui tunc temporis in Britannia potentes erant, in uocabulorum decore tenuere. Mater porro Conches, filia Ocmis, et soror Liupida[19] barbariem Britan: sonant. Nec minus ipse,[20] Succet cog: a patrię appellationis more degenerare `potuit´. Natus haud procul a mari, per quod in Hiberniam transmittitur. Locus exortus Banauen uicus in Taberniæ campo, ex metatione tabernaculorum Romanorum, ut constans, nec a uero dissimilis, fama est, tale nomen sortito. **<§2>** Ostenditur lapis puerperii conscius, in quo connixa mater sobolem effudit in lucem. Magna in diem modernum accolarum circa lapidem frequentia.

<§3> Iam uero in sortem Christi regenerandus puerulus exhibitus est uiro sancto, cui Gornias nomen.

De basilica loquens fabricata eo loco, ubi baptizatus erat S. Patritius.

Fons miraculo ortus, in quo Patritius baptizatus fuit.

Aiunt, qui uiderunt, ad altaris partem dexteram fontem esse quadratum, in crucis modum uitreis undis perlucidum, cuius haustu nihil iucundius intuitu, nihil purius.

Banauen uicus, alias Nenchor dict*us*.

<§4> In Banaue*n* igitur uico, qui et Nenchor,[21] educatus sanctiss: ut par erat, disciplina, et in

19 Leland interlined *-ui-* above the *-iu-* of this word and underlined *iu* for deletion.
20 *Patrit.* is interlined above *ipse*.
21 *Nantchor* (*-ant-* ?over erasure) is interlined above *Nenchor*.

ephębum, ęuo crescente, prouectus, religioni parentum non defuit.

Gul: Meld: frequenter citat librum Patritii de confessione, in quo[22] res a se gestas, et uitam suam scripsit.

Assistit ipse sermoni meo astipulator idoneus his uerbis in confessione sua.

<§5> Habebat sororem, ut ante dixi, Lupidam, uenerabilium posthæc meritorum fęminam, cuius nunc reliquiæ \`pausant´ in Ardmacha, urbe[23] Hiber: pręcipua.

Patritius a Scottis Hiberniensibus, qui littus Britannię a Circio infestabant, captus.

<§6> Cum enim Hiberniensium classis, prædę allecta facilitate, Britanniam, more suo, adnauigasset, inter cęteros captiuos et Patritium, iam .xvi^{m}. annorum adolescentulum, abduxit.

Ipse certe in confessione caussam[24] captiuitatis adscribit peccatis populi et suis.

<§7> Latrunculorum ergo pręda factus Patritius ueniit in seruum, trans aquilonares remotioris Hiberniæ partes distractus. Comparauit regioni[s] illius \`regulus´ Milcu, filius Boin, pro paucorum nummorum commercio ingenuo potitus, et superbus spolio. Denique, ut splendorem natalium eius obfuscaret, subuicum instituit.

alias Miluc.

<§8> Ut inuento thezauro Patritius se a seruitute redemerit.

Patritius manumissus.

Ille,[25] metalli fulgore perstrictus oculos, simul et pondere captus, se exorabilem prębuit, et adolescentem manumissum seruituti emancipauit.

Patritii reditus in Britan:

<§9> Felicibus ergo uentis in altum prouecti, post triduum continentem attingebant, etc. De erroribus Patritii per deserta loca.

Octauo ergo \`et´ .xx$^{o}$. postquam appulerat \`die´ post errores multiuagos, quos deuius secutus inciderat, Patritius terram habitalem uidit. **<§10>** Sed nec longum uisu letatus est, paulo post iterum a pręদonibus interceptus, et abductus.

Sexagesimus postea dies uidit Patritium ab omni captiuitatis [in]iuria exemptum.

<§11> Ita mag: laboribus perfunctus, tandem in patriam, tandem in domum paternam receptui cecinit.

22 Leland originally wrote *quo uidetur* but then crossed the verb through, for deletion.
23 *-e* altered from *-i*.
24 Leland originally wrote this word twice; the second was then crossed out.
25 *.s. Miluc* is interlined above *ille*.

Patritius sancti Germani discipulus.

<§12> Cuius disciplinatui duobus de uiginti annis non segniter insudans[26] scripturarum diuinarum lectione quicquid deerat plenitudi[ne][27] scientię.

Patritius, Segetio comitatus, Romam petit.

<§13> Missus cum eo ab episcopo[28] Segetius presbyter spetiosiorem fecit com[. .][29]

<§14> Inuenit gratiam in conspectu domini papæ. Is erat Cęlestinus [anno] incarnat: .ccccxxiiº. papatum ingressus. Ab eo Patritius Hiberniam [in o]pus [euan]gelii missus, datus est illis gentibus doctor et apostolus. **<p. 237>**

<§15> Idem sane Cęlestinus paulo ante Palladium quendam Hiberniam ad prędicandum miserat; ut uero autor est Beda anno domini .ccccxxxº. etc. ut Palladius, pertęsus barbariei, reuersus sit in Britanniam, ubi mortuus est.

Unde colligitur, Patritium eodem anno, quo Palladium, uel certe sequenti, Hiberniam missum, quia non ultra nouem annos Cęlestinus protendit pontificatum.

Et hęc Gul: Meld: ex libro Confessionis Patritii decerpsit.

Patritius in uinculis.

Nec non et pręmia dabam regibus[30] et filiis eorum, qui, propter securitatem meam, mecum ambulabant. Sed tamen ipsi me auidissime uolebant interficere, et quicquid inuenerunt nobiscum rapuerunt, et me ferro uinxerunt. Quartodecimo autem die absoluit me dominus de potestate eorum.

Ex .2º. libro de uita Patritii.

<§16> De puero Hu*n*na nomine, in Temoria, regione Hibernię in qua regnum erat Loegarii, qui nullo modo a Patritio abesse uoluit.

Hic est Benignus, qui sepultus est Glessoburgi.

Eum et dignatus est lecto, et insigniuit Benigni uocabulo. Iussit ergo baptizatum in currum suum leuari, pronuntians illum futurum hęredem regni sui.

<§17> Unus erat id temporis ex Britannorum regibus, dubium an adhuc paganus, certe ferocitate deterrimus, nomine Cereticus. Is ani`m´um sancti multis conficiebat angoribus hac, quę sequitur, caussa. Crebris enim, ut supra dixi, con-

26 *insudans Patricius*, Slover ('William of Malmesbury's *Life of St. Patrick*', p. 15); but there is no space for the second word.

27 *plenitudine adiecit*, Slover (*ibid.*); but again there is no space for the second word.

28 *Germano* is interlined above *episcopo*.

29 Only *-n-* of the *-m* is now visible; there is space for two letters, following this.

30 *sup. Hibernię* is interlined above *regibus*.

flictibus Britanni et Scotti summa ui utrinque decertabant, et, ut sunt incerta bellorum, modo illis, modo his uincentibus, prędæ insignes agebatur.[31] Hinc fiebat, ut Hibern: captiui, qui cecidissent in sortem Ceretici, miseris excruciati modis, anticiparent mortem suppliciis. Hanc cum in omnes exerceret[32] carnificinam, tum maxime in eos, quos Patritius baptizasset, totam fatigabat sęuitiam, sępius infrendens, quod homo Britannus Britannorum inimicis prędicaret uerba salutis etc. Ut Patritius Cereticum tantæ crudelitatis admonuerit.

<§18> De Maguilio quodam potenti homine Hiberniæ, ad fidem conuerso prædicatione et miraculis Patritii.

Maguilius autem, inuolucris mundi expeditus, ad mare contendit. Ibi, ut iussum erat, naui conscensa, regente obedientia, cui parebat, felicibus auris in Meuaniam insulam euectus, duos episcopos, assidentes littori, miraculo sui perculit.

<§19> Qui[33] mirati simul et miserati hominem, marinis iactatum periculis, simul et compeditum, de profundo leuatum asciscunt, mense participant hospitio, ubi et eorum charitate confotus, et dei gratia adiutus, ita in bonum breui conualuit, ut non solum diuinitus expeditus,[34] sed et episcopus factus, religiosam sui memoriam usque hodie insulanis reliquerit.

<§20> Rex Britonum Munessam nomine, filiam unicam, cui ętatis maturitas, et spetiositas formæ suffragabatur, nuptum dare uolebat, etc. Ut illa nullis minis adduci potuerit ad nuptias, quamuis adhuc pagana, utque parentes Patricium de hac re consuluerint, qui statim puellam baptizauit. Quo facto, paulo post obiit uirgo.

<§21> De talibus quippe [signis et miraculis] sexaginta sex libros compegit antiquitas, sicut ea exercebat per singulas regiones.

Finis .2ⁱ. libri.

Nunc ad eius in patriam gratiosum reditum, et ad cęlum gloriosum transitum, dirigam mentem et stilum.

31 Altered from *agebātúr*.
32 Written twice; the first example was crossed out.
33 *.s. episcopi* is interlined above *Qui*.
34 *s. a compedibus* is interlined above *expeditus*.

Lelandus.

Pollicetur hic Gulielmus scripturum se `de´ reditu Patritii in Britanniam. Sed hactenus in nullo exemplari `de´ reditu scriptum aliquid uidi, nescio an quod ille opus forsan imperfectum reliquerit, an quod codices, in quos incidi, mutili[35] fuerint, quorum duos Glessoburgi `in´ueni,[36] ubi Patritium[37] pręd̨icant monachi sepultum esse, reclamante hoc disticho, ex Bede (nisi fallor) epigrammatibus desumpto:

Calpurnius genuit istum, alma Britannia misit,
Gallia nutriuit, tenet artus Scottia felix.

[35] Altered from *mutuli*.

[36] *-ueni* over erasure?

[37] *esse* originally followed here, but was crossed through for deletion.

THE ARMAGH LIST OF 'COARBS OF ST PATRICK'

In 1919 H. J. Lawlor and R. I. Best published from four manuscripts of twelfth- to fifteenth-century date a list of the coarbs – viz, heirs (in effect, successors) – of St Patrick.[1] Their combined evidence produced some sixty-two names, of whom the latest belonged to twelfth-century clerics. The form of the list was in general very simple – a name, followed by a number indicating the years of rule. In one manuscript fairly consistently, and in the others sporadically, the numeral is followed by notes which give (largely in Irish) details of the ancestry of each coarb. There is no indication that the list is other than a product of the church of Armagh.

The manuscript witnesses are as follows.

B Dublin, Royal Irish Academy, MS. 23.P.16 (1230), known as 'Leabhar Breac',[2] *saec.* xv *in.*

L Dublin, Trinity College, MS. 1339 (H.2.18), the 'Book of Leinster',[3] *saec.* xii *med.*

O Oxford, Bodleian Library, MS. Laud misc. 610 (*S.C.* 1132),[4] *saec.* xv *med.*

Y Dublin, Trinity College, MS. 1318 (H.2.16), the so-called 'Yellow Book of Lecan',[5] a composite codex of which the relevant section belongs to *saec.* xiv *ex.*

These four copies represent two distinct lines of transmission – in effect, two recensions – which display many variations one from the other, particularly in respect of the numerals. BOY represent one group, L the other.[6] The last coarb named in L is Tommaltach Ua Conchobair (1181–4; *ob.* 1201); of the other witnesses, B ends with Domnall (1091–1105),[7] O with Mael Muire (1001–20), and Y with Gilla Meic Liac (1137–74). However, the last coarb to be provided with a reign-length in LY (the only witnesses still continuing to give evidence) is

1 'The ancient list'.

2 See *Leabhar Breac*, ed. Ferguson, p. 220. Cf. Ó Concheanainn, 'The scribe of the Leabhar Breac'. The text was printed separately in *The Tripartite Life*, ed. & transl. Stokes, II.546–9.

3 *The Book of Leinster*, edd. Best *et al.*, I.199–201.

4 For the text see 'The Laud synchronisms', ed. Meyer, pp. 478–9, 481–2; for description of the manuscript see Dillon, 'Laud misc. 610', and Dumville, 'The textual history of "Lebor Bretnach" ', pp. 263–4.

5 See *The Yellow Book of Lecan*, facs. ed. Atkinson, p. 327c4–50 (MS., col. 338). For cols 281–344, written in A.D. 1398/9, see Ó Concheanainn, 'The scribe of the Leabhar Breac', p. 67.

6 Lawlor & Best, 'The ancient list', p. 317, with stemma.

7 If that is what is to be deduced from the apparatus *ibid.*, p. 330, n. 1. That it is is shown in *The Tripartite Life*, ed. & transl. Stokes, II.548.

Domnall.[8] There is accordingly some presumption that the common ancestor of all the witnesses, given the overall relationship already stated, dated from the *comarbus* of Domnall's successor, Cellach (1105/6–29); his name appears to be the last in the original hand in MS. L.[9]

Unless elements of contemporaneity and a long line of transmission can be demonstrated, it is in principle unlikely that a twelfth-century list would contain material of historical value about the earliest era of Armagh history. The first head of the church of Armagh who is visible from sources external to that institution is Tomméne, found in correspondence with the papacy in 640;[10] according to the 'Annals of Ulster', Tomméne, bishop of Armagh, died in 661,[11] his predecessor being Mac Laisre who died in 623.[12]

The Irish chronicles, and particularly the 'Annals of Ulster', have provided the principal comparandum for the reign-lengths offered in this coarbial list.[13] There are two difficulties of procedure, however. It is a well recognised aspect of form-criticism that succession-lists and chronicles may be interdependent:[14] annals may be created from a succession-list, while such a list may be made by extracting the relevant matter from a chronicle; the direction of dependence is not necessarily clear in any given instance. Secondly, for a lengthy period before the deduced date of the archetypal list, the church of Armagh seems to have been the principal centre of record for the contemporary annals which underlie the fifteenth-century chronicle known as the 'Annals of Ulster'.[15] It is therefore far from certain that these two forms of record are, or could be, independent of one another. They may agree in truth, but their agreement in error because of a direct dependence of one upon the other for a part or parts of the record is a possibility by no means to be overlooked.

It was the opinion of Lawlor and Best that a first section of the list, down to Fer da Chrích (758–68), stood in the closest relationship to the 'Annals of Ulster'.[16] Thereafter it offers evidence for conflict among more than one source.[17] After Fer da Chrích there are relatively few discrepancies between the witnesses in respect of the numerals, whereas it is very striking that up to that point very considerable divergences are to be noted. What is more, the reign-lengths offered by L, the twelfth-century witness, are often considerably out of

8 Lawlor & Best ('The ancient list', pp. 354–5) took O's stopping-point to be significant for dating.

9 *Ibid.*, p. 358.

10 Bede, *Historia ecclesiastica gentis Anglorum*, II.19 (ed. Plummer, I.122–4; cf. II.112–14). Cf. most recently Ó Cróinín, ' "New heresy for old" '.

11 His death is also recorded in chronicles of the Clonmacnoise group and was therefore noticed in the common source of all these texts, the 'Chronicle of Ireland'. The date in the 'Annals of Inisfallen' (ed. & transl. Mac Airt, p. 94) has been computed as 660.

12 In the 'Annals of Inisfallen' the date has been computed as 624 (*ibid.*, p. 86), thus giving Tomméne two years' fewer rule. Neither the thirty-six years implied by that source nor the thirty-eight of the 'Annals of Ulster' agrees with figures transmitted by copies of the coarbial list (cf. 'The ancient list', edd. Lawlor & Best, p. 320 and n. 9).

13 Cf. *ibid.*, pp. 318–32.

14 Cf. Dumville, 'Kingship, genealogies', pp. 96–102 (especially 101–2), for discussion.

15 Cf. Hughes, *Early Christian Ireland*, pp. 129–35.

16 'The ancient list', pp. 336, 338–40.

17 *Ibid.*, pp. 333–4, 340–55.

step with the annalistic evidence and were frequently rejected by the editors of the list. The total number of years recorded by L for the period from the first coarb in the list (Sechnall) to Fer da Chrích is 353, which would return us to A.D. 415 as the date of the succession to St Patrick; if we suppress the first letter of L's incredible reign-length (.lxxxiii.) for Tomméne, we are returned to 465 and the implication of acceptance of an early death-date for St Patrick.[18] Such a calculation is well out of step with the chronicle-texts, however, for the coarbs' dates do not then come approximately into line with the annalistic ones until the end of the sixth century. The figures provided by BOY keep broadly in step with the 'Annals of Ulster', as we shall see.

In the part of the list referring to the early mediaeval centuries, there is one fundamental discrepancy with the chronicle-evidence: this divergence may provide us with very important evidence. All copies of the list contain a coarb named Fiachra who would seem to be being attributed to the middle years of the sixth century.[19] (The 'Annals from the Book of Leinster', which appear to stand in some relationship to the coarbial list, record his obit in that period, and stand alone among Irish chronicles in naming him as a ruler of the church of Armagh.[20]) Unlike L, BOY fail to give him (or his predecessor Duach) a reign-length, a unique collective treatment of any figure in this part of the list.[21] We can take the death-dates of the surrounding coarbs, as presented by the 'Annals of Ulster' (Du[bth]ach in 548, Feidilmid in 578), together with the reign-length for Feidilmid presented by BOY (twenty years), to give a notional death-date for Fiachra, consistent with the annalistic evidence, of A.D. 558. But it is hard to have confidence in Fiachra's historicity. What is more, it is difficult to overlook the repetitions of names among the coarbs assigned to the earlier sixth century: Dubthach, Ailill, Ailill, Du[bth]ach.[22] One is bound to suspect that Feidilmid (*ob.* 578, according to the 'Annals of Ulster') stands at the horizon of historical record. That before his time lies the mid-century plague-era and the disruption which it is thought to have caused,[23] as well as the possible origins of contemporaneity of record in the 'Chronicle of Ireland' *ca* 550,[24] gives further colour to such a deduction.

18 Or to A.D. 460 if we allow the apparently historical thirty-eight years indicated by the 'Annals of Ulster' (cf. n. 12, above). The fifty-eight years assigned to St Patrick by the L-text of the list might then seem to have to be counted from A.D. 403/4 as proposed by Bury, *The Life*, pp. 383–4 (cf. Lawlor & Best, 'The ancient list', pp. 338–9), notwithstanding the possibility of a calculation 432 + 58 = 490 as noted by Carney (*Studies*, p. 394): but which did the writer of list L really intend?

19 'The ancient list', edd. Lawlor & Best, p. 320 (cf. p. 337), no. 12.

20 For this chronicle, otherwise *Do fhlaithesaib ocus amseraib Hérend iar creitim*, see *The Book of Leinster*, edd. Best *et al.*, I.94–9; for an older edition, with facing translation, see *The Tripartite Life*, ed. & transl. Stokes, II.512–29. There are later copies in the 'Book of Ballymote' and 'Book of Lecan'. In terms of the chronology of the 'Annals of Ulster', the surrounding events are datable 550 and 561.

21 List B has *.xx.* for Fiachra, but (as shown by Lawlor & Best, 'The ancient list', p. 320 and n. 1) the figure pertains to his successor, Feidilmid.

22 He is *Duach* in the coarbial list, *Dubtach* in the 'Annals of Ulster' 548.1.

23 Cf. Hughes, *The Church in Early Irish Society*, pp. 65–7, and Mac Niocaill, *Ireland before the Vikings*, pp. 101–6, for some discussion.

24 Cf. Smyth, 'The earliest Irish annals'.

James Carney studied the section of the list referring to the fifth century.[25] His treatment is at once important and problematic. Following T. F. O'Rahilly who thought that 'we may infer with probability that before the end of the seventh century the Armagh community had drawn up a list of their bishops',[26] Carney proposed to restore the list 'to the form in which it existed before being corrupted by the "diverse opinions" which were held concerning Patrick in the seventh and subsequent centuries'; he continued by expressing the opinion that 'Unless this can be done the list at this point is virtually useless for any historical purpose'.[27]

The lost 'Chronicle of Ireland', whose condition in the year 911 can be partially reconstructed,[28] described Iarlaithe as the third ruler of Armagh.[29] (Developing this position, the author of the 'Annals of the Book of Leinster' referred to Benignus, his predecessor in the list, as the second bishop.[30]) On the evidence provided by the list, Benén (Benignus) would thus be the second, and Sen-Phátric (Senex Patricius) the first. If we were to allow that Senex Patricius was merely a doublet of the historical St Patrick, the British apostle would thus be presented to us as the first bishop of Armagh (though hardly as a successor of himself, as being the first coarb would imply!). On the other hand, if Sen-Phátric were seen as a manifestation of Bishop Palladius, then Pope Celestine's agent would enjoy this distinction. But this is to deal with shadows. While there is no doubt that the 'Chronicle of Ireland' at the beginning of the tenth century contained an obit for Benén, there is no indication that he was named in that text as (arch)bishop (or abbot) of Armagh.[31] Sen-Phátric seems to have belonged, among Irish chronicles, to the Clonmacnoise group,[32] his occurrence in the 'Annals of Ulster' probably representing a first phase of borrowing from such a text.[33] If Sen-Phátric be deemed a late accretion to the coarbs of Patrick, Sechnall (Secundinus) must then be reckoned the first: again, there is no doubt that his death was recorded in the 'Chronicle of Ireland'; in the 'Annals of Ulster' this is placed at A.D. 447.[34]

The evidence of the witnesses to the list seems to suggest the following for the first ten coarbs. The dates given are the obits in the 'Annals of Ulster'.[35]

25 *Studies*, pp. 394–402.

26 *The Two Patricks*, pp. 64–7 (at p. 65, n. 41).

27 *Studies*, p. 394.

28 For discussion see Grabowski & Dumville, *Chronicles and Annals*, chapters I–II.

29 He is called 'bishop' by the 'Annals of Ulster', 'abbot' by the 'Annals of Inisfallen'.

30 In this text neither Benén nor Iarlaithe is given a named see: *The Book of Leinster*, edd. Best *et al.*, I.94, lines 3006–7.

31 His obit is given both in the 'Annals of Ulster' and in Clonmacnoise-group texts.

32 He is found in *Chronicum Scotorum* (ed. & transl. Hennessy) and the 'Annals of Roscrea' (edd. Gleeson & Mac Airt) at A.D. 457, with a reference to Glastonbury attached: on the latter connexion see Lesley Abrams, above, pp. 233–42. One is also bound to wonder whether the entry in the 'Annals of Inisfallen' [496] (ed. & transl. Mac Airt, p. 64), giving the date also as A.P. 432 (= A.D. 459 or 464) is further evidence for the presence of Sen-Phátric or an early death-date in this group of chronicles.

33 The entries at 457 and 461 are both attributed to *alii*.

34 In the 'Annals of Inisfallen' the editorially calculated date is 448 (*ibid.*, p. 58).

35 I draw these from *The Annals of Ulster*, edd. & transl. Mac Airt & Mac Niocaill.

Sechnall	.xiii.	(.vi. O)	447 (Secundinus *sanctus*)
Sen-Phátric	.x.	(.ii. L)	457 (*alii*) (cf. 461 [*alii*]) (Senex Patricius)
Benén	.x.		467, bishop (Benignus)
Iarlaithe	.xiiii.	(.xviii. O)	481, *tertius episcopus Ard Machai*
Cormac	.xv.	(.xii. L)	497, *heres Patrici*
Dubthach	.xvi.	(.xxiii. B; .xiii. L; .xiiii. Y)	513, bishop of Armagh (*espoc Aird Machai*)
Ailill	.xiii.		526, bishop of Armagh (*espoc Ard Macha*)
Ailill	.x.		536, bishop of Armagh
Duach	.xii.	(L only)	548, abbot of Armagh (Dubtach)
Fiachra	.x.	(L only)	–

It is striking that if Secundinus was reckoned as successor of Patrick and founder of Armagh he was nonetheless placed before any known death-date for St Patrick and before any alleged date for the foundation of Armagh.[36] The notice of Cormac's death in the 'Annals of Ulster' follows by four years that of Patrick's, and this may be why he – alone of this group – is given the title *heres Patrici*, perhaps in this instance therefore meaning 'the immediate heir' of the saint.[37] Likewise in the hagiography, as O'Rahilly pointed out,[38] Benignus was referred to by Muirchú and Tírechán as Patrick's *heres* and *successor*;[39] and, in the annalistic texts, his is the first of these names to occur after Patrick's early death-date.

What is clear about the twelfth-century list of coarbs is that, as it stands, it implies a fifth-century situation whose historicity is unimaginable: Patrick had successors already before the middle of the fifth century. The only doctrine which would allow Sechnall to be first ruler of Armagh would be if Patrick was not the founding bishop of that church. While we can accept such a deduction with equanimity,[40] the same cannot be said for the mediaeval clergy of Armagh. Sechnall could be heir to Patrick at Armagh but only if that founder had relinquished his rule there to a successor while he enjoyed a pan-Irish archiepiscopate: however, this situation was not envisaged by the authors of mediaeval *Patriciana*, for whom Patrick was the source of Armagh's authority.

Unless we are to suppose that the list of coarbs offers us a historiographic statement dating from a period before the seventh-century development of Patrick's association with Armagh,[41] then we must allow (with O'Rahilly) that the names of Sechnall and Sen-Phátric were added 'to increase the prestige of

36 'Annals of Ulster' 444; 'Annals of the Four Masters' 457 (*Annala Rioghachta Eireann*, ed. & transl. O'Donovan, I.142/3). Cf. O'Rahilly, *The Two Patricks*, pp. 64–5, for discussion.

37 Cf. O'Rahilly, *ibid.*, p. 67, who quoted a chronological tract from *Leabhar Breac* (cf. n. 2, above), facs. p. 220a (the same page as the list of coarbs), to the effect that Patrick died in A.D. 493, 'in the nineteenth year of the abbacy of Cormac, coarb of Patrick, and he is the first abbot who went into Patrick's chair'.

38 O'Rahilly, *The Two Patricks*, p. 65, n. 41.

39 Tírechán, §§5 (both), 24 (*successor*), 30 (*heres*); Muirchú, I.28 (27) (*successor*).

40 As Carney (*The Problem*, pp. 31–48) and Sharpe ('St Patrick and the see of Armagh') have done.

41 On that process, see Sharpe, *ibid.*, and 'Armagh and Rome'.

Armagh by leaving none of the notable early Christian missionaries unattached to it'.[42] At the time when Iarlaithe came to be regarded as the third ruler of Armagh, his two predecessors were perhaps allowed to have been Patrick and Benignus: either Patrick was then admitted as having an early death-date or else the absolute chronological consequences of the sequence were ignored. There is little or nothing here to help us with fifth-century history; neither is it clear when the sequence found in the extant list took shape or what doctrines (if any) about the history of Armagh and St Patrick it reflected.

[42] O'Rahilly, *The Two Patricks*, p. 66; but the point is overstated, for Palladius, Auxilius, and Iserninus were not so associated.

ST PATRICK, THE *ANNALES CAMBRIAE*, AND ST DAVID

In 1955 James Carney brought into the discussion of Patrician chronology a piece of Welsh evidence which he held to be of the greatest importance as a source concerning the fifth century.[1] The related group of Welsh Latin chronicles known collectively as *Annales Cambriae* comprises three principal witnesses.[2] 'A' is a set of annals extending from A.D. 445 to 977, but surviving in a non-Welsh transcript of *ca* A.D. 1100 in which *Annales Cambriae* and a following collection of Welsh royal genealogies (also of the second half of the tenth century) have been interpolated into the middle of the *Historia Brittonum.*[3] 'B' survives in a manuscript of the beginning of the fourteenth century, written in southwestern Wales:[4] the annalistic chronicle extends from 60 B.C. to A.D. 1286, but prefixed to it is a chronicling account of the ages of the world. 'C' was written at St Davids towards the end of the thirteenth century: its last annal is for A.D. 1288, and the chronicle can be seen to be still in a process of development.[5] It too begins with a chronicle of the ages of the world but a different join is effected with the Welsh annals.[6] In these three witnesses we seem to have a Welsh annalistic chronicle kept at St Davids from not earlier than *ca* 800, which was extended backwards to A.D. 445 with the help of Irish and North-British chronicles and then again to Creation with the help of universal-history texts. At a date perhaps in the thirteenth century two different fusions of the world-history and British elements were achieved: from the chronological point of view both attempts were failures.

Knowledge of the textual history of *Annales Cambriae* is now much more substantial than was the case in 1955. This allows us to make an informed response to Carney's ideas of the development of this group of chronicles. The matter is of some importance, since he offered this Welsh evidence as a decisive support for his theory that Bishop Patrick arrived in Ireland on 5 April, 456.[7]

1 Carney, *Studies*, pp. 339–50, 359, 371–3, 407.
2 For study of *Annales Cambriae*, see Hughes, *Celtic Britain*, pp. 67–106.
3 London, British Library, MS. Harley 3859: for edition of all three texts together, see Faral, *La Légende arthurienne*, III.1–62; for translation, see Wade-Evans, *Nennius's "History of the Britons"*, pp. 35–121 (from which the Patrician annal, A.D. 457, has been omitted by an oversight; the 'Nennian' preface on p. 35 is Wade-Evans's interpolation).
4 London, Public Record Office, MS. E.164/1.
5 London, British Library, MS. Cotton Domitian A.i; into the chronicle the main scribe inserted leaves bearing extracts from a Worcester chronicle.
6 For remarks on this process of juncture, see Hughes, *Celtic Britain*, pp. 73–4, 85; Dumville, *Histories and Pseudo-histories*, chapter III; Brett, 'The prefaces'.
7 Carney, *The Problem*, pp. 7–13, 21–30 (cf. 31–3). For comment, see Binchy, 'Patrick and his biographers', pp. 98–9.

While his specific views on this point were never well received, it cannot be said that they – or the Welsh evidence in question – have been properly discussed. Carney's star-witness was an entry, in the B-text of *Annales Cambriae*, which he thought to apply to the year 456. It reads, 'Sanctus Patricius, monente angelo, Hiberniam petiit'.[8] It seems to have no precise counterpart in texts A and C, although Carney argued that behind references to Patrick in all three main texts of *Annales Cambriae* lay a single common entry shared also with lost Irish chronicles.[9]

We should perhaps begin, therefore, by considering briefly the entries in texts A and C of *Annales Cambriae* before giving detailed attention to the complex evidence of version B.

A, *s.a.* 13 [= A.D. 457] Sanctus Patricius ad Dominum migratur.

C, fo 139va38–40 Archadius annis .xiii.
Iohannes Crisostomus claruit.
Et Patricius in Domino pululauit.

As I have observed above,[10] the A-text entry seems simply to be a reflex of the notice of the death of *Senex Patricius*, Sen-Phátric, found in Irish chronicles under this date. The doctrine of the two Patricks presumably had no significance for a Welsh chronicler who therefore smoothed over the apparent oddity of the Irish record.

The C-text, on the other hand, presents information organised by the reigns of Roman emperors. (Annalistic entries begin only in the late seventh century.)[11] It is one such section which is given here. Arcadius was Emperor from A.D. 395 to 408. If we extract surrounding entries of Welsh provenance, however, a rather different chronology becomes apparent.[12]

Gratianus annis .vi. regnauit.
Aduentus Anglorum in Angliam, id est Hors et Hengist anno ab incarnatione Domini .ccccº.xxxviiiº., Gurtheirno existente rege Britonum.
Alter Ualentinianus annis .vii. regnauit.
Et pascha mutatur super diem Dominicum a Leone papa.
Theodosius annis .iii. regnauit.
Et sancta Brigida nascitur.
Archadius annis .xiii.
Et Patricius in Domino pululauit.
Honorius annis .xv. regnauit.
Theodosius rufus annis .xxvii.
Ebur episcopus quieuit.

8 London, Public Record Office, MS. E.164/1, p. 6c16–17.
9 *Studies*, pp. 340–1.
10 See pp. 29–30.
11 For an edition of the transitional passage, see Dumville, *Histories and Pseudo-histories*, chapter III.
12 These excerpts are drawn from London, British Library, MS. Cotton Domitian A.i, fo 139va24–vb5.

Into a Roman chronology which, in this short excerpt, runs from A.D. 379 to 450 have been inserted Insular entries which extend from A.D. 438 to 500, the first of whose dates contradicts the synchronism being made by the Welsh chronicler. There is a dislocation of at least fifty-two years between the two series of events. The proper place of the Patrician entry is therefore approximately in the range (395 + 52 =) 447 to (408 + 52 =) 460. It seems to correspond to an entry found in Irish chronicles.

AI[13] [443]	Patricius in Christi doctrina floruit.
ARC[14] §90	Patricius episcopus ardore fidei et doctrina in nostra prouincia floruit.
AU[15] 443	Patricius episcopus ardore fidei et doctrina Christi florens in nostra prouincia.

Nothing comparable is, however, attested in the other Cambro-Latin texts.[16]

When we turn to the B-text, we find St Patrick receiving a somewhat fuller treatment. I give the relevant section of the chronicle in full.[17]

[391]	Anus.[18]	Martianus imperat. Calcedonense consilium geritur.
	Anus.	
	Anus.	
	Anus.	
	Anus.	
[396]	Anus.	Sanctus Patricius monente angelo Hiberniam petiit.
	Anus.	
[398]	Anus.	Leo maior imperat. Egiptus errore Dioscori latrat.
	Anus.	
	Anus.	
	Anus.	
	Anus.	
	Anus.	
	Anus.	
	Anus.	
	Anus.	
	Anus.	
	Anus.	

13 *The Annals of Inisfallen*, ed. & transl. Mac Airt, pp. 58/9.

14 'The Annals of Roscrea', edd. Gleeson & Mac Airt, p. 150.

15 *The Annals of Ulster*, edd. & transl. Mac Airt & Mac Niocaill, I.40/1.

16 There are possible implications here for the question of the relationship of *Annales Cambriae* and the 'Clonmacnoise Chronicle', for the use of an entry for 443 might imply continuing contact between the two texts after the first impact of the Irish source (cf. Grabowski & Dumville, *Chronicles and Annals*, chapter IV) or early borrowing beyond the chronological bounds of the A-text of *Annales Cambriae* (with consequent further implication that version A is merely an extract from a longer text which must therefore already have existed in the second half of the tenth century).

17 London, Public Record Office, MS. E.164/1, pp. 6c–7a.

18 This unfortunate spelling of *Annus* is almost universal in the annal-markers of MS. B.

Anus.
[410] Anus. Aduentus Anglorum Horsi et Hengisti tempore Wortigerni regis.
Anus.
Anus.
Anus.
Anus.
Anus.
[416] Anus. Dies tenebrosa sicut nox.
Anus.
Anus.
Anus.
Anus.
[421] Anus. Pascha commuta<t>ur `super´ diem dominicam a Leone papa Rome.
[422] Anus. Sancta Brigida nascitur.
Anus.
Anus.
[425] Anus. Sanctus Patricius obit. **(7a)**
[426] Annus. Sanctus Dewy nascitur anno .xxx. post disessum Patricii de Meneuia.
Anus.
Anus.
Anus.
Anus.
[431] Annus.
Anus.
Anus.
Anus.
Anus.
Anus.
Anus.
[438] Anus. Quies Benigni episcopi.

Three different chronologies are apparent in the forty-eight-year section printed above. The annalistic chronicle was begun at 60 B.C., with the Bedan date for Julius Caesar in Britain,[19] and continued relentlessly thereafter with a minimum of one line per year, even if there was no entry to record. The formal chronological structure delivers the square-bracketed dates printed above (A.D. 391–438), although the dates so achieved are not stated overtly. Secondly, a chronology is presented by the Roman emperors named. In this respect, this section of the B-text begins where the quoted extract from version C ended. On that basis, these years are A.D. 450–497, a discrepancy of about sixty years from that maintained by the formal annalistic structure. Thirdly, we have the evidence of the Insular and largely ecclesiastical element for dating. Taking the reference to Pope Leo and the date of Easter as a fixed point (A.D. 453), the quoted section

[19] Hughes, *Celtic Britain*, p. 74.

covers A.D. 432–470. To recapitulate, the chronologies established by the various procedures are:
annalistic structure, A.D. 391–438, with Patrick at 396, 425, 426;
Insular annals, A.D. 423–470, with Patrick at 428, 457, 458;
Roman emperors, A.D. 450–497, with Patrick at 456, 485, 486.
Clearly there are fundamental confusions here. As in the case of the C-text, fusion of world-history and Insular information has produced false synchronisation. In this instance the Insular events are twenty-seven years *behind* their Roman counterparts, while in version C Insular history was at least fifty-two years *in advance of* the Roman chronology. There is no doubt that two separate processes of juncture have occurred in the creation of these two chronicles.[20]

It is far from clear which chronology, if any, the scribes and compilers of these chronicles intended to be understood by their readers. James Carney showed no hesitation when he had to assign A.D. dates to the events in this section of *Annales Cambriae* (B). He took the Roman emperors as determinative of chronology and accordingly assigned Patrick's move to Ireland to A.D. 456.[21] In so far as the first priority of criticism of the texts of *Annales Cambriae* must be to understand their relationship to one another, we should note that the record in 'B' of Patrick's death corresponds exactly in date with that in 'A' if one allows the Insular entries to speak for themselves. On these grounds alone, Carney's attribution of the B-chronicle's annal 396 to A.D. 456 must be rejected as misleading: it is more naturally assignable to A.D. 428. However, we need to note that there is another context within which the B-text's Patrician entries must be considered. *Sub anno* 426 we read, 'Sanctus Dewy nascitur anno .xxx. post dis<c>essum Patricii de Meneuia'. Precisely thirty years before that is the annal which so excited James Carney, 'Sanctus Patricius monente angelo Hiberniam petiit'.[22]

Reference to the hagiography of St David of *Meneuia* (Mynyw, St Davids, in Dyfed) makes abundantly clear the chronicler's sources and methods. We may begin with a mediaeval summary of the relevant information found in a Mass for St David occurring in a Welsh hagiographical manuscript written *ca* A.D. 1200, probably at Monmouth.[23] I quote from Silas Harris's edition and translation.[24]

Deus qui beatum confessorem tuum DAUID atque pontificem angelo nuntiante Patricio prophetante triginta annis antequam nasceretur predixisti: quesumus ut, cuius memoriam recolimus, eius intercessione ad eterna gaudia perueniamus.

O God who didst foretell thy blessed confessor and bishop, Dauid, by the message of an angel to Patrick, prophesying thirty years before his birth: we beseech thee that by his intercession, whose memory we are keeping, we may attain to eternal joys.

20 Cf. the conclusions of Brett, 'The prefaces'.
21 Carney, *Studies*, pp. 341–6.
22 For Carney's brief discussion of this connexion see *ibid.*, pp. 346–7.
23 London, British Library, MS. Cotton Vespasian A.xiv, fos 1–105: see Hughes, *Celtic Britain*, pp. 53–66, for analysis.
24 Harris, *Saint David in the Liturgy*, pp. 13–14 and accompanying plate; I have made a couple of minor changes in the presentation of the text.

This collect, which relates very directly to the annalistic information,[25] is effectively a summary of §3 of Rhigyfarch's Life of St David, a text written in the late eleventh century and surviving in numerous manuscripts.[26] I give texts and translations of the two principal versions from the editions of J. W. James and A. W. Wade-Evans.[27]

'Rhigyfarch'

Deinde Patricius, Romanis eruditus disciplinis, comitantibus uirtutum turmis, pontifex effectus, gentem qua exulauerat petiuit. In qua fructuosi operis lucernam oleo geminę caritatis infatigabili reficiens labore, non sub modio sed super candelabrum imponere uolens, ut cunctis glorificato omnium patre roraret, Cereticę gentis regionem adiit. In qua per aliquantulum temporis conuersatus, Demetica intrat rura: ibique perlustrans, tandem ad locum qui Vallis Rosina nominabatur peruenit, et gratum agnoscens locum, deuouit Deo ibi fideliter deseruire. Sed cum hęc secum meditando reuolueret, apparuit ei angelus Domini; 'Tibi', inquit, 'non istum locum Deus disposuit, sed filio qui nondum est natus, nec nisi peractis xxx^{ta} annis nascetur.' Audiens autem hęc, Sanctus Patricius merens *stupensque uolutat, deliberans et corde* dicens. 'Cum ante Domini mei conspectum incassum labor meus redigitur et mihi qui nondum est natus superponitur, uadam et tali labori amodo non subiaceam.' *Hec autem secum cogitans, talibus blandiciis ab angelo uerba consolationis accepit. 'Non ita fiet, sed Hibernensium*

'Vespasian' recension

Deinde Patricius, Romanis eruditus disciplinis, comitantibus uirtutum turmis, pontifex effectus, gentem a qua exulauerat petiuit, in qua fructuosi operis lucernam oleo gemine karitatis infatigabili reficiens labore, non sub modio sed super candelabrum imponere uolens ut cunctos, glorificato omnium Patre, roraret. Ceretice gentis regionem adiit, in qua per aliquantulum temporis conuersatus Demetica intrat rura, ibique perlustrans tandem ad locum qui Uallis Rosina nominabatur peruenit, et gratum agnoscens locum deuouit Deo ibi fideliter deseruire. Sed cum hec secum meditando reuolueret, apparuit ei angelus Domini, 'Tibi' inquit 'non istum locum Deus disposuit, sed filio qui nondum est natus nec nisi peractis prius triginta annis nascetur.' Audiens autem hec sanctus Patricius merens *et stupens iratusque dixit, 'Cur Dominus despexit seruum suum ab infantia sua sibi seruientem cum timore et amore, elegitque alium nondum in hac luce natum sed neque ante .xxx^{ta}. annos nascetur?' Parauitque fugere, et dominum suum Iesum Christum deserere*, dicens, 'Cum ante Domini mei conspectum incassum

[25] For an adaptation of the story which substitutes St Carannog for St David, see *Vita I S. Carantoci*, §2 (ed. & transl. Wade-Evans, *Vitae*, pp. 142–3).

[26] For discussion of this work, see Brooke, *The Church and the Welsh Border*, pp. 6–7, 27–8.

[27] For an attempt to present Rhigyfarch's original text by collating all the manuscripts, see *Rhigyfarch's Life of St. David*, ed. & transl. James: for §3 see pp. 2–3, 29–30. For the later recension from London, British Library, MS. Cotton Vespasian A.xiv, see *Vitae*, ed. Wade-Evans, pp. 150–70 (text: §3 on pp. 150–1), and *Life of St. David*, transl. Wade-Evans (§3 on pp. 2–3).

insulę principem constituit te Dominus, nondum enim uerbum uitę accepit. Ibi prodesse debes, ibi parauit tibi Dominus sedem, ibi signis et uirtutibus radiabis, totamque gentem Deo subiugabis. Ego ero tecum, sit tibi hoc in signum: totam tibi insulam ostendam; curuentur montes, humiliabitur pelagus, oculus trans omnia erectus, ex loco prospectans, uidebit promissum.' His dictis, erectisque oculis, ex loco in quo stabat, qui modo Sedes Patricii dicitur, totam prospexit insulam: *ac protinus paratis omnibus, nauim petit; resuscitatoque mortuo qui ante duodecim annos defunctus fuerat, promissam patriam intrat. Cetera autem uitę eius in Hibernensium litteris scripta, qui uoluerit, reperiet.*

mei conspectum incassum labor meus redigitur, et mihi qui nondum est natus preponitur, uadam et tali labori amodo non subiaceam.' *Sed Dominus multum diligebat Patricium, misitque ad eum angelum suum ut illum uerbis familiaribus blandiretur, cui ait, 'Patrici, letare, Dominus enim misit me ad te ut ostendam tibi totam Hiberniam insulam de sede que est in Rosina Ualle', que modo Sedes Patricii nominatur. Aitque angelus ei, 'Exulta, Patrici, tu enim eris apostolus illius totius insule quam cernis, multaque propter nomen Domini Dei tui in ea patieris, sed Dominus erit tecum in omnibus que facturus sis*, nondum enim uerbum uitę accepit; ibique prodesse debes, ibi parauit tibi Dominus sedem, ibi signis et uirtutibus radiabis, totamque gentem Deo subiugabis. Sit tibi hoc in signum: totam tibi insulam ostendam, curuentur montes, humiliabitur pelagus, oculus trans omnia euectus ex loco prospectans uidebit promissum.' His dictis, erectisque oculis ex loco in quo stabat, qui modo Sedes Patricii dicitur, totam prospexit insulam. *Tandem animus Patricii sedatus libenter dimisit locum sanctum Dauid agio; paransque nauem in Portu Magno suscitauit quendam senem nomine Criumther per .xii. annos iuxta litus illud sepultum; nauigauitque Patricius in Hiberniam habens secum nuper suscitatum, qui postea episcopus factus est.*

'Rhigyfarch'

Later, Patrick, who was learned in the Roman arts, and also possessed his own countless virtues, was made bishop, and then set out for the people amongst whom he had lived in exile. There, through unwearied toil, by refurbishing the lamp of fruitful endeavour with the aid of the oil of twofold charity, and then seeking to set it on a lamp-stand and not under a meal-tub, in order that it might be a shining light to all men, to the glory of the Father of all, he came to the country of the people of Ceredigion, where he remained a short time, and then entered the territory of Dyfed. This he traversed, and finally reaching the place called Rosina Vallis, and seeing that it was a pleasant spot, he vowed to serve God faithfully there. But as he was turning this over thoughtfully in his mind, an angel of the Lord appeared to him and said; 'Not to you has God assigned this place, but to a son who is not yet born, and will not be born until thirty years have passed.' St. Patrick was grieved and perplexed to hear this; and turning it over and pondering it in his heart, he said; 'Since in my Lord's sight my work is reduced to fruitlessness, and one not yet born is set above me, I will depart, and henceforth not submit to it.' As he was thus reflecting, he received from the angel this soothing message of encouragement; 'Not so, but the Lord has appointed you the chief one in the island of Ireland. It has not yet received the Word of Life. It is there that you must be of service, and there the Lord has prepared you a seat; and you will be radiant with signs and virtues, bringing the whole nation in subjection to God. I will be with you; and let this be a sign to

'Vespasian' recension

Then Patrick, polished with Roman learning and teeming with excellences, having been made a bishop, sought the people from whom he had lived in exile, among whom he might by unwearied toil replenish the lamp of fruitful endeavour by a double portion of the oil of charity, unwilling to place the same under a bushel, but on a stand that it might shine on all to the glory of the universal Father. He came to the country of the people of Ceredigion, wherein he sojourned a little while. He enters *Demetica rura*, the country of Dyved, and there wandering about arrived at length at the place which was named Vallis Rosina; and perceiving that the place was pleasant, he vowed to serve God faithfully there. But when he was revolving these things in his mind, an angel of the Lord appeared to him. "God," said he, "hath not disposed this place for thee, but for a son who is not yet born, nor will he be born until thirty years are past." On hearing these words Saint Patrick grieved and was confounded, and in anger he exclaimed, "Why hath the Lord despised his servant who has served him from his infancy with fear and love? Why hath he chosen another not yet born into this light nor will be born for thirty years?" And he prepared to fly, and to abandon his Lord, Jesus Christ, saying, "Inasmuch as my labour is reduced to nothing in the sight of my Lord, and one is preferred before me, who is not yet born, I will go and submit no longer to such toil." But the Lord loved Patrick much, and sent to him his angel to coax him with kindly words, saying to him, "Rejoice, Patrick, for the Lord hath sent me to thee that I you. I will show you the whole island: the mountains shall be turned aside, the sea shall be brought low, and your gaze, raised over everyting, and looking out from this place, shall view the promised land.' This said, Patrick raised his eyes, and surveyed the whole island from the place whereon he stood; it is now called Patrick's Seat. And straightway, when all things were made ready, he sought his ship; and after he had raised to life a man who had died twelve years previously, he entered the promised land. As for the remainder of his life, anyone desiring to read it will find it written down in the literature of Ireland.

may show thee the whole of the island of Ireland from the seat which is in Vallis Rosina" which now is named "the Seat of Patrick." And the angel says to him, "Exult, Patrick, for thou shalt be the apostle of the whole of that island which thou seest, and thou shalt suffer many things in it for the name of the Lord thy God, but the Lord will be with thee in all things which thou shalt do, for as yet it has not received the word of life; and there thou oughtest to do good; there the Lord has prepared a seat for thee; there thou shalt shine in signs and miracles, and thou shalt subdue the whole people to God. Let this be to thee for a sign. I will show thee the whole island. Let the mountains be bent; the sea shall be made smooth; the eye bearing forth across all things, looking out from [this] place, shall behold the promise." At these words he raised his eyes from the place in which he was standing, which now is called "the Seat of Patrick," and beheld the whole island. At length the mind of Patrick was appeased, and he cheerfully quitted the sacred spot for holy David; and preparing a ship in Porth Mawr, he raised from the dead a certain old man, Criumther by name, who for twelve years had lain buried by that shore; and Patrick sailed for Ireland, taking with him the man he had just raised from the dead, who afterwards was made a bishop.

Rhigyfarch gave to St David a life-span of 147 years, ending on 1 March, a Tuesday.[28] We have two obits for him, one preserved in Irish chronicles and represented by the date 589 in derivatives of the 'Clonmacnoise Chronicle':[29] in

28 §§58, 62.

29 *The Annals of Inisfallen*, ed. & transl. Mac Airt, pp. 78/9 (at [589].2); 'The Annals of Roscrea', edd. Gleeson & Mac Airt, p. 149 (§71); 'The Annals of Tigernach', ed. Stokes, p. 158 (*s.a.* K.iiii); *Chronicum Scotorum*, ed. & transl. Hennessy, pp. 62/3 (*s.a.* K.iiii). This was

589, 1 March was a Tuesday. *Annales Cambriae* (A) give A.D. 601: the nearest Tuesday, 1 March, fell in 606.[30] David's death is recorded in the same annal as that of Pope Gregory the Great which fell in 604 but in the early middle ages was often attributed to 606.[31] (In version B of *Annales Cambriae* David's death is placed 143 years after his birth, presumably showing the same deviation from Rhigyfarch's figures as does the A-text.) We should probably therefore admit a chronological dislocation in the extant text of *Annales Cambriae*. All this was worked out by Molly Miller, apparently in ignorance of *Annales Cambriae* (B): she showed that Rhigyfarch's calculation was of 147 years between a death-date in 606 and a birth-date in 459.[32] As we have seen, *Annales Cambriae* (B) seem to place David's birth in 458, the year after St Patrick's death; the angel's prophecy to Patrick about David was therefore placed in 428, which was consequently the date of Patrick's departure to evangelise Ireland.

It is apparent, therefore, that the chronology of St Patrick as found in the B-text of *Annales Cambriae* is, except for the date of his death (457 was inherited from the 'Clonmacnoise Chronicle' in the mid-tenth century),[33] wholly part of that for St David. It seems unlikely that these calculations originated anywhere other than at St Davids: if that deduction is correct, they belong to a period before 1202 when an ancestor of the B-text left St Davids;[34] if they originated with Rhigyfarch, then the chronology of Patrician events found in *Annales Cambriae* (B) belongs more or less to the twelfth century. The entry embraced by James Carney should be dated 428 (or 429),[35] not 456, and recognised as dependent on the hagiography of St David. It can therefore hardly be used as a source, much less a determinative source, for fifth-century history.

---

probably a borrowing of information sent from St Davids in the first half of the tenth century: for discussion of the context, see Grabowski & Dumville, *Chronicles and Annals*, chapter IV.

30 Miller, 'Date-guessing and Dyfed', pp. 47–8, noted these points.

31 As for example in the 'Annals of Ulster' and other Irish chronicles.

32 For her full discussion, see 'Date-guessing and Dyfed', pp. 41–50. She thought, however, that the 'Irish' date for David's death resulted from a 'wish to contradict the St. Davids assertion' (p. 48); I should prefer to think that the date was revised at St Davids in the course of the tenth century. For another discussion of St David's dates, not known to Miller, see Wade-Evans, 'The death-years'.

33 Cf. above, pp. 29–30, and Grabowski & Dumville, *Chronicles and Annals*, chapter IV.

34 Hughes, *Celtic Britain*, pp. 74, 85; Dumville, *Histories and Pseudo-histories*, chapter III; Brett, 'The prefaces'.

35 429 would be the figure resulting from Molly Miller's calculations (cf. 'Date-guessing and Dyfed', p. 48). It is perhaps to be preferred in that Celtic hagiographers were by no means innocent of the British visit of St Germanus of Auxerre in 429 and sometimes attributed to it (as have some modern writers) an unusual organisational and personal significance in the history of the Insular Churches. It is conceivable that St Davids chronographers and hagiographers thus saw Patrick's mission to Ireland in relation to other events of that year. There is already a dislocation in the chronology of *Annales Cambriae* (B) – as of the A-text over a corresponding period – and it is not unimaginable that a further year should be allowed. Neither, of course, can we be certain that David's life-span of 147 years originated with Rhigyfarch: if not, it could already have been corrupt; but, as far as we can tell at present, the faults of chronology are in the annalistic texts which survive. Indeed, we must wonder whether the later date for David's death (606 rather than 589) implies that the figure of 147 years had already been worked out in the tenth century.

BIBLIOGRAPHY

This makes no pretence to be a thorough Patrician bibliography. It is merely a finding list for bibliographical items cited in the body of the book. A comprehensive bibliography of St Patrick was begun by David Dumville in 1979, continued by Richard Sharpe, and has been heroically brought to conclusion by Anthony Harvey. It will be published this year by the Royal Irish Academy in *Clavis Patricii, II*.

ABRAMS, Lesley & CARLEY, J. P. (edd.) *The Archaeology and History of Glastonbury Abbey. Essays in Honour of the Ninetieth Birthday of C.A. Ralegh Radford* (Woodbridge 1991)

ADAMS, G. B. 'Some linguistic problems', in *The Bishops' Synod ("The First Synod of St. Patrick")*, ed. M. J. Faris (Liverpool 1976), pp. 19–22

ADRIAEN, Marc (ed.) *S. Gregorii Magni Moralia in Iob* (3 vols, Turnhout 1979–85)

AITCHISON, N. B. 'The Ulster Cycle: heroic image and historical reality', *Journal of Medieval History* 13 (1987) 87–116

ANDERSON, Alan Orr & ANDERSON, M. O. (edd. & transl.) *Adomnán's Life of Columba* (2nd edn, Oxford 1991)

ANDRIEU, M. 'Quelques remarques sur le classement des sacramentaires', *Jahrbuch für Liturgiewissenschaft* 11 (1931) 46–66

ANSCOMBE, A. 'The pedigree of Patrick', *Ériu* 6 (1911/12) 117–20

ASHE, Geoffrey (ed.) *The Quest for Arthur's Britain* (London 1968)

ATKINSON, Robert (ed. & transl.) *The Passions and the Homilies from Leabhar Breac* (Dublin 1887)

ATKINSON, Robert (facs. ed.) *The Yellow Book of Lecan, a Collection of Pieces (Prose and Verse) in the Irish Language, in part compiled at the End of the Fourteenth Century* (Dublin 1896)

AUTENRIETH, Johanne & BRUNHÖLZL, F. (edd.) *Festschrift Bernhard Bischoff zu seinem 65. Geburtstag dargebracht von Freunden, Kollegen und Schülern* (Stuttgart 1971)

BAILLIE, M. G. L. 'The central post from Navan Fort. The first step towards a better understanding of the Early Iron Age', *Emania* 1 (1986) 20–1

BAMMESBERGER, Alfred & WOLLMANN, A. (edd.) *Britain 400–600: Language and History* (Heidelberg 1990)

BANNERMAN, John *Studies in the History of Dalriada* (Edinburgh 1974)

BANTING, H. M. J. (ed.) *Two Anglo-Saxon Pontificals (the Egbert and Sidney Sussex Pontificals)* (London 1989)

BARLEY, M. W. & HANSON, R. P. C. (edd.) *Christianity in Britain, 300–700. Papers presented to the Conference on Christianity in Roman and Sub-Roman Britain held at the University of Nottingham 17–20 April 1967* (Leicester 1968)

BARTRUM, P. C. (ed.) *Early Welsh Genealogical Tracts* (Cardiff 1966)
BATTISCOMBE, C. F. (ed.) *The Relics of Saint Cuthbert* (Oxford 1956)
BERNARD, J. H. & ATKINSON, R. (edd. & transl.) *The Irish Liber Hymnorum* (2 vols, London 1898)
BEST, R[ichard] I[rvine] & BERGIN, O. (edd.) *Lebor na hUidre. Book of the Dun Cow* (Dublin 1929; 2nd rev. imp., 1992)
BEST, R. I. 'Palaeographical notes, III, the Book of Armagh', *Ériu* 18 (1958) 102–7
BEST, R[ichard] I[rvine] & MACNEILL, E. (facs. edd.) *The Annals of Inisfallen reproduced in Facsimile from the Original Manuscript (Rawlinson B 503) in the Bodleian Library* (Dublin 1933)
BEST, R[ichard] I[rvine], *et al.* (edd.) *The Book of Leinster formerly Lebar na Núachongbála* (6 vols, Dublin 1954–83)
BEST, Richard Irvine & LAWLOR, H. J. (edd.) *The Martyrology of Tallaght from the Book of Leinster and MS. 5100–4 in the Royal Library, Brussels* (London 1931)
BIELER, L. 'Bethu Phátraic. Versuch einer Grundlegung des Verhältnisses der irischen Patriciusviten zu den lateinischen', *Anzeiger der österreichischen Akademie der Wissenschaften*, philosophisch-historische Klasse, 111 (1974) 251–73
BIELER, Ludwig *Codices Patriciani Latini. A Descriptive Catalogue of Latin Manuscripts relating to St. Patrick* (Dublin 1942)
BIELER, L. 'Der Bibeltext des heiligen Patrick', *Biblica* 28 (1947) 31–58 *and* 236–63
BIELER, L. (ed.) 'Eine Patricksvita in Gloucester', in *Festschrift Bernhard Bischoff zu seinem 65. Geburtstag dargebracht von Freunden, Kollegen und Schülern*, edd. J. Autenrieth & F. Brunhölzl (Stuttgart 1971), pp. 346–63 + plate 16
BIELER, Ludwig (ed.) *Four Latin Lives of St. Patrick. Colgan's* Vita Secunda, Quarta, Tertia, *and* Quinta (Dublin 1971)
BIELER, L. 'Interpretationes patricianae', *Irish Ecclesiastical Record*, 5th S., 107 (1967) 1–13
BIELER, Ludwig *Ireland and the Culture of Early Medieval Europe* (London 1987)
BIELER, L. (ed.) 'Libri epistolarum sancti Patricii episcopi', *Classica et Mediaevalia* 11 (1950) 1–150 *and* 12 (1951) 79–214
BIELER, L. 'Patrick's Synod: a revision', in *Mélanges offerts à Mademoiselle Christine Mohrmann* (Utrecht 1963), pp. 96–102
BIELER, Ludwig *Studies on the Life and Legend of St Patrick* (London 1986)
BIELER, L. 'The "creeds" of St. Victorinus and St. Patrick', *Theological Studies* 9 (1949) 121–4
BIELER, L. (ed.) 'The Hymn of St. Secundinus', *Proceedings of the Royal Irish Academy* 55 C (1952/3) 117–27
BIELER, L. 'The Irish Book of Hymns: a palaeographical study', *Scriptorium* 2 (1948) 177–94 + plates 23–25
BIELER, Ludwig & BINCHY, D. A. (edd. & transl.) *The Irish Penitentials* (Dublin 1963)

BIELER, L. & CARNEY, J. (edd.) 'The Lambeth Commentary', *Ériu* 23 (1972) 1–55

BIELER, Ludwig *The Life and Legend of St. Patrick. Problems of Modern Scholarship* (Dublin 1949)

BIELER, L. 'The Lives of St. Patrick and the Book of Armagh', in *Saint Patrick*, ed. J. Ryan ([Dublin] 1958), pp. 53–66

BIELER, L. 'The mission of Palladius. A comparative study of sources', *Traditio* 6 (1948) 1–32

BIELER, Ludwig & KELLY, F. (edd. & transl.) *The Patrician Texts in the Book of Armagh* (Dublin 1979)

BIELER, L. 'The problem of "Silua Focluti" ', *Irish Historical Studies* 3 (1942/3) 351–64

BIELER, L. 'Was Palladius surnamed Patricius?', *Studies* 32 (1943) 323–6

BIELER, Ludwig (transl.) *The Works of St. Patrick; St. Secundinus, Hymn on St. Patrick* (Westminster, Md 1953)

BINCHY, D. A. 'A pre-christian survival in mediaeval Irish hagiography', in *Ireland in Early Mediaeval Europe*, edd. D. Whitelock *et al.* (Cambridge 1982), pp. 165–78

BINCHY, D. A. 'Patrick and his biographers, ancient and modern', *Studia Hibernica* 2 (1962) 7–173

BINCHY, D. A. [review of K. H. Jackson, *Language and History in Early Britain* (1953)], *Celtica* 4 (1958) 288–92

BINCHY, D. A. 'St Patrick's "First Synod" ', *Studia Hibernica* 8 (1968) 49–59

BINCHY, D. A. 'The Fair of Tailtiu and the Feast of Tara', *Ériu* 18 (1958) 113–38

BIRKHAN, Helmut *Germanen und Kelten bis zum Ausgang der Römerzeit. Der Aussagewert von Wörtern und Sachen für die frühesten keltisch-germanischen Kulturbeziehungen* (Wien 1970)

BISHOP, E. & WILMART, A. 'La réforme liturgique de Charlemagne', *Ephemerides liturgicae* 45 (1931) 186–207

BLUME, Friedrich (ed.) *Die Musik in Geschichte und Gegenwart. Allgemeine Enzyklopädie der Musik* (17 vols, Kassel 1949–86)

BOLLAND, Iohannes, *et al.* (edd.) *Acta Sanctorum* (Antwerpen, etc. 1643–)

BONNER, Gerald, *et al.* (edd.) *St Cuthbert, his Cult and his Community to AD 1200* (Woodbridge 1989)

BOUMAN, C. A. *Sacring and Crowning. The Development of the Latin Ritual for the Anointing of Kings and the Coronation of an Emperor before the Eleventh Century* (Groningen 1957)

BOURQUE, Emmanuel *Étude sur les sacramentaires romains* (2 parts in 3 vols, Roma/Québec 1948–58)

BOWEN, E. G. *The Settlements of the Celtic Saints in Wales* (2nd edn, Cardiff 1956)

BRADLEY, D. R. 'The doctrinal formula of Patrick', *Journal of Theological Studies*, N.S., 33 (1982) 124–33

BRANIGAN, Keith *Latimer. Belgic, Roman, Dark Age and Early Modern Farm* (Bristol 1971)

BRANIGAN, Keith (ed.) *Rome and the Brigantes. The Impact of Rome on Northern England* (Sheffield 1980)

BRANIGAN, Keith *The Roman Villa in South-west England* (Bradford-on-Avon 1976)

BRANIGAN, Keith & FOWLER, P. J. (edd.) *The Roman West Country. Classical Culture and Celtic Society* (Newton Abbot 1976)

BRANIGAN, K. 'Villa settlement in the West Country', in *The Roman West Country*, edd. K. Branigan & P. J. Fowler (Newton Abbot 1976), pp. 120–41

BRANIGAN, K. 'Villas in the North: change in the rural landscape?', in *Rome and the Brigantes*, ed. K. Branigan (Sheffield 1980), pp. 18–27

BREEN, A. 'The text of the Constantinopolitan creed in the Stowe Missal', *Proceedings of the Royal Irish Academy* 90 C (1990) 107–21

BRETT, C. 'The prefaces of two late thirteenth-century Welsh Latin chronicles', *Bulletin of the Board of Celtic Studies* 35 (1988) 63–73

BROOKE, Christopher N. L. *The Church and the Welsh Border in the Central Middle Ages* (Woodbridge 1986)

BROOKS, D. A. 'Gildas' *De excidio*. Its revolutionary meaning and purpose', *Studia Celtica* 18/19 (1983/4) 1–10

BROOKS, Nicholas (ed.) *Latin and the Vernacular Languages in Early Medieval Britain* (Leicester 1982)

BURKITT, F. C. 'On two early Irish hymns', *Journal of Theological Studies* 3 (1901/2) 95–6

BURNHAM, Barry C. & WACHER, J. *The 'Small Towns' of Roman Britain* (London 1990)

BURROW, I. C. G. 'Tintagel – some problems', *Scottish Archaeological Forum* 5 (1973) 99–103

BURY, J. B. *The Life of St. Patrick and his Place in History* (London 1905)

BURY, J. B. 'The origin of Pelagius', *Hermathena* 13 [nos 30–31] (1904/5) 26–35

*BYRNE, Cyril J., *et al.* (edd.) *Celtic Languages and Celtic Peoples. Proceedings of the Second North American Congress of Celtic Studies* (Halifax, Nova Scotia 1992)

BYRNE, F. J. 'A note on Trim and Sletty', *Peritia* 3 (1984) 316–19

BYRNE, Francis John *Irish Kings and High-kings* (London 1973)

BYRNE, F. J. 'Seventh-century documents', *Irish Ecclesiastical Record*, 5th S., 108 (1967) 164–82

BYRNE, Francis John *The Rise of the Uí Néill and the High-kingship of Ireland* (Dublin [1970])

CAPPUYNS, M. 'L'auteur du "De uocatione omnium gentium" ', *Revue bénédictine* 39 (1927) 198–226

CAREY, J. 'The two laws in Dubthach's judgment', *Cambridge Medieval Celtic Studies* 19 (1990) 1–18

CARLEY, J. P. & DOOLEY, A. (edd.) 'An early Irish fragment of Isidore of Seville's *Etymologiae*', in *The Archaeology and History of Glastonbury Abbey*, edd. L. Abrams & J. P. Carley (Woodbridge 1991), pp. 135–61

CARLEY, James P. & TOWNSEND, D. (edd. & transl.) *The Chronicle of Glastonbury Abbey. An Edition, Translation and Study of John of Glastonbury's* Cronica sive antiquitates Glastoniensis ecclesie (2nd edn, Woodbridge 1985)

CARNEY, J. 'Early Irish literature: the state of research', in *Proceedings of the Sixth International Congress of Celtic Studies held in University College, Galway, 6–13 July 1979*, edd. G. Mac Eoin *et al.* (Dublin 1983), pp. 113–30
CARNEY, James *Studies in Irish Literature and History* (Dublin 1955)
CARNEY, J. 'The date and authorship of *Saltair na Rann*', *Celtica* 23 (1993)
CARNEY, J. 'The dating of early Irish verse texts, 500–1100', *Éigse* 19 (1982/3) 177–216
CARNEY, James *The Problem of St. Patrick* (Dublin 1961)
CARNEY, J. (ed. & transl.) 'Three Old Irish accentual poems', *Ériu* 22 (1971) 23–80
CASEY, P. J. (ed.) *The End of Roman Britain. Papers arising from a Conference, Durham 1978* (Oxford 1979)
CASPAR, Erich *Geschichte des Papsttums von den Anfängen bis zur Höhe der Weltherrschaft* (2 vols, Tübingen 1930/3)
CHADWICK, H. M. *Early Scotland. The Picts, the Scots & the Welsh of Southern Scotland* (Cambridge 1949)
CHADWICK, Nora K. (ed.) *Studies in the Early British Church* (Cambridge 1958)
CHADWICK, Owen *John Cassian* (2nd edn, Cambridge 1968)
CHAMBERLIN, John (ed.) *The Rule of St. Benedict: the Abingdon Copy edited from Cambridge, Corpus Christi College MS. 57* (Toronto 1982)
CHARLES-EDWARDS, Thomas & KELLY, F. (edd. & transl.) *Bechbretha* (Dublin 1983)
CHATILLON, F. 'Sur le thème *alpha-oméga*. Variations complémentaires ou supplémentaires', *Revue du moyen âge latin* 11 (1955) 319–57
CHAVASSE, Antoine *Le Sacramentaire gélasien (Vaticanus Reginensis 316), sacramentaire presbytéral en usage dans les titres romains au VIIe siècle* (Tournai 1958)
CHAVASSE, Antoine (ed.) *Sancti Leonis Magni Romani Pontificis Tractatus Septem et Nonaginta* (2 vols, Turnhout 1973)
CLEMOES, Peter & HUGHES, K. (edd.) *England before the Conquest. Studies in Primary Sources presented to Dorothy Whitelock* (Cambridge 1971)
CLOVER, Helen & GIBSON, M. (edd. & transl.) *The Letters of Lanfranc, Archbishop of Canterbury* (Oxford 1979)
COCCIA, E. 'La cultura irlandese precarolingia. Miracolo o mito?', *Studi medievali*, 3rd S., 8 (1967) 257–420
COLGAN, John (ed.) *Triadis Thaumaturgae seu Diuorum Patricii Columbæ et Brigidæ, trium ueteris et maioris Scotiæ, seu Hiberniæ sanctorum insulae, communium patronorum acta* (Leuven 1647)
COLGRAVE, Bertram & MYNORS, R. A. B. (edd. & transl.) *Bede's Ecclesiastical History of the English People* (Oxford 1969; rev. imp., 1991)
COLLINGWOOD, R. G., *et al.* *The Archaeology of Roman Britain* (2nd edn, London 1969)
COLLINGWOOD, R. G. & WRIGHT, R. P. (edd.) *The Roman Inscriptions of Britain* (Oxford, etc. 1965–)
CORISH, Patrick J. *The Christian Mission* (Dublin 1972) [*A History of Irish Catholicism*, gen. ed. Patrick J. Corish, vol. I, pt 3]

CRICK, Julia C. *The Historia Regum Britannie of Geoffrey of Monmouth,* III, *A Summary Catalogue of the Manuscripts* (Cambridge 1989)

CRICK, J. [C.] 'The marshalling of antiquity: Glastonbury's historical dossier', in *The Archaeology and History of Glastonbury Abbey*, edd. L. Abrams & J. P. Carley (Woodbridge 1991), pp. 217–43

CROSS, J. E. 'The influence of Irish texts and traditions on the *Old English Martyrology*', *Proceedings of the Royal Irish Academy* 81 C (1981) 173–92

CURRAN, Michael *The Antiphonary of Bangor and the Early Irish Monastic Liturgy* (Blackrock 1984)

D'ARBOIS DE JUBAINVILLE, H. 'Saint Patrice et Sen Patricc', *Revue celtique* 9 (1888) 111–17

DARK, K[enneth] R[ainsbury] *Civitas to Kingdom: British Political Continuity 300–800* (Leicester 1993)

DARK, Kenneth Rainsbury 'High Status Sites, Kingship and State Formation in Post-Roman Western Britain A.D. 400–700' (unpublished Ph.D. dissertation, University of Cambridge 1989)

DARK, K. R. 'The plan and interpretation of Tintagel', *Cambridge Medieval Celtic Studies* 9 (1985) 1–17

DAVIS, Raymond (transl.) *The Book of Pontiffs (Liber Pontificalis). The Ancient Biographies of the First Ninety Roman Bishops to AD 715* (Liverpool 1989)

DEANESLY, Margaret *Augustine of Canterbury* (London 1964)

DE BRÚN, Pádraig & HERBERT, M. *Catalogue of Irish Manuscripts in Cambridge Libraries* (Cambridge 1986)

DE BÚRCA, S. 'The Patricks: a linguistic interpretation', *Lochlann* 3 (1965) 278–85

DE CLERCQ, Carlo (ed.) *Concilia Galliae, A. 511–A. 695* (Turnhout 1963)

DE COURSON, Aurélien (ed.) *Cartulaire de l'abbaye de Redon en Bretagne* (Paris 1863)

DE PLINVAL, G. 'Prosper d'Aquitaine interprète de saint Augustin', *Recherches augustiniennes* 1 (1958) 339–55

DEROLEZ, R. (ed.) 'Dubthach's cryptogram. Some notes in connexion with Brussels MS. 9565–9566', *L'Antiquité classique* 21 (1952) 359–75

DESHUSSES, Jean (ed.) *Le Sacramentaire grégorien: ses principales formes d'après les plus anciens manuscrits. Edition comparative* (3 vols, Fribourg en Suisse 1971–82)

DESHUSSES, J. 'Les sacramentaires. État actuel de la recherche', *Archiv für Liturgiewissenschaft* 24 (1982) 19–46

DEVINE, Kieran *A Computer-generated Concordance to the* Libri Epistolarum *of Saint Patrick* (Dublin 1989)

DEWICK, E. S. & FRERE, W. H. (edd.) *The Leofric Collectar* (2 vols, London 1914/21)

DICKINSON, Francis Henry (ed.) *Missale ad usum insignis et præclaræ ecclesiæ Sarum* (Burntisland 1861–83)

DIEHL, Ernest (ed.) *Inscriptiones latinae christianae ueteres* (3 vols, Berlin 1924–31; supplement, Dublin 1967)

DILLON, M. 'Laud misc. 610', *Celtica* 5 (1960) 64–76 *and* 6 (1963) 135–55

DILLON, Myles (ed. & transl.) *Lebor na Cert. The Book of Rights* (London 1962; 2nd edn, by D. N. Dumville, 1993)
DILLON, M. 'On the date and authorship of the Book of Rights', *Celtica* 4 (1958) 239–49
DOBLE, G. H. 'Saint Congar', *Antiquity* 19 (1945) 32–43 *and* 85–95
DOHERTY, C. 'The basilica in early Ireland', *Peritia* 3 (1984) 303–15
DOHERTY, C. 'The cult of St Patrick and the politics of Armagh in the seventh century', in *Ireland and Northern France AD 600–850*, ed. J.-M. Picard (Blackrock 1991), pp. 53–94
DOHERTY, C. 'The use of relics in early Ireland', in *Ireland and Europe*, edd. P. Ní Chatháin & M. Richter (Stuttgart 1984), pp. 89–101
DREVES, Guido Maria, *et al.* (edd.) *Analecta Hymnica Medii Aevi* (55 vols, Leipzig 1886–1922; index, 3 vols, Bern 1978)
DRINKWATER, John & ELTON, H. (edd.) *Fifth-century Gaul: a Crisis of Identity?* (Cambridge 1992)
DRISCOLL, Stephen T. & NIEKE, M. R. (edd.) *Power and Politics in Early Medieval Britain and Ireland* (Edinburgh 1988)
DUBOIS, Jacques (ed.) *Le Martyrologe d'Usuard. Texte et commentaire* (Bruxelles 1965)
DUCHESNE, L. *Fastes épiscopaux de l'ancienne Gaule* (3 vols, Paris 1894–1915)
DÜMMLER, Ernst, *et al.* (edd.) *Epistolae Merowingici et Karolini Aevi,* I (Berlin 1892)
DUMAS, A. & DESHUSSES, J. (edd.) *Liber sacramentorum Gellonensis* (2 vols, Turnhout 1981)
DUMVILLE, D. N. 'A seventeenth-century Hiberno-Breton hagiological exchange', in *France and the British Isles in the Middle Ages and Renaissance*, edd. G. Jondorf & D. N. Dumville (Woodbridge 1991), pp. 249–54
DUMVILLE, D. N. ' "Beowulf" and the Celtic world: the uses of evidence', *Traditio* 37 (1981) 109–60
DUMVILLE, D. N. 'Beowulf come lately. Some notes on the palaeography of the Nowell Codex', *Archiv für das Studium der neueren Sprachen und Literaturen* 225 (1988) 49–63
DUMVILLE, David N. *Britons and Anglo-Saxons in the Early Middle Ages* (Aldershot 1993)
DUMVILLE, D. N. 'Cath Fedo Euin', *Scottish Gaelic Studies* 17 (1993)
DUMVILLE, D. N. 'Celtic-Latin texts in northern England, c. 1150–c. 1250', *Celtica* 12 (1977) 19–49
DUMVILLE, D. N. 'Early Welsh poetry: problems of historicity', in *Early Welsh Poetry*, ed. B. F. Roberts (Aberystwyth 1988), pp. 1–16
DUMVILLE, D. N. '*Echtrae* and *immram*: some problems of definition', *Ériu* 27 (1976) 73–94
DUMVILLE, David N. *English Caroline Script and Monastic History: Studies in Benedictinism, A.D. 950–1030* (Woodbridge 1993)
DUMVILLE, D. N. 'English Square minuscule script: the background and earliest phases', *Anglo-Saxon England* 16 (1987) 147–79 + plates I–VII
DUMVILLE, D. N. 'Gildas and Maelgwn: problems of dating', in *Gildas:*

New Approaches, edd. M. Lapidge & D. Dumville (Woodbridge 1984), pp. 51–9
DUMVILLE, D. N. 'Gildas and Uinniau', in *Gildas: New Approaches*, edd. M. Lapidge & D. Dumville (Woodbridge 1984), pp. 207–14
DUMVILLE, David N. *Histories and Pseudo-histories of the Insular Middle Ages* (Aldershot 1990)
DUMVILLE, D. N. 'Kingship, genealogies and regnal lists', in *Early Medieval Kingship*, edd. P. H. Sawyer & I. N. Wood (Leeds 1977), pp. 72–104
DUMVILLE, D. [N.] 'Language, literature, and law in medieval Ireland: some questions of transmission', *Cambridge Medieval Celtic Studies* 9 (1985) 91–8
DUMVILLE, D. [N.] 'Late-seventh- or eighth-century evidence for the British transmission of Pelagius', *Cambridge Medieval Celtic Studies* 10 (1985) 39–52
DUMVILLE, D. [N.] 'Latin and Irish in the *Annals of Ulster*, A.D. 431–1050', in *Ireland in Early Mediaeval Europe*, edd. D. Whitelock *et al.* (Cambridge 1982), pp. 320–41
DUMVILLE, David N. *Liturgy and the Ecclesiastical History of Late Anglo-Saxon England: Four Studies* (Woodbridge 1992)
DUMVILLE, D. N. 'St Patrick in Cornwall? The origin and transmission of *Vita tertia S. Patricii*', in *A Celtic Florilegium in Memory of Brendan O Hehir*, edd. K. Klar & E. Sweetser (Boston, Mass. 1993)
DUMVILLE, D. N. 'St Teilo, St Cadog, and St Buite in Italy?', *Journal of Welsh Ecclesiastical History* 4 (1987) 1–8
DUMVILLE, D. N. 'Some aspects of the chronology of the *Historia Brittonum*', *Bulletin of the Board of Celtic Studies* 25 (1972–4) 439–45
DUMVILLE, D. N. 'Some British aspects of the earliest Irish christianity', in *Ireland and Europe*, edd. P. Ní Chatháin & M. Richter (Stuttgart 1984), pp. 16–24
DUMVILLE, D. N. 'Sub-Roman Britain: history and legend', *History*, N.S., 62 (1977) 173–92
DUMVILLE, D. N. (ed.) 'The Anglian collection of royal genealogies and regnal lists', *Anglo-Saxon England* 5 (1976) 23–50
DUMVILLE, David [N.] & KEYNES, S. (gen. edd.) *The Anglo-Saxon Chronicle. A Collaborative Edition* (23 vols, Cambridge 1983–)
DUMVILLE, D. N. 'The chronology of *De excidio Britanniae*, Book I', in *Gildas: New Approaches*, edd. M. Lapidge & D. Dumville (Woodbridge 1984), pp. 61–84
DUMVILLE, David N. (ed.) *The* Historia Brittonum (10 vols, Cambridge 1985–)
DUMVILLE, D. N. 'The textual history of "Lebor Bretnach": a preliminary study', *Éigse* 16 (1975/6) 255–73
DUMVILLE, D. N. 'Ulster heroes in the early Irish annals: a caveat', *Éigse* 17 (1977–9) 47–54
EDWARDS, Heather *The Charters of the Early West Saxon Kingdom* (Oxford 1988)
EKWALL, Eilert *English River-names* (Oxford 1928)
*ELLIS, Simon P. 'An Archaeological Study of Urban Domestic Housing in

the Mediterranean A.D. 400–700' (unpublished D.Phil. dissertation, University of Oxford 1983)

ESMONDE CLEARY, A. S. *The Ending of Roman Britain* (London 1989)

ESPOSITO, Mario *Latin Learning in Mediaeval Ireland* (London 1988)

ESPOSITO, M. 'Notes on a Latin Life of Saint Patrick', *Classica et Mediaevalia* 13 (1952) 59–72

ESPOSITO, M. 'Notes on Latin learning and literature in mediaeval Ireland', pt I, *Hermathena* 20 [nos 44–45] (1926–30) 225–60

ESPOSITO, M. 'The Patrician problem and a possible solution', *Irish Historical Studies* 10 (1956/7) 131–55

EVANS, J[ohn] Gwenogvryn & RHYS, J. (edd.) *The Text of the Book of Llan Dâv reproduced from the Gwysaney Manuscript* (Oxford 1893; rev. imp., Aberystwyth 1979)

FAHY, D. 'The historical reality of Saint Ninian', *Innes Review* 15 (1964) 35–46

FARAL, Edmond (ed.) *La Légende arthurienne: Études et documents, Les plus anciens textes* (3 vols, Paris 1929)

FARIS, M. J. (ed.) *The Bishops' Synod ("The First Synod of St. Patrick"). A Symposium with Text, Translation and Commentary* (Liverpool 1976)

FARMER, D. H. (facs. ed.) *The Rule of St Benedict. Oxford, Bodleian Library, Hatton 48* (Copenhagen 1968)

FERGUSON, Samuel (ed.) *Leabhar Breac, the Speckled Book, otherwise styled Leabhar Mór Dúna Doighre, the Great Book of Dún Doighre; a Collection of Pieces in Irish and Latin, compiled from Ancient Sources about the Close of the Fourteenth Century: now for the First Time published from the Original Manuscript in the Library of the Royal Irish Academy* (Dublin 1872–6)

FINBERG, H. P. R. *West-Country Historical Studies* (Newton Abbot 1969)

FLOWER, Robin *The Irish Tradition* (London 1947)

FOOT, S. 'Glastonbury's early abbots', in *The Archaeology and History of Glastonbury Abbey*, edd. L. Abrams & J. P. Carley (Woodbridge 1991), pp. 163–89

FREEMAN, A. M. (ed.) 'The annals in Cotton MS. Titus A. XXV', *Revue celtique* 41 (1924) 301–30; 42 (1925) 283–305; 43 (1926) 358–84; 44 (1927) 336–61

FRERE, Sheppard *Britannia. A History of Roman Britain* (3rd edn, London 1987)

FRERE, Walter Howard (ed.) *The Use of Sarum* (2 vols, Cambridge 1898/1901)

FRITZE, W. H. 'Universalis gentium confessio. Formeln, Träger und Wege universalmissionarischen Denkens im 7. Jahrhundert', *Frühmittelalterliche Studien* 3 (1969) 78–130

FROS, Henri *Bibliotheca hagiographica latina antiquae et mediae aetatis. Novum supplementum* (Bruxelles 1986)

FRYDE, E. B., *et al.* (edd.) *Handbook of British Chronology* (3rd edn, London 1986)

GAMBER, Klaus *Sakramentartypen. Versuch einer Gruppierung der*

Handschriften und Fragmente bis zur Jahrtausendwende (Beuron in Hohenzollern 1958)

*GARVIN, Joseph N. (ed. & transl.) *The Vitas Sanctorum Patrum Emeretensium* (Washington, D.C. 1946)

GASQUET, F. A. & BISHOP, E. *The Bosworth Psalter. An Account of a Manuscript formerly belonging to O. Turville-Petre Esq. of Bosworth Hall now Addit. MS. 37517 at the British Museum* (London 1908)

GAUDEMET, Jean (ed. & transl.) *Conciles gaulois du IVe siècle* (Paris 1977)

GERCHOW, Jan (ed.) *Die Gedenküberlieferung der Angelsachsen, mit einem Katalog der* libri vitae *und Necrologien* (Berlin 1988)

GIBSON, Margaret *Lanfranc of Bec* (Oxford 1978)

GLEESON, D. F. & MAC AIRT, S. (edd.) 'The Annals of Roscrea', *Proceedings of the Royal Irish Academy* 59 C (1957–9) 137–80

GNEUSS, H. 'Liturgical books in Anglo-Saxon England and their Old English terminology', in *Learning and Literature in Anglo-Saxon England*, edd. M. Lapidge & H. Gneuss (Cambridge 1985), pp. 91–141

GOETINCK, G. 'Lifris and the Italian connection', *Bulletin of the Board of Celtic Studies* 35 (1988) 10–13

GOUGAUD, L. 'Les plus anciennes attestations du culte de saint Patrice', *Ephemerides liturgicae* 45 (1931) 182–5

GRABOWSKI, Kathryn & DUMVILLE, D. *Chronicles and Annals of Mediaeval Ireland and Wales. The Clonmacnoise-group Texts* (Woodbridge 1984)

GRANDGENT, C. H. *An Introduction to Vulgar Latin* (Boston, Mass. 1907)

GRANSDEN, Antonia *Historical Writing in England* (2 vols, London 1974/82)

GRANSDEN, A. 'The growth of the Glastonbury traditions and legends in the twelfth century', *Journal of Ecclesiastical History* 27 (1976) 337–58

GRANT, Raymond J. S. (ed.) *Cambridge, Corpus Christi College 41: the Loricas and the Missal* (Amsterdam 1978)

GRATWICK, A. S. 'Latinitas britannica: was British Latin archaic?', in *Latin and the Vernacular Languages in Early Medieval Britain*, ed. N. Brooks (Leicester 1982), pp. 1–79

GREEN, D. H. *The Carolingian Lord. Semantic Studies on Four Old High German Words: Balder, Frô, Truhtin, Hêrro* (Cambridge 1965)

GREENE, D. 'Some linguistic evidence relating to the British Church', in *Christianity in Britain, 300–700*, edd. M. W. Barley & R. P. C. Hanson (Leicester 1968), pp. 75–86

GREENE, D. 'The making of Insular Celtic', in *Proceedings of the Second International Congress of Celtic Studies, held in Cardiff 6–13 July, 1963*, ed. H. Lewis (Cardiff 1966), pp. 123–36

GRETSCH, M. 'Æthelwold's translation of the *Regula Sancti Benedicti* and its Latin exemplar', *Anglo-Saxon England* 3 (1974) 125–51

GRETSCH, Mechthild *Die Regula Sancti Benedicti in England und ihre altenglische Übersetzung* (München 1973)

GRILLMEIER, Aloys & BACHT, H. (edd.) *Das Konzil von Chalkedon. Geschichte und Gegenwart* (3 vols, Würzburg 1951–4)

GROSJEAN, P. (ed. & transl.) 'An early fragment on Saint Patrick in Ui

Briúin Breifne contained in the Life of Saint Benén (Benignus) of Armagh', *Seanchas Ardmhacha* 1, no. 1 (1954) 31–44

GROSJEAN, P. 'Cyngar sant', *Analecta Bollandiana* 42 (1924) 100–20

GROSJEAN, P. (ed.) 'Édition et commentaire du *Catalogus sanctorum Hiberniae secundum diversa tempora* ou *De tribus ordinibus sanctorum Hiberniae*', *Analecta Bollandiana* 73 (1955) 197–213 *and* 289–322

GROSJEAN, P. 'Les inscriptions métriques de l'église de Péronne', *Analecta Bollandiana* 78 (1960) 369–70

GROSJEAN, P. 'Les Pictes apostats dans l'Épître de S. Patrice', *Analecta Bollandiana* 76 (1958) 354–78

GROSJEAN, P. 'Notes chronologiques sur le séjour de S. Patrice en Gaule', *Analecta Bollandiana* 63 (1945) 73–93

GROSJEAN, P. 'S. Patrice à Auxerre sous S. Germain. Le témoignage des noms gaulois', *Analecta Bollandiana* 75 (1957) 158–74

GROSJEAN, P. 'S. Patrice d'Irlande et quelques homonymes dans les anciens martyrologes', *Journal of Ecclesiastical History* 1 (1950) 151–71

GROSJEAN, P. 'S. Patrice et S. Victrice', *Analecta Bollandiana* 63 (1945) 94–9

GROSJEAN, P. 'The Confession of Saint Patrick', in *Saint Patrick*, ed. J. Ryan ([Dublin] 1958), pp. 81–94

GUENTHER, Otto (ed.) *Epistulae Imperatorum Pontificum aliorum inde ab a. CCCLXVII usque ad a. DLIII datae: Auellana quae dicitur collectio* (Wien 1895–8)

GÜTERBOCK, Bruno G. *Bemerkungen über die lateinischen Lehnwörter im Irischen*, I, *Zur Lautlehre* (Leipzig 1882)

GWYNN, Aubrey & HADCOCK, R. N. *Medieval Religious Houses: Ireland* (London 1970)

GWYNN, A. 'The origins of the see of Dublin', *Irish Ecclesiastical Record*, 5th S., 57 (1941) 40–55 *and* 97–112

GWYNN, Aubrey *The Twelfth-century Reform* (Dublin 1968) [*A History of Irish Catholicism*, gen. ed. Patrick J. Corish, vol. II, pt 1]

GWYNN, Edward (facs. ed.) *Book of Armagh: the Patrician Documents* (Dublin 1937)

GWYNN, John (ed.) *Liber Ardmachanus. The Book of Armagh* (Dublin 1913)

HADDAN, Arthur West & STUBBS, W. (edd.) *Councils and Ecclesiastical Documents relating to Great Britain and Ireland* (3 vols, Oxford 1869–78)

*HAMILTON, G. F. *In Patrick's Praise. The Hymn of Saint Secundinus (Sechnall)* (2nd edn, Dublin 1920)

HAMP, E. P. '**isa* in British Celtic', *Études celtiques* 18 (1981) 109–11

HAMP, E. P. 'Latin *er* in British Celtic', *Études celtiques* 17 (1980) 161–3

HANSON, R. P. C. 'Dogma and formula in the Fathers', *Texte und Untersuchungen zur Geschichte der altchristlichen Literatur* 116 [= *Studia Patristica* 13] (1976) 169–84

HANSON, R. P. C. 'Patrick and the *mensura fidei*', *Texte und Untersuchungen zur altchristlichen Literatur* 107 [= *Studia Patristica* 10] (1970) 109–11

HANSON, R[ichard] P. C. *St. Patrick, a British Missionary Bishop* (Nottingham [1966])

HANSON, Richard P. C. & BLANC, C. (edd. & transl.) *Saint Patrick: Confession et Lettre à Coroticus* (Paris 1978)
HANSON, R[ichard] P. C. *Saint Patrick, his Origins and Career* (Oxford 1968)
HANSON, R. P. C. 'The Church in fifth-century Gaul: evidence from Sidonius Apollinaris', *Journal of Ecclesiastical History* 21 (1970) 1–10
HANSON, R. P. C. 'The date of St. Patrick', *Bulletin of the John Rylands University Library of Manchester* 61 (1978/9) 60–77
HANSON, R. P. C. 'The D-text of Patrick's *Confession*: original or reduction?', *Proceedings of the Royal Irish Academy* 77 C (1977) 251–6
HANSON, R[ichard] P. C. (transl.) *The Life and Writings of the Historical Saint Patrick* (New York 1983)
HANSON, R. P. C. 'The omissions in the text of the Confession of St. Patrick in the Book of Armagh', *Texte und Untersuchungen zur Geschichte der altchristlichen Literatur* 115 [= *Studia Patristica* 12] (1975) 91–5
HANSON, R. P. C. 'The *Profession* of Patricius and Aetius', *Proceedings of the Royal Irish Academy* 89 C (1989) 67–70
HANSON, R. P. C. 'The rule of faith of Victorinus and of Patrick', in *Latin Script and Letters A.D. 400–900*, edd. J. J. O'Meara & B. Naumann (Leiden 1976), pp. 25–36
HANSON, R[ichard] P. C. *The Search for the Christian Doctrine of God. The Arian Controversy 318–381* (Edinburgh 1988)
HANSON, R[ichard] P. C. *Tradition in the Early Church* (London 1962)
HANSON, R. P. C. 'Witness from St. Patrick to the creed of 381', *Analecta Bollandiana* 101 (1983) 297–9
HARRIS, Silas M. *Saint David in the Liturgy* (Cardiff 1940)
HARRISON, K. 'Epacts in Irish chronicles', *Studia Celtica* 12/13 (1977/8) 17–32
HARRISON, K. 'Episodes in the history of Easter cycles in Ireland', in *Ireland in Early Mediaeval Europe*, edd. D. Whitelock *et al.* (Cambridge 1982), pp. 307–19
HARVEY, A. 'Early literacy in Ireland: the evidence from ogam', *Cambridge Medieval Celtic Studies* 14 (1987) 1–15
HARVEY, A. 'Latin, literacy and the Celtic vernaculars around the year AD 500', in *Celtic Languages and Celtic Peoples*, edd. C. J. Byrne *et al.* (Halifax, Nova Scotia 1992), pp. 11–26
HARVEY, A. 'Some significant points of early Insular Celtic orthography', in *Sages, Saints and Storytellers*, edd. D. Ó Corráin *et al.* (Maynooth 1989), pp. 56–66
HARVEY, A. 'The ogam inscriptions and their geminate symbols', *Ériu* 38 (1987) 45–71
HARVEY, A. 'The significance of *Cothraige*', *Ériu* 36 (1985) 1–9
HAWKES, S. C. 'The South-east after the Romans: the Saxon settlement', in *The Saxon Shore*, ed. V. A. Maxfield (Exeter 1989), pp. 78–95
HEALY, John *The Life and Writings of St. Patrick* (Dublin 1905)
HEARNE, Thomas (ed.) *Joannis Lelandi antiquarii De rebus britannicis collectanea* (2nd edn, 6 vols, London 1774)
HEATHER, P[eter] J. *Goths and Romans 332–489* (Oxford 1991)

HEATHER, Peter [J.] & MATTHEWS, J. *The Goths in the Fourth Century* (Liverpool 1991)

HEIST, W. W. 'Over the writer's shoulder: Saint Abban', *Celtica* 11 (1976) 76–84

HEIST, William W. (ed.) *Vitae Sanctorum Hiberniae ex Codice olim Salmanticensi nunc Bruxellensi* (Bruxelles 1965)

HENNESSY, William M. (ed. & transl.) *Chronicum Scotorum. A Chronicle of Irish Affairs from the Earliest Times to A.D. 1135, with a Supplement, containing the Events from 1141 to 1150* (London 1866)

HENNIG, John *Medieval Ireland, Saints and Martyrologies. Selected Studies* (Northampton 1989)

HENNIG, J. 'The literary tradition of Moses in Ireland', *Traditio* 7 (1949–51) 233–61

HERBERT, Máire *Iona, Kells, and Derry. The History and Hagiography of the Monastic* Familia *of Columba* (Oxford 1988)

HERMAN, E. 'Chalkedon und die Ausgestaltung des konstantinopolitanischen Primats', in *Das Konzil von Chalkedon*, edd. A. Grillmeier & A. Bacht (3 vols, Würzburg 1951–4), II.459–90

HERREN, M. [W.] 'Mission and monasticism in the *Confessio* of Patrick', in *Sages, Saints and Storytellers*, edd. D. Ó Corráin *et al.* (Maynooth 1989), pp. 76–85

HERREN, M. W. 'The stress systems in Insular Latin octosyllabic verse', *Cambridge Medieval Celtic Studies* 15 (1988) 63–84

HIGHAM, Nicholas *Rome, Britain and the Anglo-Saxons* (London 1992)

HINES, J. 'Philology, archaeology and the *adventus Saxonum vel Anglorum*', in *Britain 400–600*, edd. A. Bammesberger & A. Wollmann (Heidelberg 1990), pp. 17–36

HINGLEY, Richard *Rural Settlement in Roman Britain* (London 1989)

HOGAN, Edmund *Onomasticon Goedelicum Locorum et Tribuum Hiberniae et Scotiae. An Index, with Identifications, to the Gaelic Names of Places and Tribes* (Dublin 1910)

HOHLER, C. [E.] 'Les Saints insulaires dans le Missel de l'Archevêque Robert', in *Jumièges. Congrès scientifique du XIIIe centenaire, Rouen, 10–12 juin 1954* (2 vols, Rouen 1955), I.293–303

HOHLER, C. E. 'Some service-books of the later Saxon Church', in *Tenth-century Studies*, ed. D. Parsons (Chichester 1975), pp. 60–83 *and* 217–27

HOHLER, C. [E.] & HUGHES, A. (edd.) 'The Durham services in honour of St. Cuthbert', in *The Relics of Saint Cuthbert*, ed. C. F. Battiscombe (Oxford 1956), pp. 155–91

HOLDER, Alfred *Alt-celtischer Sprachschatz* (3 vols, Leipzig 1891–1913)

HOLDSWORTH, Christopher & WISEMAN, T. P. (edd.) *The Inheritance of Historiography 350–900* (Exeter 1986)

HOOD, A. B. E. (ed. & transl.) *St. Patrick: His Writings and Muirchu's Life* (Chichester 1978)

HOPE, D. M. *The Leonine Sacramentary. A Reassessment of its Nature and Purpose* (London 1971)

HOWLETT, D. R. 'Biblical style in early Insular Latin', in *Sources of Anglo-*

Saxon Culture, edd. P. E. Szarmach & V. D. Oggins (Kalamazoo, Mich. 1986), pp. 127–47

HOWLETT, D. R. 'Ex saliva scripturae meae', in *Sages, Saints and Storytellers*, edd. D. Ó Corráin *et al.* (Maynooth 1989), pp. 86–101

HÜBNER, Emil (ed.) *Inscriptiones Britanniae Latinae* (Berlin 1873)

HUGHES, Kathleen *Celtic Britain in the Early Middle Ages. Studies in Scottish and Welsh Sources* (Woodbridge 1980)

HUGHES, Kathleen *Church and Society in Ireland A.D. 400–1200* (London 1987)

HUGHES, Kathleen *Early Christian Ireland: Introduction to the Sources* (London 1972)

HUGHES, K. 'Evidence for contacts between the Churches of the Irish and the English from the Synod of Whitby to the Viking Age', in *England before the Conquest*, edd. P. Clemoes & K. Hughes (Cambridge 1971), pp. 49–67

HUGHES, Kathleen *The Church in Early Irish Society* (London 1966)

HUNTER BLAIR, Peter *The World of Bede* (London 1970; rev. imp., by M. Lapidge, Cambridge 1990)

HUWS, D. 'A Welsh manuscript of Bede's *De natura rerum*', *Bulletin of the Board of Celtic Studies* 27 (1976–8) 491–504

JACKSON, Kenneth Hurlstone *A Historical Phonology of Breton* (Dublin 1967)

JACKSON, K. [H.] 'Final syllables in "Padraig" loanwords', *Études celtiques* 9 (1960/1) 79–91

JACKSON, Kenneth [Hurlstone] *Language and History in Early Britain. A Chronological Survey of the Brittonic Languages, 1st to 12th c. A.D.* (Edinburgh 1953)

JACKSON, K. H. 'The date of the Tripartite Life of St. Patrick', *Zeitschrift für celtische Philologie* 41 (1986) 5–45

JACKSON, Kenneth Hurlstone (transl.) *The Goddodin. The Oldest Scottish Poem* (Edinburgh 1969)

JACKSON, K. H. 'The sources for the Life of St Kentigern', in *Studies in the Early British Church*, ed. N. K. Chadwick (Cambridge 1958), pp. 273–357

JAMES, J. W. (ed. & transl.) *Rhigyfarch's Life of St. David. The Basic Mid Twelfth-century Latin Text* (Cardiff 1967)

JAMES, Montague Rhodes *A Descriptive Catalogue of the Manuscripts in the Library of Corpus Christi College, Cambridge* (2 vols, Cambridge 1909–12)

JONDORF, Gillian & DUMVILLE, D. N. (edd.) *France and the British Isles in the Middle Ages and Renaissance. Essays by Members of Girton College, Cambridge, in Memory of Ruth Morgan* (Woodbridge 1991)

JONES, A. H. M., *et al.* *The Prosopography of the Later Roman Empire* (3 vols, Cambridge 1971–)

JONES, Barri & MATTINGLY, D. *An Atlas of Roman Britain* (Oxford 1990)

JONES, Charles W. (ed.) *Bedae opera de temporibus* (Cambridge, Mass. 1943)

JONES, D. M. 'Etymological notes', *Transactions of the Philological Society* (1953) 43–51

KAJANTO, Iiro *Onomastic Studies in the Early Christian Inscriptions of Rome and Carthage* (Helsinki 1963)

KAJANTO, Iiro *The Latin Cognomina* (Helsinki 1965)

KENNEY, James F. *The Sources for the Early History of Ireland: Ecclesiastical. An Introduction and Guide* (New York 1929; rev. imp., by L. Bieler, 1966)
KER, N. R. *Catalogue of Manuscripts containing Anglo-Saxon* (Oxford 1957; rev. imp., 1990)
KER, N. R. *Medieval Libraries of Great Britain. A List of Surviving Books* (2nd edn, London 1964)
KINSELLA, Thomas (transl.) *The Táin, translated from the Irish Epic Táin Bó Cuailnge* (2nd edn, London 1970)
KLAR, Kathryn & SWEETSER, E. (edd.) *A Celtic Florilegium in Memory of Brendan O Hehir* (Cambridge, Mass. 1993)
KNOTT, Eleanor & MURPHY, G. *Early Irish Literature* (London 1966)
KNOWLES, David, *et al.* *The Heads of Religious Houses: England and Wales, 940–1216* (Cambridge 1972)
KOCH, J. T. '**Cothairche*, Esposito's theory, and Neo-Celtic lenition', in *Britain 400–600*, edd. A. Bammesberger & A. Wollmann (Heidelberg 1990), pp. 179–202
KOCH, J. T. 'The cynfeirdd poetry and the language of the sixth century', in *Early Welsh Poetry*, ed. B. F. Roberts (Aberystwyth 1988), pp. 17–41
KOCH, J. T. 'The loss of final syllables and loss of declension in Brittonic', *Bulletin of the Board of Celtic Studies* 30 (1982/3) 201–33
KOCH, J. T. 'When was Welsh literature first written down?', *Studia Celtica* 20/21 (1985/6) 43–66
KOTZOR, G. 'St. Patrick in the Old English "Martyrology": on a lost leaf of MS. C.C.C.C. 196', *Notes and Queries* 219 [N.S., 21] (1974) 86–7
KRUSCH, Bruno (ed.) *Ionae uitae sanctorum Columbani, Vedastis, Iohannis* (Hannover 1905)
KRUSCH, B[runo] & LEVISON, W. (edd.) *Passiones Vitaeque Sanctorum Aevi Merovingici*, VII (Hannover 1919/20)
LAMBKIN, B. K. 'Patrick, Armagh, and Emain Macha', *Emania* 2 (1987) 29–31
LAPIDGE, Michael (ed.) *Anglo-Saxon Litanies of the Saints* (London 1991)
LAPIDGE, M. 'Columbanus and the "Antiphonary of Bangor" ', *Peritia* 4 (1985) 104–16
LAPIDGE, Michael & DUMVILLE, D. (edd.) *Gildas: New Approaches* (Woodbridge 1984)
LAPIDGE, Michael & GNEUSS, H. (edd.) *Learning and Literature in Anglo-Saxon England. Studies presented to Peter Clemoes on the Occasion of his Sixty-fifth Birthday* (Cambridge 1985)
LAPIDGE, M. (ed.) 'Some remnants of Bede's lost Liber Epigrammatum', *English Historical Review* 90 (1975) 798–820
LAPIDGE, M. (ed.) 'The cult of St. Indract at Glastonbury', in *Ireland in Early Mediaeval Europe*, edd. D. Whitelock *et al.* (Cambridge 1982), pp. 179–212
LAPIDGE, M. (ed. & transl.) 'The Welsh-Latin poetry of Sulien's family', *Studia Celtica* 8/9 (1973/4) 68–106
LAPIDGE, Michael & WINTERBOTTOM, M. (edd. & transl.) *Wulfstan of Winchester, The Life of St Æthelwold* (Oxford 1991)

LAWLOR, H. J. & BEST, R. I. (edd.) 'The ancient list of the coarbs of Patrick', *Proceedings of the Royal Irish Academy* 35 C (1918–20) 316–62

LE BLANT, Edmond (ed.) *Inscriptions chrétiennes de la Gaule antérieures au VIIIe siècle* (2 vols, Paris 1856/65)

LEVISON, W. 'An eighth-century poem on St. Ninian', *Antiquity* 14 (1940) 280–91

LEVISON, W. 'Zu den Versen des Abtes Cellanus von Péronne', *Zeitschrift für celtische Philologie* 20 (1933–6) 382–90

LEWIS, Henry (ed.) *Proceedings of the Second International Congress of Celtic Studies, held in Cardiff 6–13 July, 1963* (Cardiff 1966)

LIEBERMANN, F. (ed.) *Die Heiligen Englands; angelsächsisch und lateinisch* (Hannover 1889)

LINDSAY, W. M. *Notae Latinae. An Account of Abbreviation in Latin MSS. of the Early Minuscule Period (c. 700–850)* (Cambridge 1915)

LORENZ, R. 'Der Augustinismus Prospers von Aquitanien', *Zeitschrift für Kirchengeschichte* 73 [4th S., 11] (1962) 217–52

LOT, Ferdinand (ed.) *Nennius et l'Historia Brittonum. Étude critique suivie d'une édition des diverses versions de ce texte* (2 vols, Paris 1934)

LOTH, J. *Chrestomathie bretonne (Armoricain, Gallois, Cornique), Première Partie, Breton-Armoricain* (Paris 1890)

LOWE, E. A. (ed.) *Codices Latini Antiquiores. A Palaeographical Guide to Latin Manuscripts prior to the Ninth Century* (11 vols & supplement, Oxford 1934–71; 2nd edn of vol. II, 1972)

LYNN, C. J. & MCDOWELL, J. A. 'Muirchú's Armagh', *Emania* 4 (1988) 42–6

LYNN, C. J. 'Navan Fort. A draft summary account of D.M. Waterman's excavations', *Emania* 1 (1986) 11–19

MAC AIRT, Seán (ed. & transl.) *The Annals of Inisfallen (MS. Rawlinson B.503)* (Dublin 1951)

MAC AIRT, Seán & MAC NIOCAILL, G. (edd. & transl.) *The Annals of Ulster (to A.D. 1131)*, I (Dublin 1983)

MAC CANA, P. 'Mongán mac Fiachna and *Immram Brain*', *Ériu* 23 (1972) 102–42

MCCONE, K. [R.] 'Dubthach maccu Lugair and a matter of life and death in the pseudo-historical prologue to the *Senchas Már*', *Peritia* 5 (1986) 1–35

MCCONE, Kim [R.] *Pagan Past and Christian Present in Early Irish Literature* (Maynooth 1990)

MCCONE, K. R. 'Werewolves, cyclopes, *díberga*, and *fíanna*: juvenile delinquency in early Ireland', *Cambridge Medieval Celtic Studies* 12 (1986) 1–22

MAC DONNCHA, F. 'Dáta Vita Tripartita Sancti Patricii', *Éigse* 18 (1980/1) 125–42 *and* 19 (1982/3) 354–72

MAC DONNCHA, F. 'Medieval Irish homilies', *Proceedings of the Irish Biblical Association* 1 (1976) 59–71

MAC EOIN, G. [S.] 'Observations on Saltair na Rann', *Zeitschrift für celtische Philologie* 39 (1982) 1–28

MAC EOIN, Gearóid [S.], *et al.* (edd.) *Proceedings of the Sixth International Congress of Celtic Studies held in University College, Galway, 6–13 July 1979* (Dublin 1983)

MAC EOIN, G. S. 'The date and authorship of Saltair na Rann', *Zeitschrift für celtische Philologie* 28 (1960/1) 51–67
MAC EOIN, G. [S.] 'The dating of Middle Irish texts', *Proceedings of the British Academy* 68 (1982) 109–37
MACINERNY, M. H. 'St. Mochta and Bachiarius', *Irish Ecclesiastical Record*, 5th S., 21 (1923) 468–80 *and* 618–32; 22 (1923) 153–65 *and* 573–91
MCMANUS, D. 'A chronology of the Latin loan-words in early Irish', *Ériu* 34 (1983) 21–71
MCMANUS, Damian *A Guide to Ogam* (Maynooth 1991)
MCMANUS, D. '*Linguarum diversitas*: Latin and the vernaculars in early medieval Britain', *Peritia* 3 (1984) 151–88
MCMANUS, D. 'Ogam: archaizing, orthography and the authenticity of the manuscript key to the alphabet', *Ériu* 37 (1986) 1–31
MCMANUS, D. 'On final syllables in the Latin loan-words in early Irish', *Ériu* 35 (1984) 137–62
MCMANUS, D. 'The so-called *Cothrige* and *Pátraic* strata of Latin loan-words in early Irish', in *Ireland and Europe*, edd. P. Ní Chatháin & M. Richter (Stuttgart 1984), pp. 179–96
MACNEILL, E. 'Beginnings of Latin culture in Ireland', *Studies* 20 (1931) 39–48 *and* 449–60
MACNEILL, E. 'Colonisation under early kings of Tara', *Journal of the Galway Archaeological and Historical Society* 16 (1934/5) 101–24
MACNEILL, J. [= E.] 'Early Irish population-groups: their nomenclature, classification, and chronology', *Proceedings of the Royal Irish Academy* 29 C (1911/12) 59–114
MACNEILL, E. 'Mocu, maccu', *Ériu* 3 (1907) 42–9
MACNEILL, Eoin *Saint Patrick* (Dublin 1964)
MACNEILL, E. 'The Hymn of St. Secundinus in honour of St. Patrick', *Irish Historical Studies* 2 (1940/1) 129–53
MACNEILL, E. 'The native place of St. Patrick', *Proceedings of the Royal Irish Academy* 37 C (1925–7) 118–40
MAC NIOCAILL, G. (ed.) 'Fragments d'un coutumier monastique irlandais du VIIIe–IXe siècle', *Scriptorium* 15 (1961) 228–33 + plate 22
MAC NIOCAILL, Gearóid *Ireland before the Vikings* (Dublin 1972)
MACQUARRIE, A. 'The career of Saint Kentigern of Glasgow: *vitae, lectiones* and glimpses of fact', *Innes Review* 37 (1986) 3–24
MACQUARRIE, A. 'The date of Saint Ninian's mission: a reappraisal', *Records of the Scottish Church History Society* 23 (1987–9) 1–25
MACQUEEN, John *St. Nynia. A Study of Literary and Linguistic Evidence* (Edinburgh 1961)
MACQUEEN, W. W. (ed. & transl.) 'Miracula Nynie episcopi', *Transactions of the Dumfriesshire and Galloway Natural History and Antiquarian Society*, 3rd S., 37 (1959/60) 21–57
MCSHANE, Philip A. *La Romanitas et le pape Léon le Grand. L'apport culturel des institutions impériales à la formation des structures ecclésiastiques* (Tournai 1979)
MALONE, S. 'Sen (old) Patrick, who was he?', *Irish Ecclesiastical Record*, 3rd S., 12 (1891) 800–9

MANDOUZE, André *Prosopographie chrétienne du bas-empire*, I, *Prosopographie de l'Afrique chrétienne (303–533)* (Paris 1982)

MANSI, Giovanni Domenico (ed.) *Sacrorum conciliorum nova et amplissima collectio* (35 vols in 37, Firenze, etc. 1759–1903)

MARKUS, R. A. 'Chronicle and theology: Prosper of Aquitaine', in *The Inheritance of Historiography 350–900*, edd. C. Holdsworth & T. P. Wiseman (Exeter 1986), pp. 31–43

MARKUS, R. A., 'Pelagianism: Britain and the Continent', *Journal of Ecclesiastical History* 37 (1986) 191–204

MARKUS, R. A. *Saeculum: History and Society in the Theology of St Augustine* (Cambridge 1970)

MARKUS, R. A. 'The legacy of Pelagius: orthodoxy, heresy and conciliation', in *The Making of Orthodoxy*, ed. R. Williams (Cambridge 1989), pp. 214–34

MARROU, Henri Irénée (gen. ed.) *Recueil des Inscriptions chrétiennes de la Gaule antérieures à la Renaissance carolingienne* (Paris 1975–)

MARTIMORT, Aimé-Georges *La Documentation liturgique de Dom Edmond Martène. Étude codicologique* (Roma 1978)

MARTIMORT, A.-G. [review of D. M. Hope, *The Leonine Sacramentary* (1971)], *Bulletin de littérature ecclésiastique* 73 (1972) 267–8

MATHISEN, R. W. 'The last year of Saint Germanus of Auxerre', *Analecta Bollandiana* 99 (1981) 151–9

MAXFIELD, Valerie A. (ed.) *The Saxon Shore. A Handbook* (Exeter 1989)

MEYER, Kuno (ed. & transl.) *Cáin Adamnáin. An Old-Irish Treatise on the Law of Adamnan* (Oxford 1905)

MEYER, Kuno *Learning in Ireland in the Fifth Century and the Transmission of Letters* (Dublin 1913)

MEYER, Kuno (facs. ed.) *Rawlinson B.502. A Collection of Pieces in Prose and Verse in the Irish Language, compiled during the Eleventh and Twelfth Centuries, now published in Facsimile from the Original Manuscript in the Bodleian Library* (Oxford 1909)

MEYER, K. (ed.) 'The Laud Synchronisms from Laud 610, fo. 112a1–116b1', *Zeitschrift für celtische Philologie* 9 (1913) 471–85

MEYER, K. (ed.) 'Verses from a chapel dedicated to St Patrick at Péronne', *Ériu* 5 (1911) 110–11

MEYER, Wilhelm *Gesammelte Abhandlungen zur mittellateinischen Rythmik* (3 vols, Berlin 1905–36)

MEYVAERT, P. 'Towards a history of the textual transmission of the *Regula S. Benedicti*', *Scriptorium* 17 (1963) 83–110

MIGNE, J.-P. (ed.) *Patrologiæ [latinæ] cursus completus* . . . (221 vols, Paris 1844–64)

MILLER, M. 'Date-guessing and Dyfed', *Studia Celtica* 12/13 (1977/8) 33–61

MILLER, M. 'Date-guessing and pedigrees', *Studia Celtica* 10/11 (1975/6) 96–109

MILLER, M. 'The final stages in the construction of the Harleian *Annales Cambriae*', *Celtica* 23 (1993)

MILLETT, Martin *The Romanization of Britain. An Essay in Archaeological Interpretation* (Cambridge 1990)

MOHLBERG, Leo Cunibert, *et al.* (edd.) *Liber sacramentorum romanae aeclesiae ordinis anni circuli (Cod. Vat. Reg. lat. 316 / Paris Bibl. Nat. 7193, 41/56) (Sacramentarium Gelasianum)* (Roma 1960)

MOHLBERG, Leo Cunibert, *et al.* (edd.) *Sacramentarium Veronense (Cod. Bibl. Capit. Veron. LXXXV [80])* (Roma 1955/6)

MOHRMANN, Christine *The Latin of Saint Patrick. Four Lectures* (Dublin 1961)

MOMMSEN, Theodor (ed.) *Chronica minora saec. IV. V. VI. VII* (3 vols, Berlin 1891–8)

MORRIS, J. 'The dates of the Celtic saints', *Journal of Theological Studies*, N.S., 17 (1966) 342–91

MORRIS, Richard *Churches in the Landscape* (London 1989)

MORRIS JONES, J. *A Welsh Grammar, Historical and Comparative. Phonology and Accidence* (Oxford 1913)

MRAS, K. [review of L. Bieler (ed.), 'Libri epistolarum sancti Patricii episcopi' (1950/1)], *Anzeiger für die Altertumswissenschaft* 8 (1955) cols 73–74

MRAS, K. 'St. Patricius als Lateiner', *Anzeiger der österreichischen Akademie der Wissenschaften*, Philosophisch-historische Klasse, 90 (1953) 99–113

MUIR, Bernard James (ed.) *A Pre-Conquest English Prayer-book (BL MSS Cotton Galba A.xiv and Nero A.ii (ff. 3–13))* (London 1988)

MULCHRONE, Kathleen (ed.) *Bethu Phátraic. The Tripartite Life of Patrick* (Dublin 1939)

MULCHRONE, K. 'Die Abfassungszeit und Überlieferung der Vita Tripartita', *Zeitschrift für celtische Philologie* 16 (1926/7) 1–94

MULCHRONE, K. 'The Old-Irish form of *Palladius*', *Journal of the Galway Archaeological and Historical Society* 22 (1946/7) 34–42

MULCHRONE, K. (ed.) 'The Tripartite Life of Patrick. Fragments of Stowe copy found', *Journal of the Galway Archaeological and Historical Society* 20 (1942/3) 129–44

MULCHRONE, K. (ed. & transl.) 'The Tripartite Life of Patrick. Lost fragment discovered', *Journal of the Galway Archaeological and Historical Society* 20 (1942/3) 39–53

MURPHY, Denis (ed.) *The Annals of Clonmacnoise, being Annals of Ireland from the Earliest Period to A.D. 1408, translated into English A.D. 1627 by Conell Mageoghagan* (Dublin 1896)

MURPHY, G. 'The two Patricks', *Studies* 32 (1943) 297–307

NELSON, Janet L. *Politics and Ritual in Early Medieval Europe* (London 1986)

NEWELL, W. W. 'William of Malmesbury on the antiquity of Glastonbury, with especial reference to the equation of Glastonbury and Avalon', *Publications of the Modern Language Association of America* 18 [N.S., 11] (1905) 459–512

NÍ CHATHÁIN, Próinséas & RICHTER, M. (edd.) *Ireland and Europe. The Early Church* (Stuttgart 1984)

NIEKE, M. R. & DUNCAN, H. B. 'Dalriada: the establishment and maintenance of an early historic kingdom in northern Britain', in *Power and Politics in Early Medieval Britain and Ireland*, edd. S. T. Driscoll & M. R. Nieke (Edinburgh 1988), pp. 6–21

NORBERG, Dag *Introduction à l'étude de la versification latine médiévale* (Stockholm 1958)

NORBERG, Dag (ed.) *S. Gregorii Magni Registrum Epistularum* (2 vols, Turnhout 1982)

Ó BRIAIN, M. 'Studien zu irischen Völkernamen, 1. Die Stammesnamen auf -rige', *Zeitschrift für celtische Philologie* 15 (1924/5) 222–37

O'BRIEN, M. A. (ed.) *Corpus Genealogiarum Hiberniae*, I (Dublin 1962; rev. imp., by J. V. Kelleher, 1976)

O'BRIEN, M. A. (ed.) *Irish Origin Legends* (Dublin n.d.)

O'BRIEN, M. A. (ed. & transl.) 'The oldest account of the raid of the Collas (circa A.D. 330)', *Ulster Journal of Archaeology*, 3rd S., 2 (1939) 170–7

Ó CONCHEANAINN, T. 'The scribe of the Leabhar Breac', *Ériu* 24 (1973) 64–79

Ó CORRÁIN, Donncha[dh] *Ireland before the Normans* (Dublin 1972)

Ó CORRÁIN, Donnchadh, *et al.* (edd.) *Sages, Saints and Storytellers. Celtic Studies in Honour of Professor James Carney* (Maynooth 1989)

Ó CRÓINÍN, D. 'A seventh-century Irish computus from the circle of Cummianus', *Proceedings of the Royal Irish Academy* 82 C (1982) 405–30

Ó CRÓINÍN, D. ' "New heresy for old": Pelagianism in Ireland and the papal letter of 640', *Speculum* 60 (1985) 505–16

Ó CRÓINÍN, D. 'New light on Palladius', *Peritia* 5 (1986) 276–83

Ó CRÓINÍN, D. 'Rath Melsigi, Willibrord, and the earliest Echternach manuscripts', *Peritia* 3 (1984) 17–42

Ó CRÓINÍN, D. 'The Irish provenance of Bede's computus', *Peritia* 2 (1983) 229–47

Ó CUÍV, B. 'Aspects of Irish personal names', *Celtica* 18 (1986) 151–84

Ó CUÍV, B. (ed. & transl.) 'St Gregory and St Dunstan in a Middle-Irish poem on the origins of liturgical chant', in *St Dunstan, his Life, Times and Cult*, edd. N. Ramsay *et al.* (Woodbridge 1992), pp. 273–97

O'DONOVAN, John (ed. & transl.) *Annala Rioghachta Eireann. Annals of the Kingdom of Ireland, by the Four Masters, from the Earliest Period to the Year 1616* (2nd edn, 7 vols, Dublin 1856)

O'GRADY, Standish Hayes, *et al.* *Catalogue of Irish Manuscripts in the British Museum* (3 vols, London 1926–53)

OLMSTED, G. 'The earliest narrative version of the *Táin*: seventh-century poetic references to *Táin bó Cúailnge*', *Emania* 10 (1992) 5–17

O'MEARA, John J. & NAUMANN, B. (edd.) *Latin Script and Letters A.D. 400–900. Festschrift presented to Ludwig Bieler on the Occasion of his 70th Birthday* (Leiden 1976)

O'RAHILLY, Thomas F. *Early Irish History and Mythology* (Dublin 1946)

O'RAHILLY, Thomas F. *The Two Patricks. A Lecture on the History of Christianity in Fifth-century Ireland* (Dublin 1942)

Ó RIAIN, P. 'St Finnbarr: a study in a cult', *Journal of the Cork Historical and Archaeological Society* 82 (1977) 63–82

Ó RIAIN, P. 'The Psalter of Cashel: a provisional list of contents', *Éigse* 23 (1989) 107–30

Ó RIAIN, P. 'The shrine of the Stowe Missal, redated', *Proceedings of the Royal Irish Academy* 91 C (1991) 285–95

Ó RIAIN, P. 'The Tallaght martyrologies, redated', *Cambridge Medieval Celtic Studies* 20 (1990) 21–38

OULTON, John Ernest Leonard *The Credal Statements of St. Patrick as contained in the Fourth Chapter of his* Confession. *A Study of their Sources* (Dublin 1940)

PAGE, R. I. 'The lost leaf of MS. C.C.C.C. 196', *Notes and Queries* 219 [N.S., 21] (1974) 472–3

PARSONS, David (ed.) *Tenth-century Studies. Essays in Commemoration of the Millennium of the Council of Winchester and* Regularis Concordia (Chichester 1975)

PEARCE, S. M. 'Church and society in south Devon, AD 350–700', *Devon Archaeological Society Proceedings* 40 (1982) 1–18

PEARCE, S. [M.] 'Estates and church sites in Dorset and Gloucestershire: the emergence of a christian society', in *The Early Church in Western Britain and Ireland*, ed. S. M. Pearce (Oxford 1982), pp. 117–38

PEARCE, S. M. 'The early church in the landscape: the evidence from North Devon', *Archaeological Journal* 142 (1985) 255–75

PEARCE, Susan M. (ed.) *The Early Church in Western Britain and Ireland. Studies presented to C.A. Ralegh Radford arising from a Conference organised in his Honour by the Devon Archaeological Society and Exeter City Museum* (Oxford 1982)

PEDERSEN, Holger *Vergleichende Grammatik der keltischen Sprachen* (2 vols, Göttingen 1908–13)

PERCIVAL, J. 'The fifth-century villa: new life or death postponed?', in *Fifth-century Gaul*, edd. J. Drinkwater & H. Elton (Cambridge 1992), pp. 156–64

PERCIVAL, John *The Roman Villa. An Historical Introduction* (London 1976)

PETSCHENIG, Michael (ed.) *Iohannis Cassiani Conlationes XXIIII* (Wien 1886)

PFAFF, R. W. *New Liturgical Feasts in Later Medieval England* (Oxford 1970)

PHILLIMORE, E. (ed.) 'The *Annales Cambriæ* and Old Welsh genealogies, from *Harleian MS.* 3859', *Y Cymmrodor* 9 (1888) 141–83

PICARD, Jean-Michel (ed.) *Ireland and Northern France AD 600–850* (Blackrock 1991)

PLUMMER, Charles (ed.) *Venerabilis Baedae opera historica* (2 vols, Oxford 1896)

PLUMMER, Charles (ed.) *Vitae Sanctorum Hiberniae partim hactenus ineditae* (2 vols, Oxford 1910; rev. imp., 1968)

PORTER, H. M. *The Celtic Church in Somerset, with a Chapter on North Devon* (Bath 1971)

POWELL, D. 'St Patrick's Confession and the Book of Armagh', *Analecta Bollandiana* 90 (1972) 371–85

POWELL, D. 'The textual integrity of St. Patrick's Confession', *Analecta Bollandiana* 87 (1969) 387–409

POWELL, T. E. 'Christianity or solar monotheism: the early religious beliefs of St Patrick', *Journal of Ecclesiastical History* 43 (1992) 531–40

QUIN, E. G., *et al.* (gen. edd.) *Dictionary of the Irish Language based mainly on Old and Middle Irish Materials* (Dublin 1913–76)

RADFORD, C. A. R. 'Glastonbury Abbey', in *The Quest for Arthur's Britain*, ed. G. Ashe (London 1968), pp. 97–110

RAMSAY, Nigel, *et al.* (edd.) *St Dunstan, his Life, Times and Cult* (Woodbridge 1992)

RAND, Edward Kennard *Studies in the Script of Tours*, I, *A Survey of the Manuscripts of Tours* (2 vols, Cambridge, Mass. 1929)

REES, B. R. (transl.) *The Letters of Pelagius and his Followers* (Woodbridge 1991)

RHYS, John *Lectures on Welsh Philology* (2nd edn, London 1879)

RICHARDSON, Ernest Cushing (ed.) *Hieronymus, Liber de Viris inlustribus; Gennadius, Liber de Viris inlustribus* (Leipzig 1896)

RICHTER, Michael (ed.) *Canterbury Professions* ([London] 1973)

ROBERTS, Brynley F. (ed.) *Early Welsh Poetry: Studies in the Book of Aneirin* (Aberystwyth 1988)

ROBINSON, J. A. 'A fragment of the Life of St Cungar', *Journal of Theological Studies* 20 (1918/19) 97–108

ROBINSON, J. A. 'St Cungar and St Decuman', *Journal of Theological Studies* 29 (1927/8) 137–40

ROBINSON, J[oseph] Armitage *Somerset Historical Essays* (London 1921)

ROBINSON, J[oseph] Armitage *The Saxon Bishops of Wells. A Historical Study in the Tenth Century* (London [1918])

ROLLASON, D. W. 'Lists of saints' resting places in Anglo-Saxon England', *Anglo-Saxon England* 7 (1978) 61–93

ROLLASON, D. [W.] 'St Cuth[b]ert and Wessex: the evidence of Cambridge, Corpus Christi College MS 183', in *St Cuthbert, his Cult and his Community to AD 1200*, edd. G. Bonner *et al.* (Woodbridge 1989), pp. 413–24

RUSSELL, P. 'Recent work on British Latin', *Cambridge Medieval Celtic Studies* 9 (1985) 19–29

RYAN, John (ed.) *Saint Patrick* ([Dublin] 1958)

RYAN, J. 'The Cáin Adomnáin', *apud* R. Thurneysen *et al.*, *Studies in Early Irish Law* (Dublin 1936), pp. 269–76

RYAN, J. 'The two Patricks', *Irish Ecclesiastical Record*, 5th S., 60 (1942) 241–52

RYNNE, E. 'Celtic stone idols in Ireland', in *The Iron Age in the Irish Sea Province*, ed. C. Thomas (London 1972), pp. 79–98

SAWYER, P. H. *Anglo-Saxon Charters. An Annotated List and Bibliography* (London 1968)

SAWYER, P. H. & WOOD, I. N. (edd.) *Early Medieval Kingship* (Leeds 1977)

SCHIEFFER, Theodor *Winfrid-Bonifatius und die christliche Grundlegung Europas* (Freiburg im Breisgau 1954)

SCHMIDT, K. H. 'Late British', in *Britain 400–600*, edd. A. Bammesberger & A. Wollmann (Heidelberg 1990), pp. 121–48

SCHWARTZ, Eduard & STRAUB, J. (edd.) *Acta Conciliorum Oecumenicorum* (First series, 4 vols in 16, Berlin 1914–82)

SCOTT, John (ed. & transl.) *The Early History of Glastonbury. An Edition,*

Translation and Study of William of Malmesbury's De antiquitate Glastonie ecclesie (Woodbridge 1981)

SHARPE, R. 'Armagh and Rome in the seventh century', in *Ireland and Europe*, edd. P. Ní Chatháin & M. Richter (Stuttgart 1984), pp. 58–72

SHARPE, R. 'Gildas as a Father of the Church', in *Gildas: New Approaches*, edd. M. Lapidge & D. Dumville (Woodbridge 1984), pp. 193–205

SHARPE, R. 'Hiberno-Latin *laicus*, Irish *láech* and the devil's men', *Ériu* 30 (1979) 75–92

SHARPE, Richard *Medieval Irish Saints' Lives. An Introduction to Vitae Sanctorum Hiberniae* (Oxford 1991)

SHARPE, R. 'Palaeographical considerations in the study of the Patrician documents in the Book of Armagh', *Scriptorium* 36 (1982) 3–28

SHARPE, R. 'Quatuor sanctissimi episcopi: Irish saints before St Patrick', in *Sages, Saints and Scholars*, edd. D. Ó Corráin *et al.* (Maynooth 1989), pp. 376–99

SHARPE, R. 'Saint Mauchteus, *discipulus Patricii*', in *Britain 400–600*, edd. A. Bammesberger & A. Wollmann (Heidelberg 1990), pp. 85–93

SHARPE, R. 'St Patrick and the see of Armagh', *Cambridge Medieval Celtic Studies* 4 (1982) 33–59

SHARPE, R. 'Some problems concerning the organization of the Church in early medieval Ireland', *Peritia* 3 (1984) 230–70

SHARPE, R. 'The origin and elaboration of the *Catalogus praecipuorum sanctorum Hiberniae* attributed to Fr Henry FitzSimon, S.J.', *Bodleian Library Record* 13 (1988–91) 202–30

SHARPE, R. 'The Patrician documents', *Peritia* 1 (1982) 363–9

SHAW, F. 'The myth of the second Patrick A.D. 461–1961', *Studies* 50 (1961) 5–27

SHEEHY, M. P. 'Concerning the origin of early medieval Irish monasticism', *Irish Theological Quarterly* 29 (1962) 136–44

SHEEHY, M. P. 'The relics of the apostles and early martyrs in the mission of St. Patrick', *Irish Ecclesiastical Record*, 5th S., 95 (1961) 372–6

SHEEHY, Maurice [P.] *When the Normans came to Ireland* (Cork 1975)

SIMS-WILLIAMS, P. 'Dating the transition to Neo-Brittonic: phonology and history, 400–600', in *Britain 400–600*, edd. A. Bammesberger & A. Wollmann (Heidelberg 1990), pp. 217–61

SIMS-WILLIAMS, P. 'Gildas and the Anglo-Saxons', *Cambridge Medieval Celtic Studies* 6 (1983) 1–30

SLOVER, C. H. 'Glastonbury Abbey and the fusing of English literary culture', *Speculum* 10 (1935) 147–60

SLOVER, C. H. 'William of Malmesbury and the Irish', *Speculum* 2 (1927) 268–83

SLOVER, C. H. 'William of Malmesbury's *Life of St. Patrick*', *Modern Philology* 24 (1926/7) 5–20

SMYTH, Alfred P. *Celtic Leinster. Towards an Historical Geography of Early Irish Civilization A.D. 500–1600* (Blackrock 1982)

SMYTH, A. P. 'Húi Failgi relations with the Húi Néill in the century after the loss of the plain of Mide', *Études celtiques* 14 (1974/5) 503–23

SMYTH, A. P. 'The earliest Irish annals: their first contemporary entries, and the earliest centres of recording', *Proceedings of the Royal Irish Academy* 72 C (1972) 1–48

SMYTH, A. P. 'The Húi Néill and the Leinstermen in the Annals of Ulster, 431–516 A.D.', *Études celtiques* 14 (1974/5) 121–43

SOUTER, Alexander *A Glossary of Later Latin to 600 A.D.* (Oxford 1949; rev. imp., 1957)

SOUTER, Alexander (ed.) *Pelagius's Expositions of Thirteen Epistles of St Paul* (3 vols, Cambridge 1922–31)

SPAREY GREEN, C. 'The cemetery of a Romano-British christian community at Poundbury, Dorchester, Dorset', in *The Early Church in Western Britain and Ireland*, ed. S. M. Pearce (Oxford 1982), pp. 61–76

STÄBLEIN, B. 'Präfation', in *Die Musik in Geschichte und Gegenwart*, ed. F. Blume (17 vols, Kassel 1949–86), X, cols 1535–7

STANCLIFFE, C. E. 'Kings and conversion: some comparisons between the Roman mission to England and Patrick's to Ireland', *Frühmittelalterliche Studien* 14 (1980) 59–94

STENTON, F. M. *The Early History of the Abbey of Abingdon* (Reading 1913)

STEVENSON, Jane Barbara '*Altus Prosator*: a Seventh-century Hiberno-Latin Poem' (unpublished Ph.D. dissertation, University of Cambridge 1985)

STEVENSON, J. [B.] 'The beginnings of literacy in Ireland', *Proceedings of the Royal Irish Academy* 89 C (1989) 127–65

STOKES, Whitley (ed. & transl.) *Félire Húi Gormáin. The Martyrology of Gorman, edited from a manuscript in the Royal Library, Brussels* (London 1895)

STOKES, Whitley (ed. & transl.) *Félire Óengusso Céli Dé. The Martyrology of Oengus the Culdee, critically edited from Ten Manuscripts* (London 1905)

STOKES, Whitley (ed.) *On the Calendar of Oengus* (Dublin 1880)

STOKES, W. (ed. & transl.) 'The Annals of Tigernach', *Revue celtique* 16 (1895) 374–419; 17 (1896) 6–33, 119–263, 337–420, 458; 18 (1897) 9–59, 150–98, 267–303, 390–1

STOKES, Whitley & STRACHAN, J. (edd. & transl.) *Thesaurus Palaeohibernicus. A Collection of Old-Irish Glosses, Scholia, Prose and Verse* (2 vols, Cambridge 1901/3; supplement, Halle a.S. 1910)

STOKES, Whitley (ed. & transl.) *The Tripartite Life of Patrick, with Other Documents relating to that Saint* (2 vols, London 1887)

STRACHAN, J 'Contributions to the history of the deponent verb in Irish', *Transactions of the Philological Society* (1891–4) 444–568

STREITBERG, Wilhelm (ed.) *Die gotische Bibel* (4th edn, 2 vols in 1, Heidelberg 1965)

STROBEL, August (ed.) *Texte zur Geschichte des frühchristlichen Osterkalenders* (Münster i. W. 1984)

STROBEL, August *Ursprung und Geschichte des frühchristlichen Osterkalenders* (Berlin 1977)

*STROHEKER, Karl Friedrich *Der senatorische Adel in spätantiken Gallien* (Tübingen 1948)

STUBBS, William (ed.) *Memorials of Saint Dunstan, Archbishop of Canterbury* (London 1874)

STUBBS, William (ed.) *Willelmi Malmesbiriensis monachi De gestis regum Anglorum libri quinque; Historiæ novellæ libri tres* (2 vols, London 1887/9)

SZARMACH, Paul E. & OGGINS, V. D. (edd.) *Sources of Anglo-Saxon Culture* (Kalamazoo, Mich. 1986)

TANGL, Michael (ed.) *Die Briefe des heiligen Bonifatius und Lullus* (Berlin 1916)

TEMPLE, Elzbieta *Anglo-Saxon Manuscripts 900–1066* (London 1976)

THOMAS, C. 'Beacon Hill revisited: a re-assessment of the 1969 excavations', *Lundy Field Society Annual Report* 42 (1991) 43–54

THOMAS, Charles *Christianity in Roman Britain to AD 500* (London 1981)

THOMAS, C. 'East and West: Tintagel, Mediterranean imports and the early Insular Church', in *The Early Church in Western Britain and Ireland*, ed. S. M. Pearce (Oxford 1982), pp. 17–34

THOMAS, C., *et al.* 'Lundy, 1969', *Current Archaeology* 2 (1969/70) 138–42

THOMAS, C. '*Rosnat*, *Rostat*, and the early Irish Church', *Ériu* 22 (1971) 100–6

THOMAS, C. 'Saint Patrick and fifth-century Britain: an historical model explored', in *The End of Roman Britain*, ed. P. J. Casey (Oxford 1979), pp. 81–101

THOMAS, C. 'The Irish settlements in post-Roman western Britain: a survey of the evidence', *Journal of the Royal Institution of Cornwall*, N.S., 6 (1969–72) 251–74

THOMAS, Charles (ed.) *The Iron Age in the Irish Sea Province. Papers given at a C.B.A. Conference held at Cardiff, January 3 to 5, 1969* (London 1972)

THOMAS, R. J., *et al.* (edd.) *Geiriadur Prifysgol Cymru. A Dictionary of the Welsh Language* (Cardiff 1950–)

THOMPSON, E. A. 'Gildas and the history of Britain', *Britannia* 10 (1979) 203–26 *and* 11 (1980) 344

THOMPSON, E. A. *Saint Germanus of Auxerre and the End of Roman Britain* (Woodbridge 1984)

THOMPSON, E. A. 'St. Patrick and Coroticus', *Journal of Theological Studies*, N.S., 31 (1980) 12–27

THOMPSON, E. A. *The Visigoths in the Time of Ulfila* (Oxford 1966)

THOMPSON, E. A. *Who was Saint Patrick?* (Woodbridge 1985)

THOMPSON, E. A. 'Zosimus 6.10.2 and the letters of Honorius', *Classical Quarterly* 76 [N.S., 32] (1982) 445–62

THOMSON, Rodney *William of Malmesbury* (Woodbridge 1987)

THORNTON, D. E. 'Glastonbury and the Glastening', in *The Archaeology and History of Glastonbury Abbey*, edd. L. Abrams & J. P. Carley (Woodbridge 1991), pp. 191–203

THURNEYSEN, Rudolf *A Grammar of Old Irish* (Dublin 1946; rev. imp., 1975)

THURNEYSEN, R[udolf], *et al.* *Studies in Early Irish Law* (Dublin 1936)

TODD, James Henthorn *St. Patrick, Apostle of Ireland. A Memoir of his Life and Mission with an Introductory Dissertation on Some Early Usages of the Church in Ireland, and its Historical Position from the Establishment of the English Colony to the Present Day* (Dublin 1864)

TODD, M. 'The vici of western England', in *The Roman West Country*, edd. K. Branigan & P. J. Fowler (Newton Abbot 1976), pp. 99–119

TRAUBE, L. 'Perrona Scottorum, ein Beitrag zur Ueberlieferungsgeschichte und zur Palaeographie des Mittelalters', *Sitzungsberichte der königlichen bayerischen Akademie der Wissenschaften*, philosophisch-philologische und historische Klasse (1900) 469–538

TREITLER, L. 'Reading and singing: on the genesis of Occidental music-writing', *Early Music History* 4 (1984) 135–208

TURNER, D. H. (ed.) *The Missal of the New Minster, Winchester (Le Havre, Bibliothèque municipale, MS 330)* (London 1962)

USSHER, James *The Whole Works* (17 vols, Dublin 1847–64)

*VALENTIN, R. *Saint Prosper d'Aquitaine. Étude sur la littérature latine ecclésiastique au Ve siècle en Gaule* (Toulouse 1900)

VENDRYES, J. *De hibernicis vocabulis quae a latina lingua originem duxerunt* (Paris 1902)

VENDRYES, J. *Lexique étymologique de l'irlandais ancien* (Dublin 1959–)

VOGEL, Cyrille *Medieval Liturgy: an Introduction to the Sources* (Washington, D.C. 1986)

VON WINTERFELD, Paul & STRECKER, K. (edd.) *Poetae Latini Aevi Carolini*, IV (Berlin 1899–1923)

WADE-EVANS, A. W. (transl.) *Life of St. David* (London 1923)

WADE-EVANS, A. W. (transl.) *Nennius's "History of the Britons" together with "The Annals of the Britons" and "Court Pedigrees of Hywel the Good"; also "The Story of the Loss of Britain"* (London 1938)

WADE-EVANS, A. W. 'The death-years of Dewi Sant and Saint Dubricius', *Anglo-Welsh Review* 10, no. 26 ([1960]) 63–4

WADE-EVANS, A. W. (ed. & transl.) *Vitae Sanctorum Britanniae et Genealogiae* (Cardiff 1944)

WAILES, B. 'The Irish "royal sites" in history and archaeology', *Cambridge Medieval Celtic Studies* 3 (1982) 1–29

WALKER, G. S. M. & BIELER, L. (edd. & transl.) *Sancti Columbani Opera* (Dublin 1957)

WALLACE-HADRILL, J. M. *Bede's* Ecclesiastical History of the English People. *A Historical Commentary* (Oxford 1988)

WALLACE-HADRILL, J. M. *The Frankish Church* (Oxford 1983)

WALSH, Maura & Ó CRÓINÍN, D. (edd. & transl.) *Cummian's Letter* De controuersia paschali *together with a Related Irish Computistical Tract* De ratione conputandi (Toronto 1988)

WALSH, Paul *The Placenames of Westmeath* (Dublin 1957)

WARD, P. L. (ed.) 'An early version of the Anglo-Saxon coronation ceremony', *English Historical Review* 57 (1942) 345–61

WARNER, George F. (facs. ed.) *The Stowe Missal. MS. D.II.3 in the Library of the Royal Irish Academy, Dublin* (2 vols, London 1906/15)

WARREN, F. E. (ed.) *The Antiphonary of Bangor. An Early Irish Manuscript in the Ambrosian Library at Milan* (2 vols, London 1893/5)

WARREN, F. E. (ed.) *The Leofric Missal as used in the Cathedral of Exeter during the Episcopate of its First Bishop, A.D. 1050–1072, together with Some Account of the Red Book of Derby, the Missal of Robert of Jumièges, and a Few Other Early Manuscript Service Books of the English Church* (Oxford 1883)

WARREN, F. E. *The Liturgy and Ritual of the Celtic Church* (2nd edn, by J. Stevenson, Woodbridge 1987)

WASSERSCHLEBEN, Hermann (ed.) *Die irische Kanonensammlung* (2nd edn, Leipzig 1885)

WHATMOUGH, Joshua *The Dialects of Ancient Gaul. Prolegomena and Records of the Dialects* (Cambridge, Mass. 1970)

WHITE, N. J. D. (ed. & transl.) 'Libri sancti Patricii. The Latin writings of St. Patrick', *Proceedings of the Royal Irish Academy* 25 C (1904/5) 201–326

WHITE, N. J. D. 'The Paris manuscript of St. Patrick's Latin writings', *Proceedings of the Royal Irish Academy* 25 C (1904/5) 542–52

WHITELOCK, Dorothy (transl.) *English Historical Documents,* c. *500–1042* (2nd edn, London 1979)

WHITELOCK, Dorothy, *et al.* (edd.) *Ireland in Early Mediaeval Europe. Studies in Memory of Kathleen Hughes* (Cambridge 1982)

WILLIAMS, Hugh (ed. & transl.) *Gildas* (2 vols, London 1899/1901)

WILLIAMS, Ifor (ed.) *Canu Aneirin* (Cardiff 1938)

WILLIAMS (AB ITHEL), John (ed.) *Annales Cambriæ* (London 1860)

WILLIAMS, Rowan (ed.) *The Making of Orthodoxy. Essays in Honour of Henry Chadwick* (Cambridge 1989)

WILSON, H. A. (ed.) *The Missal of Robert of Jumièges* (London 1896)

WILSON, P. A. 'St. Ninian and Candida Casa: literary evidence from Ireland', *Transactions of the Dumfriesshire and Galloway Natural History and Antiquarian Society*, 3rd S., 41 (1962/3) 156–85

WILSON, P. A. 'St. Ninian: Irish evidence further examined', *Transactions of the Dumfriesshire and Galloway Natural History and Antiquarian Society*, 3rd S., 46 (1969) 140–59

WINTERBOTTOM, Michael (ed. & transl.) *Gildas: The Ruin of Britain and Other Works* (Chichester 1978)

WOOD, I. N. 'Continuity or calamity?: the constraints of literary models', in *Fifth-century Gaul*, edd. J. Drinkwater & H. Elton (Cambridge 1992), pp. 9–18

WOOD, I. N. 'Gregory of Tours and Clovis', *Revue belge de philologie et d'histoire* 63 (1985) 249–72

WOOD, I. [N.] 'The end of Roman Britain: Continental evidence and parallels', in *Gildas: New Approaches*, edd. M. Lapidge & D. Dumville (Woodbridge 1984), pp. 1–25

WOOD, I. [N.] 'The fall of the Western empire and the end of Roman Britain', *Britannia* 18 (1987) 251–62

WORMALD, F. 'Decorated initials in English MSS. from A.D. 900 to 1100', *Archaeologia* 91 (1945) 107–35

WORMALD, Francis (ed.) *English Kalendars before A.D. 1100* (London 1934)

WRIGHT, N. 'Gildas's geographical perspective: some problems', in *Gildas: New Approaches*, edd. M. Lapidge & D. Dumville (Woodbridge 1984), pp. 85–105

ZELZER, M. 'Zum Osterfestbrief des heiligen Ambrosius und zur römischen

Osterfestberechnung des 4. Jahrhunderts', *Wiener Studien* 91 [N.F., 12] (1978) 187–204
ZETTEL, P. H. 'Saints' Lives in Old English: Latin manuscripts and vernacular accounts: Ælfric', *Peritia* 1 (1982) 17–37
ZIMMER, Heinrich *Nennius Vindicatus. Über Entstehung, Geschichte und Quellen der* Historia Brittonum (Berlin 1893)
ZIMMER, Heinrich *The Celtic Church in Britain and Ireland* (London 1902)

INDEX OF SCHOLARS WHOSE WORK IS NAMED IN THE TEXT

INDEX OF CITATIONS OF THE WORKS OF ST PATRICK

INDEX OF MANUSCRIPTS

GENERAL INDEX